(33) PEMBROKE COLLEGE CHAPEL. W. front. 1663–65

ROYAL COMMISSION ON THE HISTORICAL MONUMENTS OF ENGLAND

An Inventory of the
Historical Monuments in the

CITY OF
CAMBRIDGE

PART II

LONDON
HER MAJESTY'S STATIONERY OFFICE

First published 1959
Second impression 1988

ISBN 0 11 300023 5

Printed in the United Kingdom for Her Majesty's Stationery Office
Dd. 240062 10/88 C30

TABLE OF CONTENTS

PLANS of King's, St. John's and Trinity Colleges are presented separately.

(32) MAGDALENE COLLEGE stands on the E. side of Magdalene Street, between the river and Chesterton Lane. The walls generally are of clunch with an external facing of red brick, now for the most part faced with stucco; the dressings are of clunch. Only the W. front of the Pepys Building is of Ketton stone ashlar. The roofs are slate and tile-covered. For descriptive purposes in the following account the Chapel is taken to be orientated due E. and W.

As the result of representations made to Henry VI that monks from Crowland (or Croyland) were sent to Cambridge to study canon law and theology but, because of the lack of a hostel for the Benedictine order, were compelled to lodge with seculars, the Abbot in 1428 obtained Letters Patent for the establishment of a hostel for them in two houses on the far side of the Great Bridge, on the site of the present college (L.P. 6. H VI, 2, m 21). Abbot Litlyngton, the applicant for the grant, died in 1469 and, according to the continuator of the Croyland Chronicle writing seventeen years later, his successor John de Wisbech (Abbot 1470–76) 'erected chambers convenient for repose and study in the monks' college of Buckingham' ('Historiae Croylandensis Continuatio' (1458–9) in T. Gale and W. Fulman *Rerum Anglicarum Scriptorum Veterum* (Oxon. 1684), I, 560). A condition of the grant was that other Benedictine houses should be able to build rooms for their monks.

The establishment, though named the 'hostel called Monks' place' in a deed of 1472, was known as Buckingham College certainly from 1483, as then recorded in the Cambridge Borough accounts, but the exact connection with Henry Stafford, 2nd Duke of Buckingham (executed 1483), or possibly his grandfather the 1st Duke, and the indebtedness to the family is unknown; the Dukes of Buckingham are reputed to have been benefactors of Crowland.

Dr. Caius (1510–73, student 1529–33) states that it was this Duke Henry who 'made a beginning' of the buildings of the college, in brick, which were continued by the monks, 'different monasteries building different portions; thus Ely one chamber, Walden a second, and Ramsey a third'. The date the sister monasteries contributed is not recorded.

As a result of this combined effort and with aid from the 3rd Duke of Buckingham, by the time of the dissolution of the College in 1539 a court with ranges on at least three sides had been completed, with the Hall in the E. range, a Chapel in the E. half of the N. range with perhaps chambers, including the Prior's room, in the rest and chambers occupying the S. range; probably the N. part of the W. range also was built. These buildings survive and form the major part of the existing *First Court*. Subsequent alterations have endowed them with greater architectural unity than they at first perhaps possessed, but it seems that the separate monastic *camerae* never had the diversity of appearance of those built in similar circumstances, and which survive largely unaltered, at Worcester College, Oxford.

The *North Range*, containing the Chapel, is of the late 15th century. The *South Range* is of similar date; here the blocks served by the separate staircases vary slightly from one another and appear to have been built as separate entities, thus corroborating Caius' statement. Further, the former existence of a doorway in the N.W. corner of the Court carved with the arms of Ely Cathedral priory, as recorded by Cole in 1777, seems to indicate a like origin for the N. part of the W. range.

According to an account of the College prepared for the visit of Queen Elizabeth to Cambridge in 1564, the Hall in the *East Range* was built in 1519 by Edward, 3rd Duke of Buckingham (executed 1521). The structural evidence indicates a rather earlier date for the remainder of the range, where the Kitchens formerly stood, though this has been considerably altered from time to time. It seems that the space available immediately S. of the Chapel was restricted and that a Hall of the size required could be built there only by projecting the bay containing the screens-passage into the northern end of the part of the range already standing.

Endowment of the College ceased at the Dissolution in December 1539. The grant to Thomas, Lord Audley of Walden, Lord Chancellor, to refound the College was made on 3 April 1542; the new dedication was to St. Mary Magdalene. Audley died in 1544 and a Return of the King's Commissioners of 1546 shows the foundation to have been in a state of extreme poverty, precluding any building activity (P.R.O. E 315/440).

On the occasion of Queen Elizabeth's visit in 1564, Thomas Howard, 4th Duke of Norfolk, Audley's son-in-law and great-grandson of Edward, 3rd Duke of Buckingham, promised the College £40 a year towards completion of the Court. This must apply to the incomplete *West Range* (see above). How far building had progressed by the time of his execution in June 1572 is unknown and the evidence of the stylised representation of the College in Richard Lyne's plan of 1574 is ambiguous. Hamond in 1592 shows the Court entirely enclosed. In 1585 Sir Christopher Wray, Thomas Parkinson and Edward Lucas had contributed some £18 towards the cost of the new gates; at the same period, expenses recorded in the Audit Books for paving the *Gatehouse* suggest that it was incomplete. Tradition attributes to Wray the Renaissance surround to the W. archway of the Gatehouse.

In an agreement dated 16 July 1587 between Wray and the College it is stated that he had lately at his own expense 'erected and new builded a portion of building' in the College; the terms of the agreement imply three storeys with four chambers each, twelve chambers in all. Tradition locates them in the E. range, S. of the Hall, but, further to the evidence of an earlier date for that fabric, exigences of space point rather to completion of the W. range and a remodelling of the existing N. end of the same.

Between 1733 and 1756 the interior of the late 15th-century *Chapel* was transformed to the Classical style, chiefly during the last two years of the period and under contract with Jeremiah Robinson, who prepared the designs. In 1754 the E. window had been blocked and in 1756 William Collins was paid for the relief panel, now in the Library, for the reredos. Between 1847 and 1851 the interior was again restored and most of the 18th-century additions were abolished; the flat plaster ceiling and the sets of attic-rooms contrived above were removed, the E. window was reopened and the wainscoting renewed. The work was supervised by John Buckler and cost some £2,000. At the same time a vestibule, with the Master's pew above, was converted into the present Ante-chapel by removing the S. entrance-doorway and replacing the E. wall of the vestibule by an oak screen. A new approach-passage was made by shortening the room to the W. now containing part of the College Library.

The *Hall* of 1519 was wainscoted in 1585 and a louvre built between 1586 and 1588. In 1714 £265 was spent on almost complete internal renovation, including a new ceiling, which may indicate that at this time the sets of rooms still over the Hall were first contrived between the original trusses.

The *Combination Room* is first recorded in 1712 when the floor above the Kitchen and Butteries was fitted to accommodate it. It was refitted in 1757; after 1810 the sash-windows in the W. wall, and on the floor below, were replaced by a single large four-light window. The *Library* is shown by Loggan in *c.* 1690 in the roof over the Chapel, but the date it was placed there is unknown; in 1733 it was moved to the room in the external N.W. angle of First Court and *c.* 1850 to the present position W. of the Chapel, in the dining-room and drawing-room of the old Master's Lodge.

The *Master's Lodge* was formerly in the N.W. corner of First Court; considerable extensions to it on the N., no longer standing, of which the dates are not recorded, are shown in Loggan's engraving of the College; they enclosed a small courtyard and a stable-yard beyond; the N. boundary-wall of the last in part survives. The accommodation was also extended by appropriating the rest of the N. range of First Court eastward as far as the Chapel. In 1834 it was decided to build a new Master's Lodge and Edward Blore was asked to prepare designs, but in the event John Buckler was the architect employed. Work was begun in 1835 to the N. of the site, adjoining Chesterton Lane; the foundation-stone was laid by H.R.H. Prince George of Cambridge.

The changes in the appearance of First Court between the late 17th century, see Loggan's view, and the present time were effected in 1702, in 1759–60 when the walls were faced with stucco, and between 1812 and 1815. In this last period, though the stucco was renewed, the recorded expenses are disproportionately heavy, and this fact, together with the known survival of plain eaves to within a short time before (see Harraden's view of the College dated 1810), suggests that it was also the period when the eaves were replaced by battlements, no change of this kind being recorded at a subsequent date. In 1955,[1] removal of the stucco facing and the battlements was begun; the E. side has been stripped and made good and the roof, now tiled, continued down to a slight eaves-cornice; this last is of stone and entirely new; similar work on the S. side is half completed (Summer 1956). The S. front to the river and the W. front to Magdalene Street were restored in 1873 and 1875 respectively by F. C. Penrose, the first after demolition of cottage properties standing between it and the river.

Beyond First Court only two buildings still surviving were added to the College in the 17th century, the Pepys Building forming the E. side of Second Court and, between it and the river, the timber-framed brewhouse, the latter built in 1629 and subsequently much altered. The *Pepys Building*, originally called the New Building, houses the Samuel Pepys library. Subscriptions for an extension to the College were solicited as early as 1640. No records of the beginning and completion of the Pepys Building survive and the evidence for dating it is largely incidental. By tradition it was begun during the Mastership of John Peachell, 1679–90, and completed during that of Gabriel Quadring, 1690–1713. A letter of 29 November 1679 to Pepys from John Maulyverer, Fellow, reads 'we had made a tender of it before this

[1] After this account had been set up in galley-proof.

time' if subscriptions had not been so slow in coming in. 'We have not yet finished the inside, and I know not when we shall'. Thus it may have been begun while James Duport was Master, 1668–79, who is said to have given £235 towards it. In 1698–9 considerable payments were being made to Francis Percy, contractor and carver. Pepys contributed during Duport's Mastership, and subsequently, and in his will in 1703 bequeathed his library conditionally to Magdalene, to 'be in the New Building there', which seems to imply completion.

The architect also of the Pepys Building is unknown, but in 1677 Robert Hooke prepared a 'draught of Maudlin College' for Dr. Burton (Hooke's Diary in *Walpole Soc. Papers* (1936–7) xxv, 25 March 1677). It may be that he redrafted only the W. front of an older design prepared some time after *c.* 1640, the inference being that money then solicited was for this building; this would explain the curious dichotomy between the front and the rest of the building.

Pepys' library, contained in his own bookcases, was installed in the room occupying the whole of the first floor of the central block in 1724. In 1834 it was moved to the old Master's Lodge, to the ground-floor room next W. of the Chapel; about 1847 it was transferred to the new Master's Lodge and in 1853 back to the Pepys Building, to the first-floor room in the S.E. wing made fire-proof in 1879, where it remains.

Work done in the present century includes the addition in 1908–9 of a Kitchen block S. of the original Kitchen and *Bright's Building* designed by Sir Aston Webb on the S. side of Second Court. In 1911 A. C. Benson, then President and later (1915–25) Master, formed the *Old Lodge*, N. of the old Master's Lodge, by combining a number of small early 19th-century buildings and adding to them Benson Hall along the street front; in the same year the ceilings of the Hall and Combination Room were elaborated.

The *Junior Combination Room* was formed in the S.W. corner of First Court in 1923 and extended westward in 1935 but this area has recently been entirely remodelled and a new stair inserted. In 1926 the passage-way between the Ante-chapel and the Library was panelled and in 1928 carved shields-of-arms of Benedictine monasteries were inserted over the doorways in First Court from the designs of Kruger Gray.

Further accommodation provided in the present century on the opposite side of Magdalene Street includes *Benson Court* and *Mallory Court*. The former was designed by Sir Edwin Lutyens, but only the W. range was built, between 1930 and 1932. Mallory Court consists of a miscellany of buildings largely of the 19th century, some remodelled in 1924 and others recently. The Magdalene Street houses are now (1957) being converted into undergraduates' rooms.

Magdalene College in the 15th-century foundation was the only house of regular studies in Cambridge provided at first exclusively for Benedictine monks; the buildings of this period survive although to some extent obscured by later refacing and refitting. The S. range of First Court retains an exceptional example, almost intact, of the mediaeval arrangements of students' rooms, consisting of one large chamber with small studies opening from it. Stucco and battlements gave to First Court the appearance, unique among Cambridge colleges, of a work of the early 19th-century Romantic movement; they are now being abolished (1956). The heraldic painting and the staircase in the Hall are unusual. The Pepys Building is of considerable architectural interest and the Pepys library within is most notable, apart from its historical, literary and bibliographical importance, for the quality of the fittings. The relief-panel formerly in the Chapel reredos is a notable piece of plasterwork.

Architectural Description—In First Court (112½ ft. by 80 ft.) the *West Range* contains the Gateway well to the S. of centre. It is of two storeys with attics. The E. wall is mostly faced with Roman cement and has clunch dressings; the W. wall, to the street, is of red brick entirely refaced in 1875, with freestone dressings. The roofs are slate-covered. Entrance to the College has been from this direction certainly since 1574 and no doubt from the foundation, and the development of the range so far as it is ascertainable is outlined above. A thick cross-wall immediately N. of the Porter's Lodge may indicate the extent of the building of the first foundation. The rest of the range to the S. is of the second half of the 16th century and financed in building probably by the 4th Duke of Norfolk and Sir Christopher Wray, the earlier northern part being remodelled at the same time.

The W. arch of the *Gateway* is largely original, of *c.* 1585, with a chamfered semicircular arch on square responds with moulded imposts; the stone surround has flanking Roman Doric pilasters with enriched caps on pedestals supporting a full entablature with triglyphs and flower-like paterae in the metopes. The oak door, for which contributions were received in 1585, is hung on old strap-hinges; it is in two leaves, of thirteen and twelve linenfold panels on the face and lattice-framed behind, with a wicket in the N. leaf. The E. arch has chamfered freestone jambs and a moulded four-centred head of clunch with a restored label (p. 394); over it is an achievement-of-arms of Richard Neville-Griffin, 3rd Lord Braybrooke, added between 1852 and 1854 (Plate 202). The Gatehall (22¼ ft. by 11¼ ft.) has a modern doorway and modern three-light window in the N. wall and a modern doorway in the S. wall.

The E. side of the W. range has a plain plinth and embattled parapet. On the ground floor the doorway to staircase 'A' has been completely restored and over it is a modern shield-of-arms of Ely Cathedral priory; the original doorway was probably some 4 ft. further S. where is a blocking below the adjacent window. The doorway to staircase 'B' has much weathered square jambs, a hollow-chamfered four-centred arch in a square head and a label; over it is a modern shield-of-arms of Crowland Abbey. The four windows of two and three lights, as shown on the plan, have four-centred openings in square heads with sunk spandrels and labels and are all of the second half of the 16th century; the glazing of the northernmost is set in modern oak framing. On the first floor is a range of seven two and three-light windows of similar character to the foregoing, the three to the S. being symmetrically placed over the three southern openings below. On the roof are five 18th or 19th-century flat-roofed dormer-windows.

The W. side, to Magdalene Street, retains almost exactly the fenestration shown in Loggan's view of the College, *c.* 1690. On the ground floor is a range of ten two-light windows and a single-light window, and on the first floor of twelve two-light windows, all similar in character to those on the E. but entirely renewed externally. The changes since Loggan, excluding intermediate changes, among them the insertion of a Gothic doorway opposite doorway 'A', are the replacement of three small single-light windows on the ground floor by the third two-light window from the N., the abolition of a fourth small single-light window further S., and the entire rearrangement and renewal of the dormer-windows; these last, eight in number, are of 1873. The great shafted chimney-stacks were rebuilt in the same period.

The N. and S. ends are gabled; the brickwork and stone dressings were very extensively renewed in 1875 and 1873. In the N. end is a modern doorway, under a modern porch, set in an area of 15th-century brickwork extending up to include on the first floor a restored 15th-century two-light window with cinquefoiled openings and a pierced spandrel in a four-centred moulded head with original relieving-arch. Further W. are two altered and restored windows of the 16th century set in brickwork of the same period; the first, on the ground floor, is of four lights, and the second, on the first floor, of three lights; both are of similar character to those of similar date described above. In the S. end, which retains original brickwork showing only up to the first-floor level, are four windows and a loop-light; the two on the ground floor, of one and two lights both transomed, are similar to the other 16th-century windows in the range but smaller and entirely restored externally; the oriel-window on the first floor and the window in the gable are of 1873.

The *Interior* of the W. range contains the Porter's Lodge N. of the Gateway, college offices at the S. end of the first floor and, for the rest, sets of chambers. Alterations at the N. end including readjustment of the staircase may account for the displacement of doorway 'A' and this, as indicated above, occurred either during or before the late 16th-century work on the range; further, the blocked light adjoining the second W. window from the N. on the first floor suggests either a displacement northward in 1875 of one of the two-light windows shown by Loggan or, accepting an earlier date for the alteration, the existence here of a three-light window antedating Loggan's view. Most of the rooms have been modernised, but they retain a number of exposed chamfered ceiling-beams; some 18th-century flush-panelled doors to the sets remain. In the N.W. corner of the northernmost room is a late 15th or 16th-century doorway with chamfered jambs and moulded four-centred head opening into a cupboard, perhaps originally a garderobe. In the N. wall of the room next S. of the Gateway are traces of a former doorway with four-centred head, now blocked, opening into the Gatehall.

On the first floor the northernmost room has the greater part of the E. wall lined to within about 2 ft. from the ceiling with panelling of *c.* 1600, in five heights with enriched frieze-panels. The main room N. of staircase 'B' has an 18th-century panelled dado and six-panel doors. The timber-framing of the partition between this staircase and the room to the S. is exposed on the S. side.

The *North Range* contains the Chapel and Ante-chapel to the E. divided by a narrow passage-way from the Library next to the W. on the ground floor. It is of one and two storeys with attics. Over the Library are a Fellow's rooms and, in the attics, sets of undergraduates' rooms. The walls are of brick very extensively refaced in the 19th century and with the S. side of the range, W. of the chapel, faced with Roman cement. It was built in the second half of the 15th century, after 1470, and has subsequently been much altered. In addition to the alterations to the Chapel already described, in 1876 the upper part of the W. gable was entirely rebuilt, incorporating a niche containing a figure of the patron saint. After the completion in 1835 of the new Master's Lodge, a staircase-wing of unknown date projecting northward from the old Master's Lodge in the W. half of this range was demolished; the Library was transferred to the present position, into the former dining-room and drawing-room, and new windows to light it were inserted towards the Court; further, the first floor of the old Lodge was converted into sets of chambers.

The *Chapel* (63½ ft. by 20 ft. including the Ante-chapel 10 ft. wide) has restored stone quoins to the N.E. angle. The E. end is gabled and the whole of the upper part has been refaced or rebuilt. The E. window is entirely renewed; it is of five cinquefoiled ogee lights with tracery in a four-centred head and replaces that, presumably of similar design, bricked up in 1754 and uncovered again in the restoration of 1847–51. The N. and S. walls have plain plinths and eaves; on the S. a modern two-stage buttress marks the W. end. The Chapel is lit from each side by three three-light windows; they replace mediaeval windows and are all of the mid 19th century except perhaps most of the jambs of the N.E. window.

The *Interior* of the Chapel, as a result of the mid 18th and mid 19th-century restorations, retains no original features except the roof. In 1847 removal of the 18th-century plaster ceiling exposed the roof to the Chapel. Removal of the panelling at the same time revealed four niches at the E. end with remains of canopies. The *Roof* is divided into eight bays by collar-beam trusses with braces forming high four-centred arches; these last spring from moulded wall-plates and have pierced tracery-panels in the spandrels; standing on the collars are king-posts supporting longitudinal braces forming four-centred arches below the ridge-piece. The principals, up to the collar, the collar-beams, the braces and the single purlins are moulded. The rafters are laid flat and have the extra support of tall vertical ashlar-pieces.

Fittings—*Door:* in W. entrance, of oak, in two leaves, front with window-tracery panelling, latticed and enriched back, 1847–51. *Floor-slab:* In Ante-chapel, of William Gretton,

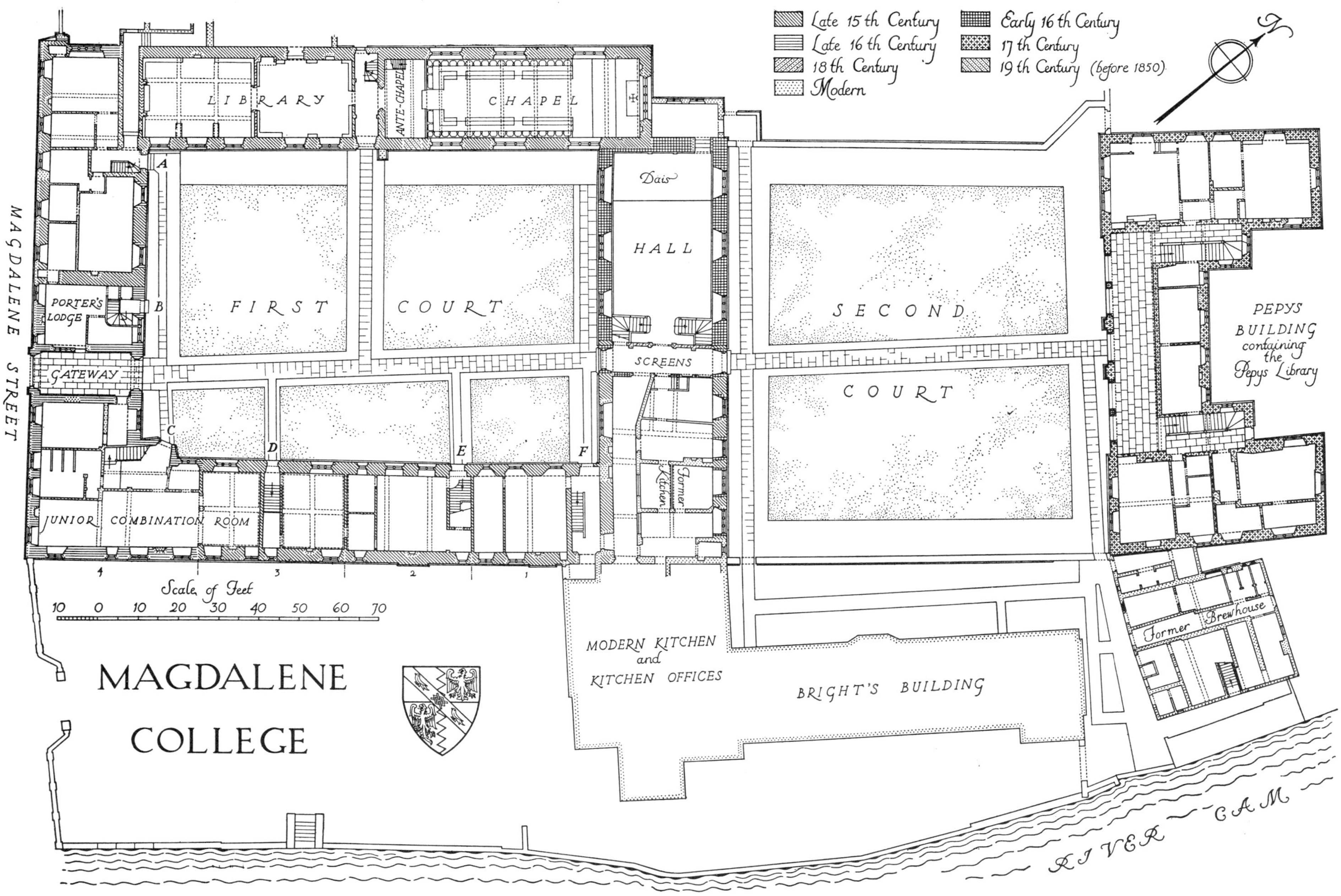

Late 15th Century
Late 16th Century
18th Century
Modern
Early 16th Century
17th Century
19th Century (before 1850)
MAGDALENE STREET
PORTER'S LODGE
GATEWAY
JUNIOR COMBINATION ROOM
LIBRARY
ANTE-CHAPEL
CHAPEL
FIRST COURT
A
B
C
D
E
F
Dais
HALL
SCREENS
Former Kitchen
SECOND COURT
PEPYS BUILDING containing the Pepys Library
Former Brewhouse
MODERN KITCHEN and KITCHEN OFFICES
BRIGHT'S BUILDING
Scale of Feet
10 0 10 20 30 40 50 60 70
1
2
3
4
MAGDALENE COLLEGE
RIVER CAM

S.T.P., 1813, Master, black marble. *Glass:* In E. window, figure subjects in each light, (1) St. Mary Magdalene anointing the feet of Christ (Plate 36), (2) The Deposition, (3) St. Mary Magdalene, (4) the three Maries and St. John, (5) 'Noli me tangere', all with kneeling angels below bearing inscribed scrolls referring to the respective scenes, and canopies and geometrical patterns above, given in 1850, designed by Pugin and made by Messrs. Hardman of Birmingham. *Niches:* four; two flanking E. window, with side-standards, three-sided canopies and tall gabled and crocketed spires; two in N. and S. walls, at E. end, similar to the foregoing, but with lower spires, 1847–51, containing modern statues. *Panelling:* on N. and S. walls over the stalls, of oak, panels with cinquefoiled heads divided into bays by buttress-like standards and with continuous cornice carved with paterae, 1847–51, in the Gothic style. *Reredos:* see *Library* below. *Screen:* between Chapel and Ante-chapel, of oak, central opening with cusped and crocketed four-centred arch with pierced traceried panels above containing carved shields of France and England quarterly and Stafford, rest of E. side with two return-stalls under elaborate traceried canopies and all surmounted by a cornice carved with Royal and Stafford heraldic devices and brattishing, W. side panelled in two heights of tracery-headed panels, 1847–51, in the Gothic style. *Stalls:* against N. and S. walls, with return-stalls for the Master and President against screen, arranged as shown on plan, of oak, with shaped and moulded arm-rests with moulded cappings, desks with tracery-panelled fronts and panelled ends with carved poppy-heads, 1847–51, in the Gothic style. (see *Screen*). *Pavement:* of stone flags set diagonally with small black marble squares at the corners, the payment of £47 was made to Thompson, 2 September 1755; at E. end, modern.

W. of the Chapel-block, approximately in the centre of the S. side of the N. range, is a doorway renewed in 1925; this replaced a window in the mid 19th-century alterations; beyond are five rectangular windows lighting the Library, with splayed heads and jambs, inserted either in or about 1834 when the Pepys library was moved here or 1847 when the College library was installed. On the first floor are seven much-weathered windows of the second half of the 15th-century, with some repairs; the first, third and fifth are of a single two-centred light, the others of two lights with a pierced spandrel in a four-centred head; any cusps they may have had have been removed. On the roof are four flat-roofed dormer-windows renewed in the 18th or 19th century.

On the N. side, W. of the Chapel-block, the door to the passage-way and the window above are modern and set in patchings of brickwork later than the rest. Much of the wall further W. is hidden by later additions; these are partly of one storey only, and in the exposed upper wall-face are traces of the W. jamb and springing of an original window close W. of a modern two-light window; further W., beyond a modern window set in a recess and impinging upon the blocking of an old doorway is a much restored original window of two pointed lights with a pierced spandrel in a four-centred head. The three late 16th-century chimney-stacks have had the upper parts rebuilt in the 19th century.

The *Library* (51¾ ft. by 20½ ft. overall), next W. of the passage-way adjoining the Chapel-block and occupying the drawing-room and dining-room of the former Master's Lodge has an extension of 1927 entered through a doorway in the N. wall of the E. room. The modern fireplace in the E. room has slips of 19th-century blue and white tiles; the overmantel is made up of fragments of carved 'Jacobean' woodwork, including arabesques, a perspective-arched panel, terminal figures and enriched and coupled attached columns. The wide doorway between the two rooms is of reset 18th-century material, with fluted Ionic pilasters *in antis* supporting a plain frieze and dentil-cornice; the double doors are each of six fielded panels. The W. room contains against the W. wall much of the reredos of 1756 (Plate 203) removed from the Chapel in the restoration of 1847–51, including the plaster relief-panel of the Maries at the Sepulchre after the Resurrection, for which William Collins was paid £31 10s. on 21 May 1756. The panel is flanked by fluted Ionic columns supporting an entablature with guilloche-ornament on the soffit, scrolled acanthus on the frieze and a dentil-cornice. The fireplace has an overmantel made up of carved fragments, some perhaps old, with four panels containing cartouches painted in modern times with shields-of-arms.

The S. windows of the Library contain heraldic and other glass reset in 1916. It is presumably that (except 4 below) mentioned by Cole in the windows of the Gallery in the Master's Lodge, probably the long building shown by Loggan with an oriel-window. The arms etc. are as follows: E. window, (1) quarterly of sixteen, Neville, Clarence, Pole, Hastings, Earl of Warwick, Beauchamp, Monthermer, Montagu, Peverel, Hungerford, Clare, Spencer, Moels, Moleyns, Botreaux and Cornwall, for Henry Hastings, 3rd Earl of Huntingdon, K.G., but with the quarters misplaced and some back to front, all in a strapwork cartouche with a coronet; (2) five apparently unrelated quarterings including the arms of William Bruges, Garter King of Arms, 1415–50, and (unidentified 17), in a strapwork cartouche with a coronet. Second window, (3) of Edward Seymour, Duke of Somerset, quarterly of six, Seymour marriage augmentation, Seymour, Beauchamp of Hache, Esturmi, Mackwilliam, and Coker, in a strapwork cartouche with a coronet; (4) the Tudor Royal arms in a strapwork cartouche with a crown above and two ostrich feathers below, and motto, 19th-century. Third window, (5) the figure of St. Lawrence in chasuble and amice holding book and gridiron; (6) kneeling angel in robe holding sceptre, book above. Fourth window, (7) quarterly of eight, Vere, Trussell, Colbrooke, Archdeacon, Sergeaux, Badlesmere (damaged), Sanford, and Bulbeck; (8) of William Somerset, 3rd Earl of Worcester, Somerset quartering Herbert and Woodville, with Garter and coronet. Fifth window, (9) nimbed figure of a king holding a cross; (10) nimbed figure of St. Edmund the Martyr, with book and arrow. The above, (5), (6), (9) and (10) late 15th-century, much restored, the remainder, except (4), late 16th-century.

The passage-way immediately E. of the Library is lined with modern panelling incorporating four 18th-century Corinthian pilasters on pedestals from the English church of St. Mary at Rotterdam.

On the first floor, the E. room is lined with mid 18th-century panelling with a moulded dado-rail; the contemporary doors are of two panels. Adjoining it on the W. are a bedroom and lobby and, beyond, a sitting-room, which has the N. and W. walls and part of the S. wall lined with reset oak panelling of *c.* 1600. A late 16th-century clunch fireplace in the N. wall has moulded jambs and a four-centred arch in a square head with a cornice-shelf above; the overmantel is made up of 17th-century and modern materials. W. of the sitting-room, in the adjoining bedroom and passage, the 15th-century moulded wall-plates on the outer walls are exposed.

The *East Range* is of one and two storeys with attics, with the N. half containing the Hall, the S. half the Butteries with the Combination Room on the first floor, and a continuous run of attics from end to end. It is of red brick, consisting of bricks of $9 \times 4\frac{1}{2} \times 2$ ins., four courses measuring 11 ins., with clunch dressings and ashlar quoins to the S.E. angle. The roofs are slate and tile-covered. The Hall is said to have been built in 1519 in an account of the College written some forty-five years later; the part S. of the Hall is of a different build and slightly earlier. In 1586 the Hall was wainscoted at the expense of Edward Lucas and was repanelled in 1714, when 'new ceiled and paved and glazed'; the Combination Room having been formed in the present position in 1712, the double staircase to it from the Hall was contrived in the same period.

The *Hall* (25 ft. by $56\frac{1}{2}$ ft. including the Screens $6\frac{1}{4}$ ft. wide) has brick plinths continued from the adjoining buildings but stepped up from the Chapel, a simple stone eaves-cornice to the E., a gabled N. end, and an embattled parapet to the W. (but see historical introduction). On the N. is a single-storey modern annexe. The Hall is lit by three windows on each side. Those on the E. are of early 16th-century style, being of three cinquefoiled lights in a four-centred head with a label, but much restored. Those on the W. are in the main original; the northernmost is of four cinquefoiled and transomed lights in an elliptical head with a label with carved headstops, that to the S. defaced; the other two windows are similar in design to those opposite but shorter and with 19th-century carved headstops to the labels. The original W. doorway to the screens-passage has moulded and shafted jambs with moulded caps and bases and a moulded four-centred arch under a square label with trefoiled spandrels carved with paterae; over it is a 17th-century carved achievement of the Audley arms within a Garter with lion supporters and the motto 'Garde ta foy' in a panel with flanking scrolls (Plate 202). The restored doorway at the opposite end of the screens-passage has moulded jambs, four-centred arch and label; above it, formerly lighting the gallery over the screens and now blocked by panelling inside, is a late 15th-century window of two four-centred lights with a pierced spandrel in a four-centred head. Just N. of these two features a change in the kind of brick used for the walling is marked by a distinct almost vertical mortar joint; this doubtless indicates the end of the earlier part of the range. Removal of the stucco facing of First Court (1955) has revealed a gallery window and mortar joint, generally similar to the foregoing, in the W. wall.

On the ridge of the Hall roof, centrally over the screens-passage, is a lead-covered timber lantern built after 1810, probably between 1812 and 1815. It is in three rectangular diminishing stages surmounted by an octagonal spire with a weathervane. In the lowest stage are clock-faces to E. and W. and in each face of the two upper stages four and three-light windows respectively, in part blocked with boarding

The *Interior* of the Hall (Plate 199) has a flat plaster ceiling with enrichments of 1911. Above the ceiling the original timber roof remains largely intact; it is in seven bays, the seventh representing the penetration into the earlier building. The six N. bays are divided by pairs of principals with cambered collar-beams stiffened by arched braces; the principals, collars, braces and two purlins on each side are moulded (p. 396) and the collar in the fifth truss is embattled. Dividing the sixth and seventh bays, is a seventh truss similar to those just described but built against and forming a fascia to a robust plainer truss belonging, with the truss now in the S. wall, to the earlier building beyond to the S. The centre part of the Hall floor is paved with stone flags set diagonally with small square blocks of slate at the angles, the sides with plain paving, laid in 1714. The walls are lined up to sill-level and to some 3 ft. higher on the N. wall behind the dais with panelling of 1714; this has a plain panelled dado, a moulded dado-rail, and large bolection-moulded and fielded panels between the rail and the crowning cornice. Behind the dais it is divided into three bays by reused late 16th or early 17th-century carved fragments made up into Ionic pilasters with carved cherub-heads and pendent bunches of fruit on the shafts; in the bays, fixed to the head-rail, are modern cartouches painted with the arms of (a) Crowland Abbey, (b) Audley, for the College, (c) Stafford. The whole of the face of the N. wall above the panelling, up to the ceiling, is painted with an elaborate armorial (Plate 202) with *trompe l'œil* marbled Corinthian columns at the sides supporting a draped cornice. Centrally placed in a painted framing is an achievement of the Royal arms of 1707–14; to each side are two smaller achievements, one above the other: E., upper, of Thomas, Lord Audley of Walden, with a coronet and Audley beast supporters, lower, of Sir Christopher Wray; W., upper, quarterly of Stafford, i Woodstock, ii Bohun of Hereford, iii Bohun of Northampton, iv Stafford, in a Garter with a coronet and swan supporters, lower, of Howard, with a coronet and lion supporters. The painting was cleaned and restored in 1949.

The double staircase at the S. end of the Hall (Plate 199) is arranged as shown on the plan, with short returns of the panelling from the side walls screening the half-landings and upper flights. The stairs have close moulded strings, turned balusters, moulded handrails and square newels. The *Screen* and gallery-front contained between the staircases have an elaborate central feature made up in part of reused materials of the late 16th or early 17th century and incorporating a single doorway. This last is set in panelling contained within an arch with rounded head, moulded archivolt and imposts and a tympanum carved with ribbons and a cartouche containing the painted arms of the See of Ely. The arch is flanked by enriched Ionic pilasters, similar to those behind the dais, and elaborate foliage carving of the early 18th century in the spandrels. The elaboration of the gallery-front above consists of fragments including terminal figures, niches and a central cartouche. The flanking bays of both screen and gallery have bolection-moulded panelling similar to that of 1714 elsewhere in the Hall and repeated on the reverse of the gallery-front.

The gallery over the screens-passage has an open screen of

three bays between it and the Hall, with the pilasters dividing the bays based, structurally, on the gallery-front already described. The pilasters support a deep cornice below the ceiling. The wide centre bay contains an elliptical arch and the narrow side bays, at the head of the stairs, contain semicircular arches, all with moulded archivolts, keyblocks, moulded imposts and plain responds. The whole may be later than the woodwork below and represent a remodelling of 1757 when the Combination Room beyond was refitted. The gallery itself is lined with bolection-moulded panelling, similar to that in the Hall, with dado, dado-rail and entablature; flanking the doorway in the centre of the S. wall are pilaster-strips with fielded panels in the shafts, and reset above the doorway is a late 16th-century carved achievement-of-arms of Edward Lucas.

The Hall windows are mostly filled with 19th and 20th-century heraldic glass, but in the centre E. window is a small 16th-century shield of the arms of Audley impaling Grey quartering Hastings, Valence, Quincy, Astley, Woodville, Bonville, and Harrington for Thomas, Lord Audley, and his second wife Elizabeth, daughter of Thomas, 2nd Marquess of Dorset; this was given to the College by Cole in 1776 (*Monumental Inscriptions from Cambridgeshire*, edit. Dr. W. M. Palmer, 278). In the N.W. window is the shield of Cust quartering Brownlow dated 1833, for John Hume, son of John, 1st Earl Brownlow.

The screens-passage is lined with 18th-century panelling in two heights of panels. The N. side is divided into bays by panelled pilasters and additional supports to the superstructure; over the doorway in the centre is a carved cartouche, perhaps modern, with a faded painting of the College arms.

S. of the Hall-block, the external brickwork of the E. wall is much patched. The plinth and eaves are continuous from the Hall. S. of the doorway to the screens are two modern cellar-windows interrupting the plinth and on the ground floor five one, two and three-light windows, all of the 16th century except the southernmost, which is modern; they have four-centred or elliptical openings in square heads with sunk spandrels and moulded labels. On the first floor are three irregularly spaced windows, the first two similar to that over the screens doorway, the third similar to those below but of four paired lights with a heavy centre mullion. The W. side has the plinth and embattled parapet continued from the Hall (but see historical introduction) and contains one large four-light transomed window; the latter is a 19th-century copy of the N.W. window in the Hall, with the upper part lighting the Combination Room, the lower part a service-passage. Traces of earlier windows show in the newly exposed brickwork.

The S. end of the E. range has the ground floor concealed by modern additions; the red brick upper part has been refaced in modern times and the large chimney-stack at the apex of the gable rebuilt. On the first floor are two restored late 15th-century two-light windows with four-centred heads and similar to the others of the same date in the N. and E. ranges; on the second floor are three late 19th-century windows.

The *Interior* of the E. range S. of the Hall block has been almost entirely modernised on the ground floor and rearranged; only the ceiling-beams remain to show the position of the Butteries and the central passage between them. The kitchen-fireplace formerly against the S. wall has been removed and the fireplaces above supported on steel joists. The Kitchen is now in the modern annexe on the S.

The *Combination Room* (Plate 201) ($24\frac{3}{4}$ ft. by $21\frac{1}{4}$ ft.) on the first floor, adjoining the gallery over the Hall-screens on the S., is first referred to in this position in 1712. In 1757 it was completely refitted at a cost of £166. Newling was paid £93 for the wainscoting and floor, and Woodward for carving scrolls and the moulding round the fireplace. The plaster ceiling is of 1911. The walls are entirely lined with wainscoting with a moulded dado-rail, tall ovolo-moulded panels, and a modillion-cornice with dentil-like fret. The doorcase in the centre of the N. wall has an architrave, pulvinated frieze and pedimented cornice; the cases to the doors in the E. wall are with plain friezes and modillion-cornices. The fireplace has Portland stone slips within an enriched wood architrave-moulding with scrolled frieze and cornice-shelf. The overmantel contains a modern oil-painting on copper of the College, after Loggan, in a framing with foliated side-scrolls and a pedimented cornice. The subsidiary cornices in the room generally match the main cornice in design and enrichment. The woodwork throughout is of 1757. The windows contain early 19th-century heraldic glass consisting of four shields-of-arms surmounted by coronets; from the N., of (a) Lord Audley of Walden; (b) Lord Braybrooke, quarterly (i) Griffin, (ii) Brotherton, (iii) Howard, (iv) Audley of Walden; (c) Stafford, Duke of Buckingham, Woodstock quartering Stafford; (d) Griffin quartering Neville of Raby quarterly with Neville of Bulmer, for Richard Neville-Griffin, 2nd Lord Braybrooke.

The remainder of the S. end of the E. range is divided into two rooms. The *Small Combination Room* ($14\frac{1}{4}$ ft. by $18\frac{1}{2}$ ft.) to the E., approached through a narrow wall-passage from the Combination Room, has an open timber ceiling with a chamfered beam running N. and S. and a second of heavy scantling against the E. wall; the joists have been widened in modern times by the addition of roll-mouldings on either side. The walls are lined to within 2 ft. of the ceiling with panelling of *c.* 1600, of five panels in the height with an enriched frieze and small cornice; it is made up with some modern work. The clunch fireplace in the S. wall has stop-moulded jambs and four-centred arch in a square head with sunk spandrels. The oak overmantel supported on fluted Doric side-pilasters on panelled pedestals is in three bays divided and flanked by terminal figures; in each bay is a round-headed panel enriched with arabesque and the bracketed frieze is similarly enriched. The panelling, previously in No. 25 Magdalene Street (Monument (205)), was inserted in 1919.

The cloakroom adjoining the Small Combination Room on the W. retains a clunch fireplace with ovolo-moulded jambs and flattened three-sided head.

The main roof is original, in six bays divided by trusses simpler than those over the Hall, with the main timbers plain or only chamfered and the alternate trusses without braces. Only the E. half of the southernmost truss and part of the next survive. A seventh bay on the N. is now in the Hall block, over the screens-passage, and the trusses flanking it are referred to above with the Hall roof.

The *South Range* is of two storeys with attics. The N. side is faced with Roman cement and has clunch dressings; the river front is of red brick with entirely renewed stone dressings; the infilling of the walls is clunch. The roofs are slate-covered. It contains sets of chambers and was built in four sections in the second half of the 15th century, after 1470, the features of windows, doorways and fittings varying slightly from one section to another. The westernmost section was remodelled or rebuilt with the W. range in the 16th century. The attic rooms were added probably in the 18th century. At an unknown date all the external heads of the windows towards First Court were raised by the insertion of another stone-course at the springing, but leaving the rear-arches undisturbed.

The N. side has the plinth and embattled parapet continued from the flanking ranges (but see historical introduction). In the S.W. corner of the Court is a projecting stair-turret. The extent of the differing sections is indicated on the plan. The E. doorway has chamfered jambs and a moulded four-centred arch with a moulded label (p. 393), the second doorway moulded jambs and four-centred arch with traceried spandrels, the third doorway moulded jambs and segmental-pointed arch with traceried spandrels, and the fourth doorway, in the stair-turret, with chamfered jambs and four-centred arch with sunk spandrels in a square head; the last three are under square moulded labels. The windows are of one, two and three lights as shown on the plan; they have two or four-centred openings in square heads with sunk spandrels and labels, unless otherwise described below. The E. three windows had reveals of two hollow-chamfered orders, but the inner order has been cut away on the reveals thus creating eccentric openings. The next four have moulded reveals; the last of the four being in a different section of building has ogee heads to the lights. The eighth window has ogee lights similar to those in the preceding window.

Since the previous paragraph was written, removal of the stucco-facing in 1956 has revealed over the entrance to staircase 'F' a blocked opening, nearly square, with a rough segmental brick head, and over the entrance to staircase 'E' a small recess with a 15th-century clunch cinquefoiled head, possibly reset, and a Roman cement panel in the back with the modelled initial and date A 1813. Furthermore, a rough vertical joint in the brickwork has been disclosed close E. of the latter staircase.

In the first floor is a range of thirteen windows, including that to the stair-turret, placed above the openings below, except the ninth, tenth and eleventh which are set closer together; these last have elliptical openings whereas the rest have four-centred openings; all have moulded heads and reveals under square labels. The reveals and heads of the ground and first-floor two-light windows in the second section are being wholly renewed (1956).

The stair-turret is of two stages externally and three storeys, the uppermost stage rising above the adjacent parapets and embattled. The ground and first-floor wall-openings are described above; in the third stage is a single light window similar to that below.

The S. side was restored by Penrose in 1873, the wall heightened and the upper part of the chimney-stacks rebuilt. It has a chamfered plinth. Straight joints in the brickwork between the two chimney-stack projections towards the E. and in the plinth further to the W., where indicated on the plan, show the extent of the four sections of the building. The windows in the S. ends of the E. and W. ranges are described above; for the rest, all the windows are of one and two lights, except a four-light window on the first floor immediately W. of the E. projecting chimney-stack, mostly with four-centred openings in square heads with labels, and all entirely restored externally; four of those on the ground floor at the western end are transomed. At first-floor level, close E. of the second projecting chimney-stack from the E., is a stone outlet from the lavatory-recess described below.

The *Interior* of the S. range has been extensively modernised on the ground floor. Some of the two-centred rear-arches to the N. windows, at a lower level than the outer heads, as already described, remain visible. The open timber ceiling (p. 396) of the room E. of staircase 'D' is divided into four panels by heavy moulded cross and longitudinal beams mitred with similarly moulded wall-plates; the heavy joists are roll-moulded and laid flat. The main room on the opposite side of the staircase and approached from the entrance to staircase 'C' is similarly ceiled; the room opening from it on the W. contains a fireplace of the mid 18th century, with eared surround, plain frieze and cornice-shelf and modern eared overmantel enriched with rosettes and garlands.

On the first floor, the set W. of staircase 'F' has been modernised. The set W. of staircase 'E' was restored in 1952 and the original features left exposed. It retains the original arrangement of one large common room, with lavatory and garderobe, with small studies opening from it, one on the E., two on the W.; one of the last is now incorporated in the adjoining set.

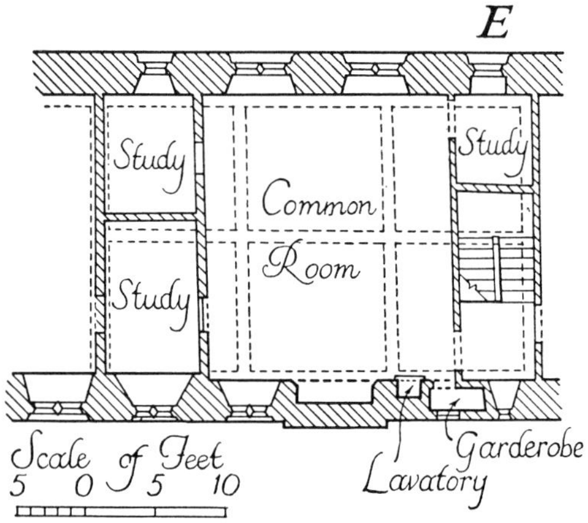

The partitions are timber-framed and retain their doorways to the studies and staircase and much of the original plaster filling between the studs; the plaster is decorated with a simple geometrical patterning scored on the surface. The doorways have slightly restored elliptical heads. The clunch infilling of the outside walls is exposed and the fireplace on the S. wall has chamfered jambs and a square moulded head under a brick relieving-arch. Immediately E. of the fireplace is a lavatory-recess with chamfered jambs and four-centred head with sunk spandrels; the sill, $2\frac{1}{4}$ ft. above floor-level, has a dishing with a central knob protecting the drain-holes; the sill, which

Interior, looking N. Panelling, 1714

Staircase, at S. end. 1714 and later

(32) MAGDALENE COLLEGE. Hall. 1519

W. front.

Exterior, from N.E.

(32) MAGDALENE COLLEGE. Pepys Building. Late 17th-century

(32) MAGDALENE COLLEGE. Combination Room, looking S.E. Fittings, 1757

(36) ST. CATHARINE'S COLLEGE. Panelled room in W. range. *c.* 1685

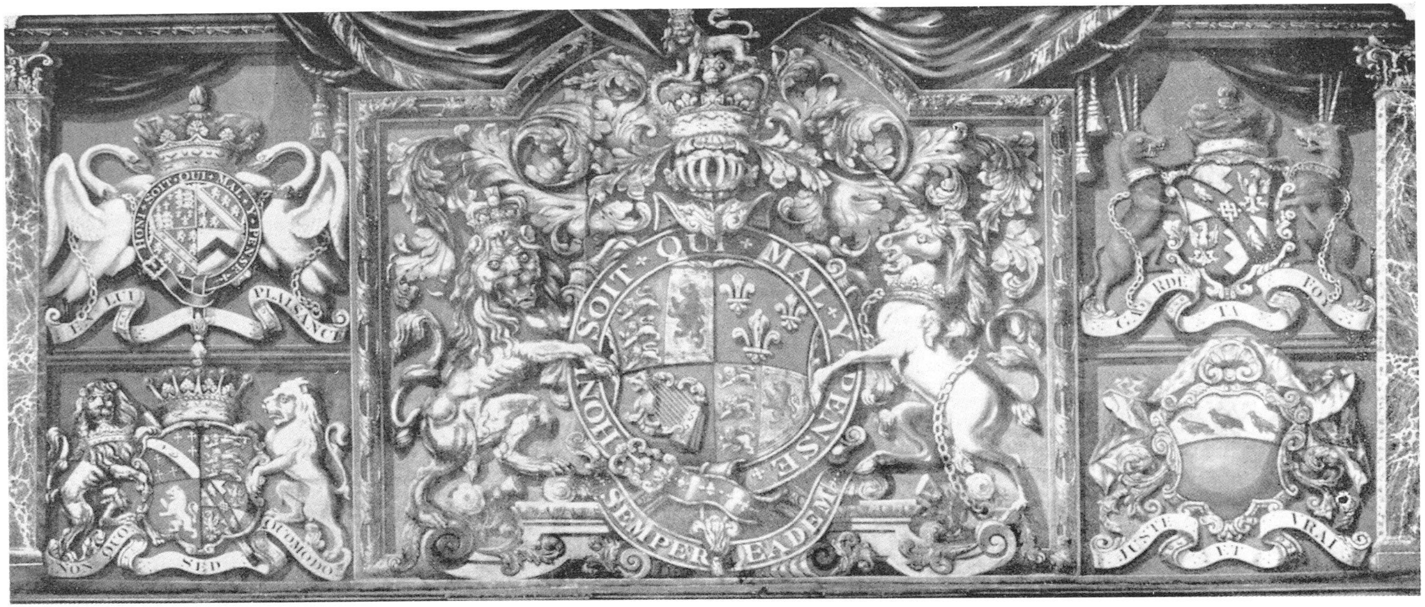

Hall. Painting on N. wall. 1714, restored

First Court. Achievement on W. range. 19th-century

First Court. Achievement on E. range. 17th-century

(32) MAGDALENE COLLEGE. Heraldic details.

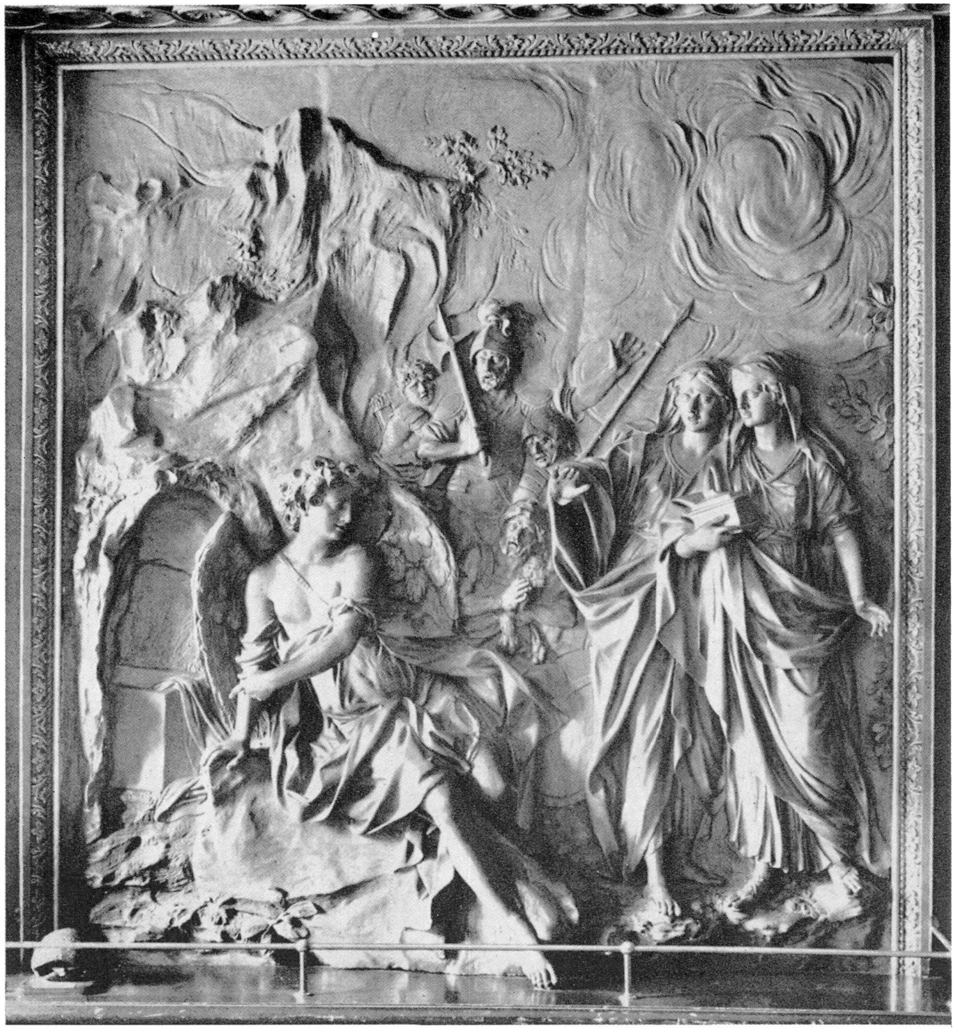

(32) MAGDALENE COLLEGE. Library. Reredos from Chapel. By W. Collins. 1756

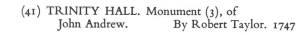

(41) TRINITY HALL. Monument (3), of John Andrew. By Robert Taylor. 1747

Ivy Court; N. range, from S. 1614–16 and 1670

Front to Trumpington Street. Late 14th-century, refaced, and later

(33) PEMBROKE COLLEGE.

(33) PEMBROKE COLLEGE. Chapel. Interior, looking W. 1663–65

(33) PEMBROKE COLLEGE. Chapel ceiling. 1664–65

originally projected, is now hacked back flush with the wall-face; the outlet shows externally. Close E. of the recess is a doorway to a garderobe in the thickness of the wall; it has been damaged but retains a chamfered elliptical head and iron staples for door-hinges fixed in the S. end of the adjoining timber-framed partition.

Over the whole set is an open timber ceiling with moulded cambered cross-beams supporting a simply moulded longitudinal beam (p. 396). The N. and S. wall-plates are moulded and embattled, the E. and W. plates only moulded.

During the restoration of these rooms and behind the later wall-plaster were found miscellaneous Latin exercises in black-letter on vellum and paper and also fragments of late 17th-century wall-paper with a figure of a man in contemporary dress. The splays of the N. windows are covered with graffiti, mostly mediaeval, including names, often repeated, and some imperfect verses. Among the names are John Comberton, John Clopton, Bryngton, W. Walsingham, John Fryer, T. Highfield, Webster (Augustine Webster was B.A., 1509, possibly the Prior of Beauvale), Nicholas Merley five times, once in Greek, (a Nicholas Marley or Morley, B.D. 1506–7, D.D. 1516–7, is recorded). Among the verses are '[Thomas] hoc ca[m]po de celso' (Highfield), 'q[ui] bon[us] e[st] vir,' (illegible) 'tertio [com]posuit anglic[us] e[st] p[ro] gene[re], mu[n]do monachu sic (?) compar i[n] isto ne[m]pe joco'; and 'O q[uam] formosu[m] Robert[us] e[st] lep[os] Antru[m]' (Cave), 'om[n]ib[us] i[n] reb[us] nullus ei s[e]c[un]dus (?)'.

The rooms in the third section, each side of staircase 'D', have open timber ceilings lower than that of the preceding section. Each ceiling has a stop-chamfered longitudinal beam and moulded wall-plates. The fourth, westernmost, section has been remodelled and in part rebuilt. The bedroom to the N.E. now encroaches into the third section but the wall-plates defining the original extent of the latter show in the ceiling; immediately W. of the cross wall-plate is a late 16th-century chamfered ceiling-beam. The room adjoining on the S. and the room at the S. end of the W. range contain chamfered ceiling-beams; between these two rooms is a narrow store-room, which perpetuates the position of a former staircase.

In Second Court (95 ft. by 104½ ft.), the *Pepys Building* (Plate 200), on the E., is of three storeys with attics and a cellar under the central block. It is a half-H on plan with the two wings extending eastward and rectangular stair-towers in the two re-entrant angles. The main W. front is of finely finished ashlar and the other walls are of red brick with stone dressings; the roofs are tiled. The little known of the building is outlined above, it is in the main a work of the last quarter of the 17th century. Loggan's view of *c.* 1690 shows none of the existing carvings on the W. front, and although it is to be inferred from the title that the engraving anticipated completion of the building (cf. Loggan's view of Clare College), some of the enrichments would seem to be later additions. The Pepys Library was not installed here until 1724 after the death of John Jackson, Pepys' nephew, and then largely at the expense of Arthur Annesley, 5th Earl of Anglesey.

The W. front (Plate 200) is in effect symmetrical although with slight irregularity in the setting-out, a peculiarity present in the layout of the whole building. The face of the central block is in five bays with an open arcade on the ground floor, an accentuated middle bay, plat-bands at first and second-floor levels, the lower moulded, a crowning frieze and cornice, and a balustraded parapet. On each flank are gabled projections both with rusticated quoins at the angles, a continuation of the moulded plat-band, and a chimney-stack at the apex; these projections express architecturally the wings lying behind; immediately over their inward facing slopes are secondary three-quarter gables flush with the face of the central block and with stacks at their apices.

The arcade (Plate 213) consists of a semi-elliptical arch in the centre and semicircular arches to each side springing from columns and half-round responds with moulded caps and bases; the archivolts are moulded and have very shallow keystones carved with animal and human masks. The six centre spandrels between the arches and the lower plat-band are carved in bold relief with elaborate acanthus foliage and two blank cartouches all applied and attached to the wall by iron dowels. Flanking the centre arch are Roman Doric pilasters, their caps mitred across the bay as an entablature with 'Bibliotheca. Pepysiana. 1724' painted on the frieze; superimposed on the Doric pilasters are plain Ionic pilasters on panelled pedestals rising the full height of the two upper storeys and supporting architraves and returns of the main frieze and cornice. At either end of the back wall of the arcade-walk are plain openings to staircases.

The first-floor windows of the central block are of two rectangular stone-mullioned and transomed lights with narrow moulded architraves, entablatures and sills. The middle window has extra elaboration of side-scrolls, a pulvinated frieze with central panel, console-brackets supporting the cornice and a curved pediment containing a cartouche painted with the arms of Pepys quartering Talbot and flanked by swathes of flowers. The second and fourth windows have male busts, after the antique, in light-coloured stone standing on the flat cornices. The end windows have pulvinated friezes and tall triangular pediments containing cartouches painted with the arms of Wray on the N. and Peckard quartering Ferrar (Master 1781–97) on the S. The aprons below these five windows are elaborately carved with drapery, garlands and cherub-heads, that under the centre window, of rather different character from the others, enclosing a panel inscribed with Samuel Pepys' motto 'Mens cujusque is est quisque'; all have the appearance of being cut on shallow slabs and reset. The painted heraldry and the motto are of the late 18th or early 19th century. The second-floor windows, of two rectangular stone-mullioned lights, have narrow architraves and sills; they are contiguous to the main frieze and cornice, which break forward over them. The main balustraded parapet above, which is divided into six bays by narrow pedestals with panelled dies, stops against the secondary gables.

The gabled flanking projections are alike; both have two windows on each floor, all of two rectangular stone-mullioned and transomed lights with architraves similar to those described above and with entablatures over the first-floor windows. The kneelers of the gables are cut to the section of a coved classical cornice.

The brick E. side has continuations of the plinth and first-floor plat-band returned from the W. front, but in brick with stone dressings, flush stone quoins at all salient angles, stone window-openings and a coved eaves-cornice in plaster. The wall-face above the plat-band is set back behind that below. The two wings, the two stair-towers and the middle part of the wall of the central block are gabled to the E., but the walls of the last three rise well above eaves-level before the start of the gables; below the middle gable at eaves-level is a relieving-arch two courses deep and of shallow curve spanning the whole width of the bay. On the ground floor, the windows in the wings, as shown on the plan, are of two rectangular transomed lights; the others are of two lights placed high in the wall; in the E. wall of the S. stair-tower is a modern doorway. All the first-floor windows, over those below, are similar to those just described in the wings. Those in the top stages of the stair-towers and the pair in the middle gable again are of two lights. All these windows have narrow architraves. In the roofs are four dormer-windows.

The N. and S. ends are alike, with continuations of the plinth and first-floor plat-band from the E. side, and a coved plaster cornice; in the centre the main wall is continued up through the roof to form the front wall of a gabled dormer-window. The arrangement of the ground-floor windows shown on the plan is repeated on the first floor; the windows are similar to those in the E. end of the wings. In both the dormers is a four-light stone-mullioned window.

The *Interior* was extensively modernised in the 19th century. After the removal of Pepys' library in 1834, the first floor of the central block (21 ft. by 55 ft.) was divided by the insertion of partitions to form sets of rooms. The original fittings remaining *in situ* in the building include the two staircases, some chamfered ceiling-beams and a fireplace-surround. The staircases have close moulded strings, turned balusters, moulded handrails and square newels. The fireplace-surround in the N.W. ground-floor room has the slips faced with English 18th-century blue and purple delft tiles; it is of stone, with an architrave flanked by small panels of alternating design and mitred round a single panel in the head, a frieze with modern inscription 'Fay bien crain rien', and a cornice. The late 17th-century wood overmantel has a bolection-moulded panel with panelled side-pilasters. The walls of the same room are lined with pieced-out panelling with dado-rail and heavy cornice. In the S. wing, the windows in the N.E. room have 18th-century panelled soffits, splays and seats and in the S. wall is a glazed door hung in two leaves on old hinges; the S.W. room has a panelled dado, small wood cornice and six-panel door, all of the 18th century.

On the first floor, in the N. wing, the E. room is lined with 18th-century panelling in two heights of panels with a cornice; the early 19th-century fireplace has a reeded surround with rosettes in squares at the corners. The W. room contains a mid 18th-century fireplace-surround brought from Elsworth and inserted in modern times: it has grey marble slips, a carved wood architrave-moulding and scroll-brackets supporting a cornice-shelf. In the central block, the N. room is lined from floor to ceiling with late 17th-century bolection-moulded panelling with moulded dado-rail and cornice; that on the N. wall is in three heights of panels, on the other walls in two heights. The fireplace-surround in the same room is an addition and probably modern. In the S. room is a wood bolection-moulded surround to the fireplace, probably of the late 17th century.

The *Pepys Library* is in the S. wing, in the E. first-floor room. It contains twelve bookcases, of red oak, in all probability those referred to in Pepys' diary under 24 August 1666, 'then comes Sympson to set up my other new presses for my books'. They are all alike, with a squat lower section for folios and a tall upper section with shelving for quarto and octavo books, both with glazed doors hung in two leaves. Each case has a plinth-mould, a moulded offset between the two sections and a cornice, all elaborately carved and the last with a cartouche in the centre, painted with a class number. Two of the cases have angle-pieces, both consisting of a Corinthian pilaster surmounted by a small urn, to fill the gap between the upper sections when two cases are placed together at a right angle; to fill similar gaps when the cases are placed together in line, four tall bevelled mirrors in wood frames with shaped and carved heads are preserved. Matching the cases is Pepys' flat-topped, pedestal writing-desk, with drawers, glazed doors to the pedestals, and enriched mouldings. The fireplace in the same room has a wood bolection-moulded surround and the windows have shutters of fielded panelling.

Extending N. from the N.W. angle of First Court are a number of two-storey buildings arranged round a small courtyard, which incorporates parts of 19th-century cottages etc. previously on the site. Their building, remodelling and unification in 1911–12 was the work of A. C. Benson (President). They now contain sets of chambers. They include a length of some 60 ft. of 17th-century brick walling running parallel with and 78 ft. from the N. wall of the N. range of First Court.

The *Master's Lodge* stands beside Chesterton Road. It is of three storeys, with walls of grey-brown bricks and stone dressings. The foundation-stone was laid on 8 July 1835; John Buckler was the architect. It is built in a spare Tudor style. The plinths and parapets are plain. The stone-mullioned windows have square heads and labels; those to the principal rooms on the ground floor and to the staircase are transomed. The main front is to the S. while the main entrance is through a porch on the W.; over the porch entrance are carved a Tudor Rose and a portcullis.

Inside the house the rooms are lofty and well-proportioned. In the Drawing-room, to the S.E., over the double-doors to the Dining-room, is a reset early 17th-century overmantel in two bays divided and flanked by coupled Doric columns supporting a dentil-cornice with scrolled cresting; in the bays are geometrical panels and, below, the shelf and frieze are enriched with arabesques. On each leaf of the double-doors are fixed two cartouches, probably of the 19th century, painted with the arms of (a) the 1st Lord Braybrooke, quarterly of Griffin, Brotherton, Howard and Audley, (b) the 3rd Duke of Buckingham, Woodstock quartering Stafford, (c) Audley, (d) the 2nd Lord Braybrooke, quarterly of Griffin, and Neville of Raby and Neville of Bulmer quarterly. In the base-panels are linked addorsed profile-busts of women and angels, probably also 19th-century. In the Dining-room is a mid 19th-century fireplace-surround in the French taste of the mid 18th century.

The high *Boundary-walls*, perhaps of the late 16th century, enclosing Second Court on the N. and S., are of rough ashlar and rubble, largely reused, with chamfered plinths on the outer sides, that on the N. ragged, and the upper parts rebuilt in brick. The E. end of the N. wall has been rebuilt at an angle to leave access to a late 17th-century doorway adjoining the Pepys Building; this has rusticated head and jambs, moulded architrave, and plain frieze and cornice surmounted by a ball-finial on a pedestal flanked by ramped scrolls. In the W. end of the N. wall and in either end of the S. wall are three doorways, all alike and that to the S.E. probably of the late 18th century, with square heads, moulded architraves and stone panels above. The three panels contain recut inscriptions, 'Unum sufficit', 'Omnes honorate fraternitatem diligite', and 'In dies ad diem' the first and last apophthegms, the second from the Vulgate (*I Peter ii, 17*).

The wall continuing N. from the W. front of New Building, dividing the Master's Garden from the Fellows' Garden, and shown by Loggan in *c.* 1690, is of rubble; it extends about half-way to Chesterton Lane and is then continued by a modern wall.

In the boundary-wall to Magdalene Street, 24½ ft. N. of the N.W. external angle of First Court, is a late 16th or early 17th-century doorway with moulded jambs, four-centred head and square label; it is in the position of that shown by Loggan and no doubt the same, but reset in a length of rebuilt wall.

For the *Range* of houses on the W. side of Magdalene Street owned and partly in use by the College, see Monuments (201–211).

For the *Earthwork* in the Fellows' Garden, see Preface p. lxii.

(33) PEMBROKE COLLEGE stands on the E. side of Trumpington Street bounded on the N. by Pembroke Street, on the E. by Tennis Court Road and on the S. by the Master's Lodge and Garden of Peterhouse and Tennis Court Terrace. The walls are of ashlar and brick; the roofs are tile, slate and lead-covered. The Hall of Valence Marie or Pembroke Hall, now Pembroke College, was founded by Mary de St. Pol, Countess of Pembroke, Baroness of Wexford in Ireland, and of Montignac, Bellac and Rançon in France, daughter of Guy, Count of St. Pol, and widow of Aymer de Valence, Earl of Pembroke. The Royal Licence of foundation was granted by Edward III on 24 December 1347.

Already, in 1346, the Foundress had bought a narrow strip of land in the N.W. part of the present site and in 1351 this was nearly doubled in extent by the purchase of the adjoining strip on the S., making a total area measuring some 250 ft. from E. to W. by 110 ft. from N. to S. The date of the commencement of the College buildings is not definitely known and subsequent alterations have obliterated the architectural evidence for it, but the oldest part, Old Court, which occupied the N. half of the present First Court, was compressed within the short N. to S. dimension, suggesting that building was begun before the acquisition in 1389 of more land to the south. By 1363 reference is made to Pembroke Hall; further, permission was granted to the Society by Innocent VI in 1355, and by Simon Langham, Bishop of Ely, in 1365, to build a chapel, and again by Urban V in 1366 more specifically for a chapel with bell-turret within the walls of the Hall. A licence to celebrate in the vestry 'of the Chapel annexed to the College' granted by John Fordham, Bishop of Ely, in 1398 implies that the Chapel was at least far advanced, if not already completed. Thus the period covering the building of Old Court was perhaps at most from 1351 to 1398. The Foundress died in 1377.

Only the *West Range*, containing the *Gateway*, and the *North Range*, with the Chapel, now the Old Library, in the W. end, survive of Old Court and bound the present First Court on the N. and N.W. The Hall was in the E. range, with the butteries and the *Kitchen*, in part surviving, in the N.E. external angle. The Master's Lodge was in the S. range. In 1452 a Library was added over the Hall, the random relation of the windows to the Hall-buttresses below, which is so conspicuous in Loggan's engraving of the College, demonstrating that it was no part of the original scheme. The Hall was extensively refitted in 1634 and the Renaissance doorway to it shown by Loggan, now the entrance to the Fellows' Garden, is probably of that time.

In the 17th century the College was much enlarged by the addition of Ivy Court to the E. and Chapel Court to the S. of Old Court. In *Ivy Court* the N. range was begun in 1614 and finished in 1616 (A. Attwater, *Pembroke College* (1936), 63); in 1670 it was extended 32 ft. to the E. at a cost of £301. In 1653 the Court of Chancery confirmed to the College property bequeathed by Sir Robert Hitcham in 1636 and, in 1659, during the Mastership of William Moses (1654–60), the S. range, *Hitcham Building*, was begun; John

Young was chief mason and William Allenby chief bricklayer. Loggan shows that previously it was more uniform with the range opposite than now appears, before the gabled dormer-windows on the S. side of the latter were removed. The three western bays of the N. front to the Court are designed as a self-contained architectural composition and they and the adjoining bay differ from the others to the extent that a different period of construction has been postulated for them. However the relation of their floor-levels with the windows suggests only a remodelling, and it may be that this end was earmarked for the Master and so given greater distinction, an explanation that is supported by a College order of 1679 appropriating it to him. The change was made early, if not during building; Moses' disbursements (College Muniments, Framlingham Box I. 4) includes the entry, 'March [1660–1], spent on Mr. Mills when he came to take measure of the building and on Young and Allenby when they came to adjust their accounts, £11', and the style of the composition is comparable with the work elsewhere of Peter Mills, bricklayer, of London.

The *New Chapel* bordering First Court on the S. was built at the sole expense of Matthew Wren, Bishop of Ely 1638–67, partly on land previously occupied by St. Thomas' Hostel. Wren, a Fellow of the College and formerly a protégé of Launcelot Andrewes (Master 1589–1605), was released from the Tower after seventeen years' imprisonment in March 1659–60, and with little delay arrangements for providing the new building were begun. The land S. of Old Court had been acquired earlier, in 1389 and 1549, together with the lease in perpetuity of St. Thomas' Hostel in 1451. In 1662 the College redeemed a forty year lease of the last and thereafter the new Chapel was begun, to the designs of Christopher Wren, nephew of Bishop Wren. A contemporary model of it (Plate 37) is preserved in the College (see under Chapel fittings). On 16 May 1663 Mark Frank (Master 1662–4) contracted with George Jackson and Thomas Hutton of Cambridge, bricklayers, for the brickwork. In 1664 the roof was covered, and on 10 January 1664–5 Robert Mapletoft (Master 1664–77) entered into an agreement with Cornelius Austin and Richard Billopps and William his son of Cambridge, joiners, for the wainscoting. The building was consecrated by Bishop Wren on St. Matthew's day 21 September 1665. Subsequently it was extended eastward. A general bill for £3,658 was given in to the Bishop in December 1665 but the *Parentalia* (ed. 1750, pp. 44, 45) says that he spent over £5,000 upon the building. The old Chapel was not converted into the Library, now the *Old Library*, until 1690 when in all probability the present windows were inserted and the N. wall refaced, if, indeed, the building was not more extensively reconstructed; the books were transferred to it from over the Hall in 1693–7.

In 1664 the College decided to connect Old Court to the Chapel, then in building, by a cloister with chambers over, and applied to Bishop Wren for money for the project from Hitcham's bequest, of which he was supervisor. Work on *Sir Robert Hitcham's Cloister* was completed in 1666 at a cost of £467; meanwhile the cloister had been consecrated for burials at the time of the consecration of the Chapel.

At the same period the older buildings were in need of repair and work was done on them in 1664 and 1689. The dilapidation was such that in 1712 the College decided to expend Mr. Banckes' legacy upon refacing the side of Old Court to Trumpington Street with ashlar; in 1717 £283 was subscribed towards refacing the inner sides and £28 for ashlaring the Gatehouse. Subsequently and before 1733 a further £953 was spent on repairs. Later in the same century rebuilding was considered and a building-fund started in 1776, in memory of Thomas Gray, the poet. It was again seriously considered in 1862; instead £4,000 was spent on repairs, under the supervision of the architect, J. A. Cory, mostly on the Hall and offices, but this proved an interim measure. In 1874 the S. range of Old Court was entirely demolished and not rebuilt, the enlarged area so formed being the present *First Court*, and in 1875 Alfred Waterhouse was authorised, not without protest, to demolish and rebuild the whole of the E. range, including the Hall, screens and butteries, and the Combination Room adjoining the Hall on the S.

Most of the reconstruction and extensive additions in the College at this time were the work of Waterhouse, including the Old Master's Lodge, E. of Ivy Court, 1871–3, the *Range* S. of the Chapel, 1871–2, the new *East Range* containing the Hall, screens and dais begun in 1875, and the *Range* containing the *Library* and *Treasury*, S.E. of the Chapel, completed in 1877.

In 1880 the Chapel was extended one bay eastward by George Gilbert Scott and all the stucco removed from the outside and from the E. side of the cloister and the whole repointed and made to match. The way through to the Chapel from Old Court, by the cloister, being no longer used, the N. end was partitioned to form a vestry and about one-third of the width of the cloister divided off for stairs and offices. In connection with this work, the doorway opening into the cloister from Trumpington Street, shown by Loggan in the second bay from the S. and by subsequent artists further N., was removed and, at the same time, the chambers in the range were entirely replanned.

It appears that the College had in 1879 ordered the demolition of the Old Library, the original Chapel, but the order was rescinded upon strong representations from

G. G. Scott. New ranges in the French Renaissance style were built by Scott on the N. and E. sides of the former Paschal Yard, now *New Court*, E. of the old Master's Lodge, between 1880 and 1883; they front on Pembroke Street and Tennis Court Road. He also added the turret in the N.E. angle of First Court.

Alterations and additions undertaken in the present century include a new block of chambers between Ivy Court and the old Master's Lodge, by W. D. Caröe, the heightening of the Hall Range by a storey and attic containing chambers, and a new *Master's Lodge*, in the S.E. corner of the Fellows' Garden, completed in 1932, both by Maurice Webb.

Pembroke College, by including a College chapel in the 14th-century buildings enclosing the court, is an early example of the typical collegiate plan at Cambridge; but the architectural evidence of it has been almost destroyed by demolitions made within the last eighty-five years. The character of the surviving mediaeval ranges has been altered by 17th and 18th-century restorations. The New Chapel of 1663–5 is of much interest, being the first completed work of Sir Christopher Wren, and both it and the old Library contain notable 17th-century plaster ceilings and carved woodwork. The 17th-century cushions in the Chapel are rare survivals.

Architectural Description—*First Court* (92 ft. average by 130½ ft.) includes the areas of Old Court and Chapel Court and of the S. range of Old Court, as indicated on the plan. (For clarity this nomenclature is adopted here, although 'Old Court' is modern College usage for the whole area.) The ranges are of one and two storeys with attics, and with cellars below the N. range. The N. half of the W. range and the N. range are of the second half of the 14th century, but the walls have been entirely refaced and no features certainly of that date survive. The S. half of the W. range was built between 1664 and 1666.

The *West Range* (Plate 204) contains the *Gateway* towards the N. end. The mediaeval walls were ashlared early in the 18th century but Loggan's late 17th-century engraving of the College shows that the earlier design of the W. side was preserved. The W. entrance, perhaps of late 14th-century origin but entirely restored, has jambs and four-centred head of two orders, the inner moulded and the outer chamfered, and a moulded label. Over the arch and flanked by oriel-windows is a square stone panel carved with the arms of the College, Valence dimidiating St. Pol, flanked by scrolls and surmounted by an achievement of the Royal arms of George I. The two early 17th-century oriel-windows are three-sided, on deep moulded corbelling, and with embattled parapets and parapet-strings returned from the main wall; the S. corbelling may be original. They both have three stone-mullioned lights on the face and one light in each canted side. The E. archway has a segmental head of two chamfered orders springing from the abutting walls and may be mediaeval. The *Gatehall* (17¾ ft. by 10½ ft.) is plain; in the N. wall is a doorway, perhaps mediaeval but entirely restored, with chamfered jambs and wave-moulded four-centred head; the openings in the S. wall are modern.

The rest of the W. range has, to the street, an embattled parapet and parapet-string interrupted at about the centre by a gabled bay aligned on the S. range, now destroyed, of the mediaeval court and stopped on the N. by the gabled end of the Old Library and on the S. by the W. end of the New Chapel. The whole extent of the front is of ashlar and without a plinth or any continuous vertical return, except at the junction with the New Chapel; the heraldic feature and the paired oriel-windows alone serve to accentuate the Gateway. The only variations from the features shown by Loggan are in the W. window of the Old Library, described below with the N. range, and in the substitution of a window in the second bay from the S. for a doorway. The mediaeval walling faced with ashlar early in the 18th century was previously plastered; the 17th-century wall S. of the central gable was probably of ashlar from the first; a straight joint is visible at the juncture of the two works. The windows, as shown on the plan, are of two lights with four-centred openings in square heads and with deep casement-moulded reveals; they are without labels; the second and third windows from the S. are of the late 19th century and the others appear to have been restored in the same period. On the first floor are ten windows with segmental openings, otherwise similar to those just described. They are placed vertically above the windows below except in the gabled bay where, centrally above the fifth and sixth ground-floor windows, is a large three-light window with vertical tracery in a two-centred head with a label; this last window is modern but corresponds with that shown by Loggan and may be of mediaeval origin; the northernmost window is blocked. In the roof are eleven rebuilt dormer-windows. On the ridge are four stone chimney-stacks each of four conjoined octagonal shafts on a square base; the two to the N. are in the positions of those shown by Loggan, but all are of the late 19th century.

The side to First Court has a central gabled bay, corresponding to that on the W., representing the butt-end of the destroyed original S. range of Old Court and entirely faced in the 19th century. The mediaeval wall to the N. was refaced in 1717; it has a plat-band at first-floor level and an embattled parapet with moulded parapet-string. The wall-openings are shown on the plan. The doorway at the N. end to the vestibule to the Old Library, with continuously moulded jambs and round head under a moulded label, has an early to mid 17th-century oak door; this last probably indicates the date of the doorway before the refacing. The door is in two leaves, with a central pilaster and side half-pilasters on panelled pedestals supporting a full entablature enriched with a cherub-head and cartouches on the frieze; the sunk face of the pilasters is carved with knotted cords and cartouches and on the boarded tympanum is a late 17th-century cartouche with the carved arms of the College. The original wrought-iron keyhole-plate is fretted. The doorway to the Porter's Lodge and the next doorway to the S. have two-centred heads and moulded labels and they and the windows of this part may represent mediaeval features, although almost wholly refaced. The windows are of two lights, except one of a single light over the entrance to the Porter's Lodge, and all similar to

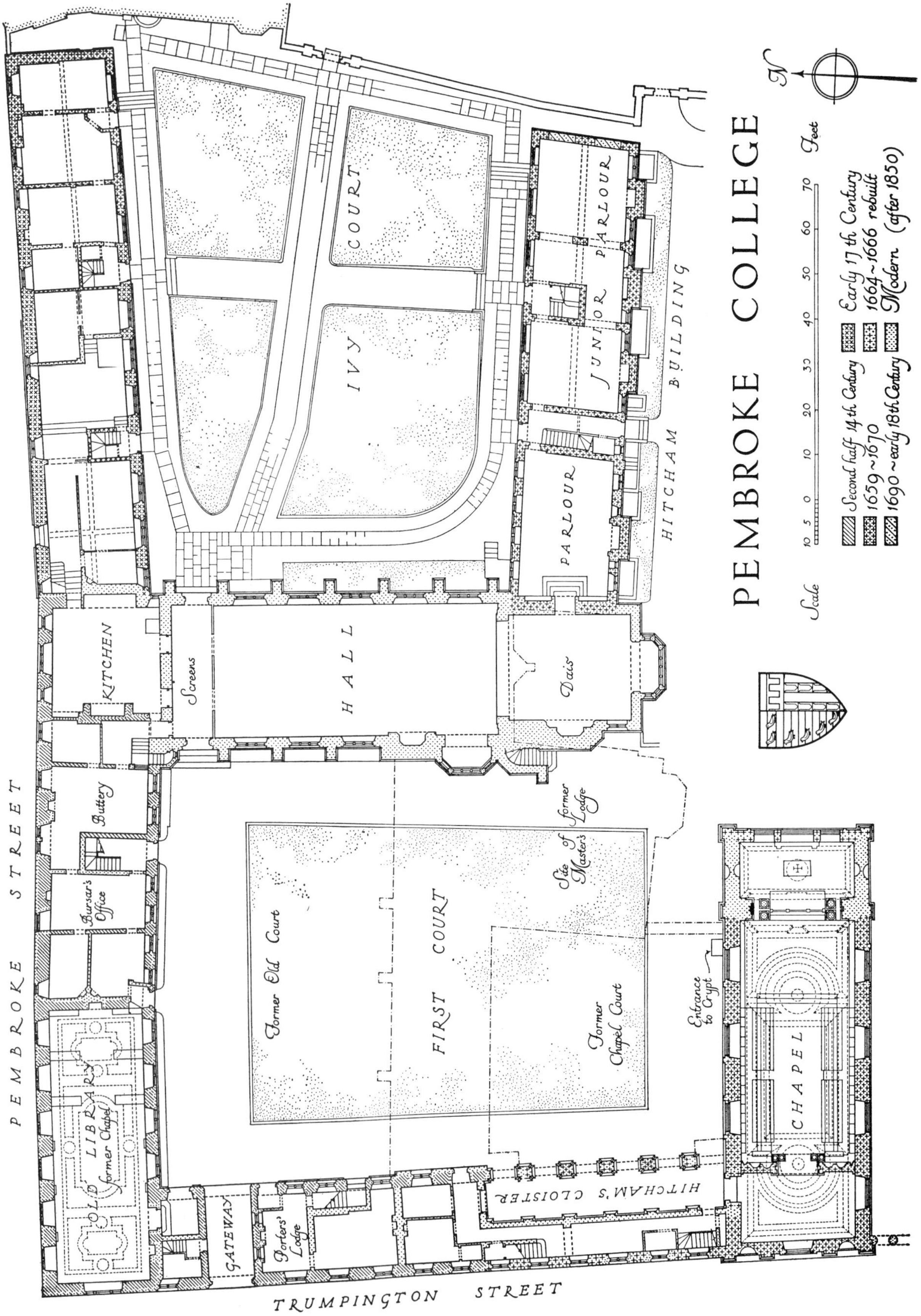
PEMBROKE COLLEGE
N
Scale
10 5 0 10 20 30 40 50 60 70 Feet
Second half 14th Century
Early 17th Century
1659~1670
1664~1666 rebuilt
1690~early 18th Century
Modern (after 1850)
IVY COURT
JUNIOR PARLOUR
PARLOUR
HITCHAM BUILDING
KITCHEN
Screens
HALL
Dais
Buttery
Bursar's Office
Former Old Court
FIRST COURT
Site of Master's former Lodge
Former Chapel Court
Entrance to Crypt
CHAPEL
OLD LIBRARY (former Chapel)
HITCHAM'S CLOISTER
GATEWAY
Porters' Lodge
PEMBROKE STREET
TRUMPINGTON STREET

those on the W. side. In the roof above are five rebuilt dormer-windows.

S. of the central gabled bay, *Hitcham's Cloister* has the arcading on the ground floor ashlared, brickwork above, a plain brick parapet-wall and a moulded stone parapet-string and coping; the arcade is of six bays divided by squat Tuscan pilasters; the pilaster-caps, which support nothing, are continued as a plain plat-band. The openings have segmental heads with moulded archivolts, keystones, moulded imposts and plain responds with bases returned from those of the pilasters. Only the four centre bays are original; the two flanking bays are late 19th-century extensions made possible by the removal of small forebuildings. On the first floor are five one and three-light modern or restored windows with square heads; between the third and fourth and centrally over the middle pilaster is a square stone panel carved with the achievement-of-arms of Hitcham. On the roof are five dormer-windows in late 17th-century character but probably of the late 19th century. The chimney-stack on the external wall has been rebuilt.

The *Interior* of the W. range has been altered and largely modernised. (For vestibule to Old Library, see below.) On the first floor, the walls of the room over the Gateway are lined with early 17th-century panelling with some modern material divided into three bays on the N. wall by panelled Ionic pilasters enriched with foliated scrolls and supporting brackets carved with beasts' masks below a cornice. The modern fireplace in the centre bay has scrollwork panels above and similar panels in the frieze of the overmantel; the flanking bays are recessed for bookcases. The panelling on the other three walls stops at window-head level. The room adjoining on the S. has a dado made up with reused panelling; the fireplace-surround and overmantel are also made up, the reused material including pilasters similar to those just described. Most of this miscellaneous woodwork is probably from the old Hall and of 1634.

The round-headed doorway in the S. wall of the S.E. room over the Cloister that formerly gave access to the gallery in the Chapel has been blocked and made into a cupboard; it was probably approached by a stair in a small forebuilding in the S.W. corner of Chapel Court, of which the gabled roof is just visible in Loggan's engraving.

The *North Range* of First Court survives from the original College buildings, being the N. range of Old Court, but it has been so much repaired and refaced that for the most part only the core of the original walls remains.

The original Chapel, now the *Old Library* (60 ft. by 21¼ ft.) was remodelled upon conversion into the Library in 1690; the W. window inserted probably between 1534–7 and the S. buttress both shown by Loggan in *c.* 1681–2 have gone. The N. side is faced with brickwork with stone dressings probably of 1690; at the wall-head is a plaster cove and timber cornice, both restored. The S. side and W. end are faced with early 18th-century ashlar; the former has a plain parapet; the latter is gabled. It is lit by late 17th-century windows, six in the N. wall and four in the S., each of two tall stone-mullioned lights with four-centred heads and sunk spandrels in a rectangular moulded architrave. The gabled W. end has a flat coping and renewed finial at the apex; the W. window is of three lights in an architrave as before, but with a semicircular head to the centre light flanked by plain stone transoms in the side lights at the springing level. In the gable is a window of two lights divided by a shell-headed niche and all of the late 19th century; N. and S. lighting to the attics over the Old Library is provided by six and four gabled dormer-windows in late 17th-century style but probably entirely of the late 19th century.

The *Interior* of the Old Library has an enriched modillion-cornice and ceiling ((Plate 207) by Henry Doogood, plasterer. The ceiling is in three compartments with moulded borders (Plate 62), enclosing elaborate foliation in the boldest relief interspersed with putti, a centaur, birds and beasts, framing large panels with semicircular ends. The main central panel (Plate 62) has figures of putti at each end, one riding an eagle, the other proffering a basket of flowers, and at random on the field flying birds modelled almost in the round; centrally at the sides are roundels containing putti, one with a water jar and rod, the other with a cup and ball. The end panels, placed crossways, have shields in the ends bearing the date 1690 and are flanked by roundels modelled with piles of books.

High in the centre of the E. wall is a plaster achievement of the Royal arms of William and Mary flanked, on the N., by a shield-of-arms (faulty) of Valence, on the S., by a lozenge-of-arms of St. Pol, both in cartouches. Original bolection-moulded oak panelling with a crowning entablature lines the walls to half their height; it rises to a similarly panelled centrepiece against the E. wall to form a setting for the fireplace. This last has a late 19th-century Frosterley marble bolection-moulded surround in the late 17th-century style. The centrepiece has a curved broken pediment framing a cartouche containing the arms of the College and flanked by foliage festoons. The frieze, cartouche and festoons are cut in high relief and finely carved and pierced.

The two E. wall-cases and the two E. pairs of projecting oak bookcases are original and *in situ* (Plate 209, p. 152); the others have been dismantled and the ends reset against the wall-panelling, presumably in 1880–1 when the room was adapted for lectures. The bookcases have low moulded plinths, five heights of shelving in two bays on each side, and entablatures. The ends are each divided into two heights of bolection-moulded panels by a moulded dado-rail, the lower panel being flanked by elaborately carved and scrolled side-wings; the entablature has a curved pediment containing a cartouche and carving in high-relief on the frieze. The S. doorway, moved some feet to the E. in the late 19th century, is hung with a door in two leaves, each of three bolection-moulded panels. It opens into a vestibule in the W. range containing on the W. wall an early 17th-century slate tablet with Latin inscription commemorating William Herris, [1631], 'former Fellow of Pembroke College . . . now of the College of Heaven', in an alabaster frame carved with cherub-heads, a skull, scrollwork and an oval panel with the arms of Herris.

The brick cellars have been modernised, the attics also, but the latter contain, reset in the W. room, a wood elliptical tympanum with radiating fluting from the old Hall screen of 1634.

The rest of the N. range, E. of the Old Library, is faced on the N. up to the eaves with 19th-century tooled random rubble, some of it reused material, with ashlar dressings;

previously, Willis and Clark record, it was of old brickwork, roughcast as far E. as the Buttery and perhaps rather earlier than the clunch walling of the latter and the Kitchen. The S. side is of early 18th-century ashlar, but most of the dressings are subsequent renewals. The S. side has a plat-band at first-floor level and a parapet with moulded string and coping. A step down from W. to E. in the parapet at the junction with the Old Library reflects a slight alteration in the pitch of the roof

Bookcase in the Old Library, Pembroke College

behind, indicating the retention and remodelling of the old Chapel in 1690 upon conversion, as suggested above, rather than complete rebuilding. The ground-floor openings are shown on the plan; the doorways in the third and eighth bays have jambs and two-centred heads of two chamfered orders with moulded labels. In each of the six other bays and in each bay on the first floor, except the westernmost, is a two-light window with four or three-centred openings in a square head. The bay excepted contains a small loop-light, which lit the former vice adjoining the S.E. angle of the old Chapel. On the roof are six 19th-century gabled dormer-windows. The N. side has ground and first-floor windows of one, two and three lights generally similar to those in the W. range to Trumpington Street; only that next the westernmost on the upper floor varies, and it is largely original, with a single cinquefoiled opening in a square head. Lighting the cellars are four 19th-century windows. Rising above the plain eaves are three brick chimney-stacks; they have each a square shaft set diagonally on a weathered pedestal-base with crow-stepped gable to the front; the shafts have been rebuilt but the bases are of the early 17th century, restored. On the roof are four late 19th-century gabled dormer-windows, and two others with flat tops entirely modern.

The *Interior* of the N. range, E. of the Old Library, contains at the E. end the old *Kitchen*, which was modernised and heightened by taking in the first-floor room in 1880–1; the rest of the range is occupied by the Buttery and buttery-offices on the ground floor and sets of chambers above. In the cellars are some exposed chamfered ceiling-beams. The ground floor has been remodelled. On the E. wall of the Bursar's office is hung an 18th-century cartouche carved with the achievement-of-arms of Robert Trefusis, Fellow, died 1742. On the first floor, the W. room (Plate 210) is lined with oak panelling of *c.* 1630 extensively made up with modern panelling to match; it is of five panels in the height, with a frieze and dentil-cornice, and projects on the W. wall between fluted Doric pilasters on panelled pedestals. The two doors on the E. are in projecting cases with broken pedimented entablatures enriched with jewel-ornament on the frieze, with brackets with small turned pendants supporting the dentil-cornice, and pierced strapwork scrolls in the tympanum flanking a small central pedestal. A third door with similar doorcase in the centre of the W. projection opens into a cupboard. Further N., a small recess suggests the presence of an original loop opening into the Chapel, but the splays etc. are lined and entirely concealed by panelling. The surround to the fireplace in the N. wall is largely modern. In the S.W. corner of the same room is a circular recess, now with a domed head, lit by a loop-light, already described, just above floor-level; it is the only vestige of the vice from the old Chapel. The attics have been modernised.

The *East Range* of First Court is occupied by the late 19th-century *Hall* (29 ft. by 74¼ ft. including the Screens 9¼ ft. wide) and dais (23¼ ft. by 27¾ ft.) to the S. Reset in the latter is some of the 17th-century woodwork from the old Hall pieced out with modern material. The lower half of the walls is lined with panelling, in two heights, with carved frieze-panels and dentil-cornice. The lower panels, which are sub-divided into a geometrical pattern of panels, and the frieze are largely original. A panelled pilaster in the S.W. corner is dated 1634. Over the E. doorway is a carved shield-of-arms of the College enclosed in strapwork cresting, and incorporated in the modern doorcase are two panels with stylised foliage and, on one, Father Time and a second male figure. Over the dais fireplace is an oak overmantel in three bays divided and flanked by enriched Corinthian pilasters standing on a panelled

(33) PEMBROKE COLLEGE. Old Library ceiling. By H. Doogood. 1690

(34) PETERHOUSE. Chapel, interior looking N.W. 1628–32

(33) PEMBROKE COLLEGE. Old Library. Woodwork, 1690

(34) PETERHOUSE. Perne Library. Woodwork, 1641–48

(33) PEMBROKE COLLEGE. President's Room. Woodwork, *c.* 1630

(35) QUEENS' COLLEGE. President's Lodge; Dining-room. Woodwork, early 17th-century

W. range, W. side. 1674–79

Chapel, S. doorway. *c.* 1695

W. range, E. side. 1674–79

(36) ST. CATHARINE'S COLLEGE.

(40) TRINITY COLLEGE. Bishop's Hostel; exterior. 1670–71

(33) PEMBROKE COLLEGE. Hitcham Building; exterior. 1659

(32) MAGDALENE COLLEGE. Pepys Building. W. front. Late 17th-century

(40) TRINITY COLLEGE. Nevile's Court. N. range. *c.* 1610; remodelled 1755–6

(33) PEMBROKE COLLEGE. Chapel. Reredos. 1665

(36) ST. CATHARINE'S COLLEGE. Chapel. Reredos. 1699–1703

plinth carved with scrolls and monsters' heads and supporting an enriched entablature; each bay contains a shallow niche with a geometrical arrangement of small panels in the back and splays carved with arabesques, the semicircular concave shell-head having radiating fluting, all in a faceted frame with cherub-heads in the spandrels.

Fragments of woodwork from the old Hall and elsewhere, other than those already described, are preserved in different parts of the College. They include: in the Hall-block, on the first floor, in the S.E. room, an overmantel incorporating pilasters with foliated scrolls, grotesque mask brackets, etc., 1634, scrolled side-wings from the bookcases in the Old Library, *c.* 1690; in the adjoining room on the W., an overmantel incorporating a carved style, early 17th-century, scrolled side-wings from bookcases, as before, *c.* 1690, and two carved panels perhaps from the same source. Other side-wings are in a room on the first floor of staircase 'M' of Caröe's building.

The *New Chapel* (88 ft., including the E. extension 12¼ ft. and the Ante-chapel 14¾ ft. average, by 25¾ ft.) has Ketton and Portland stone ashlar E. and W. ends; the original N. and S. walls are of brick with stone dressings and the extensions of ashlar. The roof is lead-covered. The history of the building is given in detail above. It was designed by Christopher Wren, begun in 1663, roofed in 1664 and consecrated in September 1665. In 1880 it was extended by one bay eastward, the original E. end being moved and re-erected; the new work was consecrated on 25 March 1881; at the same time the N. doorway was moved a short way to the E. and all the plaster rendering stripped from the external brickwork, the last being given a spurious regularity by means of much false pointing.

The Chapel is classical in style, with a Corinthian order, and consists of a rectangular temple-like building pedimented to E. and W. It has a Portland stone ashlar stylobate projecting to support the pilasters, their Portland bases returning against a plain stone plinth. The entablature is continuous round the building; it comprises an ashlar architrave with two fasciae, a plain frieze of brick to the original side walls, ashlar elsewhere, and a timber modillion-cornice. On the ridge of the low-pitched roof, near the W. end, is a timber cupola. The form of the W. front (Plate 198, Frontispiece Part II) is based upon that of a pedimented tetrastyle portico but the Corinthian order consists of pilasters only set against the main W. wall; the architrave offends classical rule by being almost flush with the wall-face instead of the pilaster-face. The pilasters are irregularly spaced, leaving a wide centre bay containing a semicircular-headed window and narrower flanking bays containing plain semi-domed niches; the astragal below the pilaster-caps is returned across the full width of the front. The composition is perhaps inspired by Serlio's reconstruction of the 'temple by the river at Tivoli' (Sebastian Serlio, *Architecture*, ed. London, 1611, Bk. III, cap. IV, f. 15). The window has a continuous architrave and a moulded sill, this last capping a projecting panelled apron. Above and below the niches are plain rectangular recessed wall-panels. In the main tympanum is a cartouche flanked by fruit garlands and at the foot of the pediment are freestanding flaming urns on low pedestals.

The hexagonal cupola has a panelled base, a boldly projecting cornice supported on scroll-brackets flanking a rectangular window nearly filling each face, and a lead-covered dome. At the apex of the dome is a slender pedestal supporting the turned shaft to a wrought-iron weathervane. It is identical with that shown by Loggan and, no doubt, substantially original.

The rebuilt E. end has Corinthian pilasters clasping the angles; between them, the centre part of the wall projects slightly and contains the E. window which is tripartite, with a centre semicircular-headed light with moulded architrave flanked by shorter rectangular lights, the latter with plain sunk wall-panels above. The window has a moulded sill capping a large fielded panel in the apron below. In the main tympanum is a round window with moulded architrave; on the pediment are, at the apex, a late 19th-century cross on an enriched base, and, at the foot, two flaming urns.

The N. side has the western end concealed by the adjoining building of Hitcham's Cloister; the eastern bay, being the late 19th-century extension, is flanked by Corinthian pilasters and contains a pedimented niche; in the intervening length of brick wall are three original windows. These have semicircular heads, moulded architraves with keystones, and flanking scroll-brackets supporting straight cornices, all of stone. The sills cap panelled aprons which extend down to the plinth and have stone surrounds to brick filling; the apparent thinness of the surrounds is no doubt the effect of the contrast of materials revealed by removal of the plaster, the original appearance being indicated in the model (see Fittings). Below the W. jamb of the N.E. window is a brick segmental relieving-arch which doubtless indicates the position of the doorway to the annexe shown by Loggan and now destroyed. The lead rain-water pipes have original heads cast with the letter W. The S. side of the building is similar in detail to the N. but with four original windows.

The *Interior* has a lofty arched opening demarcating the original building from the extension, the two now forming the body of the Chapel and the Sanctuary respectively. The arch springs from the entablature of free-standing Sarravezza marble Corinthian columns, with stone caps, bronze bases and black Dent marble sub-bases, and their pilaster-responds; the whole structure is of 1880. The lower part of the W. bay is screened to form the Ante-chapel, the upper part remaining open to the Chapel as the organ-gallery. The elaborate plaster ceiling is original (Plate 206); the middle part, which is raised to a higher level than the shaped end panels by a deep cove, has rounded ends of rather greater circumference than the semicircle and in it is a recessed rectangular centre panel surrounded by a modillion-cornice and a framing of scrolled foliage, the framing being continued round circular panels at the extremities; the shaped end panels contain branches of bay-leaves. The side walls are modelled above sill-level with plaster panels in enriched bolection-moulded frames and, over the semicircular rear-arches to the windows, with elaborate compositions of ribbons and festoons surrounding female masks. The ceiling of the Ante-chapel, perhaps of the 19th century, is divided by plaster mouldings into three rectangular panels, the centre one containing a circular laurel wreath and both the end ones an elliptical wreath of leaves and flowers.

The timber screen between the Chapel and Ante-chapel (Plate 205) has a main entablature continued from the panelling on the side walls (see Fittings) and supported by free-standing coupled Corinthian columns flanking the central entrance-opening and by coupled pilasters at each end. The return-stalls are an integral part of the screen and consist of paired semi-domed niches with a large carved cartouche applied to the central spandrel and flanked by swags extending over each niche (see also Fittings). The main entablature breaks forward over the columns, less over the pilasters, and supports a panelled gallery-front with enriched capping similarly articulated. The responds of the rectangular entrance-opening consist of Corinthian pilasters supporting a lintel with a panelled soffit enriched with laurel wreaths.

Below the Chapel is a crypt, normally inaccessible, where lie the coffins of several Masters, including Bishop Wren, and others.

Fittings—The fittings are all of *c.* 1665 unless otherwise described. *Chair* (Plate 44): of elm and beech, with turned posts and rails, the spaces in the back, below the elbow-rails and between the front rail and stretcher containing numerous turned spindles, 16th-century, said to have belonged to Bishop Ridley (martyred 1555) bequeathed to the College in 1928 by the widow of W. H. Ridley. *Communion-rails* (Plate 7): across the archway to the E. bay—of oak, with moulded and foliated top-rail, moulded base-rail, and enriched turned and twisted balusters divided into bays by dies with pendants of flowers carved on the face and sides, shortened and reset in the late 19th century, parts are now in the church at Tarrant Hinton, Dorset. *Cushions* (Plate 230): twenty-eight, of turkey-work with the arms of the See of Ely impaling Wren in a cartouche sur-surmounted by a mitre, coloured. *Doors* and *Doorcase:* To N. doorway—outer door, in two leaves each of three bolection-moulded panels, inner door of six bolection-moulded panels and hung in panelled doorcase. *Gallery:* (for front, see description above). *Model* (Plate 37): kept in College Treasury—of New Chapel, in pinewood, apparently constructional, the roof-cover, now missing, being removable to show roof structure, found in 1923 in the organ-gallery, probably contemporary with the building, badly damaged and with much missing. *Organ:* on W. gallery—in gallery-front, case with two small towers of pipes with deep entablatures divided by twin panels of pipes, all with carved and pierced pelmets and spandrels; main organ-case, with tall central tower of pipes linked by panels of pipes and by pierced and scrolled cresting to shorter flanking towers, the towers with deep angular entablatures and they and the panels with pierced pelmets and spandrels, both cases made by agreement dated 6 December 1707, to be completed in eight months for £210 and the original organ to be removed to Framlingham church, organ reconstructed in 1863 when 'Bernard Smith fecit' was found inside one of the pipes. *Painting:* In reredos—on canvas ($5\frac{3}{4}$ ft. by $4\frac{1}{4}$ ft.) in gilded frame, the Entombment (Plate 223), after Baroccio, given by Dr. Richard Baker, 1797; from the collection of Sir Joshua Reynolds; the original of 1582 an altar-piece at Senigallia. *Panelling* (Plate 33): In Chapel—lining E., N. and S. walls to sill-level and incorporating stalls, succession of plain tall and narrow semicircular-headed panels only slightly recessed in plain framing with continuous deep crowning entablature with modillion-cornice, in the body of the Chapel the alternate spandrels with large and elaborately carved applied cartouches incorporating cherub-heads and masks and linked by festoons to foliated pendants in every other spandrel, in the Sanctuary the cartouches omitted and the festoons and pendants, of rather finer detail, repeated; the seats, one to each panel where shown on the plan, with shaped and scrolled arm-rests projecting from the panel-framing; by Cornelius Austin, Richard Billopps and William his son, agreement dated 10th January 1664–5, except the lengths of eight late 19th-century panels E. of the N. and S. stalls replacing the panelling moved and reset in the Sanctuary. In Ante-chapel—lining the walls from floor to ceiling, in three heights of moulded panels with a frieze between the two upper heights, with Corinthian pilasters flanking the E. opening and in the middle of the W. wall and quarter-pilasters in the angles. *Paving:* In body of Chapel—of black and white marble squares set diagonally, black marble steps, laid after 10 January 1664–5 and before 21 September 1665. In Ante-chapel—of square flagstones set diagonally with small slate or black marble square insets. *Piscina:* In Sanctuary—reset in S. wall, of clunch, with moulded jambs, sub-cusped cinquefoiled two-centred head, trefoiled spandrels, and square dishing to drain, late 14th or early 15th-century, much weathered. *Prayer-desk:* of oak, with acanthus-enriched framing to sloping desk, square legs carved with pendent flowers and ending in dolphin-masks spouting beast-paw feet, the sides and ends with infilling of elaborately pierced carving, matching the communion-rails but possibly of later date. *Reredos* (Plate 214): of oak, with flanking Corinthian pilasters on pedestals supporting an entablature with modillion-cornice and broken pediment framing a cartouche and swags, all framing the painting of the Entombment (see above) bordered by carved garlands of fruit and flowers, the whole removed from the original E. end and reset. *Seating:* Stalls and desks, as shown on the plan (see also above), in two blocks in two tiers on each side, the back stalls opposite the four passage-ways with misericorde-seats carved with acanthus-leaves, desks with panelled fronts and shaped ends with carved scrolls at feet, modern desks added in front; return-stalls with panelled fronts to desks, as before. *Tapestry:* In Sanctuary, on N. wall—head of Christ, perhaps cut from larger scene, 17th-century, inscription below added to form composition reminiscent of the group of English representations of the emerald *intaglio* portrait sent by the Great Turk to Innocent VIII (1482–94).

Ivy Court (118 ft. by 90 ft. average) lies to the E. of First Court and is bounded on the N. and S. by ranges of chambers and offices extending E. from the Hall-block; the greater part of the E. side is bounded by the wall of the Fellows' Garden. The two ranges are of two storeys with attics and lofts above; the walls are of red brick in mixed bond with Ketton stone dressings; both brick and stonework have been in part renewed; the roofs are tile-covered.

The western two-thirds of the *North Range* (Plate 204) was built probably between 1614 and 1616 and the E. third added in 1670 in matching style. The builder of the addition was John Howard, bricklayer; Thomas Silk was the carpenter; Robert Grumbold, mason, supplied the stone, worked and set it (Treasury Accts. II, 157, transcript). In 1768 the range was damaged by fire. The S. side to the Court has a plinth with moulded stone weathering and plain eaves. The earlier bricks average 9 × 4 to $4\frac{1}{2}$ × 2 ins., four courses measuring 10 to $10\frac{1}{2}$ ins. in height; the later bricks are very slightly larger. The arrangement of doorways and windows is shown on the plan; on the first floor, windows are set centrally over each opening below except over the E. doorway where the wall is unpierced. The stone doorways have semicircular heads, plain keystones and imposts, stop-chamfered jambs and rectangular labels; the ovolo-moulded stone-mullioned windows have square heads and labels and are of three lights except the westernmost on each floor, of two lights. The relieving-arches over the earlier windows are high and pronounced, on the ground floor nearly semicircular, above, four-centred; those over the later windows are less conspicuous and of segmental form. Near the wall-head are six S-shaped wrought-iron wall-anchors; they and the eleven hipped dormer-windows with timber casements of two and three lights are of the 18th or 19th century.

The E. end is gabled and has a plinth similar to but at a higher level than that on the S. side. On both the first floor and in the gable is a three-light window, similar to those on the S., with a single light, to the loft, in the gable apex and now blocked.

The N. side to Pembroke Street has a plinth, which is concealed towards the E. by the rise of the ground. The arrangement of the openings shown on the plan is repeated on the first floor, a window occurring over the door, and with the addition of a single-light window between the third and fourth openings; all the windows are similar in detail to those on the S., but the westernmost are modern or rebuilt. Carried up flush with the main wall-face are seven two-light stone-mullioned and gabled dormer-windows; the gablets are of brick with flat stone copings returned horizontally over shaped stone kneelers and with restored finials at the apices. Between the dormers and also flush with the wall-face are five brick chimneys with tall rectangular bases and lofty rebuilt stacks.

The *Interior* of the N. range contains stop-chamfered ceiling-beams. On the ground floor, the second room from the E. contains an old fireplace with moulded stone jambs and square head; the oak overmantel is made up with carved panels and a fluted tympanum from the Hall screen of 1634. The room next W. has a stone fireplace with moulded jambs, much worn, and four-centred opening in a square head. The rest of this floor westward contains kitchen-offices and has been modernised. The containing walls of the two staircases are original and have the timber-framing exposed.

On the first floor, the E. room has the walls lined with bolection-moulded panelling of the late 17th century, with dado-rail and cornice; the section of the mouldings is similar to that of the panelling in the Old Library. The two doorways in the W. wall have bolection-moulded architraves and contain two-panel doors; between them is a third doorway, similar in detail but larger and with the door in two leaves. Against the S. wall is a cupboard made up with panelling from the Old Hall. The fireplace in the N. wall, of the mid 17th century, has a stone surround with panelled side-pilasters, a panelled frieze and a cornice. The bedroom next N.W. has a wood bolection-moulded fireplace-surround of *c.* 1700 and the adjoining vestibule contains a cupboard composed of reused late 16th or early 17th-century panelling. The room W. of the E. staircase has the E., S. and W. walls lined with mid 17th-century panelling, four panels high, divided into bays by enriched Ionic pilasters supporting an entablature with blocks and rosettes in the frieze and a dentil-cornice. On the N. wall is 18th-century panelling, with an eared panel over the flat stone fireplace-surround. The first-floor rooms to E. and W. of the W. staircase both contain original stone fireplaces with moulded jambs and four-centred arches in square heads. The former room contains reused early 17th-century woodwork and two mid 17th-century doorcases with entablatures with frieze-panels, flanking drapes and dentil-cornices. The latter room has a mid 17th-century fireplace-surround with coupled side-pilasters flanking semicircular-headed panels with frames chamfered to give a false effect of perspective and a similar treatment between pilaster-strips in the overmantel; elsewhere the walls are lined with 18th-century panelling with a dado-rail and dentil-cornice. In the attics are three original stone fireplaces similar to those just described, and some 17th-century four and six-panel doors. In the roof of the lofts are vestiges of the upper tier of small dormer-windows shown by Loggan and comparable with those existing over the S. range.

The *South Range* of Ivy Court was built in 1659. The N. side has a flush wall-face and is apparently of one build from end to end. The bays containing the doorways separate the front into three parts, symmetrical in extent, but the W. part with a self-contained architectural composition differing from the others; these last are uniform; the W. entrance-bay, being at the point of change, partakes of both designs. The external difference is the expression also of an internal difference in floor-levels, the rooms to the W. being loftier than those to the E. The six easterly bays have a plinth with stone weathering and plain eaves and contain openings as shown on the plan; the doorway and windows are similar to those in the opposite range; the windows on the first floor are uniform in style and disposition with those below, with a two-light window occurring over the doorway. The stone dormer-windows are similar in detail but shorter than those on the floor below and in the same sequence; they are set in brickwork carried up flush with the main wall-face and surmounted by gablets with shaped stone kneelers, flat copings and finials, all similar to those on the N. side of the opposite range. High up in the roof, alternating with the main dormers, is a range of six small dormer-windows lighting the lofts. The seventh bay repeats the fourth but with a two-light transomed window set high on the first floor.

The W. part (Plate 212) contains four windows in the width, the two centre coupled, projecting slightly, pedimented and elaborated to form a centrepiece. Much of this last and all the dressings are of stone, recently much refaced. The plinth is continuous from further E.; a plat-band over the ground-floor windows and an eaves-cornice extend the width of the four windows. The windows to the ground and first floors are of two transomed lights with architraves; mullions, transoms and moulded architraves have sunk faces. The coupled windows, based upon an upward extension of the plinth, are linked, horizontally, by brick panels with stone semicircular-arched heads with keystones and panelled spandrels and, vertically, from ground to first floor, by a panelled apron between the plat-band crossing the head of the lower windows and the continuous sill of the upper two windows; the upper windows are themselves linked by a frieze to a pediment, springing from the eaves-cornice, which surmounts the centrepiece so formed; in the tympanum is a cartouche carved and painted with the arms of Hitcham. The centrepiece is continued up into an ashlar-faced dormer with segmental crowning pediment, the dormer-window being of three stone-mullioned lights of unequal width. To each side, over the flanking bays, are smaller steeply pedimented dormers of brick and ashlar flush with the main wall-face and containing two-light windows.

The S. side has a plinth, as on the N., and moulded eaves. It is divided unequally by boldly projecting chimney-stacks surmounted by modern shafts; a fifth stack corbelled out from the wall has been added subsequently. Set high in the third stack is a stone panel carved with the arms of Hitcham. The windows are of one and two stone-mullioned lights, transomed towards the W., and similar respectively in detail to those in the wall opposite. The doorway is modern, with the window beside it on the W.; the four ground-floor windows W. of the latter have been altered; the stonework of all the others has been renewed and the brickwork generally much patched. In the roof are six hipped dormer-windows of two and three lights.

The E. end is gabled and has a stone coping with a finial; on the ground floor are two blocked openings with segmental brick arches; on the first floor are two three-light stone-mullioned windows with some of the lights blocked; in the gable is a three-light window to the attic with a single-light above it lighting the loft. The W. end adjoins the Hall-block.

The *Interior* of Hitcham Building has the *Senior Parlour* (31 ft. average by 20½ ft.) on the ground floor lined with panelling of 18th-century character but incorporating much modern work. The stone fireplace has moulded jambs and square head. The original E. staircase is built with a solid partition between the flights. The W. staircase has turned balusters, moulded hand-rail and square panelled newels with shaped finials; it is of the mid 17th century, repaired.

On the first floor the main room between the staircases is lined with 18th-century panelling with moulded dado-rail and cornice and a bolection-moulded panel over the fireplace. The room W. of the W. staircase is lined with bolection-moulded panelling of *c.* 1700 with dado-rail and entablature and four similarly moulded doorcases hung with two-panel doors with old rimlocks; the two small rooms adjoining on the W. were originally part of the same room, that to the S.W. retaining similar panelling in part reset and made out with later 18th-century panelling. This set was occupied by Thomas Gray, the poet; the statement that it was redecorated in 1747 (Correspondence of Thomas Gray, ed. Toynbee and Whibley, III, p. 1222) may refer to the sub-division, the existing panelling being considerably earlier. On the same floor is a number of old plank doors, probably original. In the attics, in the S.E. room, is some original panelling, four panels high with frieze-panels and a small cornice. The room S. of the E. staircase contains an old stone fireplace with moulded jambs, square head and cornice. A second original stone fireplace in the next room W. has a cornice and raised panels on the side-pilasters and on the frieze. On the same floor are more moulded plank doors as before.

Reset in the wall on the E. of Ivy Court and forming the *Gateway* to the Fellows' Garden is the stone doorcase removed from the entrance to the old Hall in 1878. It was set up probably in 1634 and is shown *in situ* by Loggan. The semi-circular-headed arch supported on square columnar panelled responds has a moulded archivolt with scrolled keystone, moulded imposts and panelled spandrels below a crowning entablature with broken segmental pediment. The frieze is of ogee section and the pediment frames a cartouche carved with the College arms against a modern pedimental brick backing; superimposed on the frieze and architrave is a shaped panel supported on the arch-keystone. The whole is much restored and refaced. It is now set between the piers of the late 17th-century gateway to the garden; these, also shown by Loggan *c.* 1681–2, are of rusticated brickwork with stone cappings and ball-finials. The clunch wall to the S. is of the 16th century or perhaps earlier, with subsequent heightening in brick and a modern brick facing to the plinth. In the Fellows' garden, the rockery is largely composed of fragments of discarded masonry, including pieces of mediaeval mullions.

In the *Master's Garden* are two late 14th or early 15th-century corbels, said to have come from the original chapel, carved with monsters' heads; one is that illustrated in Willis and Clark, I, 135.

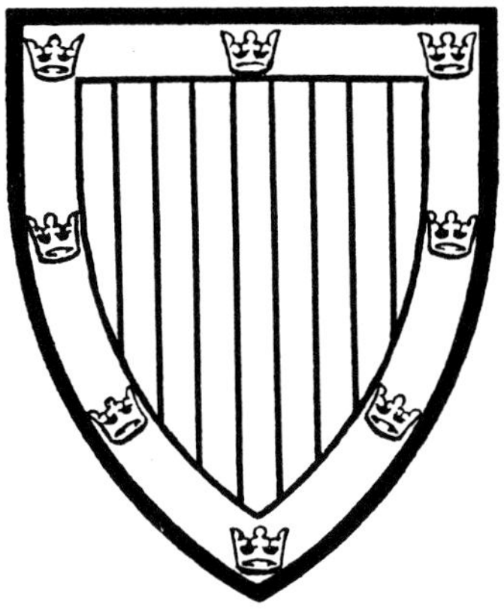

(34) PETERHOUSE stands on the W. side of Trumpington Street. It was founded in 1280 by Hugh de Balsham, Bishop of Ely, in the dwelling-place of the secular brethren of the Hospital of St. John. The College was moved to the present site, S. of the church of St. Peter (now St. Mary the Less), in 1284. When Hugh died in 1286 he bequeathed money for the purchase of land S. of the church and on this was built the existing *Hall*; the chambers were provided at first by two earlier hostels on the site and these it seems fronted on the street.

The *North Range of* Old Court, containing chambers, was being built in 1424–5. The *West Range* contained on the first floor the old Library that was contracted for in February 1430–1 by John Wassyngle of Hinton; the *Kitchen* at the S.W. angle of the Court was built in 1450. Little St. Mary's, being used by the College as the Chapel, was linked to the N. range by the existing *Gallery* about the middle of the 15th century, though the lower part of the Gallery has been assigned to *c.* 1350. The building E. of the Hall, including the Parlour, now extended to form the *Combination Room*, and Master's Lodge above, was built or rebuilt between 1460–64; the turret staircase, which gave access from the Master's Lodge to the Hall, is probably an addition made in the 16th century. The new *Library* further E., with the Master's Gallery over, was built in 1590–94 in accordance with the wishes of Dr. Andrew Perne, Master 1554–89; the extension of it eastward was begun in 1633.

Under Dr. Matthew Wren, Master 1625–35, much building was undertaken. The site adjoining Trumpington Street was cleared and the *Chapel* built on the E. to W. axis of Old Court with arcaded walks with galleries above to N. and S. The Chapel was begun in 1628 and consecrated though not completed in 1632; Dr. John Cosin, Master 1635–44 and 1660, faced the walls in stone and in 1665 gave £60 for so facing the E. end. Some damage was done to the fittings and carvings by William Dowsing in 1643. The arcaded walks and galleries were rebuilt in 1709, 'according to a paper delivered by Mr. Grumbold', and 1711.

The range N. of the Chapel built by bequest of Dr. John Richardson in 1632 was pulled down in 1738 and a new range, *Burrough's Building*, erected further to the N. from the design of James Burrough, being finished in 1742. The walling and gates towards the street were added in 1751, and in 1755 the W. porch of the Chapel was removed. The extensive refacing of the ranges of Old Court, on the courtyard side, was carried out in 1754–55 from the designs of James Burrough.

The rooms under the Perne Library were converted into a *Porter's Lodge*, Lecture Room, etc. in 1821. In 1825–26 the two ranges of *Gisborne Court*, W. of Old Court, were built to the designs of W. McI. Brooks by T. Tomson, and the W. side of the old W. range altered to accord with them; this was done from funds supplied by the Rev. Francis Gisborne. In 1870 the oriel and buttresses were added to the Hall together with the screen, panelling and a new roof from the designs of Gilbert Scott; the decorations and windows of the Hall are by William Morris, Burne-Jones, Ford Madox Brown and Philip Webb. *Fen Court* W. of Gisborne Court was erected in 1939.

The house now the *Master's Lodge* on the E. side of Trumpington Street, opposite the College, was built in 1702 by Dr. Charles Beaumont, Fellow, who, dying in 1726–7, left it for this purpose to the College.

The Hall and Buttery of Peterhouse retain remains of the original building of *c.* 1290 and are structurally the oldest college buildings in Cambridge. The Chapel, built during the ascendancy of Archbishop Laud, is of considerable architectural interest. The Perne Library contains bookcases by William Ashley that are the prototype of others in the University; among the other fittings, the panelling and the staircase to the Library are noteworthy. The interior of the Hall is a remarkable example of the Gothic Revivalism of the Pre-Raphaelite brotherhood.

The early 18th-century Master's Lodge is a largely unaltered example of the best builders' domestic architecture of the period.

Architectural Description—The College buildings are grouped round three courts, First Court to the E., Old Court in the middle and Gisborne Court to the W. The *First Court* (80 ft. average by 95 ft.) has, towards the street, two stone gateways of 1751 (Plate 218) with round-headed archways, flanking Tuscan pilasters and pedimented entablatures; the gates are of wrought-iron with plain vertical bars and scrollwork and with grilles of fan-pattern in the arch. The former wall between the gateways was removed in 1848 and replaced by railings with plain uprights and spiked cresting similar to those then existing between the N. gateway and Burrough's Building.

The *Chapel* (63¼ by 26 ft. including the Ante-chapel) stands in First Court projecting centrally and axially from the E. side of Old Court (Plate 216). It was built in 1628–32 and George Thompson was the freemason employed; the name of the designer is not known. It was originally of clunch faced with brick and was subsequently faced with ashlar, the E. end being finished soon after 1665; only in the N.W. bay, in the N. arcaded walk, is the original brickwork exposed. The E. wall (Plate 218) has octagonal turrets at the angles finished with embattled parapets and ogee cappings with carved finials; the gable has a shaped raking parapet of Flemish character and a panelled centrepiece with a pediment and a carved gable-cross; below the centrepiece is a carved cartouche with a mitre and the arms of the See of Durham impaling John Cosin. The E. window is of five trefoiled lights with vertical tracery in a two-centred head with a moulded label; flanking it are niches with enriched cartouches below the bases and rounded heads with scrolls and ogee crocketed finials; higher up, over the haunches of the window, are two small cartouches with the arms of the See of Ely and the College. The N. and S. walls, which were probably also refaced in ashlar after the Restoration, are divided into four bays by semi-octagonal buttresses similar to, but smaller than, the turrets at the E. end; the walls are finished with a moulded cornice and a plain parapet with moulded capping. Each bay has a window of similar detail to the E. window but of three lights with a four-centred head.

The W. front (Plate 217) has an arcaded lower part, rusticated in the side bays, and an upper part wholly of rusticated masonry. The arcading was presumably partly recased and altered either when the adjoining arcaded walks were rebuilt in 1709–11 or, more probably, when the porch was removed in

1755; it has three four-centred wall-arches with moulded archivolts and enriched keystones springing from attached Roman Doric columns, single at the ends and coupled between the bays. The columns stand on pedestals and the mouldings and decoration of the latter are continued across the side bays as a dado. The soffit of the middle arch has strapwork enrichment of Jacobean character and the doorway below has Gothic moulded jambs (p. 393) and a four-centred arch in a square head with plain shields in the spandrels. Above the arcade is an 18th-century entablature with bracketed projections. The upper part of the front has fluted Corinthian pilasters at either end on enriched pedestals and finished with entablature-blocks and ball-finials. The involved shaped gable has scrolled enrichments and a square-headed centrepiece with scrolled cresting, flanking ball-finials and a cherub's head at the apex surmounted by a wrought-iron weathervane. The W. window is of three trefoiled lights with vertical tracery in a four-centred head with a label; flanking it are niches with rounded shell-heads, carved brackets, pinnacles, and ogee crocketed finials; above the window is a clock-face with semicircular cornice on brackets, perhaps of the 18th century, and replacing an earlier niche.

Inside the Chapel (Plate 208), the single-storey Ante-chapel is divided from the body of the building by a screen returned to enclose two staircases to the organ-gallery above. The main roof is continuous from end to end and in four and a half bays divided by braced collar-beam trusses. It is wainscoted under the rafters and level with the collars, thus presenting a ceiling of three-sided form. The curved braces to the principals form four-centred arches with ornamental bosses and billets, carved pendants in the centres of the free trusses and moulded pendants to the wall-trusses; the wainscot in each bay comprises twelve bolection-moulded panels each enclosing a rayed oval design (Plate 25). The roof has a deep entablature against the side walls that is returned under the trusses, where it is supported on large carved consoles on wall-posts standing on moulded stone brackets, and under the intermediate ribs, where the consoles are small and plain. In 1735 the roof was examined with a view to removal or repair; it was evidently retained and repaired. The interior of the Chapel was restored in 1821–2; although the woodwork exhibits a use of both Classical and Gothic features likely during the period *c.* 1630, the extent to which it was reconstructed in the 19th century is now difficult to determine.

Fittings.—*Bell:* one, said to be inscribed 'Cum moveo Admonio 1622'. *Benefactors' Table:* Previously in Ante-chapel, now preserved in Burrough's Building—enriched and eared oak frame with cornice, broken pediment and enriched pediment in middle, with faded list of benefactors on paper, probably 18th-century. *Communion Rails:* forming three sides of rectangular enclosure, of oak, with turned balusters, moulded rails and panelled standards, probably 1731–2. *Doors:* in W. doorway—of oak, in two leaves, in upper panels a carved achievement-of-arms of Wiseman with a wyvern crest and motto 'Sapit qui Deum Sapit', and a cartouche with grapes and fruit and the inscription 'Anno D[omi]ni 1632', the lower part of the door with Gothic panelling with dentil-cornice, parts are old, including the cartouche with the date, but much is modern; in doorway in S. corridor—panelled and with cock's head hinge, 17th-century. *Gallery:* seeScreen. *Glass:* In E. window—large Crucifixion scene (Plate 215) including the two thieves and with the Virgin, Mary Magdalene, soldiers and crowd below, deep blue sky setting; in tracery, small figures of Apostles and two other saints, presumably St. Paul and St. Matthias; most probably by Bernard Van Linge, the main scene after Rubens' 'Coup de Lance'; the glass was hidden during the Commonwealth. The side windows by Professor Ainmüller of Munich were inserted 1855–8.

Monuments and Floor-slabs. Monuments: In Ante-chapel—on N. wall, (1) of Joseph Beaumont, S.T.P., 1699, Master, marbled and gilded oak wall-tablet with inscription-panel flanked by enriched Tuscan pilasters with scrolled strapwork wing-pieces and an entablature with curved broken pediment framing a pedestal supporting a later cartouche, apron carved with garlands of flowers; inscription perhaps added to earlier feature (see Monument (2)). On S. wall, (2) of Samuel Horn, M.A., 1634–5, Fellow, similar to (1). *Floor-slabs:* In Ante chapel —(1) of Joseph Beaumont, S.T.P., 1699, Master, Prebendary of Ely, with defaced achievement-of-arms; (2) of Charles Beaumont, S.T.P. 1726–7, youngest son of preceding, Fellow, vicar of Stapleford, with achievement-of-arms of Beaumont; (3) of Bernard Hale, S.T.P., 1663, Master of the College, Archdeacon and Prebendary of Ely; (4) of Thomas Richardson, S.T.P., 1733, Master; (5) of John Whalley, S.T.P., 1748, Master, provided by Edmund (Keene), Bishop of Chester, in 1770; (6) of Francis Barnes, S.T.P., 1838. *Organ:* On gallery at W. end—case, of oak, with panelled lower part and sides, front with tall central and shorter flanking towers of pipes, all on foliated corbels and with carved and pierced pelmets below deep crowning entablatures, the two intermediate panels in two heights, the lower height with pierced carving, the upper with a scrolled cornice linking the towers, on lower part of front the inscription 'Dono dedit Hor. Mann, A.M. Soc. Com. 1765', the organ built by Schnetzler and enlarged in 1871. *Panelling:* Flanking reredos and returning along N. and S. walls as far as the stalls, bolection-moulded panelling with dado, dado-rail and entablature, early 18th-century. See also Screen and Stalls. *Paving:* of black and white marble squares set diagonally, early 18th century. *Reredos:* of oak, of three bays, the middle bay projecting and with fluted Corinthian columns and pilasters on pedestals supporting an enriched pedimented entablature with scrolled cartouche in the tympanum, entablature continued over the side bays, the latter with fluted Corinthian pilasters at the outer angles and containing enriched eared panels with scrolled tops, probably erected 1731–2, with a modern tabernacle-frame in the middle bay containing a late 15th-century French wood *Pietà*, with St. Mary Magdalene and St. John, given as a memorial to Eileen (Power) Postan.

Screen and *Gallery*. Screen: at W. end—consisting of double partitions with central archways with moulded heads and ornamental key-blocks opening into a small vestibule; the semicircular E. arch with moulded imposts and Gothic traceried spandrels with carved cusp-points on the E. face and traceried spandrels with blank shields on the W. face; the elliptical W. arch with similar spandrels with shields on both faces but with thin boards, presumably modern, bearing the arms of the College and of Wren added on the W.; the cove of the stall-canopies is continued across the screen over the E. arch and has

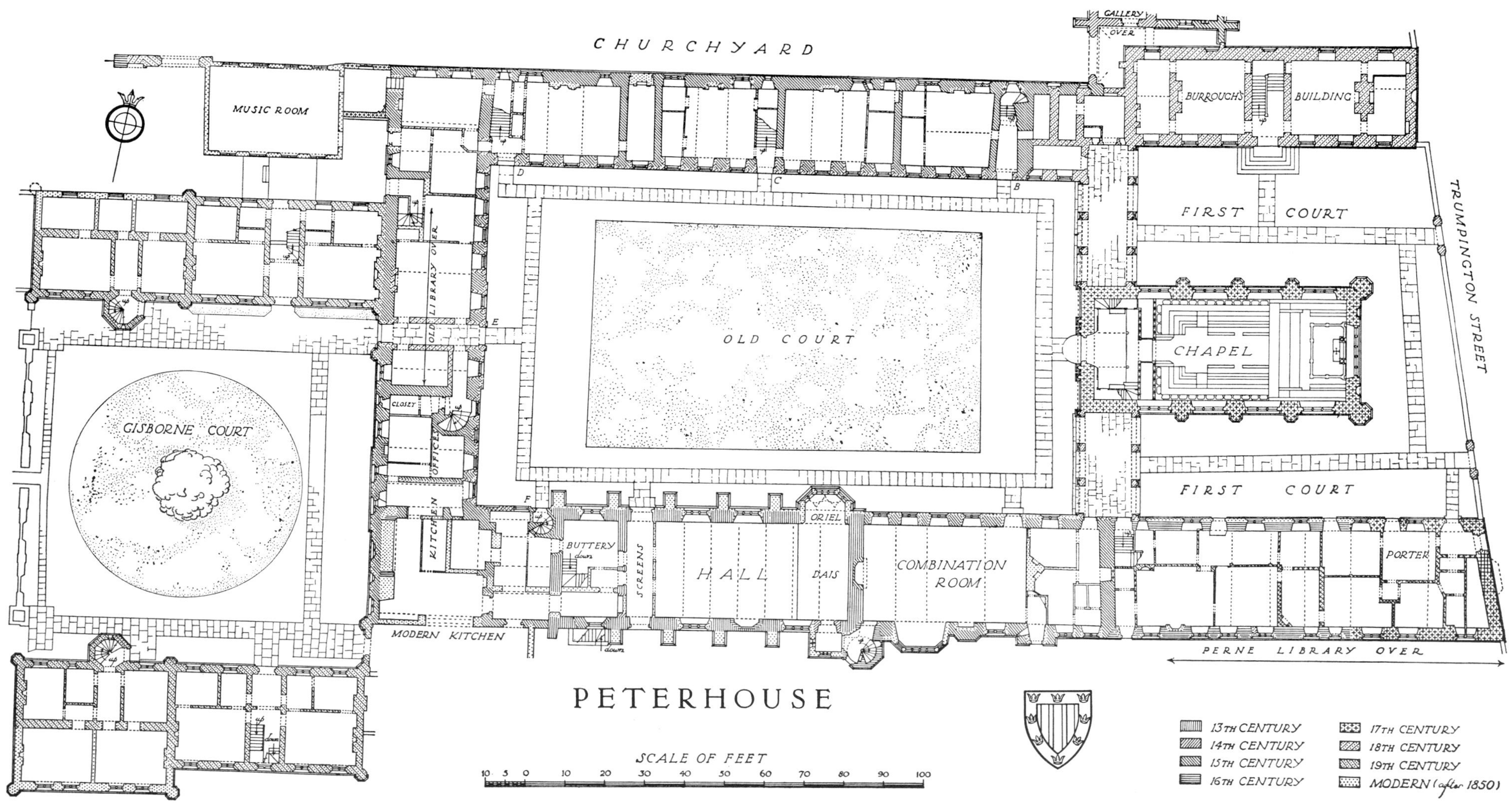
CHURCHYARD
GALLERY OVER
MUSIC ROOM
BURROUGH'S BUILDING
TRUMPINGTON STREET
FIRST COURT
CHAPEL
OLD COURT
FIRST COURT
OLD LIBRARY OVER
CLOSET
OFFICES
KITCHEN
GISBORNE COURT
BUTTERY
SCREENS
HALL
DAIS
ORIEL
COMBINATION ROOM
PORTER
PERNE LIBRARY OVER
MODERN KITCHEN
A
B
C
D
E
F
PETERHOUSE
SCALE OF FEET
10 5 0 10 20 30 40 50 60 70 80 90 100
13TH CENTURY
14TH CENTURY
15TH CENTURY
16TH CENTURY
17TH CENTURY
18TH CENTURY
19TH CENTURY
MODERN (after 1850)

carved pendants; in the same archway are gates with cinquefoiled Gothic panelling below and balusters above, seemingly largely modern. The vestibule has a panelled soffit with a carved central pendant. The W. partition returns to enclose N. and S. staircases to the Gallery; the W. face and the rest of the Ante-chapel are lined with Gothic panelling with cinquefoiled heads and carved cusp-points and spandrels; some of the cusped heads of the panels are original, of *c.* 1632. The woodwork described above contains much 19th-century work, particularly on the W. face of the screen. Gallery: The soffit, forming the ceiling of the Ante-chapel, has bolection-moulded panelling with a rose in the middle of the side bays and two more ornate panels before the opening in the Screen; the beams are supported by two oak columns with original caps and modern bases; the middle part of the soffit where presumably was a well or a ceiling at a higher level is modern. The N. Gallery-staircase has, at the top, turned balusters and newels with turned knobs incorporating a small bench with turned front legs; the S. staircase has a 19th-century enclosure at the top. The Gallery-front is formed of close panels below a moulded rail and Gothic open panels above, the latter with framing similar to that of the panels in the Ante-chapel and almost certainly of the 19th century. See also Stalls. *Staircases:* see Screen. *Stalls:* of oak, twelve on each side and three on each W. return, with shaped divisions with scrolled elbow-rests and moulded tops supporting turned and banded shafts on which rests the fascia of the ribbed and coved canopy, the fascia being in the form of an entablature with dentil-cornice and with blocks with blank shields over the shafts. The 17th-century Gothic panelling at the back, similar to that in the Gallery, is badly fitted to the stalls and may be an insertion. The desks have freestanding turned and banded shafts at the ends of the book-boards, and fronts with balusters above close panels, and fixed benches. The two stalls for the Master and the Vice-Master flanking the entrance are more elaborate than the remainder, with shaped projecting canopies and added 18th-century panelled enclosures; they have carved misericordes, on the N. a lion's head, two birds and flowers, on the S. a cherub-head, two female half-figures and flowers; the panelling behind the Master's stall has carved cherub-heads in the spandrels. The lower benches have long desks with balusters and panelling to the fronts and posts with turned knobs at each end; further W. and returned are similar benches and desks, and the latter also with original fixed benches with shaped elbow-rests. The date of the woodwork is presumably *c.* 1632 but much seems to have been repaired, reworked or renewed. Stalls and enclosures to match the foregoing have been added subsequently in front of the long desks, but before 1835 (see *Cantabrigia Illustrata*); those to the E. are modern. *Miscellanea:* On Gallery-front, gilded carved wood figure of St. Peter, late 17th-century, possibly S. German. Attached to the desks, brass candlesticks with turned stems, one and two branches, and grease-pans, early and late 18th century.

Flanking the Chapel are arcaded walks with galleries above; that on the N. was rebuilt in 1709 and that on the S. in 1711. The arcades are symmetrical towards the W. but the N. walk extends one bay further than that on the S. The ground storey has a round-headed arch in each bay with a keystone, moulded imposts and, between the arches, an attached Roman Doric column on a panelled pedestal and supporting a continuous entablature. The upper storey is ashlar-faced and finished with a small cornice and, on the W., an embattled parapet; each bay contains a square-headed two-light window with moulded architrave.

The erection of *Burrough's Building*, on the N. side of the First Court, was decided upon in 1733 and a design prepared by James Burrough, but the range was not built until 1738–42. It is of three storeys with cellars; the walls are of brick with Ketton stone facing on the S. side and the E. end and with a moulded plinth, heavy cornice and balustraded parapet; the roof is tiled. All the windows contain double-hung sashes. The S. side is symmetrically designed, with a rusticated ground storey, ashlar-faced upper storeys and a moulded plat-band at the first-floor level. The central entrance-doorway has a round head, plain keystone and moulded imposts continued across the wall-face; it is fitted with a six-panel door. The six windows have heads and imposts similar to those of the doorway. On the first floor are seven windows with eared architraves, bracketed sills and pediments, these last alternately curved and straight. On the top floor are seven square-headed windows with eared architraves and bracketed sills.

The E. end has a wall-treatment similar to that of the S. side but is finished with a pediment, which breaks through the plain parapet-wall and contains a cartouche flanked by palms in the tympanum. On the ground-floor is a round-headed niche and on the top floor a single window, both treated similarly to the window at the same level on the S. front; on the first floor is a Palladian window with Ionic pilasters and entablatures to the side-lights. The N. front is of brick in Flemish and English bond with a chamfered plinth and a plat-band, cornice and parapet, and ranges of five windows on each floor; the windows have moulded and eared architraves, except those on the ground floor, which have semicircular heads and large plain keystones. The easternmost window on the top floor has an iron fixture said to have been for a rope-ladder and set up for the poet Gray. Two of the ground-floor windows are sham.

The *Interior* of the building retains many of the original fittings; the following, unless otherwise described, are of the date of the building. The staircase is lined with moulded panelling with a panelled dado and soffits to the stairs and landings; the stairs have turned balusters, two to a step, scrolled brackets, a moulded and ramped handrail and square panelled newels. A carved cartouche painted with the College arms and surmounted by carved cross-keys, previously on the N. wall of the first landing, has recently been removed. The doorways of the staircase have eared architraves, pulvinated friezes and cornices. The rooms on the ground floor have moulded panelling and cornices; in the two main rooms the cornices are dentilled and the fireplaces each have an eared architrave, pulvinated frieze carved with bay-leaves and cornice enriched with acanthus-ornament, with an eared and enriched panel in the overmantel.

The *Ward Library*[1] consists of three rooms on the first floor; the rooms E. and W. of the staircase have moulded panelling

[1] The Ward Library was transferred to the floor above the Perne Library in 1953. The rooms here described have reverted to the use of Fellows.

and fireplaces; the fireplace in the E. room has a marble surround; the overmantels have each an enriched eared panel. The room at the E. end (Plate 49) contains two panelled partitions to form a central apartment with arches opening into closets to N. and S. The panelled walls of the apartment are divided into bays by fluted Ionic pilasters on pedestals with the capping-mouldings continued round the room; the pilasters support an entablature above which is a panelled upper frieze with scrolls over the pilasters and an enriched crowning cornice; the restored plaster ceiling is divided into panels by broad bands of guilloche-ornament and has cartouches above the Palladian window in the E. wall and the fireplace in the W. wall. The fireplace has a moulded and enriched round-headed surround and a shelf on console brackets with foliage garlands and a scallop-shell; above is an enriched panel with a shaped head breaking through the Ionic entablature, which last provides the springing for a semicircular arch-moulding over the panel. The arches in the N. and S. walls are round-headed, with panelled responds, moulded imposts and archivolts and scrolled keyblocks. The closets are panelled similarly to the main rooms of the Library. The two rooms at the W. end of the building have moulded panelling and plain cornices.

Stored in the cellars is a large panel (about 5½ ft. by 2 ft.) of early 17th-century glass, perhaps by Bernard van Linge, and possibly representing part of the subject of Christ washing the Disciples' feet. In different rooms are more of the panel-portraits described below with the Hall, including John Warkeworth, 1498, Thomas Denman, 1500, Robert Smith, 1565, Henry Wilshaw, 1578, and Edward, Lord North, 1564.

The *South Range*, containing the Perne Library, is in continuation of the S. range of Old Court and is described with it.

Old Court (151 ft. by 86 ft.) is totally enclosed (Plate 216). The main *South Range* includes the Hall and Butteries on the S. of Old Court with the Kitchen on the W. and the Perne Library block beyond on the E. The *Hall* (55¾ ft. by 25¼ ft.) was built *c.* 1290 and appears to have been originally a rubble building of five bays, including the Buttery, with freestone dressings. About the middle of the 15th century the windows, at least on the S. side, were replaced by taller ones and the Hall appears to have been considerably heightened, the heightening being faced with clunch ashlar. The N. wall was refaced in 1755 and in 1870 the whole building was restored by Gilbert Scott; to this second date belong the present facing, oriel and buttresses on the N. side, the buttresses, except the westernmost, and the small rebuilt annexe on the S. side, and the parapet and tiled roof.

The only ancient feature on the N. side is part of the jambs of the original N. doorway to the screens; the jambs are moulded and the doorway has a renewed two-centred arch with a label (p. 393). When the new windows were inserted in the N. wall in 1870 traces are said to have been found of the old windows. The lower part of the S. wall retains the original coursed rubble up to the level of the sills of the windows, with an ashlar base-course that may be seen above the ground in the first and third bays from the E. The original rubble of the first bay shows no break; the second bay shows a large modern patch; in the third bay the rubble shows no break in the lower 4 ft. but has a filling in the middle above of similar rubble. The fourth bay has original rubble flanking the doorway; in the fifth bay the rubble has been much patched and altered but on the W. is an original two-stage buttress with Barnack stone dressings and with Barnack stone quoins to the angle of the wall above. The patch below the window in the third bay is reputed to represent the blocking of an original window, but there is now no further evidence of this. On the W. side of the second buttress and on both sides of the third buttress are vertical lines of decayed ashlar which may represent the junctions of the original buttresses. The upper part of the wall is faced with decayed clunch-ashlar probably of the 15th century up to the modern parapet. The doorway at the S. end of the screens is partly original and has jambs and two-centred arch of two chamfered orders and a label similar to that of the N. doorway and partly old. The three Hall windows E. of the S. doorway are of the late 19th century.

In the *Interior* of the Hall is a S.E. doorway probably of the late 14th century with moulded jambs and two-centred arch in a square head with a label and cusped spandrels, the E. spandrel containing a blank shield; the label-stops are carved with a hart gorged with a crown couched and lodged within a paling, and a lion passant, the latter of doubtful antiquity. The fireplace is an early 16th-century insertion and has stop-moulded jambs and four-centred arch in a square head with foliated spandrels, one with a monster's head, the other with an Italianate shield; flanking it are simple upright panels and above it is a frieze of quatrefoiled and sub-cusped panels enclosing two Tudor and two rayed roses and a rayed fleur-de-lis; the cast-iron fireback bears the arms of James I and the date 1618. In the W. wall of the Hall are two doorways, both perhaps original but much restored; they have moulded jambs and segmental-pointed heads, the northern head being largely original, and renewed labels. In the same wall, further S. is a blocked serving-hatch with moulded jambs and four-centred head perhaps of the late 14th century. Below the Hall is a modern cellar.

A series of 16th-century and later panel-portraits with the names and dates of those portrayed painted on them was until between 1752 and 1756 incorporated in the panelling in the Combination Room; they are now distributed about the College and eighteen are in the Hall. Those fixed on the dais-panelling are as follows, on the N., from the top, (a) Hugh de Balsham, 1284, (b) John Whitgift, 1560, (c) John Cosin, 1634, inscription added since *c.* 1745, (d) Joseph Beaumont, 1665; on the S., (e) Edward I., 1283, (f) Andrew Perne, 1589, (g) Bernard Hale, 1660, (h) Charles Beaumont, 1726. Those fixed on the late 19th-century screen are, from the N., (a) John Holbroke, 1430, (b) Henry Hornebie, 1516, (c) Thomas Burgen, 1520, (d) Simon Montacute, 1344, (e) Robert Slade, 1616, (f) John Blithe, 1617, (g) Simon Langam, 1396, (h) John Edmondes, 1527, (i) Edward, Lord North, 1564, (j) [John] Lownde, 1519. They are more fully described in Willis and Clarke, I, 64–8. (See also Burrough's Building and Perne Library.)

The *Buttery* (13¾ ft. by 25 ft.) is included in the same building as the Hall and occupies the W. bay. The walling and buttresses are described with the Hall. The N. window is of the date of the Hall windows further E. Just E. of the S.W. buttress are

(34) PETERHOUSE. Chapel. E. window. *c.* 1630

Old Court, looking N.W.

Old Court, looking N.E.

(34) PETERHOUSE.

(34) PETERHOUSE. Chapel. W. front. 17th-century

(34) PETERHOUSE. Street front, from S.E.

17th and 18th-century

(35) QUEENS' COLLEGE. River front, from N.W.

Mid 15th-century and later

Exterior of N. range. Late 15th and late 16th-century

From N.W. Mid 15th-century and later

(35) QUEENS' COLLEGE. Cloister Court.

President's Lodge, N. side. Late 16th-century and *c.* 1790

Front Court, looking N.W. 1448–49

(35) QUEENS' COLLEGE.

The Betrayal.

The Resurrection.

Christ appearing to the Apostles.

(35) QUEENS' COLLEGE. Triptych in Chapel.

Late 15th-century

straight joints in the rubble indicating blocked openings; further E. is a 15th-century window with casement-moulded jambs and four-centred head but now without division; close W. of and partly destroyed by this window is the W. jamb of an earlier, perhaps late 13th-century, opening. Below the 15th-century window is a two-light square-headed window perhaps of the 17th century and above is a three-light square-headed window with a brick relieving-arch presumably of the 15th century, but it has been altered and, further, entirely restored. Below the building is a cellar approached through a modern doorway in the S. wall by a short stair outside. In the W. wall of the Buttery is a doorway with chamfered jambs and four-centred head, probably of the 15th century, and a modern arch opening into the kitchen-block.

A Buttery-annexe between the Buttery and Kitchen so far as it retains ancient features is of the 15th century, but earlier than the Kitchen. Traces of the former S.W. quoins remain in the S. wall and a former plinth stopped at this point. The N. wall to the Court was largely or completely rebuilt in the 18th century; it has Ketton stone ashlar facing, with a dentilled cornice and a parapet. The windows, one below and two above, have moulded architraves and sash frames with thin glazing bars; the two attic windows are of timber with hipped roofs. The N. doorway to the 15th-century spiral staircase is of that date and has hollow-chamfered jambs and four-centred head. At the W. end is an 18th-century sham doorway with eared architrave. The S. wall is of rough rubble incorporating some brick. On the ground floor is a much altered 15th-century window, now cut down to form a doorway, originally of two lights with casement-moulded jambs and three-centred head subsequently renewed in brick; the upper floor retains a window of the same date and originally of the same form but with the stone head removed and the opening carried up to the brick relieving-arch. The wall is finished with an early 19th-century brick cornice and the dormer-window is of the same period; the roof is tile-covered.

Inside the building, an opening providing access to the 15th-century staircase has been blocked and is now represented by a recess in the dividing wall; in the S.W. canted side of the same wall is a low opening, now blocked, with a four-centred head presumably to a cupboard below the stair. The staircase has an old grip-handrail to the lower part. In the W. wall of the annexe and revealed during recent alterations is a tall blocked archway with a four-centred head. On the first-floor the stone wall E. of the staircase, being the end wall of the Hall-block, has a 15th-century doorway with moulded jambs and two-centred head partly cut away. The room to the E. has 18th-century fielded panelling with a dentil-cornice, and the rooms to the W. retain two old doors.

The Kitchen-block in the angle between the S. and W. ranges of Old Court was built in 1450 and the S.W. corner retains the original quoins. On the S., the walling, brick cornice, windows and dormers are similar to those immediately to the E. in the Buttery-annexe but the two original windows on the first floor retain their mullions and pointed heads to the two lights. The *Kitchen* (formerly 22¼ ft. by 25 ft.) has recently been extensively remodelled and the whole of the S. wall, including a 15th-century doorway and two windows, removed and the open fireplaces in the E. and W. walls altered or destroyed; the accompanying plan shows the previous arrangement.

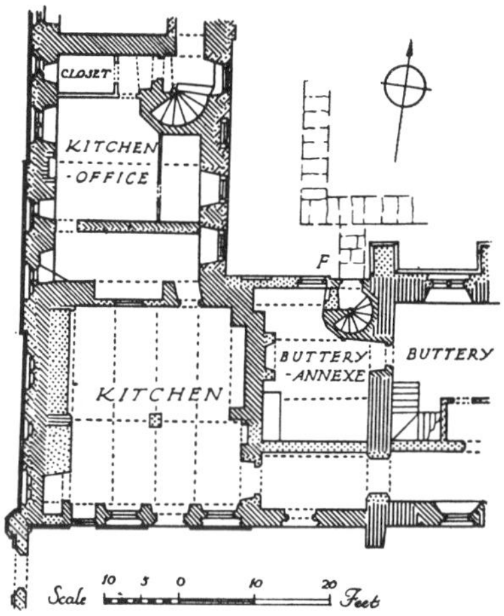

Kitchen before alteration.

Removal of the plaster from the W. wall revealed the N. jamb and springing of a small fireplace adjoining and cut in the dressings of the large fireplace and also two relieving-arches spanning the length of the wall and presumably for two original fireplaces; the two flues survived, the northernmost adapted to serve the later fireplace. In the E. wall, a tiled recess indicated the position of the blocked opening recently uncovered in the Buttery-annexe and described above. The S.E. doorway to the adjoining passage has an old segmental-pointed rear-arch. In the N. wall a doorway, probably of the 15th century, has now been blocked as has the wide opening next to it cut through the wall but perhaps once a third fireplace. In the S.W. angle of the room is a recess of doubtful purpose previously spanned by a half-arch.

The rest of the S. Range, to the E. of the Hall, is of three periods, the westernmost section of 1460, the middle of *c.* 1590 and the E. extension of 1633, all of two storeys with attics. The oldest section extends to about the middle of the arcaded walk on the N. side and to beyond the two windows E. of the rectangular projection on the S. side. The N. front is faced with ashlar of 1870 with an embattled parapet, windows and doorways of that period, except the part under the arcaded walk which has ashlar facing of 1711 and a 15th-century doorway with moulded four-centred head and chamfered jambs restored in the 18th century. The adjoining doorway (p. 393) is in the part of the building of *c.* 1590. The attics have timber dormer-windows and the roofs are tiled. The S. front has walls of small orange-coloured rubble with some brick; the copings of the embattled parapet and the dormer-windows are of the late 19th century. Next to the Hall is a small octagonal turret of brick with stone dressings, except the lower 4 ft., which are of rubble with original dressings, the dressings above being 19th-century restorations; it is carried up above the roof and finished with an embattled parapet; the 19th-century top has square openings. The date of the turret is discussed below in relation to features inside. Further E. is a two-storeyed oriel-window, entirely of 1868–70. Further E. again is a chimney-breast with splayed sides; it is original up to the parapet and carried on above the parapet in red brick with crow-stepped capping and a modern shaft. The square projecting bay containing a doorway has some original quoins; on one of them on the S.W. angle is cut a rectangular bracket with the underside splayed back to a point and, next to it, in the re-entrant angle, is a small pointed loop, now blocked. The doorway and all the windows are late 19th-century restorations except the 16th-century window over the doorway, which is of three four-centred lights, partly restored and partly of clunch, and set in a large patch of ashlar perhaps representing an earlier window. The lower window W. of the projection and the two windows E. of it have original brick relieving-arches and the window above the last retains part of the original clunch head. On the roof are four 19th-century dormer-windows.

The middle section of the range has the N. front faced in ashlar with embattled parapets and dormer-windows all of 1870, as are the two more easterly doorways and all the lower windows; the doorway under the arcaded walk is of the late 16th century and has moulded jambs and four-centred arch under a square head with restored labels. The S. front is faced with orange-coloured rubble composed of larger stones than that to the W.; the late 19th-century embattled parapet is of ashlar, the chimney-stacks are of brick and rebuilt and the three dormer-windows in the tiled roof are of the 19th century. The six windows on the ground floor of one, two and three lights have been entirely renewed externally and the doorway at the W. end is modern. On the first floor are four original clunch windows each of three four-centred lights in a square head and all partly restored with freestone.

The easternmost section, of 1633, is of red brick with stone dressings and modern or restored parapets; the roof is tiled. On the N. front the doorways and windows are of 1870 externally. The junction with the older work is immediately W. of the second window from the E. On the S. front is a chimney-stack, old up to the shafts. The ground storey has three two-light and the upper storey two three-light windows, all partly restored but similar to those in the 16th-century block; the junction with this earlier work is between the third and fourth windows. The attics have two dormer-windows similar to those further W. The E. end is set on the skew, following the street-line (Plate 218). It is gabled and has a modern doorway on the ground floor. The upper floors have a two-storeyed oriel-window, three-sided and resting on moulded brick corbelling and finished with a stone cornice; the corbelling has a dentilled top member and the top courses are continued along the wall in a label-like way, with the ends returned; the lower window is of three stone transomed lights on the face and one on each return; the upper is similar but with no transom; between the windows is a panel with the date 1633.

The *Interior* of the range contains in the block of 1460 the *Combination Room* (41 ft. by 25 ft.) on the ground floor; it was doubled in size, partly by the addition of the oriel, in 1868–70 in the course of almost complete refitting by the firm of William Morris. In 1946 the room was stripped and the floor above strengthened; the old W. moulded ceiling-beam (p. 396) was then replaced and G. G. Scott's panelling reset. The fireplace is said to have been found behind the 19th-century wainscot during alterations; it has renewed jambs but the head appears to be old though perhaps reset; it is corbelled out at the sides and the joggled lintel is continued with a small curve at the two ends. The doorway to the spiral staircase is concealed on the N. face but retains part of the old arch. It seems probable that the staircase is not part of the original 15th-century work but an early 16th-century addition; this is indicated by the fact that the doorway from the first floor (the former Master's Lodge) is partly covered by the walling of the turret and above the doorway is part of a horizontal weathering that would only relate to a roof prior to the erection of the present turret; it is possible that the doorway was approached by an open external staircase with pent roof. The windows of the staircase are old internally, and at the foot of the stairs is a deep locker with rebated reveals and segmental head. The doorway to the former Lodge has moulded jambs and two-centred head with a label and a defaced stop. The doorway to the attics is of the 16th century and has moulded jambs and lintel and an old plank door in three vertical panels on the outer face. The bell, from Malines, in the top of the turret is inscribed 'Peeter Vanden Ghein heft mi ghegoten MDXLVIII'.

The *Little Parlour* (18¼ ft. by 19¼ ft.) on the first floor is lined with panelling, mostly modern but incorporating some of the early 17th century. The corridor on this floor has an old exposed ceiling-beam. The room at the E. end of the 15th-century block has a wide recess in the projecting bay with an arched and plastered head; it is possible that this formed the oratory in the former Lodge. The late 16th or early 17th-century panelling lining the room is made up with modern work and finished with a 17th-century panelled frieze and modern cornice; above the fireplace is a restored 17th-century overmantel of two bays with panelled pilasters and an entablature. In the E. wall is a doorway with chamfered jambs and splays, which is perhaps a 15th-century window cut down to form a doorway. At the E. end of the corridor is a late 16th-century doorway of stone with moulded jambs and four-centred arch in a square head. The attic-floor has a roof of five bays with six collar-beam trusses; three retain their original chamfered and curved collars. The 16th-century doorway in the E. wall has chamfered jambs and four-centred head.

The interior of the blocks of *c.* 1590 and 1633 has at the W. end the staircase to the Perne Library (Plate 66). The staircase is of the late 16th-century and of well type with the balustrade continued round the landing of the first floor; it has panelled newels with turned finials and pendants, moulded close strings and handrails, and turned balusters linked by stretchers under the rail shaped to form three-centred or round-headed arches with foliated spandrels of Gothic character; the staircase is largely of pine, with some oak, but appears to be mostly original. The rest of the ground floor has been much modernised but has some exposed ceiling-beams and a small amount of 18th-century panelling. On the first-floor landing the late 16th-century door to the room S. of the staircase is of nail-studded battens with moulded fillets planted on and strap-hinges. The Perne Library occupies the whole of the rest of the first-floor; the doorway to it has a 17th-century panelled frieze, brackets and a dentil-cornice; the six-panel door is hung on strap-hinges.

The *Perne Library* (76 ft. by 25 ft.) (Plate 209) is of eight bays with plastered beams and a modern ceiling. In the S. wall are two stone fireplaces; the western is of the late 16th century and has stop-moulded jambs and four-centred arch in a square head; the eastern is of *c.* 1633 and similar to the foregoing but with partly chamfered jambs (Plate 40); both have 17th-century oak eared architraves and overmantels with panelled side-pilasters. Each overmantel has a large panel with moulded surround flanked by carved fruit pendants and containing an elaborate tabernacle-framing supported on a shaped apron with dentilled shelf; the tabernacle-frame has flanking pilasters enriched with roses and carved pendants on the faces, scrolled and banded side-pieces and an entablature with frieze-panel and broken pediment (cf. the panelling in the Fellows' Building,

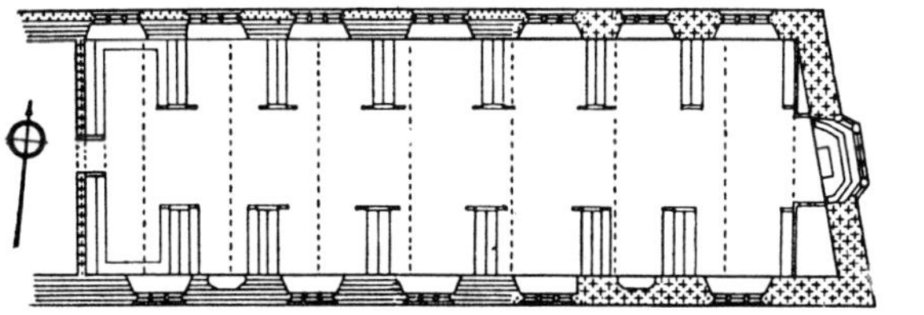

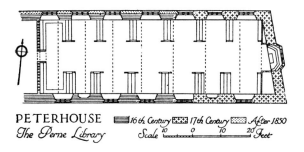

PETERHOUSE — 16th Century — 17th Century — After 1850
The Perne Library — Scale 10 0 10 20 Feet

Christ's College). The timber lobby to the entrance doorway in the middle of the W. end and the cupboards and wall-cases flanking it are designed as a unity (Plate 41); the lobby has panelled outer and inner doors and a Doric entablature surmounted by a painted and gilded cartouche containing the College arms and flanked by seed-cobs and scrollwork; on each side are bookcases divided into sections by panelled pilasters and with a continuous Doric entablature; two sections, perhaps to contain archives, are hung with eight-panel doors, the six upper panels being open and fitted with turned balusters; set against the cases are locker-seats with panelled fronts. The side walls and window-embrasures have moulded panelling, partly restored, with panelled pilasters at intervals.

The main bookcases, six on each side and projecting at right angles from the walls, are treated similarly to the W. wall-cases and the free ends are panelled. All originally had benches against them; the bench-ends consist of carved scrolls each with a pendant of fruit and leaves of varying designs. Except in the westernmost bay on both sides, the next on the S. and the second bay from the E. on the S. the benches themselves have been removed, but the bench-ends remain except in the two E. bays on the N. and the E. bay on the S. The bookcases, or many of them, were heightened at some uncertain date but all have now been restored to the original form; some cases at the W. end had curved pediments and dissevered parts of these survive. On many of the panelled pilasters are traces of former shelf-lists. At the E. end are wall-cases similar to the projecting cases but without benches or bench-ends. This end of the room is finished square with the side walls, leaving a wedge-shaped space behind the panelling. The oriel-window is flanked by panelled pilasters with pendants of leaves and fruit and supporting Doric entablatures continued into the window-reveals; the soffit of the recess is irregular and has a panelled oak ceiling, partly restored, with rosettes at the intersections of the framing and a large central pendant with a grape-cluster. Round the recess runs a bench with a panelled back finished with a plain strapped capping and bench-ends similar to those of the bookcases. In the middle is a panelled desk with panelled and carved pilasters and enriched mouldings. Triglyphs are spaced along the face of the step up into the recess. The bookcases and woodwork at the W. end of the Library were made by William Ashley and set up at intervals between 1641 and 1648 and the other panelling and overmantels are of much the same date but not to the same design.

Suspended from the ceiling are three brass candelabra, each with two tiers of six branches attached to a turned baluster with a globe at the lower end; they may be of the 18th century. Stored in the Library are more of the panel-portraits described above with the Hall, including Ralph Ainsworth, 1544, Edmund Hanson, 1516, Thomas Lane, 1472, William Martin, 1519, Widow Wolfe, 1540 (see also Burrough's Building). The attic floor has some old doors and the roof is of collar-beam type.

The *West Range* of Old Court is of two storeys with attics; the roof is slate-covered. The E. front was refaced in 1754 in ashlar and has a dentilled cornice and parapet; the middle part, comprising three bays, projects slightly and is pedimented; in the tympanum is a round opening with moulded architrave. The ground floor has ten and the upper floor eleven windows all with architraves and containing double-hung sashes; on the roof are nine hipped dormer-windows. The archway to the passage through the centre of the range has a round head, moulded imposts and flanking pilasters terminating in shaped brackets supporting a pedimented entablature. The W. front was extensively refaced in 1826, when Gisborne Court was built, and is in the revived Gothic style of the period; the opening to the central passage retains internally an 18th-century archway with segmental head. Towards the N. end of the range the original facing is preserved and is rough-cast. Here is a much weathered 15th-century doorway with jambs and two-centred arch of two chamfered orders, which probably gave access to a passage through the range; N. of it is an original window of two pointed lights in a square head. The first floor in the same area has two windows, the northern original and of three pointed lights in a square head with casement-moulded jambs, the other probably of the 16th-century and of two four-centred lights with casement-moulded jambs. The chimney projection further N. has original S.W. quoins below but the upper part is of 18th-century or modern brickwork. In the roof are two 18th-century dormer-windows.

The N. end of the W. range, which is not distinguished externally from the adjoining N. front of the N. range, is in rubble with most of the quoins of the N.W. angle remaining and with two patches of 17th-century brickwork enclosing two solid-framed two-light transomed windows. The upper floor has a late 15th or early 16th-century window of three four-centred lights in a square head with casement-moulded reveals, and in the roof is a dormer-window.

The *Interior* of the W. range, which originally contained the Library on the first floor, is substantially of the 15th century. It retains two original windows in the W. wall on the ground floor, behind the facing of 1826; these are both of a single light with segmental-pointed head; one is in the room adjoining the Kitchen, the other in the closet W. of the circular staircase; the two windows between them have recently been found to have been contrived within original splays. In 1438 Reginald Ely, 'lathamus', was employed upon the construction of the staircase to the Library. During the alterations of 1953–4 in this area, already mentioned, the circular stone staircase was found not to be bonded into the external wall of the range, though of similar material and construction, thus corroborating the two phases of building, 1424–31 and 1438, implied by the documentary evidence. The 15th-century doorway under the staircase has chamfered jambs, slightly ogee moulded head and a battened door; the staircase is carried over it on a somewhat skewed arch to the cross-wall to the N. In the Kitchen-office, removal of the modern plaster has revealed in the W. wall a late 16th or early 17th-century stone fireplace with four-centred head and, on the timber-framed N. wall, much damaged early 17th-century painted arcading of round-headed arches divided by columns supporting a frieze containing scrollwork, all in blue, black and red. The wall-painting has since been destroyed; it was similar to that preserved at Queens' College in the E. range of Walnut Tree Court built between 1616 and 1619. The room N. of the passage through the range has a fireplace with an 18th-century eared surround and a dentilled cornice.

On the first floor the middle part of the range, now divided up into rooms, formed the old Library (19½ ft. by about 46½ ft.) entered by the doorway in the middle of the cross-wall N. of the stone staircase, with hollow-chamfered jambs and four-centred head with a shield in the centre, recently painted with the College arms. The roof of the Library extended to three and a half bays, the half-bay being at the S. end; the main tie-

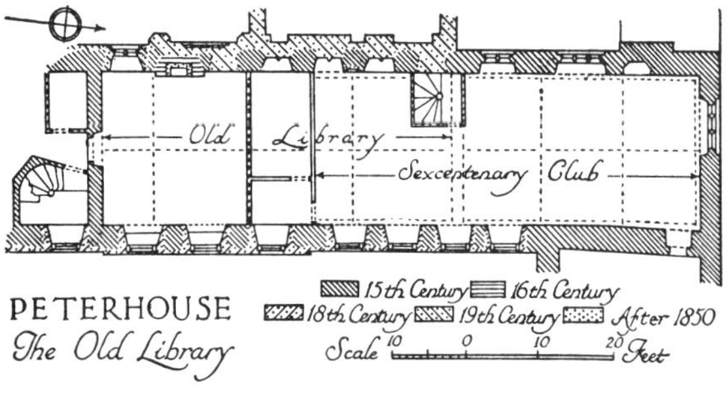

PETERHOUSE
The Old Library

beams, which are slightly cambered, are hollow-chamfered and the subsidiary longitudinal beams and wall-plates are all moulded (p. 396); the ties formerly had curved braces of which only one remains against the timber partition of the N.W. staircase. The position of the N. end of the Library is marked by a broad beam across the Sexcentenary Clubroom where a former cross-wall has been removed. Much evidence of the original arrangement of the Library windows has been preserved in the W. wall. They are placed two to a bay with one window in the half-bay; this last has been altered in the 19th century, and of the two windows in the next bay the first has been destroyed for the late 16th-century fireplace and the second is indicated only by a patch in the wall-panelling; in the next bay the splays of the first window are preserved in a cupboard and the splays and four-centred head of the second survive in the Clubroom, but the opening is blocked by the 1826 addition and the sill has been cut down to the floor; in the last bay the first window of two pointed lights in a four-centred head is preserved entire but again blocked, and the second is indicated by the splays bordering the blocking in the W. wall of the adjoining staircase.

The existing partitions in the old Library were no doubt inserted shortly after the building of the Perne Library in *c.* 1590 and the panelled room at the S. end was then formed. In the latter the panelling has a frieze carved with guilloche-ornament; the fireplace is modern but flanked by fluted and enriched pilasters supporting an overmantel of three bays and two tiers of enriched arcaded panels; the bays are divided and flanked by fluted and carved Ionic pilasters supporting an enriched entablature with guilloche frieze similar to that of the rest of the room. Immediately outside the S. wall of the old Library is part of an original truss of the roof of the S. part of the range; it has a hollow-chamfered tie-beam with a curved and hollow-chamfered brace; the brace at the W. end has been broken away. The northern three bays of the Clubroom are ceiled at a slightly lower level than the old Library and represent the extent of the room which occupied the N. end of this floor; the cross and longitudinal beams and plates are moulded and the two N. bays have an 18th-century wood dentil-cornice, the last representing a subsequent subdivision of the room. In the W. wall is a late 15th or early 16th-century clunch fireplace with hollow-chamfered jambs and four-centred arch in a square head with intersecting mouldings. The room is entered off staircase 'D' in the N. range by a 15th-century doorway with hollow-chamfered jambs and two-centred head. The attics contain some 18th-century doors.

The *North Range* of Old Court has the S. wall refaced in 18th-century ashlar and here the design, except for the doorways, is uniform with that of the side bays flanking the pedimented centrepiece on the W. side of the court. On the ground floor are sixteen windows, nineteen on the first floor and fifteen dormer-windows in the roof, all similar to those of the W. range. The three doorways have eared architraves. The composition is one of regular repetition of features without any vertical articulation of the wall-face.

The N. front has a chamfered plinth and plain eaves and the walling is a patchwork of decayed rubble and brickwork. The chimney-stacks and the whole facing of the eastern part of the wall are of reddish brick but there is no reason to suppose that these differ in date from the rest of the work, since isolated bricks and lacing-courses in the rubble are of precisely similar brick; much later patches and repairs in brick do however occur. The roofs are slate-covered. The end of the W. range forms a flush face with this front of the N. range and has been described; further E. the ground-floor windows, unless otherwise described, have square-headed lights and moulded labels and are of the 15th century; their arrangement and number of lights are shown on the plan. The first window, lighting the room under the stairs, is of the 17th century with chamfered reveals and a lowered sill and the second has a label with diagonal stops returned upon themselves. Between the next two windows is a blocked two-centred 15th-century arch with both the jambs and the W. half of the head remaining and the rest replaced by a modern chimney; it opened into a former passage through the range. The fourth window, next to the arch, has one light blocked; the next is of the 17th century and of two plain square-headed lights. The seventh window was formerly of three lights but the two western lights were lengthened in the 18th century and the mullion removed; between this window and the modern window next to the E. the wall-facing changes from rubble to brick. The two E. lights of the ninth window and both lights of the two-light window next to the E. are blocked; the next window is entirely modern externally and the two windows beyond, the first with casement-moulded reveals and pointed head, the second of one cinquefoiled light in a square head, are both blocked. Some of the other windows may have had cusped heads to the lights, if so the cusping has been removed.

On the first floor most of the windows are of the 15th century, with four-centred lights, some in square heads, and all are very much weathered. Again reading from the W., two single-light windows light staircase 'D'; one is probably of the 16th century and has an elliptical head and the other is a round-headed loop with moulded reveals, perhaps of the 17th century. The next window is of the 16th century and of two four-centred lights with casement-moulded reveals; of the next five windows, the first, fourth and fifth are each of one light, the fourth is blocked, and the second and third are each of two lights, the third with a modern mullion. The ninth window was perhaps of two lights but is now blocked and without the mullion; the next and the following are both of one light and the first is blocked; the twelfth is of the 17th century and of two lights with a solid frame; of the five remaining windows the two first and two last are of two lights; the first has been entirely restored and the third is a 17th-century light with a solid frame set in an older opening; immediately E. of the first and between the third and fourth are traces of two windows with two-centred heads. One of the chimney-projections rests on corbelling and all the chimneys are modern above the eaves. In the roof are eleven 18th-century dormer-windows, including the one over the W. range.

The *Interior* of the N. range comprises sets of rooms and in them are various heavy exposed ceiling-beams. On the ground floor the room W. of staircase 'C' is lined with early 17th-century panelling with frieze and dentil-cornice; three of the four doors have projecting cases with panelled and bracketed over-doors and dentilled cornices; the doors are panelled and two have wrought-iron cock's-head hinges. The modern fireplace is flanked by pilasters supporting a banded shelf and an overmantel in two panelled bays divided and flanked by columns on pedestals with a bracketed entablature enriched with small roses. The room E. of the same staircase is lined with simple late 16th-century panelling with a cornice. The timber-framing of the staircase-wall is exposed.

The room W. of staircase 'B' is lined with late 17th-century bolection-moulded panelling with dado-rail and cornice; the doorway in the E. wall has a bolection-moulded architrave, cornice, broken pediment and pedestal; the two doorways in the W. wall and the overmantel have bay-leaf enrichment. The inner room has 18th-century panelling with a cornice and panelled beam and a bolection-moulded fireplace-surround. The circular stone staircase 'B' has a 15th-century moulded corbel under the squinch in the S.W. angle tapered back on the underside; the staircase, in common with other early staircases in the College, extends only to the first floor in stone and the upper part is of timber with exposed timber-framing.

On the first-floor the room E. of staircase 'D' has a 17th-century panelled outer door hinged to fold. The room is lined with early 17th-century panelling with a cornice and frieze with spindle ornament; the doorcases project and have panelled entablatures with spindle ornament and are hung with eight-panel doors. The fireplace has a bolection-moulded stone surround of *c.* 1700 flanked by 17th-century wood pilasters supporting a banded shelf; the overmantel is of three enriched bays with pilasters, enriched entablature, a plain panel to the middle bay and small enriched panels to the side-bays with jewel-ornament. In the N. window are two round quarries, one painted with an apple-tree growing out of a tun, 16th-century, the other set inside out and much weathered. The room W. of staircase 'C' has early 17th-century panelled shutters to the windows. The room E. of the same staircase has 15th-century exposed moulded ceiling-beams. The room W. of staircase 'B' has some 17th-century panelling and the fireplace has an 18th-century eared surround. The room E. of the same staircase is lined with 18th-century fielded panelling with a dado-rail, cornice and three panelled doors. The *Gateway* and *Gallery* between the College and St. Mary the Less, now being inaccessible from the S., are described with the church.

Gisborne Court (Plate 39) (86 ft. by 94 ft.) lies to the W. of Old Court. It is bounded on the E. by the W. range of the latter and on the N. and S. by ranges built in 1825–6; the W. side is open. The cost of the work, including remodelling the front of the W. range of Old Court where it faces Gisborne Court, was met from funds supplied by the Rev. Francis Gisborne. The buildings are in the Tudor-Gothic style; the architect was W. McI. Brooks and the builder Thomas Tomson of Cambridge Both the N. and S. ranges were originally narrower for about half their length; in the second half of the 19th century their western halves were widened to N. and S. respectively. They are of two storeys with attics and contain sets of chambers; the walls are of white brick with stone dressings and the roofs are slate-covered.

The remodelled E. side of the Court is symmetrically designed; to preserve the symmetry, many of the windows are shams while the mediaeval windows, as described above, are screened. It has a gabled and parapeted middle bay flanked by wider bays with embattled parapets, and a narrower bay at each outer end. The narrow end bays have stepped parapets to the gables and are both flanked by semi-octagonal brick buttresses continued above the parapets as octagonal turrets with embattled caps; the S. bay consists only of a screen-wall and several of the turrets conceal chimney-flues. The middle bay projects slightly and has two windows on both the ground and first floors, the lower of two four-centred lights in a square head with a label and the upper of two four-centred lights with a pierced spandrel in a four-centred head. Between the upper pair is a canopied niche with a pedestal supported on a half-angel holding a shield of the arms of Gisborne; the gable is flanked by small octagonal stone turrets partly supported on the backs of carved beasts at the parapet-string; it has a square block at the apex, with a traceried panel inset in the face, which forms a base for two conjoined octagonal chimney-stacks. The two wider bays have windows arranged uniformly on each floor; two-light windows similar to those at the same levels in the centre bay flank a window of one two-centred light, in a square head on the ground floor and a two-centred head on the first floor, with a label. The outer bays both have, on the ground floor, a doorway with moulded jambs and a four-centred opening in a square head with blank shields in the spandrels and a moulded label and, on the first floor, a window of three four-centred lights in a square head with a label. In the two gables are shields carved with initials, on the N., F.B. and M.C. below, for Francis Barnes, Master of the College, on the S., S.T. and B.C. below, for Samuel Tillbrook, Bursar of the College.

The *North* and *South Ranges* have generally the same elevational treatment to the Court; the plinth, string-courses and the parapets are continued round from the E. side of the court; the parapet has alternate tall and short merlons. The inward-facing fronts each centre on a doorway with a large window above under a small parapeted gable. The doorway has a four-centred arch in a square head with traceried spandrels and a label with three traceried panels above, the outer with quatrefoils and the middle panel with an octofoil enclosing a shield-of-arms, on the N. range of Parke and on the S. range of the College. The window is of three transomed and four-centred lights in a four-centred head with the parapet-string carried over it as a label; in the gable is a blank shield. The two flanking two-light windows on both floors are similar to those at the same levels on the E. side of the Court. Close to the W. is a semi-octagonal buttress continued above the parapet as a turret and similar to that in the angle of the Court; the two frame the foregoing features in a symmetrical composition. Between the W. buttress and a similar buttress on the W. angle of each range is an octagonal stair-tower flanked, on the E., by a two-light window on each floor, and, on the W., by a one-light and a two-light window on each floor, all similar to those at the same levels on the E. side of the Court. The stair-tower is carried higher than the main parapet and embattled; it is lit by two square-headed single-light windows with labels, and in the E. face is a doorway with chamfered jambs and a two-centred head with a label with stops carved with leaves and a shield-of-arms, on the N. range of the See of Ely (the first arms of the College), on the S. range of the crossed keys of St. Peter (the second arms of the College).

The N. front of the N. range has brick strings at first-floor level and below the eaves; on both floors are ranges of segmental-headed windows. A semi-octagonal buttress masks the angle where the range originally narrowed.

The S. front of the S. range has plinth, strings and parapet as on the N. front; to the E. is the face of the original building; the projecting W. half is the subsequent widening. At all the angles are polygonal buttresses continued up as turrets. In the middle of the upper floor of the original building is an oriel-window with splayed sides supported on moulded corbelling; it is of three transomed lights on the face and one on each return and has a pierced parapet; on the apron-wall is a carved shield-of-arms of Hale. The main wall behind the oriel is carried up as a small gable containing a two-light window; this last, and the five windows on the ground floor and the four on the first floor are similar to those at the same levels to the Court. The later front has paired windows, four in all, on each floor and two brick dormer-windows.

The *Interiors* of the N. and S. ranges both have four sets of chambers on each floor. The easternmost staircases are each approached through a lobby with round-headed entrance-arch with plain archivolt and keystone and plain responds with moulded caps and bases. The stairs are of stone with plain wrought-iron balusters and handrails. Each set of chambers has panelled inner and outer doors and the principal rooms have simple plaster cornices, panelled window-shutters and four-panelled doors to the bedrooms. The fireplaces are of stone and have simple panelled surrounds.

The *Grove* is an open area to the S.W. of the college and the boundary-wall to the W. is said to have been rebuilt in 1501–2; it is, however, certainly not all of one date, apart from the modern repairs and rebuildings. To the W. and N.W. of the S. range of Gisborne Court the wall is much patched and rebuilt. S. from the same building is a length of reused ashlar with red brick at the top and with later work to the S. The next section is all of one date with much patching; it extends to the angle and includes the return-wall to the W. and part of the continuation to the S. The structure was originally of bands of clunch with brick lacing courses; the part S. from the return-wall must have formed part of the former tennis-court, which is undated but presumably of the 16th-century; it is supported on the W. by six later brick buttresses and two modern concrete props. The next stretch has been largely rebuilt except towards the S.; the short return-wall is mostly of the 19th century. The rest of the walling is largely of clunch but in it is a stretch mainly of red brick in which is a 16th-century stone doorway, now blocked; this has chamfered jambs and a four-centred head with a label and, above, a square cusped panel enclosing a shield-of-arms of Bishop Hotham, recently refaced in Roman cement. Reset over the door-head on the inside is part of a cusped panel with the arms of Bishop Alcock, recently entirely renewed. The S. wall is partly of stone, partly of red brick, and partly of later brick and now extends eastward as far as the area of land sold in 1823 as a site for the Fitzwilliam Museum.

On the N. boundary of the College and incorporated in the S. wall of the Museum of Classical Archaeology is a length of 16th-century brick walling containing an opening, now blocked, of which rather more than half survives; it has a four-centred arch turned in 9-inch bricks. Reset in the 19th-century boundary-wall at the N.W, angle of the College is a low 16th-century doorway, now blocked, with chamfered jambs and four-centred head with a brick relieving-arch.

The *Master's Lodge* (Plate 300) on the E. side of Trumpington Street, opposite the College, was built in 1702 by Dr. Charles Beaumont, Fellow, who, dying in 1726–7, left the house to the College as a Master's Lodge. With the exception of a small two-storey addition on the N., the house remains much as it was built. It is of three storeys with a basement; the walls are of red brick with stone dressings and the roofs are tiled. The front has a brick and stone plinth, moulded plat-bands between the storeys, rusticated stone quoins and a bracketed timber eaves-cornice with attached iron rings, perhaps aids to window-cleaning. The plain rectangular windows are symmetrically

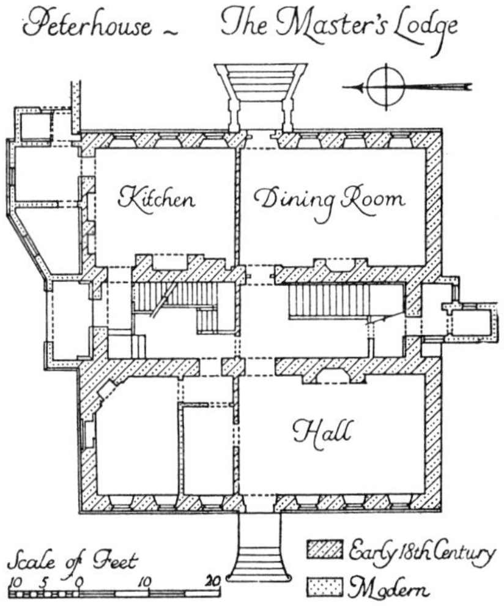

arranged and have moulded sills and flush frames with later sashes. The central doorway has a bolection-moulded surround and two-fold eight-panel doors; it is approached by a short flight of steps. The E. front is similar in treatment and detail to the W. front but on the band between the upper storeys is the date A.D. 1702. The cornice is continued round the building and the stone bands are continued across the N. but not the S. sides; on the S. is a brick band between the upper storeys. Both N. and S. walls have a central recessed bay with the main cornice mitred round it.

The *Interior* of the building contains much original panelling and two original staircases. The hall is lined with moulded and fielded panelling with a dado and cornice and a marble bolection-moulded surround to the fireplace; the floor is of stone slabs set diagonally. The arch to the staircase is semicircular and has panelled responds, moulded imposts and key-block. The N.W. room, now divided, is lined with bolection-moulded and fielded panelling with dado and cornice and moulded surround to the fireplace. The S.E. room is lined with oak panelling similar to the last described and with a panelled overmantel. The main staircase (Plate 67), the southernmost, has turned and twisted balusters, three to a step, newels of four grouped balusters and moulded and bracketed strings. The staircase-hall is lit by two identical windows in the S. wall and retains the original plaster ceiling divided into panels by bolection mouldings. The secondary staircase rises to the top floor and has heavy turned balusters, close strings and newels with turned pendants. On the first floor two rooms contain original painted deal panelling with panelled dados and cornices. In the S.W. room is a moulded surround to the fire-place and a panel above.

The forecourt of the house has two original brick gate-piers with cornices and ball-finials; the wrought-iron gate was made in 1928.

The *Outbuilding*, N.E. of the house, is of two storeys; the walls are of brick and timber-framing plastered externally. It was built probably in the 16th century and was originally of three bays. No doubt the first floor projected on the E. and W. sides, but the projection was underbuilt in brick in the 18th century when another bay was added to the N. The ground floor retains the original chamfered ceiling-beams and flat joists; in the S. room is a reset stone fireplace-surround of the early 18th century. On the upper floor the original tie-beams and wall-posts show the mortices for former braces.

(35) QUEENS' COLLEGE stands between Queens' Lane and the river. It was founded here in 1448 by Queen Margaret of Anjou on land where Henry VI by charter of 1447 had intended to place his College of St. Bernard. Andrew Docket, the first President, was primarily concerned in the foundation from its inception and was founder in all but name; he had previously been nominated President of St. Bernard's College by the king. Henry annulled his foundation-charter and Royal licence was granted to his queen to establish a College dedicated to St. Margaret and St. Bernard. It was further endowed by Queen Elizabeth Woodville in 1465. At the Suppression the area occupied by the College was greatly enlarged by the acquisition of land to the north belonging to the Carmelite friary; this was bought and conveyed to the College by the President, Dr. Mey, in 1544. Previously in 1541 Mey had bought the building materials of the friars' house.

The foundation-stone was laid by Sir John Wenlock, Queen Margaret's Chamberlain, on April 15th, 1448, at the S.E. angle of the old Chapel. The E. range, containing the *Gatehouse*, the N. range, containing the

Chapel and Library, and the E. part of the S. range of *Front Court* were built in 1448 and the rest of the S. range and the whole of the W. range, containing the *Hall* and *Kitchen*, in 1449. The strong presumption is that Reginald Ely was master-mason. The contractors for the timber-work were John Veyse, draper, and Thomas Sturgeon, carpenter, both of Elsenham in Essex, Veyse no doubt being a guarantor; their contracts include a brief specification for the existing roof over the Hall.

The range incorporating a covered walk on the W. of *Cloister Court* was built probably shortly after the middle of the 15th century and stood as a separate building until the walks on the N. and S. sides of Cloister Court were added, presumably *c.* 1494–5. In 1564 a range was built in Pump Court. At some date in the 16th century the existing timber *Gallery* and upper storey, forming part of the *President's Lodge*, were built over the N. walk of Cloister Court; there seems to be no sufficient reason for assigning this building to *c.* 1537–41; all the surviving detail is of much later date, being more appropriate to the Presidency of Dr. Humphrey Tindall (1579–1614). The range on the E. side of *Walnut Tree Court* was erected in 1616–19.

The new buildings forming the S. and W. sides of *Pump Court* were built from the designs of James Essex in 1756–60; these were the only parts completed of a scheme for rebuilding the whole of the river-front of the College. Between 1789 and 1793 a new staircase planned by Carter was added on the N. of the President's Lodge, and in 1804 an addition on the N. of the N. range of Front Court was made. In 1886 a range of chambers was built on the N. side of Walnut Tree Court, followed by the new *Chapel*, designed by Bodley and Garner, in 1890 and a further range N. of the new Chapel in 1912. The modern buildings W. of the river were erected in 1935–6 from the designs of G. Drinkwater. The old Chapel was fitted up as the *War Memorial Library* in 1951–2.

At Queens' College the Cambridge college court is seen for the first time fully developed; the buildings are amongst the best-preserved examples of mediaeval collegiate architecture in the University. The structure of the President's Lodge and the Cloister Court are highly remarkable; the covered walks round three sides of the latter are in the nature of pentices rather than true cloister-alleys.

Architectural Description—The ranges round Front Court and the W. range and the covered walks of Cloister Court are built of brick and clunch; in Front Court the brickwork is a facing to infilling of clunch or chalk rubble. The Gallery and the storey above in the President's Lodge are of timber-framing with lath and plaster panels. The E. range of Walnut Tree Court is of brick with stone dressings. The buildings by Essex and the 18th and 19th-century additions are of white brick. The roofs are covered with modern tiles and slates.

Front Court (98 ft. by 84¾ ft.) is entered through the Gatehouse placed off-centre in the E. range and which, with the rest of the range, was built in 1448. The *Gatehouse* is of brick with stone dressings and of three stages, with an octagonal turret at each angle, a chamfered plinth and restored embattled parapets. On the E. (Plate 251), the entrance has a four-centred moulded arch in a square head with the mouldings (p. 394) dying out against the plain splays of the jambs, a label with stops carved as demi-angels holding scrolls, and, at the apex of the arch, a half-length figure of a priest holding a scroll; the traceried spandrels enclose quatrefoils framing blank shields. The dressings of the arch and the sculpture have been much recut, if not renewed. The archway is fitted with original oak doors of two leaves with a wicket; a second wicket has been cut subsequently. Each leaf is in two heights of four vertical ridged panels in chamfered framing and retains the original wrought-iron strap-hinges and locking-bar. In the stage above are two windows each of one light with moulded reveals, four-centred cinquefoiled head and label and entirely restored externally; between them is a niche with a moulded bracket on a corbel carved with a leopard's head, side-standards supported on separate smaller corbels and a canopy with ribbed vault and a crocketed spire. The third stage has a single window, similar to those below, and on the parapet-string are two carved gargoyles. The turrets have single-light windows with cinquefoiled heads.

The W. face (Plate 228) is generally similar to the E. face but the turrets are larger. The archway is partly restored and has splayed jambs and a moulded four-centred arch with a label (p. 394) and grotesque head-stops. The second stage has a largely restored window of two pointed lights in a four-centred head with pierced spandrels and moulded reveals; this and the other similar windows in the Court may once have had cinquefoiled cusping similar to that remaining in the original windows on the N. side of the N. range. The third stage has a window uniform with that below but with a label. On the parapet are two gargoyles, one the head of a man, the other of a grotesque. The turrets have a number of small loop-lights and some larger openings with square heads all more or less restored. The N. doorway in the N. turret has chamfered jambs and a two-centred head with a label, all renewed.

Inside the Gatehouse, the *Gatehall* (18¾ ft. by 12 ft.) has, in the N. wall, modern openings to the Porter's Lodge and, in the S. wall, an old doorway with chamfered jambs and four-centred head. It is covered by an original ribbed stone vault (Plate 297) in two bays springing from vaulting-shafts with moulded octagonal bases and caps. The vault has moulded main, intermediate and lierne ribs with two large carved bosses, of St. Margaret and St. Bernard, at the main intersections; the remaining bosses are smaller and carved with foliage and fruits. The rooms over the Gatehall are approached by a newel-stair in the N.W. turret with original stone steps with renewed treads, except above the level of the second floor where they are of clunch and much worn.

The *Muniment Room* on the first floor is entered through a clunch doorway with four-centred head at the top of a short

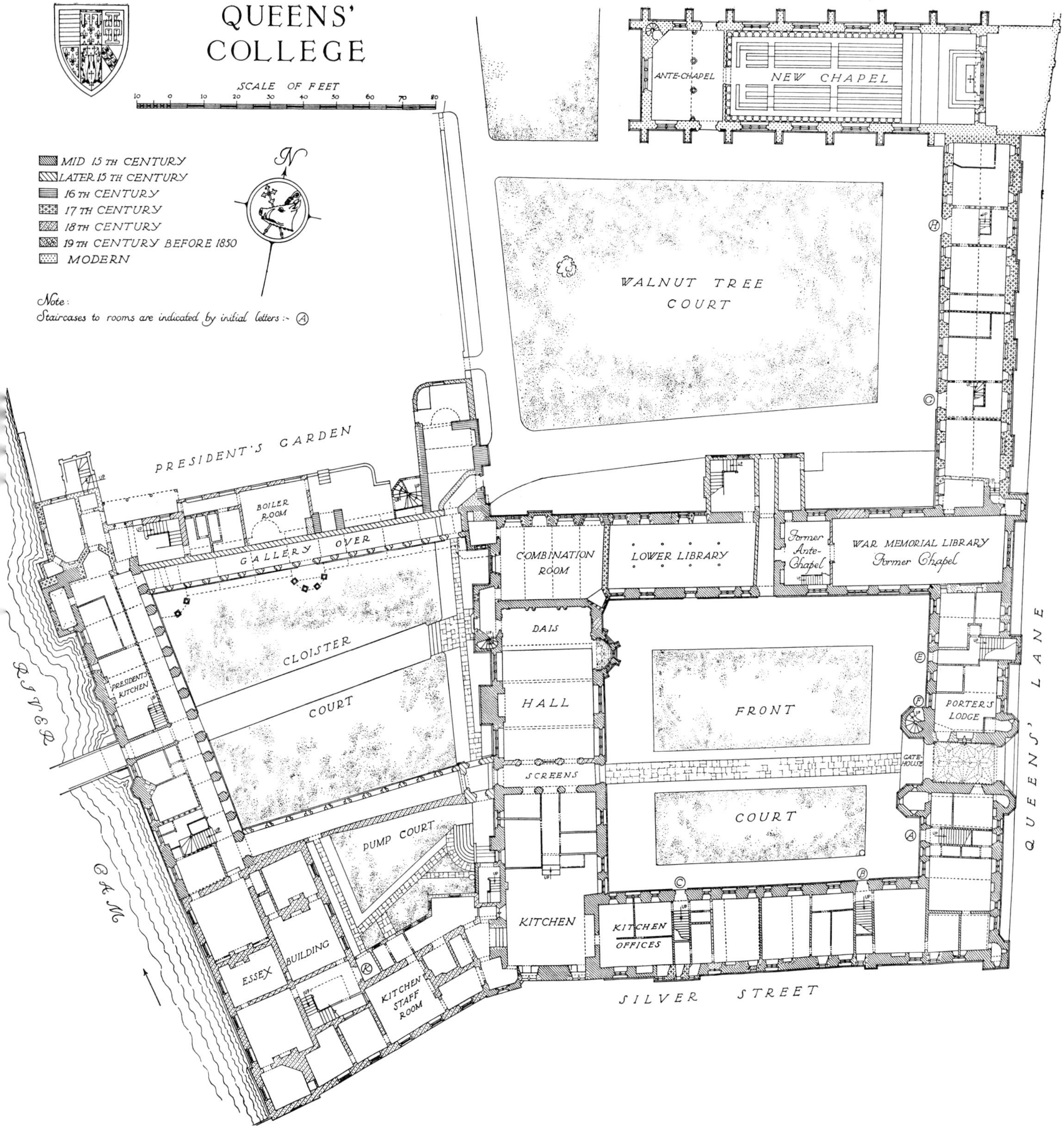

QUEENS' COLLEGE
SCALE OF FEET
10 0 10 20 30 40 50 60 70 80
MID 15 TH CENTURY
LATER 15 TH CENTURY
16 TH CENTURY
17 TH CENTURY
18 TH CENTURY
19 TH CENTURY BEFORE 1850
MODERN
N
Note:
Staircases to rooms are indicated by initial letters :- A
ANTE-CHAPEL
NEW CHAPEL
WALNUT TREE COURT
PRESIDENT'S GARDEN
BOILER ROOM
GALLERY OVER
COMBINATION ROOM
LOWER LIBRARY
Former Ante-Chapel
WAR MEMORIAL LIBRARY
Former Chapel
DAIS
HALL
SCREENS
CLOISTER COURT
FRONT COURT
PORTER'S LODGE
GATE-HOUSE
QUEENS' LANE
PRESIDENT'S KITCHEN
RIVER CAM
PUMP COURT
KITCHEN
KITCHEN OFFICES
ESSEX BUILDING
KITCHEN STAFF ROOM
SILVER STREET

flight of brick steps entered from the newel-stair through a similar doorway. The room has a quadripartite vault with chamfered plastered brick ribs springing from moulded clunch corbels and with clunch intersections; the floor is paved with original plain tiles with yellow and green glaze. It contains two 17th-century presses, one of oak and the other of pine, with panelled fronts and wrought-iron hinges, one with cock's-head terminals. Entry to the room above is similar to that below but the inner doorway is of the 18th century and the framed door has fielded panelling.

The *East Range* N. and S. of the Gatehouse is of two storeys with attics. The modern eaves-cornices here and on the other 15th-century ranges reproduce those shown in Loggan's view of the College, which were subsequently replaced by embattled parapets. The E. wall is continued to form the end wall of the N. range and contains the E. window of the old Chapel under a gable flanked, on the N., by a square turret with stone quoins and one and two-light windows with cinquefoiled openings under four-centred heads, all renewed externally. Further S. is a second square turret of three stages with a modern parapet with embrasures and an old gargoyle-face on the parapet-string. All the windows are restored externally and most of them have cinquefoiled heads; immediately N. of the second turret are two single-light windows on the ground floor, the northernmost modern, and a third window on the first floor. Between the second turret and the Gatehouse the ground floor contains a single-light modern window and a window of two cinquefoiled lights in a square head with an old relieving-arch; on the first floor is a modern window, similar to that below, and a window of two cinquefoiled lights with a quatrefoiled spandrel in a four-centred head with moulded reveals; the chimney-stack is modern. This part of the range N. of the Gatehouse has two renewed dormer-windows of timber.

The E. wall S. of the Gatehouse has on the ground floor, five windows; from N. to S., the second and fourth are modern, the northernmost is of one cinquefoiled light in a square head and the third and fifth are of two similar lights in a square head; all, except the modern windows, have been entirely restored but have old relieving-arches. On the first floor are five windows symmetrically arranged; the middle one is of two cinquefoiled lights with a quatrefoil in a two-centred head, the rest are single cinquefoiled lights and all are entirely renewed externally. The chimney-stack and two dormer-windows are modern. The turret at the S.E. angle is of three storeys with an embattled parapet; an oblique wall in the re-entrant angle on the N.E. face with a four-centred brick arch on the ground floor, now blocked, terminates and is roofed over below the main eaves. On the ground floor, in the E. face, is a small renewed light with two-centred head and, in the S. face, a light with a segmental-pointed head, chamfered reveals and a square label, all original but much weathered; on the first floor is a later rectangular light, modern externally, and on the parapet-string a lion-headed gargoyle.

The W. face of the E. range, N. of the Gatehouse, has in the centre a doorway with an original four-centred moulded head and label and renewed chamfered jambs; flanking it are single-light windows and, beyond, two-light windows, originally all with cinquefoiled lights in four-centred heads but with the cusps now removed; one of the single-light windows is entirely modern externally. The four windows on the first floor are similar but renewed; above are three 18th-century dormer-windows. S. of the Gatehouse, on the ground-floor, are four original openings set closely together, consisting of a doorway similar to that further N. between two single-light windows with a two-light window to the S., all with brick relieving-arches; the outer faces are plastered and the cusps of the windows have been removed. On the first floor are two single and one two-light windows, as before, and on the roof are two 18th-century dormer-windows.

The *Interior* of the E. range, N. of the Gatehouse, contains the *Porter's Lodge* and sets of rooms. The Lodge has an original stone fireplace with a chamfered four-centred head. In the N. end wall of the range are two plain recesses formerly opening through into the Chapel. The ceiling-beams and wall-plates are moulded and chamfered. The staircase is modern and the upper floors are without ancient features; the roof is ceiled. S. of the Gatehouse, the range contains on the ground floor an original clunch doorway with four-centred head to the S.E. turret and moulded ceiling-beams and plates. On the first floor a room is lined with early to mid 18th-century fielded panelling with dado and cornice; the fireplace has a plain clunch surround with two bolection-moulded panels over; the doors are panelled and retain their original brass locks. The part N. of the stair retains an original timbered partition and moulded wall-plates; at the head of the stairs, on the attic floor, is a late 18th or early 19th-century balustrade.

The *North Range*, built in 1448, contains the old Chapel occupying the full height of the eastern half; the remainder is of two storeys with attics and contains the Library. The E. range of Walnut Tree Court abuts on the N.E., a small rectangular 19th-century annexe projects from the centre on the N. front and the W. end of the same front is gabled.

The former *Chapel* (67 ft. by 19¾ ft. including the Ante-chapel) was licensed for services in 1454. The interior was re-fitted in 1773–5 under the direction of James Essex when a plaster ceiling was inserted and cedar panelling, which in Cole's time, 1742, was on the E. wall, was removed to the Ante-chapel; the latter has now been replaced by later panelling. In 1845 the plaster ceiling was removed and the decayed earlier roof above replaced by a modern copy. Extensive refitting was done in 1858–61 by Bodley. After 1890, when the new Chapel was built, it was used for various purposes until fitted up as the War Memorial Library in 1951–2. The E. window is of five ogee cinquefoiled lights with vertical tracery in a four-centred head with moulded reveals and a label with head-stops all renewed; a transom was removed between 1858 and 1861 and the lower part blocked with brick. In the N. wall are two completely restored windows with original relieving-arches; they have three cinquefoiled ogee lights with vertical tracery in a four-centred head with a label; immediately to the W. of the westernmost is a large relieving-arch with later brick blocking below and set in brickwork of a different character from that of the walling to the E. Loggan shows a small gabled annexe approximately in this position, now demolished, and the different brickwork is probably a refacing. The former Ante-chapel is lit from the N. by a window with three pointed lights in a four-centred head under a narrower relieving-arch; on the first floor is a blocked single-light window with a clunch head and jambs under a wider relieving-arch.

The three S. windows of the old Chapel are similar to those on the N. with a blocked doorway below the easternmost. The former Ante-chapel window is similar to that opposite, but with moulded head and reveals, and above it on the first floor are two windows, of a single light and two lights, similar to those in the W. face of the E. range and with part of a wide relieving-arch centrally over them; the E. light of the two-light window is blocked internally. It seems that the body of the Chapel was at first one bay longer and that shortly after completion a floor was inserted in the W. bay and the Ante-chapel formed; this necessitated the removal of the large westernmost windows in the N. and S. walls and the insertion of the present windows, only the original wide relieving-arches remaining to indicate the first arrangement.

The S. archway to the passage leading to the old Chapel has chamfered jambs, moulded four-centred head and a restored label; above it is a single-light window similar to that further E. over the Ante-chapel and these two, which now light an eastward extension of the Library (see below), flank a large painted sundial with the Signs of the Zodiac and tables of calculations below. The sundial is probably of mid 17th-century origin, but renewed in or shortly before 1733 and subsequently repainted. The wooden turret on the roof standing on a square base containing a clock was constructed to Hare's designs in 1910, it is octagonal with open traceried sides and ogee lead-covered dome surmounted by a wrought-iron weather-vane incorporating the College crest of a demi-eagle.

The *Interior* of the old Chapel had in the S. wall openings, now blocked, to the organ-chamber inserted into the N. end of the E. range in 1858–61. Vestry and organ-loft were formerly in a building projecting on the N., as at Christ's College. Round the room is a modern gallery. Stairs at the W. end lead to the Library-annexe over the former Ante-chapel; chambers in this position were converted for use in part as a President's pew in 1773, the rest of the space being incorporated in the Library. The mid 15th-century W. doorway has stop-moulded jambs and four-centred head. The mid 19th-century timber ceiling is five sided, boarded and panelled and with moulded and embattled wall-plates; the painting is said to reproduce the pre-existing colour-scheme. The former Ante-chapel is lined with panelling with a dado and moulded cornice fitted in 1773–5; the W. doorcase has side pilasters and a panel above; a doorway in the N.W. corner opens into a ringing-recess with plaster barrel-vault. The Chapel-passage has plaster pilasters with caps of Gothic design at the junction between the 15th and early 19th-century buildings and a plaster ceiling from end to end with a moulded cornice enriched with plaster paterae, all of 1804.

Fittings, except where stated, removed to the late 19th-century Chapel—*Bell:* on old Chapel, one, by Miles Graye, 1637. *Brasses* and *Indents:* (1) of [John Stokes], S.T.P., 1568, President, with inscription-plate, marginal inscription and indent of figure; (2) of priest in cope, head missing, with part of scroll and indent of inscription-plate, *c.* 1480; (3) (Plate 5) of Robert Whalley, 1591, Fellow, with figure in civil dress, scroll, achievement-of-arms quarterly of nine, of Whalley, Leake, Stockton, Kirton, Hatfield, Selioke, Warde, Francis, and Mallet, inscription-plate and mutilated marginal inscription with one corner-plate remaining engraved with a cockatrice displayed; (4) of figure in academic dress with indent of inscription-plate, early 16th-century, with added inscriptions: to Martin Dunstan, 'servus' to Andrew Docket, 17th-century, and to Laurence Catelyn, S.T.P., 1680, Fellow. *Glass:* In old Chapel—in tracery-lights of E. window, small figure subjects, the Annunciation, St. George, two bishops, and St. Andrew, angels and sacred monogram above; in tracery of N.E. window, St. Margaret and St. Bernard; in tracery of N.W. window, a martyr, St. Catharine, a bishop, St. Cecilia; all in similar style and probably the remains of windows by Barnett of York inserted 1846–8. In tracery-lights of S. windows, angels playing musical instruments, remnants of glazing by Hardman, mid 19th-century.

Monuments and *Floor-slabs. Monuments:* (1) of David Hughes, S.T.B., 1777, Fellow, wall-tablet of wood with painted cornice and scroll-cresting; (2) of Henry James, 1716–7, Fellow, Regius Professor of Theology, white marble wall-tablet with foliated frame and cartouche containing the arms of James; (3) of William Sedgwick, 1760, President, white marble wall-tablet; (4) of John Darell, 1771, Fellow-commoner, white marble wall-tablet with pedimental head; (5) of Thomas Sowerby, 1808, Fellow, white marble wall-tablet with pedimented cornice. *Floor-slabs:* In old Chapel, (1) of Robert Powell, 1690, Fellow; (2) of Richard Bryan, 1680, Fellow, Vice-President, slate; (3) of John May, 1749, Fellow, slate; (4) of Samuel Edwards, 1730, slate; (5) of Isaac Carew, 1742, Fellow, slate; (6) of Edward Kemp, 1671, slate; (7) of John Davies, 1731–2, President, with defaced achievement-of-arms. *Paintings* (Plate 222): In late 19th-century reredos, painted panels from triptych, of the Betrayal, the Resurrection, Christ appearing to the Apostles after the Resurrection, Rhenish, probably Cologne, late 15th-century.

Westward from the old Chapel, the N. side of the range, W. of the 19th-century annexe, shows an area of clunch masonry with traces of a projecting building now removed. The seven restored windows on the ground floor are insertions, but indications of the earlier fenestration remain; the easternmost window is of two lights and of the late 17th century, the following three are of one and two rectangular lights with chamfered reveals and mullions and of the early 17th century. Over the W. half of the fourth is the relieving-arch of an original two-light window and, proceeding westward, are the E. jamb and part of the pointed head and relieving-arch of an original single-light window cut into by a later opening now blocked and with a two-light stone-mullioned and transomed window with architrave probably of 1686 in the blocking. Two windows similar to the last flank the chimney-stack and replace wider windows. On the first floor are four original windows to the Library and a fifth further W. each of two cinquefoiled lights with a quatrefoil in a four-centred head and with chamfered reveals; two others, one of which is blocked, are masked by the 19th-century annexe. Flanking the chimney-stack on the W. are two late 17th-century mullioned and transomed windows similar to those below; in the gable, lighting the attics, are two 16th-century windows each of two four-centred lights in a four-centred head, rendered outside. On the roof over the Library are four 18th-century dormer-windows. The chimney-stacks are modern.

The annexe of 1804 is on the site of an earlier building; the latter, with a small tower or bell-turret, is shown in Loggan's view of the College. It is of white brick with stone dressings. The N. doorway has chamfered jambs and a four-centred head. The ground-floor windows are of two rectangular lights with chamfered reveals and mullions, and those on the upper floor are of two cinquefoiled lights with a pierced spandrel in a four-centred head.

The S. side of the range, W. of the old Chapel block (Plate 221), has on the ground floor one single-light and three two-light windows and a blocked doorway; all originally served sets of rooms and are similar to the corresponding features on the W. side of the E. range. The original Library is lit by a range of six two-light windows uniform with those below and faced with plaster; the two single-light windows in the E. extension (see below) have been described with the exterior of the former Chapel.

The *Lower Library* (44¼ ft. by 18¾ ft.) was formed about the middle of the last century, the pre-existing partitions being removed and the upper floor supported on cast-iron columns. It contains a number of oak presses with desk-tops and panelled ends with shaped heads given in 1819. The *Library* (67¾ ft. by 20 ft.) on the first floor is approached by a staircase in, and contemporary with, the annexe, with close-strings, turned balusters, square newels and moulded handrail. The room (plan p. 175) retains original moulded ceiling-beams and plates and the old flooring of broad oak planks. An eastward extension, marked by a step, was made from the remainder of the set of rooms converted into the President's pew in 1773. At the W. end (Plate 41) is early 17th-century shelving with a central doorway with a pierced balustraded door to a cupboard above and both flanked by tall superimposed Doric and Ionic pilasters with straight sides and the faces decorated with fluting and strapwork ornament; at the head is a plain frieze with square jewelled blocks at intervals.

The five projecting bookcases and two half-cases on either side retain in the lower parts the oak bases with heavy moulded feet and the shaped ends of the 16th century desks; the dentilled and jewelled entablatures and panelled upper portions with a return of the entablatures, shaped cresting and urns are additions assigned to Andrew Chapman, 1612–3; in the 18th century they were heightened by the insertion of plain boarding in the ends and the addition of three pinewood shelves. Under the windows are 18th-century pinewood cases.

The N. windows contain reset 15th-century glass, said to have come from the Carmelite friary, consisting of heads of friars in medallions, ten in all, set in quarries diapered with flower-sprays in silver-stain, all in borders of quatrefoils or oak-leaves, and with fragments of black-letter inscriptions, including 'otus Badrl' and 'Magr̄ Thome Wett' in Italian capitals. The range has an extensively renewed timber roof with collars and braces.

The gable towards the W. end defines the rooms contained in the external angle between the N. and W. ranges; the Combination Room is on the ground floor, with the President's Study above and a bedroom in the attics. The absence of alignment, apparent here on the plan, coincides with the juncture of the two periods of building, and may be so explained; subsequent alterations make the detailed sequence of construction difficult to determine. The rooms each have a window splayed across the N.W. angle of Front Court, the lower probably of 1686 with transom and mullion, the upper of the 16th century, of two transomed lights with four-centred head, and restored. In the W. wall on each floor is a window similar to the other late 17th-century windows on the lower floor. Off the N.W. angle is a rectangular turret probably incorporating some of the walling of an original and similar feature but apparently altered and in part rebuilt before the completion of the N. covered walk of Cloister Court in which it is incorporated; it now stands only to the height of the lower floor and contains a small room with a 17th-century two-light window in the S. wall.

The *Combination Room* (Plate 64) (31 ft. by 21¼ ft.) has an open timber ceiling with original moulded ceiling-beam and plates with applied modern cornice-mouldings. The walls are lined with bolection-moulded oak panelling with dado and moulded cornice made by Austin in 1686; over the 17th-century fireplace with square moulded head and jambs and bolection-moulded wood surround is a moulded shelf with bolection-moulded panel above flanked by panelled pilasters; the projecting moulded doorcases have moulded architraves, entablatures and frieze-panels; the doors are in two bolection-moulded panels and retain early brass rim-locks. The heraldic glass is mostly early 19th-century and probably by Charles Muss: in the N.E. window, of the Earl of Stamford, Grey quartering Booth, and of Thomas Harrison, Fellow, 1794, Harrison impaling (unidentified 18); in the centre window, of Henry VI impaling Margaret of Anjou, 15th-century, of Queens' College, 18th or 19th-century, and of the College impaling Isaac Milner, President, dated 1821; in the N.W. window, of Simon Patrick, Bishop of Ely; in the S.E. window, of Joseph Jee, B.D., Fellow, and of John Davenant, S.T.P., President 1614–21, Bishop of Salisbury; in the W. window, of the Royal Foundresses, Elizabeth Woodville and Margaret of Anjou, in quatrefoils with crowns above and inscriptions in scrolls below.

The *President's Study* on the first floor is divided from the Library by a narrow vestibule with an original timber-framed W. partition-wall. The open timber ceiling has a moulded beam and renewed moulded wall-plates. In the S. wall is a recess containing a round-headed niche with a loop opening into the Hall. The walls are lined to two-thirds of their height with panelling now made up with much modern work; some was originally in the Hall and removed presumably during the alterations of 1732–4. It consists of three heights of linen-fold panels with a deep frieze containing panels carved with antique heads in wreaths and shields-of-arms retaining much original colouring (Plate 65). Accounts dated 1531–2 for the work survive. The timber was bought from Lynn; the carvers were Giles Fambeler and Dyrik Harison and the painter John Ward. The arms on the E. wall are of (2) Holland impaling Tiptoft, (4) Green impaling Rolfe, (6) Tiptoft impaling Spencer, (9) as (6), (11) Wentworth impaling Spencer (reversed), (12) Holland impaling Tiptoft and Charlton quarterly, (13)

Roos impaling Spencer, (15) Humburlton, and (18) as (6); on S. wall, (22) as (6), (26) obscured, (27) as (2), (30) as (4), (33) as (4) and (36) as (6); on W. wall, (39) St. Aubyn, (41) St. Aubyn impaling Tilney, (44) as (13), (46) as (41), (49) as (4) and (51) as (11); on N. wall, (54) as (41), (57) Humburlton, and (61) as (11). The attic above, now called the Founder's Bedroom, was fitted up in the 16th century; the windows, both with graffiti on the splays, and the fireplace with flat three-centred head are of this date.

The *West Range*, S. of the Combination Room, contains the Hall, with the Screens, Butteries and Kitchen to the S., and was built in 1449. The *Hall* (Plate 221) (27¼ ft. by 52½ ft. including the Screens) is of five bays. In the E. wall of the N. bay, high up, is the relieving-arch of a window shown in Loggan's view of the College of *c.* 1688 and blocked probably in the 18th century. Continuing southward, the next bay contains the three-sided oriel-window, with restored three-stage buttresses, pinnacles and parapets and, in each face, a restored two-light transomed window with cinquefoiled openings and vertical tracery in a flat four-centred head with a label; extensive restorations to it were made in 1854. In each of the two following bays is a large window of three lights with tracery in a four-centred head with a label; both were designed by Thomas Johnson in 1854 to replace very similar but smaller features. The doorway to the Screens-passage has restored splayed jambs, an original moulded two-centred head (p. 393) and a modern label; it is fitted with a 15th-century oak door of four vertical panels with trefoiled ogee heads with flowers and beasts on the cusp-points, crocketed finials and blind tracery above, all surrounded by a border of quatrefoils and trefoil-headed panels partly restored. Over the doorway is a stone achievement-of-arms of the College in a tabernacle-frame with Ionic side-pilasters and pedimented entablature supported on head-corbels of the Foundresses; it was carved by Thomas Graye in 1575 and painted originally by Theodore.

On the W. side of the Hall, at the N. end, is a broad shallow projection with a stair in the S. end added probably shortly after the completion of the range and subsequently raised to the full height of the building; in it is a restored 17th-century doorway with moulded jambs and segmental head with plain spandrels; the one and two-light windows with two-centred or square heads are much restored. In the second and fourth bays are windows similar in design and origin to those in the opposite wall; they flank a boldly projecting chimney-stack of two weathered stages, which is rebuilt above eaves-level. In the fifth bay the original doorway to the Screens-passage has stop-moulded jambs, renewed at the base, and a four-centred head (p. 393); it is protected by a porch added prior to the contruction late in the 15th century of the adjoining S. covered walk of Cloister Court.

The porch has an open archway on the N. with four-centred head of two continuous chamfered orders, a doorway on the S. with four-centred head of three continuous chamfered orders and a doorway on the W. with segmental head and splayed jambs; the last two doorways are rebated for doors opening outward, presumably into pre-existing structures. The N. and S. walls have 18th-century wood cornices and the W. gable has bargeboards of the same date; in the gable is a plain round light, which is shown cusped in an engraving of 1842.

The *Interior* of the Hall was very much altered by James Burrough in 1732–4 who destroyed the arch-braces of the original roof and inserted a flat plaster ceiling, added new panelling, and simplified the windows. The roof was opened out again and restored in 1845–6 to the designs of Dawkes, architect; he also replaced the tracery in the windows, which was altered again in 1854. The original fireplace was uncovered and restored in 1861 when tiles by William Morris and Ford Madox Brown were added, the heraldic decoration above it being designed by Bodley, who, in 1875, added the wood cresting when carrying out the present colour-decoration of the Hall.

The restored mid 15th-century roof (Plate 226) is divided by trusses with moulded and embattled cambered tie-beams into three bays of which the N. and S. bays are each divided into two subsidiary bays. The tie-beams are carved on the vertical faces with roses and stylised leaf-ornament; they have mid 19th-century braces below forming four-centred arches with traceried spandrels and springing from short wall-posts supported on 19th-century stone angel-corbels. The trusses and two subsidiary pairs of principals have arch-braced collar-beams and king-posts with curved struts. Under the sub-principals are small false hammer-beams carved as angels holding crowned shields charged with the initial letters of the patrons and Foundresses of the College (Plate 226); they have been restored but are for the most part original. The wall-plates are moulded and embattled. The whole roof was coloured in 1875 on the basis of traces of original colouring said to have survived; the gilded lead stars are original.

The oriel-window is semi-octagonal internally and entered through a tall four-centred arch with moulded head and hollow-chamfered and shafted jambs, the last with moulded capitals and bases; the side walls have blind window-light stone panelling; in the angles are vaulting-shafts for a lierne vault with hollow-chamfered ribs which have foliage bosses at all the intersections. The much-restored fireplace in the W. wall of the Hall has a moulded triangular head with spandrels carved with Tudor roses and banded stylised leaf ornament, chamfered jambs and flanking colonnettes with moulded bases and caps. All the windows are filled with heraldic glass by Hardman, of 1854, with the arms of the Presidents and Benefactors of the College.

The back and side walls of the dais are lined with panelling of 1732–4 by Essex, with carving by Woodward. It consists of a centrepiece with coupled and attached Corinthian side-columns framing an eared and enriched panel and supporting a pedimented entablature with 'Floreat Domus' painted in the frieze, a modillion-cornice, and the arms of the College in a cartouche in the tympanum; the pediment is surmounted by the College crest and two urns. The side bays and the returns on the side walls contain large bolection-moulded panels and Corinthian pilasters supporting a continuation of the main entablature; the capitals of the order are linked by frieze-like panels containing looped garlands of foliage and fruit. In the W. return bay is a doorway with moulded and eared architrave, scrolled frieze, and curved pediment, which is matched by a similar but sham door in the E. return. The panelling of the E.

and W. walls, up to the window-sills, and the *Screen* are of the same date and workmanship as the foregoing; they are divided into bays by panelled pilasters on a high continuous moulded plinth with conventional acanthus capitals continued as an enriched crowning member to the rest of the panelling. In each bay is a bolection-moulded and fielded panel, except in the centre three of the five bays of the Screen; these three contain round-headed arches with panelled responds, moulded imposts, carved spandrels and archivolts with cartouches at the apices. The centre cartouche contains the third shield-of-arms of the College (a boar's head with the cross-shaft of St. Margaret and the crozier of St. Bernard), the others the College crest. The outer arches frame doorways fitted with wrought-iron scrollwork gates, contemporary with the Screen, and the centre arch contains a serving-hatch and a solid panelled tympanum. All the 18th-century woodwork is painted dark green with gilded enrichments. The S. face of the Screen is similar to the N. face but plainer. The three doorways in the back wall of the screens have been wholly renewed; the westernmost retains an original door similar in construction to that of the main gate. Over the Screens is a gallery with balustraded front; access to it is through a doorway in the middle of the S. wall with an 18th-century doorcase with eared architrave and pediment supported on console-brackets.

The remainder of the W. range is of two storeys with attics and contains the Kitchen and the Butteries on the ground floor and rooms above. The windows on each side, except those otherwise described, are original but, in common with most of those to this Court, with the cusping removed during the 18th century; some cusping has been restored subsequently. On the E. are three two-light windows to the ground floor and three, similar, on the first floor, with a single-light window with four-centred head in the S.W. angle. On the W. is a buttress-like projection flanked, on the ground-floor, by a two-light window to the N. and a wide 18th-century window under an original relieving-arch to the S. and, on the first floor, by a single-light and a two-light window to the N. and a single-light window to the S. The projecting staircase-bay next to the S. was enlarged in the 18th century in white brick; it rises above the main eaves and has a hipped roof; the openings are of the 18th century or renewed. Continuing southward is an original two-light window high up in the ground floor, a restored window on the first floor and an original chimney-stack with crow-stepped weathering; the lower part of the stack is built up against the S.W. angle-turret. On the roof-ridge of this range is a late 19th-century bell-cote over the screens; the bell is inaccessible.

The S.W. angle-turret, known as Erasmus' Turret from his occupation of it, is of four storeys, with an embattled parapet; in the ground floor, on the S., is a restored window of two pointed lights in a four-centred head with a small brick light over; in the floor above is a blocked window; the remaining one and two-light windows on each floor in the N. and S. walls are original or of the 17th century and more or less restored.

Inside, the Kitchen and Butteries have been modernised but retain one original ceiling-beam. The main room on the first floor is lined with 18th-century fielded panelling with dado and dentil-cornice; this room was fitted for use as a chapel in 1773 while the old Chapel was being altered. The Erasmus Room to the S. has a dado and doors of 18th-century fielded panelling and a restored open timber ceiling with moulded beams. The attics retain an original timber-framed partition and the collar-beam roof is exposed; they are lit by 18th-century dormer-windows.

The *South Range* contains sets of rooms served by staircases 'B' and 'C'. The junction between the two dates of building is clearly marked by a line in the brickwork between the third and fourth windows; the work of 1448 stopped at this point and was continued westward a year later. On the N. side the doorways and windows are similar to those towards the Court in the E. range; their arrangement on the ground floor is shown on the plan. On the first floor the arrangement is very similar but with the third window over 'B' doorway, the ninth over 'C' doorway, and without a window over the westernmost ground-floor window. On the roof are eight 18th-century dormer-windows.

The S. side (Plate 228) between the S.E. and S.W. angle-turrets is divided into three unequal bays by a shallow buttress in two weathered stages to the E. and a wide garderobe of shallow projection further W. The junction between the two stages of building is immediately W. of the third window W. of the buttress. In the brickwork of the lower part of the later walling are diapers of darker bricks, now scarcely perceptible. At the western end is the gable-end of the W. range of Front Court which is of the same build with the W. portion of the range. On the ground floor the original two-light windows have square heads and all are extensively restored; the two under the gable are shown by the original brick relieving-arches above to be modern replacements of smaller windows; the small rectangular lights, the fourth of which is blocked, are insertions of the 17th century, and at this time similar windows were inserted in the garderobe when it became disused, excepting one original window where shown on the plan, of one light with rounded opening and spandrels in a square head; just over the W. reveal of the latter and over the E. reveal of the fifth window are two 17th-century windows, the first now blocked. The first-floor windows are for the most part of one, two and three lights with cinquefoiled openings in four-centred heads, all almost wholly restored. They are placed over the large windows below, except the third, now blocked, rather to the W. of the corresponding window below and the sixth, immediately W. of the garderobe projection; the garderobe has at this level one small rectangular light, perhaps original, and a larger inserted 18th-century window. Under the main eaves are two small round-headed single-light windows, one immediately W. of the buttress, the other over the weathered head of the garderobe projection. In the roof are twelve 18th-century dormer-windows and in the gable two restored windows of one and two lights similar in detail to those on the first floor. The bases of all the chimney-shafts are original; the shafts were rebuilt in paler brick probably in the 18th century.

Inside the S. range the ground-floor rooms retain original moulded ceiling-beams and the staircases much of their original timbered containing-walls. Most of the doors are of 18th-century fielded panelling. In the room E. of staircase 'B' is an original stone fireplace with a chamfered four-centred head and in the room E. of the middle partition an 18th-century stone fireplace-surround with fluted key. The two rooms over the foregoing are lined with 18th-century fielded panelling with dado and dentil-cornice and eared panels over the fireplaces; in the second room are two original ceiling-beams; the bedroom and study have original timber-framed partitions E. and W., the former much renewed, and an early 17th-century pinewood panelled partition dividing them. The moulded wall-plates on the N., S. and W. walls are original; on the E. is a plain head-rail. At the head of staircase 'C', on the first floor, are the remains of the original garderobe with a barrel-vault and lamp-niche. The room on the first floor W. of the same stair is lined with 18th-century fielded panelling with dado and moulded cornice and with a bolection-moulded panel over the fireplace; the fireplace has a plain white marble surround. At the top of the early 19th-century continuation of this staircase is an opening fitted with a 17th-century panelled door with wrought-iron hinges to a floor now removed. In the attics are some old timber-framed partitions.

Cloister Court, of irregular shape (average 89 ft. by 69 ft.), lies immediately to the W. of Front Court. The *North Range* (Plate 220) contains on the ground floor a covered-walk with open arcading to the Court and on the first floor the Gallery of the President's Lodge, with rooms above. The late 15th-century arcaded walk has a brick-built S. wall; in it are seventeen openings with four-centred arches of two continuous chamfered orders; the first and ninth opening, the latter higher than the others and with a third order, are continued down to the ground to form doorways. The N. wall is of clunch and brick and the two walls together support the timber-framed building above, which is jettied out some 2¼ ft. on either side. Earlier supports to the middle and W. projecting bays on the S. were replaced by the existing free-standing oak columns in or about 1911. In the pavement of the walk is a slab inscribed 'I. Poley. Bursar 1695', presumably the date of the paving. Adjoining the walk on the N. is a low early 18th-century addition, now including the boiler-room, lit by large windows with casements containing leaded quarries.

A superstructure of some sort seems to have been erected about 1537 but no work clearly of that period is now visible. The date of the existing building containing the Gallery is not certainly determinable but the carved brackets supporting the walls and window-projections belong to a later date than 1537. All these features may be assigned to the Elizabethan period. Furthermore, the survival under the roof of a dormer-window on the E. side of the W. range of Cloister Court with mid 16th-century mouldings indicates that the roof was completed after the time, during the Presidency of Dr. John Stokes (1560–68), when the 'master's upper-chambers' in the W. range were being built. Again, much panelling is known to have been installed in the time of Dr. Humphrey Tindall (President 1579–1614). About 1911 the plaster was stripped from the timber-framing and the latter extensively restored.

The S. side of the timber-framed superstructure is symmetrical, with a semi-octagonal projecting bay in the middle and one three-sided bay at each end, the easternmost rising as an octagon above the roof. It has the jetty supported on timber console-brackets carved with foliage which are placed in total disregard of the spacing of the arcade below. Closely-set timber uprights rise from a moulded bressumer to the height of the heads of the Gallery windows where a small moulded cornice is carried across the face as a string; the studding is continued up in equal spacing and with one range of horizontal timbers to a rail at the wall-head on which is a moulded eaves-cornice. The only diagonal timbering is in the centre bay. The ornamental cappings of the projecting bays shown in Loggan's view of the College were removed and flat roofs substituted in the 18th century. The E. bay is now of three storeys and the others of two, the octagonal top storey of the E. bay finishing in a cornice and framed parapet; the windows on the S.W. face of this bay on each floor are modern replacements. The Gallery window returned round the full width of the middle bay consists of two transomed lights in each face and one on each short return, with moulded frames and mullions and all partly restored; the window on the top floor is similar but without transom. The W. bay has a S.E. window of two transomed lights on the lower floor and a restored two-light window above. Centrally between the bays and lighting the Gallery are two large projecting windows, both of four transomed lights on the face and one on each return, supported on carved console-brackets and with a cornice and modern pediment level with the wall-string; over them are similar windows, but lower and without pediments, lighting the upper floor. Between the upper windows and the bays are small two-light windows, except in the westernmost space.

The N. side (Plate 221) has at the E. end a N.E. wing and at the W. end the brick projecting bay containing the main staircase in the President's Lodge; the latter was added between 1791–3, during the Presidency of Dr. Milner, and planned by Carter; beyond is the N. end of the W. range of Cloister Court. The general treatment is similar to that of the S. side. In the re-entrant angle to the E. is a three-sided projecting staircase-bay with an early 17th-century round-headed timber doorway in the N. face. The doorway has spandrels carved with a putto and two lions and fluted Ionic side-pilasters on pedestals supporting a restored pedimented entablature; it contains a panelled and nail-studded door with 18th-century glazing in the head. In the W. face of the bay is a modern doorway and the two-light windows on the upper floors are largely modern. The main wall-face is divided unequally into two by a brick chimney-stack; towards the outer ends are projecting windows on the two floors similar to those at the same levels on the S. Centrally between the lower western window just described and the stack is a semicircular bow-window to the Gallery supported on two large scrolled brackets; it is of seven transomed lights with moulded frames and mullions. The late 16th or early 17th-century chimney-stack has, on the ground floor, a large arched recess with semicircular stone head with jewel-ornament on the key, a weathering at eaves-level and three tall octagonal shafts, the westernmost a subsequent addition.

The N.E. wing is generally uniform in treatment with the N. range. The ground floor is of 16th-century brickwork with a moulded plinth and refaced on the W. and the timber-framed superstructure stands on moulded plates. The N. end is gabled and the shaped ends of the head-rails of the side walls project at eaves-level and have pierced pendants. The projecting bay on the N. is semicircular; it starts at first-floor level, rises the height of the two upper storeys and has windows the full width on the first and second floors, each of seven transomed lights; the semicircular conical roof of slightly ogee profile against the gable-end is shingled and has a carved wood finial. The E. and W. windows are largely modern. In the E. wall is a late 17th-century doorway S. of the projecting chimney-stack; this last has had the upper part rebuilt. A number of rainwater-heads are of the 18th century.

The bay containing the main staircase in the President's Lodge rises the full height of the range and has a hipped roof. In the N. wall, on the first floor, is a double-hung sash-window with semicircular head set in a recessed wall-arch of the same form. Across the face of the ground floor is an early 19th-century loggia.

The *Interior* of the N. range contains heavy chamfered ceiling-beams across the covered walk. The *Gallery* (Plate 224) (79¼ ft. by 12 ft.) on the first floor is panelled from floor to ceiling with late 16th or early 17th-century oak panelling divided into bays by enriched and fluted Doric pilasters on pedestals, with carved lions' heads on the entablature-blocks; the panels are small, in five heights, with moulded muntins and rails, a moulded plinth and an entablature with reeded frieze. The original fireplace has moulded stone jambs and a four-centred arch with sunk spandrels in a square head; over it are two enriched oak panels divided by a strip-pilaster with scale enrichment, with a band of guilloche-ornament below. The doorways have been altered to some extent to take 18th-century doors and the panelling has been patched in pine. The windows have been much restored; in the S. oriel-window is a quantity of 16th and early 19th-century heraldic glass: in the E. light, of (1) Andrew Docket, President 1448, (2) John Jenyn, President 1519, (3) Simon Heynes, President 1528; in S.E. light, of (1) Thomas Wilkinson, President 1484, (2) Robert Bekensaw, President 1508, (3) William Mey, President 1537, (4) Grey quartering Booth, perhaps late 19th century, (5) John Stokes, President 1560, (6) Thomas Peacock, President 1557; in S. light, of (1) the College, with '1589' in a strapwork panel, and of that date, (2) Humphrey Tindall, Dean of Ely, President 1579, quartering Felbrigg, (unidentified 19), Scales and Mundeford, with 159[0]' in a strapwork panel below, and of that date, (3) achievement similar to (2) but with a sixth quarter of Tindall, (4) John Stokes; in S.W. light, of (1) John Mansel, President 1622, (2) Henry James, President 1675, (3) Robert Plumtre, President 1760, (4) Edward Martyn, President 1631 and 1660, (5) John Davies, President 1717, (6) Isaac Milner, President 1788; in W. light, of (1) William Wells, President 1667, (2) William Sedgwick, President 1732, (3) Thomas Farman (?), President 1525; many of these shields are given gold borders which are no part of the arms. The enriched modern plaster ceiling was designed by H. T. Hare in a style contemporary with the building.

The *Essex Room*, formerly the President's study, on the first floor of the N.E. wing, is lined from floor to ceiling with panelling similar to that in the Gallery. The fireplace has a bolection-moulded stone surround with keyblock of *c.* 1700; the oak overmantel with flanking pilasters is in three bays, each with two heights of enriched arched panels, all much altered and reset. In the glass of the N. window is a late 16th-century achievement-of-arms in a Garter of Robert Devereux, Earl of Essex, Chancellor 1598–1601, with sixteen quarterings, i Devereux, ii Bourchier, iii Woodstock, iv Bohun of Hereford, v Milo, vi Mandeville, vii Louvain, viii Woodville, ix Crophull, x Verdun, xi Bigod, xii Marescal, xiii Ferrers, xiv Chester, xv and xvi destroyed, and talbot and stag supporters. The original staircase adjoining on the W. has an octagonal central newel with a modern cap and a reset balustrade on the first floor with square moulded balusters set diagonally; the landing doorway, with fluted Roman Doric pilasters on pedestals set against the returns of the jambs and supporting a semicircular head with enriched soffit, carved spandrels and key-block, is original. The staircase in the S.E. projecting bay, starting at first-floor level, is a mid 17th-century insertion and cuts across the windows; it has square newels with moulded pendants, plain handrail, two shaped posts on the top landing and modern balusters. The late 18th-century main staircase to the W. rises round four sides of an open well and has a plain cut string, moulded and ramped handrail, slender square balusters and newels in the form of columns.

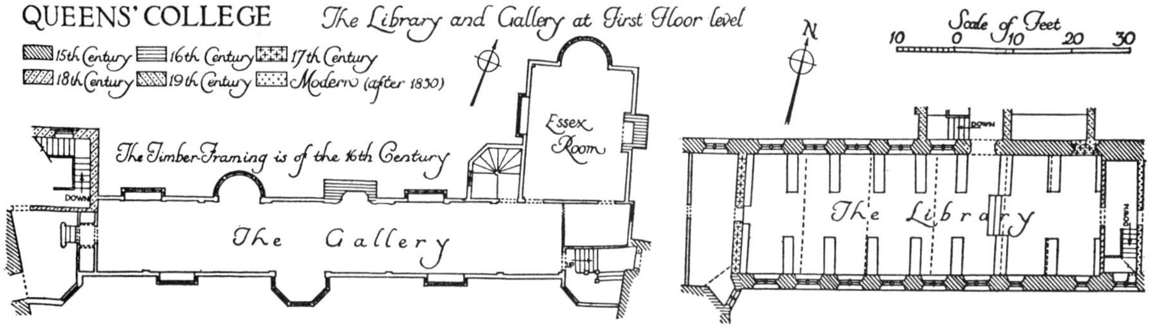

The upper floor, over the Gallery, may originally have formed one large room; all the present rooms are formed by panelled partitions generally of the 18th century. The arched braces of the original roof-trusses, surviving on the N. only, have guilloche-enrichment on the soffits. The E. half of this storey, at a period prior to the insertion of the late 18th-century partitions, formed one room which is now demarcated by the mid 17th-century enriched frieze on the N. and S. walls extending as far as the middle bay on the S. The remainder of the panelling, including some linenfold, is of the 16th, 17th, 18th and early 19th centuries, of oak and pine and all much altered and reset. The original stone fireplace in the N. wall has moulded jambs with shaped stops and a four-centred arch in a square head; the panelling of *c.* 1600 above has three enriched arched panels and frieze-panels carved with arabesques. The bedroom in the N.E. wing is lined with panelling similar to that in the Gallery with a frieze of guilloche-ornament and with pilasters flanking the window-bay. The fireplace and panelled overmantel are generally similar to those in the room below except that the restored and reset overmantel is rather simpler; the S. door is similar to that on the landing of the adjoining staircase on the floor below. In the attic the roofs have been ceiled; the 18th-century dormer-windows retain their original leaded casements.

The *West Range* of Cloister Court is of two storeys with attics and contains the private residential rooms of the President's Lodge and also sets of rooms. It was built between 1448 and before 1494, probably shortly after the earlier date, and originally continued further to the S. On the ground floor and facing the Court is an arcaded covered walk generally similar to that on the N. but of fourteen bays. Also the arches are of three orders, except the northernmost and the eighth from the N. which are of two orders; these last and the southernmost are continued down to form entrances, the N. and S. opening respectively into the N. and S. arcaded walks of the Court; the eighth has a lower and more pointed head than the rest of the arcading. On the first floor is a range of seven 15th-century windows of two four-centred lights in four-centred heads with moulded reveals; an eighth window at the N. end has been blocked and a smaller single-light window of similar character, itself now blocked, inserted.

The W. side (Plate 219), which rises sheer from the river, is divided into three unequal bays by a large rectangular garderobe on the N. and two projecting chimney-stacks with splayed sides further S. It has a chamfered plinth, a stone string at first-floor level and an 18th-century wood eaves-cornice. The original windows are generally similar to those on the E. The garderobe has been extended some 2½ ft. to the N., the original width being indicated by the length of weathered tabling over a shallow projection and by the line of the original W. gable; in the W. face, at water-level, are three two-centred arches and a fourth in the S. face, all now blocked; above is a number of small one and two-light windows with chamfered four-centred heads, all probably original; two are blocked, and of another only the relieving-arch survives. In the northernmost bay is a blocked opening to a drain near water-level and at the same level in the S. bay a large four-centred brick arch to a conduit, also now blocked. In the centre bay the restored doorway giving access to the bridge over the river has chamfered jambs and four-centred head. Of the seven ground-floor windows, six are of two lights, as shown on the plan, and original, with the exception of the middle and northernmost in the S. bay which are modern; the sixth window, in the N. bay, is a plain 18th-century rectangular window. On the first floor, the N. bay contains a large late 17th-century sash-window with moulded stone architrave immediately to the N. of a three-sided oriel-window. This last is said by Cole to have been inserted in 1711, but the style of much of the stonework is a hundred years earlier. The oriel is supported on shaped stone corbels with label-like wall-panels below and has base mouldings in the form of a cornice and frieze, the latter with panel decoration, double-hung sashes, a small stone cornice, and a rusticated and embattled parapet wall. The three first-floor windows in each of the other two bays are of one and two lights and original. The lower parts of the chimney-stacks are original; the shafts were rebuilt in the 18th century.

The N. end of the W. range is covered on the ground floor by largely modern additions. A polygonal turret on the N.E. shown in Loggan's view of the College has been destroyed except perhaps for some thick walling at the base through which the main entrance to the President's Lodge was cut late in the 18th century. The three-storey semi-octagonal bay-window in the centre is probably of the early 17th century; in the two upper floors are much restored windows of two lights on the face and one on each return and with small cornices above. The main eaves have an 18th-century wood cornice.

The *Interior* of the range contains on the ground floor heavy moulded ceiling-beams continued across the covered walk. The partition-walls to the walk and the passage to the bridge are of original timber-framing; the entrance to the passage has been renewed; near the S. end the opening to the stair has a head-beam with braces forming an elliptical arch and all of the 17th century. The late 17th-century S. staircase (Plate 66) has close strings, heavy moulded rail, turned balusters and panelled newels with moulded cappings; it was introduced presumably to give access to the principal rooms on the first floor but now serves the sets of rooms to the S. These last retain only a late 15th-century timber door-frame to the set on the first floor that extends into the Essex Building. The *President's Lodge* (see also Front Court, N. range, and Cloister Court, N. range), occupying the part of the range N. of the bridge passage on the ground floor and N. of the S. staircase on the upper floor, contains at the S. end of the Kitchen an 18th-century staircase and, in the S. wall, an original doorway with four-centred head, now blocked, to the passage. The base of the garderobe, now a small pantry, is barrel-vaulted. The N. end of the original range and the junction with the 17th-century work is marked by a heavy chamfered ceiling-beam; further N. is a later larder with a reused 16th-century door of four panels with moulded and studded framing and strap-hinges.

The President's Dining Room (Plate 210), formerly the Audit Room, over the Kitchen, is panelled throughout with early 17th-century oak panelling divided into bays by reeded and fluted Ionic pilasters on panelled bases supporting an entablature with reeded frieze and carved lions' heads; the bays generally contain seven heights of three rectangular panels in moulded framing. The original stone fireplace has moulded and elbowed jambs and a four-centred head with sunk spandrels bringing it out to a square; it is flanked by wood Roman Doric fluted pilasters supporting a jewelled frieze and shelf. The early

(39) SIDNEY SUSSEX COLLEGE. Chapel; The Nativity.
G. B. Pittoni. Acquired 1783

(33) PEMBROKE COLLEGE. Chapel; The Entombment. Given 1797

(35) QUEENS' COLLEGE. President's Lodge. Interior of Gallery, looking W. Late 16th-century; ceiling modern

1598–1602

(37) ST. JOHN'S COLLEGE. Combination Room, looking W.

(35) QUEENS' COLLEGE.
Hall roof; angel.

(17) SCHOOLS BUILDING. Council Room roof; carved figures. 1466

(35) QUEENS' COLLEGE. Hall roof, looking N. By Thomas Sturgeon. 1449

(41) TRINITY HALL. Chapel, ceiling.

1730

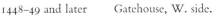

S. side, to Silver Street. 1448–49 and later

Gatehouse, W. side. 1448

(35) QUEENS' COLLEGE.

(36) ST. CATHARINE'S COLLEGE. Gateway; E. frontispiece.
1674–79

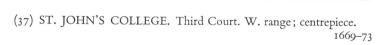

(37) ST. JOHN'S COLLEGE. Third Court. W. range; centrepiece.
1669–73

(40) TRINITY COLLEGE. Hall. Glass in W. oriel-window. *c.* 1425

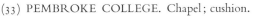

(33) PEMBROKE COLLEGE. Chapel; cushion. *c.* 1665

(37) ST. JOHN'S COLLEGE. Library; shelf-list. *c.* 1625

17th-century overmantel is in three bays divided by pilasters tapering to the base with gadroon ornament below Ionic caps and standing on pedestals with strapwork and prism-ornament and supporting a return of the main cornice from the side walls; the bays are in two heights of panels each containing a geometrical pattern of subsidiary enriched panels. The early 18th-century oriel-window contains heraldic glass: in N.W. light, of (1) the See of Salisbury impaling John Davenant S.T.P., President 1614, Bishop of Salisbury, (2) the See of Rochester impaling John Fisher S.T.P., President 1505, Bishop of Rochester; in middle light, of (1) Henry VI impaling Margaret of Anjou, (2) the College, (3) Edward IV impaling Elizabeth Woodville, (4) Roos impaling Spencer in a lozenge and inscribed 'Domina Margareta de Roos principia benefactrix circa 1478', (5) quarterly (i) Inglethorpe, (ii) Burgh, (iii) Bradston, (iv) de la Pole impaling quarterly (i) and (iv) Tiploft, (ii) Charlton, (iii) Holland, all in a lozenge and inscribed 'D[omi]na Joanna Ingaldesthorp Benefactrix 1491', (6) the See of Lincoln impaling Chaderton, President 1568, Bishop of Lincoln, with 'W.L.' below, (7) the See of Ely impaling (unidentified 20), (8) the See of Winchester impaling H. E. Ryle, President 1896, Bishop of Winchester, all in a Garter; in S.W. light, of (1) the See of Bangor impaling William Glyn, President 1553, Bishop of Bangor, (2) Antony Sparrow, President 1662, Bishop of Norwich, impaling the See of Norwich (reversed). The glass and woodwork of this window were paid for by the President, Dr. James, in 1711, and the original bevelled glass and glazing-bars survive. Most of the shields-of-arms are applied; (7) may be early 18th-century and the remainder later in the century, with the exception of (4), (6) and (8) which are perhaps 19th-century. The ceiling has three 15th-century moulded ceiling-beams and wall-plates.

The President's Drawing Room, immediately N. of the Dining Room, is lined with late 16th-century oak panelling divided into bays by fluted Doric pilasters on pedestals with an entablature with fluted frieze; the bays contain six heights of panels in framing with run-out mouldings. The fireplace is modern; above it is a reset panel containing an 18th-century landscape painting. In the E. wall is a semi-domed recess fitted with 18th-century shelving and with late 16th-century panelled doors with cock's-head hinges. The original entrance to the room was through a small doorway at the E. end of the S. wall; the present entrance-lobby embodying late 16th-century panelling was formed in 1791–3. The room on the first floor of the garderobe on the W., entered through a doorway in the panelling, has a floor of 15th-century tiles. A chute from the floor above against the S. wall has been truncated and supported on shaped brackets in the 18th century; in the wall below is a rebated opening to a small oven with brick vault. Fixed to the wall by the oven is a mid 18th-century turned wood wig-stand. The bedroom over the Drawing Room contains an early 17th-century pinewood panelled dado with a frieze of arabesque-ornament in the N. bay-window. The original N. wall-truss of this range is visible in an alcove in the W. wall of the same room. Built out on the E. slope of the roof and now concealed under the roof of the range containing the Gallery is a mid to late 16th-century dormer-window of four lights with moulded oak frame and mullions (see above under Cloister Court, N. range).

The *South Walk* (Plate 220) of Cloister Court is generally uniform in date and build with the walk incorporated in the N. range; for the greater part of the length it stands free and has a lead-covered roof. The arcade to the Court consists of eleven openings, excluding the earlier porch at the E. end already described; the arches are of two chamfered orders, except the middle one which is higher than the others and of three orders and was originally open down to the ground. The S. wall seems to have been almost entirely rebuilt in the 18th century; the lowest courses are of red brick, the remainder of white brick.

Pump Court (Plate 220), of irregular shape (average 54 ft. by 30 ft.) lies immediately to the S. of Cloister Court and is bounded on the W. and S. by an L-shaped building designed by James Essex and built between 1756 and 1760 as part of a larger scheme for rebuilding the whole of the river-front. *Essex Building* is of three storeys, with walls of white brick in English bond with dressings of Ketton and Portland stone. The W. side rises sheer from the river (Plate 219) and has a high stone plinth with roll-moulded capping. The stone plat-band at first-floor level, the cornice and balustraded parapet are continued across the outward faces; on the Court side the string is omitted and the plain parapet-wall is of brick. All the windows have moulded stone architraves and are placed at regular intervals horizontally, as shown on plan, and vertically; the tallest windows are on the first floor and the shortest, almost square, on the top floor; all contain double-hung sashes except the two blocked windows in the middle of the N. front of the E. wing. The door architraves are similar to those of the windows. One bay on each side flanking the S.W. external angle of the building projects slightly, perhaps in some measure to represent the original turret-treatment at the corners of the 15th-century Front Court; incorporated in the same angle, at ground-floor level, is a stone and cast-iron Doric quarter column. The ground-floor windows to Silver Street (Plate 228) contain original wrought-iron grilles.

The *Interior* of Essex Building contains sets of rooms, with a Kitchen-staff room on the ground floor of the E. wing. The principal staircase is of the date of the building and has moulded close strings, turned balusters, moulded handrail and square newels with moulded caps; against the wall is a panelled dado. The main room in most of the sets is lined with mid 18th-century fielded panelling with moulded dado-rail and wood cornice, some with dentils. The panelling in a room on the second floor, to the N. of the staircase, has all the members enriched with carved leaf and flower ornament and an eared panel in the overmantel. All the original doors are of six fielded panels.

Walnut Tree Court, N. of Front Court, has an E. range built in 1617–9; purchase of the building materials had been begun in 1616. Between 1778 and 1782 the two original attic-storeys were replaced by the present third storey and in 1823 the range was reroofed and the embattled parapet added. The walls are of brick with stone dressings, the latter much refaced with Roman cement. Gilbert Wigge, Henry Mann, Wilson and Pindar all appear in the few surviving accounts for the original work, and of them the two last received considerably more in payment than the others. A sum of 5s. was paid 'to two freemasons for contriving the building' but whether Wigge was in fact one of them is not clear.

The W. face to the Court, excluding the southernmost bay, is symmetrical, with two doorways and one and two-light windows of uniform design disposed as shown on the plan. The arrangement of the windows on the upper floors follows that below, with two-light windows over the doorways. The doorways have splayed jambs and moulded four-centred heads with sunk spandrels and labels. The windows have rectangular openings with splayed reveals and labels with return stops, the wider mullions cloaking internal partition-walls; the original brick relieving-arches are more rounded than those in the mediaeval walling elsewhere; those in the 18th-century walling are segmental. The E. face is symmetrical and divided into five unequal bays by four projecting chimney-stacks; the latter have renewed octagonal shafts. The fenestration is the same on each floor and the windows are similar to those on the E. front except that most of the labels run horizontally and stop against the chimney-stacks. A small loop-light has been inserted on the first floor of the S. bay.

The *Interior* contains sets of rooms. An exposed longitudinal ceiling-beam stops at the S. end of the range where the N. wall of the old Chapel vestry formerly stood. In the S. wall is the 15th-century moulded segmental-pointed rear-arch of the former doorway from the vestry to the old Chapel and in the S. end of the W. wall are parts of a doorway which gave access to the Court from the vestry. The 15th-century N.E. corner-turret of Front Court is now entered from this range through a doorway with rounded head. Three rooms on the ground floor have 17th-century stone fireplaces with moulded jambs and four-centred arches in square heads. The modern panelling on the S. side of the N. main room opens to show a pattern of arcading in blue, green, ochre and red painted on the face of the original timber-framed partition-wall and extending from above a painted dado, now almost entirely destroyed, nearly to the ceiling. It is in seven bays containing semicircular-headed arches with moulded imposts and bases in false perspective and divided and flanked by columns with Corinthian-like capitals (Plate 58). Off centre in the fifth bay a pediment with scrolled cresting appears to replace the arch and one column, but this area is much damaged and in part destroyed. The whole is probably contemporary with the building.

Evidence of the original arrangement of the rooms on the first floor remains in the studding and junction of wall-plates in some of the bedrooms. On the first floor the room S. of staircase 'G' is lined with 18th-century fielded panelling with dado and cornice, and the room to the N. has some similar panelling, much made up. The room N. of staircase 'H' has a 17th-century clunch fireplace similar to the others on the ground floor but with an early 17th-century wood surround with banded and ornamental side-pilasters and moulded shelf and an overmantel in two bays divided and flanked by small coupled columns supporting a deep entablature enriched with paired brackets and strapwork; in each bay is a panel containing an elaborate strapwork framing to a smaller square panel enclosing added shields of the University and the College. Round the same room is a 17th or 18th-century dentil-cornice. Some of the doors to the sets are original and of moulded planks with narrow vertical panels and strap-hinges; a number of 18th-century doors in the sets retain their original brass rim-locks.

Under the walnut-tree in the Court foundations of a clunch wall run E. and W. This probably marks the S. boundary of the Carmelite Convent which was on the N. side of the former lane from Queens' Lane to the river.

The *President's Garden* is bounded on the N. by an old red brick wall and by an 18th-century wall on the E. The *Fellows' Garden* has a N. wall of clunch and reused stone patched with brick; this is probably the wall built by King's College in 1551; the return-wall on the E. as far as the surviving wall of the Carmelite church is of the same character; to the S. of the junction the wall is of 18th-century buff-coloured brick with both strip and two-stage buttresses. The wall of the *Carmelite Church* extends some 165 ft. from this junction towards the new building of 1886. There seems to be little doubt that it is the lower part of the N. wall of the church. It is faced on the S. side with clunch ashlar except for two patches near the middle, which may represent cross-walls or responds. The N. face of the wall is also faced with ashlar; it is divided into seven bays by the remains of former buttresses and has a moulded plinth to the six E. bays; the seventh bay has had the plinth destroyed. In the W. bay is a 14th-century doorway, now blocked, with moulded jambs and much weathered two-centred arch. The whole wall is about 3 ft. thick and has been patched and heightened with brick; no traces of window-sills appear although it stands some 6 ft. high. It is probable from these facts that this is the N. wall of the aisleless church, with the oblong crossing usual in Friars' churches represented by the patched ends of the two cross-walls. The monastic buildings must have stood to the S. of the church and between it and the former lane.

The timber *Bridge* over the Cam was built in 1902 and is a copy of the bridge that was built in 1749–50 by Essex to the designs of W. Etheridge.

The *Brewhouse*, on the W. side of the Cam, first built in 1533–4, was recently converted for use as two junior common-rooms and extensively altered. Some of the brick walls and roof-timbers are old; the brickwork may in part be of the 16th century; the roof-timbers are later. Adjoining the brewhouse on the N. is the *Fellows' Fruit Garden* enclosed by brick walls of different dates. The S. wall, E. of the brewhouse, is of the 17th century and probably of 1667–72; it is about 10 ft. high, with a renewed capping of bricks set on arris and a brick coping. The E. wall is much patched and heightened in white brick and with added buttresses on the west; opposite the timber bridge it contains a modern doorway. The eastern part of the N. wall as far as the break is of the 19th century; the remainder westward is probably late 18th-century and contains a doorway of that date of Bath stone with a square head and moulded architrave. The W. wall is of *c.* 1800, in English bond, and with strip-buttresses on the E. at approximately 13 ft. centres. The S. wall, W. of the Brewhouse, is of modern white brick.

(36) St. Catharine's College stands on the W. side of Trumpington Street bounded on the N. by part of King's College, on the S. by part of Silver Street and on the W. by Queens' Lane. The ranges generally are of three storeys with attics. The walls are of brick with stone dressings and the roofs are tile-covered. It was started in 1473 by Dr. Robert Woodlark, the third Provost of King's College, who had begun the acquisition of the site in 1459. According to his *Memoriale Nigrum* (in College Muniment Room) he founded and built it at his own expense to the honour of God, the most blessed Virgin Mary, and St. Catharine, virgin. Until recent times it was known as St. Catharine's Hall. The original buildings were ranged round a small court adjacent to Milne Street, now Queens' Lane, on the western part of the present site, and were subsequently extended by the addition of a second court on the S.

In 1626 Dr. John Gostlin, Master of Gonville and Caius College, had bequeathed the Bull Inn to St. Catharine's Hall and in 1631–2 Dr. Gostlin's Court on part of this property where it adjoined the original court on the N. was enclosed. In the accounts for 1634–5 to 1636–7 entries occur for the building on the W. side of the new court, now *Walnut Tree Court*. This range, which is the only one of the earlier buildings of the College to survive, is that to Queens' Lane projecting northward from the N.W. corner of the existing main Court

Towards the end of the third quarter of the 17th century rebuilding the College was begun. The remarkably complete accounts for the work survive. Dr. John Lightfoot was Master at the beginning, but the inception of the scheme is attributed to Matthew Scrivener, vicar of Haslingfield (who entered Pensioner in 1639 and died in *c.*1688), and the furtherance of it to the energies and liberality of Dr. John Eachard (Master 1675–97). The ranges to the main Court, excepting Ramsden Building, were completed by the end of the century, though fitting the Chapel continued into the early years of the 18th. No architect's name is recorded but early in the work small payments were made to one Elder, surveyor, from London, and to Robert Grumbold 'for surveying'. In regard to the Chapel, £2 4s. was paid 'to Mr. Talman the King's controller for advice' in April 1696 and most of the payments for it were receipted again by Robert Grumbold.

From February 1673–4 to February 1676–7 some £3,103 was spent and the *Hall*, wainscoted by Cornelius Austin, in the *North Range* is known to have been complete and in use at Whitsuntide 1675. The Master was lodged, temporarily, in this range.

By January 1678–9, with a further expenditure of £1,524, probably most of the *West Range* and *South Range* were built. The curiously contrived change in height between the N. and S. ranges and the W. range may be explained on the N. by the incorporation of an older building, but on the S., the plan of the junction and the continuous roof and architectural unity of the S. end of the W. range indicate a difference in phases of construction and that the W. range preceded the S. range. This and the ill-arranged juxtaposition of windows in the S.W. corner of the main Court may result from a belated readjustment of the S. range to avoid any substantial encroachment upon the Queens' College property lying immediately to the S., because of lack of confidence in the terms of the lease of it sought by St. Catharine's College. Entries in the accounts for 1676 are self-explanatory: shortly after Lady Day 'payment to Howard for pulling down five weeks' work', on 18th October 'pulling down next Queens' and work done inside the second building'. The Queens' Lane front of the W. range is known to have been finished by November 1679, but this is a *terminus ad quem*, though entries for plasterers' work and joinery suggest that completion of the interior was delayed until September 1687.

From 1678–9 to November 1681 an expenditure of £1,101 included for Library fittings and furnishings for the Master's Lodge, Dr. Eachard being housed in the N. range until his Lodge in the S. range was ready. From 1681 to September 1687 £3,217 spent included retrospective payments to tradesmen, considerable interest on money borrowed, and costs of appeals for funds. Work seems to have ceased between 1687 and 1694; the further sum of £1,673 incurred after 1687 is again chiefly the interest on money borrowed.

Between 1694 and January 1696–7 the *Chapel* was structurally completed; an abstract of accounts for the latter date includes 'for finishing down the pediment of the east end of the Chapel at last'. Various expedients, including the sale of plate, were made to meet the deficit in the building-funds, but the money bequeathed by Eachard who died in 1697 and the response to an appeal for contributions in January 1698–9 resulted in a sufficient improvement in the financial position for the Chapel fitting to be begun. Taylor, a London joiner, was paid 'for a draught of the wainscot', though an agreement for it, to be exactly like that in Christ's College Chapel, to be finished before Christmas 1703, was made with John Austin. Thomas Woodward was the carver. The Chapel was consecrated on 1st September 1704 by Simon Patrick, Bishop of Ely. The present organ was installed between 1893 and 1895.

In 1743 Mrs. Mary Ramsden, who died in 1745, bequeathed her estates to the College, directing in her will that ground lying between the College and Trumpington Street should be bought for a new building for Skerne's Fellows and Scholars. *Ramsden Building*, first called Yorkshire Building, begun in July 1757 on the S. side of the Court, balancing the Chapel block, was the outcome of her bequest. By College order of February 1757 it was agreed to seek Burrough's advice on the project, but no payment to him is recorded and James Essex, who had already submitted plans some years earlier (Audit accounts, 1753–4), was the architect employed. The contract for the brickwork was with Simon Barker of Cambridge. The estimated total cost was £7,300. The building seems not to have been occupied at the earliest before July 1772.

The Court thus completed on three sides was opened out on the fourth by demolition of the adjacent Trumpington Street houses and bounded by railings with a central *Gate* some distance eastward; at the same period stables were built S. of the present Bull Hostel in a position immediately N. of the modern Hobson's Building.

Loggan's engraving of *c.* 1688 of the proposed College shows the E. side of the Court enclosed by a range containing the Library and with a central gatehouse, whereas at that time only the buildings bordering the W. half of the Court had been completed. The Chapel and Ramsden Buildings built subsequently follow in mass and position, though not in detail, the scheme adumbrated in Loggan, but the E. range was never built. In 1753, only shortly before the clearance described above, Carter indicates (Edmund Carter, *History of the University*, p. 199) that a library-building on the E. was still proposed. The reason for these proposals is indicated in Loggan's plan of Cambridge, where the E. side is shown to front a narrow lane behind the houses lining Trumpington Street. The main approach, from the beginning of Woodlark's foundation in Milne Street, had been from the W. and doubtless so remained. Thus the present vista from the E. contrived in the 18th century represents a complete re-orientation of approach.

The project for an E. range being abandoned, the upper floor of the Hall block was opened out and fitted for the *Library* between 1756 and 1763 at the expense of Dr. Thomas Sherlock, Bishop of London.

In 1868, under the supervision of W. M. Fawcett, the windows of the N. range W. of the Chapel were changed to the Tudor-Gothic style and an oriel-window in similar style added to the Hall. In the following year the Hall was newly panelled in oak. The cost of these changes was £1,770. A new *Master's Lodge* designed by the same architect was built in 1875–6 S. of the former Lodge, in the angle formed by Silver Street and Queens' Lane. The old Lodge was then used as Fellows' chambers until converted into undergraduates' sets in 1921.

No major works were undertaken again until 1930 when *Hobson's Building*, containing sets of chambers, was built some 12 yards E. of the Chapel, forming the N. side of a forecourt to Trumpington Street. In 1949 the Porter's Lodge of *c.* 1765 on the S. side of the forecourt was demolished and his accommodation provided in a new block, *Woodlark Building*, on the same site and designed in symmetry with Hobson's Building. A new *Combination Room* with a choir-room below was built in 1932 on the N. side of the Hall, on the site of the old choir-room, and at the same time the old Combination Room over the Buttery and screens-passage was opened to the Hall.

In 1933 *Gostlin's House*, a small range containing chambers, was built close N.E. of the Chapel, and in 1935 an old house, known as Sherlock Building, S. of Ramsden Building, was pulled down and replaced by *John's Building* completed in 1936, a change involving the destruction of the 19th-century swimming-pool.

Bull Hostel fronting Trumpington Street next N. of Hobson's Building consists of sets of chambers in the former Bull Hotel, which was converted to College use in 1948. The Black Bull Inn is mentioned in a conveyance of land for the College in 1460; in 1626 Gostlin gave the property to the College who entered into possession by 1630. The contract for the existing building with a Mr. Bennet was entered into in 1828; the cost was £7,683. Additions have been made subsequently.

At St. Catharine's College the unaltered ranges built between 1673 and 1687 and the Chapel finished by 1704 are good examples of the plainer work of their periods, with notable compositions forming frontispieces to the Gateway in the W. range. In designing the Ramsden Building, Essex exercised care and discretion to maintain the balance of the Court. The Chapel contains woodwork of very high quality. Much original panelling remains in the W. range of the main Court; and the W. range of Walnut Tree Court has an exceptional staircase.

Architectural Description—The main *Court* (193 ft. average by 111 ft.) is bounded on the N. by the Chapel, Hall and Buttery, on the S. by Ramsden Building and a range of chambers, formerly the Master's Lodge, and on the W. by a range containing a central Gateway and sets of chambers. To the E. is a dwarf wall with railings and central gate which now extends between modern buildings; these last present a symmetrical appearance to the street and flank a forecourt formally arranged with grass and paving.

The *Chapel* (70½ ft., including the Ante-chapel, by 25¾ft.), at the E. end of the N. range, has a loft in the roof above. The walls are of brick with rusticated stone quoins and stone dressings. In the main, the structural work was in hand from 1694 to 1697. Payments were made to Coolege and Archer, the London brickmaker, Howard the bricklayer, and Robert Grumbold for stone and mason's work. An appeal for contributions towards the cost of completing the building was issued in January 1698–9 (see historical introduction) and the consecration took place in September 1704. It has a brick plinth with moulded stone capping, a moulded string at sill-level, and a stone modillion-cornice pedimented over the E. wall. This last has a central blind window flanked by smaller niches, all with panelled side-pilasters or pilaster-strips supporting console-brackets under pediments and with brick aprons of slight projection, extending from sill to plinth, in flat stone surrounds. The window is of two transomed panels with a bolection-moulded architrave and a plain frieze and segmental pedimented cornice. The stone semidomed niches have shell heads and triangular pediments, their side-pilasters standing on pedestals that are based upon the string and flank brick panels. In the wall over both niches is a brick panel in a bolection-moulded stone surround. The slopes of the main pediment are lead-covered and extend back to meet the hipped end of the steeper-pitched roof of the Chapel. In the tympanum is a stone cartouche flanked by palm-leaves.

The Chapel and organ-gallery over the Ante-chapel are lit by four windows on each side; these are similar to the E. window-feature but with triangular pediments; the apron below the S.W. window is supplanted by the S. doorway (Plate 211). The latter is approached up four steps; it is square-headed and has an architrave with stepped keystone, attached three-quarter Ionic columns at the sides with short Ionic pilaster-like returns and an entablature with modillion-cornice but no frieze. The door is in two leaves, each of four bolection-moulded panels. In the apron below the N.W. window is a doorway smaller and simpler than the foregoing, with a plain stone architrave and containing a door of two bolection-moulded panels; close above is a two-light stone-mullioned window. In the roof are four two-light dormer-windows to the S. with triangular timber pediments, the centre two with leaded casements, the others with wood louvres; to the N. are two ventilators and a dormer-window.

The *Interior* of the Chapel is lined to sill-level with panelling; above, the walls are plastered and have modern enriched panels above the window-heads. The elaborately modelled entablature at the wall-head is largely modern, only the modillion-cornice being original. The original plaster ceiling is divided into five panels in the length and three in the width by moulded trabeations. The Ante-chapel is lined with panelling; the panelled and enriched plaster ceiling is modern. The roof of the Chapel has king-posts with struts and raking queen-posts; it is entirely plain.

Fittings—The fittings, unless otherwise described, are original. *Bell:* in roof, in W. dormer, one, inscribed 'H 1654'. *Communion-rails* (Plate 7): in two short lengths, of oak, with moulded top and base-rails carved with acanthus foliage, twisted enriched balusters, and panelled standards at the ends.

Monuments and *Floor-slabs.* Monuments: In Ante-chapel—on W. wall, (1) of Henry, son of Henry Moore, S.T.P., 1729, white marble wall-tablet with side-pieces, cornice and shaped apron with a cartouche painted with the arms of Moore; (2) of Francis (Darcy), 1705, wife of Sir William Dawes, Bt.. S.T.P., Master, standing grey marble wall-monument with long Latin inscription, flanking pilaster-strips, supporting a simplified entablature with exotic fluted enrichment in place of the architrave and surmounted by an urn flanked by garlands on a pedestal with the painted shield-of-arms of Dawes with Darcy in pretence, the whole on a pedestal-base with gadrooning and shaped side-pieces; (3) of John Eachard, S.T.P., 1697, Master, white and grey marble wall-tablet with Latin inscription extolling his benefactions and restoration of the College buildings, with scrolled side-pilasters with acanthus caps, shaped apron and cornice surmounted by flaming urns and a cartouche with the carved and painted arms of the College impaling Eachard. Floor-slabs: In Chapel—at E. end, (1) of Kenrick Prescot, S.T.P., 1779, Master, black marble paving-stone; (2) of Susanna Eyre, 1782, white marble paving-stone. In Ante-chapel—(3) of John Addenbrooke, M.D., 1719, Fellow, of slate, with shield-of-arms of Addenbrooke impaling Fisher.

Panelling, Reredos, Screen and *Stalls:* These are all integrated into the overall design for the woodwork fittings in the Chapel prepared, it seems, by Taylor of London; they are the work of John Austin and Thomas Woodward (see also historical introduction). The oak bolection-moulded Panelling, from ground to sill-level, has an enriched entablature interrupted only on the E. wall, by the reredos, and with the cornice turned in a segmental pediment over each of the two W. return-stalls; at the eastern end it is articulated over Corinthian pilasters which divide and flank the three end panels on each side-wall. The pilasters stand on pedestals; their necking-mouldings are continued across the three bays and returned over paired panels on the E. wall to enclose a band of elaborately carved, pierced and undercut foliation (Plate 33); the capping of the pedestals is continued equally as a moulded dado-rail dividing the two heights of panels. The rest of the panelling westward is in two heights above fixed benches.

The Reredos (Plate 214) has a large central panel with enriched bolection-moulded frame and coupled Corinthian columns at each side standing on pedestals and supporting a full segmental pedimented entablature; this last is articulated round entablature-blocks continued up through the pediment to form pedestals for pairs of crowning urns. The frieze is inscribed 'Sursum Corda' in the centre and enriched with palm-branches on the entablature-blocks; the recessed part of the tympanum is carved with a laurel wreath and looped palm-branches. Flanking the reredos are small scroll-brackets springing from the top of the panelling.

The Screen has the panelling continued from the side-walls

and is surmounted by the gallery-front. In the centre is the semicircular-headed arched opening from the Ante-chapel, with enriched archivolt and imposts and elaborate carved foliation in the spandrels. To each side are the Master's and President's stalls; these both have Corinthian columns and pilaster-responds supporting entablature-blocks and open segmental pediments with carved and pierced foliage in the recessed tympanum; the enriched bolection-moulded panels at the back are flanked by slender panelled pilaster-strips and the seats have scrolled arm-rests. The gallery-front flanking the modern organ-case has a top-rail carved with acanthus, symmetrically turned balusters and pedestals with panelled dies. The rest of the Stalls are arranged as shown on the plan; the front desks are modern. The benches have shaped supports and, at the easternmost ends, scrolled arm-rests projecting from the panelling. The close-panelled fronts have scrolled ends carved with foliage.

In the Ante-chapel, bolection-moulded panelling on the reverse of the screen is divided into five bays by Corinthian pilasters on panelled pedestals supporting an enriched architrave; the cornice is turned in a segmental pediment over each of the bays flanking the archway. The panelling elsewhere is modern. *Paving:* of black and white marble squares, black marble steps. *Reredos* (see Panelling). *Screen* (see Panelling). *Seating:* In Ante-chapel, two oak benches with scrolled and carved supports (see also Stalls, under Panelling).

The rest of the *North Range*, W. of the Chapel, contains the Hall rising through two storeys, with the Buttery on the ground floor and the old Combination Room on the first floor to the W. The whole of the third storey is occupied by the Library. In the attics are sets of chambers. It is part of the work begun in February 1673–4; the Hall was opened at Whitsuntide 1675 and this may mark the completion of the whole, for in the same year Cornelius Austin was paid for wainscoting the old Combination Room and the room above for Dr. Eachard, as well as the Hall.

The Hall-block has stone quoins to the S.W. angle where it overtops the lower range. The S. side has the plinth, cornice and roof continuous with those respectively of the Chapel. In the plinth are there original blocked two-light windows and a stone inscribed 'May VII MDCLXXIIII', possibly the foundation-stone, which was found 'a few years ago' (G. F. Browne, *St. Catharine's College*, 1902) under the Hall steps and, after lying loose, reset in the present position in 1936. The sills of the Hall windows are continued as a moulded string returned over the heads of the S. doorway to the Screens and the window to the Buttery; these features and all the other S. windows below the eaves are of 1868, when also the Hall oriel-window was added. Below the uppermost windows are patchings of 19th-century brickwork and below the old Combination Room and Buttery windows are remains of projecting brick aprons. In the roof are five original two-light dormer-windows with triangular and segmental timber pediments alternately and containing fixed leaded lights and casements.

The N. side has a projecting staircase-bay towards the W. end; low modern additions mask the wall to E. and W. It has a plinth and a slight stone cornice at the level of that to the Chapel. Original flat brick relieving-arches with brick plat-bands above survive over the two 19th-century Gothic windows to the Hall. The three windows to the floor above are original, of two stone-mullioned and transomed lights with moulded architraves and sills. In the main wall W. of the staircase-bay, on both the ground and first floors, is an original two-light window, the lower altered and in part blocked, and each with a flat brick relieving-arch and plat-band above; the original window on the top floor is of two lights with a transom, as before. The staircase-bay has stone quoins and continues up above the main eaves-level to finish in a hipped roof with small eaves-cornice. The doorways in the N. and E. walls have stop-chamfered jambs and four-centred heads; that in the N. wall may be an insertion. In the wall above are four original windows lighting the landings; the first two are similar to the ground and first-floor windows just described but with transoms, the third window is elliptical with a moulded stone surround and an outer ring of radiating bricks, the fourth is of two lights.

The *Hall* (39 ft., excluding the Screens 7¼ ft. to 10½ ft. wide, by 21 ft.) retains no ancient features except, fixed to the 19th-century screen, an oak cartouche carved with the arms of the College impaling Crosse, for Thomas Crosse, Master 1719–36, and, in the oriel-window, two panels of enamelled glass with figures of the Almighty and St. Paul. These are dated 1598 and 1600 respectively and have small attendant scenes, the former of the Sacrifice of Abraham and Jacob's ladder, the latter of the Good Samaritan. Both have elaborate repaired borders and are set in modern scrollwork frames. On the N. side of the N. wall of the Buttery and opposite are lengths of reset early 17th-century panelling, the first in five heights of panels with a reeded frieze, which has been copied in the 19th-century panelling in the Screens-passage, the second of miscellaneous pieces. In the *Buttery* are exposed chamfered ceiling-beams. The staircase is original up to second-floor level; it rises round an open well and has turned balusters, close moulded strings, moulded handrail and square panelled newels with moulded and carved foliated pendants; against the walls, up to the first floor, is a tall dado with two heights of panels, the lowest wall-newel similarly being doubled in height. The staircase has subsequently been continued up to the attics in pine, blocking the oval window, probably in the mid 18th century. The Hall bell in the roof over the W. end of the range is uninscribed.

The old *Combination Room* (23 ft. by 21¾ ft.), now a dining-annexe to the Hall, retains the bolection-moulded panelling for which Cornelius Austin was paid in 1675; it is of two panels in the height separated by a dado-rail, and with an entablature against the ceiling. The fireplace in the W. wall has a moulded stone surround in a later wood frame with cornice-shelf; the overmantel contains a bolection-moulded panel flanked by panelled pilasters supporting returns of the main entablature. An arcaded opening was pierced through the E. wall above the dado in 1931.

The *Library* (63½ ft. by 22¾ ft.) occupies the third storey remodelled and fitted for the purpose between 1756 and 1763, the plasterwork being by Clark, the woodwork by Woodward. It is of five bays and divided into three parts by cross-walls. The central compartment of three bays has an enriched plaster

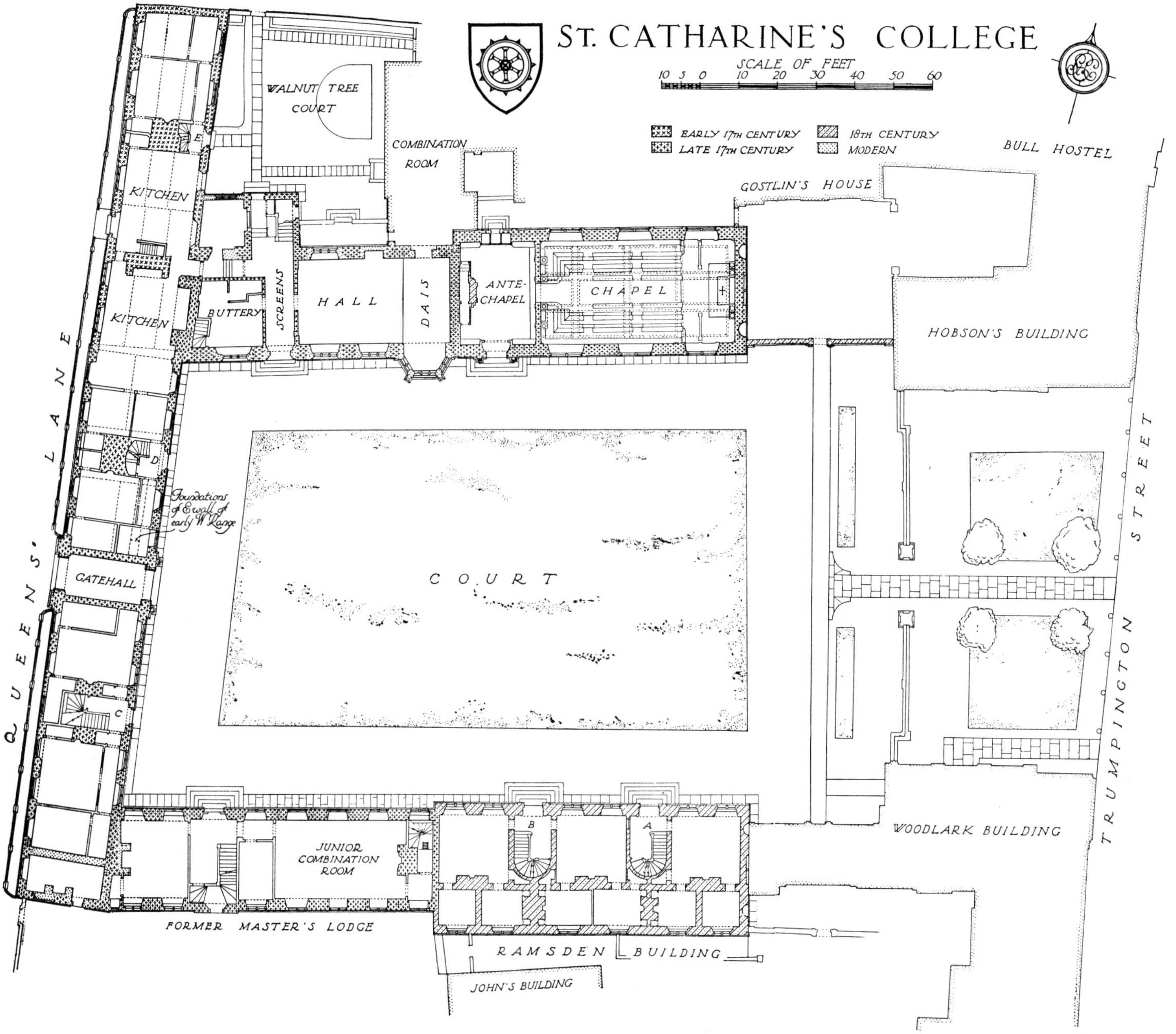

St. CATHARINE'S COLLEGE
SCALE OF FEET
10 5 0 10 20 30 40 50 60
EARLY 17TH CENTURY
LATE 17TH CENTURY
18TH CENTURY
MODERN
WALNUT TREE COURT
COMBINATION ROOM
BULL HOSTEL
GOSTLIN'S HOUSE
KITCHEN
KITCHEN
BUTTERY
SCREENS
HALL
DAIS
ANTE-CHAPEL
CHAPEL
HOBSON'S BUILDING
QUEENS' LANE
Foundations of E wall of early W Range
GATEHALL
COURT
TRUMPINGTON STREET
JUNIOR COMBINATION ROOM
WOODLARK BUILDING
FORMER MASTER'S LODGE
RAMSDEN BUILDING
JOHN'S BUILDING
A
B
C
D
E

dentil-cornice and panelled ceiling of geometrical design with the soffits of the framing containing key-pattern ornament. In the middle is a foliated boss in a rococo setting of acanthus and ribbons all within an octagonal panel surrounded by radiating panels. The walls are lined with oak bookcases which have panelled ends and entablatures with enriched cornices; cartouches reset on the architraves are painted with the class-letters. Two cases now without their cornices project at right angles from each side wall. All the wall-cases were heightened in the 19th century by the addition of five shelves. The doorway from the stair has an enriched ovolo-moulded architrave and contains a six-panel door. Each of the cross-walls contains in the centre a timber-cased archway with semicircular head, moulded and enriched imposts and archivolts, keyblock and panelled soffit and responds. The two end compartments have plaster dentil-cornices and simply panelled ceilings; the walls are lined to two-thirds of their height with bookcases with panelled ends and entablatures as before, the last returned to form the imposts of the archways just described, and with the class-letters in their original positions on the frieze. The cases on the E. and W. end walls are both divided into three bays by panelled pilasters, with the entablature pedimented over the middle bay and with leaves carved in the tympanum; in the W. tympanum is also the shield-of-arms of the College impaling Sherlock and with the remains of a pelican in piety in the place of a crest. In the flanking bays on the W. wall are doorways containing six-panel doors.

The attic-rooms extend over the two W. bays only and contain some old doors. Further E. the original roof is accessible; the trusses are of king-post type with struts to the principals. The king-posts stand on collar-beams with arched braces to the foot of the principals, these last being tied in by the beams in the ceiling of the rooms below.

The *West Range* of the main Court was begun and completed in the late 17th-century rebuilding scheme for the College. The shell was finished by 1679 at the latest but the internal fitting was probably not completed until 1687. It contains a Gateway, central to the Court, accentuated by frontispieces, and sets of chambers approached by staircases 'C' and 'D'. The walls are of red brick in English bond with stone dressings, the frontispieces of ashlar, and the roofs are tile-covered. It is of three storeys with attics but considerably lower than the N. and S. ranges. Alterations in 1955 disclosed a short length of the foundation of the E. wall of the earlier range (see plan).

The E. side (Plate 211) is generally symmetrical in effect; the W. side, demarcated by rusticated quoins, has the Gateway occupying the sixth of thirteen bays. The openings are arranged as shown on the plan and constant vertically, windows on the upper floors taking the place of the doorways on the ground floor. The *Gateway* contains a Gatehall (20 ft. by 10¼ ft.). The E. frontispiece (Plate 229) is of two superimposed orders, Tuscan and Corinthian, the columns being inset about a diameter. The archway has an elliptical head with rusticated voussoirs and scroll-keystone, moulded imposts and plain responds against the flanking attached Tuscan columns; these last have short pilaster-like lateral returns and support an entablature returned over them and over the arch keystone. The Corinthian order frames the first and second-floor windows, the lower window of two stone-mullioned and transomed lights with apron and triangular pediment on console brackets, and the upper of two stone-mullioned lights with apron and architrave. The head of the upper window rises above the level of the Corinthian architrave and this and the frieze are omitted from the crowning entablature, leaving the columns supporting entablature-blocks with short lateral returns; the modillion-cornice has a broken segmental pediment articulated over the entablature-blocks and framing an elaborate cartouche carved with the arms of the College.

The W. frontispiece (Plate 211) is in two stages, with a high rusticated lower stage with cornice forming a classical basement below a lofty Ionic order with a pediment. The basement contains the archway to the Gatehall, with elliptical head with keystone, moulded imposts and plain responds against flanking square projections forming pedestals to the two Ionic pilasters above. These last rise through two storeys and flank the first and second-floor windows. The windows are similar to those at the same respective levels in the opposite side but the lower window has a segmental pediment. Again the architrave and frieze of the crowning entablature are omitted to make way for the upper window and the main triangular pediment is articulated over the entablature blocks.

The W. archway is hung with original oak panelled doors of two leaves with strap-hinges; each leaf contains six rectangular bolection-moulded panels and three more shaped panels filling the quarter oval of the head. The Gatehall is entirely plain.

The remainder of the W. range to N. and S. has a brick plinth with moulded stone capping, a stone plat-band at first-floor level and a stone modillioned eaves-cornice surmounted, on the W., by a blocking-course; all are interrupted by the frontispieces; the wall up to and including the plat-band represents a classical basement. The ground-floor windows are of two mullioned lights, and the first and second-floor windows of two mullioned and transomed lights, all with narrow moulded architraves and sills; the first-floor windows are given main accentuation by the addition of plain stone friezes and cornices. The square-headed doorways in the E. wall, to staircases 'C' and 'D', have rusticated stone jambs and graduated voussoirs. In the roof, to E. and W., are dormer-windows with timber triangular and segmental pediments alternately leading outwards from the frontispieces and coterminous with the bays below; they contain two-light casements with the original leaded quarries. The two brick chimney-stacks on the roof-ridge although rebuilt are similar to those shown by Loggan in *c.* 1688 and have an arcading of semicircular-headed panels on the sides. The N. end of the roof is gabled, the S. end hipped; the subsidiary ridged roof linking the last to the gable-end of the S. range is a later addition. Three of the lead rainwater down-pipes are old. The S. end of the W. range overlooks the Fellows' Garden; it is a unity in design, with rusticated stone quoins at both angles and horizontal features continued round from the W. side. On the ground floor is a square-headed doorway with a stone architrave intruding into an area of brick patching, presumably in the place of a destroyed window; it is hung with an old panelled door. The windows, one remaining on the ground floor, but now blocked, and two on each of the upper floors, are similar to those at the same levels respectively on the W.; the dormer-window is flat-topped.

The *Interior* of the W. range has the N. part of the ground floor, beyond staircase 'D', given up to kitchen-offices; the original dividing-wall between it and the Kitchen in the earlier range adjoining on the N. has been removed and the upper parts supported on steel joists. One of the rooms next to the Gatehall on the N. served as the Porter's Lodge while the main entrance to the College was from the W. Rooms on all floors contain exposed stop-chamfered ceiling-beams and those on the first and second floors retain much original oak panelling.

The staircases are original, with close moulded strings, moulded handrails, turned balusters and square panelled newels, these last, in the N. stair, being capped by returns of the handrail and, in the S. stair, having ball finials and turned pendants. The doors from the landings to the sets of chambers are generally, on the ground and first floors, of six fielded panels, and on the second floor of two bolection-moulded panels.

Off staircase 'D', on the first floor, the main S. room has a timber cornice and an original fireplace with moulded stone surround flanked by wood pilaster-strips on panelled pedestals supporting an entablature with central frieze-panel; superimposed panelled pilaster-strips flanking a bolection-moulded panel and supporting a duplication of the entablature below, but with a heavier cornice, form the overmantel. On the second floor, the main N. room has a cornice, fireplace and overmantel similar to those just described.

Off staircase 'C', on the ground floor, a cupboard in the N. lobby has a reused early 17th-century door of eight panels. On the first floor, the N. room has a cornice, fireplace and overmantel similar to those described above. A closet W. of the stair has the walls partly lined with reused early 17th-century panelling with arabesques carved in the frieze. The S. room is lined with bolection-moulded panelling in two heights, with moulded skirting, dado-rail and cornice. The two doorcases flanking the fireplace in the N. wall project slightly and have bolection-moulded architraves, shaped panelled friezes, and broken segmental pediments framing small pedestals; they are hung with doors of two bolection-moulded and fielded panels. Refixed over the doorway in the S. wall is an 18th-century carved shield-of-arms of Lever (?). The projecting fireplace has a marble bolection-moulded surround and wood overmantel containing two similarly moulded panels. In the W. window are quarries painted with birds and flowers, perhaps of the 18th-century. The room adjoining on the S. is lined with panelling similar to the foregoing. The southernmost room has a dado of similar moulded panelling and a timber cornice. On the second floor, the N. room contains a fireplace and overmantel similar to that in the room below. The S. room (Plate 201) is lined with bolection-moulded panelling as before but with an entablature with bolection-moulded panelling in the frieze. The slightly projecting doorcases flanking the fireplace in the N. wall have entablatures with central panels imposed on architrave and frieze and broken pediments framing small pedestals. The wide doorway in the S. wall is hung with a door in two leaves, each leaf having a bolection-moulded base-panel and eight glazed panels above. The fireplace has a stone surround in a bolection-moulded frame with a cornice-shelf; in the overmantel is a similarly moulded panel. In the bedroom of the same set is an original built-in cupboard with glazed doors and an entablature with panelled frieze. The attics retain some old moulded plank doors. The roofs here and elsewhere, unless otherwise described, have robust cambered collar-beams.

The *South Range* of the main Court is of two periods: the narrower western half, formerly the Master's Lodge, a part of the late 17th-century rebuilding, was completed probably by 1681; the eastern half, *Ramsden Building*, was begun in 1757 and apparently not occupied until 1772. The latter, designed by James Essex, is of the same height and in similar materials to the range opposite. It is longer than the Chapel block, which it balances, and projects slightly on the Court side, more on the S. At the angles are rusticated quoins; the modillioned eaves-cornice is continuous. The N. side is symmetrical, the openings being as shown on the plan, with short flights of steps to the doorways to staircases 'A' and 'B' in the third and sixth bays; the windows on the floors above are regularly arranged over the ground-floor openings. The doorways have architraves against plain stone surrounds and cornices with segmental pediments which interrupt the stone plat-band at first-floor level. The stone-mullioned two-light windows are transomed on the ground and first floors; they have narrow architraves and moulded sills, those on the first floor with plain friezes and cornices, and conform to the pattern of the original windows elsewhere in the College. In the roof are five dormer-windows with timber triangular pediments and fitted with two-light casements. The S. side is generally similar to the foregoing but of six unequal bays, with a window in each bay on each floor. The E. end is a replica of the E. end of the Chapel.

The *Interior* of Ramsden Building contains sets of chambers, the planning of all floors being constant. The original staircases rise in continuous flights between floors and have close moulded strings, thin turned balusters, moulded handrails and square newels. The main ground and first-floor rooms retain original plaster dentil-cornices; those on the second floor and all the bedrooms have plain cornices; some contain early 19th-century fireplaces with reeded stone surrounds with roundels at the corners and plain shelves. The doorways have simple architraves and are hung with doors of six fielded panels, except in the attics where they are of four panels.

The rest of the S. range westward, which contains cellars, has a plinth continued from the adjoining buildings and rusticated stone quoins to the angles of the western end where it overtops the W. range. The N. side is of eight bays, with a plat-band at first-floor level, and a modillion-cornice returning round Ramsden Building. The stone doorway in the sixth bay has an architrave in a panelled surround and a segmental pediment; in the opening the styles of the door-frame are in the form of responds with moulded imposts supporting a semi-circular arch with panelled tympanum; the door is of six panels. In all the other bays on the ground floor and throughout above are stone-mullioned two-light windows, those on the ground and first floors transomed, similar in detail to the original windows elsewhere in the College. The cellar windows appearing in the plinth are of two lights but without projecting architraves. In the roof are eight dormer-windows similar to those on the opposite range. The chimney-stacks are similar to those of the W. range. The S. side has a square lead eaves-gutter supported on a small stone bedmould. The sixth bay, as shown on the plan, projects slightly to within approximately 3½ ft. from the eaves where it is weathered back in brick; in it is a doorway with stone architrave and, above, are two two-light mullioned and transomed windows lighting the landings. The windows on every floor in all the other bays are similar to those in the wall opposite but without the friezes and cornices over those on the first floor. On the roof are eight dormer-windows with triangular pediments. The chimney-stack is modern or rebuilt. At the junction of the wall with the end wall of the W. range is an old lead rainwater down-pipe with a moulded head below each of the two eaves-cornices.

The *Interior* now contains undergraduates' rooms. On the ground floor, the *Junior Combination Room* (33½ ft. by 19½ ft.) to the E. has an original timber cornice. The room adjoining on the W. is lined with bolection-moulded panelling of *c.* 1700 with dado-rail and cornice. The room W. of the staircase is lined with early 18th-century panelling with dado-rail and cornice, with a contemporary door of six fielded panels; in the overmantel is a bolection-moulded panel and the fireplace has a moulded and eared stone surround with roses carved in the angles. The staircase is original, with close moulded strings, turned and twisted balusters, except down to the cellar where they are only turned, moulded handrail and square newels; the last were capped by returns of the handrail and had turned pendants, but these have been displaced by the later insertion of panelled supporting posts between the newels. From ground to first floor is a dado of bolection-moulded panelling.

On the first floor the small room and passage immediately E. of the staircase are both lined with original panelling similar to that in the room next described; the fireplace in the first has an original bolection-moulded stone surround. The room W. of the staircase, now divided by a modern partition, is lined with late 17th-century panelling with dado-rail and cornice. The fireplace has a moulded stone surround in a heavy bolection-moulded wood frame with a cornice-shelf and a panelled overmantel with panelled pilaster-strips at the sides supporting an entablature; the cornice is that continued from the flanking panelling and the architrave and bed-moulding return over the pilaster-strips. The architraves of the doorways and the panelled doors are original. The panelling and framing members throughout are bolection-moulded. The second floor and attics retain some original woodwork and bolection-moulded fireplace-surrounds.

Walnut Tree Court, N.W. of the main Court, is bounded on the W. by a range extending northward from the W. range already described. This is the earliest surviving building of the College. The Court was walled in 1631–2 and the cost of materials for the 'New Building' first appears in the accounts for 1634–5 when expenses amounted to £260; the latest entries, for red ochre, sand, bricks at 1s. 10d. a hundred, and for mending the tiling, occur in 1636–7. Some structural features may indicate a heightening of the range by a full storey, but necessarily before *c.* 1688, the date of Loggan's view which shows three storeys. It is of three storeys with attics and built of red brick with stone dressings. The southern end contains the Kitchen rising through two storeys; the chambers in the rest of the range are approached from staircase 'E' in Walnut Tree Court.

The exterior has a plinth with moulded stone weathering and plain stone-capped parapets to E. and W. The E. side is symmetrical, in five bays but with the ground floor of the southernmost bay masked by a modern addition. The symmetry indicates the extent to which this side was covered by the range preceding the present late 17th-century Hall block. At the level of the first floor is a moulded stone string; above the first-floor windows is a ragged set-back of the wall-face and, it seems, a change in the brickwork. The central doorway has chamfered stone jambs and a four-centred head. In the flanking bays and in every bay on the upper floors is an original stone three-light window with hollow-chamfered head, reveals and mullions in a casement moulding; the uppermost windows have stone cornices. The ground-floor window S. of the doorway has been converted into a doorway in modern times and the southernmost is blocked by the modern addition. The two-light dormer-windows have timber entablatures and hipped roofs. The two lead rainwater-pipes with moulded heads are old.

The N. end is gabled and has plain stone quoins, except where the wall forming the N. side of the Court adjoins. It has been refaced to two-thirds of the height, presumably when the adjoining gatehouse seen in Loggan's engraving was demolished. The chimney-stack at the apex is corbelled out from the wall-face below the start of the gable; it and the two other stacks on the roof-ridge have panelled sides but only the moulded brick corbelling is not rebuilt.

The W. side, to Queens' Lane, has moulded stone strings at first and second-floor levels and returns of the quoins at the N.W. angle. It is in seven bays, with a three-light window in each bay on each floor; one has subsequently been converted into a doorway. The windows have been altered in profile of moulding, and perhaps in height to accord more nearly with the later windows further S.; they have wave-moulded heads, reveals and mullions. In the roof is a range of two-light dormer-windows with timber cornices and hipped roofs. The two lead rainwater-pipes with moulded heads are of the 18th century.

The *Interior* has been largely modernised on the ground floor where it retains only chamfered ceiling-beams and, in the N. end of the E. wall of the Kitchen, a doorway with a 17th-century timber frame. The early *Kitchen* (19½ ft. by 21 ft. average) has been enlarged in modern times by the removal of part of the S. wall and heightened by extending it through the floor above. Doubtless it has been in this position since the new Hall block was completed in 1675, but perhaps not from the first, for Hamond's map seems to show the earlier Hall much further E.

The original staircase rises in single flights between the floors, turning round a rectangular newel-post; this last stops short at the second-floor floor-level. On the ground floor, the face of the post has a base-panel and abutting-pieces at the sides with shaped tops, and, at the head, a pendant carved in relief below a frieze and dentil-cornice continued across the stair-lobby in the form of a pelmet with pendants at the ends and flanking the newel-post (Plate 42). On the first floor, on the face of the post is a diminishing Ionic pilaster on an enriched pedestal and supporting an entablature below the ceiling in the form of a pelmet as before. Some further elaboration of the staircase setting is provided by sinking the field of the inner faces of the mullions etc. of the window lighting the landing. Many of the outer doors to the sets are old; one on the first floor is original, with moulded ribs planted on the face to form panels.

On the first floor, the room N. of the stair, now with modern partitioning forming a passage on the E., has the fireplace-surround made up with Roman Doric side-pilasters with enrichment of damask-like design, brackets, a foliated frieze with carved masks and a dentil-cornice. A doorcase in the W. end of the S. wall, similar to that next described now fronts a cupboard. The entrance to the set has on the inside, and balancing the foregoing before the passage was made, a projecting doorcase with an arabesque-enriched frieze flanked by similarly enriched brackets supporting a dentil-cornice. Reset on the external wall of the passage is a length of 17th-century carved panelling. The room S. of the stair has a fireplace-surround also made up, with panelled Roman Doric side-pilasters supporting a dentil-cornice and with late 17th-century pierced scroll-finials above, not *in situ*; in a central panel over the fireplace has been placed a cartouche carved with the College arms and with reset scrolls below. The four projecting doorcases are similar to the doorcases in the set opposite, but one is partly modern. The walls are lined with 18th-century panelling and, reset in the corners immediately under the cornice, are four late 17th-century carved scrolls, similar to those over the fireplace. All the above woodwork, unless described otherwise, is contemporary with the building, but extensively reset and with modern repairs. On the top storey are some old doors. In the attics the chamfered roof-principals are exposed; the roofs are of collar-beam type. 'R.L. 1634' is cut on one of the timbers (Robert Long entered Pensioner 1633) and, accepting the probability of reuse of materials in any heightening of the range, this may indicate how early the building was occupied.

The late 19th-century *Master's Lodge* contains some old fittings reset. The Dining-room is partly lined with panelling of *c.* 1600 said to have come from Cromwell House at the Castle End, Cambridge; the overmantel incorporates some early 16th-century linenfold panels, three early 17th-century terminal figures and reeded panels. The Master's Parlour is lined to within 2 ft. of the ceiling with early 17th-century panelling at one time in the Buttery; it is five panels high with a jewelled entablature divided into bays by foliated brackets. The old door is of ten panels, each subdivided saltirewise. All the woodwork is made up with later and modern material.

The main Court is enclosed on the E. by *Railings* with a central *Gate* and on the N.E. by a screen-wall; a similar wall in line with the S. wall of Ramsden Building bounded the S.E. corner until 1949. This arrangement is perhaps attributable to James Essex and entries in the Audit accounts for 1779–80 of payments to Fuller, £169 for railings, £73 for a gate, are doubtless in connection with it. The *Gate* has two ashlar piers which have recently been entirely rebuilt to the previous design; they are square on plan, with Roman Doric pilasters clasping the angles and supporting full entablatures with small wheels, for St. Catharine, carved in the metopes, and large ball-finials; on the dies between the pilasters are lions' heads with rings in their mouths and pendent foliage. The wrought-iron gate is in two leaves hung with short fixed lengths with plain uprights, two bands of scrollwork and elaborate scrolled cresting, the last incorporating a wheel in the central pyramidal feature on the overthrow. The railings extending N. and S. rise from a brick dwarf wall with stone plinths and capping; they have plain uprights with shaped spear-finials and are divided into bays by stouter coupled uprights with urn-finials.

The N.E. screen-wall is of brick with stone dressings; it has panelled stone pilasters at either end and a central doorway with architrave and side-pilasters supporting console-brackets under a pedimented entablature.

The *Railings* and their stone plinth along the Queens' Lane boundary of the College on a strip of land first leased in 1680, were set up in 1759; they were given by Dr. Thomas Sherlock, Master 1714–9, who by codicil to his will, 1760, devised money for their upkeep. The railings consist of arrow-headed uprights threaded through a plain top-rail and are divided into bays by stouter paired uprights; these last are in the form of slender Roman Doric columns on pedestals with flaming urn-shaped finials decorated with gadrooning.[1]

The brick *Boundary-wall* to Queens' Lane, S. of the W. range, is of the late 17th or early 18th century. It has a central gateway with plain piers and, at each end, a stone doorway with architrave, pulvinated frieze and pedimented cornice; the northernmost is hung with a contemporary six-panel door.

Bull Hostel to the N.E. of the College, fronting Trumpington Street, now contains sets of chambers. The history of the property and the present building is outlined above with that of the College buildings. It is of four storeys, with attics added in 1926. The walls are of white brick with ashlar facing to the street; the roofs are slate-covered. All the windows are double sash-hung. The advertisement for tenders for rebuilding the Black Bull Inn appeared in the *Cambridge Chronicle* for 15th February 1828, and according to the issue of 17th October of the same year work was in hand.

It consists of a rectangular block to the street and a W. wing; late in the 19th century extensions were made to the latter on the S. The former yard is largely occupied by a modern dining-hall. The E. front, of eight bays, is symmetrical from the northernmost bay to the penultimate bay on the S.; these two bays project slightly the full height of the building. The whole of the ground floor, except the southernmost bay, is rusticated. At the first floor is a balcony with cast-iron balustrade extending the length of the front excepting the end bays; under the second-floor windows is a plat-band, and at the wall-head is a cornice and blocking-course. The doorway, central in the symmetrical design, is under a porch with detached square columns and pilaster-responds supporting a simplified entablature. The ground-floor windows with elliptical heads in the projecting bays and the first-floor windows above them are wider than the rest and contain tripartite timber frames; all the first-floor windows have architraves and cornices, but

[1] These fine railings were removed in 1956.

those above have architraves only. The window-feature in the S. end bay is of the later 19th century and may replace an arched carriage-way. The other sides of the building have plain sash-windows.

The *Interior* contains the main rooms on the E. with a central hall-passage on the ground floor giving access to the stairhall on the W. The S.E. room has been extended into the later addition but is now subdivided into offices. The main rooms on the first floor have also been subdivided in recent times. All contain original enriched plaster cornices. The staircase is elliptical within a rectangular hall, with cast-iron balustrades and a mahogany handrail.

The *Houses*, 68, 69a and 70 Trumpington Street, S. of Woodlark Building, were taken into the College enclosure in 1933; except for the ground-floor rooms let for shops, they contain sets of chambers. The first, rebuilt in 1852, was bought for £900 in 1821, the second in 1894, the third in 1871. W. of No. 70 is a small early 17th-century building, of two storeys, with plastered timber-framed walls and tiled roofs. In the S. wall is a 17th-century jettied window, now blocked and converted into a cupboard, with moulded bressummer and cove below, retaining the original chamfered frame of five transomed lights; it has been heightened to two storeys by the addition of a dormer-window in the 19th century. The main ground-floor room, now divided by a modern partition to form an entrance-passage on the N., is lined with contemporary panelling five panels high, with frieze-panels enriched with arabesques. Some similar frieze-panelling remains *in situ* in the shop-store further E. On the first floor is further 17th-century panelling; an original stop-chamfered tie-beam and some timber-framed partitioning are visible.

(37) ST. JOHN'S COLLEGE (see plan at end of book) (Plate 231) stands W. of St. John's Street, between Bridge Street and Trinity College. It was founded by Margaret (Beaufort), Countess of Richmond and Derby, but during the initial arrangements the Foundress died (1509) and the charter of foundation was obtained by her executor, John Fisher, Bishop of Rochester, in 1511. The buildings of *First Court* were begun at this date and opened in 1516. The brickmaker was a certain Reculver of Greenwich and the clerk-of-works Oliver Scales; Richard Wright of Bury St. Edmunds, glazier, contracted for windows in the Chapel, Hall and Master's Lodge in 1513, to be completed in 1514. Though partly in use, the buildings were evidently not finished by 1516 for in the same year Thomas Loveday of Sudbury, carpenter, contracted for work that included flooring the chambers.

The site had been occupied by the Hospital of St. John the Evangelist and of this foundation the chapel and an earlier building to the N., called the Infirmary and no doubt the first Hospital and chapel, were retained. The latter was built early in the 13th century, and surviving details of the later chapel (now destroyed) indicate that it was at least as old as the end of the same century. This later chapel was altered to serve as the College Chapel, the E. arch of the crossing being removed and the part to the W. divided between the Ante-chapel and the then Master's Lodge at the N.W. corner of the Court. Before the Reformation four chantry-chapels were added, of Hugh Assheton, built probably on his death in 1522, and Bishop St. John Fisher, under construction 1525 to 1533, on the N., of Dr. John Keyton, built probably soon after 1533, and Dr. Thomas Thompson, before 1525, on the S.

First Court has the main *Gatehouse* in the E. range and the *Hall* with the *Butteries* and *Kitchen* to the S. in the W. range. The original Library, on the first floor, S. of the Gatehouse, was converted into chambers in 1616, when the books were placed temporarily in a room over the Kitchen. A small court to the S.W., in the position indicated on the plan, was added under Dr. Nicholas Metcalfe, Master (1518–38). It was begun in 1528 and so placed that the N. range lay S. of the approach to the Hall-screens and the S. range projected beyond the S. range of First Court. Under Dr. William Whitaker, Master (1586–95), or shortly before, the 'Infirmary' was fitted up as rooms.

Second Court was begun in 1598 under Dr. Richard Clayton, Master (1595–1612); the contractors were Ralph Symons of Westminster and Gilbert Wigge of Cambridge, freemasons, and the contract, with plans and elevations, is preserved in the College Library. The cost was partly borne by Mary (Cavendish) wife of Gilbert Talbot, 7th Earl of Shrewsbury. The small court mentioned above was destroyed to make way for this new larger Court. The work was finished in 1602 and the paths paved in 1603. The W. range contains the Gatehouse now called the *Shrewsbury Tower*. The N. range provided new accommodation on the first floor for the Master, consisting mainly of a *Gallery* extending nearly 50 yards with a plaster ceiling executed in 1600 by one Cobbe and panelling set up in 1603–4. About twenty-five years later some 45 ft. at the W. end of the Gallery were absorbed in the vestibule and staircase to the new Library. Certain work was carried out on windows in the buildings of First Court when Second Court was built, and the level of the court lowered.

The new *Library* on the N. side of *Third Court* was built in 1623–5, though the staircase was not finished until 1628, at the cost of John Williams, Bishop of Lincoln and Lord Keeper of the Great Seal. The design was perhaps due to Henry Man, carpenter, who with the Bursar bought timber and bricks and who drew the 'plots for the Librarie'; but towards the end of the work a payment was made to Grumbold, freemason, presumably Thomas. The bricks were 14s. and 15s. a thousand; clunch came from Barrington, freestone from Peterborough and lead from Derbyshire; the deals were shipped from Lynn. The total cost was about £3,000. Thomas, Earl of Suffolk, writing to the Master in June 1624, having heard that the workmen for the main frame of the building had 'performed their part well', recommended for the fittings, if it was not too late, one Mathewes 'that hath wrought all my wainscot work at Audley End' (College Archives; '*Eagle*' (St. John's College, House Magazine) XXVII, 328). The books were installed in 1628.

The other two ranges of Third Court were begun in 1669 and finished in four years at a cost of £5,256. The S. range exhibits discrepancies between the windows of the N. and S. sides and a curious placing of the chimney-stacks, just S. of the roof-ridge, that suggest a change of design in the course of building, from a range of one room in thickness to a range of two rooms in thickness; but this is disproved by the arrangement of ceiling-beams inside and the positions of the stops to their chamfers. Thus it is the earliest range in the University planned in double thickness *ab initio*. The same range incorporates in the W. end a late 16th-century building, which also projects as a S. wing, retaining original features; the building is shown in Hamond's map of Cambridge of 1592.

The S. side of First Court was refaced in ashlar and the windows sashed in 1772–6 under the supervision of James Essex, architect. To the N. of the same Court, the new *Chapel* was built from the design of Gilbert Scott in 1863–9; this entailed the demolition of the old Chapel and the 'Infirmary' at the same time. The Hall was then lengthened towards the N. destroying the old Combination Room; thereupon the latter accommodation was provided in the Gallery of the old Master's Lodge, the present *Master's Lodge* having been built in 1863. The E. range also was extended N. as lecture-rooms in 1869.

The old *Bridge* over the river, to the S.W. of Third Court, with the adjoining gate-piers, was built between 1709 and 1712; expenditure in connection with it between 1696 and 1698 appears to have been for preliminary work and materials. Wren and Hawksmoor were concerned in the matter to some extent and their letters to Dr. Gower, Master, indicate that the site for the bridge was still undecided in June 1698. Both recommended a position in continuation of the E. to W. axis of the three Courts; among the Wren drawings at All Souls College, Oxford (Vol. IV, No. 76), is a ground plan demonstrating this layout (*Wren Soc.* V, pl. xxix), and a drawing in the British Museum (King's Lib. VIII, 57a), thought to be by Hawksmoor, shows the W. range of Third Court. Robert Grumbold was the freemason; John Longland, a London master-carpenter, 'and others', advised 'about a modell for the bridge', and Francis Woodward executed the carving on bridge and gate-piers (*Wren Soc.* XIX, 103–7, pl. lx). The total cost was £1,353. In the College Library are preserved alternative designs, both unsigned, one with a number of features occurring in the present structure.

On the W. side of the river, *New Court* was built in 1826–31 from the designs of Thomas Rickman and Henry Hutchinson; the covered *Bridge* over the river designed by the latter was built in 1831. The *Gates* at the entrance to the College from Queens' Road were erected *c.* 1822 when the cast iron *Bridge* carrying the High Walk over the Bin Brook was built.

In 1885 an annexe was added at the N. side of Second Court, from the design of F. C. Penrose, which involved alterations to the Library staircase. The new buildings of *Chapel Court* were completed in 1942.

At St. John's College the main Gatehouse and the unaltered ranges of First Court, 1511–6, and Second Court with the Shrewsbury Tower, 1598–1602, are important brick buildings of their periods. The Library, 1623–5, is of architectural interest for the premeditated use of revived Gothic forms in the reign of James I.

The W. and S. ranges of Third Court, 1669–73, are of elaborate but unsophisticated design, presumably by an East Anglian builder, and contain much interesting original panelling of similar character. The S. range is the first built in the University of two rooms in thickness throughout. The Hall, the Combination Room, formerly the Master's Gallery, and the old Bridge, 1696–1712, are all notable, the last with carvings remarkably Roman in character. New Court, 1826–31, and the covered Bridge, 1831, are important examples of the decorative use of the Gothic idiom; they equate closely to a stage-setting when seen from the S.

Architectural Description (See plan at end of book)—*First Court* (about 136 ft. by 192 ft.) is entered by the main Gatehouse (Plate 232) in the early 16th-century E. range. The *Gatehouse* (Plate 90) is of three storeys and of red brick with dressings of freestone and clunch; both fronts were restored in 1934–5, when the E. turrets and the upper part of the N.W. turret were entirely reconstructed and the parapets replaced in old brick. The building has an embattled parapet and octagonal angle-turrets also embattled. On the E. front, the archway has splayed jambs and moulded four-centred arch (p. 394) enriched with paterae; the ogee label is similarly enriched and has crockets, finials, and head-stops supporting side-standards with pinnacles; the paterae are carved with germanders, daisies, Lancastrian roses, ostrich feathers and portcullises and the spandrel contains a Lancastrian rose. On the label and flanking it is the coroneted shield-of-arms of the Foundress with two yale supporters; beyond the yales are a royally crowned Lancastrian rose and a coroneted portcullis, the royal crown being an 18th-century restoration. The background of the heraldic composition is carved with a rough field strewn with daisy plants and germander speedwell, rabbits and a fox with a goose; above it is a frieze of daisy-plants and a string-course carved with running vine-ornament, portcullises and Lancastrian roses (Plate 93). The carved work was repainted and regilded in 1934–5 under Professor Tristram's directions. The oak doors are in two folds with four tiers of linenfold panels, moulded styles and rails, lattice-framing behind, strap-hinges and locking-bar; the N. leaf contains a wicket. The doors would appear to be largely the work of Thomas Loveday, *c.* 1516, in spite of the record of a payment to John Adams in 1665–6 for the new great gate. The second storey has two windows, both of two cinquefoiled lights in a four-centred head with a label; between them is a niche with a corbelled base and buttressed standards supporting a three-sided canopy with pinnacles and a domical ogee capping. The niche contains a figure of St. John the Evangelist (Plate 242) carved by George Woodroff for £11 in 1662–3. Flanking the canopy are a portcullis and a rose both royally crowned; the crown over the first may be of the 17th century, that over the rose is a replacement of 1934. (Sir Charles Peers in '*Eagle*' XLIX, 1.) The top storey has two windows similar to those below and surrounded by network diaper in the brickwork.

On the W. front of the Gatehouse, the archway has splayed jambs and a moulded four-centred arch (p. 394) with a horizontal string-course above enriched with paterae, a double rose, ostrich feather plumes and daisy-flowers; in the spandrels are a rose and a portcullis. The two upper storeys have each a window of two lights similar to those on the E. front, and their brickwork retains traces of a network diaper. The turrets have each a doorway with stop-chamfered jambs, moulded four-centred arch and label.

The *Gatehall* (19½ ft. by 16 ft.) has a doorway in the N. wall with moulded jambs and four-centred arch in a square head with sunk spandrels; the early 17th-century oak door is nail-studded and has six panels with moulded ribs. The fan-vault is in two bays and springs from foliated corbels; the cells of the vault are in two tiers, the lower with cinquefoiled and the upper with trefoiled and sub-cusped heads, carved cusp-points and foliated spandrels; between the tiers is carved brattishing and in the middle of each bay is a carved boss, one with a rose and one with portcullis and daisies. The vault has modern painting and gilding. On the first floor, the ceiling has chamfered beams and exposed joists, all much restored. The Treasury on the second floor has a flat-pitched open timber roof with central and side purlins and exposed rafters. On the E. and W. walls is a dado of reused early 16th-century and later linenfold panels. The doorway has chamfered jambs and moulded four-centred head and is hung with a battened door with moulded ribs forming four panels. In the E. angles are doorways to the turrets; they have chamfered jambs and four-centred heads and retain original plank doors on strap hinges. In the room are two late 17th or early 18th-century bookcases with shaped panelled ends. The two chests from here are now in Lecture Room 5: (1) (Plate 46) is of oak, with elaborate carved tracery-panelled front with foliage and swans, 14th-century, remainder modern, (2) of oak, front in four panels with initials IR, square panelled ends, moulded top, early 17th-century. In the S.W. turret is a bell with the initial letters and date W.L. 1624, crowns, Royal arms, and inscription, probably by William Land.

The E. Range, N. of the Gatehouse, is of two storeys with attics; the walls are of diapered red brick with an embattled parapet. On the E. front the string-course below the parapet is carved with paterae and monsters' heads and pierced for rain-water pipes; much weathered lengths have been replaced in modern times with lengths of a similar and contemporary string preserved from the old Chapel ('*Eagle*', XLIX, 3). The windows on both floors are of one or two four-centred lights in square heads with labels, all more or less restored. The dormer-windows are modern. On the W. front, the central doorway has chamfered jambs and moulded four-centred arch with a label; the windows are similar to those on the E. front and almost entirely restored; the upper part of the wall, on this side, appears to have been rebuilt and the brickwork is of yellower colour. Inside the range, the staircase has timber-framed walls. The *Porter's Lodge*, N. of the Gatehouse, has exposed ceiling-beams and joists; in the N. wall is an oak doorway with moulded jambs and four-centred arch in a square head with foliated spandrels; the doorway into the N.E. turret of the gatehouse has a moulded four-centred head. On the first floor in the S. main room is a 16th-century clunch fireplace with stop-moulded jambs and four-centred opening with sunk spandrels in a square head. In the N. wall of the adjoining bedroom is an oak doorway similar to that on the floor below, giving access across over the stairs. The remains of an original stair to the garret said to be behind the cupboard in the adjoining gyproom are concealed, but raking bearers appear in the ceiling below. The attics retain parts of the wind-braces and part of a collar-brace of the original roof. The modern lecture-room, at the N. end of the range, has a ceiling incorporating 16th-century moulded timbers, curved braces, and a beam with conventional foliage-enrichment; it also contains a dome-topped iron-bound chest, late 16th-century.

The E. Range, S. of the Gatehouse, is generally similar to that N. of the same feature. On the E. front, the windows on the ground floor are of one, two and three lights and similar to those in the N. range but some of them have been enlarged and all more or less renewed. On the first floor are six much-restored windows each of two four-centred lights in a four-centred head with a label; they were formerly cinquefoiled and the foils remain internally in one window. They lighted the original Library and one further window seems to have been removed, though this must have been done before Loggan's engraving of the College was made. In the gabled end of the range are windows similar to those on the floor below. The dormers to the attics are comparatively modern. On the W. front the windows are similar to those on the E. front, including six lighting the old Library; they, in common with most of the windows throughout the range, have conspicuous relieving-arches, and all have brick rear-arches. Inside the building, most of the ground floor now forms the *Junior* further S.; they had moulded principals and collar-beams with curved braces forming two-centred, nearly semicircular, arches with traceried spandrels and, above the collars, shaped 'scissors' struts; the moulded wall-plates and lower purlins were linked by a frieze of panels with four-centred heads and foliated spandrels. Stretches of four and eight of these panels remain on the E. wall. The Hall roof has similar arcading.

The N. side of First Court was formerly occupied by the old Chapel (121½ ft. by 25 ft.) of which the foundations are marked out on the grass. The only architectural features surviving are the bases of the responds of the W. crossing-arch, which have three attached shafts, dating from the end of the 13th century.

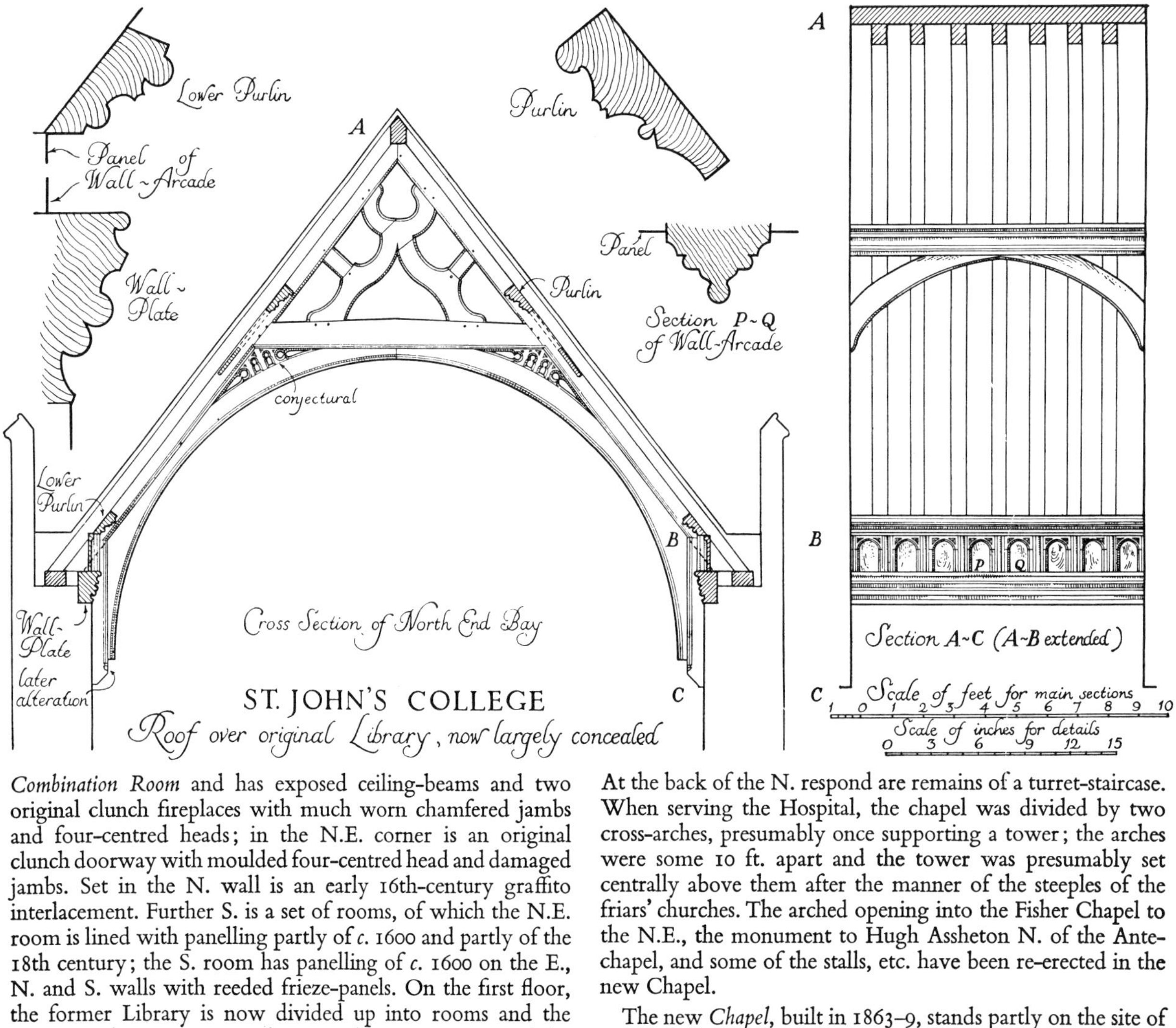

Combination Room and has exposed ceiling-beams and two original clunch fireplaces with much worn chamfered jambs and four-centred heads; in the N.E. corner is an original clunch doorway with moulded four-centred head and damaged jambs. Set in the N. wall is an early 16th-century graffito interlacement. Further S. is a set of rooms, of which the N.E. room is lined with panelling partly of *c.* 1600 and partly of the 18th century; the S. room has panelling of *c.* 1600 on the E., N. and S. walls with reeded frieze-panels. On the first floor, the former Library is now divided up into rooms and the present ceiling was inserted in or about 1616; one of the windows in the E. wall retains its panelled shutters of *c.* 1600. The inserted ceiling cuts across the original roof, of which the truss against the wall survives with parts of the three trusses

At the back of the N. respond are remains of a turret-staircase. When serving the Hospital, the chapel was divided by two cross-arches, presumably once supporting a tower; the arches were some 10 ft. apart and the tower was presumably set centrally above them after the manner of the steeples of the friars' churches. The arched opening into the Fisher Chapel to the N.E., the monument to Hugh Assheton N. of the Ante-chapel, and some of the stalls, etc. have been re-erected in the new Chapel.

The new *Chapel*, built in 1863–9, stands partly on the site of the old 'Infirmary' and contains the following pre-1850 Fittings, mostly from the old Chapel—*Brasses and Indents.* Brasses: In organ-chamber—on S. wall, (1) of [Eudo de la Zouche, 1414, Canon of Sarum, Chancellor of the University,

Archdeacon of Huntingdon, and Master of St. John's Hospital], figure of priest in academic costume, head missing, triple canopy with buttressed side-standards, roundel and shield-of-arms of Zouche, much worn and marginal inscription missing (see Indents); (2) figure of priest in mass vestments, *c.* 1430, much worn (see Indents). On N.E. tower-pier, (3) of Christopher Jackson, 1528, Fellow, inscription-plate only; on S.E. tower-pier, (4) of Nicholas Medcalf, 1537, Master, inscription-plate only, deliberately defaced. See also Monument (1). Indents: On site of old Chapel, (1) of Brass (1); (2) of Brass (2); (3) of figure and inscription-plate, much weathered. *Chair:* In choir—modern but incorporating early 17th-century arms and part of back, given in 1921. *Chest:* of oak, with moulded lid, base and necking, *c.* 1700, on later feet. *Glass:* In tower—in W. side of lantern, in the two lights and the cinquefoil of the middle window and in the cinquefoils of the side windows, mosaic of fragments, mainly tabernacle-work, with pieces of coloured glass, mostly 15th-century, from the old Chapel. *Lectern* (Plate 10): of brass, with naturalistic eagle on domical cap to tall pedestal buttressed by pinnacled and crocketed side-pieces pierced with window-tracery, all on moulded base, cap with memorial inscription, given 1840, founder Sidey, London, pedestal copied from that of lectern in Ramsey church, Huntingdon (*Ecclesiologist*, IX (1842), 143; R.C.H.M. *Hunts.* pl. 32).

Monuments and *Floor-slabs. Monuments:* In Ante-chapel—on N. side, (1) of Hugh Assheton, 1522, Archdeacon of York, altar-tomb, effigies and canopy (Plates 31, 243); altar-tomb of freestone with moulded plinth, three rounded open arches in sides with trefoiled spandrels, trefoil-headed panels on end-standards, and moulded marble slab with brass fillet-inscription; cadaver under slab in loose shroud; effigy on slab, painted, in surplice, hood and under-vestment with tails at sides, head on two cushions, hands, feet and probably face restored; canopy of freestone or clunch with moulded and shafted supports to moulded four-centred arch in a square head, with panelled octagonal attached shafts on face of supports, carved leaves in hollow-moulding of responds and head, and traceried spandrels enclosing carved and painted rebuses of an ash-tree and a tun; the whole finished with a continuous cornice carved with running foliage and a cresting; on S. side only, attached shafts finished with crocketed pinnacles above cornice and similar finial over curve of arch; ends with trefoiled ogee-headed panels and quatrefoils enclosing rebuses; soffit of canopy with similar panels and rebuses; grate of wrought-iron, with buttressed standards at each end and in the middle terminating in twisted pinnacles with restored rebuses at the tops, broad band below pinnacles containing inscription and foliated panels, intermediate uprights set diagonally and finished with spikes; all with modern recolouring. On W. side, (2) of William Wilberforce, free seated figure rather larger than life on pedestal dated 1838, plaster cast of the monument in Westminster Abbey by Samuel Joseph; S. of foregoing, (3) of James Wood, S.T.P., 1839, Master, Dean of Ely, white marble free seated figure (Plate 20), larger than life, on marble pedestal, in academic dress, holding papers on right knee, signed by E. H. Baily, R.A., 1843. On E. wall, (4) of John Smith, S.T.P., 1715, [Treasurer of Durham Cathedral], white marble wall-monument (Plate 18) with cornice and achievement-of-arms of Smith, recoloured. On N. wall, (5) of G[eorge] D[owning] Whittington, 1807, white marble neo-Greek wall-tablet on grey marble backing; (6) of Robert Worsley, 1714–5, white marble tablet (Plates 16, 18) with drapery, cherub-heads and a cartouche-of-arms of Worsley quartering Worsley with modern recolouring. On S. wall, (7) of William Wilson, S.T.B., 1800, Fellow, white marble tablet with moulded pedimental frame; (8) of Sir Isaac Pennington, M.D., 1817, white marble wall-tablet with pediment; (9) of Thomas Catton, S.T.B., 1838, white marble wall-tablet on black marble, by White, London; (10) of William Pakenham Spencer, M.A., 1845, white marble pedimented wall-tablet on black marble, by Tomson; (11) of George Langshaw, S.T.B., 1843, white marble wall-tablet. On W. wall, (12) of Charles Fox Townshend, 1817, white marble portrait bust on rectangular wall-tablet, with semi-circular backing of black marble, signed 'Chantrey'; (13) of Dr. [William] Whitaker, [1595], Master, black marble wall-tablet with alabaster side-pilasters, entablature, apron and painted clunch cresting; (14) from All Saints' church, of Henry Kirke White, 1806, poet, white marble neo-Greek tablet with profile portrait head by Chantrey, inscription by Prof. W. Smyth, bequest of F. Boott, Boston, U.S.A. *Floor-slabs:* On site of old Chapel—(1) probably of Humphrey Gower, 1711, Master, with achievement-of-arms, partly covered; (2) Robert Worsley, 1714–5, with indent; (3) John Newcome, S.T.P., 1765, Dean of Rochester and Master; (4) William Samuel Powell, S.T.P., 1775, Archdeacon of Colchester and Master; (5) John Chevallier, S.T.P. 1789, Master, letters inlaid in lead; (6) William Craven, S.T.P., 1815, Master; (7) James Wood, S.T.P., 1839, Master, Dean of Ely; (8) Thomas Baker, S.T.B., 1740, Fellow, with shield-of-arms of Baker (in 1782 Cole left £10 for a monument to Baker); (9) William Tatham, S.T.B., 1834, Fellow, and Ralph Tatham, S.T.P., 1857, Master; (10) John Palmer, 1840, Fellow, Professor of Arabic; (11) [Gawen] Brathwaite, S.T.B., 1814, Fellow; (12) William Jones, S.T.B., 1834, Fellow; (13) Joseph Taylor, S.T.B., 1836, Fellow; (14) George Langshaw, S.T.B., 1843, Fellow.

Paintings: In Ante-chapel—framed painting of the Virgin with the dead Christ, said to be a copy by Anthony Raphael Mengs, 1777, of an original by Van Dyck; presented by the Hon. Robert Henry Clive, and in 1841 hung over the altar in the old Chapel. On S. wall, fragment of painted plaster showing the right hand of Christ, 15th-century, found inside the S. wall of the Hall in 1927. *Piscina:* In S. wall of choir—reset recess of two bays with central and side-shafts of freestone with clunch caps and bases and moulded half-round intersecting arches with the mouldings crossing one another, early 13th-century, formerly in S. wall of the 'Infirmary'. (*Rood-screen:* for which Thomas Loveday, carpenter, contracted in 1516, has been re-erected in part in the S. transept of Whissendine church, Rutlandshire.) *Stalls:* In choir—the twenty-two eastern stalls on both sides, with backs, desks and sub-desks, are from the old Chapel; the backs, of late 19th-century panelling incorporating old material and with a modern cornice, have two panels to each stall with trefoiled and sub-cusped heads, foliated spandrels and carved cusp-points; stalls, with shaped and moulded divisions with shafted fronts and elbow-rests with moulded trefoiled ends and capping incorporating a carved band of running foliage. Misericordes (Plate 242), mostly carved with foliated brackets and foliage and flowers at sides; on the N., the 9th has bouched shields charged with pomegranates at the sides; the 14th has a crowned Tudor rose in the middle and the 15th shields at the sides; on the S., the 1st has an eagle and scroll in the middle, the 2nd a mask and foliage in the middle, the 9th a shield and foliage in the middle and dimidiated roses and pomegranates, for Henry VIII and Katherine of Aragon, at the sides, the 14th bouched shields charged with pomegranates at the sides, the 15th a shield charged with a rose in the middle, the 16th a fleur-de-lis and foliage in the middle and Tudor roses at the sides, one charged with a fleur-de-lis, the 19th human heads at the sides, the 20th foliage and a bat in the middle. The upper and lower desks have standards with shaped tops, carved poppy-heads and attached shafts in front; the caps support seated figures many of which seem to have been renewed perhaps in the 17th century and some subsequently; they include St. John the Divine, St. Paul and various figures with books, arks and other objects; fronts much renewed but with panels similar to those at the backs. The stalls were copied from those formerly in Jesus College Chapel, 'or better in every point', and the work of Thomas Loveday, carpenter, in 1516; made up with later work as described.

Miscellanea: The entrance into Bishop Fisher's Chantry (Plate 31) in the old Chapel has been re-erected in the S. wall of the Ante-chapel; the blind middle arch, partly restored, has moulded and shafted jambs and moulded four-centred head with traceried spandrels and shields, one defaced, one with the arms of the See of Rochester, beneath a square label supported by the outer jamb-shafts; the reveals and soffit have tiers of cinquefoiled ogee-headed panels, with bands of quatrefoils enclosing leaves, flowers, paterae, a mitre, a man's head and half-angels holding shields; the blind flanking arches are similar though narrower, but both have been renewed; their spandrels contain shields-of-arms of the See of Rochester and of Fisher quartering Fisher. The Chantry-chapel was built by Bishop Fisher between 1525 and 1533; the master-mason of Ely was paid for a draft of the tomb and for 'his avyse of the chapell'; one Lee, freemason, was paid for making and setting up the tomb; this last does not survive but a drawing of it by Essex, showing a stone chest with Classical ornament, is preserved (B.M. Add. MSS. 6768, f. 226).

The *West Range* (Plate 232) of First Court has walls of diapered red brick with embattled parapets restored in 1935. The N. part forming the Hall, extended N. in 1863–5, is of one storey; the rest of the range is of two storeys with attics and forms the Kitchen, offices and rooms. On the E. front, the parapet-string has carved paterae and beast-heads as gargoyles. The central doorway to the Hall-screens has chamfered jambs, moulded four-centred arch and ogee label (p. 393) with crockets, paterae and finial, and a rose in the spandrel; the label-stops are carved as angels, which support standards and finials, the spaces so framed on either side of the label containing panels with a rose and a portcullis. The early 16th-century nail-studded door has ribs, forming panels, and a wicket. Above the doorway and rising above the parapet is a restored late 17th-century niche with side-pilasters and scrolls and a cornice with broken curved pediment framing a lozenge of the Lady Margaret's arms with a coronet and yale supporters, much weathered; in the round-headed recess is a carved stone coroneted figure of the Foundress made in London and set up in 1674 (Plate 245). The Hall is divided into bays by two-stage buttresses, and the two bays next the screens have each a much restored window of three cinquefoiled lights with tracery in a four-centred head with moulded reveals and label. In the next bay to the N. is the original three-sided oriel-window with three transomed lights on the face and two on each return; the lights have four-centred heads and the transoms are enriched with foliated paterae. The main parapet is carried round the oriel. The window and the second oriel to the N. are of 1863–5, with brickwork refaced in 1935 (*'Eagle'*, XLIX, 78). The rest of the front has two-light windows similar to those in the E. range, all considerably restored, and a doorway with chamfered jambs and moulded four-centred arch and label. The dormer-windows in the roof are modern.

On the roof of the Hall is a hexagonal timber louvre erected in 1703 by Abraham Silk, carpenter, with carving by Francis Woodward; the lower part is lead-covered but the main stage has angle pilaster-strips and an entablature with enriched frieze and cornice; in each face is a rectangular glazed opening under a semicircular head with moulded archivolt, carved mask key-block and pierced tympanum. The small dome is lead-covered, with lofty finial and wrought-iron weather-vane (Plate 238).

The W. front is similar in materials to the E. front, but the modern extension of the Hall does not show on the elevation; the whole has been raised by the addition of seven gabled dormer-windows contemporary with Second Court. At each end of the front is a semi-octagonal stair-turret carried up above the range and embattled. The buttresses and windows of the Hall are similar to those on the E. front but less restored, and with an additional window in place of the oriel on the other side and another above the doorway. The restored doorway to the screens has chamfered jambs and moulded four-centred head and label; the nail-studded door has moulded ribs forming twelve panels, and a wicket. The windows in the S. part of the front are similar to those on the E. front but of three lights. The walling to the fifth and sixth bays from the N. has been considerably patched, where the small court, added in 1528, has been removed; the windows here and to the S. are no doubt of the date of Second Court. The gabled dormers, also of the date of Second Court, have finials and steps at the base; they each have a window of three four-centred lights in a square head but those over the Hall are not functional; between the dormers are gargoyle-masks and 17th-century lead rain-water-heads. Behind the middle dormer is a bell-cupola of timber, with two round-headed openings in each face and an ogee-shaped capping with a tall finial; there is some evidence that it was erected or re-erected in 1714. A cupola is shown in this position by Loggan. The bell, which is inaccessible, may be that cast by Richard Holdfeld in 1610 (J. J. Raven in *Camb. Ant. Soc.* (1882), p. 186, says it is of 1816).

The N. octagonal stair-turret has a rectangular projecting bay on the S. and is known as the *Master's Tower*; it gave access to the original Master's Lodge. The top storey has been

Aerial view showing ST. JOHN'S COLLEGE and TRINITY COLLEGE.

By courtesy of Aerofilms Ltd.

First Court, looking S.W. 1511–16 and 1772–76

Front to St. John's Street, from S.E. 1511–16

(37) ST. JOHN'S COLLEGE.

(37) ST. JOHN'S COLLEGE. Shrewsbury Tower, E. side. 1598–1602

Second Court, looking N.W. 1598–1602

Third Court, looking S.E. 1598–1602 and 1669–73

(37) ST. JOHN'S COLLEGE.

Library range, from S. 1623–25

W. range, from S.E. 1669–73

(37) ST. JOHN'S COLLEGE. Third Court. Exteriors.

(37) ST. JOHN'S COLLEGE. Library, W. range of Third Court and covered bridge, from N.W. 1623–25, 1669–73 and 1831

Library staircase. 1628

Library; inner E. entrance. 1623–25

(37) ST. JOHN'S COLLEGE.

(37) ST. JOHN'S COLLEGE. Cupolas on Hall range. 1703 and 1714

(29) GONVILLE AND CAIUS COLLEGE. Cupola. 1728

refaced or rebuilt. The S. entrance-doorway is a late 17th-century insertion and has a bolection-moulded surround, a high, shaped frieze with a carved crowned portcullis and a cornice and curved pediment above. The passage on the ground floor has a semi-elliptical barrel-vault of brick and two blocked doorways on the E., formerly opening into the Hall and the old Combination Room; the N. doorway has chamfered jambs and a moulded four-centred head, the S., also with four-centred head, is rebated to the W. The room over the passage, called the Silver Room and entered through a doorway with chamfered jambs and moulded four-centred head, has an early 16th-century panelled ceiling with moulded beams; the E. and W. walls have original recesses with oak shelves. The S. stair-turret was rebuilt or refaced in the 18th century and the top storey has been subsequently again refaced. The top storeys of both turrets were presumably additions of the date of Second Court.

Inside the range, the *Hall* (Plate 239) (29½ ft. by 108 ft., originally 68 ft.) was formerly of five but is now of eight bays. The original roof may perhaps be attributed to Loveday; it has hammer-beam trusses with upper and lower collars: the main timbers are moulded and rise from wooden corbels carved with half-figures holding shields. The shields are charged with the badges of the Foundress and a cross on a mount. The hammer-beams have curved braces below and shields at the ends bearing roses and portcullises alternately, both crowned. Below the lower collar-beams are curved braces interrupted by the hammer-posts, but continued down to the corbels in the form of four-centred arches. Between the lower and upper collars are queen-posts from which spring flat four-centred arched collar-braces; the roof is ceiled at the level of the upper collars. The spandrels of the main timbers have traceried fillings. Between the trusses, the bays are divided into six main heights and subdivided by the moulded rafters; between the deeply moulded wall-plate and the lowest purlin on each side is an arcading of small panels with four-centred heads (see also the roof of the original Library, p. 190). The 19th-century N. bays match the foregoing. In the third bay from the S. of the original roof is the hexagonal opening to the louvre.

The opening to the original oriel has a four-centred timber arch springing from corbels carved with half-angels holding shields charged with a Lancastrian rose and a portcullis; the spandrels have pierced tracery. The walls of the Hall are lined to sill-level with linenfold panelling in two heights finished with a modern entablature. In the old part of the Hall the panelling seems to be largely of 1528–39; a donation towards the wainscot was made in 1528 and one Lambert was paid for 'selyng the hall' in the later year; part of that in the original oriel is surmounted by late 16th-century arabesque panels. Against the N. wall is the reset panelling from the earlier N. wall, which is carried up to the level of the roof-corbels; above the plinth-panels, of 1863, are six tiers of linenfold panels divided into four bays by elaborately enriched Ionic pilasters carved with monster-heads and portcullises. The pilasters support an enriched architrave, a panelled frieze with scrolls and heads and a coved cornice; the fascia of the last is carved with two bands of monsters supporting roses, portcullises and vases, and divided into twelve short lengths by small posts with acorn finials and painted shields-of-arms of Ormesby, Cecil, Vere, Pollard, Langley (?) and Jackson. The arrangement of this panelling would seem to be of late 16th-century date, of the cove etc. of 1863. Above the panelling is a carved achievement of the Stuart Royal arms, with the motto 'Exurgat Deus dissipentur inimici', set in a panel with terminal side-pilasters and small figures supporting the entablature, the last with a carved frieze, strapwork cresting and pierced obelisks.

The *Screen*, at the S. end of the Hall, is original but extensively restored. It is of five bays with doorways in the second and fourth bays; these have moulded jambs and four-centred heads with portcullises and Lancastrian roses in the spandrels; the doors are of the late 19th century. The other bays have each three tiers of linenfold panels with moulded rails and styles and are finished with a moulded and carved cornice and modern brattishing. The Screens-passage has a partly restored open timber ceiling in eight panels with enriched and moulded beams (p. 396); the panelling on the S. wall is mostly modern but incorporates some linenfold panels seemingly of the 16th century in the lower parts; the three doorways have chamfered jambs and moulded four-centred heads and are fitted with nail-studded doors with moulded ribs forming panels, the side doors being divided horizontally into two leaves. On the S. wall above the Screens is a repainted achievement of the arms of the Foundress in an ornamental border.

The windows contain mediaeval and later glass. The main tracery-lights of the side-windows are filled with a jumble of fragments from the old Chapel, mostly of the 15th century. In the middle upper light of the original oriel is a figure of St. John under a canopy (Plate 242), probably of the 18th century and formerly in the cathedral of Regensburg; in the lower part of the light are two 17th-century shields-of-arms, of the Foundress (repaired) and of the See of Lincoln impaling Williams. Much of the rest of the heraldic glass was made for the old Chapel in 1842; it includes, in the 19th-century oriel, the arms of (a) the See of Worcester impaling Stillingfleet, (b) Durham impaling Morton, (c) St. Asaph impaling Beveridge; (d) Norwich impaling Overall; (e) St. Davids impaling Watson; (f) Edward James Herbert, Earl of Powis; (g) Chichester impaling Lake; (h) Mary, Countess of Shrewsbury, Talbot impaling Cavendish, (i) Lincoln impaling Williams; (j) Norwich impaling Lloyd; (k) Rochester impaling Fisher; (l) Peterborough impaling White, (m) the Foundress; (n) Ely impaling Turner; (o) Sarah, Duchess of Somerset, Seymour with the Royal augmentation impaling Alston, (p) Catherine (Willoughby), Duchess of Suffolk, Brandon impaling Willoughby of Eresby; (q) York impaling Sandys; (r) Canterbury impaling Morton, (s) Ely impaling Gunning; (t) Durham impaling Pilkington, (u) William Cecil, Lord Burghley, (v) Mildred, Lady Burghley; in window next S. of original oriel, (a) Thomas Linacre, (b) John Dowman; (c) Henry Hebblethwaite, (d) Roger Lupton; (e) Sir Ralph Hare, (f) Sir Marmaduke Constable; in next window S., (a) James Wood, Dean of Ely, (b) Humphrey Gower, Master; (c) Regius Professorship of Divinity impaling William Whitaker, (d) Deanery of Rochester impaling John Newcome; (e) William Craven, Master, (f) Alan Percy, Master, Percy quartering Lucy; W. wall, in second window, (a) Richard Bentley, (b) Sir John Cheke; (c) Thomas Wentworth, Earl of

Strafford, (d) Lucius Cary, Viscount Falkland, Cary quartering Spencer, Beaufort; (e) Roger Ascham, (f) Thomas Baker; in third window, (a) Peterborough impaling Marsh, (b) Peterborough impaling Dee; (c) Lichfield impaling Ryder, (d) Bath and Wells impaling Beadon; (e) Lichfield impaling Butler, (f) Salisbury impaling Fisher; in fourth window, (a) William Platt, (b) John Hulse, Hulse quartering Hinton; (c) Sir Isaac Pennington; (d) Thomas Sutton, Founder of the Charterhouse, (e) Robert Johnson, Archdeacon of Leicester. The remainder of the shields-of-arms are after 1850, mainly of 1863.

The rest of the W. range, to the S., is occupied by the *Butteries* and *Kitchen* on the ground floor; both have exposed ceiling-beams and the W. wall of the central passage has exposed timber-framing. The Kitchen (29½ ft. by 83 ft. including the Butteries) has been considerably altered; the floor over the S. part was at one period removed except for the central cross and longitudinal beams, but it has now been replaced with a modern floor and the Wordsworth Room formed above. In the N. wall of this last the timber-framing over the middle beam is exposed and incorporates, at the E. end, a small king-post truss with the date 1754, presumably a stiffening then inserted; in the S. wall of the same room is an original fireplace; it has moulded jambs and four-centred head. On the first floor of the N. part of the range, some rooms are lined with 18th-century panelling.

The *South Range* (Plate 232) is of the early 16th-century, but was raised one storey and the whole N. front refaced in ashlar in 1772–6 from the designs of James Essex; the roof is slate-covered. The N. front is symmetrically designed, with a band between the lower storeys, a dentilled cornice and a plain parapet. The sash-windows have architraves; the four doorways also have architraves, two of them with side-pilasters and console-brackets supporting cornices and pediments. Under the lintel of the doorway to staircase 'G' is inscribed 'Stag, Novr. 15 1777'. The three 18th-century stone chimney-stacks have coped tops.

The S. front has also been heightened. The main wall is of the 16th century and of red brick with restored stone dressings including a plinth refaced in the 18th century; the top storey is an 18th-century addition in yellow brick. The windows of the original part are symmetrically arranged and of one or two four-centred lights in a square head with a label; a doorway at the W. end has been remodelled in the 18th century. The 18th-century top storey has square-headed windows with cornices above. The lead rainwater pipes are of the same date.

Inside the S. range, the arrangements have been much altered in the 18th century, but some timber framing is exposed in the partitions and there are some exposed ceiling-beams. In a room on the first floor behind the easternmost staircase is an original oak doorway with moulded jambs and four-centred arch in a square head with leaves in the spandrels; the original door, hung on strap-hinges, has mouldings planted on to form four panels. A similar doorway remains at the W. end of the same floor.

Adjoining the S.E. angle of the building is a re-set early 16th-century gateway, formerly, and until 1855, standing further to the E. It has jambs and two-centred arch of two chamfered orders, and the rebuilt wall containing it has a crow-stepped gable.

Second Court (about 165½ ft. by 138 ft.) was begun in 1598 by contract with Ralph Symons and Gilbert Wigge and the original drawings are preserved in the College archives. The walls are of red and yellow mottled brick with Northamptonshire stone dressings, and the roofs are covered with green slates. The diapering of the Court fronts so conspicuous in the drawings scarcely appears in fact, and the entry in the accounts for 'painting' the brickwork is perhaps significant in this context. The ranges are of two storeys with attics. The *North Range* (Plate 234) is of ten bays on the S. front, each bay with a gabled dormer; these last are similar to those on the W. front of the Hall-range but the western four have been rebuilt in the 19th century. The four doorways have chamfered jambs and moulded four-centred heads and labels. The windows, generally, are of three four-centred lights in square heads with labels; the parapet-string is returned as the label over the dormer-windows and enriched with paterae and gargoyle-heads. The fifth bay has on the first floor a three-sided oriel-window of stone on four shaped brackets; it has three four-centred lights on the face, one on each return, and is finished with pierced strapwork cresting; the panelled apron-wall is enriched with strapwork reliefs. The lead rainwater pipes have shaped heads, two of which are inscribed, one "ANŌDŌ.", the other "1599".

The N. front of the N. range is of three storeys with a plain parapet and a series of small gables rising above it. The chimney-stacks have rebuilt diagonal shafts. The windows are of two four-centred lights in square heads with labels. The small projecting bay in the middle is largely of the late 19th century except for part of the upper western half and the reset early 16th-century N. doorway, heavily restored, which was formerly the S. doorway to the old Chapel. The early 18th-century rainwater-pipes have shaped heads.

Inside the N. range, in the rooms on the ground-floor are some exposed ceiling-beams; the central passage has exposed timber-framing. The rooms to the W. and a room on the E. contain 18th-century panelling. On the first floor is the Combination Room, originally the Gallery in the former Master's Lodge and now partitioned; the W. end has been transformed into the staircase to the Library. The modern staircase at the E. end of the range has 16th-century moulded ceiling-beams and the walls of the upper part are lined with panelling of *c.* 1600 with an enriched frieze; refixed above the ground-floor doorway in the N. wall is a carved wood achievement-of-arms of the Foundress with yale supporters and flanked by terminal pilasters supporting putti (Plate 52). The first-floor passage to the W. of the same staircase is lined with panelling, similar to that just described, and the doorway at the W. end has a late 17th-century moulded surround and an entablature with frieze-panel.

The *Combination Room* (Plate 225) (93 ft. by 19 ft.) has a plaster ceiling of *c.* 1600, executed by Cobbe, and divided into geometrical panels by moulded ribs with running vine-enrichment; the middle panel of each of the ten bays or repeats has a small boss; the plaster ceiling of the oriel-window is panelled.

The walls are lined with wood panelling of the same age, six panels high, with enriched frieze-panels; at the angles of the window-splays are fluted and enriched Doric pilasters on pedestals and surmounted by lion-masks, with many renewed. Similar pilasters flank the W. doorway, which has a panelled door on the E. side and a later panelled door on the W. side. The two fireplaces in the N. wall have entirely restored or modern stone jambs and heads. The E. fireplace (Plate 225) is flanked by enriched Doric pilasters of oak, of *c.* 1600, supporting an enriched and bracketed entablature; the overmantel is of three bays divided and flanked by terminal pilasters supporting an enriched entablature; each bay has a central and four subsidiary shaped panels. The restored W. fireplace (Plate 48) has woodwork formerly in No. 3 Sussum's Yard and part of the old Red Lion Inn and moved here in 1919; flanking the opening are fluted Doric pilasters with a frieze and an entablature with carved brackets on both the friezes; these last are enriched and the upper has shields carved with the initials and date 'I.V.' and 'E.V. 1594', said to be for Vintner, and a device of three fishes. The overmantel is of three bays divided and flanked by coupled and fluted Corinthian columns supporting an enriched entablature; each bay contains an intarsia panel depicting an architectural composition in perspective with water and swans in the foreground. In the oriel-window is a glass roundel with the portrait-head of Henrietta Maria against a yellow background, in enamel and grisaille, possibly by Richard Greenbury, *c.* 1630 (R. L. Poole, *Catalogue of Portraits* etc. *Oxford*, II, xxi, 218). Fixed to the walls are thirteen silver candle-sconces (Plate 45) each with two branches and a shield-of-arms surmounted by the College badge; two are of 1790 and made probably by John Scofield, with the arms party dexter the College sinister the See of Lincoln impaling Green, and two of 1839 by Joseph Taylor, with the College arms alone. The remaining nine, of 1868 and 1875, match the latter; another four of the same design, of 1815, by Benjamin Smith, are in the Master's Lodge. In 1790 Messrs. Rundell and Bridge were paid £88 for silver sconces. The smaller room ($22\frac{3}{4}$ ft. by $19\frac{3}{4}$ ft.), to the W., originally formed part of the Gallery and has a continuation of the main ceiling of *c.* 1600; the walls are lined with mid 18th-century panelling with dado, dado-rail and slight cornice.

The staircase to the W. (Plate 237) was inserted in *c.* 1628 when the Library was built; it cuts through part of the Gallery, the ceiling of which remains, except the N.E. quarter; along the N. and part of the S. wall is a plaster frieze of running vine-ornament. The arrangement of the lower part of the staircase has been altered in modern times by the transfer of the two lower flights to the N. It has symmetrically turned balusters, moulded grip-handrail and square newels with turned finials; the double newel between the second and third flights has an elaborate finial in three stages with scrolls and a pierced pyramidal top (Plate 42). On the E. side of the top flight is a partition and between it and the foregoing newel is an elaborate carved and pierced scroll with a stag's head cut in relief; above is a moulded half-round arch of wood supported on console-brackets and with a pierced pendant in the middle; a similar arch on the ground floor spans the entrance-passage and frames a semi-dome. On the ground floor the doorway in the W. wall has a semicircular moulded arch with a pierced pendant in the middle and a dentilled cornice above. The doorway above, on the first floor, opens into the vestibule of the Library and is of *c.* 1628; it has tapering Ionic side-pilasters on pedestals, all enriched with arabesques, with entablatures under scrolled brackets supporting a deep crowning entablature; these frame the half-round arch of the doorway, with a rose and a fleur-de-lis on the archivolt and cherub-heads in the spandrels. The door has moulded panels with arabesque enrichment and with the Ionic entablature carried across below the springing of the arch; the tympanum is carved with an oval convex shield-of-arms, of the See of Lincoln impaling Williams, in elaborate strap-work framing. Both the vestibule and the room to the N. originally formed part of the Gallery and retain the plaster ceiling similar to that in the Combination Room. The walls of the vestibule are lined with early 17th-century panelling with arabesque frieze-panels. The doorway into the Library is of stone and has moulded jambs with attached shafts and a half-round arch, of the same section, in a square head with pierced spandrels. The small room to the N. has a fireplace with chamfered jambs and moulded four-centred head; above it are two tiers of arched and enriched oak panels and an enriched frieze; the rest of the wall has panelling with an enriched frieze; against the S. wall is a large press with panelled doors, having enriched frieze and top rail; all of *c.* 1600. The staircase to the attics is of the late 18th century.

The attics have part of the main roof-timbers exposed. The easternmost room is lined with panelling, much of which is of *c.* 1600; the other rooms have 18th-century panelling, and the westernmost room has a threee-sided recess which may represent a former oriel-window in the W. wall. The interior of the Master's Tower is described with the W. range of First Court.

The *South Range* is of red brick and of two storeys with attics; it has a series of refaced gables on the N. similar to those on the opposite range. The windows and doorways on this front are generally similar to those opposite and there are lead rainwater-pipes with shaped heads. The S. front is of similar materials to the N. front and retains the quoins at the S.W. angle; it has a plain parapet-wall with small gables over most of the top-floor windows and a series of chimney-stacks. The windows, of one and two lights, are similar to those on the N. front; the third ground-floor window from the E. end has lately been cut down to form a doorway. On the second floor, towards the W. end, one window retains an original wrought-iron frame with casement and leaded quarries, and most of the windows retain original wrought-iron grilles. Some of the rainwater pipes and heads are of the 18th century, others are perhaps original.

The interior of the S. range is occupied by sets of rooms, except at the E. end where are kitchen-offices. The rooms have some exposed ceiling-beams. Staircase 'M' is of the mid 18th century, with turned balusters and newels in the form of Doric columns; it incorporates the central octagonal newel of the earlier staircase and the upper part has exposed timber framing. The ground-floor room W. of the same staircase has a panelled dado of *c.* 1600; the next room, approached from doorway 'L', has also a panelled dado of *c.* 1600. On the first floor, the principal room on Staircase 'O' has a late 16th-century fireplace with chamfered jambs and moulded four-centred head; the upper part of the E. wall is painted to represent timber-framing and on part of the W. wall real framing is exposed. The main E. room on Staircase 'M' has a panelled dado of *c.* 1600; the inner S.E. room is lined with panelling which incorporates work of *c.* 1600; the room W. of the same staircase is lined with 18th-century panelling with dado and cornice, and the small room to the N.W. has a cupboard with panelled doors with frieze-panels and 'cock's-head' hinges of *c.* 1600; above the cupboard is reused panelling of the same date, with enriched arches and frieze. The first-floor main room E. of Staircase 'K' is lined with panelling of *c.* 1600, with arabesque frieze and moulded cornice; the fireplace is flanked by enriched Ionic pilasters supporting an enriched shelf, and the overmantel is of three bays divided and flanked by pilasters supporting an enriched entablature; in each bay is an enriched arched panel; all the woodwork was adapted to the room probably towards the middle of the 18th century; there are 18th-century panelled pilasters under the ends of the cased ceiling-beam. The main first-floor room W. of the same staircase is lined with 18th-century panelling and has a semicircular recess with doors in the W. wall. The small room to the S.E. has an original moulded timber doorframe with the head cut through; the upper parts of the N. and S. walls have painted decoration on the plaster, probably of *c.* 1600. On the N. wall are two panels one with a landscape and church, the other with trees and a chained monkey with a basket of fruit (Plate 58); the long panel on the W. wall shows a landscape with fields and beasts, including a stag with a fiddle, pipes and a drum ('*Eagle*', XLIV (1926), 1). In the attics some of the roof-timbers are exposed, and a room towards the E. end has an original fireplace with chamfered jambs and moulded four-centred head. Another room, towards the W., is lined with re-used panelling, which includes some linenfold panels.

The *West Range* (Plate 234) is generally similar in design and materials to the N. and S. ranges but has a central Gatehouse, now called the *Shrewsbury Tower* (Plate 233). This is of three storeys with semi-octagonal angle-turrets carried above the embattled parapet and themselves with restored embattling. The E. front has an archway with splayed jambs and moulded four-centred arch with carved masks and paterae in the main hollow-moulding; the spandrels are carved with strapwork, shields and conventional foliage, the string-course above with heads and paterae. On the first floor are three panels of 1671, the middle one enclosing a lozenge-of-arms, with talbot and stag supporters, of Mary, Countess of Shrewsbury, Talbot impaling Cavendish, and the side-panels a double rose and portcullis; above them are two windows each of two tall four-centred lights in a square head. The windows flank a central round-headed niche containing a statue of the Countess (Plate 255) carved by Thomas Burman in 1671 at the cost of her nephew William Cavendish, Duke of Newcastle, and brought from London; returned over these three features as a label is an enriched string in continuation of the parapet-string of the flanking ranges. The second floor has a window of four four-centred lights in a square head. The turrets have single-light windows with four-centred openings in square heads and doorways with restored stop-chamfered jambs and four-centred moulded heads, all with labels. On the W. front of the Gatehouse (Plate 234) the general arrangement is similar to that on the E. front. The archway has splayed jambs and moulded four-centred arch with a label; above it is a panel carved with the arms of the College in a cartouche. The second storey has a window of three four-centred lights in a square head with a continuous string-course above. On the third storey is a similar window with a label. The Observatory added on the top of the Gatehouse in 1765 was removed in 1859.

The *Gatehall* (18½ ft. by 16 ft.) has a panelled stone vault in two bays with ribs springing from moulded corbels, pendants in the middle of each bay and a carved rose on the central cross-rib. The staircases in the E. turrets have been extensively renewed; but the original octagonal newel of oak survives in the N.E. stair. The room on the first floor, entered through a stone doorway with original oak door, is lined with early 18th-century bolection-moulded panelling with dado-rail and cornice; in the W. angles of the room are original stone doorways with four-centred heads to the turrets, now concealed behind the panelling. The room on the second floor is lined with plain 18th-century panelling with a dado-rail.

The sections of the W. range flanking the Gatehouse (Plate 234) are symmetrically designed and generally similar in character, materials and detail to the N. and S. ranges of Second Court. The gables on the E. side have been refaced or rebuilt; here the lead rainwater pipes with shaped heads are original. On the W. side, the enriched parapet-string is omitted; the windows are much restored and the chimney-stacks rebuilt; the two buttresses are additions made in 1691 by Robert Grumbold, and the lead rainwater pipes with moulded heads are of the 18th century. Inside the W. range some ceiling-beams and timber-framing are exposed. In the N. section, the S. room approached from doorway 'F' is lined with late 18th-century panelling. On the first floor, the N. room has a dado incorporating some panelling of *c.* 1600; a bedroom S.W. of this room contains an original stone fireplace with chamfered jambs and four-centred moulded head, all cut back, The room at the same level adjoining the Gatehouse is lined with mid 18th-century panelling with a bolection-moulded panel over the fireplace. In the S. section, the N. main room has some panelling of *c.* 1600 in the window-recess and an original doorway to the S.W. Gatehouse-turret with chamfered jambs and four-centred head. The S. room is lined with late 18th-century panelling, with a semicircular-headed recess in the S.W. corner. On the first floor, one room has a dado incorporating panelling of *c.* 1600 and an internal lobby and door of panelling of the same period. Some roof timbers are exposed in the attics.

Third Court (80 ft. average by 121½ ft.) has the Library range on the N. side and rather later ranges on the W. and S. The *North Range*, built between 1623 and 1625 at the cost of John Williams, Bishop of Lincoln, is of two storeys with the main Library on the first floor; the walls are mottled red and yellow brick faced with clunch on the inside; the dressings are of freestone. The first scheme, rejected by Bishop Williams, was for a Library built upon pillars extending W. from the Shrewsbury Tower. The Gothic form of the existing windows is evidently due to representations made to him by Bishop Cary of Exeter that 'the old fashion of church window' was 'most meet for such a building' (College Archives: Letter, Valentine Cary to Owen Gwyn, Master, 19 Nov. 1623).

The S. front (Plate 235) is of ten bays but the western two extend beyond the line of the W. range of the Court. The wall has a refaced plinth and continuous stone entablatures over the ground-floor and upper windows; the parapet-wall is embattled, with a wide merlon in the middle of each bay with a central ogee feature rising above it, and all with a moulded stone capping. The ground-floor has two much restored doorways with chamfered jambs, moulded four-centred heads and labels (p. 393). The windows in the other free bays are each of two four-centred lights in a square head with moulded reveals; the continuous entablature is broken forward over them to suggest individual crowning entablatures. The first floor has, in each bay, a window of two cinquefoiled ogee lights with Gothic curvilinear tracery in a two-centred head; the windows are set in slight projections of the brickwork extending below the sills, as aprons, to the entablature over the lower windows, and above the heads, where they have a narrow stone framing, to the upper entablature; this last breaks forward over each projection. The N. wall is divided into five double bays by buttresses and has a plain rebuilt parapet. Each bay has two windows similar to those on the S. but the lower ones have no cornices and entirely restored heads and the upper ones have labels, more or less restored jambs, and are flush with the wall-face. The lead rainwater pipes have shaped heads and are probably of the late 17th century.

The W. end (Plate 236) rising from the river has a stepped plinth of stone and diagonal buttresses finished with crocketed pinnacles. In the middle is a three-sided bay-window of two storeys finished with a stepped and shaped parapet-wall with moulded capping and pierced finials of stone over each face; on the face of the parapet are stone embellishments, on the front, two shields, of Griffith and of the See of Lincoln, and the initials I.L.C.S. (Johannes Lincolniensis Custos Sigilli), and on the S.W. return the date 1624. The windows in the lower storey of the bay are of three four-centred lights on the front and two on each return; above them is an entablature continued across the wall between the buttresses. The front window of the storey above is of three cinquefoiled and transomed lights with curvilinear tracery in a two-centred head; the side windows are similar but of two lights; above them is a second entablature again continued across from buttress to buttress. The wall is finished with ramps against the bay and with a large cresting of pierced wave-ornament.

Inside the N. range, the ground floor originally contained sets of rooms, but the space was taken for extensions to the Library, in 1858, 1874–5, and later; it has no ancient features except, in the bay-window at the W. end, glass shields-of-arms of Thomas Baker, Fellow, died 1740, and the Deanery of Ely, impaling Wood, for James Wood, Master, Dean of Ely, died 1839, both 19th-century, the second with older glass in the border. On the first floor the *Library* (106 ft. by 27¼ ft.) has a roof of ten bays with arch-braced collar-beam trusses on acanthus brackets, with carved pendants at the arch apices; along the side-walls runs a panelled and bracketed entablature and the whole is ceiled below the collars and rafters with large rectangular wood panels, twelve in a bay. The roof

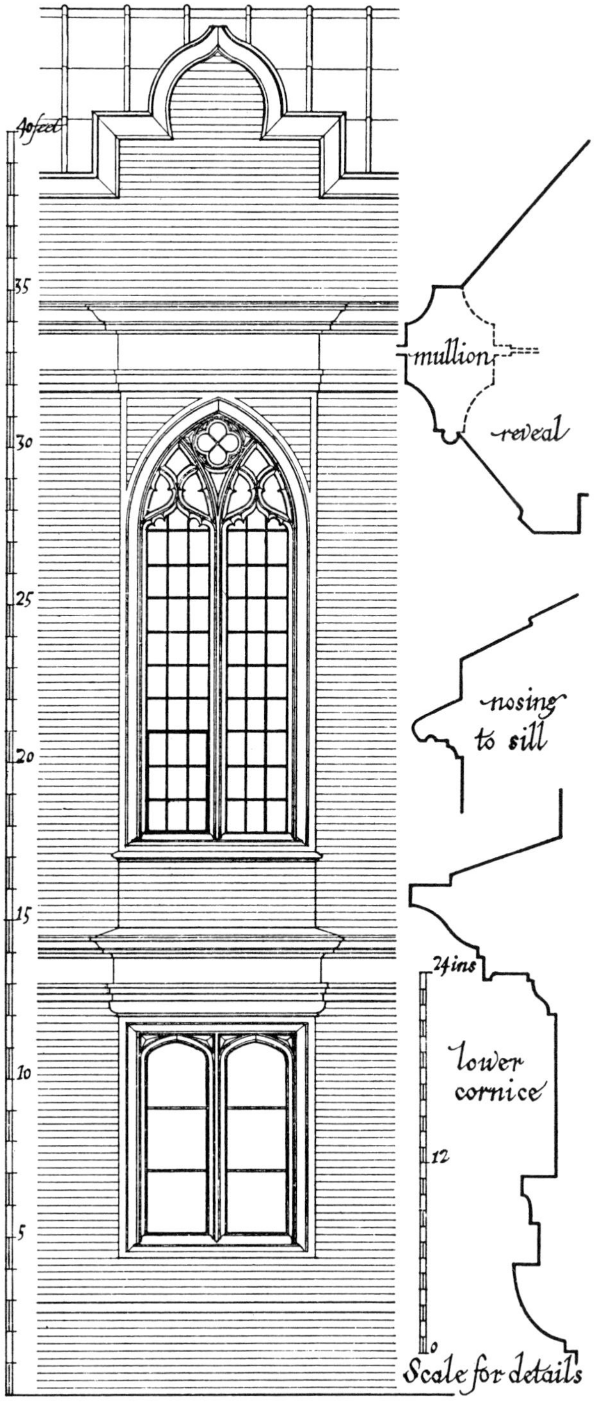

St. John's College Library design of typical bay

was restored in 1783 by James Essex and later reconstructed, largely with steel and concrete, though the original form and visible timbers were so far as possible retained, by Professor Beresford Pite in 1927 and 1928. On the E. wall, above the entrance, is a large shield-of-arms tierced in pale of the See of Lincoln, Williams quartering Griffith, and the Deanery of Westminster, with a mitre and croziers and all in a strapwork frame (Plate 237). Between the side-windows are projecting bookcases (Plate 40) which have been reconstructed and in part altered; the ends are in two main stages, the lower with a panelled plinth and two enriched arched panels above, and the upper with enriched side-pilasters supporting an entablature with a bracketed frieze and Jacobean cresting enclosing shields; between the pilasters are two ranges of grouped panels divided by small hinged panels closing the shelf-lists (Plate 230). The shields on the cresting bear the arms of the following persons, the dates being those of their deaths: N. side, E. to W., (a) Thomas Gisborne, 1806; (b) William Lloyd, Bishop of Norwich, 1709; (c) Thomas Morton, Bishop of Durham, 1659; (d) Sir Isaac Pennington, 1817; (e) Thomas Baker, 1740; (f) Sir Soulden Lawrence, 1814; (g) Edward Bendlowes, 1676; (h) Mildred (Cooke), Lady Burghley, 1589; (i) John Cary, 2nd Viscount Rochford, Cary with a crescent gules for difference in chief quartering Spencer, Beaufort, Boleyn, Rochford, Morgan, over all a label gules, 1677; (j) Thomas Whytehead, 1843; (k) Richard Duffield, 1863; S. side, (a) Humphrey Gower, Master, 1714; (b) James Wood, Master, Dean of Ely, 1839; (c) John Hacket, Bishop of Lichfield, 1670; (d) Sir Ralph Hare, K.B., 1624; (e) John Newcome, 1765; (f) Peter Gunning, Bishop of Ely, 1709; (g) Henry Wriothesley, K.G., 3rd Earl of Southampton, Wriothesley quartering Dunstaville, Lushill and Drayton, 1624; (h) Matthew Prior, 1721; (i) Hugh Percy, 3rd Duke of Northumberland, Percy quartering Percy ancient, 1847; (j) Lord William Howard of Naworth, Howard quartering Brotherton, Warren and Mowbray, 1640; (k) Robert Metcalf, 1652. The sides of the cases were formerly divided into two bays, but the pilasters now remain only at each end; the base and entablature, as described above, are continued along the sides. The cases against the E. wall have been extended at some period, but the original arrangement of two bays has been retained. A lower case (Plate 42) stands in the middle of each bay; the tops are gabled and designed for reading desks, but all except the two easternmost have been heightened about 1 ft. They are of similar character to the main cases; those unaltered have the ends in two stages, the lower with enriched arched panels and the upper with enriched pilasters and grouped panels, a carved frieze, cherub-heads and scrolls in the gabled ends and enrichments in the form of crockets, including fleurs-de-lys, on the slopes; each side has pilasters and a cornice. The heightened cases have an additional plinth. Against the side-walls are cases of *c.* 1800 and behind them is 17th-century panelling. Opening into the bay-window at the W. end is an arch with chamfered responds and four-centred head. In the window is heraldic glass set up after 1850, except perhaps the shield-of-arms tierced in pale of the See of Lincoln, Williams quartering Griffith and Westminster Deanery with a strapwork surround surmounted by a mitre and the initials I.W. with a crozier. The 19th-century accounts regarding the latter are ambiguous; if of the 17th century, it has been much restored.

The *West Range* was built in 1669–73 and is of three storeys with attics; the walls are of red brick with stone dressings and the roofs are covered with green slates. The E. front (Plates 229, 235) has a projecting centrepiece flanked by an open arcaded walk of six bays on either side extending to a seventh bay on the extremities, that on the N. with a repetition of the arcading framing a 19th-century doorway and perhaps of that date, that on the S. of plain brickwork containing a window. On the floors above the seven bays to the S. of the centrepiece are maintained, but to the N. the building terminates beyond the fifth bay, in order to leave access for light to the Library, the front alone being linked to the Library range by a lofty open arch.

The centrepiece is in three main stages, coinciding with the height of the storeys in the range, with an attic consisting of a deep frieze and broken curved pediment. Most of the lowest stage and all the pediment are of ashlar, the upper stages and frieze of brick with ashlar quoins and dressings. It contains a semicircular-headed archway in the ground stage with imposts, archivolt and scrolled keystone, flanked by attached Tuscan columns supporting an entablature. Above this last, rising into the second stage, is a cartouche carved with the arms of the College, surmounted by a demi-eagle and flanked by swags of fruit and flowers. In the second stage is a two-light transomed window with eared architrave, side-scrolls, and apron, flanked by pilaster-strips on pedestals and with oval panels superimposed on the shafts; the pilasters support a cornice pedimented over the window. In the third stage is a two-light window with architrave and apron flanked by pilasters similar to those below, but with a portcullis and a Lancastrian rose respectively on the shafts, and supporting an entablature. On this last, against the attic frieze, is a large carved lozenge-of-arms of the Foundress with yale supporters and flanked by draped urns. The pediment contains a central pedestal supporting a ball-finial and weathervane.

The arcading flanking the centrepiece is of ashlar; each bay contains an open semicircular-headed arch, similar to that already described, and the bays are divided by Tuscan pilasters; the pilasters support an entablature returned from, and in continuation of, that to the ground stage of the centrepiece. Each floor above contains a window in each bay, the windows being linked vertically by brick aprons. All the windows are of two lights, those on the first floor transomed, with moulded architraves and sills, friezes and cornices; the friezes over those on the second floor are of inverted scroll form in profile. The upper entablatures align with the entablature to the third stage of the centrepiece, and are returned and continued to form a parapet-string. The parapet is similar to that of the Library range but smaller in scale and with threequarter-circular extensions of the merlons. The dormer-windows have been rebuilt. The stone arch at the N. end, forming an open screen linking the N. and W. ranges, has a four-centred head with scrolled imposts and keystone and sunk spandrels below an entablature and parapet-wall in continuation of those of the W. range. The arch was altered to its present form by James Essex in 1777, who evidently retained and reused as imposts the 17th-century keystones indicated in the view of the earlier oval opening shown here in Loggan's engraving of the College from the E.

The W. front (Plates 236, 244), on the river, is divided into five main bays by chimney-projections, which rise from the stone plinth; it has brick plat-bands between the storeys, a moulded parapet-string, and an embattled parapet similar to that on the E. front. At the N. end is a deep diagonal-buttress added in the 18th century. The windows are of one or two square-headed lights, those on the ground and first floors transomed and with flat brick arches; all have stone architraves. Projecting from the middle bay to the height of two storeys is the Gothic bridge of 1831, and close S. of it on the ground floor is a Gothic window of the same date. Concealing the lower part of the northern bays is a grey brick annexe built and extended in the 19th century standing on the 17th-century quay, or 'Foot-wharf', and with the lower part of that date. In 1777 and 1841 the main foundations were strengthened, and in the latter year the front was restored and the chimney-stacks rebuilt. The roof has rebuilt square-topped dormer-windows. Two of the rainwater pipes have heads dated 1672 and two 1799.

The N. and S. ends of the W. range are finished with shaped gables surmounted by finials; the S. wall, rising from a skewed plinth with broad water-tabling, has plat-bands returned from the W. front and a third plat-band below the gable, a two-light window, as before, on each floor, and a round window with stone architrave in the gable.

Inside the W. range, the ground floor is occupied by the arcaded walk, store-rooms etc. and the approach to the 19th-century Bridge, the approach being described below with the last. The two staircases are largely original, though the lower flights of that to the N. are much altered; they have turned balusters, plain strings, grip handrails and rectangular newels, the lowest panelled, the inner continuous and the outer with ball-terminals and turned pendants; some of the terminals and pendants are missing. On the first floor, the main room N. of staircase 'C' is lined with original panelling with three flat-topped projecting doorcases; the doors are original. The main room S. of the same stair is lined with original oak panelling with dado and cornice etc.; the projecting doorcases are rather more elaborate than the foregoing, but the doors are modern; the overmantel has a bolection-moulded panel and side-pilasters. The main rooms N. and S. of staircase 'D' are lined with original panelling with dado-rail and cornice; it has been much restored in the former, which contains an early 19th-century stone fireplace. On the second floor, the main room S. of staircase 'C' has original panelling, rather plainer than that below; that in the N. room was completely renewed in a similar style in 1955 when the date 1673 and initials W.B. were found cut in the brickwork behind. The moulded stone fireplaces, with rectangular openings, are original. The main rooms N. and S. of stair 'D' are lined with panelling similar to the foregoing, that in the S. room with three projecting doorcases with central frieze-panels; the N. fireplace has a heavy bolection-moulded stone surround, probably original; the S. fireplace may be later. Many of the oak outer doors to the sets are contemporary with the building; they have long wrought-iron strap-hinges with fleur-de-lys terminals.

The *South Range* of Third Court, of three storeys with attics, is of the same date, except where otherwise described, and general character as the W. range; the walls are of red brick with stone dressings. It incorporates an older building in the western end, which, remodelled, projects as a S. wing; thus the whole plan is L-shaped. The N. side towards the Court, is of eight bays with a plat-band at first-floor level and a continuous entablature and parapet-wall similar to those of the W. range. In the third bay from the E. on the ground floor is a doorway with an eared architrave, triple keystone, slender flanking pilaster-strips and slim console-brackets supporting a cornice. In the sixth bay is the archway to the passage through the range; it has a semicircular head with moulded imposts and is flanked by Tuscan pilasters supporting an entablature. The other bays on this level and all the bays on the two floors above have each a two-light window similar to those at the same levels in the W. range and set in similar articulations of the wall-face, the aprons extending downwards only to the plat-band. At the E. end is a rainwater pipe with head dated 1671. In the roof are flat-topped dormer-windows.

The S. side of the main block is of five bays and similar in character to the S. front of the S. range of Second Court but with a continuous parapet-wall and no gablets. In the W. bay is an archway with chamfered jambs and semicircular head with a label and containing an original oak door of nine panels. The windows on all floors are of two four-centred lights in a square head and the parapet-string acts as a label to those on the second floor; all have been restored. The form of these windows may perhaps be explained by a desire for uniformity in the College frontage to the adjoining lane and, presumably, the presence of such features available for reuse from the older building on the W. evidently remodelled, not 'plucked down' as recorded in the Prizing Books, in 1670. The four lead rain-water pipes and heads are old. The square-topped dormer-windows have been rebuilt. The W. end of the range, towards the river, has plat-bands, windows, and a shaped gable similar to those of the adjoining S. end of the W. range, but the gable is larger, spanning three bays, and contains a carved stone cartouche with the College arms and the date 1671 flanking the round window. The shaped head of the lead rainwater pipe is dated 1762 (*sic*). The W. side of the S. wing continues flush with the wall-face of the foregoing and is uniform with it, but the height of the two upper storeys is less, one plat-band is stepped down, and a parapet-string replaces the uppermost, at a lower level. The parapet-wall is similar to that of the W. range. The windows are similar to those at the same levels further N.; in the roof are two rebuilt square-topped dormer-windows. The head of the lead rainwater pipe is dated 1800. The S. end of the S. wing has a shaped gable with finials similar to that at the S. end of the W. range; the whole wall is blind and the lower part has been refaced. The E. side of the wing is generally similar in character to the adjoining S. side of the main block of the S. range but with relieving-arches to the ground-floor windows only.

Inside the main block, the central staircase 'F' is similar to those in the W. range of the Court. Some of the rooms have exposed stop-chamfered ceiling-beams. The main room W.

of the staircase on the ground floor is lined with original panelling with dado-rail and entablature and pilaster-strips in the centre of the E. and W. walls. The fireplace is flanked by panelled pilaster-strips supporting an entablature with panelled frieze; superimposed strips flank a bolection-moulded panel in the overmantel and support an upper entablature with central frieze-panel. The room E. of the stair has similar panelling etc., but with a bolection-moulded frieze over the fireplace. On the first floor, the main room W. of the stair is lined with panelling as before but with a later or modern fireplace-surround. The E. room retains only part of the original panelling. On the second floor, one room is lined with similar panelling with dado-rail and cornice; the S.E. room of the same set has an early 19th-century white marble reeded fireplace-surround with carved paterae at the angles. The S. wing fronting the river is entered through the stone doorway to staircase 'E', which has chamfered jambs and semicircular head. The staircase is similar to that in the main block. Much readjustment of the plan and the floor-levels has occurred where the N. part of the older building intrudes into the main block. In the less altered S. wing some 16th-century ceiling-beams are exposed. One room on the first floor has a 16th-century fireplace of clunch with chamfered jambs, a four-centred head with sunk spandrels, and a timber overmantel of 1672. A room on the second floor has a similar fireplace. Further N., the second-floor room at the W. end of the main block also contains a 16th-century clunch fireplace; it is probably reset; the width of the older building is indicated by a diagonal ceiling-beam inserted presumably when the old external wall at this point was demolished in the remodelling of 1670.

The *Old Bridge* (Plate 247), S.W. of Third Court was built between 1709 and 1712 (see above). It is of Weldon stone and of three spans, with a semi-elliptical central arch and semi-circular side arches all rusticated and with triple keystones; they spring from cut-water piers and plain abutments and are surmounted by a cornice, which breaks forward over the piers and keystones, and a balustraded parapet with panelled pedestals over the same (Plate 244); the balustrade is returned a short distance along the W. bank. The panels above the central arch are carved with achievements-of-arms of the Foundress and those over the side arches with a Tudor rose and a portcullis. The panels above the piers have groups of Neptune and young tritons, and Father Cam with the bridge and College in the background; the N. panel over the E. abutment has sea-horses. The *Gateway* (Plate 56) at the E. end of the bridge has panelled stone gate-piers with cornices surmounted by carved yales holding shields charged with eagles; the W. panels have carvings of the Tudor rose and portcullis. The gate-cheeks have moulded cappings and small scrolled brackets. One staple survives for the original timber gates; these were replaced by the existing 18th-century wrought-iron gates, which have side-standards with ornamental cresting and an elaborate overthrow with a monogram of the letters S.J.C. (St. John's College). A second *Gateway*, further E., was erected in 1711–2; the panelled stone piers have cornices surmounted by eagles carved by Nicholas Bigée and John Woodward; Robert Grumbold was the mason. The piers are hung with heavy timber gates, possibly of 1766.

The *Master's Lodge* of 1863 stands away to the N. of Third Court and contains a considerable amount of timber and panelling removed from the first Master's Lodge, when the Hall was extended, and from elsewhere. The vestibule has an early 16th-century open timber ceiling in six panels with moulded beams and plates, and the walls are lined with panelling including some linenfold panels, some 18th-century fielded panelling, and some work of *c.* 1600, probably part of a former overmantel; this last includes enriched arcaded panels. Over the vestibule door is a fragment of lead guttering of the early 16th century. The Hall has an early 16th-century open timber ceiling in ten panels with moulded beams, plates and joists, and the walls are lined with restored panelling of the late 16th or early 17th century. The early 17th-century overmantel in the Hall came from the old Combination Room and is said to have been brought from Audley End between 1669 and 1701; it is of four bays divided and flanked by paired tapering and fluted Ionic pilasters supporting an entablature with carved enrichment including fleurs-de-lys and portcullises; the bays have enriched panels; it stands on an enriched and partly restored entablature; later cresting was removed in 1952. The former Ante-room has a 16th-century fireplace of clunch with moulded jambs and four-centred arch in a square head with foliage and shields in the spandrels; one shield has a merchant's mark and the initials H.S. and the other the looped initials I.I.; the top is embattled and inscribed "Anno D. 1560". The same room has a 16th-century open timber ceiling. In the Drawing-room and Dining-room are eight angel-corbels with bouched shields charged with the letter M; they are of uncertain date, possibly early 16th-century and from the old Chapel. The open timber ceiling in eight panels over the staircase-hall has a moulded and enriched centre beam and moulded subsidiary beams and joists.

On the first floor, the Oak Room is said to preserve the dimensions of the Study in the old Master's Lodge. The reset oriel-window (Plate 92), restored in its upper part, formerly opened on First Court, where it is shown in Loggan's engraving of the College in a position comparable to that of the similar window surviving *in situ* at Christ's College. It is three-sided, rests on enriched moulded corbelling, and has a sill carved with foliated paterae and a portcullis; the apron is carved on the front with a coroneted achievement-of-arms of the Foundress with yale supporters against a thicket of germander speedwell, and on the returns with a royally crowned rose and a coroneted portcullis. The room has a 16th-century open timber ceiling similar to that over the stairs. The walls are lined with linenfold panelling with enriched frieze-panels carved with foliage, a rose, a portcullis and panels inscribed "Cocus Secundus", the initials R.L., for Richard Longworth, Master (1564–9), and the date 1567. The present Study has a restored early 16th-century open timber ceiling and is lined with early 18th-century bolection-moulded panelling with a dado and moulded dado-rail. The corridor has 16th-century moulded ceiling-beams and contains an oak double doorframe of the same age with four-centred openings in square heads with foliated spandrels.

New Court (Plate 240) (229 ft. by 83 ft.), on the W. side of the river, was begun in 1826 and finished in 1831. In February

(37) ST. JOHN'S COLLEGE. Hall, looking S. 1511–16

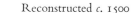

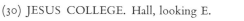

(30) JESUS COLLEGE. Hall, looking E. Reconstructed *c.* 1500

(37) ST. JOHN'S COLLEGE. New Court, from S.W.

1826–31

Gatehall and cloister-walk.

Court, looking N.W.

(37) ST. JOHN'S COLLEGE. New Court.

1826–31

Gatehouse. Statue of St. John. 1662–63

N. side (9).

S. side (1).

S. side (15).

Chapel. Misericordes. 1516

Hall. Glass in oriel-window; St. John. 18th-century

(37) ST. JOHN'S COLLEGE. Miscellanea.

Lettering on grate.

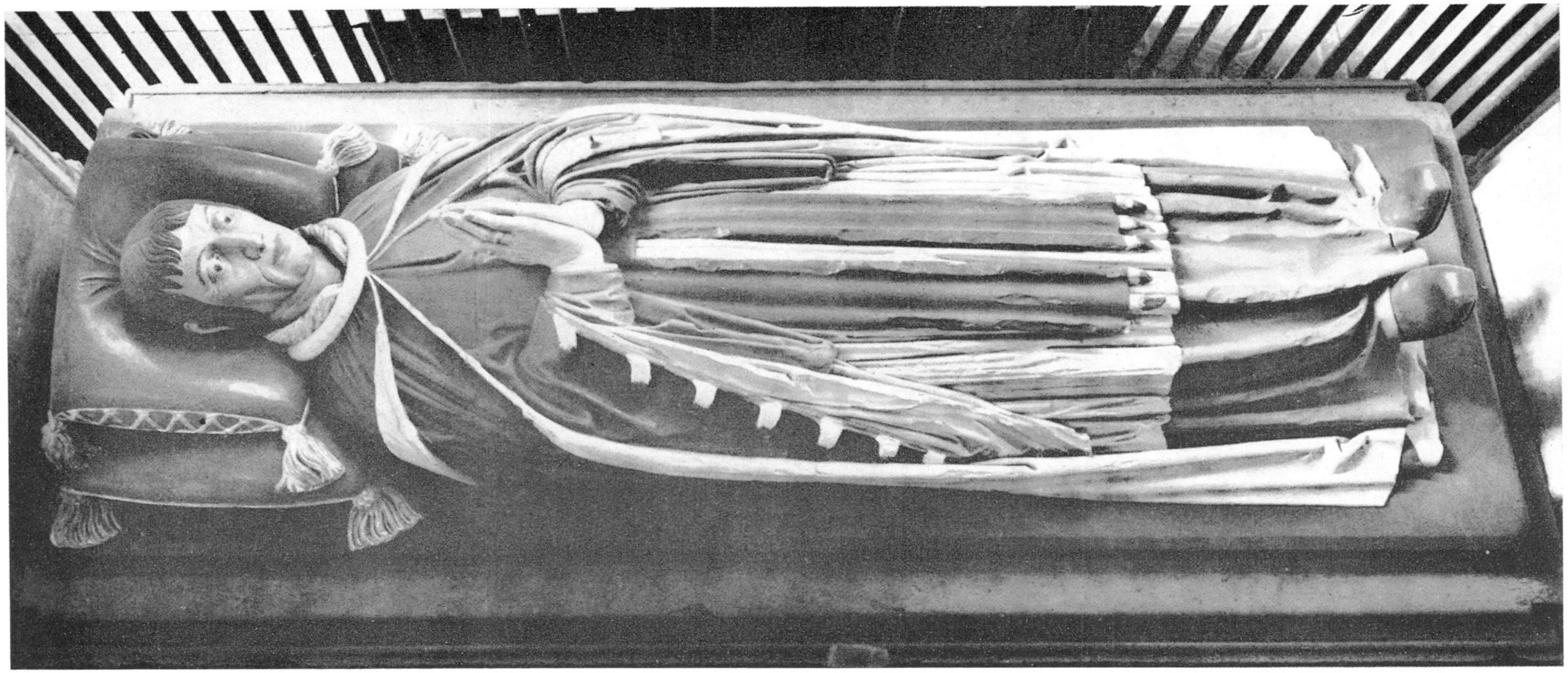

Effigy, restored and recoloured.

Lettering on brass inscription-fillet.

(37) ST. JOHN'S COLLEGE. Chapel. Monument (1), of Hugh Assheton; details.

1522

(37) ST. JOHN'S COLLEGE. Third Court. W. range, from S.W. 1669–73

(37) ST. JOHN'S COLLEGE. First Court. W. range; statue of the Foundress. 1674

(39) SIDNEY SUSSEX COLLEGE. Gateway in Jesus Lane. 1749

(76) MUSEUM OF ARCHAEOLOGY AND ETHNOLOGY. Choir-screen from Winchester Cathedral; centrepiece. *c.* 1638

1825 the College agreed to approach Wilkins, Browne and Thomas Rickman for designs, but in March 1826 Rickman and Henry Hutchinson were the architects chosen and five months later permission was given to accept the tender of T. and J. Bennett, contractors, for the basement. Until at least February 1827 the intention was to build in red brick with stone dressings, but in June Thomas Phipps' estimate for stone facing was accepted; further, in 1829 clunch was decided upon for the vault of the cloister-walk, instead of the wood and plaster proposed. The cost of the Court was £77,878, much work and expense being involved in providing sure foundations.

The Court is built on an E plan, with the end wings connected by a cloister-walk to provide enclosure on the S.; in the centre of the walk is a Gatehouse. The ranges are of four storeys; the walls are faced with stone, except the N. elevation which is of gault brick with stone dressings. The roofs are slate-covered. The style is in the main Tudor-Gothic. The building is symmetrically designed, with a central tower-structure, connected by rather lower ranges with short S. returns to larger pavilion-like blocks. The *Gatehouse* in the centre of the cloister-walk linking these last is four-square, with diagonal and angle-buttresses ending in pinnacles, and low-pitched N. and S. gables. The S. archway is two-centred with an ogee label ending in a pedestal supporting an eagle above the apex of the gable; the wall-surface above the arch is enriched with stone panelling. The original painted deal door of two leaves has each leaf divided into fifty-three panels containing cast-iron paterae and Tudor badges. The two-centred N. archway is in a square head with shields-of-arms in the spandrels, of Craven and of Pennington; the face of the gable-end above is panelled and frames the arms of the Deanery of Ely impaling Wood (for James Wood, Master 1815–39). The *Gatehall* ($23\frac{1}{2}$ ft. by $23\frac{1}{2}$ ft.) is covered by a fan-vault springing from moulded and enriched corbels and with a large central conoid ending in an octagonal pendant. In the E. and W. walls are two-centred archways to the cloister-walk set in taller wall-arches with pierced quatrefoils in the apices.

The embattled *Cloister-walk* is in seven bays to each side of the Gatehouse. On the S., the bays are divided by two-stage buttresses ending in pinnacles and contain each a three-light window with vertical tracery in a two-centred head with a label; on the N., the dividing three-stage buttresses end at the parapet and in each bay is a two-centred archway. The walk is covered with ribbed vaulting (Plate 241).

The *Ranges* generally are embattled. On the N., the tower-structure (Plate 241) has turrets at the corners, octagonal on the S. and square to octagonal on the N., rising high above the main parapet-walls and with the top stage enriched with Tudor badges and the upper part with quatrefoiled panels in each face. Between the turrets, the S. front is in three bays; the middle bay projects slightly between four-stage buttresses and contains the entrance with four-centred arch and, above, an oriel-window rising through three storeys and ending in a quatrefoiled parapet. The oriel is supported on corbelling carved with shields-of-arms of (a) the See of Peterborough impaling Marsh, (c) the College, (d) the See of Rochester impaling Fisher, (e) Percy; the shield (b) is charged with Assheton's rebus of an ashtree growing from a tun. Rising above the centre of the tower-structure is a large octagonal stone clock-tower and lantern, with vertical-traceried windows in each face, diagonal and flying buttresses at the angles, all ending in pinnacles, and a crocketed flared roof of stone ending in a finial supporting a vane. The windows generally, except those with two-centred heads on the first floor of the turrets, are of one and two cinquefoiled lights in square heads with labels. The flanking ranges are for the most part symmetrically arranged, as shown on the plan; the doorways have four-centred openings and the windows are similar to those just described.

The pavilion-like blocks forming the greater part of the E. and W. wings have pinnacled diagonal buttresses and embattled parapets. The S. fronts have each four single-light windows on the ground floor, a central oriel-window rising through the first and second floors, and a central two-light window with vertical tracery in a two-centred head on the top floor; above, is a small gable with a canopied niche at the apex. Each oriel has moulded corbelling and an embattled parapet and is flanked by single two-light windows on the first floor; on the floors above are one-light windows. The inward-facing fronts have windows and doors as before, the latter in square heads with traceried spandrels.

The E. front of New Court, N. of the bridge, is symmetrically grouped from end to end. It has a battered plinth rising directly from the river. The rectangular projecting end bays are carried up above the main parapet; they and the three-sided projecting bay in the centre have oriel-windows to the second and third floors. The other windows are as elsewhere. From a doorway in the N. bay steps lead up from water-level and then down to the cellars; N. of the doorway is an arched outlet from a culvert, now blocked, that left the Bin Brook opposite the N.W. corner of the Court and served for sanitation. The two openings are flanked by mooring-rings.

The W. front is tripartite; the S. part, being the frontage of the main W. block, is broadly similar to the opposite side of the last, facing the Court, but with a central projecting bay with angle-buttresses carried up through three storeys and with four-light windows on each floor linked by wall-panelling. On the panelling between the lower windows are carved shields-of-arms of Rickman and Hutchinson. The rather lower centre part is divided into five unequal bays by buttresses. The N. part is higher than the rest of the range, being of five storeys; it has an oriel-window rising through the three middle floors.

The brick N. side is symmetrically grouped; the taller centre and end blocks have embattled parapets; the ranges between have plain parapets. All the windows are of a single light; the heads are either two-centred or four-centred. The chimney-stacks generally have grouped octagonal shafts, rectangular bases and moulded cappings.

The *Interior* is divided into sets of rooms mostly following the normal plan of a main room, entered from the stair, looking into the court and with two small rooms opening off it. This plan is modified in the E. and W. blocks and also in the tower-structure where is a central circular stone staircase lit by the lantern. Some of the rooms entered from this stair have ribbed plaster ceilings of Tudor-Gothic character, with geometrical and shaped panels containing Tudor badges. The stone and plaster roof of the lantern is similarly treated. All the doorways have four-centred heads and moulded timber architraves. Most of the original fireplaces remain; those in the rooms formerly Fellows' rooms are of white, grey or black marble, those in Undergraduates' rooms of freestone. At the S. end of the E. block, on the ground floor, is a passage with depressed four-centred ribbed vault in three bays that links the cloister-walk with the covered bridge.

The covered *New Bridge*, known as the 'Bridge of Sighs' (Plate 236), between the W. range of Third Court and the S.E. corner of New Court, is of stone ashlar and consists of a single segmental span with traceried spandrels on the S. side carved with a portcullis and a fleur-de-lys. It was designed by Henry Hutchinson in 1827 and presumably finished, with New Court, by 1831. The two sides of the superstructure are similar in arrangement. At each end are plain abutments; the length between is in three unequal bays divided and flanked externally by shallow buttresses ending in crocketed pinnacles above the embattled parapet; the S. parapet-string is carved with paterae. In the centre bay is one and in the flanking bays are two unglazed windows containing wrought-iron lattices; each window is of three cinquefoiled lights, the centre one ogee, with vertical tracery in a four-centred head with a continuous label; the tracery is original, the mullions were renewed in 1952; the spandrels between the label and parapet-string on the S. side contain tracery-panelling. The interior has at each end a doorway, that at the E. end with moulded four-centred head and an elevated rear-arch with panelled soffit, that at the W. end with a moulded two-centred head; in the wall above each is a niche with a cinquefoiled ogee head under a crocketed label and a shaped corbel supporting a tall pedestal. The plain plaster ceiling is divided into seven bays by four-centred plastered metal arches with pierced spandrels.

Physical approach to the bridge and the architectural requirement of centralising the entrance to an off-centre feature involved some remodelling of the interior of the W. range of Third Court. A centred internal arcade of three bays was inserted, opening on a landing. In the W. wall of the latter, the entrance to the bridge is balanced by the three-light window with a four-centred head already described; centrally placed in the wall between them is a niche with cinquefoiled ogee head and crocketed label. The landing is covered by a plaster ribbed vault. All the foregoing are contemporary with the bridge.

The *Bridge* carrying the High Walk from the old Bridge to Queens' Road over the Bin Brook is of cast-iron; the entry in the College Conclusion Book agreeing to the material is dated July 1822. It has ashlar abutments and is in one segmental span, with pierced tracery spandrels, enrichments of portcullises and a frieze of roses. The railing consists of a diagonal iron latticework divided into three unequal bays by slender round standards with knob finials.

The '*Field*' *Gate* to Queens' Road consists of an ornamental wrought-iron gate hung between stone piers; the College agreed that it should be built in 1822 (Conclusion Book 4 July) though the style of the piers is of *c.* 1700. If the stonework is not reused, then the style of Grumbold's gateway futher E. must have been copied. The gate is in two leaves, the northern with a wicket, with side-standards and an overthrow incorporating an embossed and painted shield-of-arms of the College. The panelled piers have crowned portcullises carved on the dies, enriched cornices and gadrooned pedestals supporting eagles. Flanking the piers are stone dwarf-walls, ogee-shaped on plan, surmounted by railings and ending in smaller panelled piers; the last are carved with roses and have ball-finials. The high red brick wall to the S. is contemporary with the foregoing.

S.E. of the 'Wilderness' is a wrought-iron *Gate* to Trinity Piece. It is in two leaves hung between scrollwork piers with spire-like finials linked by an elaborate overthrow incorporating the College badge of a rising demi-eagle; lengths of railing to each side extend to smaller flanking piers. It was probably in the Horseheath Hall sale of 1777. Set up in 1780, it was removed some 80 yds. S. to the present position in 1822 (C.A.S. *Procs.* XLV, 28).

(38) Selwyn College, at the corner of Grange Road and Sidgwick Avenue, was begun in 1881. The early 20th-century Hall contains, on the back wall of the dais, reset woodwork given in 1914 in memory of E. W. Benson, Archbishop of Canterbury, by A. C. Benson. It consists of the reredos from the English church of St. Mary at Rotterdam and was brought over by Benson in 1913, the year the church was demolished.

Description—The reredos extends the width of the W. wall; it is of oak, with coupled pilasters at each end and a central pedimented feature with freestanding columns, all of the Corinthian order, on low pedestals. The pilasters support a plain entablature, the columns an enriched entablature with dentils and modillion-cornice; on the pediment are two urns. The lining is of fielded panelling, with short returns on the side walls flanked by plain pilasters with stylised capitals and carrying simple entablatures. The rest of the 18th-century panelling in the Hall is partly fielded, partly plain, with a cornice. The woodwork is considerably restored and much of the panelling is modern.

A pamphlet, *An Account of the Money Collected for the English Church at Rotterdam*, published in two parts, in 1702 and 1706 (University Library), records that in 1702 the draft for 'erecting a convenient and ornamental building' was submitted to the Duke of Marlborough and the Magistrates. The list of contributors is headed by Queen Anne. The last page has a list of contracts but concludes, the 'inward work not yet contracted for'. The reredos is stylistically of the early 18th century.

(39) SIDNEY SUSSEX COLLEGE stands on the E. side of Sidney Street, between Jesus Lane on the N. and Sussex Street on the S. It occupies the site of the Franciscan friary dissolved in 1538. The land and the Greyfriars' buildings were conveyed to Trinity College in 1546 but by then, although in the meantime the University had made efforts to obtain the buildings for ceremonial use, their destruction had been begun, the material being taken for the King's new foundation. By about the end of 1547 the friars' church had been destroyed; Fuller believed that it stood just N. of the N. range of Hall Court of the present College. The cloister, as will be shown was probably S. of the church.

The College was founded in July 1594 under the terms of the will of Frances Sidney, Countess of Sussex, who died in 1589, the Letters Patent of foundation being obtained by her executors who, with difficulty, acquired the present site in September 1595. Henry, 6th Earl of Kent, and Sir John Harrington executed their deed of foundation in February 1595–6 and building was begun in May 1596. Ralph Symons, freemason, is said to have been the architect, on the evidence of the inscription on his portrait at Emmanuel College, though the picture is of very much later date. With the exception of the Chapel and Library, the College buildings, comprising the three ranges to *Hall Court*, were completed by the end of the 16th century. In the early years of the 17th century the Chapel with the Library above was contrived in an older surviving range lying at an angle S.E. of Hall Court. The evidence of James Essex's survey of this range during demolition in 1776 to make way for the new Chapel suggests that it was the hall of the Warden's Lodging in the friary.

During the Mastership of Samuel Ward, in 1628 Sir Francis Clerke founded four Fellowships and eight Scholarships; the deed records his intention of adding to the College buildings to provide chambers for his beneficiaries. The range built presumably soon afterwards is that on the S. of *Chapel Court*.

The College as it then appeared is shown by Loggan; built of brick with stone dressings, it had two adjoining courts, both closed only by a wall on the W., the earlier with a small but elaborate W. gateway. Hall Court was symmetrical, with the Hall etc. and the Master's Lodge in the E. range and chambers in the N. and S. ranges. In the re-entrant angles were small towers, one containing the entrance to the Master's Lodge, the other the entrance to the Parlour. In Chapel Court, the E. Chapel range met and just overlapped Sir Francis Clerke's S. range.

During the second quarter of the 18th century repairs were made to the building and in the period between 1747 and 1750 the original *Hall* was refitted and the original timber roof concealed by a flat plaster ceiling; at the same period the old W. gateway was replaced by a new *Gateway* which itself was removed in 1831 to the N.E. corner of the College grounds, where it still is. The style of these alterations suggests the hand of James Burrough, though no architect's name is recorded. Subsequently Cole records that the Chapel and Library were becoming structurally dangerous; in 1776 they were demolished and rebuilt in approximately the same position to the designs of James Essex; the last payment to him for supervising the work was made in 1782. The *Chapel* is at the S. end of the block, extending as far as the S. wall of Sir Francis Clerke's range, with the Antechapel to the N. and offices beyond; over the last two is the *Library*, which still retains the fittings of 1778. The appearance of the College at this stage is preserved in an early 19th-century drawing by Wyatt (College Muniments) (Plate 248).

Charles Humfrey, architect, of Cambridge, submitted proposals for alterations to the buildings in the Tudor style in drawings, preserved in the College, dated 1820, but they were evidently not accepted, and the present Tudor-Gothic appearance of the College is due to a series of alterations begun in 1821 under the direction of Jeffry Wyatt (Wyatville 1824, knighted 1828) and financed from an early 18th-century bequest by Samuel

Taylor. The comparative illustrations (Plates 248 and 249) are eloquent of the measure of the work. The Hall range was the first begun. The upper part of the leaning E. wall was rebuilt, and buttresses and an E. porch were added; the dormers were linked and the parapet embattled. On the W. a forebuilding with a W. porch was inserted in the space between the corner towers; to make way for it the original central porch-tower was demolished. The forebuilding contains the *Taylor Library* on two floors to the N. In 1831 and 1832 the attics and garrets of the N. and S. ranges of Hall Court were raised in height to a full storey and attics, and the W. end of the latter range was transformed into a *Gate-tower*. The outside of Sir Francis Clerke's range was altered and a Combination Room, since demolished, was added N.W. of the Hall. In 1833 the Chapel was remodelled, though not exactly as in Wyatville's drawing illustrated, at the expense of the Master, William Chafy, and at the same time the *Master's Lodge*, still in its original position on the first floor S. of the Hall, was partly rearranged. The walls for the most part were faced with Roman cement in the course of these alterations, except the Gate-tower which was rebuilt in stone, and all the windows and minor features more or less remodelled to accord with the new style. Much refacing in stone was undertaken in 1954–57.

A range of chambers added in 1890 N.E. of Hall Court and incorporating an arcaded walk returned westward was designed by J. L. Pearson, who also refaced with brick part of the N. wall of the adjoining range and added chimney-stacks. Work in the present century includes the southward extension of the Chapel in 1910–12 by T. H. Lyon and the completion of the entire refitting, then begun, in 1920–5. The same architect rearranged the ground floor immediately N. and E. of the Chapel and Ante-chapel in 1919–20; he also designed the block of chambers, *Garden Court*, built in 1923–5 at the S. end of the Master's Garden. The range of chambers to Sussex Street is of 1937–9.

At Sidney Sussex College the drabness of the cement facing of the buildings belies the qualities evident in the early 19th-century drawings of them. Wyatville's ingenious alterations of 1821–33 have created, out of an unresolved duality of two adjacent courts differing in date and style, a unified design on an E-plan, with the Gatehouse as the central feature. The Hall roof, now concealed, is an interesting example of timber construction of the late 16th century. The interior of the Hall, refitted *c.* 1750, and the Gateway of the same age, both of the Roman Doric order, are notable examples of the neo-Classical work of the period. The *Presepio* in the Chapel by G. B. Pittoni (1687–1767) is an early and accomplished example of Italian rococo painting. The important 15th-century chest preserved in the Library exhibits unusually elaborate smith's work.

Architectural Description—*Hall Court* (94 ft. by 78½ ft.) is entered from Sidney Street by the Gatehouse in the W. end of the S. range. The E. range contains the Hall to the full height and the rest is in three storeys with attics over part. The walls are of brick faced with Roman cement and with stone dressings; the roofs are slate-covered. These materials are constant throughout the older buildings, except where stated below. Other than the rooms shown on the plan, the Master's Lodge is over the Butteries and the Kitchen and in the S. part of Wyatville's forebuilding.

The history of the *East Range* is given above; the main block and the towers, now recessed, in the E. angles of the Court are of the last years of the 16th century; the additional thickening of the range on the W., the forebuilding, is part of Wyatville's work begun in 1821.

The W. side to Hall Court is symmetrical, with a two-storey stone porch in the centre and octagonal buttresses, continued up as turrets above the embattled parapets, dividing the front into five bays. In the gablet over the middle bay is a stone lozenge-of-arms of the Foundress, Radcliffe quartering Fitzwalter all impaling Sidney, with a coronet above. The wall in the end bays is canted back to meet the 16th-century towers; these last were remodelled and heightened by Wyatville and given embattled W. gablets; over the doorway in the N. tower is a reset late 16th-century shield-of-arms of Harrington. The porch has three archways with pointed-segmental heads on the ground floor and square three-light transomed windows on the upper floor; the parapet is embattled. The windows elsewhere are of two and three lights with square heads, those flanking the porch on the first floor having transoms.

The E. side is also symmetrical, in nine bays divided by 19th-century buttresses, with semicircular bay-windows two storeys high in the wider end bays, and a central single-storey porch screening the lower half of the four middle buttresses. The front is three full storeys in height, with embattled parapets rising in embattled gables over the bay-windows. The extent of Wyatville's remodelling is shown by the comparative illustrations (Plate 249). Only four of the original first-floor windows and the two bay-windows are retained in form; the first are renewed and the second rebuilt and with balustraded parapets added. Several of the more northerly windows are shams. The porch is of stone, with archways similar to those in the W. porch, but now closed. The bay-windows are of nine lights in the width; the N. window, lighting the Hall dais, is divided by transoms into four tiers of lights rising the full height of the bay; the S. bay has a window on each floor, both transomed, and four blank shields on the apron-wall between them.

The N. end of the range is of dark red brick. It is gabled, and the lower part is covered by a late 19th-century arcaded walk. At the first-floor level, lighting the Hall, is a five-light window with two transoms remodelled and enlarged in the 19th century. The S. end has a stepped gable; on the first floor is a six-light transomed window to the Master's Dining-room; above are one, two and four-light windows; all are of the 19th century.

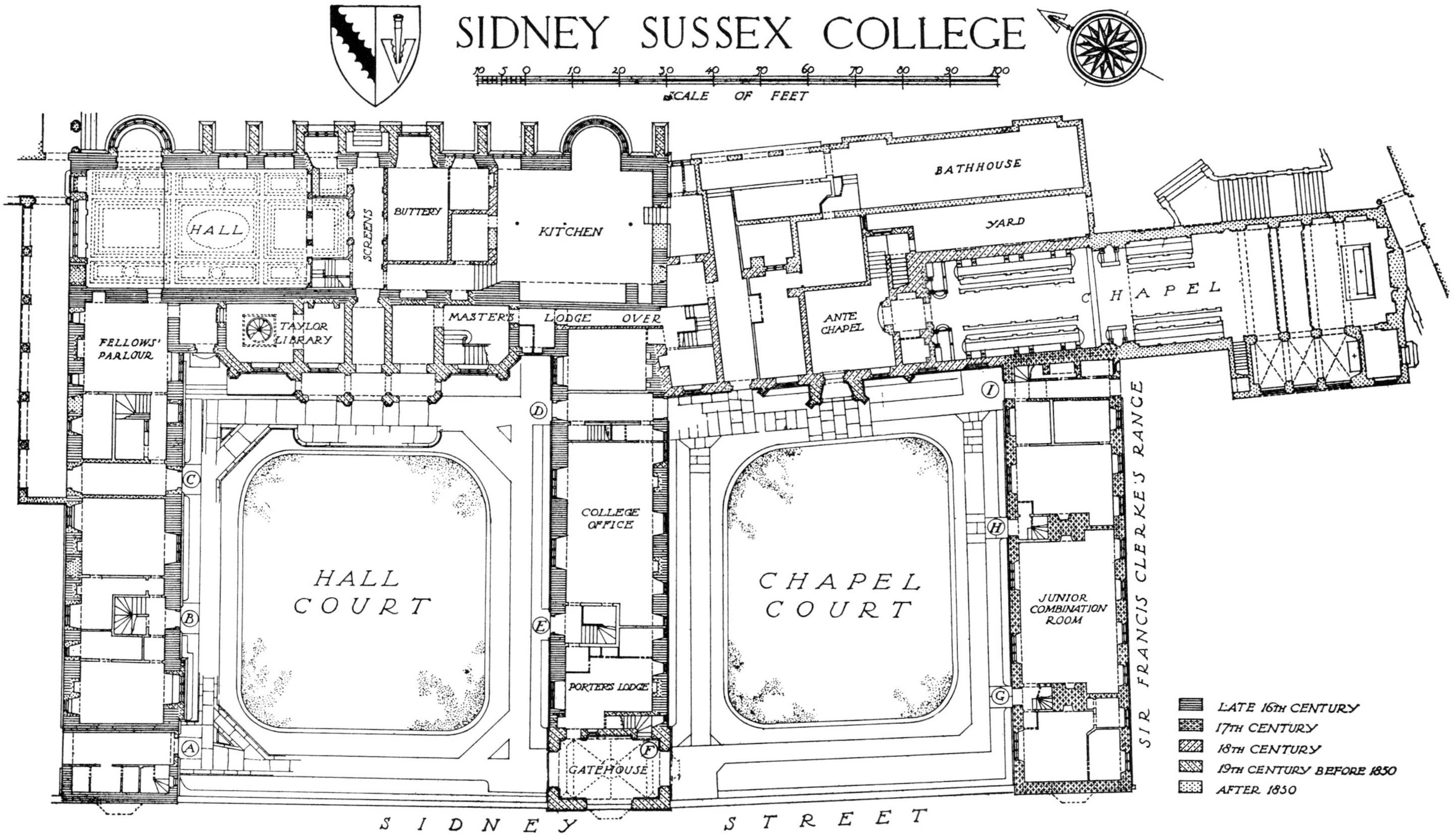
SIDNEY SUSSEX COLLEGE
10 5 0 10 20 30 40 50 60 70 80 90 100
SCALE OF FEET
HALL
SCREENS
BUTTERY
KITCHEN
BATHHOUSE
YARD
CHAPEL
ANTE CHAPEL
FELLOWS' PARLOUR
TAYLOR LIBRARY
MASTER'S LODGE OVER
COLLEGE OFFICE
PORTER'S LODGE
GATEHOUSE
HALL COURT
CHAPEL COURT
JUNIOR COMBINATION ROOM
SIR FRANCIS CLERKE'S RANGE
SIDNEY STREET
A
B
C
D
E
F
G
H
I
LATE 16TH CENTURY
17TH CENTURY
18TH CENTURY
19TH CENTURY BEFORE 1850
AFTER 1850

The *Hall* (26 ft. by 63½ ft., including the screens-passage) was refitted between 1747 and 1750 and the following plaster and woodwork were inserted. The plaster ceiling is divided into nine panels by trabeations decorated with guilloche ornament on the soffits. The central panel contains in an oval an elaborate rococo centrepiece of scrolls and acanthus foliage, and the remaining panels contain foliate bosses of simpler character. At the wall-head is an enriched dentil-cornice. The soffit of the window-bay has a large shell design.

The N., E. and W. walls are lined nearly to sill-level with panelling consisting of large moulded panels between a plinth and an enriched cornice carved with Greek wave ornament. On the N. the cornice is returned over pilasters dividing the panelling into five unequal bays; in the middle bay, the panel-mouldings are eared, carved and enriched with pendants below the upper ears. The windows have small plaster architraves and the remaining wall-faces at the upper level have plaster panelling to uniform scale; between the windows are foliage pendants, also repeated on the opposite wall, and all appearing in A. Pugin's view of the Hall in R. Ackermann's *History of the University* etc., 1815.

The *Screen* at the S. end is advanced sufficiently to incorporate a vestibule, staircase and servery adjoining the screens-passage on the N. The front is of the Roman Doric order and in three unequal bays divided by pilasters; the wide central bay is open to the vestibule and subdivided by two fluted columns in antis; the end bays are panelled. The continuous and unbroken entablature has triglyphs, rosettes in the panelled metopes, and a dentil-cornice, and supports a balustraded parapet to the gallery above. The vestibule is panelled throughout and with pilaster-responds on the back partition; it is entered centrally from the screens-passage through a timber doorcase with semi-circular head, moulded archivolt and imposts, panelled jambs and carved spandrels. In the doorway is an elaborate wrought-iron gate contemporary with the panelling. The end bays of the screen contain panelled recesses in surrounds similar to the central doorcase and with key-blocks in the form of small cartouches; they enclose the servery on the E. and the gallery-staircase on the W., the latter transposed from the position of the former in 1948 and both entered from the screens-passage. This last is fitted with woodwork uniform with that in the vestibule. The staircase has close strings, turned balusters and moulded handrail. The blocked doorway in the middle of the back wall of the gallery, formerly giving access to the Master's Lodge, has a timber doorcase with eared architrave, flanking panelled pilaster-strips, and console-brackets supporting a curved pediment; it is surmounted by a lozenge-of-arms of the Foundress in an elaborate rococo framing with bull and porcupine supporters, a coronet above and the motto below, nearly wholly in the round.

Most of the original timber roof of the Hall survives above the ceiling. It is in five bays divided by trusses identical in form and closely similar in detail to those over the Hall at Emmanuel College, and similarly mutilated, (see Monument (27) and figure p. 67); further, the central pendants have been removed.

The *Buttery* and *Kitchen* (26 ft. by 56 ft.) have been modernised; the recess in the W. wall of the latter represents the original fireplaces.

The *Master's Lodge* is approached by the staircase in Wyatville's forebuilding; it includes, in addition to the whole of the upper part of the Hall range S. of the Hall and most of the forebuilding other than the Taylor Library, the easternmost room on each floor of the S. range of Hall Court and a secondary staircase in the Chapel range. The Drawing-room, the N.E. room on the first floor, has a plaster cornice enriched with acanthus and corn and vine foliage and contains a mid 19th-century marble fireplace-surround; the fluted marble surround to the fireplace in the adjoining room on the S.E. is of the early 19th century. The Dining-room is lined with mid 18th-century fielded panelling, with dado, moulded dado-rail and dentil-cornice, all painted white; the fireplace is flanked by panelled pilaster-strips supporting returns of the main cornice and has an eared and enriched surround to marble slips; in the overmantel is an eared panel with a carved shell and flanking scrolls above. The cast-iron grate has a circular shell-like opening and cast shells and scrolls in the spandrels; it is of the early 19th century (see Monument (302)).

The bay-window in the Dining-room contains early 19th-century heraldic glass, including shields-of-arms of (a) Sir John Brereton, with a crest, (b) Sir Francis Clerke, with a crest, (c) Sir John Hart (?), with a crest, (d) Henry (Grey), 6th Earl of Kent, with a coronet, (e) the Foundress, with bull supporters and a coronet, (f) Sir John Harrington, with a cap of estate, (g) Shelley-Sidney quarterly, with two crests, (h) James Montagu, Master, Bishop of Winchester, quartering Monthermer, with a mitre, (i) William Chafy, Master, with a crest. On the upper floors is a number of old fittings, including 18th-century plain panelling and doors, a door of *c.* 1600, early 19th-century marble fireplaces, and a length of mid 18th-century balustrading with moulded handrail at the head of the attic stairs. The main staircase is modern; the secondary staircase is of the second half of the 18th century, rises round a rectangular well, and has close moulded strings, turned balusters, square newels and a moulded handrail.

The *Taylor Library* (12¾ ft. by 25 ft.) is in the N. part of Wyatville's forebuilding and rises through two floors, with a gallery at first-floor level; access to the gallery is now by an iron circular stair, but originally was through a doorway on the S.E. It is fitted with simple original wall-cases and a Derbyshire marble fireplace-surround with four-centred head, panelled spandrels and hollow-chamfered canted jambs.

The *North Range* of Hall Court is of three storeys with attics. The fabric is of the end of the 16th century, heightened and remodelled, as described above, in 1831–2. J. L. Pearson formed the passage through the range at 'C' to his arcaded walk on the N. added in 1890. The S. side to the Court is of seven bays, with a narrower eighth bay on the W.; the sixth bay from the E. projects slightly, the thickening being in effect a buttressing, added by Wyatville. The second, fourth and sixth bays are continued above the embattled parapet in stepped gablets flanked by octagonal pinnacles carried on corbels at the parapet-string and enclosing two-light windows to the attics; a chimney-stack counterfeits one of the pinnacles. The doorways have four-centred arches with sunk spandrels under square labels. The windows are of one, two and three rectangular lights and uniform with the others without transoms in the College.

The N. side has the lower part of the E. half concealed by the arcaded walk; the wall above was refronted in 1890, by Pearson, and the W. half in the present century, all in red brick with stone dressings. Apart from the addition of a storey, the general character of this front shown in the *Cambridge University Almanac* of 1809 is retained; readjustments of the ground floor openings are indicated on the plan, by deduction from Wyatville's drawings preserved in the College. The wall is continued up flush into gabled dormers containing the attic windows, and at varying intervals between the dormers rise chimney-stacks with grouped shafts set diagonally. The one and two-light windows are similar to those on the S. but without labels.

The W. end on the street has a stepped gable. The ground floor is of red brick, the rest rendered. Corbelled out on the first floor is a stone oriel-window of two transomed lights on the face and one on each canted side; the parapet is embattled and the apron-wall panelled with quatrefoils framing shields, the front shield being carved with the arms of Harrington. On the floors above are two windows, of three and two lights respectively. The whole is Wyatville's remodelling, based essentially upon the original arrangement; but the comparative illustrations (Pl. 249) show in the steepening of the gable one of the effects from the revived Gothic repertory. The original carving of the Harrington arms has been reset in the E. range and is described above.

The Fellows' Parlour (19½ ft. by 17¾ ft.) in the N. range is lined with mid 18th-century fielded panelling with moulded dado-rail and dentil-cornice. The fireplace (Plate 277) has stone slips, and an eared and enriched architrave moulding, a pulvinated frieze carved with rosettes in ovals, and an enriched cornice-shelf with a feature above in low relief in the form of a broken scroll-pediment surmounted by a shell; in the tympanum is a cartouche containing a lozenge-of-arms of the College and flanked by palm leaves; on the wall above are foliage swags. (Cf. Trinity Hall, fireplace etc. in Library-annexe.) The colouring is modern. Staircase 'C' is dog-legged, turning on a central newel from ground to second floors, and represents the original stair; from the second floor upwards it is of the early 19th century, with close strings, turned balusters and moulded handrail. Staircase 'B' is similar to the foregoing but with the newel cut down nearly to first-floor level and the 19th-century stair beginning so much lower. On the first floor, the main room E. of staircase 'C' is lined with mid 18th-century fielded panelling with dado-rail and cornice; in the main room opposite is a cast-iron fire-grate of shell form of the first half of the 19th century. The main room E. of staircase 'B' has the E. and S. walls lined with panelling of *c.* 1600, of five panels in the height; the fireplace contains another shell-like grate, with shells modelled in the spandrels. The main room opposite is lined with plain 18th-century panelling. On the second floor, the main room E. of staircase 'C' and the W. main room off staircase 'B' are lined with mid 18th-century panelling, the first with dado-rail and cornice, the second plain; further, the first room retains in the E. end of the S. wall the jambs of an original stone doorway, with hinge-pins, to the angle-tower.

The *South Range* of Hall Court has a history similar to that of the range opposite on the N. except that the whole of the W. end was rebuilt by Wyatville to form a Gatehouse and tower. The *Gatehouse* is of ashlar and of three storeys. The three exposed sides have stepped gables flanked and surmounted by octagonal pinnacles. On the ground floor are three archways with four-centred openings with panelled spandrels under square labels. The S. and W. sides have three-sided oriel-windows corbelled out on the first floor and with embattled parapets and a single transomed light in each face. In the equivalent position on the N. side is a two-light transomed window. Above, is a three-light window on the W., a two-light window on both the N. and the S., and, in each gable, a blank shield. The *Gatehall* (13 ft. by 21¼ ft.) is covered by a ribbed vault of a main and two half bays springing from moulded corbels. The early 19th-century gate in the W. archway is of oak, in two leaves, with a wicket in the S. leaf; the vertical panels on the front have four-centred heads.

The rest of the S. range is of three storeys with attics but lower than the Gate-tower; the S. wall is carried up to an embattled and gabled parapet above the attic windows and presents the effect of four full storeys. The N. side is of six, the S. of seven, irregularly spaced bays; the former is generally uniform in treatment with the S. side of the range opposite. The details of the S. side are also similar, but the parapet, already described, has three stepped gables with grouped diagonal chimney-shafts between and flanking them.

The *Interior* of the S. range has the easternmost ground-floor room, belonging to the Master's Lodge, lined with panelling of *c.* 1600, five panels high and with a shallow cornice. The overmantel is in two bays, with gadrooned mouldings enclosing shaped secondary panels. The rest of the ground floor, including the College office and *Porter's Lodge*, contains no ancient features. Staircase 'E' is similar to those opposite but, from the first floor upwards, of the mid 18th century, with close strings, turned balusters and newels, and moulded handrail. On the first floor, the room adjoining staircase 'D' on the W. is lined with mid 18th-century fielded panelling with a dado-rail and small cornice. The main room E. of staircase 'E' is lined with similar panelling, but without a dado-rail. In the W. wall of the second room is a large recess fitted with shelves. The room W. of staircase 'E' contains panelling similar to that just described, with a dado-rail; the fireplace has a stone eared and enriched architrave. In the room over the Gatehall is an early 19th-century reeded fireplace-surround of grey marble.

Chapel Court (90 ft. by 72 ft. average) adjoins Hall Court on the S. The *East Range*, of one and two storeys, is on the site of the hall of the Greyfriars' Warden's Lodging that was converted into the College Chapel and Library in the early years of the 17th century and demolished in 1776. The range built forthwith in replacement, designed by James Essex, is the present one, though almost wholly remodelled by Wyatville in 1833 (Plate 39). The Chapel at the S. end was extended some 63 ft. to the S. in 1910–12.

The W. side, to the Court, is symmetrical in arrangement, of seven bays, with the three middle bays accentuated by pinnacled diagonal buttresses issuing from a nearly flush wall-face and the centre bay projecting slightly to form a centrepiece.

This last is of ashlar; it has a projecting porch on the ground floor, a shield-of-arms and crest of Chafy over the first-floor window, and an open bell-turret of stepped gable form with a clock-face in the base. The porch has diagonal buttresses ending in pinnacles and an obtuse gable with tracery-panelled battlements; the four-centred entrance archway is deeply splayed and panelled. Flanking the centrepiece, the main parapet-walls are embattled and panelled. All the unaltered windows are of two transomed lights with four-centred openings in square heads with labels; several are shams. The second window on the ground floor and the southernmost on the first floor have been altered in the present century; the former is now a doorway. The windows, the porch-entrance and the bell-turret differ from those shown in Wyatville's drawing (Pl. 248), but they represent variations upon the design and are not later alterations.

The E. side is largely concealed by modern additions, but the lower part of the N. wall of the Chapel designed by Essex and built between 1776 and 1782 is visible, being of white brick and containing three shallow recesses. The upper part was remodelled by Wyatville, and the fenestration again in 1910–12. On the parapet of the staircase-bay is a coroneted lozenge-of-arms of the Foundress.

The *Chapel* (21¾ ft. by 96½ ft.) is orientated approximately N. and S. The fittings of the S. extension are contemporary; refitting the original N. part was completed between 1920 and 1922. It contains no ancient Fittings other than the following—*Monuments:* In Ante-chapel, on N. wall, (1) of Francis Sawyer Parris, S.T.P., 1760, Master, round white marble tablet with cartouche carved with the quarterly arms and crest of Parris, erected by his sister Eleanor Parratt; (2) of William Elliston, S.T.P., 1807, Master, similar to (1), erected by his sister Martha Martyn, with arms only of Elliston; (3) of William Chafy, S.T.P., 1843, Master and Maria his wife, 1831, similar to (1), with the arms and crest of Chafy with an escutcheon of Westwood, by Tomson & Son; on W. wall, (4) of Robert Field, 1836, rectangular white marble tablet with semicircular-headed recess containing the shield-of-arms and crest of Field, by S. Manning, London. *Painting:* Over altar, the Virgin and Child and St. Joseph at the manger, with cherubs above (Plate 223), by G. B. Pittoni (1687–1767), on canvas, acquired in 1783 by the Rev. Thomas Martyn through John Strange, British Resident at Venice, for 20 guineas.

The *Library* (22¾ ft. by 36¼ ft.), on the first floor, stands between the Chapel and the Master's Lodge and is entered from the organ-gallery in the former and the secondary staircase in the latter; it is symmetrically designed, with four windows in each of the side walls and central doorways in the N. and S. ends. The timber outer S. doorcase, on the gallery, has side-pilasters with carved roundels in the heads supporting a pedimented entablature with dentil-cornice. The W. windows, overlooking Chapel Court, are described above with the exterior of the E. range; the E. windows, largely screened from outside, are similar to those opposite, being insertions of 1833 doubtless in the original openings in the brick walling of Essex's building. The room has a late 18th-century plaster dentil-cornice. The oak projecting doorcases have moulded architraves, horizontal panels over the doors and pedimented dentil-cornices; these last are continued to mitre round the flanking wall-cases as capping members, at a level about two-thirds the height of the walls. The same wall-cases have the central sections projecting and fitted with simply panelled doors. The standing bookcases projecting from between the windows, six in all, have panelled ends in four heights, the topmost panel alone being elaborated with extra mitres. All the woodwork is of 1776 and designed presumably by James Essex. Preserved in the room is a 15th-century iron-bound chest with domed top with traceried edge, long and elaborately contrived hasps, loop-handles, and buttress-like wrought-iron pieces applied to the lock-plate and corners (Plate 46).

Sir Francis Clerke's Range, bordering Chapel Court on the S., was built in or shortly after 1628 and, like the other College buildings, remodelled outside in the second quarter of the 19th century by Wyatville. He added parapets in place of eaves. It is of three storeys with attics. The N. side is in eight bays and the ground-floor openings are shown on the plan. The three doorways have 19th-century four-centred heads and the windows each three square-headed lights. On the floors above are repetitions of the three-light windows below and two light windows over the doorways and in the attics; those to the last are in assymetrically placed stepped gables in the parapet-wall. The S. side has a plain parapet; at the E. end is a doorway with four-centred head and a single-light window on each floor above it; westward are ranges of nine two-light windows on each floor. On the ridge are three chimney-stacks with grouped diagonal shafts.

The gabled W. end is similar to the W. end of the N. range of Hall Court but entirely rendered. The arms on the oriel-window are of Sir Francis Clerke. The *Interior* has in the E. wall at ground-floor level, and now within a cupboard opening off a later passage, parts of an original brick fireplace. On the first floor, the wall below the window in the closet off the main room W. of staircase 'H' is lined with a piece of early 17th-century panelling. E. of staircase 'G', reused panelling of the same date, possibly originally doors, divides the bedroom and closet. The main room W. of this staircase is lined with mid 18th-century fielded panelling with dado-rail and cornice; the two smaller S. rooms of the set have cornices of the same date and are divided from one another by a panelled partition. On the second floor, both the main rooms off staircase 'G' contain early 19th-century reeded fireplace-surrounds of wood; in the eastern of these sets is an early 17th-century eight-panel door.

The *Gateway* (Plate 246) built probably in 1749 to replace the original entrance to the College was removed and rebuilt in the E. end of the wall to Jesus Lane when Wyatville built the present Gatehouse in 1831. It is a structure of wrought stone ashlar, rectangular on plan, with rusticated walls and a continuous pedimented Roman Doric entablature. The semi-circular-headed archways in the front and back walls have moulded imposts; the side walls contain similar blind arches with panelled stone filling. The entablature includes triglyphs, and carved rosettes in the metopes; in the tympanum to the street is a cartouche carved with the arms of the College and flanked by scrolls, in the opposite tympanum a coroneted lozenge-of-arms of the Foundress between palm-leaves. Inside the Gateway is a plaster ceiling and entablature enriched with

Carved panels: Father Neptune and tritons.

Father Cam and the College.

N. side.

(37) ST. JOHN'S COLLEGE. Old Bridge; general view and details. 1709–12

Before the alterations begun in 1821.

Wyatville's proposed alterations.

(39) SIDNEY SUSSEX COLLEGE. Early 19th-century drawings of W. front.

(39) SIDNEY SUSSEX COLLEGE. E. side of Hall-range. Late 16th-century, remodelled 1821

E. side.

W. side.

(40) TRINITY COLLEGE. Great Gate.

Begun *c.* 1490

(40) TRINITY COLLEGE. Great Gate. N. archway, E. side. *c.* 1490

(35) QUEENS' COLLEGE. Gatehouse, E. side. 1448

(40) TRINITY COLLEGE. Great Court, looking S.E.

(40) TRINITY COLLEGE. Hall. Exterior, from S.W. 1604–05

(40) TRINITY COLLEGE. King Edward's Tower; S. side. 1428–32; rebuilt 1600–01

fret ornament. The original oak door of fifteen fielded panels is hung within a panelled framing, the rail at impost-level being carved with Greek key-pattern ornament; most of the wrought-iron door-furniture is original.

The clunch *Boundary-wall* on the E. of the College grounds, though largely faced with later brickwork, is probably mediaeval.

Reset over the S. doorway of the bathhouse yard is a carved stone achievement-of-arms of Grey quartering Hastings, David of Scotland, Blundeville, Cantelupe and Valence, for Henry Grey, 6th Earl of Kent, with wyvern supporters; it also is said to be from one of the original oriel-windows on the street front of the College (see Hall Court, N. range).

In 1955–56, after this account was written, the W. side of the Chapel range was stripped of stucco and refaced with stone and staircase 'B' was reconstructed.

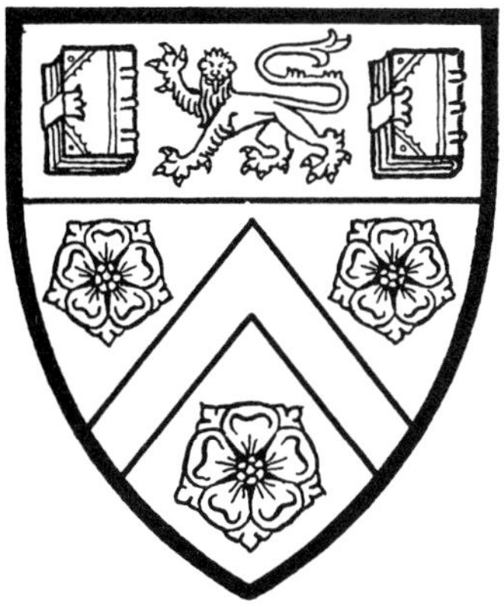

(40) Trinity College (see plan at end of book) is bounded on the E. and S. by Trinity Street (formerly High Street), Trinity Lane (formerly St. Michael's Lane), Trinity Hall Lane (formerly Milne Street) and Garret Hostel Lane, on the N. by St. John's College, and on the W. by the River Cam (Plate 231).

The College was founded in 1546 by King Henry VIII for a Master and about sixty Fellows and scholars. On the site stood Michael House, King's Hall and several private hostels, of which the most important was Physick Hostel. The two colleges surrendered, with their possessions, to the king, while Physick Hostel was acquired from Gonville Hall. The distribution of the land owned or leased by the three establishments is indicated in the accompanying diagram. The lanes that bisected the area, in so far as they affected the position of the buildings of the earlier foundations, will be shown to have had an important influence upon the disposition of the buildings of Trinity College. The king doubtless chose King's Hall as the nucleus of his royal College because of the connection since 1337, traditionally since 1317, with the Court through admission of boy scholars, 'the King's childer', destined for public service.

Michael House was founded by Hervey de Stanton, Chancellor of the Exchequer to Edward II, in 1324. It was in the vicinity of the S.W. corner of the present Great Court of Trinity College. Chambers stood to N. and S. and the Hall, as will be shown, was orientated N. and S.; such disposition suggests three sides of a court. Some of the buildings were demolished in 1550–2, but the Hall and probably the S. range were retained; the Hall was subsequently incorporated in the S. end of the W. range of Great Court but only fragments of the walling survive *in situ*. Opposite Michael House stood *Physick Hostel*, on the E. side of Milne Street; it was bequeathed to Gonville Hall in 1393. Little is known of the buildings, but a N. part and a S. part, perhaps ranges, were built in 1481. They too were to some extent demolished in 1550–2. That the S. ranges of both Michael House and Physick Hostel were however retained seems to be indicated by the entry in the accounts of 1550–1 for making a gate between them and for walling up their own gates. The N. section of Milne Street was closed and the new gate was evidently placed across the entry to it from St. Michael's Lane. This is taken to have predetermined the site of the present Queen's Gate of Trinity College, but some doubt has been expressed of the broken alignment here of Milne Street accepted by Willis and Clark (A. E. Stamp, *Michaelhouse*, privately printed 1924); instead, axial planning upon King Edward's Tower has been adduced to explain the siting. The total demolition between 1594 and 1597 of all the buildings in the way of Nevile's S. range of Great Court has hitherto been assumed; but John Hamond's view of Cambridge of 1592 shows an almost continuous sequence of ranges and tenements here and this, together with the fact that the masonry of the S. wall of the present S. range varies, suggests that some older walling was again retained. The masonry indicates the retention of the S. wall of a building extending the length of the centre third of the range, curtailed on the W. by the insertion of Queen's Gate. This length approximates very closely and could have coincided with that, known documentarily, of the E. to W. extent of the Physick Hostel property. Thus identification with the S. wall of the S. range of that Hostel may be hazarded. This would also imply a lesser break in the line of the former Milne Street and axial siting of Queen's Gate.

King's Hall was founded by Edward III in 1337, in continuation of Edward II's benevolence in supporting students at Cambridge, for a Master and thirty-two scholars. The house and land of Robert of Croyland had been bought for them the year before; the house is presumed to have stood immediately N. of King's Childer Lane and close W. of the present Great Gate; it has been entirely destroyed. By 1351 all the land further N., to the wall of the Hospital of St. John, W. to the river, and N.E. to the High Street had been acquired, but the property at the corner of King's Childer Lane and High Street was not obtained until 1376; this, and the facility of approach to the College afforded by the convergence of King's Childer Lane and Milne Street that it indicates, influenced the Society, after the initial expansion of Croyland's house, to extend their buildings at first to the N. and N.W. The work begun in 1375 and continued for nearly 50 years included a Court, of which the W. range in part survives in *King's Hall Range*, or '*King's Hostel*', in a position N.W. of the present Chapel. In consequence of the preponderance of buildings thus being to the W. rather than to the E., when a monumental gatehouse, *King Edward's Tower*, was added (some 90 ft. S. of its present position) it was placed towards Milne Street, not towards High Street. It was begun in 1428 and finished structurally in 1432. At much the same time a range of chambers was built linking King Edward's Tower with the S. end of the W. range of the Court already described; this is shown in John Hamond's view of 1592, eight years before its demolition and the removal

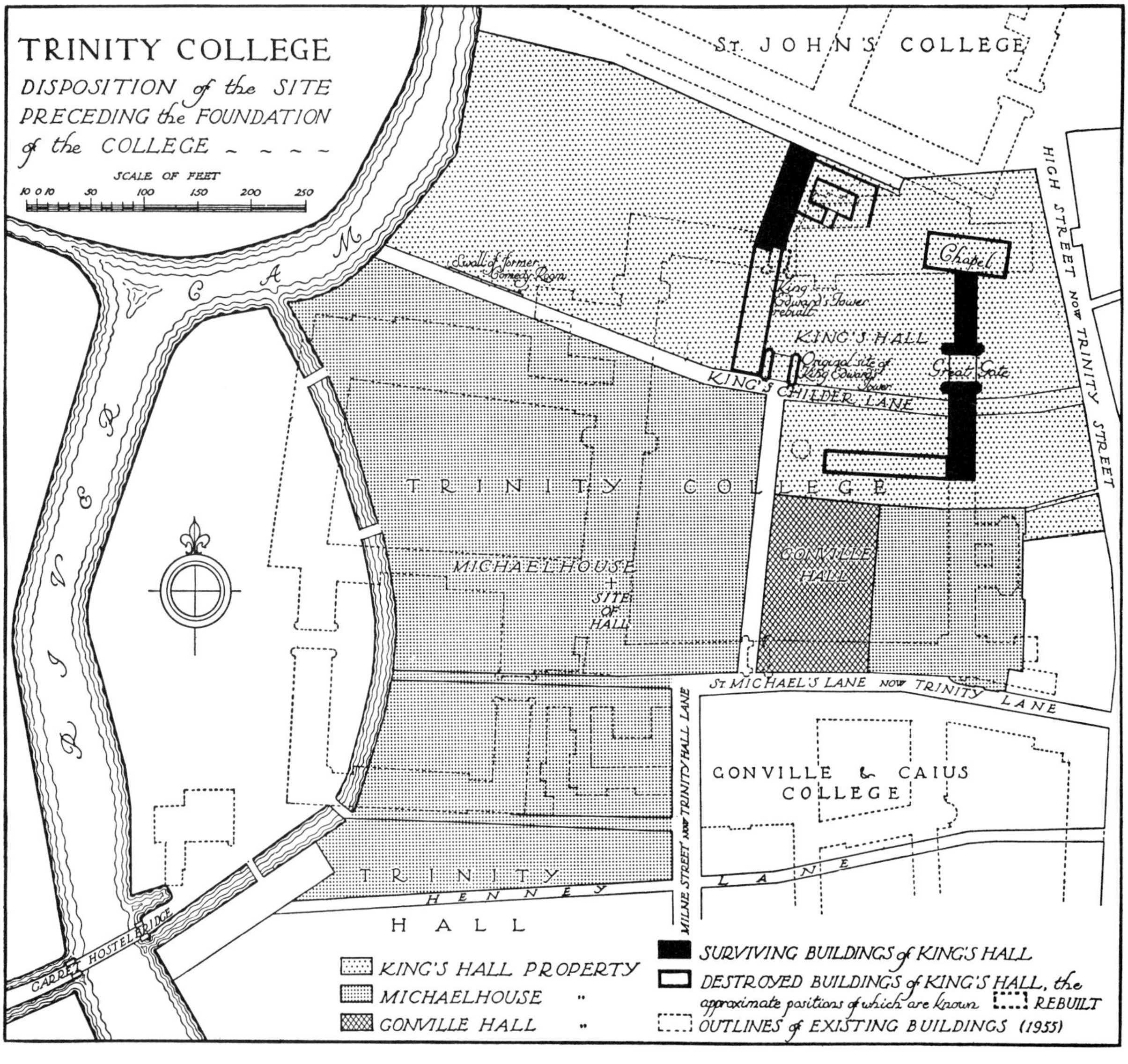

northward of King Edward's Tower. The accommodation of Henry VI and his retinue in College in 1445 is some indication of the development of the King's Hall buildings.

In 1433 the eastern part of King's Childer Lane was acquired by the College, after the acquisition of land lying to the S. of it to a depth of some 90 yds. (see diagram, p. 210). In 1449 a building of some size was begun; the accounts, though incomplete, include for over two hundred loads of clunch for it, but its position is unknown. It may have been the range on this newly acquired land shown by Hamond projecting at right angles into the present Great Court; it was demolished probably in or shortly before 1599, but its position is established by the close alignment shown by Hamond of the S. wall with the S. end of the later 15th-century E. range; for the latter is marked by the thick wall surviving, though only to first-floor height, incorporated in the prolonged E. range of the Great Court of Trinity College (see plan).

The Chapel was begun in 1464–5 and not completed until twenty years later; it stood to the N.E. of the site, approximately in the position of the eastern five bays of the present Chapel of Trinity College.

By the middle of the 15th century King's Hall had extended its land eastward to include the whole frontage to High Street from the Hospital of St. John property on the N. for a distance of some 114 yds. southward. Thus, while closure of the E. part of King's Childer Lane, by preventing direct access to King Edward's Tower, must have created the need for main approach to the College from the E., from High Street, all obstacle to such approach had been removed. Not unexpectedly therefore in, or shortly before, 1490, a new building was begun which with reasonable certainty may be identified with the ground stage of the present *Great Gate* and the adjacent N. part of the E. range. In the accounts a porter's lodge with walls and turrets are named (K.H. Accts. xviii, 296 (1491–2), 'Nova edificacio: It.' pro coopertura pro le porters logge cum muris et turribus' etc.) and payments are included to John Wastell, freemason. Wastell was responsible for the Angel Tower of Canterbury Cathedral, 1494–7, where the wall-panelling is identical in design with that over the small arch of Great Gate (Plate 251). Similarities in the parts of the E. range flanking Great Gate show them to be contemporary, and a further agreement for roofing was made in 1495.

From the foregoing, although, as indicated, the evidence is not conclusive, it would seem that the E. range begun in 1490 extended from the Chapel on the N. as far as the line of the S. wall of the range of 1449 on the S., with the Great Gate near the centre, so presenting a balanced elevation to E. and W. Unspecified ranges of chambers were taken down in 1428 ('subtractione antiquarum camerarum') and 1490, and if these referred mainly to Croyland's house, then Great Gate gave impressive easterly access to a Court approximately quarter the size of the present Great Court of Trinity College. This is essentially the arrangement appearing in J. Hamond's view of this area, but presumably with some enclosure on the S.W. provided by 'the wall near the new gate' (King Edward's Tower) mentioned in the accounts for 1433–4.

The upper stages of Great Gate were not added until between 1528–35, though expenses 'circa novum turrim' begin sporadically with the accounts for 1518–19. The masonry occurring in the N. and S. walls above the adjoining roofs shows that some predominance in height was intended from the very first, but this is the earliest documentary evidence of a scheme to raise over the gate a 'great tower' (so named in K.H. Accts. 1528–9, xxiv, 68, 'Expense circa magnam turrim'), and structural evidence that it was an afterthought appears from the eastern turrets being demonstrably additions set against the earlier ground stage and the western turrets being perhaps replacements of smaller turrets that were set closer in towards the W. archway. The facts however that the main gates were not supplied until 1522 and the stone vault of the Gatehall was never completed show that the whole resulted rather from a prolonged and irregular building operation than from a series of remodellings.

The history of the buildings of King's Hall after assimilation into Henry VIII's new foundation, other than that already given, may be summarised here. In the N.W. Court, the S. range, containing the late 14th-century Hall, and the S. part of the E. range, containing the early 15th-century Pantry and 'Squyer's Chamber', with the buildings eastward of it, including the 15th-century Chapel, were pulled down between 1554 and 1561 to make way for the new Chapel of Trinity College. The rest of the E. range, containing the 14th-century Kitchen, and most of the N. range, containing the 15th-century Library, were demolished in 1694.

A 'first plott' of *Trinity College within the Town and University of Cambridge of King Henry VIII's foundation*, that is, a report on the financial requirements and constitution of the proposed College, was prepared for the king by the Court of Augmentations, probably in consultation with John Redman and early in 1546. In April or early May possession was taken of the site. Although upon it stood a chapel and three halls, of King's Hall, Michael House and Physick Hostel, with their chambers, and the premises of some six of their subordinate hostels, already in May the buildings of the Franciscan friary (see Monument (39), Sidney Sussex

College), were being demolished and the materials taken to provide 'toward the building of the King's Majesty's new College'. In December the Court of Augmentations was directed to pay £2,000 to Redman, the first Master, 'towards the establishment and buildings' and in recompense of a year's loss of revenues pending issue of letters patent for their donation. The formal dissolution of the older Colleges took place in October and December and the Charter of Foundation of Trinity College is dated 19 December 1546. The endowment granted was valued at £1,640 net a year; the annual income of King's Hall was £214 and of Michael House just over £141.

The indications of work of adaptation being begun immediately have been described. Costs of repairs, alterations and new buildings recur in the accounts, generally without detailed specification; but in 1547 work was being done on the Hall. The position of this last, and thus the probable identification of it with the Hall of Michael House, is shown by a 16th-century plan of Great Court preserved in the College Library and the corroborative evidence of the entry in the building accounts of 1604–05 for the present Kitchen, 'digging the foundation of the kitchen wall that goes through the old Hall', which is the stage of development shown in the early 17th-century Smithson drawing of Great Court (R.I.B.A. Drawings AE5/28). A great lobed oriel-window, clearly the dais window, occurs in these plans and in the views of the College by Hamond (1592) and Loggan (*c.* 1688); the foundations of it and of the flanking buttresses were revealed by excavation in 1892 (C.A.S. *Proc.* VIII, 234) and are indicated on the plan. The buttery etc. of the old Hall were on the N.

The northward extension of this *West Range* as far as, and including, the present Entrance-hall of the Master's Lodge, and the right-angle turn of it eastward to link with King Edward's Tower (in its original position) were in hand in 1554, and that they formed part of a general project appears from a Commission issuing in that year under the great seal of Philip and Mary authorising the assembly of craftsmen, labour and materials for 'new edifying, building, rearing and setting up' the College. Other contemporary works are described below. Chief among them is the *Chapel*; the contract was made in 1555 and the walls were finished in 1564. The circumstances of the ceiling of its western end between 1561 and 1563, with the subsequent preponderance of masons over carpenters and, in 1564, the references to preparation of roof timbers and to the supply of ironwork for the E. window, tend to confirm the possibility alluded to below in the description of the building that completion of three bays, and these to the E., was reserved until towards the end of the building operations. The entry in the accounts so late as 1560–1 for taking down the roof of the old Chapel, on the eastern part of the same site, suggests that this sequence was followed to enable part at least of the latter to be used while the new Chapel was being built. Entries in the Junior Bursar's accounts for 1556–7 for minor work to the floor and roof of the chamber at 'the new chapel end' may refer to the adjustment necessary to link either 'King's Hostel' or the E. range of King's Hall with the new building; the second is less probable since the old Chapel was still in use in January 1556–7. Repairs to and refitting the Chapel were begun in 1706 and continued throughout much of the first half of the century; the reredos, screen, organ, stalls and panelling are mostly of this period. Between 1868 and 1876 the E. and S. sides were newly ashlared, the vestries and S. porch added, and the interior redecorated, all under the supervision of A. W. Blomfield. Other alterations are described in the detailed account below.

The present appearance of Great Court and the inception of Nevile's Court are due to 'the splendid, courteous and bountiful' Dr. Thomas Nevile, Master 1593–1615. Before 1598 at least £1,453 had been spent on the buildings; but no details of the expenditure survive. The Junior Bursar's accounts for 1598–9 indicate that the continuation of the *East Range* S. from the northern King's Hall section of 1490–5, and the *South Range*, including the *Queen's Gate* and the turret in the S.E. angle, were approaching completion; the Gate is dated 1597. Incidental expenses in the 1601–02 accounts imply that they were being finished. Meanwhile demolitions were proceeding and the Court was levelled; the former included removal of the 1449(?) S. range of King's Hall, and, in the N.W. area of Great Court, of the ranges forming a salient angle with King Edward's Tower at the point.

The *North Range*, the old Library range, continuing W. from the Chapel, and the West Range continuing N. from the old Hall range were built at much the same time as the foregoing. The extension of the W. range more than replaced the Master's previous accommodation in the demolished return range. Payment to Mr. Hall for freestone for the old Library range occurs in the 1589–90 accounts and by 1600 the library had been built but not completed; in 1601 it and the staircase to it were finished. In 1600 the foundations of the W. range were laid and the building completed the following year. The same years saw the removal of King Edward's Tower and its re-erection in the present position.

Provision early in the 17th century of the present Hall, Buttery and Kitchen involved the demolition of the former W. range from within the N. end of the old Hall northward to the N. containing-wall of the further staircase shown in the 16th-century plan of Great Court preserved in the College (Willis and Clark, II, fig. 10, facing p. 465). The *Hall* was begun in 1604; Ralph Symons was paid for a model of the building. The Bursar and John Symes, the builder, had inspected divers halls in London and the dimensions of Middle Temple Hall were those adopted here. Symes began work in April and the roof was slated by October 1605. The *Kitchen*, which intruded laterally into the old Hall, and the *Buttery* were begun in July 1605; the roofs were slated by November the same year.

Dr. Nevile embellished Great Court with the *Fountain*. This was begun in 1601–02 and rebuilt, with some alteration, in 1715–16. The *Sundial*, further N., was set up in 1704. Nevile's Court, the gift of the eponym in the form it stood until 1676, is referred to below.

Great Court remained without alteration of note until the Mastership of Richard Bentley (1700–42). Between 1700 and 1709 the *Master's Lodge* in the W. range, of 1554 and 1600–01, was remodelled; sash-windows were inserted, except in the oriel, the interior was extensively refitted, and a grand staircase added. By custom royal visitors to Cambridge, and by custom and concession the sovereign's Judges on Assize, are lodged at Trinity College; for them Bentley refitted the state bedrooms in the King's and Judges' suites. In 1842 and 1843 the Lodge was restored; on the E., the sash-windows were replaced by the present stone-mullioned windows and the oriel-window, destroyed some time after 1740, was rebuilt; on the W., the sashes were left but the oriel was rebuilt, all to the designs of A. Salvin. Other alterations are described below in the detailed account of the Master's Lodge. In 1920 the S. rooms on the ground and first floors became the *Fellows' Parlour* and *Senior Combination Room.*

In 1750–1, under the direction of one Denston, from Derbyshire, most of Great Court was plastered. Three years later, the E. side of the Hall was extensively repaired and the S. side of the Court, including Queen's Gate and the S.E. angle-turret, in part refaced with new ashlar. This latter refacing was far less extensive than the accounts of 1753–4 at first suggest, for the greater area of the front retains reused mediaeval ashlar and it is known that stone from Cambridge castle was being reused for Nevile's buildings in *c.* 1600; furthermore the masonry is totally unlike the mid 18th-century stonework elsewhere in the College. In 1771 the S.W. angle-turret was demolished and the W. range thence northward to the Hall, but excluding Nevile's Kitchen, almost entirely rebuilt to the designs of James Essex, primarily to provide finer accommodation for the Combination Room and Parlour on the first floor. Work was completed in 1774 and the rooms occupied the following year; they are now the *Old Combination Room* and *Junior Combination Room.* Thereupon, it appears the possibility of rebuilding the whole Court was suggested but progressed no further. In 1810 the W. side of the E. range N. of Great Gate was repaired; as Bernasconi was employed the reparation probably consisted of a refacing in Roman cement, and in 1812–13 more work definitely of this nature was completed on the rest of the E. range and the N. range. In Queen's Gate the sash-windows inserted in 1723 on the first floor were replaced with the present stone-mullioned windows in 1866. Other 19th-century alterations to the ranges of Great Court include the refacing of the E. side of the E. range N. of Great Gate and rebuilding in stone the small annexe to it, both in 1856, under the supervision of Anthony Salvin. The W. side of the same part of the range was entirely refaced in 1935. On the N., the chambers on the third floor of the old Library range were improved in 1873 by the renewal of the S. windows and the insertion of some elaborate plasterwork.

W. of Great Court, *Nevile's Court* was built at Dr. Nevile's own expense, with the result that the charges for it are not entered in the College books and no accounts have survived. The only oblique references to it are in Orders of 1612 and 1614 in the College Conclusion Book that refer to adjustments to be devised by Symes and Pearce in the Kitchen and Buttery and to completion of a gable to be 'in concurrence with our Master's building'. The Kitchen had been completed in 1605; therefore Nevile's Court may probably be dated between 1605 and 1612. Again, from the history of St. John's College (Thomas Baker, *History* etc. (ed. J. E. B. Mayor, 1869), I, 208), it is known that the N. and S. ranges each cost £1,500

The N. and S. ranges were originally but three-fifths of their present length, the W. side of the Court being closed only by a wall with a gateway in the centre. With little doubt this last was the elaborate gate, *Nevile's Gate,* now at the entrance to the College by Bishop's Hostel. The extent of the buildings is indicated in the roughly-drawn view of Cambridge dated 1634 in Thomas Fuller's *History of the University* and the position of the W. wall is preserved in two ground plans of the Court in the Wren drawings at All Souls College, Oxford (Vol. IV, 50, I, 43). The extension of the ranges westward was undertaken in connection with the Library building next described.

The *Library* at the W. end of Nevile's Court was begun in February 1676–7; Isaac Barrow, Master 1672–7, promoted the scheme after damage by fire to the old Library, which was already inadequate. Sir Christopher Wren was the architect and gave his services without charge. The first proposal was for a free-standing centrally-planned domed building, reminiscent of Palladio's Villa Capra, 'La Rotonda', linked only by dwarf walls and railings to the ends of Nevile's ranges.

The final scheme was for a long rectangular building with staircases on the N. and S. ends; this was to close the Court, in its original dimensions, on the W. The work was carried out, except for the omission of the S. staircase, almost exactly in accordance with the drawings, which are preserved in the Library at All Souls College (Wren drawings, Vol. I, 45–8, 50, 51), but the whole was placed some 27 yds. further W. than intended when the drawings were made, so extending the E. to W. depth of Nevile's Court. Enclosure on the N.W. and S.W. was then obtained by prolonging Nevile's N. and S. ranges in uniform style to meet the new building. The extension of the N. side was begun after April 1676 and the eastern half completed before 1679, at the charge of Sir Thomas Sclater, Bt., the western half before May 1681; the S. side was begun after May 1681 and finished the following year, the eastern half at the expense of Dr. Humphry Babington. Meanwhile the Library building was proceeding; the plastering stage was reached in 1686–7, and the whole completed *c.* 1695. The original fittings and furniture are to Wren's designs. Robert Grumbold, mason, was in charge of the work; other workmen employed are named below in the detailed account of the Library. Grumbold also supervised the extension of the S. range of the Court, and thus perhaps of the N. range.

The *Tribunal* at the E. end of Nevile's Court, against the W. wall of the Hall, was built in 1682; it endows the irregularity of this side of the Court with a measure of symmetry suited to the regularity of the other three sides. Robert Grumbold, who supervised the work, was in close touch with Wren at the time.

By 1755 the fronts of Nevile's ranges had weathered and become unstable and the decision was then made (Conclusion Book, 7 April 1755) to rebuild them; a 17th-century elevational drawing in the Victoria and Albert Museum (Drwg. E 408/1951), incorrectly titled 'Gresham's College', preserves their appearance. James Essex was entrusted with the work. He retained the arcade design and the main vertical and horizontal articulation of the fronts but omitted much of the Jacobean detail and raised the attics to a full storey, replacing the ranges of gabled dormers with larger windows and a horizontal balustraded parapet. This surface treatment was continued across the late 17th-century W. extensions of both ranges. The front of the N. range was the first begun and the cost of stone supplied before Michaelmas 1755, £330, indicates the extent of renewal. The S. side was in worse condition, 'so that a considerably greater quantity of new stone was used', (Junior Bursar's Day Book, 1755–6), while the back wall of the older part was reconstructed of new stone and with new dressings; thus Nevile's S. range was virtually entirely rebuilt, for the internal refitting was equally extensive. The whole work was finished in 1758; that to Nevile's ranges cost £5,486, to the later western extensions £578. The S. wall of the S. range was in part remodelled in the 19th century when New Court was built.

In 1669 John Hackett, Bishop of Lichfield and Coventry, gave £1,200 towards rebuilding Garret Hostel to the S.W. of Great Court, the new building to be named *Bishop's Hostel.* A substantial part was built before October 1670 though it was not finished until late in 1671. The contract, with a plan for the building, is preserved in the College; it is dated January 1669–70 and is with Robert Minchin of Bletchingdon, Oxfordshire, carpenter, who had worked for Wren at Trinity College, Oxford. Wren's brother-in-law was rector of Bletchingdon. The total cost exceeded Hackett's gift by some £357. It was restored by A. W. Blomfield in 1877.

The rapid increase in the number of admissions of undergraduates early in the 19th century and the policy of the Master, Christopher Wordsworth (1820–41), in accommodating more students within the College led to the building of the 'King's Court', generally called *New Court,* S. of Nevile's Court. It was designed by William Wilkins, begun in July 1823 and occupied in October 1825. The style is Tudor Gothic, but Wilkins also prepared a design in part at least Classical. The scheme adopted included a cloister-walk on the N. extending between the staircase-bays, but this was demolished in 1868. In 1833–4 *Lecture Room Court* was added on the S.E. of Great Court under the supervision of Charles Humfrey at a cost of £5,500.

Later additions to the accommodation include *Whewell's Court* (William Whewell, Master 1841–66), on the E. side of Trinity Street opposite Great Gate. The first part, to the W., was completed in 1860, the second, between the first and Bridge Street, was begun in 1865 and finished in 1868; both were designed by Anthony Salvin and remodelled to some extent in 1908 by W. D. Caröe. The ranges S. and W. of Bishop's Hostel were added between 1876 and 1878, the architect being A. W. Blomfield, who also added the Library extension against the N. range of Nevile's Court in 1892 and the W. extension of the Master's Lodge in the same year.

Restriction of space has led in recent years to the occupation of private houses, 2 and 37 Trinity Street, and the building of *Bevan Hostel* in 1949 some way from the College, in Green Street.

Among the architectural features in the College grounds, *Trinity Bridge* over the river, W. of New Court, was rebuilt to the designs of James Essex in 1764–5. The cost, £1,500, was defrayed from a bequest of Dr. Hooper, whose arms it bears. The materials from the old bridge of 1651–2 were used in the substructure. The 'High Walk' over the bridge leads to the *Field Gate*, to Queens' Road, which was given to the College in 1733 by Henry Bromley and came from the donor's house, Horseheath Hall; it replaced Nevile's Gate, which had been rebuilt in this position probably in 1681 where it appears in Loggan's view of the College. *Trinity College Walks* retain the arrangement shown by Loggan, *c.* 1688; the avenue E. of the Bridge was replanted in 1716–17, then continuing eastward where New Court now stands. The *Bowling Green* W. of 'King's Hostel' was laid in 1647–8.

At Trinity College, Great Court devised by Dr. Thomas Nevile *c.* 1600 is the most spacious College court in existence totally enclosed by buildings of dates varying from 1428 to the present century. King Edward's Tower of 1428–32, though rebuilt in 1600 with some alterations, is the prototype of the Cambridge gate-towers. Great Gate, begun as a structure of a different form in *c.* 1490 and largely completed as it now stands between 1528 and 1535, is the most monumental building of the kind in the University. The Chapel, though perhaps lacking in inspiration, is historically interesting as a building initially of the counter-Reformation almost wholly in the Gothic style. Dr. Nevile's Hall of 1605 contains one of the most remarkable timber roofs and one of the more elaborate screens of the period; the early 18th-century cast-iron brazier is a very rare survival. Nevile's Fountain in Great Court of 1601–02, rebuilt early in the 18th century, is the only important example of the kind remaining in this country.

Nevile's Court with N. and S. ranges built between 1605 and 1612, extended between 1676 and 1682 and reconstructed in the mid 18th century, is a refreshingly Italianate conception and on a more ambitious scale than are the surviving examples of the fashion elsewhere in England. The Library range, begun in 1676 and finished structurally by 1695, enclosing the same court on the W., is a mature and noble work of Sir Christopher Wren; the design is essentially Roman, with influences from France. A spaciousness within the Library greater than the exterior would suggest is obtained by an expedient, described below, typical of Wren's ingenuity.

The buildings of the College contain many fittings of note, in particular the contemporary woodwork of the Library and early 18th-century woodwork in the Chapel. These two buildings contain one of the most important assemblages of 18th and 19th-century sculpture in England.

Architectural Description (See plan at end of book)—*Great Court* (Plate 252) (273 ft. by 325 ft. average) has the entrance range on the E., the Chapel on the N., the Hall and Master's Lodge on the W., and ranges of chambers on the S. 'King's Hostel', adjoining the N. range and approached through King Edward's Tower, is described below after the buildings of Great Court.

The *East Range* is of two periods, the N. length, containing Great Gate, as far S. as the thick wall by the Bursary being a surviving part of King's Hall, the S. length as far as Trinity Lane, being part of Dr. Nevile's work in extension of Trinity College.

The lower part of *Great Gate* (Plate 250) and the flanking sections of the E. range formerly of King's Hall are probably those buildings begun in or shortly before 1490; from 1490 to 1492 £158 was spent. William Swayn 'lathamus' was paid for doors and windows and stone and seems to have been regularly employed as master-mason until 1505. 'Expenses concerning the new building' also include fees to John Wastell, freemason, in 1491–2 and 1496–7; the significance of his employment is suggested in the historical introduction above, the presumption being that he was peripatetic while Swayn was resident master-mason. Payments for covering the part of the range containing the Porter's Lodge were made in 1492. An agreement with the carpenter for roofing was made in 1495. The name of John Salter, carpenter, first appears in the accounts for 1496–7, for timber 'beyond his first agreement'. Payments to him in the accounts for 1497–8 include for a new door in the new wall to High Street. After *c.* 1505 thirty years elapsed before the upper stages of Great Gate were completed. The accounts for 1518–19 include a minor purchase of stone from King's Cliffe and payments to a small number of masons, including William Burdon, presumably master-mason. In the Audit book for 1522–3 is the cost of the new gates, by contract with Buxton, carpenter, in the sum of £6 13*s.* 4*d.*, the timber being from Chesterford, Essex.

Work was fully renewed in 1528–9, when John Shereff, mason, was paid an earnest of 10/- and a first instalment of £10 on sealing the indentures. Thomas Loveday, carpenter, was paid £8 for making the upper floor and roof. The turrets are additions, subsequent to the building of the late 15th-century ground stage; a summary of accounts dated 1535 includes for payment to Loveday for floors in four turrets, showing that they had by then been added. The cost, mainly of materials, of this second phase of building was £109 10*s.*; bricks were bought from Browne of Ely.

In the last years of the century, under Dr. Nevile, some minor work of heightening, difficult to identify, was put in hand and the exterior was plastered. John Symes was master-mason and the work included cutting quoins and window-jambs. Shortly afterwards Paris Andrew was paid for carving Henry VIII's statue (Bursar's Accts. 1600–01), but he appears not to have completed it. All the four statues, of Henry VIII, James I, Queen Anne, and Prince Charles (Plate 255), were carved in London. The accounts of 1614–15 include payments to Cure (William Cure, jun.) for the Queen, Prince, and Henry, and the Queen's and Prince's shields-of-arms, to John Smythe for going to London to help with carving James I, and for transport of all the statues and their shields-of-arms to Cambridge. Surprisingly, the stone for the Stuarts came from Barrington and Eversden. The Royal arms on the W. are by Smythe. Thorpe wrought the metal crowns on the E. Finally the whole of Great Gate was whitened and the carvings painted and gilded.

The enriched embattling on the E. has been replaced since the measured drawing of Great Gate was made for publication by Willis and Clark (*Architectural History of the University* etc. (1886) II, 484, fig. 13). Corbels in the Gatehall indicate that a stone vault was intended, but it was never built, and a flat ceiling existed until 1845 when the present timber vault was inserted at the expense mainly of William Whewell, Master 1841–66, and designed by him in collaboration with Professor Willis.

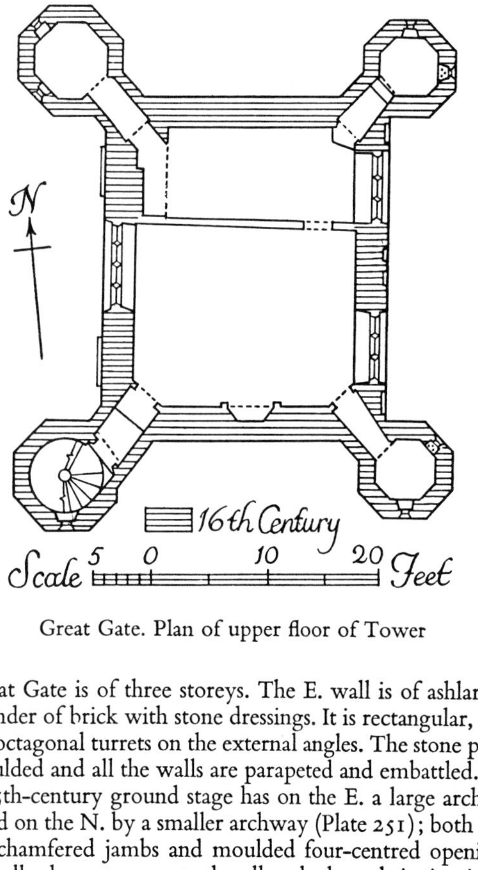

Great Gate. Plan of upper floor of Tower

Great Gate is of three storeys. The E. wall is of ashlar, the remainder of brick with stone dressings. It is rectangular, with taller octagonal turrets on the external angles. The stone plinth is moulded and all the walls are parapeted and embattled. The late 15th-century ground stage has on the E. a large archway flanked on the N. by a smaller archway (Plate 251); both have plain chamfered jambs and moulded four-centred openings; the smaller has a two-centred wall-arch above bringing it to a uniform height with the larger where both have square heads with traceried spandrels. The wall-arch contains an ogee crocketed finial over the opening, carved with a crown in glory in the spandrel, and a field enriched with elaborate tracery-panelling including quatrefoiled and subcusped roundels enclosing Tudor roses. The moulded cornice above is carved with paterae and on the frieze are 17th-century metal plates with renewed painted inscriptions in Roman characters, that in the centre with 'Edvardvs Tertivs Fvndator Avle Regis MCCCXXXVII', the rest identifying shields-of-arms in the wall-arcading above. This last is of three bays to each side of a wide central panel carved with the Royal arms of old France and England quarterly with lion supporters and a small shield-of-arms below of John Blyth, Master of King's Hall 1488–98, Henry VII's chaplain. The arcading consists of bays of window-light tracery-panelling with crocketed ogee heads in cinquefoiled subcusped arches divided by pinnacled standards and framing carved and painted shields-of-arms surmounted by gilded 17th-century wrought-iron crowns. The arcading continues and disappears behind the turrets. The arms are of the sons of Edward III, from the N., (a) Thomas of Woodstock, Duke of Gloucester, (b) John of Gaunt, Duke of Lancaster, (c) (blank) 'William of Hatfield' on the panel below, (d) Edward, Prince of Wales, with two shields charged with ostrich feathers painted on the stonework below, and 'Ich Dien', (e) Lionel, Duke of Clarence, (f) Edmund, Duke of York. All the foregoing is surmounted by a string enriched with spiral leaf ornament interrupted in the centre by a corbel carved with a demi-angel supporting the statue of Henry VIII in a niche above (Plate 255). The niche has a three-sided canopy with domical ogee top and pinnacled side-standards and is flanked by superimposed wall-panels with ogee heads; to each side are three-light windows with two-centred openings, once cusped, in square heads with moulded labels, and, at the extremities, between the windows and turrets, wall-panels with cinquefoiled heads. Much of this zone and the stage above belong to the work begun in 1518–19 but pressed on more actively from 1528 and finished by 1535; contemporary with them are the turrets.

The king's statue (Plate 255) begun by Paris Andrew *c.* 1600 and finished by William Cure was set up in 1615 and is now much weathered. He wears cloak and tunic with the Garter sash, from which the metal George has gone, and a modern gilded tin crown. In one hand is an orb, in the other a sceptre consisting of a wooden chair-leg. The top stage, demarcated by a string carved with paterae, has two windows similar to those below, but with rather rounder heads, from which also the cusps have been removed, and wall-panels at the extremities. In the centre wall-space is a subcusped quatrefoiled panel framing a shield of the Royal arms of new France and England quarterly. The enriched embattled parapet and parapet-string are restorations of the late 19th century based upon those shown in Loggan's view of the College.

The main gate of oak is that made by Buxton, with iron-work by a smith of Thaxted, and hung in 1523. It is in two leaves, each leaf being framed in three heights of five linenfold panels with a deep base rail enriched with carved quatrefoils; two of the last in each leaf contain shields charged with (a) the cross of St. George, (b) a saltire. The smaller archway contains an 18th-century oak screen of fielded panelling with a central wicket.

The E. turrets have high moulded stone plinths, different from the main plinth, and enriched strings dividing them into four stages. They are lit by loops with moulded jambs and two-centred openings in square heads. The lowest stage of the S. turret has been refaced and both parapets have been rebuilt in modern times; for the rest, the walling is pecked for plaster facing.

The W. side of Great Gate (Plate 250) has a large 15th-century stone archway the full height and most of the width

(40) TRINITY COLLEGE. Anne of Denmark. Prince Charles. 1614–15

(40) TRINITY COLLEGE. Henry VIII. 1614–15

(37) ST. JOHN'S COLLEGE. Mary, Countess of Shrewsbury. 1671

(40) TRINITY COLLEGE. Hall. Interior, looking N. 1604–05

N. side, with the shutter-boards removed.

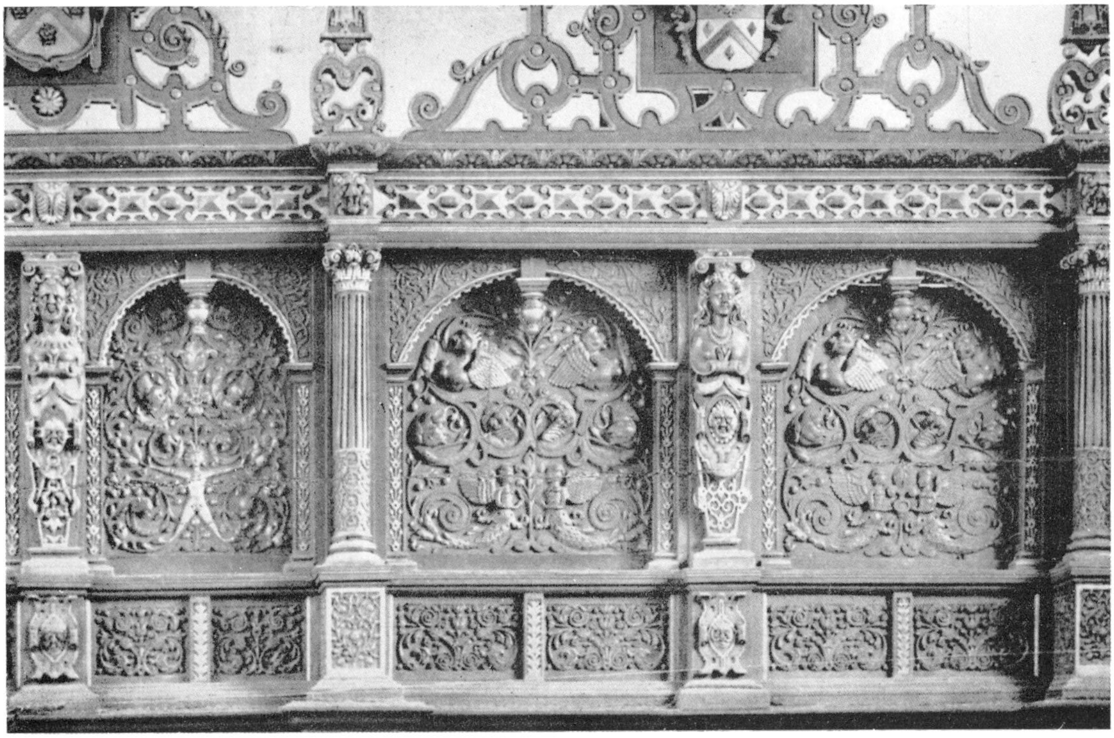

Detail, showing the shutter-boards.

(40) TRINITY COLLEGE. Hall. Screen. *c.* 1605

Screen and organ-case from W. *c.* 1735

Reredos. Early 18th-century

(40) TRINITY COLLEGE. Chapel.

(79) HOBSON'S CONDUIT. Fountain. 1614

(40) TRINITY COLLEGE. Nevile's Gate, E. face. c. 1610

(40) TRINITY COLLEGE. Chapel. Monument (1), of Sir Isaac Newton, 1727. Set up 1755

John Ray. 1751

Francis Willoughby. 1751

Richard Bentley. 1756

Sir Robert Cotton, Bt. 1757

(40) TRINITY COLLEGE. Library. Sculptured busts by L. F. Roubiliac.

Isaac Newton. Marble bust, by Roubiliac. 1751

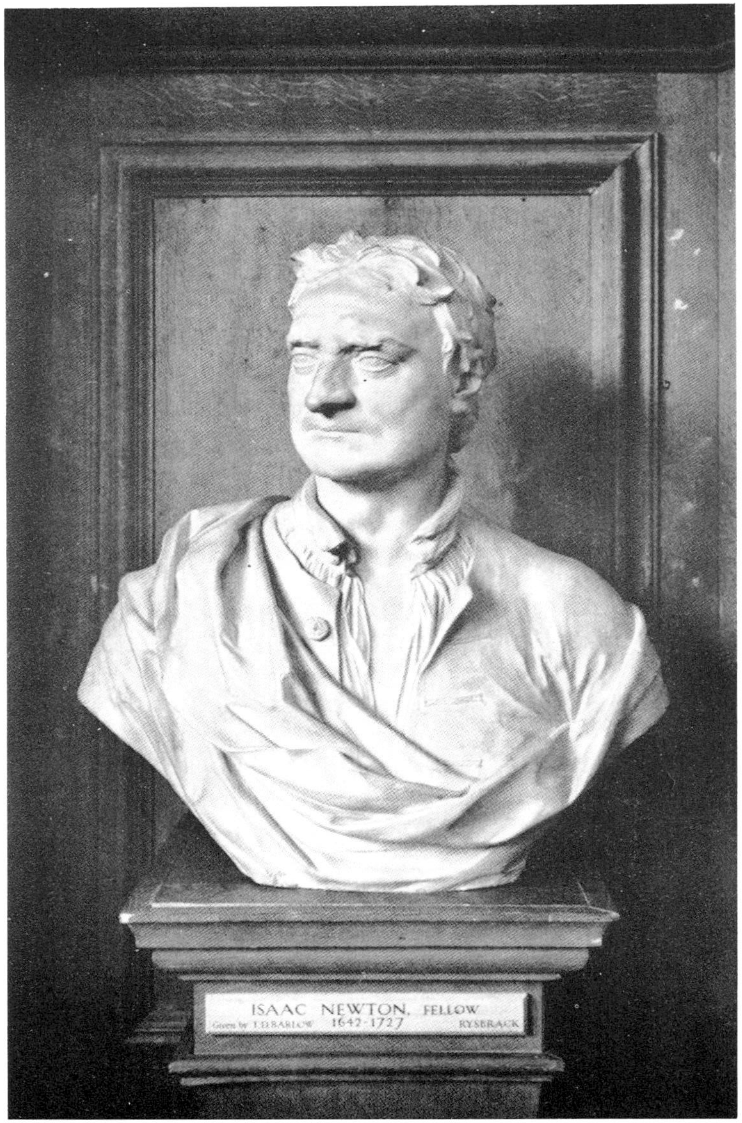

Isaac Newton. Terra-cotta bust, by Rysbrack. 1739

(40) TRINITY COLLEGE. Library.

of the ground stage between the turrets. It has plain chamfered jambs with moulded bases and a moulded four-centred head (p. 394) with elaborate tracery-panelled spandrels bringing the last out to the square; the outer ends of the jamb-dressings are ragged, as if originally concealed. Above the archway is a moulded string carved with paterae extending between the flanking turrets and broken in the centre by a renewed square traceried panel with label containing a blank shield. The two courses of clunch facing in this area may be remains of the upper part of the late 15th-century building; for the rest the brickwork is of the 16th century. In the second stage is a four-light stone-mullioned window of similar character to those on the E. at the same level; the label is interrupted by a niche above. Flanking the window are two stone traceried panels with blank shields and similar to the panel just described. The central niche and those to each side of it are insertions of *c.* 1615 and are similar to that on King Edward's Tower wrought by Paris Andrew *c.* 1600. They have at the sides, on pedestals carried on scrolled brackets, free-standing Ionic columns supporting cornices; to the shallow rounded niches are shell heads. They contain the statue of King James I in the centre, of Queen Anne (Plate 255) to the N. and Prince Charles (Plate 255) to the S., all much weathered and with renewed heads. The upper string is carved with paterae and runs at the sill-level of the four-light window of the third storey. This window is similar in character to those opposite and surmounted and flanked by carved stone achievements, now badly decayed, of the Royal arms of James I above in a Garter with lion and unicorn supporters, of Queen Anne to the N. with wild men supporters, and of Prince Charles to the S. with the Royal supporters; all are crowned. The Royal arms extend up through the parapet-string and into the embattled ashlar parapet. The date and carvers of the statues and arms have already been quoted.

The W. turrets are similar to those on the E. except that the S.W. turret has in the S. wall a stone doorway with continuous chamfered jambs and four-centred head under a moulded label. The re-entrant angle between the turrets and the W. wall of the two upper stages is splayed, the splays being carried on moulded stone corbels just above the ground stage. The quoins of the turret-angles adjoining the flanking ranges are continued down to the level reached by the former eaves of the latter, before they were replaced by battlements. All the quoins are pecked for a plaster facing.

The N. and S. walls of the tower rising above the E. range are of plain brickwork with stone parapet-walls but they incorporate some stonework in the lower exposed areas. The angles between them and the turrets are splayed as on the W.

The *Gatehall* (19 ft. by 23 ft.) has in the N. wall an original but much restored doorway to the Porter's Lodge with continuous chamfered jambs and four-centred head; the hatch to the E. of it is entirely plastered. The doorway in the S. wall is modern. The timber vault of 1845 rises from original stone springers on moulded corbels enriched with paterae; it is in two bays, with moulded ribs with carved and coloured shields-of-arms and foliage bosses at the intersections. The arms are, at the main intersections, of Edward III and the Tudors; elsewhere, of all the Masters (except Thomas Hill and John Arrowsmith) from John Redman to Montagu Butler inclusive, W. H. Thompson's and Butler's shields being later additions. The upper floors, which have been modernised, are reached by a stair in the S.W. turret approached only by the external S. doorway described above; a doorway into the lobby from the E. range is blocked. The floors of the N.W. turret have been cut through for a lift-shaft.

The rest of the E. range is of two storeys and attics and in part with a small cellar. It retains original or restored eaves on the E.; those on the W. were replaced by embattled parapets probably *c.* 1600; the roofs are covered with stone slates and tiles. The length N. of Great Gate has been entirely refaced on both sides, on the E. in 1856 by Salvin, who altered the former character, and on the W. in 1935, but here the measured drawing in Willis and Clark (II, 505, fig. 19) shows that at least the moulding of the original doorway to staircase 'E' was reproduced. This has chamfered jambs, moulded bases and a moulded four-centred head with a label and is similar to that to staircase 'G', both being in the late 15th-century part of the range; the doorways further S. differ from them. Inside, staircase 'E' is flanked on the N. by a set of chambers, on the S. by the Porter's Lodge; the first floor contains chambers. The ground floor retains a number of exposed late 15th-century ceiling-beams and wall-plates, stop-moulded in the N. set and stop-chamfered in the Porter's rooms. The room N. of the staircase is lined with early 18th-century fielded panelling with a dado-rail and cornice. The doorway from the Porter's N. room into the E. annexe is cut through an original window with moulded jambs and square head; the annexe is Salvin's replacement of the earlier arcaded annexe, presumably of the 17th century, shown in Loggan's engraving. The doorway to the N.W. turret of Great Gate has stop-chamfered jambs and a four-centred head; that to the N.E. turret has a four-centred head but is now largely concealed. The first floor has been modernised but retains in the N. wall a recess, presumably a blocked single-light window, with wide plain splays and chamfered segmental-pointed rear-arch.

The length of the E. range S. of Great Gate is of the late 15th century as far as some 6 ft. S. of the sixth W. window; the rest, as far as Trinity Lane, was begun in the last decade of the 16th century and finished probably in 1602. The walls, where not covered by later additions or cement, are of rubble with patchings of brick and with clunch and freestone ashlar dressings. On the E., the addition of Lecture Room Court and other buildings later has concealed or destroyed most of the original features. At the N. end some original walling faces on a small yard; it has a plinth and two three-light ground-floor windows, both entirely renewed. The three first-floor windows of clunch are original; the northernmost is of three lights, the others are of two, all with moulded reveals and two-centred openings in square heads with sunk spandrels. The dormer-windows have been renewed and the stack has been rebuilt. More original walling faces the small court further S.; the window on the ground floor and one of the two on the first floor are of two lights and similar to those just described but with plain chamfered and hollow-chamfered reveals; the third window is of three lights, with the centre light cut down to form a doorway to a balcony. The wall facing Lecture

Room Court was remodelled when the Court was formed in 1833–4 and is described with it.

The W. side has an ashlar plinth and an embattled parapet; the Roman cement facing of the entire area between them conceals all features of the walling. It is in twenty-three bays and, though variations occur in the horizontal spacing and details, the effect is one of uniformity from end to end. On the ground floor are doorways to staircases 'G' and 'H' and at entry 'I', in the fifth, eleventh and eighteenth bays respectively; the windows, of two and three lights, are as shown on the plan. On the first floor two and three-light windows occur over the openings below. The doorways have chamfered jambs and moulded four-centred heads; the mouldings of 'G' consist of an ogee and a casement, of 'H' and 'I' of reversed ogees. The window-openings are two-centred, under square heads with sunk spandrels. The two northern ground-floor windows are entirely renewed and the next four differ in detail from the rest southward. In the roof are eighteen renewed gabled dormer-windows. The lead rainwater pipes have shaped heads and are of the 18th century.

At the S. end, in the S.E. angle of Great Court, is an octagonal stair-turret, 'Mutton Hall Turret', rising well above the main parapet. It is of ashlar, entirely renewed in the mid 18th century, and has a plinth, a string at first-floor level and an embattled parapet. The doorway in the N. face has chamfered jambs and a depressed four-centred head under a square label. The staircase is lit by four single-light windows on the N.W. with four-centred openings in square heads with labels.

The S. end of the range was refaced in brick in the late 19th century and the windows are of the same date.

Inside the E. range, S. of Great Gate, the ground-floor rooms N. of staircase 'G' now contain the Bursar's offices, with the Bursary next S. of the same staircase. The former contain some exposed chamfered ceiling-beams; the exposed joists are laid flat, those in the second and third bays from the N. being painted red with a white stencilling of the sacred monogram 'ihc' in black-letter. Similar stencilling extends to a third bay in the next room S. The walls of the N. room are lined with panelling of *c.* 1600 with a fluted and arabesque-enriched frieze and incorporating, on the N. wall, round-headed panels enclosing enriched diagonal panels and, on the E. wall, geometrical panels over the fireplace; round-headed panels form the window-shutters. The *Bursary* is lined with early 18th-century fielded panelling with a dado-rail and modillion-cornice, the panelling on the E. wall being divided into three and a half bays by Ionic pilasters supporting entablature-blocks. The fireplace has an eared surround and shaped, fluted and enriched entablature.

The room next S. of the entry 'I' is lined with panelling of the same period as the foregoing, with a dado-rail and cornice and a bolection-moulded panel over the fireplace. The doors retain two original brass rim-locks. The rooms further S. contain some exposed chamfered ceiling-beams. Where later additions have been made on the E. the windows have been blocked to form recesses and cupboards.

On the first floor are exposed ceiling-beams including a moulded longitudinal beam in the room N. of staircase 'G', otherwise little old work remains except in the middle room of the set between staircases 'G' and 'H'. Here are two reused moulded and embattled ceiling-beams of the 15th century and a central longitudinal moulded beam with large leaf stops; the decorative plaster ceiling between of early 17th-century design has been inserted in modern times. The walls are lined with early 18th-century fielded panelling with dado-rail and cornice. Reset in the S.E. window are six roundels of heraldic glass of the late 17th or 18th century, mostly foreign, of (a) (unidentified 21), (b) probably a rebus, (c) Cronenburg of Utrecht, (d) Pyke quartering Upton, with the crest of Upton, (e) (unidentified 22), and (f) Neville of (?) Holt quartering Neville of Bulmer.

The *North Range* of Great Court contains the Chapel and Ante-chapel to the E., the former projecting three bays beyond the E. range, King Edward's Tower towards the middle and the old Library range to the W. The Master's Tower in the N.W. corner of the Court serves the Master's Lodge in the W. range.

The *Chapel* (204½ ft., including the Ante-chapel 69½ ft. long, by 34 ft.) was begun in replacement of the Chapel of King's Hall in the reign of Mary I. It was not completed until 1567 and the date of consecration is unknown. The walls are of rendered brick, stone and flint with ashlar dressings and much 19th-century ashlar facing; the roofs are covered with modern slates. An agreement in the sum of £80 for the walls was made with Perse, mason, at Michaelmas 1555. Large quantities of stone again came from the Franciscan friary and Ramsey Abbey, including nearly three thousand loads from the friary in the first year, and from the Cliffe, Barrington and Weldon quarries. The accounts that survive show that about eleven masons and labourers were at first employed, mounting later to thirty, and four carpenters. Timber was selected from Thorney Park. On 30 April 1556 Stephen Wallis, burgess and joiner of Cambridge, contracted for the fittings and decorative woodwork. The last payment to him was not made until April 1566.

The walls, unlike those of King's College Chapel, seem to have been raised uniformly excepting, as will be shown, towards the E. The inference from the accounts and Wallis' contract is that three bays were completed subsequently to the rest: at the end of the accounts for 1556–7 is the entry for ironwork for nineteen windows, below the transoms, which suggests that only some three-quarters of the Chapel had been carried to half the height; the contract includes for fretwork for a timber roof 34 ft. by only 157 ft. Again, much extra timber was bought and men other than Wallis were employed in the later years. The inference, and the identification of the bays with the three E. bays, seems confirmed by the circumstances already briefly described in the historical introduction to the College.

In 1559-60 Russell, probably John Russell of Westminster, came from London to 'devise the chapel work', Forde, the carpenter, consulted with him, and Henry Dickinson came to inspect the stonework. John Brewster was master-carpenter. By 1561 the building had progressed to the stage of some of the corbel-table being worked and glass being bought for the 'new [W.] window at the end of the new Chapel'. Between 1561 and 1563 Wallis was ceiling the W. end and William Blithe of Thaxted and Miles Jugg began the glazing with white and 'painted' glass, which continued into 1565; the date of glazing the E. and N.E. windows is not recorded. In 1564 more of the Chapel was roofed and ironwork for the E. window was bought, while the Junior Bursar's accounts for 1564–5 include for painting the inscription on the coping of the E. gable and for ironwork for the E. finials. Presumably the structure was then completed.

In 1565 and 1566 the stalls, screens and panelling at the E. end were being set up, the stalls by Wallis and the panelling by Arnold Pinckney, and in September 1567 the entries in the accounts of payments for the Chapel end. None of the original glass and only fragments of the 16th-century woodwork survive.

The internal arrangements until the early 18th century are described by Willis and Clark (II, 574–8). The work of repair and refitting envisaged at the beginning of that century was started in 1706, and by 1717 nearly £5,500 had been spent upon it, but the cost was met largely by subscription and no detailed accounts survive. The date of the woodwork is not recorded; Woodward the carver was paid £79 between 1719 and 1721, over the Vice-Master's stall is carved the name of Dr. Richard Walker, who was elected in 1734, and the greater part of the refitting was completed during the Mastership (1700–42) of Richard Bentley. The carving in 1756 by John Woodward of twenty-six shields-of-arms, presumably of the thirty-four still on the stalls and screen, would seem to have been a later embellishment, perhaps of blank shields. Most of Bentley's fittings survive in position.

In 1832 the fabric was restored, the ceiling elaborated and the seating extended under the supervision of Edward Blore, at a cost of £2,511. In 1867 the roof was repaired and the earlier 19th-century elaboration removed; and between 1868 and 1873 the E. end and the S. side of the building were ashlared. Meanwhile the screen was reduced in width and it and the stalls were moved 7 ft. to the W., more seating was installed, and the *Vestry*, *Choir-room*, and *South Porch* were added, all to the designs of A. W. Blomfield; at the same period the organ was enlarged. Thereafter, under the supervision of the same architect, the painted decoration of the Chapel and the new glazing to a theme devised by Westcott and Hort were undertaken. The cost of the repairs and decoration was nearly £20,000. The roof above the panelled ceiling is entirely of the 19th century.

The Chapel has a moulded plinth, an embattled parapet, and diagonal and plain four-stage buttresses surmounted by panelled and crocketed pinnacles. The ashlar of the E. end is of the 19th-century except that of the low-pitched embattled parapet-wall, which has an original inscription in Roman capitals and Arabic numerals, 'Anno 1564' and 'Domus Mea domus orationis vocabitur' (*Matthew xxi, 13*), and parapet-string with carved bosses, one of a bearded man's head, the rest foliage. The transomed E. window, blocked in 1706, is of nine ogee cinquefoiled lights with subarcuated vertical tracery in a four-centred head with a label with fleur-de-lys and rose stops. Principal mullions articulate the lights into three groups of three; the transom is embattled and the lights below have cinquefoiled heads. The dressings are all renewed.

The N. and S. walls (Plate 254) are each in twelve bays of slightly differing lengths. The N. wall between the buttresses is faced with Roman cement and other rendering from plinth to parapet-string. Projecting between the eighth and ninth bays is an octagonal stair-turret with loop-lights with square and two-centred heads in the N. and W. sides; it has a rebuilt top stage containing an original doorway opening on the roof with square head, moulded and stop-chamfered jambs and pediment; the domical ogee roof is of stone, with crockets and finial. The parapet-string of the S. wall is enriched with bosses carved with foliage, a lion and the demi-figure of a bishop. In every bay except the westernmost on the N. and the fourth on the S., where the E. range adjoins, is a transomed window of four cinquefoiled lights in a four-centred head with a label; on the S. this last has returned diagonal stops. The S. door, in the eleventh bay, with shafted jambs and moulded four-centred head, is entirely renewed. The blocked W. window retains the mullions and tracery showing inside the building; outside only the blocking and part of the damaged label appear. It is similar in division to the E. window and has unusual vertical cusping to the lights and narrow vertical tracery in a high four-centred head. A small late 14th-century window looking into the Chapel by the N. angle of the foregoing, of two cinquefoiled two-centred lights under a frieze of trefoiled curvilinear tracery-panelling, has been removed to make way for the modern war-memorial. It opened from an E. extension of the S. first-floor set of rooms in 'King's Hostel', at one time the Master's *camera*.

The roof, continuous from end to end, is in twenty-four bays with a flat timber ceiling at the level of the tie-beams. From wall-posts on moulded and carved stone corbels spring short shallow braces with pierced tracery in the spandrels. On the tenth tie-beam are the letters R B Mr. (Robert Beaumont, Master 1561–7) and a roughly-cut face. Each bay is subdivided into four panels from N. to S. by longitudinal beams, which also bear initials and dates, a beam in the seventh bay IT and NS, the eight bay Rh (or RK) twice, and the tenth bay 1561 twice with ER on the S. wall-plate. HR is on both the wall-plates in the twelfth bay. All the main timbers are moulded and carved with folding leaf, vine and other running foliage ornament; they and the panels are enriched with late 19th-century painting and gilding.

Fittings—*Brass:* In Ante-chapel, of John Beaumont, 1565, rectangular plate with black-letter inscription. *Communion Rails* (Plate 7): forming a three-sided enclosure, of oak, with moulded base-rail, moulded and enriched top-rail, pedestals with panelled and carved dies, and infilling with elaborate pierced foliation, early 18th-century.

Monuments and *Floor-slabs. Monuments*: In Ante-chapel—free-standing centrally towards W., (1) of Sir Isaac Newton, [1727], of veined white marble, full-length standing figure (Plate 260) in academic dress holding small prism, on base resting on tall pedestal with black marble step; the base inscribed, on the E., 'Newton. Qui genus humanum ingenio superavit.', on the W., 'Posuit Robertus Smith S.T.P. Collegii hujus S. Trinitatis Magister MDCCLV. L. F. Roubiliac inv^it^ et sc^it^.' Freestanding to S.E., (2) of Francis Bacon, 1626, white marble seated figure on pedestal with inscriptions including, on the E., 'H. Weekes. Sc. 1845'; a copy of that in St. Michael's, St. Albans, and presented by Dr. William Whewell, Master 1841–66. On N. wall, (3) of Thomas Kynaston Selwyn, A.B., 1834, white marble tablet with pedimental head containing bay-leaves, on black marble backing, by Tomson and Son, Cambridge; (4) of Francis Hooper, S.T.P., 1763, white marble bust (Plate 19) standing against veined marble pyramidal backing and flanked by books, all on the cornice of a black marble inscription-tablet, signed 'N. Read int. et sct.'; (5) of Richard Porson, 1808, Fellow, Regius Professor of Greek, white marble bust, signed 'Chantrey, sculptor', with inscription-tablet below; (6) of Daniel Lock, 1754, white marble bust (Plate 19) flanked by books and attributes of Painting, Sculpture and Music, all against a black marble shaped backing and on a shelf with inscription-tablet below, of similar material, signed 'L. F. Roubiliac sculpt.'; (7) of Peter Paul Dobree, A.M., 1825, Fellow, Regius Professor of Greek, white marble bust against black marble backing (Plate 20), on foliated corbel incorporated in inscription-tablet below signed 'Baily, R.A. sct. London', inscription by Bishop Kaye. On S. wall, (8) of Richard Stevenson, A.M., 1837, white marble oval tablet flanked by laurels, signed 'W. G. Nicholl, Scult., London'; (9) of the Rev. Thomas Jones, A.M., 1807, white marble bust A.M., 1830, Fellow, white and grey marble neo-Greek tablet; on buttress on S. wall, (16) of John Davies, S.T.B., 1817, Vice-Master, square white marble tablet (Plate 17) with wreathed inscription-roundel with cup and paten below and border with Greek fret, all on grey marble backing; (17) of Samuel Hawkes, A.M., 1829, Fellow, white marble sarcophagus-shaped tablet; (18) of James Lambert, A.M., 1823, Regius Professor of Greek, white marble sarcophagus-shaped tablet, corbel below signed 'Crake, London'; against S. wall, (19) of Thomas Seckford, 1624, painted stone canopied tomb-chest with effigy, removed from N. wall of Ante-chapel in 1831–2, much damaged and mutilated, chest with panelled front with inscriptions, hour-glass, and two shields-of-arms, of Seckford impaling Brewster and of Seckford, effigy of boy in academic dress lying on side with head originally propped on right arm, forearm and head missing, canopy in two stages each of two bays, the lower stage with Corinthian columns and panelled responds supporting an ovolo-moulded cornice carved with cherub-heads, now defaced, the upper stage with flanking Corinthian columns on pedestals and a central corbel

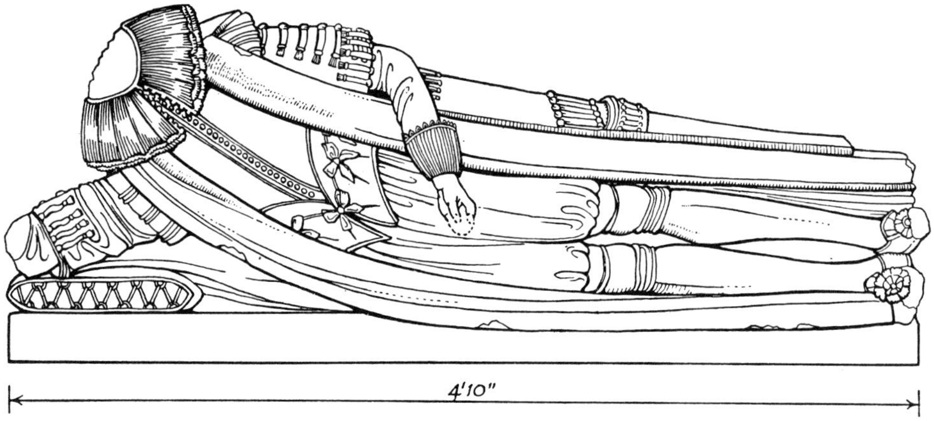

against dark marble backing, with inscription-tablet below supported on corbels, one signed 'Nollekens Ft.'; (10) of Isaac Hawkins Brown, A.M., 1760, white marble tablet with semicircular top containing three female figures, roundel above with portrait head, signed on the tablet 'Flax[man] R.[A]. scul[psit]', set up 1804; (11) of Roger Cotes, 1716, Fellow, Lucasian Professor, white marble cartouche with acanthus, scrolls, cherub-heads and shield-of-arms of Cotes, inscription by Dr. Bentley. In Choir-room—on E. wall, (12) of John Wordsworth, A.M., 1840, Fellow, white marble bust against black marble backing (Plate 20), cornice of inscription-tablet below signed 'H. Weekes sc. 1840'; (13) of George Chare, 1676–7, white marble draped cartouche (Plate 16) with flaming urn and smaller cartouches above and below, the upper with the carved arms of Chare, all on a scroll-corbel signed 'I. Latham', set up by Albion Chare, his brother. In Vestry—on E. wall, (14) of the Hon. Charles Fox Maitland, A.M., 1818, son of James, 8th Earl of Lauderdale, white marble tablet with two mourning angels, corbel below signed 'Richard Westmacott, R.A., invt. et fecit'; on N. wall, (15) of Frederick Malkin, supporting round-headed arches below a plain ovolo-moulded cornice, the corbel being in the form of a horizontal robed figure, now headless; painted on the back wall of the lower stage are three quotations, one in Greek from *I Thessalonians, iv, 16*, the others, on roundels below, in Latin from *Job xix, 25*, and *II Timothy i, 12*; on the tomb-chest is carved 'Henricus Sekford patruus nepoti posuit, Gulielmus Hardwik curavit, Edwardus Woodrofe exculpsit'; fragments lying on the monument include the small figure of a woman, part of an obelisk and three pedestals, the last with six shields-of-arms on the dies, of Seckford impaling (a) (unidentified 23), (b) Jenny, (c) Cranwell, (d) Goldingham, (e) Purry and (f) Harlow.

Floor-slabs: In Chapel—at E. end, of (1) Richard Bentley, S.T.P.R., 1742; (2) William Lort Mansel, S.T.P., 1820, Bishop of Bristol, Master; (3) Robert Smith, S.T.P., 1768, Master. In Ante-chapel—(4) Humphrey Babington, S.T.P., 1691–2, Vice-Master, with shield-of-arms of Babington; (5) Elizmar Smith, 1758, sister of Robert Smith, Master, with shield-of-arms of Smith; (6) William Lynnet, S.T.P., 1699–1700, Vice-

Master; (7) George Chare, M.A., 1676–7, Fellow, with shield-of-arms of Chare; (8) Peter Courthope, 1695, with shield-of-arms of Courthope; (9) Richard Porson, 1808; (10) Daniel Brattell, S.T.P., 1694–5, Fellow; (11) Dionysius Lisle, LL.B., 1727, auditor and registrar of the College, etc., with shield-of-arms of Lisle; (12) Edward Walpole of Houghton, A.M., 1688–9, Fellow, with achievement-of-arms of Walpole; (13) Thomas Rotherham, A.M., 1702, with shield-of-arms of Rotherham; (14) William Corker, A.M., 1702, Fellow and benefactor, laid down by the College in 1709, payment of £14 10*s*. being made to Robert Grumbold (see Bursar's Accts. 1709–10); (15) Thomas Bainbrig, S.T.P., 1703, Vice-Master, with shield-of-arms of Bainbrig; (16) Sir Thomas Sclater, Bt., 1684, Fellow, with achievement-of-arms of Sclater; (17) Thomas Smith, S.T.P., 1713–14, Fellow, Vice-Master; (18) John Wordsworth, 1839; along W. end (19–32), small paving-stones with 19th-century inscriptions: W. H., S.T.B., 1715, Fellow; J.B., 1598; H.P., 1697; E.B., A.M., 1718–19, Fellow; J.C., S.T.B., 1714, Fellow; Moore Meredith, S.T.B., 1789; J.N., 1683, Master; John Wilson, S.T.P., 1754; P.C., A.M., 1717–18, Fellow; Stephen Whisson, S.T.B., 1783; N.C., 1633; W.G., 1702–03; W.D., M.A., 1713, Fellow; A.H.

Organ and *Organ-case*. On Screen between Chapel and Ante-chapel: organ, begun by Bernard Smith, completed by Christopher Schrider (Conclusion Book, 3 May 1708) and subsequently enlarged; organ-case (Plate 258), of oak, in two stages, the lower close panelled, the upper jettied on carved console-brackets and in two main bays to E. and W. divided and flanked by four towers of pipes, the shorter middle two paired and flanking a narrow subsidiary central bay; the towers supported on paired cherub-heads and with crowning entablatures and pierced pelmets; the main bays with three panels of exposed pipes with carved pelmets etc., the middle panel extending up into a high entablature and flanked by scrolls to the towers, the entablature having a broken curved pediment with central pedestal supporting an elaborate foliate feature; the narrow central bay with lofty elaborately carved cresting; centre part *c*. 1710, the remainder, that is the flanking towers and adjoining panels, represent a late 19th-century enlargement to N. and S. by Messrs. Hill. Choir-organ, over E. face of Screen, case with central tower flanked by two panels of exposed pipes with cornices and pierced pelmets etc., the outer panels higher than the inner, all the members and the plinth with carved foliated enrichment, *c*. 1710 (see also Screen, under *Panelling*).

Panelling, Screen and *Stalls*: In Chapel, lining the N. and S. walls to sill-level and returned on the E. and W., bolection-moulded panelling in one tall height above a dado, or fixed benches, and divided into bays by coupled attached Corinthian columns and pilasters on pedestals supporting an entablature; the six E. bays and the E. returns are those demarcated by columns, the W. ten bays and the W. returns by pilasters; the necking mouldings are continuous and the space above, between the pilaster caps, is filled with elaborate carving (Plate 33) partly in the round of garlands, drapery, cherub-heads and shields-of-arms with the names of the bearers below on scrolls; the enriched entablature has console-brackets the full depth of the frieze supporting a cornice of wide projection with coffered soffit and surmounted, on the Screen, by a gallery-front of bolection-moulded panelling. The square-headed doorway in the middle of the Screen is flanked by attached Corinthian columns on pedestals supporting paired brackets under a canopy-like projection of the main cornice, on which stands the choir-organ (see above); symmetrically to S. and N. of the doorway, the Master's and Vice-Master's stalls have detached side columns and responds supporting open curved pediments with cherub-heads carved on the frieze of the entablature-blocks; the seats are within semi-domed niches with shell heads with 'R. Bentley Mr. Coll.' and 'R. Walker V-Mr.' respectively carved in Roman capitals on the moulded archivolts; above the niches are carved foliage, garlands and shields-of-arms, and beside them are elaborate scrolled arm-rests; the close-panelled desk-enclosures have enriched members. The remainder of the stalls, arranged as shown on the plan, have desks with plain close-panelled fronts. The shields, reading from N.E., by W., to S.E., are of (i) Rud, (ii) Knight; (iii) Trevor, (iv) Campion; (v) Hacket, (vi) James; (vii) Newton, (viii) Montagu; (ix) Stubb; (x) Cotes; (xi) Burrell, (xii) Eden; (xiii) Bathurst; (xiv) Cressar, (xv) Barrington; (xvi) Perry; (xvii) Walker; (xviii) Bentley (Master's stall); (xix) Pierpoint; (xx) Montagu; (xxi) Bacon, (xxii) Modd; (xxiii) Chamberlayne, (xxiv) Miller; (xxv) Jurin; (xxvi) Ekins; (xxvii) Ayloffe, (xxviii) Hutchinson; (xxix) Middleton, (xxx) Moyle; (xxxi) Smith, (xxxii) Colman; (xxxiii) Fuller, (xxxiv) Banks. The woodwork described, except the desks, is enriched with modern gilding. The W. face of the Screen (Plate 258) is uncoloured; it is of the Doric order and in five unequal bays divided and flanked by fluted columns, those on the flanks being square, supporting a continuous entablature; the end columns are engaged and flank tall semi-domed niches with panelled seats and moulded imposts and archivolts; the two middle columns are free-standing, the back wall being recessed; the three recessed bays are divided and flanked by attached half and quarter columns and contain the doorway to the Chapel in the middle and niches similar to those just described to each side. The full Doric entablature supports a gallery-front of bolection-moulded panelling divided into bays by panelled pedestals. Within the thickness of the S. end of the Screen is a stair to the organ-gallery above. The limiting dates for the woodwork are given above; stylistically it is *c*. 1735; twenty-six of the shields were not carved until 1756. Extra rows of seating and wrought-iron desks in front of the centre blocks of stalls are late 19th-century. In Ante-chapel, lining N., S. and W. walls to a height of 7 ft. above fixed benches, oak panelling divided into narrow bays by attenuated pilasters and with carved 'antique' heads flanked by foliated scrolls over the segmental top of each panel and below the main cornice, parts perhaps mid 16th-century, largely late 19th-century; supporting the 19th-century benches, parts of moulded and shaped arm-rests cut from oak stalls, 16th-century.

Reredos (Plate 258): against the E. wall, of oak, painted and gilded, of baldachino form, with four grouped Corinthian columns at each side on panelled pedestals supporting enriched entablature-blocks with modillion-cornices; from the last springs a semicircular arch with moulded archivolt and wide coffered soffit, each coffer containing a carved rosette; flanking the arch and rising from the entablature blocks, elaborately carved scrolls with urns upon the volutes support an open pediment with all the members enriched; the tympanum and the rest of the space above the arch and between the scrolls are filled with palm-leaves and foliation of much complexity with, in the centre, a triangle supported by cherub-heads and painted with AΩ on a rayed roundel; the back wall of the arch has a dado of bolection-moulded panelling and short returns of the order etc. framing late 19th-century paintings, a *Pietà* below, the Ascension above (see Library, for the painting formerly here); the E. window was being blocked in 1706 presumably to provide the setting for this reredos, early 18th-century. *Screen*: see under *Panelling*. *Stalls*: see under *Panelling*.

King Edward's Tower (Plate 254), sometimes known as the 'Clock Tower', adjoining the Chapel on the W., formerly stood some 90 ft. further S. where it was the gatehouse, preceding Great Gate, to King's Hall. Begun in 1428, the master-mason was probably John (?) Dodington; John Brown and Henry Jekke of Barrington supplied the clunch for it; stone came from Burwell and Hinton. John Douse was the chief carpenter and the accounts of 1428–9 include payments to him for the centering of the gateway. Timber came from Haverhill. The battlements and vaults were added and the stonework evidently finished in 1432; thereafter the gates were made and mounted and the carving, which included a statue of the king, coloured. The date of removal to the present position is shown by the accounts for 1599–1600, which include for digging the new foundations and for carrying the stonework to store pending rebuilding the following year. A number of alterations were made during re-erection; the N. turrets were superimposed and neither the staircase in the N.W. turret nor the main vault of the gate-hall retained; furthermore, compression seems to have been necessary to fit the laterally constricted space between the two buildings, the Chapel and Old Library, to E. and W. A number of decorative additions are noted below. In 1610 the clock and bell were inserted, but the former was renewed and a new clock-face made in 1726–7, when also two more bells were added. The timber bell-turret is of the mid 19th-century, though following in form and silhouette that, probably of 1610, shown by Loggan; it was taken down, repaired and re-erected in 1945. In 1752-3 Charles Bottomley was paid £88 for repairing 'and beautifying the turrets and great gate of the Clock' and for stone, presumably for some refacing.

The Tower is of coarse shelly oolite, except the brick N. wall. It is rectangular on plan with octagonal angle turrets on the S. continued above the main parapets and embattled; the turrets on the N. now rise from within the fourth storey, their N. faces being flush with the N. wall-face. Of the four storeys, the first and second floors are reached from the Old Library stair and the top floor by a stair in the S.W. turret. The Tower has a moulded plinth, strings dividing the front into three and the S. turrets into four stages, and, except on the E., a main parapet embattled on the S. and W., plain on the N.

The S. archway has chamfered jambs and moulded high four-centred head with a moulded label (p. 394) with returned stops, that to the W. carved with a shield now much decayed charged with a saltire for Nevile.[1] Over the head of the arch is a strapwork panel of *c.* 1600 enclosing the carved and painted arms of the College with a painted inscription below, 'Tertivs Edwardvs fama svper æthera notvs', extending between two 15th-century shields in cusped panels over the haunches of the arch; the shields are carved and painted with the arms of England on the E. and new France and England quarterly on the W.

The niche in the middle of the first floor, for the columns of which payment to the carver Paris Andrew occurs in the Junior Bursar's accounts of 1600–01, has a shell head and flanking Ionic columns on pedestals supporting a cornice with strapwork cresting incorporating a roundel painted with the arms of England impaling old France. In the niche is a statue of *c.* 1600 of Edward III, with metal crown, holding an orb and metal sword, the last encircled by three crowns; on the sill is the painted inscription 'Pvgna pro patria 1377'. The windows each side of the niche are of two lights with two-centred openings in square heads with sunk spandrels and moulded labels; the labels butt against the flanking turrets on the extremities. The four-light window on the second floor has openings with polygonal heads and sunk spandrels; most of the upper-half is concealed by the clock-face. To each side of the window are crowned strapwork roundels of *c.* 1600 containing the arms of new France and England quarterly on the E., and of England on the W., each in a Garter. The two windows on the third floor are similar to those on the first floor but with ill-fitting carved crestings instead of labels. Level with the cresting, splayed across the angles between wall and turrets, are carved lions' masks below the main parapet-string; this last is enriched with paterae and surmounted by a band of curvilinear tracery-panelling. The band has been compressed to fit the space between the turrets; above it, the embattled parapet is panelled.

The turrets have a S. window in each stage consisting of a single light with four-centred opening in a square head with a label; additional oval windows low in the second stage are both of *c.* 1600.

The rebuilt timber bell-turret is hexagonal and in two diminishing stages with open arcaded sides, the arcading in the upper stage being in two heights; the lead-covered dome, of reversed ogee profile, has a tall timber and iron finial and weathervane. It contains three bells: 1st inscribed and dated 'Trinitas in unitate resonat 1610 Ricardus Holdfeld me fecit'; 2nd inscribed 'Cum voco venite Thomas Osborn Downham Norfolk fecit 1795'; 3rd dated 1726; all were recast in 1910.

The N. side has the two lower floors largely concealed; on the ground floor towards the E. is a 15th-century archway with moulded four-centred head; it opens to a passage to 'King's Hostel' with a rendered pointed-segmental barrel vault. On the second floor is a two-light window similar to those to the S. on the first floor; the small rectangular two-light window on the third floor has a timber frame and mullion. The E. side is concealed. The W. side, where it rises above the adjoining range, is faced with Roman cement; on

[1] The arms of Nevile are those of Thomas Nevile (Master 1593–1615); those of Neville refer to other branches of the Neville family. See Armorial.

the top floor is a two-light window similar to those at the same level on the S. but with a label and no cresting.

The Gatehall ($15\frac{1}{2}$ ft. by $15\frac{3}{4}$ ft.) and the rest of the interior have been modernised. The doorway from the Old Library staircase to the *Treasury* on the second floor has chamfered jambs and a high four-centred head and retains an old nail-studded plank door with original wrought-iron embattled lockplate.

The *Old Library Range*, towards the W. end of the N. side of Great Court, is of three storeys. The Library formerly occupied most or all of the top floor; the books were removed from it in 1694–5. The range will be seen to occupy one of the two positions suggested for it in the 16th-century plan of the College reproduced by Willis and Clark (II, fig. 10 facing p. 465), but it follows English tradition in style, not the colonnaded plan there proposed. The accounts of 1589–90 include for stone bought from one Hall. By 1600 the range was built but not completed. In 1601 the N. parapet was rendered, the staircase was plastered, the ironwork bought for the interior, and the lead flashings of the roof adapted to the 'new tower' (King Edward's Tower). The N. extension of the Master's Lodge on the W. of Great Court was built at much the same time, but the Old Library range, through to the external W. wall, was completed first. The whole exterior is described here in the correct architectural context but part of the interior is allocated to the Master and accordingly, with the exception noted below, is described with the Lodge.

Entries in the accounts of 1665–6 show that the Library had been burnt and the roof destroyed; the damage seems to have necessitated rebuilding much of the N. and W. walls of the range and the addition of buttresses on the N. Subsequently the conversion of the top floor into chambers involved some alterations to the windows. In 1812–13 the S. side was faced with Roman cement by James Clabbon, and in 1873 five of the S. windows on the top floor were renewed.

The rendered S. side is in eight bays, with a plinth and an embattled parapet. In the second and sixth bays are doorways with chamfered jambs, moulded four-centred arches in square heads enriched with shaped dentils and moulded labels; the more easterly doorway has blank shields in the spandrels. The windows generally are of two and three lights, those on the ground and first floors with polygonal openings, those on the second floor with two-centred openings, all in square heads with sunk spandrels and moulded labels. The turret, the Master's Tower, overlapping on the W. is described with the Master's Lodge.

The N. side is of clunch, rubble and brick, with a plinth and a white brickwork parapet, the last renewed in 1756–7. It is divided unequally by five 17th-century four-stage buttresses of white brick with Ketton stone dressings. In the E. division are two bays of windows, in the next three, and in the third two; in the fourth a modern two-storey addition has been built between the buttresses; in the fifth is one bay of windows. Except in the end bay the ground-floor windows are of one, two and three lights with two-centred openings in square heads with sunk spandrels and in part restored; presumably many windows from the demolished buildings were available in 1590–1600 and the foregoing are probably earlier features reused; the seventh window, of three lights, may be wholly modern; the end window is of the early 18th century with rectangular sash-hung opening and moulded stone architrave. On the first floor are two windows similar to that last described, a third taller and a fourth of the same date but with a timber frame, three of one, two and three lights similar to the older ones described but the three-light window over that below again perhaps wholly modern, and one modern two-light window. On the second floor one original but much restored three-light window with four-centred openings in a square head remains at the E. end; of the nine other windows, three are of the early 18th century, as described above, though one is now blocked, and the rest modern.

The W. end has a plinth and parapet-wall continued from the N. side; the latter rises in the middle in a low-pitched gable. The wall up to about half the height is of rough clunch ashlar with small patches of brick and, above, of brick with some Ketton ashlar patches. The windows on the ground and first floors are both of the early 18th century and similar to those of the same date on the N. already described; flanking the head of the lower and the sill of the upper window are traces of blocked windows relating to the original floor-levels inside (see Master's Lodge). On the second floor are two windows and the patching where a third window has been removed; those surviving are of three and two lights with four-centred openings in square heads; the first is entirely restored, the second perhaps original.

The interior contains Fellows' and undergraduates' rooms, except the westernmost room on the ground floor and the W. half of the first floor; these are part of the Master's Lodge. The first floor room next W. of staircase 'B', which was added to the Lodge in exchange for the Master's S. rooms taken over by the College in 1920, is the Master's Library; being a modern allocation, it is here described.

On the ground floor are exposed chamfered ceiling-beams. Staircase 'B' rises only to the first floor, staircase 'C' to the full height; the latter is that finished in 1601. On the first floor, the E. room has an oak fireplace-surround made up of materials of *c.* 1600, with flanking enriched coupled and fluted Doric pilasters supporting an entablature forming an overmantel in three bays with frieze-panels containing arabesques. The small room adjoining on the N.W. is lined with 18th-century fielded panelling with a dado-rail and cornice. The *Master's Library* has only a secondary approach from staircase 'B'; the floor is at the original level and lower than that in the westernmost room. The walls are lined with modern bookcases and panelling, but the latter incorporates six enriched arched panels of *c.* 1600 in the overmantel. On the second floor, the middle room is lined with late 18th-century panelling with a dado-rail and has a plaster dentil-cornice; the fireplace has a wood surround with a traceried frieze, cornice-shelf, and eared panel in the overmantel. The large room next W. has an elaborate cellular plaster ceiling probably of 1873. The self-contained W. set is approached by the Master's Tower and entered through a small lobby partly lined with reused panelling of *c.* 1600 and containing a flight of 17th-century stairs with close strings, turned balusters, square newels and moulded handrail. The set contains more reused panelling of *c.* 1600 and a bolection-moulded fireplace-surround of *c.* 1700.

The *West Range* of Great Court contains the Hall in about the middle with the Kitchen etc. to the S., and the Master's Lodge to the N. The Hall and all to the S. are almost wholly of *c.* 1605 and *c.* 1775, the earlier being part of Dr. Nevile's great rebuilding scheme. Some account of the former buildings on the site, of which only fragments survive, is given in the historical introduction to the College.

The *Hall* (Plate 253) (40½ ft. by 101¼ ft., including the Screens 9¾ ft. wide overall), begun in 1604 and slated the following year, was designed by Ralph Symons and built by John Symes. Thomas Yates was paid for the slating and Gilbert Wigge for the paving. Clunch came from Barrington and Eversden and limestone from King's Cliffe; ragstone was reused from Cambridge Castle. Francis Carter was master carpenter; an agreement with him for the timberwork in the Hall, Buttery and Kitchen, but not the roof of the last, was made in February 1603–04 in the sum of £212, the first payment being made to him in June 1604 and the last recorded in September 1605.

The wainscoting was made by Andrew Chapman by agreement dated February 1604–05; the wood was brought from King's Lynn. Both Carter and Chapman, the former by evidence of the accounts, the latter by inference, were responsible for the Screen. The windows were not glazed until 1607–08. The total cost of the work has been computed at £1,994. In 1651 the arms of the Commonwealth were set up over the dais panelling but were replaced by the Stuart Royal arms, carved by George Woodroffe, in 1660. The cellars below the Hall were dug in 1751–2. In 1866 the interior was restored and the dais increased in depth. In 1955 the dais panelling and the Royal arms were taken down, restored, recoloured and regilded and in the following year the screen was similarly renovated, *in situ*. The 'Tribunal' against the outside of the W. wall is described with Nevile's Court.

The Hall is open to the roof. The walls have been largely refaced outside in modern times with Ketton and Clipsham stone ashlar; the infilling is brick, four courses measuring 10 ins. The N. wall is of modern brickwork. The roofs are slate-covered. The E. and W. sides have plinths and embattled parapets; they are generally similar; both are in seven bays, with oriel-windows filling the second bay from the N. and the other bays divided and flanked by three-stage buttresses, those on the E. with pinnacles rising above the parapet-wall, those on the W. stopping just below the parapet-string. In each free bay, above a high moulded string, is a stone-mullioned window. The windows in the N. bay are of three and the rest are of four transomed lights with four-centred openings in square heads below horizontal labels continued as strings that butt against the buttresses and return round the oriel-windows. These last are of four lights on the face, three on each canted side and two on the straight returns, all being divided into equal heights by four transoms. The lights have four-centred openings, below each transom as well as at the head, and sunk spandrels. The main embattled parapet is returned round the oriels, that on the E., and possibly that on the W., supplanting the strapwork cresting shown in both Loggan's and West's engravings of the College, of *c.* 1688 and 1740.

The porch bounded by the buttresses in the S.E. bay is one storey high and approached up eight steps, elliptical on plan. The outer arch has a semicircular head with moulded archivolt and keystone, enriched network diapering on the soffit, and enriched responds with moulded caps and bases; flanking it are attached Roman Doric columns on pedestals supporting an entablature surmounted by a modern strapwork cresting, reproducing that shown by Loggan, incorporating a square panel carved with the College arms. The steps were given their present form between *c.* 1688 and 1740.

The reset E. and W. doorways to the Screens-passage are of the 15th century; they have moulded jambs and two-centred arches in square heads with traceried spandrels and a 17th-century horizontal string above; both are extensively restored; that to the W. has a segmental-pointed rear-arch, some brickwork in the splays and a four-centred brick relieving-arch. The oak doors are of the early 17th century, with applied nail-studded mouldings forming rectangular and radiating panels, wrought-iron strap-hinges, two with fleur-de-lys terminals, and wickets.

The N. and S. ends of the Hall are gabled. The gables rise clear of the adjoining buildings; each contains a restored window of five mullioned and transomed lights with four-centred openings in a square head with a label. The copings and finials are modern and the S. gable has been refaced with white brick, probably in 1862 when the window was re-opened after being blocked since 1774.

The timber lantern at the roof-ridge is hexagonal and in three stages, with a shaped lead-covered dome rising to a gilded ball and slender obelisk-finial supporting a wrought-iron weathervane; the vane is pierced with the arms of the College. Almost filling each face of each stage is a glazed window, and at the corners of the upper stages are gilded wrought-iron scrolls rising from squat pedestals on the cornices of the stages below. The lantern is generally similar to that shown by Loggan except that the heads of the openings in the two lower stages are now two-centred and that scrolls replace small vanes on the top stage. The accounts for the original louvre include for 'the great and the lesser' vanes and the 'spire'; thus, although the structure is much repaired, and glazed, the original form is probably perpetuated. John Atkynson was paid for the original boarding.

The interior (Plate 256) retains the original double-framed timber roof in seven bays divided and flanked by hammer-beam trusses with three collars. The arched braces from the shaped corbels to the hammer-beams and from the hammer-posts to the lowest collars are rusticated; at the junctions, below posts and collars, are shaped pendants. Longitudinal plates across the heads of the hammer-posts support the principals and intermediate principals and are stiffened by curved longitudinal braces from the posts, again with pendants at the junctions. In each roof-slope are four purlins. All the spandrels and the spaces between the first and second collars are filled with open arcading of semicircular arches springing from square and turned Ionic columns tapering to the base; the arches have keyblocks with small turned pendants. Between the second and third collars are shaped posts only. The roof is ceiled above the third collar and below the common rafters. Between the wall-plate and the lowest purlin is close-panelled arcading. Most of the timber mouldings are of Classical profile. The lantern-opening in the middle bay is hexagonal.

Cross-Section through Hall
TRINITY COLLEGE

The panelling behind the dais and returned into the oriel-windows is seven panels in the height and divided into five bays on the N. wall, one on each return, and one on the N. sides of the oriels by Ionic pilasters on pedestals supporting an entablature just below window-transom level. The pilasters are panelled and enriched with arabesques; the pedestals contain lozenge-shaped panels; the entablature has arabesque frieze-panels separated by foliated and mask-brackets, the middle bracket being carved with the arms of Nevile. All the main panels are subdivided into a geometrical pattern of smaller panels. Surmounting the three middle bays on the N. wall is an elaborate pyramidal strapwork cresting flanked by obelisk-finials and incorporating terminal figures supporting an entablature to frame the Stuart Royal arms; these last are carved in high relief and with the motto 'Semper eadem' on a ribbon below, the motto being imposed to adapt the arms to Queen Anne (before 1707). In the end bays are projecting door-cases with fluted pilaster-strips supporting entablatures with mask-brackets and strapwork cresting flanked by spiked ball-finials. The doors are uniform with the rest of the panelling. The whole is painted and heightened with gilding. Except the Royal arms by Woodruffe, the woodwork is doubtless part of the work of Andrew Chapman for which he was paid £40 and an earnest of £3 6*s.* 8*d.* in 1605. The panelling on the S. sides of the oriels and on the E. and W. walls is renewed but incorporates some early 17th-century arabesque frieze-panels and some old grotesque masks.

The *Screen* (Plate 257) is in two stages and in five symmetrical but unequal bays divided and flanked by superimposed Ionic and Corinthian columns on pedestals. The middle and end bays of the lower stage and all the bays of the upper are divided into two subsidiary bays by terminal figures. The entablatures of both orders are continuous, returning over the columns. Surmounting the Corinthian entablature is a pyramidal strapwork cresting to each main bay divided and flanked by pierced strapwork obelisks over the columns. The second and fourth bays of the lower stage contain segmental-headed doorways with fanlights; the rest, that is, the six subsidiary bays are close panelled. The ten subsidiary bays of the upper stage have, above a panelled dado, arched openings with removable shutter-boards (Plate 257). The Ionic columns and responds are carved with arabesques to one-third their height and fluted above; their pedestals contain lozenge-shaped panels and their entablature has carved masks on the entablature-blocks, arabesques and roses in the frieze, and a dentil-cornice. The terminal figures in this stage have baskets of fruits on their heads and spring from tapering shafts enriched with arabesques, strapwork, etc.; the close panelling is framed in a geometrical pattern. The doors and fanlights are of the late 19th century, but the enriched keyblocks and spandrels are original. In the upper stage, the columns are diapered and fluted, the terminal figures support Ionic caps, and the pedestals of both are continued as a dado and the whole carved with elaborate foliation, cartouches and fruits. The Corinthian entablature is enriched with grotesque masks and jewel ornament on the frieze and acanthus on the cornice. The arched openings have keyblocks with turned pendants, enriched responds with caps and bases and foliated spandrels. Incorporated in the cresting over the three middle bays are the carved arms of the College in the centre, and achievements of Nevile quartering Neville, Albany, Middleham, Albany, Middleham, Clavering, (unidentified 24) on the E., Hide on the W. The shutter-boards (Plate 257) are covered with carved foliation, grotesques, masks, winged mermaids, human figures with extremities ending in scrolls etc. of the highest elaboration; the fourth shutter from the E. includes the arms of Nevile.

The S. side is in five bays divided by Ionic pilasters, enriched as before, on pedestals; the arches of the doorways spring from terminal figures on pedestals; the other bays are close panelled. In April 1605 Francis Carter was paid £5 for part of 'his bargain for the workmanship of a screen for the hall'. In 1607–08 Andrew Chapman was paid £6 10*s.* in full discharge of his bill for the Hall wainscoting; three years before he had been paid, as noted above, and Willis and Clark (II, 492) conclude that the later payment was for a share in the workmanship of the screen.

In the S. wall of the Screens-passage are three clunch doorways with chamfered jambs and four-centred heads. Elsewhere in the College is preserved the Hall brazier (Plate 273) bought for £12 in 1702–03 and discarded in 1866; it is of wrought and cast-iron, with a lobed-square fireplate, some 2 ft. 10 ins. across, on shaped feet and with a perforated dome in the middle surrounded by a balustrade, 8¼ ins. high, with ball terminals.

The Hall windows contain much heraldic glass, which in the following account is divided into two groups: first, that of the late 16th and early 17th centuries; second, that of later date to 1850. The first also includes two mediaeval fragments, and the second an 18th-century portrait-head of Queen Anne. Group A: in N.E. window, upper N. light, (a) See of Ely; in second light, (b) Wilmer quartering Lumley. In E. oriel, top tier: second light, (a) Henry Bellasis, K. and B., of Newbrugh, Bellasis quartering (unidentified 25), Lespring, Cardigan, Billingham, Errington; third light, (b) See of Bath and Wells impaling (John) Still; fourth light, (c) Russell quartering two blanks, Herring, Froxmore, Wyse, blank, Seamark, Barnack, Tilly, Tame, Tilly, Laxham, Oldham, (unidentified 26 and 27); fifth light, (d) Coke quartering (unidentified 28, 29 and 30), damaged; sixth light, (e) Thomas Howard, K.G., 1st Earl of Suffolk, Howard quartering Brotherton, Warren, Mowbray, within a Garter with an earl's coronet; seventh light, (f) See of Canterbury impaling (Richard) Bancroft, with motto, faded; eighth light, (g) Egerton quartering Bassett within an engrailed sable border; ninth light, (h) Devereux, Earl of Essex, K.G., Devereux quartering Bourchier, Woodstock, Bohun of Hereford, Milo, Mandeville, Louvain, Woodville, Crophull, Verdun, Bigod, Marescal, Ferrers, blank, Quincy, Blanchman, within a Garter with an earl's coronet; eleventh light, (i) Jenour quartering (unidentified 31), Fitzherbert, Zouch of Leicester, Molineux, Segrave, (unidentified 32 and 33), blank, (unidentified 34, 35, 32, 36 and 37), Segrave, blank; second tier: sixth light, (j) Sir Francis Barrington, Barrington quartering Mandeville, Clarence, Neville, Montagu, Holland, Beauchamp, Spencer, Clare; ninth light, (k) Parker of Herstmonceux quartering Morley, (unidentified 38), Morley, blank, Marescal, (unidentified 39), de la Pole, Latham, Isle of Man, Warren, (unidentified 40–42), Parker; tenth light, (l) See of Ely impaling Heton quartering

More, faded; eleventh light, (m) Fulke Greville, Lord Brooke, Greville quartering Ufford, Beke, Latimer, Cheney, Stafford, Maltravers, Beauchamp, Ufflet, with a label below inscribed 'Fulco Greville', with a crest, faded and damaged. In middle E. window, upper N. light, (a) Smith of Suffolk; upper fourth light, (b) Jermyn, reset in reverse and partly upside down, in nine quarters, blank, Rushbrooke, Jermyn, Redesham, blank, Gissing, Bosun, Burgon, Reppes, damaged. In fifth window, upper N. light, (a) Richard Lovelace reset in reverse and much patched, in four quarters, St. Barbe, Hengham (twice), Lovelace; upper fourth light, (b) Harcourt quartering (unidentified 43), Marmion, Kilpeck, Fundin, (unidentified 44), blank, (unidentified 45), Zouche, (unidentified 46–48). In sixth window, upper N. light, (a) Deanery of Canterbury impaling Nevile quartering Neville, Albany, Eudo; upper S. light, (b) Nevile quarterly as in sixth (a) impaling Mantell quartering Heyford, Wood, Cantelupe.

In N.W. window, upper N. light, (a) Stanhope quartering (illegible), Longvillers, Lexinton; upper middle light, (b) (unidentified 49), achievement in oval panel; upper S. light, (c) Elwes of Stoke quartering Garbett, a crescent for difference in fess point, achievement. In W. oriel, lowest tier: second light, (a) Furtho; third light, (b) Keyes, (c) Weld quartering Button, (unidentified 50); fourth light, (d) Fotherby with motto, (e) Nevile quartering Neville, Albany impaling Eudo, Middleham; fifth light, (f) Stanhope quartering Malovell, Longvillers, Lexinton, much renewed and first quarter reversed, (g) Harcourt, dated 1610, achievement, (h) Thorold quartering Hough, Burnell, Brerehaugh, Touchet, Audley, Hough, blank; sixth light, (i) (unidentified 51) quartering Norton, (j) Sir John Cutts, Cutts quartering Esmerton, with scutcheon of pretence of Brocket quartering Neville, (unidentified 52), two blanks, Lytton, inscribed 'Ioh Cuts', achievement, (k) Henry Bellasis of Newbrugh, Bellasis quartering (unidentified 25), Lespring, Cardigan, Billingham, Errington; seventh light, (l) Sir Robert Wroth, (m) Howard quartering Brotherton, Warren, Mowbray, within a Garter, with earl's coronet and motto, (n) Zouche quartering Cantelupe, Brewes, Milo, Marescal, Segrave, blank, St. Maur, Lovell, Zouche, Quincy, (unidentified 53, 54), Segrave, Segrave, Dynham, Arches, (unidentified 55), Welby, (unidentified 56–58); eighth light, (o) Robert Rich, Earl of Warwick, Rich quartering Baldry, (p) Cecil quartering Echington, Wynston, Echington, Walcot, Cecil, within a Garter, with an earl's coronet, (q) Sir Percival Hart, Hart quartering Peche, [Hadley?], blank, Bray, Bray, blank, [Wright?], Butler, Hussey, (unidentified 59, 60), Crosier, D'Abernon; ninth light, (r) Radcliffe, (s) Stanhope quartering Malovell, Longvillers, Lexinton, inscribed 'Ed. Stanhope', achievement, (t) Duckett quartering impaled coats of Stopham and Vavasour, Bellingham, Burnishead; tenth light, (u) William Thornhill, Thornhill quartering Eland quartering Tankersley, (v) Stanhope quartering three damaged coats impaling Macwilliams quartering blank, Easton, Caunfield, Wingham, Ingloss, Gestingthorp, Eston, Hartishorn, Nernvit, Ley, (w) Metcalf quartering blank, Pigott, Leeds, Normanville, Metcalf; eleventh light, (x) small figure in plate armour, inscribed 'Ricardus Dux', *c.* 1425 (Plate 230), (y) Tudor Royal arms, 15th-century; twelfth light, (z) (unidentified 61), (aa) Gray quartering Hastings, Valence, Quincy, Astley, Woodville, Bonville, Harrington, with an ermine label overall, with inscription below 'Joh Gray Miles', and crest, (bb) Banning quartering Norden; thirteenth light, (cc) Hall, formerly inscribed 'W.HA', (dd) Radcliffe quartering Fitzwalter, Burnel, Mohun, Lucy, Egremont, Mortimer, Coulchiefe, inscribed 'W. Radcliffe Miles Comensal Col 1567', (ee) Toddington impaling Throckmorton; fourteenth light, (ff) Falconer, (gg) John Hammond, Fellow, doctor to James I and Prince Henry, inscribed with name, titles and date 16[08], damaged, (hh) Barrow. In middle W. window, upper N. light, (a) Whalley, the first quarter blank, quartering Leeke, (unidentified 62, 63), blank, Kirton, Stockton, Hatfield, Selioke, Warde, Francis, Mallet, much faded; upper S. light, (b) Bill. In fifth window, upper S. light, (a) Goodyear. In sixth window, upper N. light, (a) Bill; upper S. light, (b) Nevile quartering Neville, Albany, Middleham. In S.W. window, upper N. light, (a) Clifton quartering Constable, all reset in reverse, in four grand quarters, Frechville, Constable, (unidentified 64), Newmarch quartering Rode, Clifton, (unidentified 65), Cresby, on a scutcheon over all (unidentified 66); upper S. light, (b) Kercher, faded.

Group B: the later heraldic glass to 1850 consists generally of achievements-of-arms, with names and dates below. Those of the late 18th-century have foliated wreaths or naturalistic flowers, those of *c.* 1830 have cusped Gothic framing. In N.E. window, upper S. light, (a) head of Queen Anne, in grisaille, early 18th-century; lower middle light, (b) Augustus Frederick, Duke of Sussex, 1830, with Gothic canopy-work and inscription on scroll. In E. oriel, top tier, first light, See of Peterborough impaling Hinchliffe. In third window, top row, (a) George John, Earl Spencer, Spencer quartering Bingham quartering Turberville, with supporters, motto, and earl's coronet above, 1787, (b) More Meredith, B.D., with crest, 1786(?), (c) James Backhouse, B.D., with crest, 1786(?), (d) Charles, Lord Compton, with supporters and motto, 1787; second row, (e) Sir William Bolland, with crest, 1830, (f) John Singleton Copley, Lord Lyndhurst, with motto and crest, (g) Sir Nicholas Conyngton Tyndale, with crest, 1830, (h) Sir James Parke, with motto and crest, 1830; third row, (i) John Henry Manners, Duke of Rutland, with supporters and crest, 1835, (j) Thomas Pelham Holles, Duke of Newcastle, arms of Clinton with supporters, motto and crest, 1830, (k) Augustus Henry Fitzroy, Duke of Grafton, with supporters and crest, 1830, (l) John Jeffreys Pratt, Marquess Camden, Pratt quartering Jeffreys, with Molesworth in pretence, 1835; fourth row, (m) See of Hereford impaling Thomas Musgrave, (n) George, Lord Lyttleton, with motto and crest. In middle E. window, top row, second light, (a) William Collier, M.A., Professor of Hebrew, with crest; third light, (b) Lord Gray of Groby, Gray quartering Booth, with baron's coronet above, 1786; second row, (c) James Henry Monk, S.T.P., Bishop of Gloucester, 1830, (d) Charles Grey, Earl Grey, with crest, 1832, (e) Lawrence, Lord Dundas of Aske, with crest, (f) See of London impaling Charles James Blomfield, 1828(?); third row, (g) William Pitt, with motto and crest, 1830, (h) Philip Yorke, Earl of Hardwicke, with supporters and crest, 1830, (i) William Lowther, Earl of Lonsdale, with supporters and crest, (j) William Spencer Cavendish, Duke of Devonshire,

Cavendish quartering Boyle, Clifford, with supporters, motto and crest, 1830. In fifth window, top row, second light, (a) George Henry Fitzroy, Earl of Euston, Fitzroy with a silver label, with earl's coronet, 1786, (b) Henry Legge, Lord Stawell, Legge quartering Stawell, 1786; second row, (c) John Henry Smyth, Smyth quartering (unidentified 67), Foxley, Wood impaling Fitzroy, with a scutcheon of Ibbetson, with crest, 1830, (d) Charles Manners Sutton, LL.D., Sutton quartering Manners, with crests of Sutton and Manners, 1830, (e) Sir James Scarlett, (f) Sir Thomas Coltman, Justice of the Common Pleas, with crest, 1837(?). In sixth window, top row, second light, (a) William Henry Lambton, with crest, 1786; third light, (b) Lord Henry Fitzroy, Fitzroy with a silver mullet, with baron's coronet, 1786; second row, (c) John Cust, Earl Brownlow, Cust quartering Brownlow with baronet's badge over all, with supporters and crest, 1833, (d) S. Peck, Senior Fellow, with crest, 1786, (e) I. Tharp, Fellow-Commoner, of Jamaica, with crest, 1786, (f) Sir John Williams, tierced in pale, Richardson (for Williams), Davenport quartering Ward, and Davenport quartering Calveley, Hazelwall, (unidentified 68), [1835]. In S.E. window, (a) Millecent, with crest, and cartouche below with family names and dates and 'W. Price Lon[don] pinxit 1703'; upper third light, (b) Robert Hitch, oval shield in cartouche with putti and inscribed with paternal descent and 'Henricus Gyles Eborac pinxit 1690'.

In N.W. window, lower middle light, William Frederick, Duke of Gloucester, with Gothic canopy-work, 1830. In W. oriel, in lowest fourth light, See of Peterborough impaling John Hinchliffe, D.D., 1785, shield renewed. In middle W. window, top row, second light, (a) Posslethwaite, with crest; third light, (b) Thomas Horton, Horton quartering Horton and Scott. In fifth window, top row, first light, (a) Darley; second light, (b) Richard Newbor, Senior Fellow, with crest, [1786]; third light, (c) Lord Charles Fitzroy, Fitzroy with a silver crescent, 178[6]; second row, fourth light, (d) William John Bankes, Bankes quartering Wynne, (unidentified 69), with crest, 1822. In sixth window, top row, second light, (a) William Lowther, Lowther quartering Quale, Stapleton, Lucy, Strickland, Warcop, (unidentified 70), Lancaster, with crest, 1786; third light, (b) Ralph John Lambton, Lambton with a crescent for difference, 1786. In S.W. window, upper second light, (a) Thomas Spencer, M.A., with crest, 1786; upper third light, (b) John Higgs, B.D., with crest, 1786(?).

Opening off the Hall on the N.W. and contemporary with it is a rectangular staircase-turret, which gave access to the Master's Lodge; after being partly covered by the N. range of Nevile's Court, it was altered in the 19th century and remodelled in 1920.

The Buttery adjoins the Hall on the S. and the Kitchen stands S.W. of the Buttery. Both were contemporary with the Hall, but the former, with the rooms over, has been almost wholly remodelled to accord with the rest of the range to the S. and is described with it. The *Kitchen* (32 ft. by 28 ft.) is equivalent to three storeys in height and open to the roof. The walls are of ashlar to the N. and ashlar and brick to the W.; small areas still unmasked on the S. are of rubble incorporating 'herringbone' masonry. The foundations were begun in July 1605; Francis Carter's contract of February 1603–04 for carpenter's work has been mentioned with the Hall; a second contract with him, of September 1605, was for the roof of the Kitchen. The last payment to the slaters was made in November 1605. The spacing of the roof-bays is now irregular; this and the early 17th-century Smithson drawing of the College (R.I.B.A. Drwgs. AE 5/28) leave little doubt that the Kitchen originally extended another bay eastward. Thus the significance emerges of the entry in the accounts of 1604–05, quoted in the historical introduction, for digging the foundation of the Kitchen wall 'that goes through the old Hall'.

The exposed W. part of the N. wall has been remodelled superficially to accord with the treatment of the S. range of Nevile's Court. The entablatures, main cornices and balustraded parapet are continued across it and the three-light windows at first and second-floor levels are both uniform with those further W. The S. wall, now almost entirely concealed by modern kitchen-offices, has in the upper part two windows of two lights with casement-moulded jambs; that to the E. has two-centred openings in a square head, the other has four-centred openings in a four-centred head with a pierced spandrel and both are earlier features reused. The W. wall, partly covered by the S. range of Nevile's Court, shows the projection of the W. fireplace, with a moulded plinth, and has at the S. end a modern doorway cut through an original window. The exposed upper S. part is largely of brick; of the two clunch windows high in the wall and in the gable, the lower is of four lights with polygonal openings in a square head with a label, the upper of three similar lights and without a label. The hexagonal timber louvre at the roof-ridge has a lead-covered flared roof.

The interior has large fireplaces in the N., S. and W. walls; the first and last have been entirely encased with modern tiles; the S. fireplace, now partly blocked, is of stone, with chamfered jambs and segmental head with a plain keystone. The roof is in three bays; a fourth bay was probably destroyed in the 18th century by the insertion of the arcaded wall forming the E. service-passage. The hammer-beam roof-trusses are original; they rise from wall-posts on plain stone corbels and are similar in form to those of the Hall but much rougher, with only two collars, three purlins, one with curved wind-braces, and without the arcaded infilling, queen-posts alone occurring between the collars. The timbers are unmoulded except on the ends of the hammer-beams. The louvre is supported by struts rising from the lower collar beams. The dormer-windows are later insertions. The service-passage of 1771–4 has two large elliptical-headed arches in the W. wall and is covered by a groined vault now in two and a half bays.

The *Buttery* and rest of the W. range S. of the Hall underwent a remodelling, begun in 1771 and finished in 1774, so extensive as to amount almost to rebuilding. James Essex was the architect. In 1927 the W. side of the Buttery was refronted, in Clipsham stone. The range is of three storeys with cellars. The E. wall is of Ketton stone ashlar; the W. wall, except of the Buttery, and the S. wall are of white brick. The roofs are slate-covered. The E. side, extending from the Hall to the S. range of Great Court, is symmetrical, in seven bays with the middle three projecting slightly. It has a plinth, a plat-band at first-floor level and a modillion-cornice surmounted by a balustraded parapet. The doorway in the middle and the windows in the flanking bays and in every bay on the floors above have rectangular openings with architraves; the entablatures restricted to the first-floor windows give them the main emphasis in the composition. All the windows have plain sills except the three in the middle of the top floor, which have returns of the architraves.

The S. end has a plinth, a stone cornice and brick parapet-wall. On the ground floor are two and on both the upper floors three 18th-century windows with flat brick arches; the bay-window is modern. The W. side, where now visible, is of similar character to the foregoing.

Inside, the ground floor is occupied largely by kitchen-offices; at the S. end is a Porter's Lodge. The entrance-passage and flanking rooms have groined plaster vaults; the W. wall of these is in, or close to, the position of the original E. wall of the Kitchen, while the thick S. wall is perhaps a survival from Michael House.

The late 18th-century staircase approached through the E. doorway in the S. wall of the Hall rises to the first floor in three flights; it has open bracketed strings, thin turned balusters, square newels and a moulded ramped handrail. Against the walls is a panelled dado. The staircase further S. is similar but with close strings and without ramps to the handrails.

On the first floor, the *Old Combination Room* (Plate 274) (30 ft. by 36 ft.), occupying the whole of the middle three bays and extending westward to the wall inserted in the Kitchen, rises through two storeys. It has a plaster dado with wood dado-rail enriched with Greek key-pattern ornament. At the wall-head is a frieze modelled with honeysuckle flowers and foliation and an enriched dentil-cornice. The plaster ceiling has a recessed circular panel in the middle and restrained decoration of foliage-festoons, pendants and scrolls, urns, ribbons, etc. The N. doorcase has an enriched architrave and entablature, with delicate festoons and ribbons in the frieze; the mahogany door is in six panels. All the decoration except the fireplace-surround is contemporary with the building. From the ceiling-panel hangs a glass and ormolu oil light-fitting (Plate 55) with a central vase and two tiers of crystal pendants, the lower hung from a metal band inscribed in applied Roman capitals and numerals 'D.D. Ca[r]olus Shaw Lefevre hujus Collegii quondam socius pietatis ergo A.D. 1809'.

The part of the W. range of Great Court N. of the Hall is of two storeys with attics. The side to the Court is of ashlar; the W. side is of clunch rubble, ashlar and brick. The roofs are slate-covered. Next to the Hall are the Fellows' Parlour and Combination Room on the ground and first floors respectively; these rooms formerly belonged to the Master and were exchanged in 1920 for the room, now the Master's Library, described above, in the Old Library range. The rest of the range northward contains the *Master's Lodge* with rooms for H.M. Judges on Assize at the N. end. The oldest part of the building, from the Hall to the thick wall N. of the Master's Entrance-hall, was in hand in 1554; the Entrance-hall was then the room ('conclave magistri') in the external angle of the Court, the range continuing eastward from it to link up with King Edward's Tower. Nevile's porch is in the position of the former turret in the angle between the two ranges. The arrangement is shown in J. Hamond's view of Cambridge (1592) together with the mid 16th-century Master's Gallery, which extended at an angle on the N.W. towards the river and was replaced in 1892 by a new wing designed by Arthur Blomfield.

In 1599, as part of Nevile's rebuilding scheme, the E. return range was taken down, and in 1600 the foundations were laid of the N. extension of the W. range, that is, from the Entrance-hall to the Old Library range, the fabric of which was then in process of completion. Both were finished in 1601. The interior fitting of the extension of the Lodge seems to have been completed slowly; work was still proceeding in 1612–13. Chapman was again employed for the wainscoting.

Dr. Bentley, shortly after becoming Master in 1700, began an extensive scheme of improvement, replacing the stone-mullioned windows with sash-hung windows, inserting new ceilings and fireplaces, panelling the rooms, and adding a spacious new staircase on the W. Cornelius and John Austin were paid for panelling, Robert Grumbold for window-dressings and for setting up marble chimney-pieces. By 1703 at least £1,193 had been spent. By 1705 the staircase was nearing completion, and by 1710 the work and the expenditure had become a matter for such acrimonious dispute with the College that the Senior Fellows drew up an indictment, 'Articles against Dr. Bentley', for submission to the Visitor. A summary of expenses to 1723 shows that the work had cost the College £2,086.

Sometime after *c.* 1740 (see West's engraving of the College) the semicircular E. oriel was demolished, and in 1785–6 the roof was renewed. During the Mastership of Dr. Whewell (1841–66) changes were made under the supervision of Anthony Salvin with the aim of reinstating something of the earlier external appearance of the Lodge, at least towards the Court. In April 1842 rebuilding the E. oriel and insertion of mullioned windows in the E. wall were begun, and in September the conversion of the shallow single-storey bay-window on the W. into the present oriel was decided upon; these works were finished early in 1843, at a cost of £3,766. The ground plan of the Lodge as it remained to the present century is reproduced by Willis and Clark (II, 605, fig. 41). In 1920, when the S. end between the Master's Entrance-hall and the College Hall was taken over by the College, the party-walls between the two S. rooms on ground and first floors were demolished and an entrance-vestibule and staircase contrived adjoining the Hall; these last, which may recreate some such earlier arrangement, involved a remodelling of the Master's staircase-turret at the N.W. angle of the Hall. The W. side of the Lodge was restored in 1941 when the Master's Dining-room was reconditioned.

The E. side, from the Hall to the Master's Tower, is now largely the work of Salvin of 1841 to 1843. It has a plinth and embattled parapet; the windows, all of the 19th century, are of two and three lights with four-centred openings in square heads with labels. The two-storey semioctagonal oriel-window, replacing the semicircular oriel depicted by Loggan, has windows of four lights on the face, two on each canted side and one in each return; it is surmounted by an enriched continuation of the main parapet with a weathered inscription, 'Munificentia fultus Alex. J. B. Hope generosi hisce aedibus antiquam speciem restituit W. Whewell Mag. Collegii A.D. MDCCCXLII'; the College paid two-thirds of the cost. The acute gable above the oriel, containing a window of three stepped lights and three much weathered shields-of-arms, with a lofty finial, is Salvin's innovation. On the roof are eight 18th-century flat-topped dormer-windows.

The Master's porch is a work of Nevile, *c.* 1600, though restored. It has canted angles with attached Ionic columns on pedestals supporting an entablature with elaborate strapwork cresting incorporating the crowned arms of new France and England quarterly in the middle. The outer arch has a semi-circular head with moulded archivolt, carved soffit and jewelled keystone; it springs from jewelled and enriched responds with moulded imposts that are continued to divide enriched flanking pilaster-strips into two stages. In the side walls are single-light windows with four-centred openings.

The stair-turret, the *Master's Tower*, in the N.W. angle of Great Court, is contemporary with the adjoining ranges; it is three-sided to the height of the last, polygonal above and divided into two stages by a string; the embattled parapet with parapet-string has been renewed. The S. entrance has chamfered jambs and a four-centred opening in a renewed square head with a moulded label. In the front wall are five single-light windows of similar form to the foregoing, except the second and third, which have polygonal openings. It contains a bell of 1811.

The W. side, between the Old Library range on the N. and the W. wing of 1892 on the S., has a preponderance of clunch in the lower part and of brickwork above; it has a plastered plinth and a plain parapet and contains two 18th-century sash-hung windows on each floor. Towards the S. is Salvin's semioctagonal oriel-window of 1842–3 rising through two storeys and with the main wall behind it gabled. In the roof are two 18th-century hipped dormer-windows. S. of the W. wing the lower part of the wall is covered by modern additions as far as Bentley's staircase bay; this last is of red brick, gabled to the W., and with a large semicircular-headed W. window divided into small panes by heavy timber glazing-bars. The rest of the wall visible southward has the lower part of rubble, the upper of ashlar, but both have been much refaced. On the ground floor are three two-light windows with polygonal openings in square heads with labels; the middle window replaces a doorway, the other two are of *c.* 1600 but entirely restored. On the first floor are two two-light windows with four-centred openings and otherwise similar to those below; they also are entirely restored. The chimney-shafts are of 18th-century red brickwork flush with the main wall-face and rebuilt later where they rise clear.

Inside, the *Fellows' Parlour* (29 ft. by 36 ft.), converted from the former Master's kitchen and housekeeper's room, has been modernised but retains an old clunch fireplace with moulded jambs and four-centred head. The *Combination Room* above (28¾ ft. by 47¼ ft.), converted from the Master's bedroom and study, was fitted in 1920 but has an old clunch fireplace, now partly defaced, in the N. wall with four-centred opening in a square head. The reset overmantel of *c.* 1600 is divided into three bays by enriched Ionic pilasters supporting an entablature with lions' masks and guilloche ornament in the frieze and a modern cornice; in the middle bay, over an enriched panel inscribed '1546 H8R Fundator', is a strapwork cartouche with the crowned Tudor Royal arms in a Garter with lion and dragon supporters flanked by the crowned initials 'H' and 'R' and by Tudor roses; in the side bays are round-headed panels. The small room W. of the foregoing is lined with reused panelling of the 16th century and *c.* 1600 incorporating modern work. The doorway to it has a reset timber frame in part original, with stop-moulded jambs and a square head.

The Master's *Entrance-hall* (28¾ ft. by 29 ft.) has two original chamfered ceiling-beams running N. and S., now encased. At the W. end of the N. wall is a reset clunch doorway of *c.* 1600 with stop-moulded jambs, flat four-centred head and sunk spandrels. The room is lined with panelling of the 16th century on the E., N. and S. walls, of *c.* 1600 elsewhere, incorporating some later repairs, in six and seven heights with a cornice of *c.* 1700; in the overmantel the panels have round heads, enriched responds and carved spandrels. The bolection-moulded fireplace-surround is of gray marble and of *c.* 1700; the cast-iron fireback is dated 1596 and displays the arms of the Holy Roman Empire. The Junior Bursar's accounts for 1600–01 include £26 to Chapman for labour and materials in the Master's Lodge, including fitting the wainscot in two of the old chambers and adding new wainscot to it. For the following year the Senior Bursar's accounts include £115 to him for wainscot work in the Library and Master's Lodge.

Dr. Bentley's *Staircase* (Plate 67) (27 ft. by 14 ft.), in process of completion in 1705, opens off the W. side of the Entrance-hall through an exceptionally wide doorway with glazed door of the same date. It has a bolection-moulded panelled dado, open bracketed strings, turned and twisted balusters, two to a step, and a moulded ramped handrail. The first-floor landing is lined with bolection-moulded panelling incorporating four doorcases with architraves and cornices consisting of returns of the panelling entablature and hung with eight-panel doors. The plaster ceiling is coved.

The *Dining-room* (28 ft. by 38 ft.), next N. of the Entrance-hall, has three chamfered ceiling-beams running E. to W., now encased. The walls are lined with early 18th-century bolection-moulded panelling with moulded dado-rail and cornice, the last now in part encased; the doors are of six moulded and fielded panels. In the overmantel are two fruit and flower festoons finely modelled in plaster. The bolection-moulded fireplace-surround is modern. The cast-iron fireback displays the Tudor Royal arms with lion and dragon supporters. The room was restored in 1941 when the oak panelling was stripped of paint and found to be heavily restored and supplemented with deal, particularly on the N.; no doubt this was done to provide the partitioning for the narrow passage projected into the room on the N., probably late in the 18th century; similar panelling, part of that described, remains lining the passage. Further repairs in 1952 revealed part of an old clunch fireplace with four-centred arch in a square head close N. of the present fireplace.

The rest of the ground floor of the range northward comprises the *Judges' Suite*. Both bedrooms are lined with early 18th-century bolection-moulded panelling similar to that already described; the marble bolection-moulded fireplace-surround in the Junior Judge's bedroom is of the same period.

The dressing-room at the S. end is lined with plain panelling. The passages on the E. are a 19th-century arrangement.

On the first floor, the room over the entrance-hall has an enriched plaster cornice of *c.* 1840; the fireplace-surround incorporates 17th-century carved woodwork. The Master's *Drawing-room* (Plate 274) over the Dining-room has an original plaster ceiling with canted angles. A network of narrow moulded ribs divides it into a geometrical pattern of panels radiating from fifteen moulded and enriched pendants. The elaborate stone fireplace-surround, of the same period, has at the sides twisted pilasters with quarter-length blackamoor terminal figures supporting Ionic caps; the entablature has a frieze of ogee section carved with arabesques; the overmantel, flanked by scroll-like pilasters based on the cornice-shelf and enriched on the face, is in three bays, that in the middle containing a cartouche with the carved and painted arms of the College, those at the sides with strapwork surrounds to roundels containing painted shields-of-arms of Nevile on the N., and of the See of Canterbury impaling Whitgift on the S. Surmounting the crowning dentil-cornice is a pyramidal cresting with obelisk and ball-finials painted blue with gilt stars framing a rectangular panel carved with an achievement of the Tudor Royal arms in a Garter with mantling and lion and dragon supporters. The enrichments of ceiling and fireplace are part gilded and coloured. The surviving accounts suggest that fitting this room was prolonged from 1601 to 1613, but loss of some of the Bursars' books prevents definite allocation of expenditure.

The rest of the first floor northward comprises the *King's Suite*; the arrangement and fittings of the rooms are similar to those of the Judges' suite below.

The difference between the floor levels of the King's Suite and the rest of the Old Library range, and the position of the blocked windows in the W. end of the latter, show that the rooms of the Judges' Suite have been heightened. The change may be connected with the incorporation, at an unknown date, of these rooms in the Master's Lodge, in order to obtain uniformity throughout. Dr. Bentley's responsibility seems indicated but, against this, appropriation of rooms in the Old Library range is not an item in the Fellows' indictment of him. Further, the arrangement of the ground-floor ceiling-beams suggests that any heightening of the N. rooms would involve a heightening throughout the 1600–01 extension of the Lodge and thus that the change may have taken place in the 17th century.

Access to the N. rooms and, as described, to the top floor of the Old Library range is by the lobby and staircase in the Master's Tower through doorways in the W. and N. walls with chamfered jambs and four-centred heads. The doorway to the first floor of the Old Library range, into the Master's Library, is now blocked.

The *South Range* of Great Court incorporates the Queen's Gate rather to the W. of centre; the rest contains sets of chambers. It is of two storeys with attics, except the three-storey Gate. The N. wall is of ashlar, mostly reused material, the S. wall of rubble, both random and in 'herringbone' courses. The roofs are slated and tiled.

Some evidence for the retention and use of older walling is given in the historical introduction to the College, but the range in the form it now stands was not begun before 1594. Most of the structural timber is reused material. The Queen's Gate is dated 1597, which may mark completion of the fabric; but work on the range continued into the 17th century when the accounts of 1601–02 indicate that it was finishing. A variation in the building progress E. and W. of the Gate, which minor differences in the fabric suggest, seems to be confirmed by the expenses: these include for boarding over the upper chambers overlooking Gonville and Caius College in 1598, for making the gutters between the Hall and the Queen's Gate in 1601–02. In 1753–4 the N. side was repaired and 'new faced' but, as shown in the historical introduction, this amounted chiefly to retooling, while refacing with new ashlar was confined to the plinths, much of the door and window-dressing, and the upper part of the wall from above the first-floor window heads. The N. face of the Queen's Gate, which had sash-windows inserted on the first floor in 1723, was included in this work, with only rather more refacing and new or renewed arms carved by Woodward; stone-mullioned windows were reinstated in the 19th century. James Essex's work S. of the Hall necessitated the rebuilding of a short length of the W. end of the range between 1771 and 1774. The whole N. front was repaired again and cleaned during the period 1945 to 1947.

Queen's Gate is approximately square outside, with octagonal turrets at the corners so inset that the Gatehall ($18\frac{3}{4}$ ft. by 23 ft.) has irregular canted angles. It has moulded and chamfered plinths and embattled parapets, the turrets being carried up well above the main parapet. The ashlar N. side has an archway with chamfered jambs and high four-centred moulded head with a label (p. 394); over the apex and haunches are three sunk rectangular panels, the first cusped, containing respectively the arms of the College, the See of Canterbury impaling Whitgift on the E., and Nevile quartering Neville, Neville of Bulmer, Bulmer, Eudo, Middleham, Clavering, Glanville, Albany on the W. In the middle of the first floor is a niche, entirely renewed, similar to that opposite on King Edward's Tower, but without the cresting and with 'Dieu et mon droit' inscribed on the sill, containing a seated statue of Queen Elizabeth, crowned and holding orb and sceptre, brought from London in 1597; crown, sceptre and cross on orb are of metal, gilt. Flanking the niche are late 19th-century two-light stone-mullioned windows with four-centred openings in square heads with labels. At second-floor level is a moulded string stopping against the sides of the turrets, and on the second floor is a four-light window, of similar detail to those below, flanked on the E. by a Tudor rose, on the W. by a fleur-de-lys. The parapet-string above is enriched with paterae and lions' masks, the parapet with flutings and roundels flanking the carved date 1597, and the face of the merlons with vertical tracery-panelling. The N. turrets are divided into three stages by moulded strings; in the N. face of each stage is a single-light window and, in addition, low down in the second stage, a small oval window. The oval windows are similar to those opposite in a comparable position in King Edward's Tower.

The S. side, of random rubble with restored ashlar dressings, has an archway similar to that in the opposite wall but with a chamfered head and hung with an original nail-studded oak door. This last is in two leaves, each leaf with the face divided into two heights of four panels by moulded rails and muntins and with the back lattice-framed; the panels are ridged and in the E. leaf is a small wicket. On the first floor is a four-light window and on the second floor are two two-light windows, all similar in detail to those in the opposite wall and restored. The turrets are generally similar to those on the N. but so inset that only three faces project from the main wall-face; the S. windows are all, except the oval lights, more or less 19th-century renewals and now without labels. Two similar windows are in the W. side of the top stage of the W. turret.

In the Gatehall is a chamfered ceiling-beam; the doorway to the N.W. turret has chamfered jambs and four-centred head. No old work is apparent on the first floor; the second-floor room is lined with plain 18th-century panelling with a timber cornice.

E. of Queen's Gate, the N. wall of the S. range is of reused ashlar masonry, some being of the 13th century, retooled and in part refaced. It has a moulded plinth and embattled parapet, both refaced, and is in fourteen bays, with ground-floor openings as shown on the plan and two and three-light windows correspondingly on the first floor. The doorways in the fourth, eighth and twelfth bays have chamfered jambs and moulded four-centred arches in square heads with labels. The stone-mullioned windows also have four-centred openings in square heads with labels. The dressings were very extensively renewed in 1753–4, but the original clunch inner order of many of the windows survived until 1945, though much decayed. The lead rainwater-heads and downpipes are of the 18th century. On the roof are seventeen flat-topped dormer-windows.

The S. wall is of 'herringbone' masonry for some 75 ft. W. from the brick gable of the E. range; thereafter, to Queen's Gate, it is of large random rubble with many reused dressed blocks in the upper part. It has a plinth, in part renewed in brick, and plain eaves. The chimney-flues have been repaired in red brick flush with the wall-face; above, the stacks have been rebuilt in the 18th century and later in white brick. The windows on ground and first floors, placed above as below, are of one and two lights with four-centred openings in square heads. They are of much-weathered clunch, with renewed mullions and sills of freestone, or entirely renewed, and some are blocked, but they mainly represent the original fenestration. In the roof are twenty-six restored gabled dormer-windows.

Inside, staircases 'L', 'M' and 'N' rise to the first floor in straight flights between original timber-framed partitions. The sets generally consist of a large room, a small room opening from it on the side away from the staircase, and a gyp-room below or above the stairs. The longitudinal ceiling-beams on ground and first floors are chamfered and some of the timber-framed partitions incorporate central posts supporting them. The wall below the window-seat in the ground-floor room E. of staircase 'M' is lined with panelling of *c.* 1600 and the room opposite is lined to two-thirds of the height with panelling of the same date.

On the first floor, an original stone fireplace with chamfered jambs and depressed four-centred head remains in the S. wall of the easternmost main room. The main room E. of staircase 'L' is lined nearly to the ceiling with panelling of *c.* 1600, four panels high with enriched but defaced frieze-panels. The main room opposite retains an original stone fireplace now much mutilated. The main room W. of staircase 'N' has the E. and W. walls lined with panelling of *c.* 1600, five panels high with fluted frieze-panels, and the N. and S. walls, except below the windows, with 18th-century panelling with a cornice; this last is continued round the room; below the windows the panelling is of *c.* 1600. Small cupboards with 18th-century panelled doors are contrived in the blocked S. windows. The two-panel door from this room to the N.E. turret of Queen's Gate is of the 18th century; it masks an original stone doorway with chamfered jambs and four-centred head. The similar doorway to the S.E. turret retains an original door of six panels hung on 'cock's-head' hinges. In the attics some of the main chamfered roof timbers are exposed.

W. of Queen's Gate, the N. and S. walls of the S. range are composed of ashlar and 'herringbone' rubble respectively; the first, where not refaced, differs from the ashlar E. of the Gate only in the use of rather smaller blocks of stone, probably almost wholly of the 13th century; the second is much patched and repaired in random rubble. The chimney-stacks on the S. are similar to the others eastward. The N. side has a plinth, three courses at the wall-head and an embattled parapet renewed in the 18th century. It is in ten bays with doorways in the third and seventh bays and an archway in the westernmost bay. This last projects and is an 18th-century rebuilding; the archway is of the same date and has chamfered responds and a four-centred head. For the rest, the doorways and windows are similar to those E. of Queen's Gate but all placed approximately 1 ft. lower. In the roof are nine flat-topped dormer-windows.

On the S. side, the windows differ from those further E. only in the profile of their mouldings. The westernmost bay was rebuilt in the 18th century; in it, the contemporary S. archway has chamfered responds and a four-centred head and the first-floor window is of two lights. On the roof are nine gabled dormer-windows.

Inside, the exposed chamfered ceiling-beams run N. and S., otherwise the arrangement is similar to that in the E. part of the range. On the ground floor, in the partitions of staircase 'P' and E. of staircase 'Q' are original oak-framed doorways with stop-moulded posts and moulded lintels. On the first floor, the main room E. of staircase 'P' is lined to 2 ft. from the ceiling with panelling of *c.* 1600, incorporating modern work, with a reeded frieze and cornice. In the attics some of the chamfered principals and purlins of the roof are exposed.

The octagonal *Fountain* (Plate 278) (17 ft. from side to side), standing in the middle of Great Court, is of Cliffe and Clipsham stone ashlar. It was begun in 1601–02. Wyat and Thorpe were paid £5 for carving eight beasts and the lion at the apex; Robert Masson 42*s.* for the enriched plaster soffit; Lyllie and Baylie £4 10*s.* for six thousand bricks for the foundations and vaults, among other works. The water-cocks were of brass. The recorded expenses in 1614–15 for painting the Fountain as part of the decorations for the visit of James I show that it was then, at the latest, complete. It was repainted and gilded and twice extensively repaired before being completely rebuilt in 1716 by Robert Grumbold at a cost of nearly £184.

Exterior, from S.W.

Interior of 'Cloister', from S.

(40) TRINITY COLLEGE. Library Range. 1677–90

(40) TRINITY COLLEGE. Library Range. Exterior, from E.

1677–90

1677–99

(40) TRINITY COLLEGE. Library. Interior, looking S.

(40) TRINITY COLLEGE. Library; panelled alcove in N.E. corner. *c.* 1690

Detail of limewood carvings on N.W. alcove. 1691–95

Wood busts on bookcases. 1691–95

(40) TRINITY COLLEGE. Library.

(2) Arms of Robert Drake.

(3) Cypher of Sir Henry Puckering, Bt.

(40) TRINITY COLLEGE. Library. Limewood carvings. 1691–95

(12) Arms of Dr. Isaac Barrow.

(13) Arms of Dr. John Pearson, Bishop of Chester.

(40) TRINITY COLLEGE. Library. Limewood carvings. 1691–95

(40) TRINITY COLLEGE. Library Range. Ceiling in staircase-pavilion.

1687

Jeffs and Bentley made further repairs in 1766–7 costing £136; in 1821–2 the steps and in 1842 the pipes were repaired.

The water-supply is obtained from the aqueduct first laid in 1327 to bring water from a source some 300 yds. W. of the Observatory (Monument (19)) to the Franciscan friary formerly on the site of Sidney Sussex College (Monument (39)). The supply led under King's Childer Lane, and thus, after 1433, through King's Hall land; thereafter the aqueduct was held jointly by the friars and the scholars until granted by Henry VIII in its entirety to Trinity College.

In spite of repairs and rebuilding the Fountain retains the form and detail, so far as the last is identifiable, shown in Loggan's view of the College in *c.* 1688, except that the steps have been reduced in number, the crowning flying-ribs are now embellished with intermediate finials, and the main basin is no longer in part covered; further, Masson's enriched plaster soffit has been replaced by a flat boarded ceiling.

The Fountain is raised on three steps. A solid panelled base with chamfered plinth, which contains the main basin, has attached pedestals at each corner on which stand Ionic columns. From the columns spring semicircular arches with solid spandrels supporting an entablature. The entablature has an elaborate pierced strapwork cresting incorporating pedestal-bases to seated beasts at the corners. From behind the beasts rise flying chamfered ribs of ogee form meeting in a finial surmounted by a crowned lion holding a shield of the Royal Tudor arms. The total height of the building is 39¾ ft. Standing in the middle of the main basin and rising to the ceiling is a stone shaft supporting two smaller basins.

In each face of the panelled base is a much-weathered carved terminal figure; in the abdomen of the W. figure is a tap, but all the figures appear once to have been so fitted with water-cocks; below the tap is a lead-lined basin cut in the chamfer of the plinth. The Ionic columns have five-sided capitals and a deep necking enriched with varied paterae, knots, rosettes, etc. The arches have continuous moulded archivolts, mask keystones, and spandrels carved with strapwork incorporating small shields-of-arms and cartouches as follows: N. by W., clockwise, to N.N.W., (a) See of Canterbury impaling John Whitgift (Archbishop 1583–1604), (j) (unidentified 71), (m) See of York, (n) the College, (o) Thomas Nevile (Master 1593–1615), (p) See of Canterbury, (b, c, f, g, l) decorative cartouches etc., (d, e, h, i, k) blank shields. The frieze of the entablature contains elaborate interlacement of tendrils and foliage. The strapwork cresting incorporates shields-of-arms and blank roundels alternately over each face; the shields, at the cardinal points, are: N., See of Canterbury impaling Whitgift; E., Nevile; S., See of Chester impaling Henry Ferne, Master (Bishop of Chester 1662); W., the College. The Junior Bursar's accounts of 1661–2 include payment to Spakman for carving the arms of the Bishop of Chester. The seated beasts include lions, greyhounds, dragons and griffins.

The central shaft, which, in the lower part, is in the form of a Corinthian column, is fluted up to a foliated band beneath four much decayed demi-figures supporting a large hemispherical fluted basin with eight carved masks on the underside fitted with lead spouts; above, the Corinthian capital supports another basin similar to that below but smaller. The upper part of the shaft is four-sided, panelled and with four naked putti below a foliated cap supporting the timber ceiling. Applied on the last are radiating moulded ribs that mitre with a stone cornice round the perimeter.

About midway between the Fountain and King Edward's Tower is a stone *Sundial* set up in 1704 at a cost of £6 19*s.* 8*d.* The dial was renewed in 1795. It stands on two circular steps and has a broad baluster-stem with moulded base and capping, the last with the upper members octagonal. The engraved bronze dial is by Troughton of London.

'*King's Hostel*', being the W. range of the former inner court of King's Hall, stands close N.W. of the Chapel, extending N.N.E. from King Edward's Tower to the College boundary. It is of two storeys with attics. The walls are of brick and rubble with dressings of clunch; the roofs are slate-covered. The range is the work of two periods and the oldest surviving building in the College. In 1375 the ranges round the Court were begun and the Rolls series of accounts, 1375–7, refer to a solar, evidently the Master's *camera* and on the first floor of the S. half of the surviving 'Hostel'; the garderobe at the N.W. corner of it is referred to in the College accounts of 1416–17. The S. and E. sides of the Court were completed before the Library range on the N. and the chambers between it and the Master's rooms were begun in 1417; these chambers thus comprised the N. half of the surviving 'Hostel'. A contract for roofing the new chambers was made in 1418, the last payment being made to the contractor in 1420, and the Library was finished by 1422. In the 1416–17 accounts Dodington is shown to have received payment, probably as master-mason.

Subsequent demolitions have already been noted in the historical introduction to the College. In 1791 'King's Hostel' was cased in brick and given regular fenestration. In 1905 the brickwork was removed and the original building restored and reroofed under the supervision of W. D. Caröe, who published an account of the work (*King's Hostel, Trinity College, Cambridge*, for the Cam. Ant. Soc., 1909).

A projecting bay about the centre of the E. side of the range, shown in Loggan's map of Cambridge, may have contained an Oratory. Adjoining it on the S. was a stair to the Master's *camera* entered from the dais of the Hall, which lay to the S., through a doorway that survives *in situ*. A walk, 'claustrum', in the position of the modern E. passage, had, N. of the bay, an upper storey, 'deambulatorium', providing access to the Library on the first floor of the N. range. Both walks seem to have been prolonged through to the N. wall of the N. range, which here survives and contains a doorway on the first floor that opened into a 'latrina prope librarium'.

The buildings now standing between the 'Hostel' and the Chapel are all of the second half of the 19th century and modern.

Access to the King's Hall range is from a modern passage on the E. closed at the S. end by an old cross-wall containing the 15th-century clunch doorway mentioned above. The doorway has stop-moulded jambs and a two-centred arch in a square head with quatrefoiled traceried spandrels. A block of masonry uncovered in 1905 in the angle formed by the N. side of this cross-wall and the range was found by Caröe to be the base of a staircase and the N.E. angle of the containing wall, now destroyed, lay a short way N.E. of the doorway (Willis and Clark, II, 463 and fig. 6).

In the E. side of the range are the following old features on the ground floor, from N. to S., a much-weathered clunch archway with moulded jambs, four-centred head and high chamfered rear-arch opening to a passage through the range; a small rectangular window with chamfered reveals and a four-centred rear-arch; a doorway, much renewed, with stop-chamfered jambs and four-centred arch opening on a circular stair; two early 15th-century casement-moulded windows each of two cinquefoiled lights in a square head with sunk spandrels and retaining old wrought-iron grilles and rebated inside for shutters, the hinge-pins for which survive; and an early 15th-century doorway with stop-chamfered jambs, four-centred arch, carved foliated spandrels and a square moulded label with decayed stops, the S. spandrel including a human mask and the S. label-stop being in the form of a demi-angel holding a shield. The foregoing open into the early 15th-century half of the range. The following are in the earlier half, a doorway probably of the late 14th century with chamfered jambs and four-centred arch, the lower part of the jambs being rebated for a door, and with a small light above with chamfered reveals and fitted with an old wrought-iron grille, and a two-light window, modern externally but with original splays.

On the first floor are two mediaeval doorways both with chamfered jambs and four-centred arches; that to the N., now blocked, is approximately over the second ground-floor window from the N. That to the S. is over the early doorway below, and retains an old plank door hung on strap-hinges; immediately N. of it is a small blocked loop with chamfered reveals. The other openings at this level are ostensibly of 1791 or modern.

The W. side of the range has been completely restored. The N. half is of brick interspersed with rubble; the S. half has a modern brick facing. In the middle is a tall recess, with a rough triangular arched head, which is the remains of the Master's garderobe. The ground-floor openings are shown on the plan. The N. archway has moulded jambs and four-centred head but only the lower courses of the dressings are old. The next three two and three-light windows with cinquefoiled openings in square heads incorporate some reused original dressings. S. of the garderobe recess, the first two-light window, similar to the windows further N. but smaller, retains old dressings in the head and reveals. The doorway, now blocked, with moulded jambs, partly old, and a renewed head, is a 17th-century conversion from a window. The next two windows are completely renewed outside, and the recess at the S. end retains an old square head and N. reveal.

On the first floor, in the N. end of the wall are the splays and rear-arch of a doorway, which presumably originally opened on an external stair; the chamfered jambs and four-centred head show inside the N. room. Continuing southward, the first two windows are modern, but close S. of each is the moulded S. reveal of an original window; next is an original window, now blocked, with restored reveals and four-centred arch in a square head with sunk spandrels, followed by the N. reveal of an original window, and two modern windows; the second of these last is flanked by the N. reveal and the S. reveal of original windows. The garderobe-recess retains a stone doorway, now blocked, with chamfered jambs and square head; over the S. haunch of the recess is the N. reveal of a small original light. S. again are three modern windows, with the S. reveal of an original window S. of the second. All the modern windows replace 18th-century sash-hung windows.

The N. end of the range contains two small single-light windows with four-centred rear-arches set high in the ground floor and a single cinquefoiled light on the first floor, all original, but only that on the first floor remaining unblocked. The S. end is covered by adjacent buildings.

Inside, on the ground floor, the second room from the N., formerly the Senior Bursar's Room, is probably that converted into an 'elegant chemical laboratory' by Dr. Bentley. It has an open timber ceiling with a moulded beam supported on modern wall-posts and braces. The N. doorway and fireplace are original, the first with clunch stop-chamfered jambs and high four-centred head, the second with defaced clunch jambs and depressed four-centred brick arch. The rest of the range southward is now divided into small rooms by 18th-century and modern partitions; in the N.E. corner is a wall-recess with a half-arch to allow for the swing of the N.E. door. The *Muniment Room* (18¼ ft. by 21 ft.) has part of an old fireplace in the S. end of the E. wall.

On the first floor, the N. room has an open timber ceiling with moulded wall-plates and central cambered beam, the last with mortices for braces; the joists are laid flat. The old S. fireplace has chamfered jambs corbelled to support a moulded lintel; it has been restored and narrowed on the E.; to the W. of it is the stone base course with stop of a destroyed doorway. The second room is lined with early 18th-century bolection moulded panelling with moulded dado-rail and cornice. The doorcases have bolection-moulded architraves and doors of six panels. The fireplace has a flat moulded surround of coloured marble contemporary with the panelling. The main approach to the first-floor set of chambers formed in the 18th century in the S. half of the range, in the Master's former *camera*, is now by the staircase in King Edward's Tower. The N. room of the set is lined with 18th-century fielded panelling with dado-rail and cornice; E. of it is a narrow lobby, entered through the S. mediaeval doorway already described with the E. side of the range, giving access through an altered opening to a modern stair to an attic bedroom. The main room next S. contains panelling, doorcases and doors similar to those previously described in the second room on the same floor. The S. entrance-passage next King Edward's Tower is lined with plain 18th-century panelling with a cornice; it gives access also eastward into a wedge-shaped gyp-room, between the 'Hostel' and the Chapel, which has in the E. wall the rear-arch of the destroyed window already described that opened into the Ante-chapel.

Part of the N. wall of the early 15th-century Library range survives extending some 8 yds. from the N.E. corner of 'King's Hostel' and incorporated in the boundary-wall to St. John's College. It contains on the first floor remains of four 15th-century openings, all now blocked and visible only from the S.; these include the chamfered jambs and four-centred arch of a doorway nearly on the axis of the modern E. passage adjoining the 'Hostel', further E. the reveals of a single-light window, and E. again, the splays and the W. splay and four-centred rear-arch respectively of paired doorways.

Nevile's Court (228 ft. by 131 ft. on the E., 144½ ft. on the W.) is enclosed by the Hall and Buttery already described on the E., the Library on the W., and uniform ranges on the N. and S. containing cloister-like arcaded walks on the ground floor and sets of chambers above.

Towards the Court, the *North* and *South Ranges* are of three storeys and faced with Ketton stone ashlar repaired in the present century with synthetic stone. The N. rear wall is of 'herringbone' rubble to the E. and brick with stone dressings to the W. The S. rear wall is now rendered. The roofs are slated and tiled. The ranges are, for three-fifths of their length from the E., part of a single building scheme, paid for by Dr. Nevile, begun and completed between 1605 and 1612. This, the extension of the ranges westward between 1676 and 1682, and their remodelling and part rebuilding between 1755 and 1758 are described in the historical introduction to the College. Subsequent alterations to the S. side of the S. range are connected with the building of New Court, which adjoins on the S. The N. side of the N. range is obscured in the lower part by A. W. Blomfield's Library-extension of 1892.

The *North Range* has the whole of the ground floor devoted to the cloister-walk, without interruption by any projecting feature. The thickening of the N. wall indicates the beginning of the late 17th-century W. extension. The S. side (Plate 213) is divided into three stages, coinciding with the storeys, by two continuous entablatures and a continuous cornice below the balustraded parapet, and into five main bays by panelled pilaster-strips to the full height; the link with the Hall range is provided by a plain part-bay projecting to the same extent as the pilaster-strips, and with the Library range by a wide plain pilaster-strip. Each main bay is subdivided into four bays. The continuous open arcade of twenty bays on the ground floor consists of round-headed arches with moulded archivolts, plain keystones and fielded spandrels springing from Roman Doric columns and half-columns on square sub-bases. Across the head of the arches and across shaped post-like brackets in the spandrels runs the lower entablature, already mentioned, with triglyphs and diapered panels in the frieze. On the first floor, over each of the arches, is a rectangular three-light transomed window without architrave or label; similarly on the second floor are short three-light windows. The parapet is divided into bays uniformly with those below by main and subsidiary pedestals, panelled over the pilaster-strips and plain between. In the E. part-bay are six windows, generally similar to the foregoing, of two and three lights; those of two lights on the ground floor and that above them on the first floor are modern.

Apart from the considerable renewal of stonework in 1755–6, the pilaster-strips are Essex's transformation of superimposed pilasters on pedestals originally in their position; he omitted short Ionic columns corbelled out between the first-floor windows and thus repetitive returns of the upper entablature (see drwg. E 408/1951 in V. and A. Museum), and discarded cartouches containing the arms of Nevile, Sclater and Babington, which are now reset near the Brewhouse (see below). The front of the second floor is an entire innovation replacing gabled and finialed dormer-windows; in this at least James Burrough was again in some measure concerned with Essex, for he set the price of the stonework.

The N. side is of two storeys with attics and garrets and the earlier wall exhibits a notable expanse of 'herringbone' masonry. From it project three rectangular staircase-towers, those to Nevile's building being smaller than the one to the W. and original though refitted inside. The wall above the late 19th-century Library is extensively masked by numerous additions against the towers, while the appearance of the upper part has been much altered by the heightening of some of the attic rooms involving carrying up the main wall and linking the original dormer-windows and chimney-stacks. The windows were mostly of two transomed lights but many of the mullions and transoms have been removed. The unaltered attic and garret dormer-windows are gabled, the second being much smaller than the first. The staircase-towers are continued above the main eaves and gabled; they each have three windows, largely original, in the N. wall, the lower two of three transomed lights, the third in the gable, smaller and of two lights; windows of one and two lights also occur in the side walls. The chimney-stacks, flush with the wall-face, are of brick; the upper parts have been rebuilt in white brick, some with additional shafts.

The interior of the N. range has the back wall of the walk unpierced except by six doorways to the staircases etc.; these have chamfered jambs and semicircular heads with plain imposts and keystones all contained within shallow rectangular stop-moulded wall-recesses. They are of early 17th-century character. Staircase 'L' is of the mid 18th-century, with close moulded strings, thin turned balusters, square newels and moulded handrails. The timber door-frames on the first-floor landing with flat triangular heads are original, of 1605–12, and retain their oak plank doors with nail-studded mouldings forming nine panels. The doorways on the second-floor landing are original, 1605–12, with stone chamfered jambs and four-centred heads; one retains an original oak door. Staircase 'I' is modern; one original doorway on the first floor and two on the second are similar respectively to those just described. Staircase 'G' is of the date of the structure, 1676–81, with close moulded strings, heavy turned balusters, square panelled newels with turned pendants, and moulded handrail.

The chambers served by the first two staircases, that is, in Nevile's range, have been modernised; only in the E. first-floor set are some mid 18th-century doors with fielded panels remaining. The attics have been altered as described, but some of the principals and purlins of the original timber roof are exposed. In the late 17th-century extension, in the E. half, paid for by Sir Thomas Sclater, Bt., the main first-floor room is lined with oak bolection-moulded panelling with dado-rail and enriched entablature; the three bolection-moulded doorcases have entablatures with enriched cornices, central panels and broken pediments; the doors are of two bolection-moulded panels and retain old rim-locks. The original bolection-moulded fireplace-surround is of marble. The plaster ceiling (Plate 61) has a central oval wreath of leaves and flowers, roundels at the sides modelled with helms with crests of wreaths and at the ends with shields-of-arms of Sclater, and shaped panels in the spandrels filled with elaborate scrolled foliation, wreaths and flowers. Sclater's building was completed by 1679 and occupied before May 1681. In the W. half of the extension, the main first-floor room has a dado of bolection-moulded panelling and a simple 19th-century timber cornice. The outer doors to these last two sets are of two bolection-moulded panels. In the attics some old panelled doors remain and some of the main timbers of the original roof are exposed.

In the *South Range* virtually nothing of Nevile's period other than the form and basic design, and some panelling, survives. Of the E. extension, the E. half, paid for by Dr. Babington, was begun in 1681 and completed in 1682 under the supervision of Robert Grumbold; Cornelius Austin was paid for the wainscoting in the first-floor main room at 6*s*. a yard with £16 10*s*. for the carving; the W. half was built at much the same time, by agreement with Robert Grumbold, Thomas Silke and Matthew Fitch. Nevile's front was entirely rebuilt in 1756–7 and a similar extent of the S. wall at the same time; in the following year the interior of Nevile's range was refitted, with new floors, new ceilings and plastering throughout, new wainscoting on the first floor and the old wainscoting reset above. These fittings mostly survive. Essex was paid £213 for the new wainscoting in the four sets; in December 1758 the rent of these rooms was increased.

The S. range is similar in form to the N. range, and the design of the Court side repeats that opposite except that the part-bay on the E., a refacing of the earlier Kitchen, is longer and with windows, as described earlier, only in the two upper stages, the ground stage being blank. The S. wall is now masked by buildings and Roman cement added in the 19th century to complete the Tudor Gothic unity of New Court (1823–5). The parapets were embattled, octagonal turrets added to the two more westerly staircase-towers, and the windows of the last greatly enlarged and elaborated. An arcade of six four-centred arches with semicircular rear-arches was pierced in the wall between the towers, regular fenestrations of mullioned and transomed windows opened on the floors above, and a niche with canopied head added as a central feature. Beyond the towers, single-storey additions with embattled parapets were made and the main wall-face above remodelled to accord with the rest.

Inside the S. range the ground floor is devoted to the cloister-walk, as in the N. range, and the five doorways in the back wall are also similar to those opposite; they are renewals of 1756. Staircase 'A' is of the late 17th century, with close moulded strings, turned balusters, square newels and moulded handrails. Staircase 'C' is similar to the foregoing. Staircase 'D' is of the date of the structure, 1681–2, with close moulded strings, turned balusters, square panelled newels with ball finials and turned pendants and moulded handrail.

The first-floor main rooms each side of staircase 'A' are lined with fielded panelling of 1758 with dado-rail and dentil-cornice and retain contemporary six-panel doors; the smaller rooms are lined with plain panelling of the same date with a cornice. The E. main room has an early 19th-century marble fireplace-surround. On the second floor, the outer doors of the sets are of the mid 18th century and of six panels. The main E. room is lined with plain panelling as before, and the room N.E. of it is lined with reused early 17th-century panelling incorporating some arched panels enriched with arabesques; both rooms contain flat moulded stone fireplace-surrounds of the mid 18th century. The main W. room is lined with reused early 17th-century panelling and the fireplace is similar to those just described; both the smaller rooms contain similar reused panelling.

The first-floor rooms off staircase 'C' are lined with panelling similar to that in the corresponding rooms of staircase 'A'. The fireplace in the E. main room is also similar to those just described above; that in the W. main room is of the early 19th century, with reeded surround with roundels at the angles. In the partition between the small rooms in the W. set are double doors under a semi-elliptical arch with, on one side, a moulded archivolt springing from pilasters. The second-floor rooms again contain reused early 17th-century panelling, incorporating two fluted pilasters on panelled pedestals. The E. main room has three mid 18th-century doors and a flat moulded stone fireplace-surround of the same date. The modern fireplace in the W. room has a surround made up of early 17th-century fragments; in the adjoining N.W. room is a mid 18th-century fireplace-surround similar to those described.

The outer doors to the first-floor sets off staircase 'D' are of the date of the building, 1681–2, each of two bolection-moulded panels. The main room in the E. set, the *Old Guest Room*, is lined with bolection-moulded panelling supplied by Cornelius Austin with dado-rail and enriched entablature. The two doorcases have carved entablatures and contain doors of two bolection-moulded panels. The late 19th-century ornamental plaster ceiling with heraldic devices was added by Sir William Vernon Harcourt and the overmantel is modern. The adjoining bedroom is lined with reused early 17th-century panelling, extended with modern material, with a frieze of arabesques and a gadrooned cornice; the fireplace-surround and overmantel are made up of miscellaneous enriched woodwork of the same period; the ceiling is of the date and character of that in the main room. In the W. set, the main room is lined with mid 18th-century panelling with dado-rail and dentil-cornice; the doors are of six fielded panels except in the W. wall where a large opening formed in the early 19th century is hung with a door of two panelled leaves. The enriched wood surround to the fireplace is eared and has a frieze carved with acanthus foliage; in the overmantel is an eared panel with cornice and broken pediment, all enriched. On the second floor, the E. set has an old plank outer door, and the W. set an 18th-century door of four fielded panels. Some of the principals of the original timber roof are exposed.

The *Library Range* (Plate 264), enclosing Nevile's Court on the W., contains the Library on the first floor. The ground floor, forming an open undercroft, has an open arcade to the Court, a row of columns down the centre and open fenestration and doorways on the W. At the N. end projects a rectangular staircase-pavilion. Clunch from Hinton and Barrington was used in the foundations, as well as brick, and in the wall infilling. Brickfields named in the accounts are Stow and

Trumpington. The walls are of Ketton stone ashlar except of the pavilion, which are of red brick. The hipped roofs are lead-covered.

The inception of, and Sir Christopher Wren's proposals for, the Library are described in the historical introduction to the College. Work was begun on the building on 23 February 1676–7 and the accounts show that Wren, already Surveyor-General of the King's Works, kept in constant touch with it either by sending agents to Cambridge or through Robert Grumbold, the mason in charge, coming to London; further, Matthew Banckes (Master-carpenter in the Office of Works 1683–1706) was employed as surveyor in 1676 and 1685–6, and craftsmen were engaged who worked for Wren in London. A full descriptive, but undated, letter by Wren accompanies the drawings of the building that are preserved at All Souls College, Oxford (Wren drawings Vol. I, 44, 45–48, reproduced in Wren Society V, 32–44, pls. xxii–xxiv); when it was written, the intention was to place the range against the ends of Nevile's N. and S. ranges. At this stage the site had apparently not been fully surveyed and the drawings show a building even longer than the existing one, which itself, owing to the wedge shape of Nevile's Court, is longer than would have fitted further E. Two of the working drawings are also at All Souls (Wren drawings, Vol. I, 50, 51; Wren Soc., V, pls. xxv, xxvi) and another is in the College Library.

Wren uses continuous superimposed orders towards the Court and contrives the Library floor at the springing of the arches between the lower columns. He describes his motives: 'I chose a double order rather than a single because a single order must either have been mutilated in its members, or have been very expensive, and if performed would not have agreed with the lownesse of the porches which would have been too darke and the solids too grosse for the openings. I have given the appearance of arches as the order required fair and lofty; but I have layd the floor of the Library upon the impostes, which answer to the pillars in the Cloister, and the levels of the old floores, and have filled the Arches with relieves of stone, of which I have seen the effect abroad in good buildings and I assure you where porches are low with flat ceilings is infinitely more graceful than lowe arches would be, and is much more open and pleasant: nor need the mason feare the performance, because the arch discharges the weight, and I shall direct him in a firme manner of executing the designe. By this contrivance the windowes of the Library rise high and give place for the deskes against the walls, and being high may be afforded to be large. I have given noe other Frontispiece to the middle than Statues, according to ancient example because in this case I find any thing else impertinent, the Entrances being endwise, and the roofe not suiting it.' In addition to this letter and the drawings mentioned, there survive in Trinity College Library circular letters from Barrow and North appealing for subscriptions to the building fund, a list of the subscribers, the Senior Bursar's accounts for the relevant years and Robert Grumbold's account book. Extracts from the Bursar's accounts are printed in *Designs of Sir Chr. Wren for Oxford, Cambridge* etc. in Wren Society, V (1928), 34–44.

Isaac Barrow, Master, died in 1677 when, according to Roger North the biographer of the Hon. Dr. John North, who succeeded to the Mastership, 'the library was advanced about three-quarters of the height of the outward walls'. Dr. North (Master 1677–83) is said to have seen the finishing of it, except the classes, but the shell only must be meant. In 1680 lead for the roof was bought and a contract made with John Kendall, plumber, and in May 1681 Gabriel Cibber was paid £80 for carving the four statues on the parapet. More than £18 was paid for his and his men's board and so, with little doubt, the figures were cut in Cambridge. Percy was one of the carvers paid for the architectural sculpture. In January 1684 the scaffolding, presumably the external scaffolding, was struck. Timber for the roof had been provided in 1683–4, for the flooring in 1685–6, and the internal plastering and ceiling were completed in 1687; Doogood and Grove were the London plasterers. The most ingenious floor-construction supervised by Banckes is illustrated and described by H. M. Fletcher, 'Sir Christopher Wren's Carpentry', in R.I.B.A. *Journal*, xxx, 3rd Ser. (1923), 388. In 1688 the marble paving was laid by agreement of March 1687, with Grumbold, at 2*s*. 3*d*. a foot. Before the end of 1690 all mason's work was finished. Partridge, a London smith, provided the iron gates on the ground floor and the staircase balustrading for £400, and these were installed in 1691–2.

Regarding the woodwork etc., other than the structural timberwork, between 1685 and 1691 Cornelius Austin was paid for boarding, planks, including cedar, carving and bookcases. By the later year he had made nineteen bookcases, for £28 each. Subsequently he made a pair of doors for one of the MS. classes for £22 10*s*. Apparently in connection with a visit of his to London between March 1691 and February 1692, a guinea was paid to Hawksmoor. Grinling Gibbons and Cornelius Austin supplied the achievements etc. on the ends of the cases between March 1691 and December 1695; for his part of these, the busts above, the statue of the Duke of Somerset, and other carvings unspecified the former was paid over £400; only two of the original busts survive. In May 1695 the Library was still not furnished, according to Ralph Thoresby, although books were moved in in that year (*The Diary of Ralph Thoresby*, ed. Hunter, 1830, 435). In 1698–9 John Austin and Francis Woodward made two more pairs of doors for the MS. enclosures and in 1699 more books were moved in. The subscription-lists were already closed and the building may be regarded as then complete. Some uncertainty must remain about the cost, but it was of the order of £15,000.

The glass now in the N. and S. windows was added subsequently. In 1850 additional small oak bookcases were made in consultation with C. R. Cockerell and in 1850–1 the trabeations of the ceiling, omitted in the building, though shown in Wren's drawing, were added.

The E. side (Plate 264), to Nevile's Court, is strictly symmetrical; it is of two correct superimposed orders, Roman Doric and Ionic, with contained arches in eleven bays within the confines of the N. and S. ranges and with two flanking astylar bays across the ends of these last and rising clear of them. The whole has a balustraded parapet with plain pedestals, of which the middle four support statues (Plate 271). The attached three-quarter columns of the lower order have square sub-bases and support an uninterrupted entablature returned to end just short of the N. and S. ranges, so setting the architectural bounds of the composition fronting the Court, returns of the Ionic entablature being vertically above. The Doric architrave is plain, the frieze contains a triglyph centred over each column and three between in every bay. The contained arches have plain responds with moulded bases and imposts; these last support flat arches in the form of moulded lintels from which spring semicircular arches with moulded archivolts and keystones. The keystones project as scroll-brackets rising to the soffit of the main entablature. The tympanum of each arch is solid and contains a sculptured relief, that in the middle a figure-subject, Ptolemy II receiving the Septuagint from the Translators (Plate 271), for which a payment in April 1679 to 'the carver at London for cutting of the middle piece in the middle arch for stone and other things' is thought to refer, the others with elaborate cartouches flanked by garlands on broad pedestals with foliate side-pieces (Plate 271).

The attached three-quarter Ionic columns have plain shafts and capitals with swags slung from the volutes; they stand on low pedestals returned as apron-walls across each bay and support a plain crowning entablature returned at the end columns and continued across the end bays. The contained arches rise from the apron-walls and have plain responds with moulded bases and enriched imposts, moulded archivolts and keystones carved with masks. They contain three-light windows with square stone mullions and a moulded transom at the springing; the glazing consists of rectangular leaded quarries. The astylar end bays are both panelled and contain a window in an arched frame, similar to the foregoing but without the keystone, screened in the lower part by the adjoining ranges, and with a human mask flanked by swags immediately over the archivolt.

The payments for these enrichments of the upper part are recorded in detail: 'Mr. Percy and carver. Dec. 1678 to Mr. Percy for cutting the impost mouldings in part £8 10*s*. March 1679 for the thirteen great heads £13, for twelve capitals £25 10*s*., for four festoons £8.'

On the parapet, on the middle pedestals, stand Cibber's statues personifying Mathematics, Physics, Law, and Divinity (Plate 271), all female figures, the first counting on her fingers, the second holding a staff encircled by a serpent, the third holding a scroll inscribed 'Ivbet et Prohibet', the fourth shrouded, holding a book; each is accompanied by her emblem, a globe, a cock, books, an eagle. Cut on the die of the southernmost pedestal on this side are the name and date 'John Yaxly' and 'turner 1712'.

The W. side (Plate 263) is in two stages, divided as described below, and with a balustraded parapet. The lower stage is designed as a monumental base, with a great expanse of ashlar pierced by three doorways and ten windows symmetrically arranged. The openings are low in order to clear the Library floor, which is not expressed architecturally on this side. The surrounds to the doorways are similar to one another; they are of the Roman Doric order, with attached three-quarter columns with short pilaster-like returns at the sides supporting full entablatures, all on a very large scale. The entablatures are returned and continued across the building, the architrave and frieze together as a slight projection of the wall-face, entirely plain, the cornice in full. The doorways rise only some three-fifths of the height of the order; flat arches in the form of moulded lintels are there supported on responds with moulded caps and bases and the blind spaces above panelled. In the openings are original wrought-iron gates, hung in 1691–2, with plain uprights and two deep bands of scrollwork (Plate 273). The windows have architraves, friezes and cornices, and square sills, elaboration being restricted to the simplest of moulding; they contain original wrought-iron grilles.

The Doric cornice described divides the stages. Above it is an unbroken masonry course with moulded capping-string forming a plinth to tall rectangular wall-recesses containing the Library windows, thirteen in all, opposite those on the E. and generally similar to them but without keystones and enrichment on the imposts; the end windows, being in wider bays, are flanked by narrow blind recesses. At the wall-head is a plain unbroken frieze and cornice. The parapet balustrade is divided into seventeen bays, corresponding to the recesses below, by pedestals.

The N. end is largely covered by the staircase-pavilion, but the upper part, rising clear, is of ashlar with a return of the top cornice and balustraded parapet; in it is a window similar to the W. windows in the Library. 'I made the pavilions of the stairs so as I might not lose my end lights' (Wren's letter quoted above). On the E. is a small rectangular projection of red brick with stone quoins containing a staircase to the roof; the cornice and parapet, here plain, return round it. The pavilion is of similar materials to the foregoing and with stone window-dressings. Half the length of the N. wall has been refaced and the N.W. angle rebuilt; the lower part of the latter is now splayed and the angle above supported on plain splayed corbelling. In the N. wall are four rectangular windows, of two lights with architraves. The shaped, lead-covered roof rises in a convex curve to a short vertical face with a cornice from which it continues in flat ogee form.

The S. end is partly covered by the W. range of New Court. High in the middle of the lower stage is a square-headed doorway with eared architrave opening on a small balcony with a wrought-iron railing. William Grizell was paid £20 for this last, which was set up between March 1693 and July 1695. The staircase-pavilion at this end proposed by Wren, of similar design to that on the N., was never built, but this doorway, which would have given access to it, shows that the proposal was not abandoned until comparatively late. The Doric cornice alone returns from the W. side, but only a short way, and then continues as a plat-band. The frieze and cornice at the wall-head and the balustraded parapet are continuous. The window in the middle of the upper stage is similar to the W. windows of the Library but without mullions and transom.

Inside the Library range, the 'cloister' (Plate 263) on the ground floor is open from end to end, excluding the staircase-pavilion. Down the middle, from N. to S., is a row of fourteen Roman Doric columns, the two towards each end coupled; on the side and end walls and in the angles are responds in the form of attached half-columns and quarter-columns. They support a heavily trabeated plaster ceiling. The columns, responds and E. wall are of ashlar; the N., S. and W. walls are plastered. 'I have chosen middle pillars and a double portico and lights outward rather than a middle wall, as being the same expense, more graceful, and according to the manner of the ancients who made double walks (with three rows of pillars, or two rows and a wall) about the forum'. (Wren's letter quoted above, All Souls College, Wren drawings, Vol. I, 44). The openings to the walks in the N. and S. ranges of Nevile's Court are similar to those of the rest of the E. arcade as viewed from inside the 'cloister'. In the N. wall, the doorway to the staircase has a stone architrave and contains an original oak door in two leaves, each of five bolection-moulded panels.

The *Staircase-pavilion* (27 ft. by 21 ft.) has a black and white marble pavement. The staircase rises to the first floor in three flights. The wrought-iron balusters are alternately square and twisted, the twisted ending in scrolls, and support a moulded wrought-iron handrail. On the containing walls is a dado of bolection-moulded panelling. The inner ends of the black marble steps are supported on stone walls; in the W. wall of these last are two semidomed niches, one incorporating a doorway to a cupboard, flanking a white marble bust on a corbel, of Edward Wortley-Montagu signed 'P. Scheemakers Ft, 1766'. The landing also is paved with black and white marble squares, and the doorway to the Library has a stone doorcase with eared architrave, pulvinated frieze and cornice; the door is original, in two leaves, each of five bolection-moulded panels. The plaster ceiling (Plate 270) has deep coves rising to a modillion-cornice surrounding a rectangular panel containing an oval wreath framing a small plain domical recess. The coves are enriched with panels containing elaborate scrolled foliation with incidental beasts and birds flanking wreaths containing achievements-of-arms, on the N., of the Hon. Dr. John North (Master 1677–83), the S., of the See of Chester impaling John Pearson (Master 1662–73, Bishop of Chester 1673–86), the E., of the Hon. John Montagu (Master 1683–1700) Montagu quartering Monthermer, the W., of Dr. Isaac Barrow (Master 1673–7). Flanking the Library door, on modern pedestals, are white marble busts of Charles, Lord Whitworth of Galway, and Thomas, 2nd Lord Trevor, both signed 'L. F. Roubiliac sculpit 1757'. On the E. wall is a large oil painting by Benjamin West of St. Michael binding Satan, formerly in the Chapel reredos, given by Dr. John Hinchliffe, Master 1768–89.

The *Library* (Plate 265) (38 ft. by 191½ ft.) consists of one great compartment. It has panelling on the end walls and projecting bookcases and wall-cases down each side, all rising to about 2 ft. below window-sill level. The walls above and the trabeated ceiling are plastered. The broad central walk is paved with black and white marble squares. On the ends of the projecting bookcases are pedestals carrying wood and plaster busts; Wren proposed statues in these positions but in fact Gibbons was paid for busts. Standing against the ends of the cases are white marble busts on pedestals; these were not part of the original scheme but have been collected and so placed at different times, to become part of the architectural aspect of the building.

The side walls above the bookcases are each divided into thirteen bays by Composite pilasters supporting a continuous enriched entablature with modillion-cornice; the wider end bays are divided from the rest by coupled pilasters. Between these last are carried the mouldings of the enriched imposts to the great windows. The inside surrounds to the windows are of similar form to those outside, without keyblocks. The end walls above the panelling are each divided into three bays by

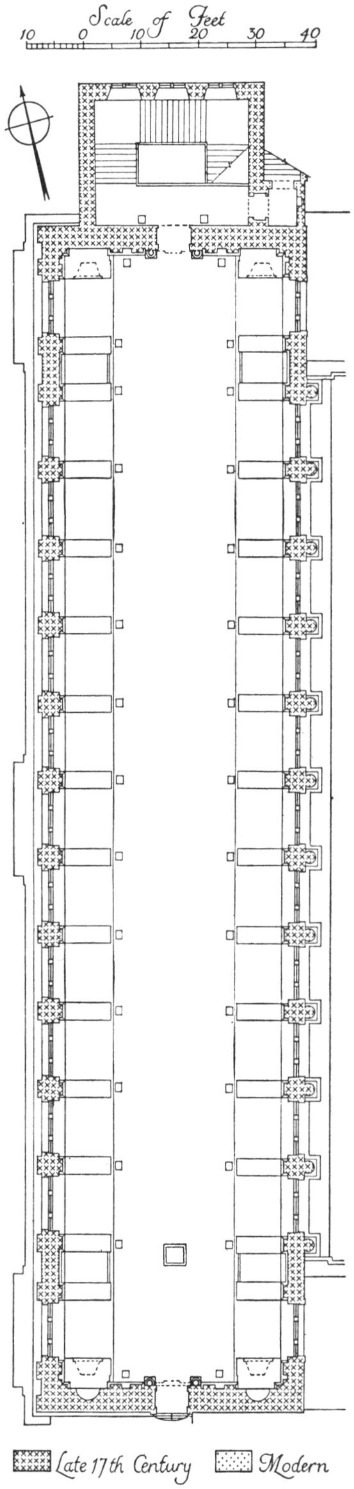

TRINITY COLLEGE LIBRARY

coupled Composite pilasters. In the middle bay is a great window similar to the foregoing. The enriched imposts of the window and the necking-mouldings of the pilaster-caps are continued across the flanking bays, and below the first are semidomed niches in the S. wall and above the second swags of fruit and flowers. The niches are an afterthought; they were inserted by Grumbold in 1692, after the plastering, for which John Grove was paid in full in 1687. The S.W. niche contains a white marble standing figure of Charles Seymour, 6th Duke of Somerset (Chancellor 1689–1748) (Plate 272) in Roman armour, for which Grinling Gibbons was paid in 1691.

The glass in the head of the N. window includes an achievement of the arms of Queen Anne, before 1707, with the initials A.R., the motto 'Semper eadem' and lion and unicorn supporters. The Junior Bursar's accounts 1705–06 include for 'carriage of the Queen's arms'. They were made by Henry Gyles of York in 1704 and set up in 1707; he refers to them in a letter to Ralph Thoresby (*Letters addressed to Ralph Thoresby* (ed. Hunter, 1832), II, 63). The supporters may have belonged to the arms of Charles II referred to in the accounts, 1682–3: 'Samuel Price, goldsmith in Lombard Street, gave the king's arms in painted glass'. The glass in the S. window (Plate 272) shows the University, personified by a female figure, in the left foreground presenting Sir Isaac Newton to George III. The king is enthroned, with Britannia beside him and Fame and cherubs in the clouds above. Seated in the right foreground is Lord Bacon in Lord Chancellor's robes. It was fixed in 1774–5; Cipriani was paid £105 for the design and Peckitt of York £315 for making it.

The N. and S. doorways have oak doorcases with enriched architraves, Corinthian columns at the sides supporting entablature-blocks and broken segmental pediments. Applied on the frieze and the pediment are limewood garlands of fruit and flowers exquisitely carved in the round; similarly in the pediments are roundels of the Royal arms of William III in a Garter, crowned and flanked by wings and palm-leaves. The inner N. door is modern; the inner S. door is original and of bolection-moulded panels. Similarly moulded panelling with applied limewood swags lines the walls to each side of the doorcases and returns to form projecting cupboards containing panelled alcoves in the corners of the room. The alcoves (Plates 266, 267), facing N. and S., are three-sided and have semicircular heads with most elaborate carved limewood flowers and foliation in place of archivolts; two of the carvings are missing. The semi-conoidal soffits have radiating panels and in the small tympanum formed in the back of each recess is a limewood whorl of foliage. The alcoves are flanked by pilaster-strips with paired cherub-heads and garlanded drapery instead of caps supporting a broken segmental pediment with enriched members. The return-panelling to the ends of the cupboards is on the plane, and repeats the design, of the ends of the projecting bookcases next described, except that the limewood shields-of-arms are omitted and the panels contain metal grilles; above are pedestals and busts, as on the bookcases (see below).

The fourteen projecting oak bookcases on each side are centred on the wall-pilasters above, thus the penultimate bays are narrower than the others; the narrow recesses so formed are closed by doors. The reason for the spacing and the use of it are described by Wren, 'The necessity of bringing windows and doors to answer to the old building' of Nevile's Court 'leaves two squarer places at the ends and four lesser cells not to study in but to be shut up with some neat lattice doors for archives'. The projection of the alcove features described above, presumably Wren's own revision of the scheme he describes, has reduced 'the squarer places' to the normal bay width, and doorways were never in fact opened through to the N. and S. ranges of Nevile's Court.

The bookcases, returned across the back of each recess, have cupboards in the base behind a high plinth with bolection-moulded panels, open shelves above and a continuous enriched entablature; the ends, between the plinth and the entablature, are in two heights of bolection-moulded panels, the lower panels each enclosing a smaller hinged panel containing book-lists and with a foliated cartouche for the class-letter above and carved swags below, the upper for the most part with achievements-of-arms and cyphers (see below) in wreaths of foliage, fruit and flowers hung upon them. The last described are carvings of remarkable virtuosity; they are cut from blocks composed of 2½-in. planks of pale limewood glued together. The pedestals on the entablatures are original, but the busts they support are, except two, later. The doors to the archive enclosures are in two leaves, close-panelled below and with carved and pierced panels above and scrolled top-rails. Before the ends of the bookcases and between the N. and S. doorways and the alcoved cupboards are white marble busts on pedestals (see below).

The series of limewood achievement-of-arms etc. and the two series of busts are here listed, first on the E. side, from N. to S., then on the W. side, from N. to S.; by including the cupboards and blank spaces in each series the numbering is constant for each group:

Arms etc. of (1) (cupboard), (2) Robert Drake (Plate 268), (3) cypher H.P., for Sir Henry Newton Puckering, Bt. (Plate 268), (4) Newton and Puckering quarterly, (5) crest, of Puckering, (6) William Lynnet, D.D., (7) Humphry Babington, D.D., Babington quartering Cave, (8) Sir George Chamberlaine, (9) Sir Robert Hildyard, Bt., (10) Sir Thomas Sclater, Bt., (11) the Hon. John Montagu, Montagu quartering Monthermer, (12) Isaac Barrow, D.D. (Plate 269), (13) See of Chester impaling John Pearson (Plate 269), (14) See of Lichfield and Coventry impaling John Hackett, (15) (blank), (16) (cupboard); on the W., (17) (cupboard), (18) decorative swag, (19–30) devices of Charles Seymour, 6th Duke of Somerset, Chancellor 1689–1748, (19) achievement, quarterly of six, the Seymour augmentation, Seymour, Beauchamp of Hache, Esturmy, Macwilliam, Prynne, all in a Garter with crest and unicorn and bull supporters, (20) Seymour crest, a demi-phoenix in flames issuing from a coronet, (21) cypher C.S. in a Garter, coroneted, (22, 25, 28) as (19), (23, 26, 30) as (20), (24, 27, 29) as (21), (31) (blank), (32) (cupboard). Payments are recorded in the accounts between March 1691 and December 1695 to Grinling Gibbons for (6–14) and (19–30) inclusive at £5 each, and to Cornelius Austin for (2) at £5.

Busts on the bookcases etc. of (1) Joseph Nollekens, R.A., aged 84, signed 'L. A. Goblet fecit 1821', (2) Homer, (3) Democritus, (4) Demosthenes, (5) Socrates, (6) Julius Caesar,

Divinity.

Ptolemy II receiving the Septuagint from the translators.

Law.

Mathematics.

E. tympanum.

Physics.

(40) TRINITY COLLEGE. Library. Stone sculpture.

Reliefs, 1677–78; statues, 1680–81

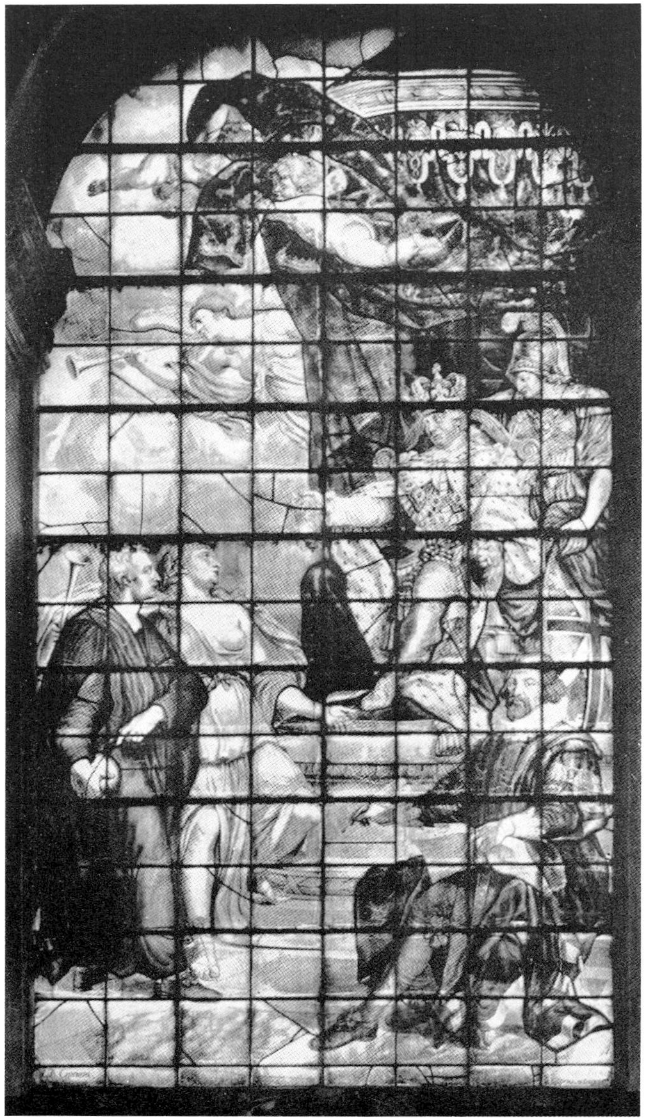

S. window. Designed by Cipriani. Installed 1774–75

Statue of Charles, 6th Duke of Somerset. By Grinling Gibbons. 1689–91

(40) TRINITY COLLEGE. Library.

(40) TRINITY COLLEGE. Library. Gate to 'Cloister'. 1691–92

(40) TRINITY COLLEGE. Hall brazier. 1702–03

(41) TRINITY HALL. Chapel. Lectern. c. 1730

Master's Lodge. Drawing-room. *c.* 1610

Old Combination Room. 1774

(40) TRINITY COLLEGE.

Dr. Eden's Room, looking N.W. 14th-century and later, reconstructed 1929

Library. Interior, looking W. Late 16th-century

(41) TRINITY HALL.

(41) TRINITY HALL. Fireplace in Library-annexe, former Combination Room. 1730

(41) TRINITY HALL. Hall. Fireplace. *c.* 1745

(39) SIDNEY SUSSEX COLLEGE. Fellows' Parlour. Fireplace. *c.* 1730

(40) TRINITY COLLEGE. The Fountain. Begun 1601–02; rebuilt 1716

(7) Marcus Aurelius, (8) Horace, (9) Cicero, (10) Marcus Brutus, (11) Seneca, (12) Virgil, (13) Anacreon (Plate 267), (14) Plato, (15) Shakespeare, (16) Hooper; W. side, (17) Newton, (18) Shakespeare, (19) Spenser, (20) B. Jonson (Plate 267), (21) Beaumont, (22) Fletcher, (23) Inigo Jones, (24) Sydenham, (25) Milton, (26) Dryden, (27) Locke, (28) Tillotson, (29) Addison, (30) Pope, (31) Porson, (32) Coleridge. (13) and (20) may well be two of those for which Gibbons was paid; they are of wood painted white.

Busts before the bookcases etc. of (1) Francis Willoughby (Plate 261), 'L. F. Roubiliac. Sct. 1751', (2) Sir William Bolland (1772–1840), 'Sievier Sc.', (3) Adam Sedgwick, '1860, T. Woolner, Sc. London.', (4) Anthony Shepherd, 'J. Bacon R.A. Sculpt. 1790', given 1796, (5) John Mitchell Kemble, 'T. Woolner. Sc. London., 1865', (6) Roger Cotes, 'P. Scheemakers Fecit: 1758', given the same year, (7) Arthur Caley, 1821–95, 'Henry Wiles Sc. Cambridge', (8) Lord Houghton, 1809–85, by W. W. Story, (9) Sir Robert Cotton, Bt. (Plate 261), 'L. F. Roubiliac 1757', given the same year, (10) William George Clark, 'T. Woolner Sc. London. 1879', (11) Julius Charles Hare, 'T. Woolner, Sc. London, 1861', (12) Connop Thirlwall, 1797–1875, 'E. Davis Sc. London', (13) Richard Bentley (Plate 261), 'L. F. Roubiliac Sct. 1756', given the same year, (14) Joseph John Thomson, 'Derwent Wood R.A. 1923', (15) (blank), (16) Francis Bacon, 'L. F. Roubiliac Sculpit 1751'; W. side, (17) John Ray (Plate 261), 'L. F. Roubiliac Sct. 1751', (18) Alfred Tennyson, 1857, 'T. Woolner, Sc. London.', (19) Arthur Henry Hallam, 1811–33, 'F. Chantrey Fecit', (20) James Jurin, 'P. Scheemakers Ft. 1766', (21) Coutts Trotter, 'T. Woolner Sc. London 1888', (22) Robert Smith, 'P. Scheemakers Fecit: 1758', given 1758, (23) Robert Leslie Ellis, 'T. Woolner. Sc. London. 1867', (24) John Ferguson McLennan, 'J. Hutchinson R.S.A. Edinburgh 1892', (25) Sir Edward Coke, 'L. F. Roubiliac 1757', given the same year, (26) Johnstone Munro, 'T. Woolner Sc. London 1886', (27) William Whewell, 'E. H. Baily, R.A. Sculp. 1851', (28) William Clark, by Timothy Butler, London, given 1882, (29) Isaac Barrow, signed twice 'L. F. Roubiliac Sct. 1756', given the same year, (30) Lord Lyndhurst, 'W. Behnes Sculpt. 1844', given 1876, (31) (blank), (32) Isaac Newton (Plate 262), 'L. F. Roubiliac Sculpit. 1751'. Ray (17) and his pupil Willoughby (1), F. Bacon (16) and Newton (32) flanking the N. and S. doorways respectively were the first to be set up; they have original marble pedestals; most of the rest are on oak pedestals copied from the last. (See also Staircase-pavilion above). A terracotta bust of Newton (Plate 262), signed 'M. Rysbrack 1739', has recently been placed near (32); it was at Teddesley Hall, Warwickshire, from 1756 to 1932.

Centrally placed towards the S. end of the room is a large white marble seated figure of Lord Byron on a pedestal (Plate 81) signed 'Thorvaldsen Fecit', given in 1843 and set up here in 1845. The feet rest on a fragment of a Doric column, and he holds a pencil and a copy of *Childe Harold*; in the pedestal is a relief of the Genius of Poetry, a winged youth playing a lyre, with his foot on the prow of a ship. It was carved in Rome in 1831. A committee of Byron's friends offered it to Westminster Abbey.

In the recesses between the bookcases are original reading-tables and stools. Wren's suggestion for these appears in his sketch dated 1686 at All Souls College for one of the bookcase bays, and the final design in a dimensioned drawing in the same collection (Wren drawings, Vol. I, 48 and 49; Wren Soc., V, 44 and pl. xxiv). The oak tables have square tops, panelled bearers, and four turned legs with carved braces; turning on central posts threaded through the tops and steadied by diagonal stretchers below are flattened pyramidal bookrests. The oak stools have rectangular seats, panelled bearers and turned legs.

The *Tribunal*, a classical composition on a raised terrace, stands against the W. side of the Hall, centred on Nevile's Court. Payments for it to Robert Grumbold occur in the building accounts for the Library in 1682 and 1683. Built of Ketton stone ashlar, it consists of a screen with the W. face in five unequal bays divided and flanked by attached Roman Doric columns on square sub-bases supporting a full crowning entablature. This last is discontinued over the middle bay, which is spanned by an open pediment surmounted by three urns containing carved flowers. The order frames a large round-headed segmental niche in the middle bay and smaller niches in the flanking bays; the narrow end bays are panelled. The niches rise from stone benches and have moulded archivolts with keystones and continuous imposts extending between the columns. Grumbold was paid £7 10*s.* for the 'flowerpots upon the pediment' in October 1683. The terrace, arranged as shown on the plan, has a rusticated ashlar retaining-wall on the W. surmounted by stone balustrading between pedestals. On four of the pedestals are 18th-century wrought-iron lamp-standards. The paving is of rectangular stone slabs.

Bishop's Hostel (Plate 212) is a detached building standing 10 yds. S.W. of Great Court, with the E. side bordering Trinity Hall Lane. It is of two storeys with attics. The walls are of red Stow brick, in Flemish bond, with freestone dressings, and the roofs are tiled. Dr. John Hackett, Bishop of Lichfield and Coventry 1661–71, was the donor and Robert Minchin, carpenter, of Bletchingdon, Oxfordshire, the builder. The agreement between the Master and Fellows and Minchin is dated 15 January 1669–70; the contract survives, and the present Hostel differs only slightly from the plan attached. It was finished in 1671 and cost £1,200. The original dormer-windows were altered in the late 18th century. In 1874 the proposal to demolish the building suggests that it was in bad condition, but in the event it was restored under the supervision of A. W. Blomfield between then and 1878.

The building is symmetrically planned in the form of a half-H, with the wings extending northward. It has a brick plinth with moulded stone weathering, stone quoins, a stone plat-band at first-floor level and a plaster coved eaves-cornice springing from a stone necking-mould. The windows, except the dormers, are uniform, with moulded stone architraves and sills; none of the original two-light and transomed timber frames survives, and the present 19th-century ones are very slight reproductions of them. The hipped dormer-windows have two-light timber frames with 18th-century leaded glazing. The main roofs are hipped, 'a sufficiently strong French roof to be made after the best manner hipped and with handsome Lutheran windows in the roof answerable to the fashion of the same roof' (Minchin's contract).

On the N., the recessed entrance-front is in three bays. The middle bay presents an Ionic pedimented composition; it projects and is carried up a short way above eaves-level; all the horizontal features described above, plinth, plat-band, and cornice, stop against it; flanking the central entrance-doorway and inset from the quoins are two colossal Ionic stone pilasters on stepped sub-bases supporting a full pedimented entablature with short returns. In the tympanum is a freestanding cartouche carved with the arms of the See of Lichfield and Coventry impaling Hackett. The doorway has a stone architrave, pulvinated frieze and cornice; over it is a flat stone inscribed 'Bishops Hostel 1670' and surmounted by a horizontal rectangular panel of carved foliage. The central window above on the first floor is of the pattern already described. In each side bay is a window on each floor and a dormer-window axially above.

The N. wings and E., W. and S. sides have openings as shown on the plan. The doorways near the re-entrant angles are similar to that already described but rather smaller and with simpler mouldings. On the first floor a window occurs over each ground-floor opening. On the roof, the dormer-windows number two on each of the inward facing sides, one on each of the N. ends, two on the E., two on the W., and five on the S. The three chimney-stacks rising from the roof-ridges have square bases, arched panels in the sides and moulded brick cappings; they are similar to those shown by Loggan though rebuilt above the bases in modern times.

Across the base of the recessed front is a low, paved terrace approached up three steps and with a brick retaining-wall with flat stone coping.

The interior has been much modernised; some of the partitions between studies and bedrooms have been removed, but otherwise the original arrangement remains. 'Upon the ground floor there shall be five outward chambers, and each of those chambers to have made and belonging thereunto two bedchambers and two studies', each bedchamber to be 7 ft. by 5½ ft., and each study 6 ft. by 5 ft., and the first floor to repeat this arrangement (Minchin's contract). Only one departure was made from the revised contract plan, presumably during building: the chimney-stack shown projecting from the middle of the S. wall was placed within the S. block, centrally against the E. cross-wall.

Both staircases are original and divided from the adjoining corridors by open screens of turned balusters in timber framing. On the first floor, the middle room of the S. block is lined with bolection-moulded panelling in two heights surmounted by an entablature; this last crosses small panelled pilasters flanking a square panel in the overmantel of the modern fireplace. Some old moulded plank doors and others of two panels survive.

Nevile's Gate (Plate 259) is now between Bishop's Hostel and the S. range of Great Court, at the W. end of Trinity Lane; this is certainly the third and probably the fourth position in which it has stood.

It is of the early 17th century and conjectured to have been originally in the cross-wall that closed Nevile's Court on the W. In *c.* 1688 a gate recognisable as Nevile's Gate is shown by Loggan at the W. end of the avenue crossing Trinity College Meadow; the leases of the land beyond had only been acquired after the middle of the same century. In 1733 it was moved to the entrance to the College from Trinity Hall Lane, then close S. of Bishop's Hostel, and, in 1876, during the Mastership of W. H. Thompson, to its present position.

The gateway is of ashlar, much refaced. The two sides are similar in design. The arch has a semicircular head with moulded archivolts and imposts, scrolled keystone with prism pendant, carved spandrels containing shields, and stop-moulded responds. Against the flanking piers are Roman Doric half columns on tall panelled pedestals supporting an entablature. This last is surmounted by a large central achievement-of-arms in a strapwork frame and by carved badges, roses and thistles, and obelisks over the columns. The wall-faces flanking the shafts of the order have shields-of-arms on the inward sides and oval sinkings on the outward sides.

The large achievement is of the Stuart Royal arms on the E. flanked by rose and thistle badges, the Nevile arms in six quarters on the W. flanked by Neville crests of a bull's head and a ship on a chapeau; the Nevile arms quarter Neville, Bulmer, Eudo, Middleham, Clavering. If the conjecture of the original position of the Gate be accepted, then the achievements are probably those carved by G. Woodroffe (Junior Bursar's accounts 1659–60) to replace those of the Commonwealth, which themselves replaced the Royal arms in 1650–1. The other arms are, on the E., in the spandrels, both of Nevile, on the piers, of Magdalene College impaling Nevile, and the College impaling Nevile; on the W. similarly, of the College, and Thompson impaling Selwyn, and of the Deanery of Canterbury impaling Nevile, and the Deanery of Peterborough impaling Nevile.

'King's Court' (151 ft. by 164 ft.), known as *New Court* (Plate 39), adjoining Nevile's Court on the S., was designed by William Wilkins in 1821, begun in 1823 and occupied in 1825. George IV contributed £1,000 towards the total cost of £50,444. Spicer Crowe, builder, of London, was the contractor. It is in the Tudor-Gothic style. The N. range is a part of the S. range of Nevile's Court and described accordingly above, the 19th-century work being a remodelling only of that part of the S. side towards New Court. The other ranges are of three storeys with attics and contain sets of chambers.

The river front is faced with Ketton stone ashlar and that to Garret Hostel Lane with white brick with Ketton dressings; the rest of the walling is for the most part cement-rendered. The buildings have moulded plinths, strings at first and second-floor levels and embattled parapets with parapet-strings embellished with carved bosses. On most of the salient angles are octagonal buttresses carried up above the main parapets and embattled. Unless otherwise described, the windows are of two lights with cinquefoiled openings in square heads on the ground floor and four-centred heads with pierced spandrels on the floors above, all with labels. Except in the N. range, the inner order of the windows to the Court is of cast-iron painted to simulate stone.

The *East* and *West Gatetowers* are very similar; the first is placed axially upon the Court in the E. range, the second asymmetrically in the W. range but axially upon Trinity Bridge. They rise above the flanking buildings and have taller octagonal buttresses at the corners. Both have E. and W. gateways with moulded jambs and four-centred arches in square heads with carved spandrels containing shields-of-arms of the College. The original timber gates are both in two leaves of three tiers of four linenfold panels. On the first floor are two windows as described, but transomed, separated and flanked by wall-panelling; on the second floor, except in the W. face of the W. Gatetower, similar windows, without transoms, are separated but not flanked by wall-panelling. The differing W. tower has two two-light windows with vertical tracery in square heads flanking a central niche with traceried canopy and a corbel supported on an angel holding a shield of the Tudor Royal arms. Below the E. and W. parapet-strings are friezes of quatrefoiled panels enclosing blank shields; the embattled parapets are plain except again on the W. side of the W. tower where the wall is elaborated with pierced quatrefoiled panels and a central octagonal pinnacle. The *Gatehalls* (27¼ ft. by 17 ft. and 27 ft. by 16¾ ft.) have pointed-segmental plaster vaults with tracery-panelling on the soffits.

The fenestration of the W. side of the *West Range*, excluding the N. bay and the two S. bays, is arranged in four groups, each group being of three bays and symmetrical in itself; the Gatetower occurs between the first and second group from the N. Each centres upon a first-floor oriel-window supported on moulded corbelling, with three transomed lights on the face, one on each canted side and a pierced parapet. Centrally above the foregoing is a large second-floor window of three lights with vertical tracery in a four-centred head rising above the main parapet-string into a small gable. The gable is elaborated with a blank shield and an octagonal pinnacle at the apex. The ground-floor windows and the flanking windows on the upper floors are similar to those described but with transoms on the first floor. The northernmost bay is of two storeys only and divided from the rest by an octagonal buttress; in it are paired archways with moulded jambs and four centred heads on the ground floor and two windows on the first floor similar to the window next to the S. at the same level. The two S. bays contain windows on all floors similar to those at the same levels next to the N. The dormer-windows, largely screened, are flat topped, and the plain chimney-stacks are rendered.

The E. side of the W. range is without the elaboration of the W. side. All the features are as generally described above. The ground-floor openings are shown on the plan, the doorways having continuously moulded jambs and four-centred heads with labels, and windows occur regularly over them on both floors above. Again the northernmost bay is marked by a buttress and of two-storeys only, being largely screened by a single-storey forebuilding of the N. range. In the S.W. angle of the Court is a projecting turret rising as an octagon above the adjoining ranges and embattled; it is entered through a doorway similar to those just described but smaller and lit by single-light windows.

The *East Range* has much of the lower part of the E. side concealed by later additions. Most of the ground floor S. of the Gatetower is of exposed brick to a height of 6 ft.; here the windows are as shown on the plan, those without mullions containing double-hung sashes, and with dummy windows opposite the staircases and smaller lights inserted subsequently below. The single-light windows each have three others closely spaced in the height of wall above them. With these exceptions, the windows on all floors are similar to those described generally above, the larger with cast-iron inner orders. The W. side is of similar detail and character to the W. side of the Court.

The N. side of the *South Range*, again similar in detail to the E. and W. sides of the Court, is elaborated with a grouping of three bays in the centre similar to the individual tripartite grouping described on the W. side of the W. range with, in addition, tall niches beyond the flanking windows; the niches contain pedestals and have canopies surmounted by wall-arches containing crowned Tudor roses. The symmetry is accentuated by projecting the middle nine of the total of thirteen bays on this side and placing buttresses on the salient angles. The recessed faces contain tiers of single-light windows at the extremities. The S. side, to Garret Hostel Lane, has buttresses at each end, that to the E. cut away on the ground floor; all the windows have flat brick arches and double-hung sashes.

Inside, the E., S. and W. ranges contain stone staircases with plain iron balustrades. The sets opening from them on each side contain a sitting-room overlooking the Court, a bedroom behind and a gyp-room; some of those adjoining the Gatetowers and the S.E. and S.W. turrets are slightly more ingeniously planned and contain an extra room. The fireplace-surrounds, mostly original, have flanking panelled pilaster-strips and plain shelves; those in the larger sets are mostly of marble or wood, the rest of stone. A late 18th-century surround on the first floor of the E. range comes from elsewhere. The original main doors are of four panels with a central bead-moulding. Most of the plaster ceilings are original, segmentally vaulted on the second floor of the Gatetowers and with simple cornices elsewhere.

Lecture Room Court (43 ft. by 53 ft.) was added on the S.E. of Great Court in 1833–4. It is of two and three storeys, with walls of gault brick, rendered towards the Court, and slated roofs. The building, according to the Conclusion of 15 June 1833, was to be superintended by Humfry (Charles Humfrey). It consists of a N. range, elongated from N. to S. to fit into the constricted space between the E. range of Great Court and the old boundary-wall dividing the College from the houses on Trinity Street, and a S. range in continuation of the S. range of Great Court. The S. range, which may incorporate a rather earlier building on the S., was extended S.E. after 1864. In 1953–4 the N. range was heightened, the upper lecture room being demolished and replaced by two floors of chambers.

The Court is in the Tudor-Gothic style, the E. side of that part of the E. range of Great Court facing it being remodelled accordingly. The ranges have low plinths, discontinuous strings at first-floor level and embattled parapets to the original walls. The windows generally are transomed, with four-centred openings above and below the transom, square heads and labels. The doorways have continuous moulded jambs and four-centred heads with labels.

The *North Range* has large oriel-windows to N. and S. rising the full height of the building, the upper parts being modern; on the S. oriel is a shield-of-arms of the College, on the N. of Wordsworth impaling Lloyd. The recessed S.W. wall contains a doorway and three windows, of one, two and three lights; over the doorway is a cusped panel with the date 1834.

The N. side of the *South Range* is symmetrical, with small rectangular towers at each end rising above the main parapets and embattled. Over the central doorway is a cusped panel containing a blank shield. Three-light windows occur on the first floor over those below, and a single-light window over the doorway. The S. side, excluding the late 19th-century extension, is in red brickwork incorporating some gault bricks. The centre bay projects slightly. The windows are of two and three lights and insertions. Remodelling of the W. side of the Court consists of the addition of two two-stage buttresses to the late 16th-century wall and the adjustment of the windows symmetrically in each bay.

Inside, the stone staircase in the N. range has a plain wrought-iron balustrade and the plaster ceiling of the stairhall is trabeated, the centre panel opening to a lantern. The mid 18th-century staircase in the S. range is of wood, with close strings, turned balusters, moulded handrail and square panelled newels.

Trinity Bridge (Plate 38) over the river W. of New Court is of old material reused in the piers and abutments and of Portland and Ketton stone ashlar above water-level. It was designed by James Essex, who supervised the building in 1764–5, in replacement of a mid 17th-century bridge, which itself replaced an earlier one. Dr. Francis Hooper bequeathed the money for it, the cost being £1,500.

It is slightly cambered from end to end and in three spans of graduated semi-elliptical arches springing from low cutwaters. The two sides are alike; the arches have moulded archivolts, and in the spandrels between the latter and a continuous modillion-cornice at road-level are carved shields-of-arms of the College and of Hooper; above is a solid parapet-wall with moulded plinth and capping. The parapet-walls stop at each end against pedestals, which have ramped and scrolled returns surmounting short ashlar continuations of the abutments. The flanking retaining-walls are of red brickwork.

The early 18th-century *Field Gates* at the W. end of the avenue leading from Trinity Bridge replace Nevile's Gate (see above), which was removed to make way for them in 1733. They were given to the College by the Hon. Henry Bromley, M.P., of Horseheath Hall, whence they came in that year. They are entirely of wrought-iron, with a central gate hung in two leaves and smaller side gates, the three being divided and flanked by wrought-iron piers supporting overthrows. The large central overthrow, containing the College arms, is composed of scrollwork of much elaboration with sheet-cut foliation and vase-shaped finials; the supporting piers have embossed sheet capitals and scrollwork spires. The side overthrows are slighter and in the form of scrolled abutments; the flanking piers have small scrollwork spires. Extending from the Gates are short lengths of railings, probably of 1733, guarding the bridge over the stream bounding the College grounds on the W.

The mid 18th-century *Gate* at the entrance to the Fellows' Garden, W. of Queens' Road, came in the present century from the Rectory Manor House, Enfield, Middlesex (see also Monument (21), the University Library). It consists of a central gate hung between piers supporting an overthrow and flanked by short lengths of railings, all being of wrought-iron incorporating decorative scrollwork and extending between modern stone piers.

Some ancient *Boundary-walls* etc. survive in the College grounds. The high wall running W.N.W. from the late 19th-century kitchen wing of the Master's Lodge probably marks one boundary of the former King's Childer Lane (see historical introduction to the College). Some 4 yds. at the E. end are modern, the next 25 yds. are mediaeval, thence to the river it is probably of the 17th century. The mediaeval length is of clunch, much patched and with brick bonding-courses in the E. part; it formed the S. external wall of a two-storey building, either part of the Master's Gallery, or the Comedy Room, and blocked doorways and windows with clunch dressings remain on both ground and first floors. The 17th-century length is of red brick.

Bounding Lecture-room Court on the E. and continuing a short way N. and S. is a length of high walling, much altered and concealed by cement rendering. It is at least as ancient as the late 17th century, being indicated in the left foreground of Loggan's engraving of the College.

At the W. end of the Master's kitchen-garden is an 18th-century brick retaining-wall beside the river. In it are four semicircular stone arches, probably to culverts, but now blocked.

Little of interest survives in the early 19th-century *Brewhouse* S.W. of New Court, but built into the W. wall and into a short length of 17th-century boundary-wall extending westward from it towards Garret Hostel Bridge are four late 17th-century stone cartouches carved with the arms of Nevile (twice), Sclater, and Babington, which were on the N. and S. ranges of Nevile's Court until these were remodelled in the 18th century. In all probability the one with Dr. Humphry Babington's arms is that for which Robert Grumbold was paid £3 (Willis and Clark, II, 527).

(41) Trinity Hall stands between Trinity Lane, formerly Milne Street, and the river and is bounded on the N. by Garret Hostel Lane and on the S. by Clare College. Henney Lane, formerly alongside the N. range of the present Front Court, was the N. boundary until 1545; thereafter it was closed and absorbed in the northern extension of the site.

The Hall of the Holy Trinity for scholars of canon and civil law was founded by William Bateman, Bishop of Norwich. He issued his statutes in January 1350 and in the following months obtained Royal Licences to acquire houses and the land for the College. The smaller site was wholly acquired by 1354, rather more than the southern half by purchase in 1350 from the Chapter of Ely, being the area comprising the hostel and grounds bought by Prior John Crauden (1321–41) for Ely monks studying in Cambridge.

The date of the commencement of building is unrecorded but Richard de Bury is known to have been employed as master-carpenter in 1352. Completion was perhaps retarded by Bateman's death in January 1355. He left only a Master, three Fellows and three scholars, for whom presumably the Ely hostel was available. Before 1374 the *Hall* and an E. range of chambers had been built, for in that year a contract was made between the Founder's executor, Simon Sudbury, Bishop of London, and John de Mildenhale, carpenter, of Cambridge, for the timberwork of offices and chambers; the work for the former is specified 'pro domibus' (*Kitchen-offices* etc., since remodelled,) 'construendis a boriali fine Aule—versus boream usque ad venellam communem vocat Heneylane', and, for the latter, to be similar in form and quality to that of the 'camerarum orientalium habitacionis dicti mansi'. This last was perhaps the *East Range*, subsequently rebuilt, of the present Front Court. The extent of the work specified in Mildenhale's contract points to the *North Range* of Front Court, which retains 14th-century features, as the chambers built in *c.* 1374. The Master's Lodge occupied the S. end of the Hall range and was presumably of the date of the Hall.

Licence was obtained from the Bishop of Ely in 1352 to build a *Chapel*, and reference to the 'chapel built' within the College occurs in 1366 in a petition to the pope for permission to celebrate therein (Granted, Avignon. *Cal. Pap. Petitions*, edn. W. B. Bliss, I, 533). The building has undergone much alteration but a piscina discovered *in situ* in 1864 is of the 14th century. The rest of the *South Range* may conjecturally be attributed to the same century.

The Court, now *Front Court*, thus completed, was the inner court of the College; the original entrance court, now *South Court*, adjoined it on the S., having a Gatehouse and Porter's Lodge in the E. range. This last, after the duplication of entrance to the College by the provision in 1742 of an entry through the E. range of Front Court, was rebuilt in 1872–3 by Alfred Waterhouse, the mediaeval entrance archways being re-erected in Garret Hostel Lane. The W. range of the same Court consisted of a S. extension of the Master's Lodge, probably of the late 16th century as described below, and older buildings.

During the Mastership of Dr. Harvey (1560–84) the College buildings, according to Dr. Caius, were extended and made more ornamental and ample. It was probably in this period or soon after that the N. range of Library Court, containing the *Library* on the first floor, was added and the storey built above the Butteries and Kitchen that incorporated the Combination Room; an early memorandum of uncertain date and authorship transcribed by Warren dated the second to 1563 (A. W. W. Dale, *Warren's Book* (1911), 65). The crow-stepped gables of these two additions are shown in Loggan's engraving of the College; their uniformity one with another and with those of the S. and W. extensions of the Master's Lodge suggests that all were works of much the same time. Loggan also shows the battlements of the wall closing Library Court on the W., now demolished, that carried a wall-walk providing direct access from the W. wing of the Master's Lodge to the Library.

During the 18th century a gradual but almost entire remodelling of the College buildings was effected and the appearance of Front Court completely altered. In 1702 sporadic insertion of sash-windows began, but the more wholesale changes were financed by Sir Nathaniel Lloyd (Master 1710–35). In March 1727–8 Christopher Cass, mason of London, agreed to replace the eaves of the N. range with a stone cornice and parapet-wall and to make two Classical doorcases of Ketton stone. He completed the work by July. In 1729 similar works on the Chapel range, with the Ketton stone cases for two windows and four round windows, were undertaken and alterations to the interior of the Chapel begun. By December 1730 the present ceiling, panelling and paving had been inserted in the Chapel, the former panelling being removed to the Ante-chapel. The cost, excluding extras not specified in the contract, was £923; the bill for extras, £63, includes the names of the following: James Jones, painter, Barker, carver, Mines, plasterer, and Carter and Essex, joiners. The bills are receipted by John Ogle for Cass and Partners, the principal partner being Andrews Jelfe, mason. The same year, 1730, the Combination Room, now and since 1890 a *Library-annexe*, was refitted and refurnished.

Cole in 1745 records the ashlaring of the entire Court since 1741, and describes the Hall as new, 'built from the ground in the place where the old one stood', James Burrough being the architect. But William Whiting of Cambridge had contracted in 1743 for the Hall and Butteries, and it is clear from the contract, 'to build with the best Ketton ashlar at 6 ins. thick', and from the account given by William Warren (*Collectanea ad Collegium sive Aulam Sanctae Trinitatis*, etc.) that refacing, not rebuilding, was involved. The interior of the Hall was remodelled, the offices altered and the whole range reroofed. Bills of quantities were to be supplied to Burrough and, in view of the design and uniformity of all the Court fronts, and Cole's statement, it is reasonable to attribute the total undertaking to him. Essex sen. was again party to a contract for the woodwork in both E. and W. ranges. A design, known from an engraving dated 1743, signed by James Burrough, 'Architect', and drawn by James Essex, jun., shows that Library Court was to be rebuilt on an impressive scale; but a bequest of £20,000 for the purpose was declined because of conditions attaching to it, and the scheme abandoned. Nevertheless, the refacing of the W. side of the Hall range, so far as it was completed, was in commencement of this new design.

In addition to the 19th-century alterations already described, the E. range of Front Court was gutted by fire in 1852 and rebuilt by A. Salvin. The Chapel was extended eastwards in 1864 by incorporating in it the Treasury adjoining on the E.; the window, already blocked, between the former Master's pew over the Ante-chapel and the Chapel was removed and the opening filled, and, in 1876–7, the walls were painted and the windows filled with stained glass; subsequently the former pew was opened out to form an organ-gallery. The original *Master's Lodge* in the S.W. angle of Front Court, with the 16th-century extensions to S. and W., was improved in 1804 and 1822; the work is unspecified, but the sum spent, £3,300, shows it to have been very extensive. The S. wing, with the rest of the W. range of South Court, was rebuilt in 1823, being completed in 1824 when Sir T. Le Blanc, Master, advanced £1,200 at 4½% to pay the cost. In 1852 the Lodge was enlarged, in part rebuilt and the interior considerably altered under the supervision of Anthony Salvin, and again altered and refronted in 1890–2, with the result that few ancient features survive. In this last period the College Hall was extended southward by incorporating in it the Master's original Parlour and room above in the S.W. angle of the Court, and the new *Combination Room* formed W. of the W. range of South Court instead of over the Butteries. At the same time an open timber roof was substituted for the 18th-century plaster ceiling in the Hall.

Latham Building, containing chambers, was built N.W. of the Library Range in 1889–90 to the designs of G. H. Grayson and E. A. Ould. Ranges in continuation of it were added in 1909 and 1927 beside Garret Hostel Lane and extending S.W. to the river. In 1928 to 1929 the interior of the N. range of Front Court was completely stripped of floors and partitions and replanned; the N. and S. walls were repaired and a number of mediaeval features exposed or restored. The 14th-century Kitchen, after extension in 1877, was remodelled and again extended northward in 1934. *North Court* is bounded on the W. by the extension just mentioned and by a contemporary range on the E., to make way for this last the Tutor's House built in 1882 being demolished; the N. range linking the two was built in 1952 and adjoins Garret Hostel Lane.

Trinity Hall possesses in Front Court the largest enclosed court on the Cambridge collegiate plan built before the end of the 14th century and the earliest of the kind to include a chapel. Little remains visible of the original buildings, which were largely refaced in the mid 18th century. This refacing extending throughout Front Court is in the Classical style; the design, probably by James Burrough, is small in scale and unspectacular, but harmonious and pleasing. The Elizabethan Library retains the original fittings and is important as an almost unaltered building of the period. The Chapel contains a remarkable plaster ceiling of 1730, and a rococo wall-monument of 1747 of accomplished design and workmanship. The fireplace and panelling of 1730 in the Library-annexe are notable.

Architectural Description—*Front Court* (114 ft. by 79 ft.), originally the inner court, is bounded on the E. by a range containing the main entrance to the College and sets of chambers, on the S. by a range containing the Chapel in the W. half and chambers in the rest, on the W. by the Hall range, and on the N. by a range of chambers. The walls, except where otherwise described, are faced with Ketton stone ashlar and the roofs are slate-covered.

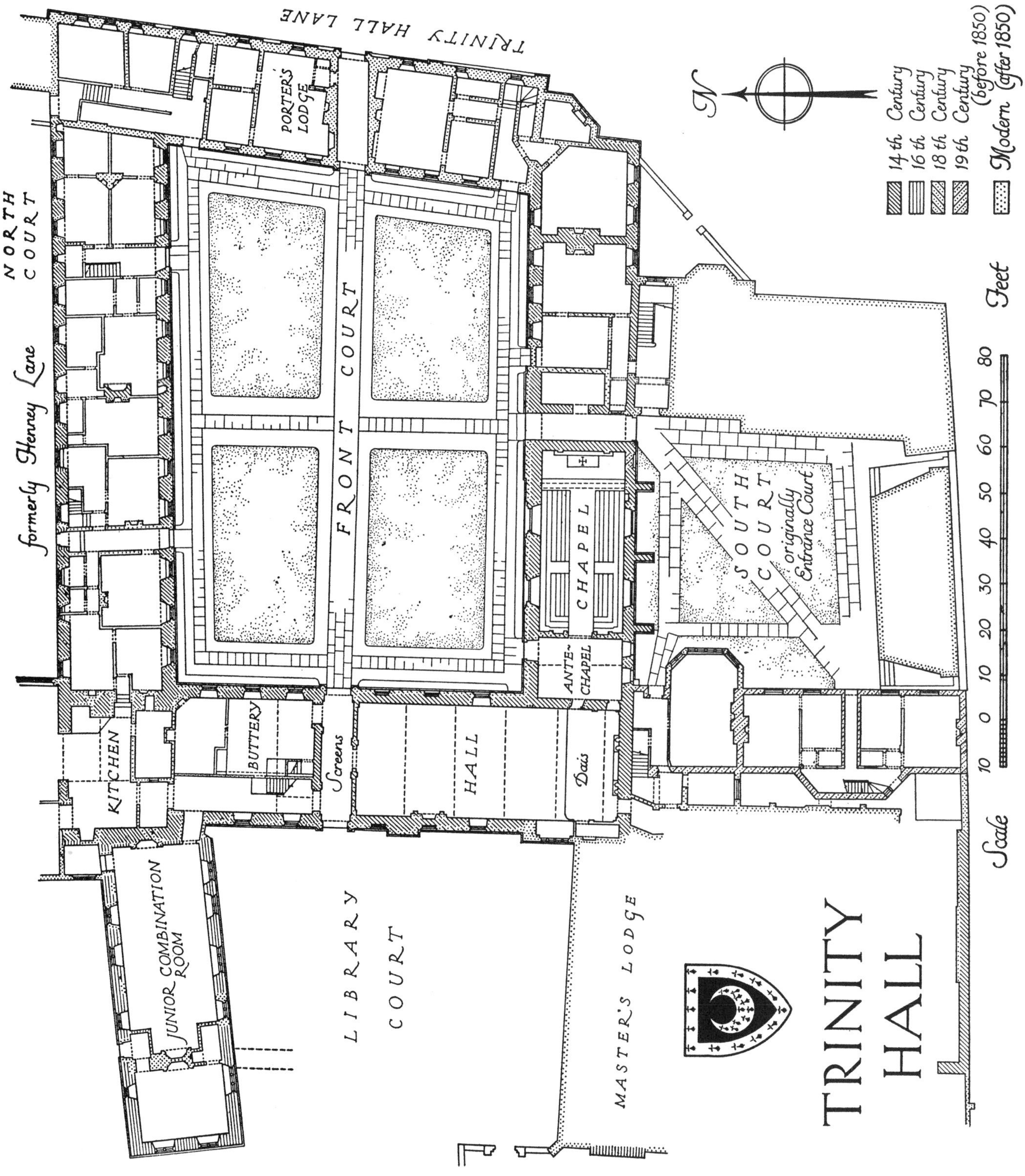
TRINITY HALL LANE
PORTER'S LODGE
NORTH COURT
formerly Henney Lane
FRONT COURT
CHAPEL
ANTE-CHAPEL
SOUTH COURT
originally Entrance Court
KITCHEN
BUTTERY
Screens
HALL
Dais
JUNIOR COMBINATION ROOM
LIBRARY COURT
MASTER'S LODGE
N
14th Century
16th Century
18th Century
19th Century (before 1850)
Modern (after 1850)
Scale
10 0 10 20 30 40 50 60 70 80
Feet
TRINITY HALL

The *East Range* is of three storeys. The original range, probably built in the third quarter of the 14th century, was entirely refaced between 1741 and 1745. In 1852 it was burnt out and rebuilt at a cost of about £4,800 to the designs of Salvin who retained the former stone surrounds of the openings to the entrance-passage. He also reproduced the 18th-century two-storey W. front, adding a third storey above the cornice. The 18th-century E. entrance has a semicircular arch on plain responds, with moulded archivolt and imposts, keystone, probably of 1852, carved with a bearded mask and a shell above, and panelled spandrels, all flanked by plain pilasters with console-brackets supporting a pedimented entablature; set in the arch-tympanum is an 18th-century wrought-iron grille with an applied cartouche displaying the arms of the College. The W. front of 18th-century character incorporates reused ashlar and dressings of this date; it is generally similar to the E. front of the W. range opposite, described below, but with 19th-century arched doorways at each end. The 18th-century central archway to the entrance-passage has a semicircular head and flanking pilasters with console-brackets supporting a pedimental entablature. The interior of the range is of 1852 and later.

The *South Range* of Front Court has, near the middle, a passage through to South Court. It is of one and two storeys with attics under a continuous roof. The S. side is of brick rough-cast, and with stone dressings. The Chapel was built in the second half of the 14th century and the rest of the range presumably at the same time; as described in greater detail above, the former was remodelled inside in 1729–30 and the whole refaced, towards the Court, between 1741 and 1745. The Treasury, W. of the passage, incorporated into the body of the Chapel in 1864, was once entered from the Chapel and was perhaps originally a sacristy.

The N. side has horizontal features continued from the E. and W. ranges, except that the plat-band is discontinued at the Chapel. In the roof are nine flat-topped 18th or 19th-century dormer-windows. The three bays centred on the passage project slightly. The semicircular-headed archway to the passage is rusticated; of the three windows on the first floor, the westernmost is blocked behind the sashes. E. of the projection are four regularly spaced windows on each floor and a doorway, shown on the plan, now blocked internally, which formerly opened on a staircase. The doorway has an architrave, pulvinated frieze and pedimented cornice, and is hung with an 18th-century door of six fielded panels. The S. side of the range seen from Trinity Lane has three windows on each floor. With the exception of those last described, which have semicircular heads, all the windows mentioned above are similar to those described on the W. side of Front Court.

The *Chapel* (54 ft., including the Ante-chapel 13½ ft., by 18½ ft.) is divided on the S. into four bays by mediaeval buttresses of four stages with gabled heads. The body of the Chapel is lit by two mid 18th-century semicircular-headed windows on each side; those on the N. have moulded architraves with plain impost-blocks and pedestal-like sills, all within a shallow casement-moulding with moulded surround and plain sill; those on the S. have architraves and plain imposts and sills. The N. doorway to the Ante-chapel has an architrave and panelled frieze with console-brackets supporting a pedimented cornice; all except the architrave is of the 19th century. In the opposite wall are two mid 18th-century round windows with moulded stone surrounds. The organ-gallery is lit from each side by a window contemporary with, and similar to, the main S. windows of the Chapel but considerably smaller. In the S.E. bay is a round window, as before, but blocked, on the ground floor and, above, a rectangular area of exposed brickwork in a flush stone frame. The S. archway to the through-passage is similar to that at the N. end and above it is a modern window.

In the interior, the Sanctuary represents the E. extension of 1864 and is demarcated by a flat panelled plaster ceiling; similarly the Master's pew at the W. end, latterly converted, has a flat ceiling. The main plaster ceiling (Plate 227) of 1730 is of segmental-barrel form. It has a continuous and unbroken entablature at the wall-head, duplicated on the end walls and turned below the vault, consisting of a frieze of Greek wave ornament and a dentil-cornice. The surface is divided into five panels in both length and width by broad bands of key ornament, with rosettes at the intersections. In the panels are cartouches containing painted shields-of-arms alternating, in the two rows of panels on either side, with large open sunflowers. The modelled enrichments are all coloured and gilded against a white ground. The arms are, from N. to S. and E. to W., of (a) the College impaling Dalling, (b) See of Norwich impaling Bateman, (c) Goodknape, (d) Spicer, (e) See of Norwich impaling Nykke, (f) Moptyd, (g) the College impaling Hewke, (h) See of Canterbury impaling Sudbury, (i) the College impaling Mowse, (j) Dunne, (k) tierced in pale, See of Winchester, Gardiner, the College, all in a Garter, (l) Busby, (m) the College impaling Harvey, (n) See of Canterbury impaling Parker, (o) the College impaling Eden. All the cartouches with the arms of bishoprics are surmounted by mitres. (For the woodwork, see Fittings.)

The Ante-chapel has in the S. end of the W. wall a mediaeval doorway with chamfered jambs and two-centred head; before the southward extention of the Hall it opened to the Master's Lodge.

Fittings—*Brasses* and *Indents*. *Brasses:* In Chapel—towards E. end, (1) of John Cowell, LL.D., 1611, Master, Regius Professor of Law, Vicar-General of the Province of Canterbury, rectangular inscription-plate with shields-of-arms of the College and Cowell in the upper corners, in black marble slabs; in floor of N. stalls, (2) of Thomas Eden, LL.D., [1645], Master, rectangular inscription-plate, second plate above with achievement-of-arms of Eden. In Ante-chapel—on panelling on S. wall, (3) of Daniel Darnelly, M.A., 1659, Fellow, inverted T-shaped inscription-plate with achievement-of-arms of Darnelly; (4) of Laurence Moptyd, S.T.B., 1557, Master of Corpus Christi College, rectangular plate with black-letter inscription; in floor, (5) of Walter Hewke, [1517, Master], figure of priest in cope over habit of Doctor of Canon Law, with lead inlay, head restored 1895, cope with Majesty on the morse and the Apostles on the orphreys, two scrolls and inscription-plate with blank for year of death; Hewke's will of 1 May 1517 reads 'and my gravestone that is ready bought and paid for—with the image and the scriptures made thereon'; (6) of Thomas Preston, LL.D., 1598, Master, set up by his wife

Alice, figure of man in civil dress, top of head missing, with inscription-plate and shield-of-arms of Preston, with lead inlay, all reset, another plate and the indent perhaps of this brass are said to be under the stalls (Mon. Brass Soc., *Trans.* II, 275); (7) priest in academic dress (B.D.?) with indent of inscription-plate, early 16th-century, perhaps recut. *Indent:* see (6) above.

Communion-table: of oak, with plain top, moulded bearers and turned legs, *c.* 1600, with modern heightening. *Doors:* see Screen. *Gallery-front:* See Screen. *Lectern:* Fitted to E. desk-end of upper S. stalls, wrought-iron hinged scrollwork bracket with smaller scrolled supports to bookrest, *c.* 1730 (Plate 273).

Monuments and *Floor-slabs. Monuments:* In Chapel—on N. wall, (1) of Thomas Eden, LL.D., 1645, Master, Chancellor of the diocese of Ely, Commissary of Westminster and Bury St. Edmunds, etc., black marble inscription-tablet in alabaster frame with gadrooned capping surmounted by urns and a cartouche with the painted arms of Eden, set up by the Master and Fellows *c.* 1708. On S. wall, (2) of Sir Nathaniel Lloyd, LL.D., [1741], Master, King's Advocate, white marble tablet with pedimented cornice and cartouche with the painted arms of Lloyd quartering Cadwgan Bacchew in the tympanum, urns, black marble shelf, shaped brackets, and apron inscribed with year of production, 1736; (3) of John Andrew, LL.D., 1747, Fellow, Master of the Faculties, Chancellor of the diocese of London, etc., white marble wall-monument (Plate 203), with portrait bust in half relief in an oval framed by palm-branches and surmounted by a cartouche with the painted arms and carved crest of Andrew, shaped inscription-plaque below with rococo border, all against black marble backing, the figure in informal dress and turban, signed 'Rt. Taylor, Fect.'. In Ante-chapel—on W. wall, (4) of the Rev. Joseph Jowett, LL.D., 1813, Fellow, Regius Professor of Law, white marble tablet with black marble shelf, capping and pedimental top. *Floor-slabs:* In Chapel—towards E. end, (1) of Robert King, 1676, Master, Chancellor of the diocese of Ely, of black marble, damaged, with achievement-of-arms of the College impaling King; in floor of N. stalls, (2) of Walter Hewke, [1517], Master, small white marble diagonal slab, laid down 1730, damaged and partly obscured; in floor of S. stalls, (3) of Sir Nathaniel Lloyd, 1741, Master 1710–35, of white marble. In Ante-chapel—(4) of the Rev. Joseph Jowett, LL.D., 1813, Regius Professor of Law, of Purbeck marble.

Painting: see Reredos. *Panelling:* In Ante-chapel—lining walls to a height of approximately 6¼ ft., plain panelling in three heights with entablature with panelled frieze, early 17th-century, removed from the Chapel in 1730, that on S. wall subsequently adapted as mount for brasses, on E. wall heightened to ceiling with 17th-century panelling and 18th-century cornice. See also Screen. *Paving:* of black and white marble squares laid to pattern, 1729–30, except in later extension of Chapel. *Piscina:* in S. wall of Chapel, behind hinged panel, with moulded jambs, cinquefoiled ogee head, sill, with octofoiled dishing to drain, cut back to wall-face, late 14th-century. *Reredos:* of oak, painted and gilt centrepiece with fluted Ionic pilasters on pedestals supporting an entablature with dentil-cornice and open pediment; the pedestals with wreaths on the dies and linked by a frieze carved with an open book, inscribed with a text from *Luke xxii, 19,* in Greek, vine swags, flowers and wreaths, all above a panelled dado; short flanking lengths with tall plain panels and sham doorways, all of 1730, reduced in height and reset against new E. wall in 1864. Painting in centre, the 'Presentation in the Temple', on canvas, given by John Chetwode, LL.D., Fellow, *c.* 1730, bought by his father, the Dean of Gloucester, in Flanders (*Warren's Book*, 71).

Screen, Panelling and *Stalls* (see plan): Screen dividing Chapel from Ante-chapel, incorporating Master's and Vice-Master's stalls, of large plain panels with continuous cornice of bold projection surmounted by modern gallery-front of fielded panelling; six-panel enriched door to doorway with architrave in centre; the two stalls with semicircular-headed recesses set in slightly projecting casings, with panelled responds, imposts and archivolts, the projections being continued upwards to form a duality in the design by forward returns of both the main cornice, over shaped side-brackets, and the gallery-front, and further accentuated by elaborate carved and coloured modern achievements-of-arms of Lloyd (Master 1710–35) and Geldart (Master 1852–77) on the cornice projections. The imposts are continued outwards from the recesses and returned along the side walls of the Chapel to form the cornice of plain panelling behind the upper N. and S. fixed benches. All the upper desks have shaped ends, panelled fronts and fixed lower benches. The foregoing, 1730, unless described otherwise, and excluding some 9 ft. of panelling, desks and seating extended eastward in 1864; desks to lower benches also modern. *Stalls:* see Screen. *Miscellaneous:* Loose fragment of vaulted niche-canopy, probably mediaeval, doubtless that found 10 ft. up in the centre of the E. wall when the latter was demolished in 1864 (*Warren's Book*, 75).

The *West Range* of Front Court is of one storey and of two storeys with attics under a continuous roof. This last is covered with slates on the E. and tiles on the W. The Hall and perhaps some 15 ft. of the range to the N. of it was built between the foundation of the College and 1374. Refacing and reconstruction of the interior have left no original features, but a plan of 1731 reproduced by Willis and Clark (IV, 9, Fig. 1) shows the earlier arrangement of the offices; for analogies with the Hall and offices at Peterhouse see Preface p. lxxx. In *c.* 1374 the N. part of the present Buttery and the Kitchen were built, probably as a single storey extension to the Hall-block. Probably between 1560 and 1584 the second storey was added, which contained the Combination Room. Between 1743 and the end of the summer of 1745 the range was refaced on both sides in Ketton stone ashlar and the interior remodelled. Sir Nathaniel Lloyd (died 1741) left £3,000 for the purpose; £2,264 was spent on the Hall, £679 on the Buttery etc., the rest, supplemented by his executors, being expended on the N. and S. ranges. The Hall was extended to the S. in 1890–1, the 18th-century plaster ceiling destroyed except for the cornice, and the 18th-century panelling of the dais reset round the new dais. Work of 1934 included, in addition to remodelling the Buttery and Kitchen, the incorporation in the Library-annexe, formerly the Combination Room, of the first-floor rooms and corridors immediately N. of the Hall.

The E. side of the W. range is symmetrical, of seven bays, with a plain plinth, a plat-band at first-floor level, a simple dentil-cornice and parapet-wall. The parapet-coping is pedimental over the centre three bays. In the tympanum is a reset cartouche flanked by scrolls carved and painted with the College arms; it was formerly on the street-front of the E. range. The central archway to the screens-passage has a semicircular head, flanking pilasters and scroll-brackets supporting a pedimented entablature. The windows, as shown on the plan, and those on the first floor, regularly spaced over the openings below, are uniform, with moulded architraves to rectangular openings, and contain double-hung sashes; two on the ground floor are blocked behind the glass. The three dormer-windows, in the N. part of the range, are flat-topped and of the 19th century or modern. In the middle of the roof is an octagonal timber cupola with lead-covered dome, pineapple finial and weathervane; it rises from a panelled base and has at the corners attached Corinthian columns on pedestals supporting a mitred entablature with dentil-cornice; in each side is a semicircular-headed window and, above, a pierced roundel within a wreath. The cupola is contemporary with the remodelling of the range, 1743–5.

The W. side of the range is of eight bays, of which seven bays were refaced in the 18th century and are similar in detail to those of the E. side. The N. bay extends behind the Library range and is obscured and penetrated on the ground floor by a later passage to the Junior Combination Room. The projecting eighth bay at the S. end is modern and has a gable extending over the Master's Lodge adjoining on the S.W. The refacing is all that was carried out of the Library Court designed by Burrough and Essex. The W. archway to the through-passage and the flanking bays completed were to be central in a symmetrical composition, with projections beyond and wings running westward on the extremities. The return of the cornice for the S. projection remains in the head of the modern S. bay. On the N., the E. end of the brick S. wall of the Elizabethan Library was demolished to allow the refacing to be continued beyond it as far as the Kitchen, no doubt the supposition being that the old Library range would soon be demolished.

The projection of the Hall chimney-stack, though not shown on Burrough's elevation, was retained and the 18th-century main cornice returned and pedimented across it; the two diagonal shafts rise from a rectangular base above parapet-level and finish with a cornice-like capping. The four dormer-windows, similar to those on the opposite slope of the roof, are again restricted to the N. part of the range. The 16th-century brick W. wall of the Kitchen, visible only from the N.W., has stone quoins at the N. angle and ends in a stepped gable largely rebuilt in modern times. In the lower part is an 18th-century window with semicircular head; in the gable are 16th-century one and three-light windows, both with four-centred openings in square heads and all much renewed.

The *Hall* ($24\frac{1}{2}$ ft. by $66\frac{1}{4}$ ft. including the screens-passage 7 ft. wide) is of six bays and open to the late 19th-century hammer-beam roof. At the wall-head the mid 18th-century plaster cornice with acanthus enrichment survives though cut into for the later roof. Close to the S. end of the E. wall, about 13 ft. from the ground, is a small mediaeval loop-light in a splayed recess with high semicircular head; it formerly opened between the Master's Lodge and the Chapel. The S. end wall is lined to three-quarters of the height with mid 18th-century panelling divided into three bays by coupled and attached Corinthian columns and flanking pilasters, all on pedestals, supporting an entablature with enriched architrave and modillion-cornice; the entablature is segmentally pedimented over the middle bay and contains in the tympanum the College arms on a carved and painted cartouche flanked by laurel branches. In the middle bay is a large painted portrait of Sir Nathaniel Lloyd, reputedly after one by James Thornhill, in an eared and enriched frame with a carved shell and scrolls above and foliage pendants at the sides. In the side bays are doorcases with eared architraves and, above, panels with enriched framing and segmental heads; the doors are of six panels. The panelling returns 6 ft. along each side wall to end in a pilaster. The stained pine panelling lining the side walls to half their height is of the date of the foregoing, with a narrow entablature carved with wave ornament on the frieze; it is one panel high, above fixed benches. The matching panelling of oak was installed when the Hall was lengthened in 1890–1. The mid 18th-century fireplace (Plate 277) has white marble slips, a pine eared architrave and side scrolls, a pulvinated frieze carved with leaves and an enriched cornice; in the overmantel scrolled pilasters supporting a return of the panelling-entablature flank a central wreath tied with ribbons and garlands.

The mid 18th-century *Screen*, of pine, is divided into three bays by panelled pilasters on pedestals supporting a return of the panelling-entablature surmounted by the balustraded gallery-front. In the middle bay is a semicircular-headed doorway with moulded archivolt, a cartouche on the key-block, and panelled responds with moulded caps and bases; the spandrels contain carved scrolls and the tympanum is filled by panelling; the contemporary wrought-iron gate is now at the entrance to the Fellows' Garden. The side bays contain eared and rectangular panels. The gallery-front, with turned balusters, is divided into three bays by pedestals with panelled dies. Access to the gallery is through a central doorway in the N. wall now and since 1952 approached by a narrow staircase from the Buttery-passage; the doorcase has an eared architrave flanked by panelled pilasters with console-brackets supporting an entablature with segmental pediment. The Screens-passage is lined with pine panelling in two heights of panels, with a dado-rail and cornice and panelled pilasters at each end on the S. In the N. wall are two semicircular-headed timber archways similar to the one in the Screen but with plain key-blocks and spandrels and open tympana; all three are flanked by panelled pilasters.

The *Buttery* and *Kitchen* and ground-floor offices N. of the Hall retain no ancient features. On the first floor, the old Combination Room, now part of the *Library-annexe*, was to some extent remodelled and the approaches to it improved in 1730 and 1731, the present oak panelling and fireplace-surround being installed, and new furniture provided, all at a cost of £419 defrayed by Dr. John Chetwode. The fielded panelling, in two heights divided by a moulded dado-rail, has a cornice against the ceiling carved with elaborate acanthus enrichment. The fireplace-surround (Plate 276) on the W. wall is of white marble, with a square opening flanked by pilaster-strips carrying console-brackets supporting an entablature and blocking-course; surmounting the last are two scrolls in the form of a pediment crowned by a shell and framing in the tympanum a cartouche carved with the College arms and flanked by foliage. The oak overmantel contains an enriched, eared and scrolled panel shaped to the pediment just described and with a cartouche containing the Founder's arms below a mitre superimposed on the top horizontal mouldings; below the cartouche is a scroll inscribed with the date 1731 in Roman numerals. Opposite Bateman's arms, on the E. wall, is a carved achievement-of-arms of Chetwode supported by man-headed bulls, which was set up by the College in 1734 at a cost of £5 10s. The rest of the Library-annexe to the S. is lined with fielded panelling with dado-rail and cornice; it is of pine and of the mid 18th century, made up with modern work. The same room contains four oak bookcases with panelled ends and cornices; they consist of parts of cases from the old University Library made up with much modern work.

The *North Range* of Front Court is of two storeys with attics. The N. wall is of clunch rubble faced, on the lower part, with old red brick. The roof is slate covered on the S. slope, tiled on the N. It is probably the range built *c.* 1374, and until 1545 bordered Henney Lane. The original outer walls only survive. The S. wall was refaced towards the middle of the 18th century, as already described, and during the same century sash-windows were inserted in the N. wall, involving mutilation or removal of earlier openings. In 1928 and 1929 the surviving mediaeval features in the N. wall were restored and stone-mullioned two-light windows substituted for most of the sash-windows; in the same years the interior of the building was entirely demolished, except for the central chimney-stack, and redesigned by Montague Wheeler.

The S. side maintains the 18th-century design of the rest of Front Court; the horizontal features are continued from the E. and W. ranges; the doorways are similar to the one, now blocked, across the Court; the windows are uniform with those in the adjoining ranges. The fenestration shown on the plan is preserved on the first floor, the blank wall-spaces over the doorways being elaborated by foliage pendants. The blank space opposite the early chimney-stack is decorated with a swag on the ground floor and a cartouche with the carved and painted arms of the See of Norwich impaling the Founder surmounted by a mitre on the first floor. At the W. end of the first floor and extending behind the E. wall of the W. range is a late 14th-century window of two lights with trefoiled openings and sunk spandrels in a square head with double-chamfered reveals and sill; this was revealed *in situ* in 1928–9 and left exposed, but blocked. On the roof are twelve modern flat-topped dormer-windows.

The N. side (Plate 114) has, from E. to W., after the modern doorway into the E. range: two modern windows with two more above them on the first floor, the western one on each floor having an earlier, perhaps original, relieving-arch; a tall transomed window of two cinquefoiled lights in a square head, the upper part of the late 14th or 15th century and blocked, the lower part modern, and a modern window above it on the first floor. The gyp-room behind the staircase is lit by a modern lancet-light inserted in an old, probably original, recess with two-centred head and rebated for a door; above is a window with square head and chamfered reveals perhaps of the 16th or 17th century lighting the stair, and on the first floor a small

14th-century pierced quatrefoil, now blocked, cut in a single stone. Continuing westward are two modern windows, the western with an old relieving-arch, and a modern doorway; above them are three restored mediaeval windows, the first of two four-centred lights with sunk spandrels in a four-centred head, *c.* 1500, the second of two two-centred lights with a cusped spandrel in a depressed two-centred head, late 14th or early 15th-century, the third as the second but with acutely pointed lights and normal two-centred head, late 14th-century; both the second and third have segmental rear-arches and rebates for shutters, the second retaining the hinge-pins. The next two ground-floor windows, though much restored are of 16th or 17th-century origin; over the second is an old relieving-arch; above them on the first floor, rather more to the W., are two modern windows; traceable in the walling E. of the E. reveals of these last are respectively the E. jamb of one and the E. jamb and part of the head of a second mediaeval window; at an equal spacing westward is an area of patching. The ground-floor window E. of the next doorway is modern. The 16th-century doorway has chamfered jambs and four-centred head; the features over it are similar to those opposite the E. staircase and lit the pre-existing staircase, but the rectangular light is now blocked. Of the remaining three windows on the ground floor and three on the first floor, all are modern except the more westerly upper two. These last are of the 18th century and fitted with double-hung sashes; the more easterly one has old relieving arches above and below and a wrought-iron balcony, perhaps of the late 18th century. None of the relieving-arches mentioned above, except the upper one last described, relates structurally to the present opening below.

The interior of the N. range, though remodelled, retains a number of ancient features *in situ* in the outside walls and others reset in different rooms. In the N.E. ground-floor room is a small wall-recess similar to that described above but unaltered, originally a cupboard or perhaps a garderobe. In the main room W. of the E. staircase is a restored mediaeval stone fireplace with chamfered jambs corbelled out to a chamfered segmental head. In the W. end of the S. wall of the same room is a cupboard contrived in a blocked mediaeval window, the W. splay being original; close W. of this, in the adjoining room, is a similar feature, the original E. splay and part of the chamfered rear-arch surviving.

On the first floor, *Dr. Eden's Room* (Plate 275), the large room between the E. staircase and the old chimney-stack, has an open timber ceiling of *c.* 1500 in three bays; the main beams and the joists are moulded, with die-out stops. The walls are lined with oak panelling of *c.* 1600 formerly in the adjoining room on the W., the Mathematical Lecture Room, and now incorporating much modern material; it is six panels in height, with a frieze of arabesque and, on the E. and W. walls, carved pilasters of *c.* 1625. The clunch fireplace is modern but incorporates 14th-century corbelling taken from the W. fireplace below. The oak overmantel of *c.* 1625, also from the adjoining room, is divided into two bays by coupled Roman Doric banded columns on pedestals supporting an entablature with carved brackets in the frieze; the pedestals are supported on similar brackets and linked by a band of carved foliage ornament; the bays are filled with panelling framed in a geometrical pattern. Over the E. doorway is a plaster panel, cut from the ground-floor room below, with restored painting of the achievement-of-arms of Redman quartering Aldeburgh.

The westernmost room on the first floor was sashed and refitted between 1725 and 1730 by Dr. Dickins (Regius Professor of Law, 1714–55); the two sash-windows in the N. wall and the fittings survive. The walls are lined with oak fielded panelling with dado-rail and simplified dentil-cornice; the doors are of six panels and fitted with brass rim-locks. Over the fireplace are two panels, the upper bolection-moulded and containing the shield-of-arms carved in bold relief of the Regius Professorship impaling Dickins with the date 1730 in Roman numerals on a scroll below. The fireplace has a rectangular opening and moulded marble slips. Flanking the chimney-breast are fitted bookcases with glazed doors.

Before the modern alterations, the timber-framed partitions retained many traces of 15th and 16th-century painted decoration, some of stylised patterns, others simulating wood panelling.

Library Court (68 ft. by 76 ft.) next W. of Front Court is now open to the W.; the Hall range is on the E., the Library range on the N., and the Master's Lodge on the S. The Library range is of two storeys; the walls are of red brick, in part in English bond, with stone dressings, and the roofs are tile-covered. On the ground floor is the Junior Combination Room, with a Fellow's set adjoining on the W.; the Library occupies the whole of the first floor. It was built and fitted probably towards the end of the Mastership of Dr. Harvey in 1584 or soon afterwards. The E. end of the S. wall was demolished to allow the 18th-century facing of the Hall range to be continued beyond, and the end refaced in brickwork on the cant. The interior of the ground floor was remodelled in 1863 and again in 1935; formerly it contained two sets of chambers entered from a S. doorway and with fireplaces in the N. wall.

The S. side of the Library range has on the ground floor five two and three-light stone-mullioned windows with four-centred openings and sunk spandrels in square heads. The fourth window from the E. is of the 19th century and set in the patching of a destroyed doorway; the other windows are entirely renewed externally. The eight one and two-light windows lighting the Library are similar in form to the foregoing and similarly renewed, except the sills, which appear to be original. Between the sixth and seventh windows is a doorway with chamfered jambs, four-centred head and brick relieving-arch which opened from the wall-walk described above; it is blocked behind the door, this last being original, of oak, with applied mouldings and original wrought-iron furniture.

The N. side has four one and two-light windows on the ground floor and eight to the Library, all of similar form to those in the wall opposite. On the ground floor the first is modern, the second and third are restored and the fourth appears to be original. The two doorways are of the late 19th century but replace original windows. The upper windows retain only the original sills. Corbelled out from the upper part of the wall are two chimney-stacks; that to the E. is destroyed above eaves-level; that to the W. continues up to a stepped base but is mostly rebuilt.

The W. end has stone quoins; the stepping of the gable has been rebuilt. On the ground floor are two two-light windows; these and the four-light W. window of the Library are as those already described, but the last is larger, has an original label and retains the old sill; below the sill is a rectangular stone panel carved with the arms and crest of the College, with modern colouring.

The E. end has a rebuilt stepped gable merging at the apex into the stepped gable of the Kitchen already described. In the upper southern part is a blocked doorway with defaced chamfered jambs and four-centred clunch head; it retains the original door with a geometrical pattern of panels formed by applied mouldings. Only the top part of this feature is visible, from the Library-annexe; it was probably the original entrance to the Library from the College, before the floor-levels were altered presumably in the 18th-century remodelling of the Hall range.

The *Library* (Plate 275) (64 ft. by 20 ft.) has a plain flat segmental plaster ceiling. Standing at right angles to the walls down either side of the room are five late 16th-century bookcases alternating with six contemporary benches, all the ends being tenoned into continuous timber sills. The bookcases have panelled plinths to the fronts, one shelf, and sloping bookrests with an enriched rail at the apex; the shaped and gabled ends terminate in square posts on carved brackets, the posts having a cornice-like capping and tall turned finials. Applied to one of the posts is a carved shield-of-arms of the College impaling

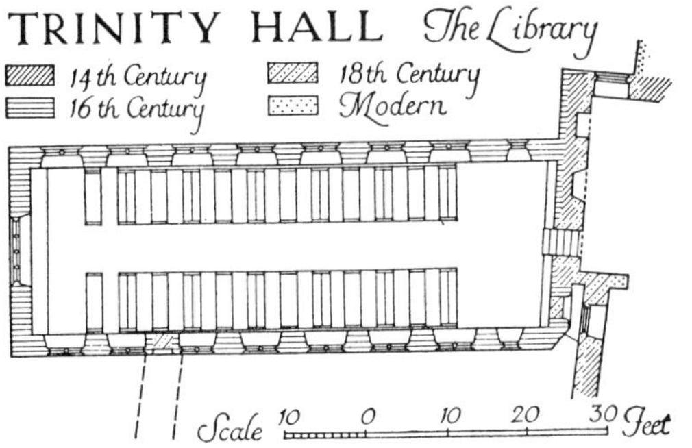

Eden. In the gable-ends are original wrought-iron lock-plates for hasps hinged to the ends of the rods for the book-chains; the plates are decorated with the crescent charge from the arms of the College. The benches have seats divided by a central panelled back; the shouldered ends terminate in rounded poppy-heads carved with rosettes. The pair of cases at the W. end, uniform with the others, are of the early 19th century. In the W. window are four original heraldic quarries, three of the College arms and one of Stokes with the crest of an arm with bedell's staff in hand (Matthew Stokes, esquire-bedell, died 1591).

The *Master's Lodge* has undergone so many alterations and part rebuildings that it now has the appearance of a modern building, externally and internally, except for a small late 16th-century gabled bay towards the N. end of the W. front, overlooking the Fellows' Garden. This is of rubble and rough ashlar, of two storeys and projecting slightly from the rest of the refronting of 1891; the gable has shaped kneelers and a chimney-stack at the apex. On the first floor is a three-light clunch window, now blocked, with square head and label, all much weathered except the mullions, which are modern. The gable may be seen in Loggan's engraving of the College.

South Court (56 ft. by 54 ft. average) formerly the entrance court, is bounded on the N. by the Chapel range, on the E. by the range rebuilt in 1872–3, on the W. by the range described below, and on the S. by a modern single-storey range against the wall to Clare College. The *West Range* is of three storeys; the walls are of grey brick and the roofs are slate-covered. It was built in 1823 in place of the former S. wing of the Master's Lodge and miscellaneous buildings; in it are sets of chambers. The five-sided bay-window on the N.E. is a modern addition. The side to the Court has a plain parapet-wall, stone copings and stone sills. The doorways and sash-hung windows have plain brick arches, semicircular and flat respectively. The interior is quite plain. In a niche in the passage from the Hall to the Combination Room is a marble bust by Nollekens of Lord Mansfield.

In the *Fellows' Garden*, the N. boundary-wall leading W. from Library Court is of red brick on a stone rubble base and probably of the 17th century. In the gateway in the modern S. return at the E. end is the mid 18th-century wrought-iron gate removed from the Hall screen; it has a semicircular head, plain uprights and scrollwork. The W. boundary-wall is of like character and date to the N. wall; the apparent heightening is in fact in part a filling-in, in part a rebuilding, of the embattling shown by Loggan. Towards the N. end of the wall, on the river side, are two stone panels with shields-of-arms of Newman with a motto below and the College in a strapwork frame; a third panel between them is inscribed 'Anno Domini 1619'; these were reset here in 1708 and came from the summer-house, where they seem to be shown by Loggan.

The *Boundary-wall* to Garret Hostel Lane, extending some 13 yards W. from the modern N. range of North Court, is presumably that built in 1545 after the land N. of Henney Lane was acquired; it is of much-weathered clunch ashlar later repaired and heightened in brick. Further W., reset in 1890 in the N. wall of the new buildings backing on the lane, is the late 14th-century main entrance to the College formerly in the E. range of the old entrance court, now South Court; it consists of a large archway flanked on the E. by a small archway; both have moulded jambs and four-centred heads of two moulded orders, but the outer order of the large archway has been almost cut away for a rebate. The small archway retains the original, though restored, door; it is nail-studded, in four vertical panels, with a wicket with two-centred head in the E. part and lattice framing at the back.

The *Boundary-wall* between the yard of the Master's Lodge and Clare College, extending some 18 yards, with a short N.

return at the W. end cut down to resemble a buttress, is of clunch rubble with a plinth of old bricks and a modern coping. It is all remaining of the building shown here by Loggan which may have antedated the foundation of the College.

In *North Court*, next N. of Front Court, reset over the first-floor doorway at the head of the modern steps against the W. wall is a small 17th-century cartouche carved with the arms of the College.

ECCLESIASTICAL BUILDINGS, ETC.

(42) Parish Church of All Saints stands on the S. side of Jesus Lane. The old church, of All Saints in the Jewry, which is first mentioned as having been bestowed upon the monks of St. Albans in the time of Abbot Paul (1077–93), stood on the E. side of St. John's Street, where the churchyard still is. In 1180 the advowson was given to St. Radegund's and at the dissolution of the nunnery it passed to Jesus College. The W. tower stood over the pavement and the building was largely of the 15th and 16th centuries with a chancel of 1726. The old church was demolished in 1865 when the hammer-beam roof of the nave was re-erected in the new church of Wendy near Royston; the latter has since been demolished and the roof is in a builder's yard. The present church was built on the new site in 1863–4 from the design of G. F. Bodley and decorated by William Morris. It contains from the old church the following:—

Fittings—*Bells:* three, 1st uninscribed and perhaps 14th-century; 2nd by Thomas Norris and with the names of the churchwardens, 1632; 3rd perhaps by Tobie Norris of Stamford, dated 1406, probably a transposition of 1604, and inscribed 'Non sono animabus mortuorum sed auribus viventium' in Lombardic capitals. *Books:* Henrie Bullinger, *Fiftie Godlie and Learned Sermons*, 1587; Bible, in black-letter, New Testament dated 1613; two prayer-books bound and presented by John Bowtell, jun., in 1821, now in University Library. *Brasses* and *Indent. Brasses:* In S. chapel—on E. wall, (1) of William Tireman, 1777, inscription only; on S. wall, (2) of Edward Salisbury, 1741, organist of Trinity College, and Margaret his mother, 1749, also Susanna Stephens, 1763, inscription only; (3) of John Edmund Lodge, 1808, inscription only. *Indent:* In old churchyard—of figure and inscription plates, much defaced, but perhaps that referred to in Cooper's *Memorials* as probably to Richard Holme, master of King's Hall, 1424, added inscription to Thomas Prince, 1782. *Font:* of clunch, octagonal bowl with quatrefoiled panels enclosing roses and shields alternately, moulded underside, octagonal stem and hollow-chamfered base, 15th-century, painting modern.

Monuments and *Floor-slab. Monuments:* In S. chapel—on E. wall, (1) of Isack Barrowe, M.D., [1616–7], and Ann his wife, [1589–90], widow of George Cotton, erected by her grand-daughter Ann, wife of Sir Philip Landen, in 1631, plain black marble slab formerly on altar-tomb; on S. wall, (2) of William Gifford, 1786, white marble slab; (3) of James, eldest son of James Gifford, 1813, and two sons, Lucius, 1812, and Theophilus, 1811, white marble wall-tablet; (4) of Elizabeth Theodora Christie, eldest daughter of Charles Claydon, 1829, white marble tablet, by Tomson; (5) of Richard Shipton, 1692, slate tablet; (6) of Alexander Scott Abbott, 1843, Jane his wife, 1844, and Charles Graham his son, 1837, white marble altar-shaped tablet on black marble backing, by King, London; (7) of John Carter, 1825; (8) of Miriam Charlotte and Mary Drage, daughters of Moses and Mary Knell Browne, 1841, this and (7) white marble tablets on black marble backings; on W. wall, (9) of Thomas Daye, [1701–2], marble tablet with flanking palm-leaves, cherub-head, cartouche and urn; (10) of Samuel Munk, 1791, white marble tablet; (11) of Ann (Newling), wife of John Lettice, 1788, white marble tablet; (12) of Henry Neve, 1768, of St. John's College, white marble tablet; (13) of Rev. Salusbury Jones, M.A., 1763, Fellow of St. John's College, white marble tablet; (14) of William Bate Strong, 1843; (15) of George Thring, 1807, and Maria his wife, 1830; (16) of Mary, 1829, and Thomas Smith her husband, 1837; (17) of Hannah Maria Syer, 1832, and others; (18) of Richard Nethercoat Cooke, 1819, altar-shaped tablet with foliage garland; (19) of Catharine Thring, 1825; (20) of Thomas Cubitt, 1841; (21) of Thomas Blundell, 1819; (22) of Henry Thring, 1834; (14–22) white marble wall-tablets. In nave—on N. wall, (23) of John Masters, 1793, white marble tablet; (24) of William Beales, 1831, Sarah his widow, 1850, and others, black and white marble tablet; (25) of Susanna Forrester, widow, daughter of Edmund Salter, 1732–3, white marble tablet; (26) of William Norfolk, 1785, and Susan his wife, 1773, white marble tablet; (27) of James Gifford, alderman, 1774, Martha his wife, 1769, Robert their son, 1755, and Harriet Elizabeth, 1775, white marble tablet with shaped frame. In old churchyard—(28) of [Ri]chard Stephenson, 1668, broken headstone; (29) of Henry Kirke White, 1806, and other headstones, now flat, much worn and illegible, but including twelve with shaped tops, carved cherubs, etc., late 18th and early 19th-century. *Floor-slab:* in old churchyard—of John W. . . . . , 1768.

Plate: includes a cup with date-letter for 1568, inscribed 'Verbum Domini manet in eternum', maker's mark I.C. in a shield, a cover-paten probably of the same age, a paten with date-letter for 1633 with a shield-of-arms of Allot impaling Wade, a cup and cover-paten with date-letter for 1706, a paten with date-letter for 1698, inscribed 'Ecclesia omnium sanctorum Cantab', two flagons with date-letter for 1734, one provided from a bequest of Dr. Robert Strachie of Bishop's Stortford, 1704, the other given by Robert Lambert, D.D., Master of St. John's College, 1735, and three alms-dishes, one of pewter and engraved with the Stuart arms, the others of base-metal and dated 1846. *Royal Arms:* In vestry—of wood, carved and painted, Stuart.

The old churchyard in St. John's Street is enclosed with a wrought-iron *Railing*, partly of the 18th century, rearranged and extended in 1821, with vases on some uprights and scrolled standards; a taller upright in the middle of the S. side, embellished with scrolls, has a cross-bar and was perhaps a lamp-standard.

(43) PARISH CHURCH OF CHRIST CHURCH stands on the S. side of Newmarket Road near Maids' Causeway. The walls are of red brick with stone dressings and the roofs are slate-covered. The church was built in the Tudor style to the designs of Ambrose Poynter, opened in May, and consecrated in June 1839; the cost was defrayed by a subscription exceeding £3,800 and grants from the Commissioners for building new churches and the Church Building Society. It is orientated N. and S. and comprises a shallow *Sanctuary* and *Nave* under one roof, *East* and *West Aisles* and a *South Vestry*. The nave (Plate 279) is of six uninterrupted arcaded bays with a clearstorey; the aisles stop some 6 ft. short of the S. end wall of the sanctuary. The form of the building is reminiscent of King's College Chapel. A *North Porch* was added in the second half of the 19th century. Minor repairs and alterations to the interior were made in 1946.

Architectural Description—The *Sanctuary* and *Nave* (28 ft. by 86 ft.) are structurally undivided. The S. and N. ends have stepped gables and the E. and W. walls have embattled parapets. At the S. end are diagonal buttresses continued high above the parapets in octagonal pinnacles with ogee-shaped domical caps; they are built in a chequer-work of brick and stone. The

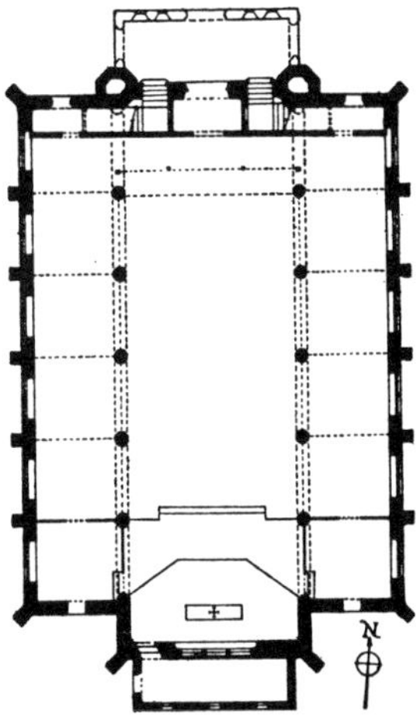

N. end has tall octagonal turrets at the angles divided by stone strings into stages, the uppermost with recessed quatrefoiled panels in each face, and with domical ogee stone caps. The transomed window in the S. wall of the sanctuary, the liturgical E. end, is of three trefoiled lights in a four-centred head. In the E. and W. walls are arcades of six bays with plain octagonal piers and moulded four-centred arches; the clearstorey has in each bay a window of two four-centred lights in a four-centred head with pierced spandrel. The N. window is similar to the S. window.

The *East* and *West Aisles* (13½ ft. wide) are uniform and divided externally into six bays by buttresses of brick and stone in two weathered stages. In each bay is a transomed window of two lights with four-centred openings in a square head with a segmental rear-arch. In the S. and N. walls are small single-light windows above doorways with four-centred heads. The panelled *Roof* of the nave (Plate 279) is contemporary with the building. It is divided into twelve and a half bays in the length by plain tie-beams on shaped wood brackets; each bay is divided into five panels by plain longitudinal beams; the painting is modern.

Fittings—*Bell:* In N.E. turret—one, by Mears, London, 1839. *Chest:* In E. aisle, of oak, with plank front and ends, panelled top with strap-hinges decorated with simple hatching, three locks, and on front a shield-shaped brass plate inscribed 'This was given by Frances Carow clark of Barnwell who dyed Ano. Do. 1635'. *Font* and *Cover* (Plate 17). Font: hexagonal, of limestone, straight-sided bowl, each face with tracery-panelling, panelled stem, moulded base. Cover: of oak, with ogee domical top, turned finial and embattled sides containing a band of carved paterae; inscription round lower edge recording purchase by penny subscriptions from 1200 children and presentation in 1839. *Galleries*: carried on traceried trusses over the E. and W. aisles and on pillars across N. end of nave, contemporary with the building but with modern fronts.

Monuments: In sanctuary—on W. wall, (1) of Rev. John Doudney Lane, M.A., 1847, Fellow of St. John's College, rector of Forncet St. Peter, white marble sarcophagus-shaped wall-tablet against a grey and black marble backing on corbels resembling triglyphs. In W. aisle—on S. wall, (2) of Frederic William Broughton, 1846, black and white marble tablet.

(44) PARISH CHURCH OF THE HOLY SEPULCHRE stands on the E. side of Bridge Street. The walls are of rubble partly ashlar-faced and the dressings are of Barnack and other freestone; the roofs are covered with Westmorland slates. Sometime between 1114 and 1130 Reinald, Abbot of Ramsey, granted the cemetery of St. George's and adjoining land to the members of the fraternity of the Holy Sepulchre to build there in honour of Christ and the Holy Sepulchre. The round *Nave* with its *Aisle* and a small chancel were built in the first half of the 12th century (Plate 282). The original form of the *Chancel* is uncertain, but the start of the N. wall was found during the restoration of 1842. At the same time remains of the base of a 13th-century W. respond are said to have been found in the same wall, under the later respond. Other remains of 13th-century work were found at the N.E. angle of the chancel. From this it appears that a N. chapel was added at this period and the chancel in part rebuilt. The church was much altered in the 15th century when a polygonal belfry was added above the clearstorey of the round nave and most of the windows

of the round were altered and enlarged; further, the *North Chapel*, with the arches opening into it from the chancel and the nave-aisle, was rebuilt together with the chancel-arch; this last involving the destruction of the vault of the E. bay of the nave-aisle. A W. porch was added at some uncertain date and is shown in Cole's sketch of 1743 together with three square-headed windows in the N. wall of the N. chapel.

Part of the aisle-vault collapsed in 1841 and a drastic general restoration was undertaken by the Cambridge Camden Society, under the direction of Anthony Salvin, which involved the following works. The 15th-century belfry was destroyed and a stone vault, based upon indications of springers then found, erected over the round nave. The clearstorey-windows were replaced by others of 12th-century character, based on one that is said to have survived. The vault of the aisle was taken down and rebuilt and where it had been destroyed over the E. bay replaced; to allow of this last being done the chancel-arch was rebuilt narrower than its predecessor. The S. wall of the aisle having tilted over owing to the thrust of the vault was taken down to within six feet of the ground and rebuilt. Windows of the 12th-century form replaced the Gothic windows of the aisle; the W. doorway was taken down and completely restored, and all the stonework, inside and out, carefully cleaned and dressed. The W. porch had been removed at an earlier date. In the chancel the E. and N. walls were rebuilt partly of old materials, except the W. arch in the N. wall, and the E. arch to the N. chapel was added. The N. chapel was rebuilt, being extended half a bay to the E., and a bell-turret added on the N.W. angle. At the same time the *South Aisle* of the chancel and the S. arcade were built and the arch inserted between the new chancel-aisle and the nave-aisle. The whole of this work took place in 1841–43 and is recorded in the *Ecclesiologist*. The *North Vestry* was added later in the 19th century. The erection of a stone altar and credence-table led to a lawsuit and the closing of the church from 1843 to 1845: the Court of Arches declared them illegal in January 1845 and they were removed.

In spite of its drastic restoration Holy Sepulchre church is of considerable interest as one of the five surviving round churches in this country. The 19th-century restorations are notable for the care taken by the Cambridge Camden Society to preserve, and where necessary to re-create, the 12th-century style of the building.

Architectural Description—The *Chancel* ($28\frac{1}{4}$ ft. by $18\frac{3}{4}$ ft.) has an E. wall rebuilt in 1841–43 incorporating old material; the E. window probably incorporates 15th-century material and is of three cinquefoiled lights with vertical tracery in a two-centred head with a label. In the N. wall is an arcade of two bays with moulded four-centred arches and shafted responds. The W. arch is of the 15th-century but the E. arch dates from the mid 19th-century restoration. In the S. wall is an arcade of 1841–43 with arches uniform with the E. arch of the N. arcade. The chancel-arch replaces a wider 15th-century arch and may incorporate material of that date; it is four-centred with shafted responds and above it are mid 19th-century openings to the triforium of the round. These openings consist of four cinquefoiled lights paired under four-centred sub-arches in a four-centred head with a pierced spandrel, which are flanked by pairs of cinquefoiled lights each in a two-centred head with a pierced spandrel, the whole group being embraced by a wide four-centred arch; the lights have square cinquefoil-headed stone panelling below a transom.

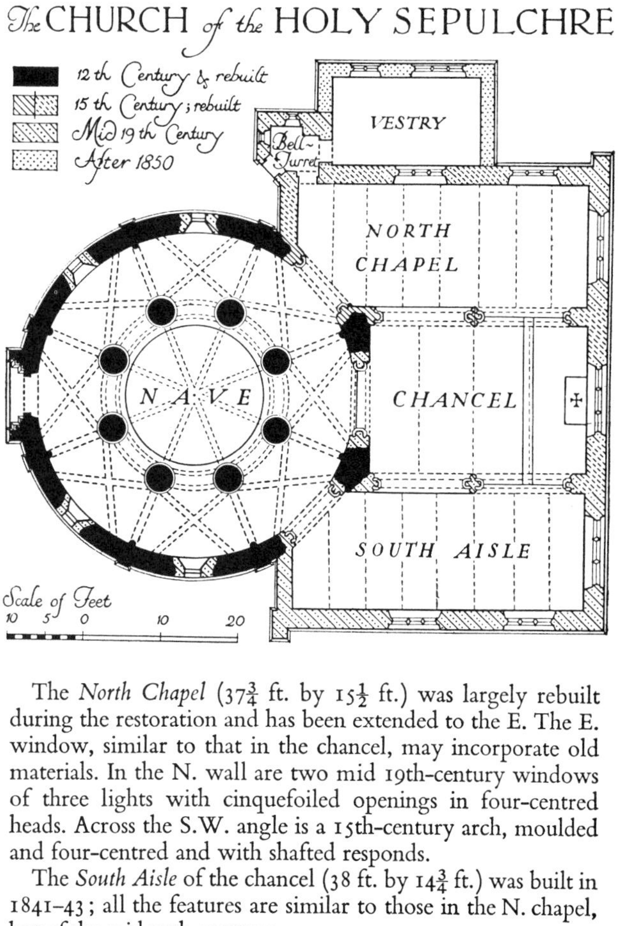

The *North Chapel* ($37\frac{3}{4}$ ft. by $15\frac{1}{2}$ ft.) was largely rebuilt during the restoration and has been extended to the E. The E. window, similar to that in the chancel, may incorporate old materials. In the N. wall are two mid 19th-century windows of three lights with cinquefoiled openings in four-centred heads. Across the S.W. angle is a 15th-century arch, moulded and four-centred and with shafted responds.

The *South Aisle* of the chancel (38 ft. by $14\frac{3}{4}$ ft.) was built in 1841–43; all the features are similar to those in the N. chapel, but of the mid 19th-century.

The *Nave* (Plate 283) ($19\frac{1}{4}$ ft. in diameter) has a much restored 12th-century arcade of eight bays with half-round arches of two plain orders and one roll-moulded order on the soffit; the arches spring from cylindrical columns with moulded bases and scalloped, fluted or otherwise enriched capitals. The triforium is divided into bays by heavy cylindrical piers with scalloped etc. capitals; each bay has a main half-round arch of two plain orders enclosing two moulded sub-arches springing

(46) ST. ANDREW THE GREAT. Interior, looking E. 1843

(43) CHRIST CHURCH. Interior. looking N. 1839

Tower, from S.W. — 15th-century

(49) CHURCH OF ST. BOTOLPH.

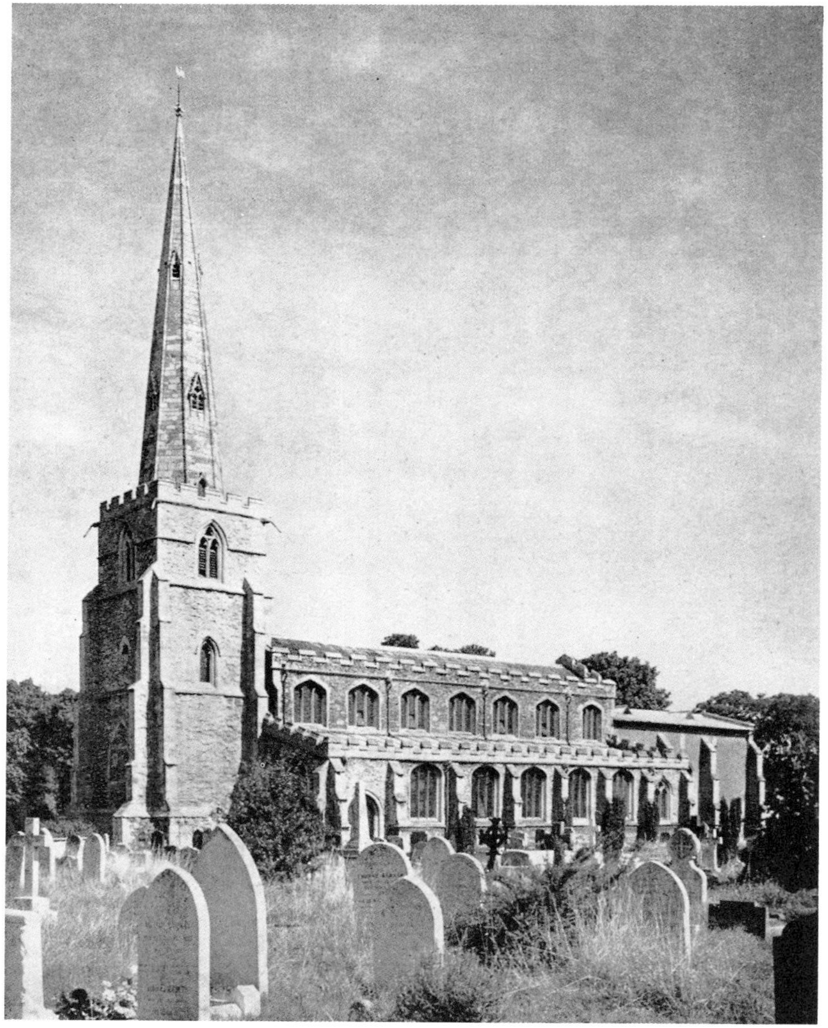

Exterior, from S.W. — 14th-century and later

(60) CHESTERTON CHURCH.

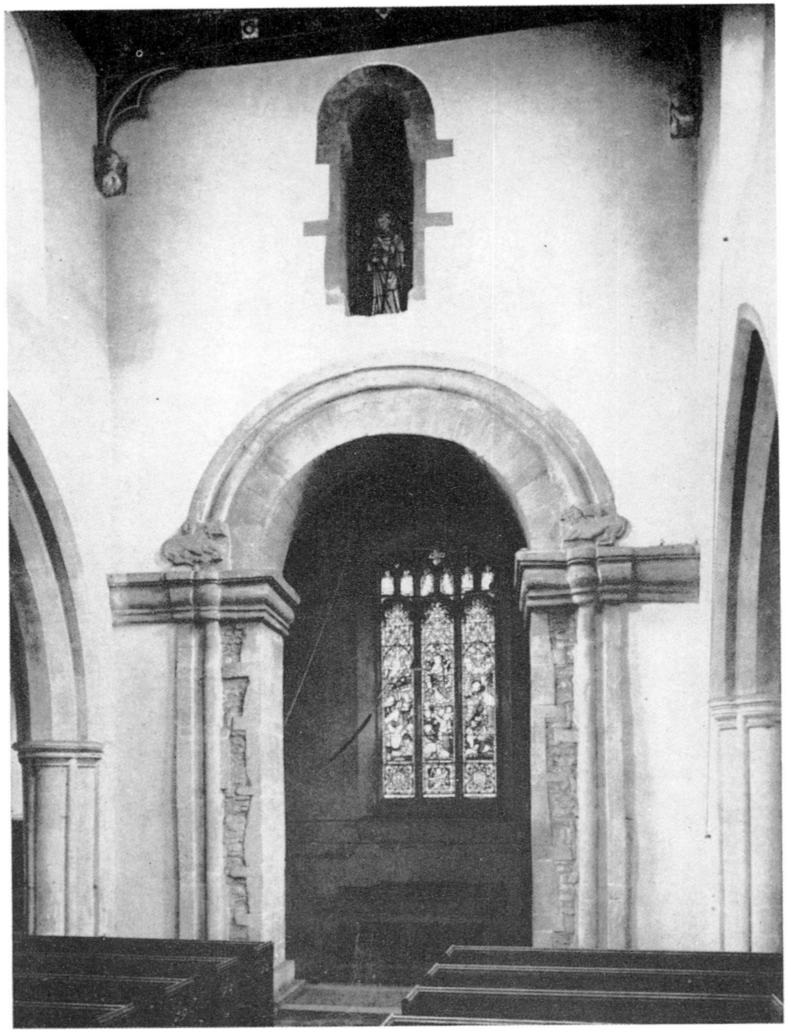

Tower-arch, from E.

Tower. Exterior, from N.W.

(48) CHURCH OF ST. BENET.

Early to mid 11th-century

(44) HOLY SEPULCHRE. Exterior, from W. *c.* 1125 and 1841–43

(62) STOURBRIDGE CHAPEL. Interior. Mid 12th-century and *c.* 1400

Nave; interior, looking S.W.

N. aisle of nave, looking W.

(44) HOLY SEPULCHRE CHURCH.

12th-century, restored 1841–3

(45) CHURCH OF THE HOLY TRINITY. Nave, looking W.

Late 14th-century and later

(51) CHURCH OF ST. EDWARD. Interior, looking N.W.

c. 1400 and later

(53) CHURCH OF ST. MARY THE GREAT. N. arcade of nave. Late 15th and early 16th-century

from one free and two attached shafts with scalloped, foliated or otherwise enriched capitals. The clearstorey now has, in each bay, a completely restored round-headed window. The stone vault, vaulting-shafts and corbels are of the mid 19th century.

The *Aisle* of the nave (Plate 283) (7½ ft. wide) is faced externally mainly with old ashlar. It has a restored stone vault with square ribs except in the W. bay, which has moulded ribs, and in the E. and S.E. bays, which have cheveron-ornamented ribs; the E. bay is entirely of 1841–43 as are apparently the head-corbels. Against the outer wall the main bays are divided by vaulting-shafts with scalloped capitals. The round-headed windows are all mid 19th-century restorations. The restored 12th-century W. doorway projects and has a half-round arch of four orders, the innermost continuous and with cheveron-ornament, the second moulded, the third with cheveron-ornament, and the outermost with embattled ornament; the three outer orders spring from shafts with scalloped caps and enriched abaci.

The *Roof* of the chancel is of the 15th century, flat-pitched and of four bays with moulded main timbers and embattled plates; the tie-beams have curved braces with restored angels below; at the main intersections are carved bosses or leaves; the E. boss has the Five Wounds, the centre three crowns and the W. a geometrical leaf-pattern. The roof of the N. chapel is similar but of eight bays and is partly mid 19th-century. The roof of the S. aisle of the chancel is similar to that in the N. chapel but of 1841–43 and with half-figures of men below the braces carrying blank shields and musical instruments.

Fittings—*Bells:* one and sanctus; former by Robart Gurney, 1663; sanctus uninscribed. *Chairs:* In chancel, two, of oak, back of each with two subcusped ogee-headed and traceried panels, moulded and embattled top-rail, octagonal front legs supporting curved arms, foliated bearers below seats, 1845. *Communion-Rails:* of oak, with moulded top and chamfered lower rails, divided into ten bays containing open panels with subcusped trefoiled ogee heads and tracery by small buttressed standards, with larger standards with moulded and embattled caps at each end and flanking the gates in the two centre bays, 1845. *Communion-Table:* in chancel, of oak, with buttressed legs, top rail carved with naturalistic vine-ornament, pierced trefoiled spandrel-pieces, 1845. Chairs, Communion-rails and Communion-table 'furnished' by Joseph Wentworth. *Font* and *Cover* (Plate 17). Font: of clunch, octagonal, straight-sided bowl with sub-cusped quatrefoiled panels in each face, flared stem, moulded base, 1843. Cover: of oak, with crocketed spire, each face in two stages with pinnacled side-standards and two cinquefoiled window-light panels under ogee crocketed gable with finial, mid 19th-century; the cover swings on a wrought-iron bracket. *Glass:* In clearstorey of nave—in E. window, Agnus Dei on altar, with inscription; in N. window, figure of the Venerable Bede; in S. window, figure of St. Etheldreda; in W. window, pelican in piety, with chalice, Tables of the Law and inscription; all by Thomas Willement, inserted at the time of the 19th-century restoration and of that date; in N.E. window, figure in red robe, made-up canopy and fragments; in N.W. window, figure of St. Peter with book and key, canopy and fragments, red seraph above; in S.E. window, figure in white robe with crozier and head of angel, made up canopy and bust of seraph above; in S.W. window, figure in red holding cup below, head not belonging, figure of the Father above with fragmentary black-letter inscription; 15th-century and later, given by H. P. Oakes of Bury St. Edmunds in 1842. In nave-aisle—S. window, Entombment and Resurrection, by Wailes; in S.W. window, Baptism (Plate 36), with sacred monograms, by Thomas Willement, with his initials; both mid 19th-century.

Monuments: In chancel—on N. wall, (1) to Samuel Ogden, S.T.P., 1778, oval marble tablet with carved and painted laurel-wreath surround. In N. chapel, on N. wall (2) to Emma Yeldon, 1800, Francis Harwood, 1811, Ann his wife, 1838, and Ann their daughter, 1843, marble tablet with mediaeval style of lettering, by Tomson; (3) to Edward Goode, 1815, marble tablet, by Tomson. In S. aisle of chancel—on S. wall, (4) to Rene Labutte, 1790, and Mary his wife, 1808, white marble tablet; (5) to John Sparke, 1759, and Deborah Sparke, 1772, grey and white marble tablet with shield-of-arms of Sparke impaling Angerton, erected by Deborah Ashby, their daughter; (6) to Mary Bond, black and white marble oval wall-tablet, early 19th-century; (7) to John Wentworth, 1818, and Daniel Wentworth, 1822, Mary, wife of Daniel Wentworth, 1817, and Susan their sister, 1830, Martha, wife of Joseph ...., 1832, and Charles their son, rectangular marble tablet, partly obscured by organ. In churchyard, W. of church, (8) of Jonathan Sharp, 1794, stone pedestal-monument with urn.

Plate: includes two cups, one with the date-letter for 1725, the other very similar, both given in 1734, two stand-patens given the same year, a flagon with the date-letter for 1768, given the following year by Samuel Ogden, D.D., and two almsdishes, one given in 1734 by Rev. Dr. Lambert, Master of St. John's College, and with the date-letter for that year, the other given the same year and with the date-letter for 1725. *Royal Arms:* In N. chapel—of Victoria, but perhaps painted on earlier carved arms. *Tables of the Creed, etc.:* In N. chapel, on W. wall, two plain round-headed panels and a rectangular panel, painted with Creed, Decalogue and the Lord's Prayer, early 19th-century. *Tiles:* in chancel and nave-aisle, slip-tiles with symbols of the Evangelists, geometrical and foliated patterns in white on red, mid 19th-century.

(45) Parish Church of the Holy Trinity stands on the W. side of Sidney Street. The lower part of the W. wall is faced externally with flint pebbles. Most of the rest of the building is covered with Roman cement, except the 19th-century chancel and the tower, which have been refaced in rough ashlar; the dressings are of freestone and the roofs are covered with lead. The Cambridge fire of 1174 is thought to have destroyed a church here; presumably it was then rebuilt. The existing flint pebbles of the W. wall may well be part of the late 12th-century building. The chancel was rebuilt *c.* 1300. Late in the 14th century extensive work was undertaken: the N. and S. arcades of the *Nave* were built and the *North* and *South Aisles* added, the work on

the N. being undertaken first; the *West Tower* was built within the W. end of the nave at the same time. In the 15th century the *North* and *South Transepts* were rebuilt; the date of the earlier transepts is unknown. The clear-storey of the nave is contemporary with this rebuilding, and in the same period the buttresses of the tower were added and the E. tower-arch was strengthened by the addition of a further order on the E.; late in the century the *North Porch* was added. The S. aisle was widened and lengthened towards the W. in the 16th century. Galleries were put up in the church, beginning in 1616, to give the extra accommodation required in connection with the Town lectureship established here; but all have been removed except one, in the S. transept, of the early 19th century, probably of 1806 and commissioned by the Rev. Charles Simeon. In 1834 the stone-vaulted *Chancel* was pulled down and replaced by a brick building. The transept-arches were rebuilt, reputedly in 1851, and in 1885 the chancel was refaced in stone and the *Organ Chamber* added. The *South-West Vestry* is modern.

The church is of some architectural interest, and amongst the fittings is a wall-monument to the Rev. Charles Simeon. After his appointment as perpetual curate and lecturer in 1782 the church became the centre of the Cambridge Evangelical revival associated with his name.

Architectural Description—The *Chancel* (30 ft. by 23 ft.) was rebuilt in 1834; the chancel-arch is of this date and similar in design to the arches between the nave and transepts. The remaining features date for the most part from 1885.

The *Nave* (Plate 284) (50 ft. by 22½ ft.) is of the late 14th century and of four bays, within the westernmost of which stands the tower. The first arch on the N., of the 15th century, has been rebuilt with much of the original material, and is considerably larger than the others; the arch is two-centred and of two moulded orders, the inner springing from attached shafts with moulded caps and bases and the outer continuous and enriched with a band of cinquefoil-headed panelling. The three other arches, of the late 14th century, are two-centred and of the two wave-moulded orders springing from a quatre-foiled pier between the second and third bays and shafted responds, all with moulded capitals and bases. The S. arcade is also of four bays; the E. arch is similar to the corresponding arch on the N., of the same date and similarly rebuilt. The other three bays have late 14th-century two-centred arches of two orders, the inner chamfered and the outer wave-moulded;

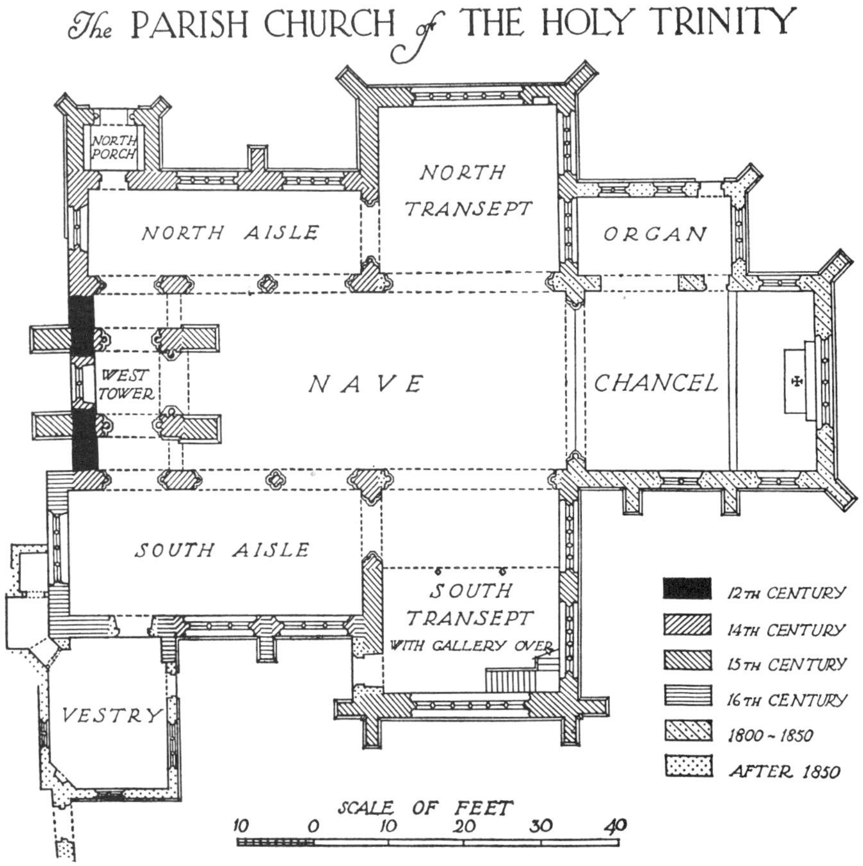

they spring from a pier and responds similar to those on the N., but some of the bases are partly covered by the modern floor. The two middle bays on both sides have three 15th-century clearstorey windows, each of three cinquefoiled lights with vertical tracery in a four-centred head with a label.

The *North Transept* (23¼ ft. by 21½ ft.) was rebuilt in the 15th century and has an embattled parapet. In the E. wall are two ranges of windows; both the lower windows are of four cinquefoiled lights with vertical tracery in a two-centred head with moulded reveals and label; the three clearstorey windows are each of three cinquefoiled lights with vertical tracery in a four-centred head with a label. In the N. wall is a large window of six cinquefoiled and transomed lights with vertical tracery in a two-centred head with a label. In the W. wall is an arch to the aisle similar to those in the middle N. bays of the nave; the three clearstorey windows are similar to those in the E. wall.

The *South Transept* (23¼ ft. by 26 ft.) was also rebuilt in the 15th century. In the E. wall are two lower windows both of five trefoiled and sub-cusped lights with vertical tracery in a two-centred head with moulded reveals and label. The three clearstorey windows are each of three cinquefoiled lights with vertical tracery in a four-centred head with a label; their sills are continued across the wall-face as a moulded string, with brattishing and stone corbels carved with half-angels holding shields between the windows. In the S. wall is a large window of six trefoiled and sub-cusped transomed lights with vertical tracery in a two-centred head with moulded reveals and label. In the W. wall is an arch to the aisle similar to the western arches of the S. nave-arcade and a modern doorway; the clearstorey has three windows similar to those in the E. wall.

The *North Aisle* (10¾ ft. wide) has, in the N. wall, two late 14th-century windows, both of four cinquefoiled lights with flowing tracery in a four-centred head with moulded reveals and label; they have been completely restored externally. The restored N. doorway, originally of the same period, has moulded jambs and four-centred head. In the W. wall is a late 14th-century window of two cinquefoiled lights with a quatrefoil in a two-centred head with a label.

The *South Aisle* (16 ft. wide) was rebuilt in the 16th century. In the S. wall are two reset late 14th-century windows, both of three cinquefoiled lights with pierced spandrels in a square head and with the middle light ogee-headed; further W. is a modern doorway. In the W. wall is a 16th-century window of four four-centred lights in a square head, all restored externally.

The *West Tower* (8½ ft. by 8 ft.) stands in the W. end of the nave and is of three stages with a plain parapet and a spire. It was built at the end of the 14th century and incorporates the late 12th-century W. wall of the nave. The ground-stage has, in the E., N. and S. walls, a moulded two-centred arch springing from chamfered and shafted responds; the E. arch has an extra order on the E. face added in the 15th century when the buttresses were built. The E. buttresses have moulded plinths and ranges of cinquefoiled panelling on the E. faces. Supporting the E. arch are two half-arches of two chamfered orders contemporary with, and springing from, the piers of the arcades and butting against the tower-walls. In the earlier W. wall is a late 14th-century window of two cinquefoiled lights with vertical tracery in a two-centred head with a label and defaced head-stops. The upper part of the tower has been refaced with modern rock-faced ashlar and the octagonal stone spire was rebuilt in 1823.

The *North Porch* (8 ft. by 5¾ ft.) is of late 15th-century origin but has been much restored and rendered in cement. The outer archway is moulded and two-centred with a label; the arch springs from chamfered and shafted responds with moulded caps and bases.

The *Roof* of the nave is of the 15th century, of six bays, flat-pitched and with moulded tie-beams, purlins, plates and rafters; curved braces form four-centred arches below the tie-beams and spring from short wall-posts carried on stone corbels carved with half-angels holding shields, except over the arches to the transepts where the corbels are omitted or have been removed. The roofs of the transepts are generally similar to the nave roof and of the same date. The 15th-century lean-to roof of the N. aisle is low-pitched and of six bays with moulded principals and purlin; two of the principals have curved braces. The 16th-century roof of the S. aisle is of four main bays, each divided into panels by a principal rafter and two purlins; the timbers are moulded and chamfered.

Fittings—*Bells:* five and sanctus; 1st, 2nd, 3rd and 4th by Thomas Newman, 1705; 5th by Thomas Newman and with the names of the churchwardens, 1705; sanctus not hung. *Books:* New Testament translated into Persian by Henry Martyn, 1815. See also *Miscellanea. Brass-indent:* In S. aisle—of small figure with inscription-plate; see also Floor-slab (1). *Chair:* see *Miscellanea. Chest:* In nave—of wood covered with sheet-iron, with flat lid, handles and two locks, 16th-century. *Consecration Cross:* In N. aisle—on N. wall, painted in red and black, formy cross in rope circle, perhaps mediaeval, damaged. *Font:* In churchyard—octagonal bowl with moulded underedge, plain stem and chamfered base, 14th or 15th-century, worn and patched. *Gallery:* In S. transept, spanning the full width, incorporating stair in S.E. corner—of wood and plaster, front with continuous succession of narrow vertical tracery-panels cinquefoiled at head and foot, supported on three moulded four-centred arches springing from quatrefoiled piers with moulded caps and moulded and foliated corbels against the walls, early 19th-century (a faculty of 1806 for the Rev. Charles Simeon to build galleries and a staircase at his own expense probably refers). *Glass:* In N. transept—in N.E. window, in four main lights figure subjects and texts, with Christ in the contexts of *Matthew viii, 13, xi, 28, xxvi, 11* and *Luke x, 42*, the last two texts transposed, and in tracery sacred monograms and lilies, by the artist and of the date of the following. In S. transept—N.E. window, in five main lights large figures of Christ flanked by the four Evangelists under canopies (Plate 17), and in tracery angel musicians with scrolls of plain-chant and angel holding symbol of the Trinity, memorial inscription to Charles Claydon, 1809, and Hannah his wife, 1796, 19th-century, signed 'W. H. Constable Stained Glass Artist in Cambridge'.

Monuments and *Floor-slabs. Monuments:* In chancel—on S. wall, (1) of Rev. T. T. Thomason, 1829, Fellow and Tutor of Queens' College, white marble tablet with pedimental head, by Swinton; (2) of Rev. Henry Martyn, 1812, Fellow of St. John's College, translator of New Testament into Hindustani and Persian, white marble tablet with pedimental head; (3) of

Rev. Charles Simeon, 1836, vicar, Fellow of King's College, white marble tablet (Plate 17) in elaborate 19th-century Gothic frame with flanking niches containing figures of a man and a woman, with shield-of-arms of Simeon, by H. Hopper, London. In nave—on tower buttresses, (4) of Edward Warren, 1722, Ann his wife, 1734–5, and Edward his son, 1734, painted stone cartouche with scallop shells; (5) of Samuel Conant, 1706, Fellow of Magdalen College, Oxford, slate tablet in alabaster frame with cherub-head, cornice, urns and cartouche containing the arms of Conant. In N. transept—on W. wall, (6) of Francis Percy, alderman, and Margaret his wife, both 1711, also commemorating their two sons Algernon, 1705, and Henry, 1706, who served in the wars against France, paired black marble tablets with moulded shelf and achievement of arms of Percy impaling (unidentified 72); (7) of Pell Gatward, 1741, white marble tablet with achievement-of-arms of Gatward quartering Pell with an escutcheon of March quartering Rowland; (8) of Elizabeth (Anderson) Peyton, [1659], black marble tablet on two moulded brackets. In S. transept—on E. wall, (9) to Charles Claydon, 1809, and Hannah his wife, 1796, white marble tablet on black marble backing; on S. wall, (10) to John Porter, 1771, white marble eared tablet with pediment, urn and cherub-heads; (11) to Mary, wife of John Porter, 1747, white marble tablet with pedimental head; on W. wall, (12) to Anna Horlick, 1852, wife of Robert Potts, M.A., of Trinity College, white marble tablet with scroll inscribed with her own verses, lilies, harp and heavenly crown, on black marble backing, by Manning, London; (13) to Hannah, widow of Robert Potts, 1845, white marble tablet with laurel branch on black marble backing; in gallery, (14) to Richard Mee, 1791, and Elizabeth (Jacob) his wife, 1778, marble tablet with pediment and cherub-heads; (15) to Maria, wife of William Jackson, 1777, white marble tablet with pediment. In N. aisle—on N. wall, (16) to Thomas Burleigh James, 1799, white and black marble tablet with pedimental head; (17) to William Wallis, 1799, and Mary his wife, 1796, rectangular marble tablet; (18) to William and Susan Mott, 1785 and 1790, white and black marble tablet erected by their children; (19) to William Mott, alderman, 1772, and Mary his second wife, 1755, white marble tablet in coloured marble frame with pediment; (20) to Mary Anne and William, children of Thomas and Rebecca Mott, small white marble tablet with urn on black marble backing, 18th-century; (21) of Sir Robert Tabor (or Talbor), physician, [1681], son of John Tabor, registrar to the Bishop of Ely, grandson of James Tabor, registrar of the University, attended Charles II, Louis XIV and Louisa Maria of Spain, slate and white marble wall-monument with fruit and flowers carved in high relief, cornice, urns and cartouche containing a blank shield. In S. aisle—on E. wall, (22) to Capt. William Jardine Purchas, R.N., 1848, and William Jardine his son, 1850, black and white marble tablet, by Tomson; (23) to Elizabeth, widow of Rev. George Paddon, M.A., 1843, black and white marble tablet, by Tomson and Son; on S. wall, (24) to Mary Ann, wife of Rev. Frederick Hose, 1841, black and white marble tablet; (25) to John Ingle, 1809, and Susannah his wife, 1832, black and white marble tablet; on W. wall, (26) to Ann Ind, 1807, and Edward Ind, alderman, 1808, white marble tablet in coloured marble frame with pediment. *Floor-slabs:* Under tower—(1) of Edward Warin, 1722, reused slab with rectangular indent and also initials and date S.C., 1706; (2) of Pell March, son of Pell Gatward and Sarah Rowland his wife, 1735, with achievement-of-arms as on monument (7); (3) and (4) of Pell Gatward, 1741, and another member of the Gatward family, both with shields-of-arms, all much worn. In S. aisle—(5) of James Godby, 1786, and Ann his wife, 1827; (6) of W.J.P., 1848, and W.J.P., 1830; (7) of Margaret, wife of Fr. Percy, 1711; (8) of Edward Lawe, 1676, and Edward his son, 1682, of slate with achievement-of-arms, much worn.

Plate: includes a cup and cover-paten with inscribed date 1569 (Plate 24), repaired in 1827, a cup and cover-paten with date-letter for 1622 given by William Rowland the same year, repaired in 1827, two cups given in 1839, copies of the two earlier cups, an almsdish with date-letter for 1631 with cinquefoiled dishing and cherub-heads on the rim, and an almsdish with the mark for 1836 and engraved view of Holy Trinity Church, Ipswich. *Pulpit:* see *Miscellanea. Recess:* In N. transept—in N. wall, tall, with chamfered jambs and four-centred head, 15th-century. *Royal Arms* (Plate 53)*:* In nave—over chancel-arch, carved and painted, 1814–37. *Miscellanea:* In Vestry—collection of relics of the Rev. Charles Simeon, including: his 'preaching Bible'; the collected edition (30 vols.) of his works, 1833; a large green umbrella; the 'Windsor' armchair used during his ministry 1782–1836, and a cabinet, about 3 ft. high, with four doors, made from the pulpit removed 1833. In churchyard—N.E. of chancel, carved stone with hand etc., probably corbel and mediaeval; N. of chancel, pilaster with drapery, probably part of 17th-century monument. In Museum of Archaeology and Ethnology, clunch image of bishop (Plate 68) in cope and mitre, blessing, with remains of crozier and of figure at foot, retaining much original colouring, 15th-century.

(46) Parish Church of St. Andrew the Great, previously known as St. Andrew without Barnwell Gate, stands on the W. side of St. Andrew's Street, opposite Christ's College. The walls are of ashlar and the roofs are slate-covered. The former church was entirely destroyed in 1842 and the present church built by subscription in the late 15th-century Gothic style from the designs of Ambrose Poynter and consecrated in 1843. It consists of an aisled *Nave* with a *Sanctuary*, the latter projecting a short way beyond the line of the E. walls of the *Aisles*, and a *West Tower*. The *South Porch* and the *Vestries* at the W. end were built in 1850 and 1897 respectively.

Structural remains of earlier date than the rebuilding are confined to details, perhaps some walling in the heating-chamber and a re-erected archway S.W. of the church. The said walling, below the western end of the S. aisle, appears to be of old material and contains the lower parts of a single-light window, perhaps of the 13th century. Built into the same wall are the double capitals of two pairs of shafts, probably half-round, of the early 12th century and carved with crude volutes; there seems to be no evidence of their provenance. The re-erected archway, made up largely of 17th-century material, has square stone jambs with moulded imposts and a semicircular arch of two square orders with a moulded archivolt and a plain keystone.

The interior of the church (Plate 279) is an elaborate and well-preserved example of the period.

Architectural Description—The *Sanctuary* (6 ft. by 21 ft.) and *Nave* (62 ft. by 21 ft.) are structurally undivided and without a clearstorey. The E. window is of five cinquefoiled and transomed lights with vertical tracery in a four-centred head; the internal splays and soffit are panelled and jamb-shafts at the angles are continued up above the head to support a straight moulded cornice enclosing traceried spandrels. The nave has N. and S. arcades each of five bays with lofty four-centred arches of two chamfered orders springing from octagonal cast-iron piers with moulded caps and bases standing on high rectangular plinths.

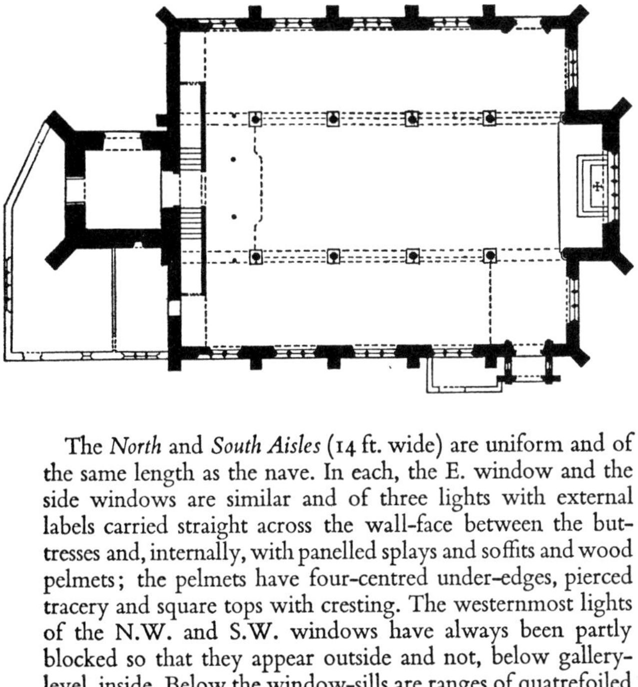

The *North* and *South Aisles* (14 ft. wide) are uniform and of the same length as the nave. In each, the E. window and the side windows are similar and of three lights with external labels carried straight across the wall-face between the buttresses and, internally, with panelled splays and soffits and wood pelmets; the pelmets have four-centred under-edges, pierced tracery and square tops with cresting. The westernmost lights of the N.W. and S.W. windows have always been partly blocked so that they appear outside and not, below gallery-level, inside. Below the window-sills are ranges of quatrefoiled panels and enriched strings. In the first bay is a doorway with a four-centred opening in a square head; that in the S. wall is now protected by a later porch. Over both aisles are galleries built up on cross-beams and raking members, with pierced tracery in the spandrels, supported on small cast-iron colonnettes immediately behind the piers of the nave arcades and standing on the same tall plinths; (see also Fittings).

The *West Tower* (13¼ ft. square) is of four stages with angle buttresses on the E., diagonal buttresses on the W. and an embattled parapet. The doorway in the E. wall has plain square jambs and a four-centred head. The N. doorway, which is the main entrance to the church, has casement-moulded jambs and a four-centred head with a label. In the W. wall is a modern door to the vestries. The second stage has single pointed lights in the S. and W. walls and a two-light window with tracery in the N. wall. In each wall of the bell-chamber is a three-light window with vertical tracery in a four-centred head.

The *Roof* over the sanctuary and nave is in five bays divided by queen-post trusses with curved braces below the tie-beams and others between the queen-posts and the collar-beams; all the spandrels are enriched with pierced tracery. The flat beamed roofs of the aisles are in ten bays, and each bay, except the westernmost, is divided into two main and eight subsidiary panels by chamfered beams with enrichments at the intersections. All these roofs are contemporary with the building.

Fittings—*Bells:* eight; 1st and 2nd, by Mears of London, 1856, with Latin inscription commemorating the Peace of Paris; 3rd, 4th, 5th and 6th, recast by Mears, 1843; 7th by Robert Gurney, 1667; 8th by Thomas Newman, 1722. *Benefactors' Tables:* In tower—two, charities of (1) Thomas Carrington, 1820, (2) Elizabeth Cook, 1841, text painted on boards, mid 19th-century. See also Brass (3). *Brasses and Indent.* Brasses: in nave—(1) to Leonard Chappelow, B.D., 1768, Professor of Arabic, Mary his widow, 1779, lozenge-shaped inscription-plate only. In tower—(2) to Edward Noyes, 1801, shield-shaped plate; (3) record of bequest by Christopher Rose, died 1661, for an annual sermon to be preached on the day of his death, mid 19th-century, similar in shape to (2). Indent: In nave, of inscription-plate, *Chairs:* In sanctuary, two with panelled backs, embattled top-rails, curved and moulded arms, mid 19th-century. In vestry—six; one, with panelled back enriched with arabesques, scrolled cresting and scrolled arms, turned legs and stretcher carved with initials A.F., modern but incorporating early 17th-century material; five 'Windsor' chairs, two with arms, splats pierced with fleurs-de-lis, *c.* 1800. *Coffin-stools:* two, with turned legs and plain stretchers, 17th-century. *Font:* octagonal, of limestone, each face of bowl with panel containing four quatrefoils, stem with buttresses at the angles and vertical tracery panelling, mid 19th-century, in the late 15th-century style, *Galleries:* Over N. and S. aisles—fronts between piers of nave-arcades with cinquefoil-headed panels, small buttresses and moulded base and top-rails. At W. end of nave—gallery with similar front, breaking forward in the centre and supported on cast-iron columns with moulded caps and bases; all contemporary with the building. *Glass:* In sanctuary—in E. window, of multicoloured interlacing geometrical design on grisaille ground with foliage borders and, in the heads of the lights, shields of the arms of Christ's College, the See of Ely, Queen Victoria, the Deanery of Ely, and Emmanuel College, in the tracery-lights, an Agnus Dei, and A and Ω. In N. and S. aisles—in tracery-lights of E. windows, sprigs of roses and made-up shields; in N. wall, in tracery of first window, six seraphim on golden wheels holding scroll of plain-chant, in tracery of second window, six children under canopies holding continuous scroll; in S. wall, in tracery of first window, canopy-work with name and date

Nathan Jennings, 1851, in tracery of second window, similar canopy-work in memory of Mary Sayle, 1850, in fifth window, angel (Plate 36) with inscription to Samuel Francis, 1840. In tower—in W. window, of geometrical design similar to that of E. window. All the foregoing of the mid 19th-century.

Monuments and *Floor-slabs. Monuments:* In sanctuary—on N. wall, (1) of Capt. James Cook, R.N., killed by natives of Owybbe in the Pacific Ocean, 1779, Nathaniel Cook, lost with the man-of-war Thunderer, 1780, Hugh Cook, 1793, Cdr. James Cook, R.N., drowned 1794, Elizabeth Cook, 1771, Joseph Cook, 1768, George Cook, 1772, Elizabeth Cook, 1835, white marble tablet (Plate 17) with flanking pilasters, trophies, a mourning woman, urn and, on the apron, a shield-of-arms of Cook; only Hugh, James and Elizabeth their mother buried here; (2) of John Wolryche, 1689, white marble tablet (Plate 14) with flanking putti, two cherub-heads, urn and blank shield; on S. wall (3) of Thomas Thackeray, surgeon, 1806, and Lydia his wife, 1830, white marble tablet with broken pediment and carved apron; (4) of James Robson, alderman, 1676, his son James, 1686–7, and Catherine Robson, 1709–10, black marble tablet (Plate 14) with gilt lettering, with side-pilasters and cherubs holding emblems of mortality, cherub-heads and achievement-of-arms of Robson; (5) of Anna Robson, 1727, oval marble tablet on corbel carved as cherub-head. In nave—on W. wall, (6) of Richard, son of Richard Humfrey, 1659, stone tablet (Plate 13) with strapwork apron and achievement-of-arms of Humfrey; (7) of Isaac, son of Giles Aleyn, 1661, very similar to (6) and with the arms of Aleyn (Plate 13). In N. aisle—on E. wall, (8) of George Fowler, 1775, Fellow-Commoner of Christ's College, white and coloured marble wall-monument with oval panel flanked by Doric pilasters supporting a pedimented entablature, with painted shield-of-arms of Fowler; (9) of Daniel Yate, 1676–7, Master of Emmanuel College, black marble tablet with alabaster side-scrolls and broken pediment supporting nude reclining angels holding emblems of mortality and framing achievement-of-arms of Yate; (10) of Robert, son of Charles Stoddart, vicar of Eglingham, 1732, rectangular marble tablet in plain slate frame; (11) of George, son of Shukburgh Ashby of Blaby, 1760, painted stone cartouche; on N. wall, (12) of John Bones, solicitor, 1813, and Mary his wife, 1786, white marble tablet surmounted by draped urn, on shaped grey marble slab, by S. Manning; (13) of Joseph Wilson, 1815, white marble tablet, by Tomson; (14) of Rev. John Edwards, 1716, Fellow of St. John's College, and Catharine his wife, 1744–5, of Mary, wife of Rev. Dr. John Newcome, Master of St. John's College, 1744, and Dorothy their daughter, 1758, white and coloured marble tablet with pedimented cornice and cartouche below; (15) of Jean Baptiste Goussel, 1832, teacher of French in the University, white marble tablet, by Tomson & Son, Cambridge; (16) of Joseph Butcher, 1814, white marble tablet on black slab, by Tomson; on W. wall, (17) of Thomas Fairmeadow, M.A., 1711, Fellow of Christ's College and rector of Ansty, black marble tablet with clunch flanking garlands, coved cornice and cartouche containing the arms of Fairmeadow. In S. aisle—on E. wall (18) of John Collins, [1618], painted stone wall-monument with bust cut in relief surrounded by inscribed fillet and scrolls flanked by pilasters, hand issuing from clouds above; (19) of Thomas Wiseman, J.P., 1764, alderman and mayor, cartouche with shield-of-arms of Wiseman impaling Butler (?); monuments (18) and (19) are difficult to see; on S. wall, (20) of Mary Humfrey, 1828, and four of her children, black and white marble tablet; (21) of John Fisher, 1795, and others later, plain tapering marble tablet; (22) of John Favell, 1804, Elizabeth his wife, 1840, and their children, George, 1798, John, died of wounds received at Baccum, 1799, buried in Leyden 'Cathedral', Capt. Samuel, killed at Salamanca, 1812, William Anthony, killed at Toulouse, 1814, James, in H.M.S. Leven at Delagoa Bay, 1823, Elizabeth, 1834, Thomas, Cdr. R.N., 1835, Edward, 1854, and seven infants, plain tapering black marble tablet; (23) of Jane, wife of G. B. White, Town Clerk of Cambridge, 1826, and two sons, white marble tablet with fluted side-columns, acroteria and urns; (24) of Frances (Redfarn), wife of Robert Barber, 1831, white and black marble tablet, by A. Swinton; (25) of Henry Cornwall, LL.D., 1699, alabaster tablet (Plate 14) flanked by palm-leaves, with cherub-heads, torches and cartouche containing the arms of Cornwall, and, immediately below, plain black memorial tablet to his sister Susanna, wife of John Baines, 1700; on W. wall, (26) of Rev. George Langshaw, B.D., 1843, Fellow of St. John's College, vicar, black and white marble tablet, by Swinton. In churchyard—S. of church, (27) of Maria Elizabeth Couldsbury, 1841, and Charlotte Elizabeth Mill, 1843, tomb with steep gabled top; about fifty headstones dated between 1715 and 1850, one to Willm Buttler, 1745, and Joan his wife, 1744, the rest later, some carved with cherub-heads, putti, angels and vases of flowers, many illegible. *Floor-slabs:* In nave —(1) of Dionsius Shales, 1718–9, Damaris his wife, 1732, and Dionsius their son, 1732–3, with achievement-of-arms of Shales impaling (unidentified 73); (2) of Elizabeth, wife of Gilman Wall, apothecary, 1760, Mary (Wall), wife of Morgan Gwynn Davies, 1782, Lydia Wall, 1789, Gilman Wall, 1790, and Mary Wall, 1796; (3) of John Barnard, 1703, with achievement-of-arms of Barnard; (4) of William, son of the Rev. William and Elizabeth (Cullum) Boys, 1722, with achievement-of-arms of Boys; (5) of Joseph Butcher, solicitor, 1814; (6) of the Rev. John Edwards, D.D., 1716, and Catharine his wife, 1744–5; (7) of William Woods, 1820; (8) of Thomas Thackeray, 1806, and Lydia his widow, 1830; (9) of Hugh, 1793, and James Cook, 1794, and Elizabeth their mother, 1835 (see monument 1). In N. aisle—(10) of A. Wall, 1798; (11) of Norris Wilson, 1821, and Mary his wife, 1822; (12) of Samuel England, 1741. In S. aisle—(13) of B. Audley, 1783.

Organ: In E. bay of S. aisle—front in two heights, the lower panelled, the upper with central group of pipes and flanking towers, W. side enclosed with shafted panelling that formerly lined the sanctuary, all mid 19th-century, in the Gothic style, reset early in the present century. *Plate:* includes a cup and cover-paten, the latter with the engraved date 1569, a flagon with the date-letter for 1732 and alms-dish, given by Ann Robson in the same year, both with shield-of-arms of Robson, and a cup, a stand-paten and two plates with the date-letter for 1844, given the following year. *Seating:* In nave, at W. end, two benches incorporating some early 16th-century material, shaped brackets below the seats, shaped ends, one terminating in a carved poppy-head. *Miscellanea:* Loose in the church—

various architectural fragments including freestone and Purbeck marble bases and caps, one cap with stiff-leaf foliage, all 13th-century and said to be from Barnwell priory, but authority not known.

(47) CHURCH OF ST. ANDREW THE LESS stands on the N. side of the Newmarket Road. The walls are of clunch rubble, extensively refaced with rough freestone ashlar, much of it reused material; the dressings are of Barnack and other freestone and the roofs are covered with tiles. The church, consisting of *Chancel* and *Nave*, was built early in the 13th century by the adjacent Barnwell Priory and, until the Dissolution, was served by one of the canons. Cole's sketch of 1745 shows a bell-turret and a S. porch. After being closed since 1846, the church was restored in 1854–6 under the supervision of the Cambridge Architectural Society when the upper part of the N. wall seems to have been rebuilt and the lower part refaced; it was reopened in the latter year.

The *Nave* (48¼ ft. by 18¼ ft.) has, in the N. wall, three lancet-windows and further E. an opening to the organ and a staircase, all of the later 19th century. The entirely restored N. doorway has jambs and two-centred arch of two chamfered orders with a label; the internal string-course is carried square over the rear-arch. In the S. wall are three completely restored lancet-windows, two of which are shown on Cole's sketch; both the larger windows in the same sketch have been removed. The S. doorway is largely original and has a two-centred arch of two chamfered orders, the inner continuous and the outer springing from attached shafts with moulded capitals and bases; the label has mask-stops. In the W. wall are two restored lancet-windows and in the gable are two modern openings for bells.

Fittings—*Bells:* two, inaccessible, with Latin inscriptions, one said to be by Taylor of St. Neots, *c.* 1800, the other probably post-1850. *Coffin-lid:* In chancel—tapering slab with moulded edge and ornamental raised cross, 13th-century. *Font:* of limestone, plain octagonal bowl and stem with moulded base, 13th-century. *Monuments:* In churchyard—

The *Vestry* and *Organ Chamber* were built in the later 19th century and the *South Porch* in 1929 on the site of the earlier porch. A *Choir-vestry* was added on the N. in 1955.

Architectural Description—The *Chancel* (22¼ ft. by 18¼ ft.) is structurally undivided from the nave. In the E. wall are three 13th-century lancet-windows, with two-centred rear-arches of two moulded orders and internal labels with mask-stops at the outer ends; the outer orders spring from Purbeck marble shafts with moulded stone capitals, bands and bases; the inner orders and the splay-mouldings stop against the abaci, which are continued into the splays. The string-course below the sills is continued round the church. In the N. wall, which sets back above the string, are two modern lancet-windows and a modern doorway. In the S. wall are two windows; the eastern is a restored 13th-century lancet-light; the western is of the late 14th century, of two transomed and trefoiled lights with a quatrefoil in a two-centred head with a label and head-stops; below the embattled transom the lights are rebated for shutters and served as a 'low-side'; the staples for the shutters remain.

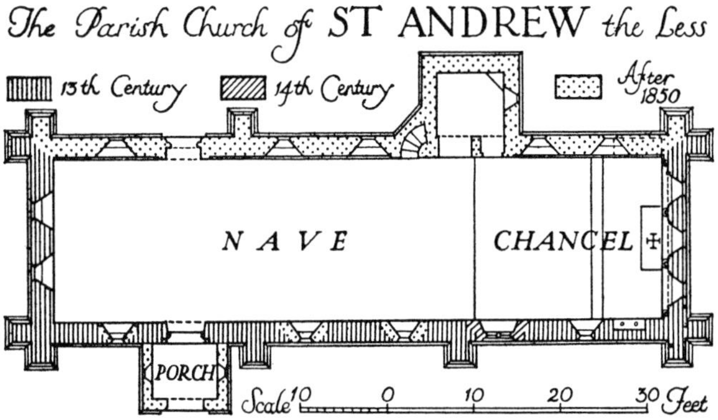

against W. boundary-wall, (1) of Jacob Butler, barrister-at-law, 1765, Rose (Clark) his wife, 1778, and with genealogy of the family including fifty-one names, six framed stone panels with pediment, removed from chancel in 1854; against E. wall of church, (2) of Elene, wife of Phill. Prigg, 169[0–1], cartouche with emblems of mortality; (3) of Philip Prigg, 1686–7, similar to (2); against S. wall of chancel, (4) of John Clarke, 1673, panel with shaped head; in S.W. corner, (5) headstone inscribed E.P., 1690–1; *Painting:* In nave—high on W. wall, large sacred monogram in a circle, in red, date uncertain. *Piscina:* In S. wall of chancel, rectangular recess with two drains, with octofoiled dishings, 13th-century, with modern wood frame. *Recess:* In chancel—in N. wall, with chamfered clunch jambs and segmental head, 13th-century, restored.

(48) PARISH CHURCH OF ST. BENET stands on the S. side of Benet Street. The walls are of rubble, with oolite and other freestone dressings, except of the vestry, which are of brick with stone dressings; the roofs are covered with tiles, slates and lead. The church, consisting of *Chancel*, *Nave* and *West Tower* was built in

the pre-Conquest period, perhaps early in the second quarter of the 11th century. Of this building the tower, the four external angles of the nave and probably much of the S. wall of the chancel survive. The base of this S. wall was uncovered in 1872 and recorded to be of large blocks of Barnack stone with a few of the quoins remaining in the S.E. angle; at the same time in the 19th century remains of a N. wall were found just within the existing N. wall of the chancel. In the 13th century, windows were inserted in the S. wall of the chancel and recesses for altars were contrived on each side of the original chancel-arch; conjecturally to the same period may be assigned the addition of aisles 10 ft. wide of which traces of the foundations were found in 1853.

During the reign of Edward I the church was badly damaged by fire (*Liber mem. ecc. de Bernewelle*, 159) and at the end of the 13th or beginning of the 14th century the chancel-arch was enlarged, the nave-arcades were rebuilt and probably also the aisles. This at the latest is when the N. wall of the chancel was reconstructed further N. The nave-roof was renewed in 1452 and a clearstorey was probably added at the same time. The church was intimately connected with Corpus Christi College, part of it being used as the College Chapel until the Chapel in the College was built in 1579; Dr. Thomas Cosyn, Master (1487–1515), built the *South Vestry* and a *Chapel* above together with the building containing a *Gateway* and a *Gallery* joining them to the College. The *North Aisle* was rebuilt wider and the *North Porch* added in 1853 from the designs of J. R. Brandon. Under A. W. Blomfield in 1872 the *South Aisle* was rebuilt and widened, the clearstorey, the E. and N. walls of the chancel and probably the chancel-arch were rebuilt, and the *Organ Chamber* was added.

The church is most notable for the survival of the pre-Conquest tower and some portions of the nave and chancel of the same date. Dr. Cosyn's building of *c.* 1500 shows an interesting and unusual arrangement providing a Gateway to Corpus Christi College and, on the first floor, access across from College to church.

Architectural Description—The *Chancel* (22¼ ft. by 16½ ft.) has a late 19th-century E. window of 14th-century character; it has shafted splays and moulded rear-arch and label. In the N. wall is an arch and, to the E., a single-light window, both of

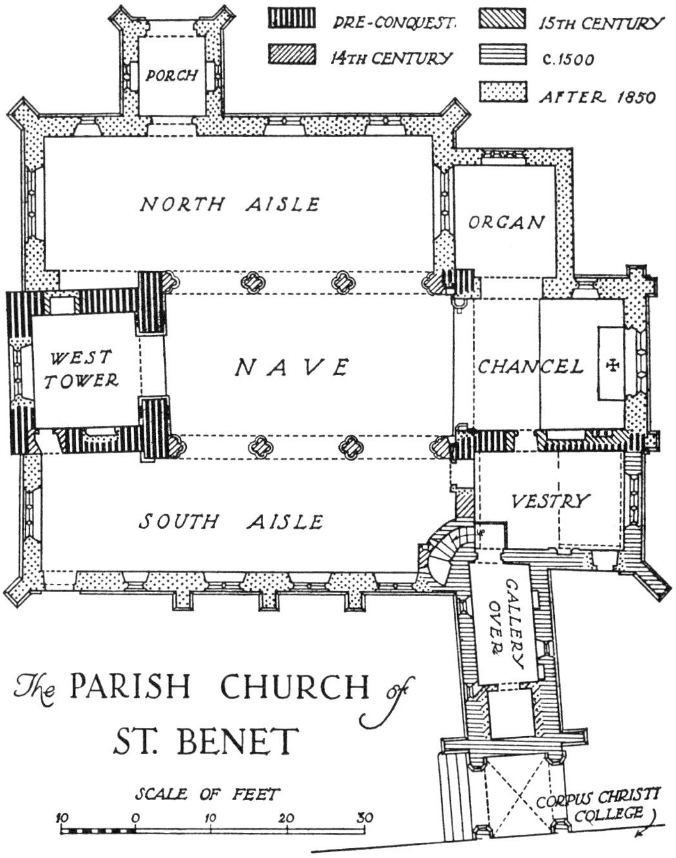

The PARISH CHURCH of ST. BENET

the late 19th century. In the S. wall is a 14th or 15th-century doorway with jambs and two-centred arch of two chamfered orders; higher up in the wall are two blocked 13th-century windows, visible internally; the eastern is of one pointed light with a segmental-pointed rear-arch; the western is wider but shows only the splays and segmental-pointed rear-arch. The E. side of the last is partly cut away by a blocked opening of *c.* 1500 with a flat segmental head formerly opening into the chapel over the vestry. The chancel-arch is of the late 19th century, but against the side-walls are the mutilated moulded bases of the chancel-arch of *c.* 1300. N. and S. of the arch, on the W., exposed in rough holes some 4½ ft. above the pavement, are remains of the springers and voussoirs of wall-arches to recesses that flanked the chancel-arch existing before the reconstruction of *c.* 1300. The requisite space for them could only be obtained, it seems, by excavating and splaying off the inner face of the pre-Conquest nave-walling on the N. and S. extremities.

The *South Vestry* (19¼ ft. by 12¼ ft.) and the former chapel above were built *c.* 1500. The walls are of brick with stone dressings. The lower floor has an E. window of three four-centred lights in a square head with a label. In the S. wall, the E. doorway is of the late 19th century; the other doorway and that to the staircase to the upper floor are partitioned off and serve Corpus Christi College. The upper floor and the adjoining building now being part of the College are described with it (p. 57).

The *Nave* (35½ ft. by 17¾ ft.) has N. and S. arcades of *c.* 1300 and of three bays with two-centred arches of two chamfered orders; the quatrefoiled piers, with subsidiary shafts, have moulded caps and bases and the responds have attached half-piers; E. of the arcades, above the haunches of the arches, are the remains of the doorways at each end of the former rood-loft. The N.E., N.W. and S.W. angles of the nave retain their pre-Conquest 'long and short' quoins and there are also a few remaining at the base of the S.E. angle. The clearstorey has three late 19th-century windows on each side.

The *South Aisle* (54¼ ft. by 14¼ ft.) is of 1872 except for the E. wall, containing a doorway of 1872 to the vestry, and, further S., the projection enclosing the staircase to the upper chapel and gallery. In the staircase-wall are three small lights, two opening into the church.

The *West Tower* (Plate 281) (14¼ ft. by 14¼ ft.) is of three stages and four floors. The walls are of rubble with 'long and short' quoins, square strings between the stages and remains of pilaster-strips in the middle of each face of the third stage rising from corbels over the windows and cut off at the reconstructed parapet; the quoins project slightly and there are some remains of a former harled outer surface. The semicircular tower-arch (Plate 281) is of one square order with a moulded surround on both faces; on the E. face this springs from two carved lions (Plate 28); the moulded imposts are continued along the wall-face; the responds are faced with long and short slabs and are of similar section to the arch, the moulding forming rectangular and half-round pilaster-strips stopping on a restored plinth; the N. respond has been partly restored. In the S. wall is a late 14th-century doorway with jambs of two chamfered orders and a two-centred head. The W. window is of three cinquefoiled lights with tracery in a four-centred head with a label and head-stops; only the arch, label and head-stops are old, of the 15th century. The second storey has, in the E. wall an original doorway with round head, chamfered imposts and jambs faced with slabs laid in 'long and short' fashion. In the W. wall is a restored 15th-century window of one elliptical-headed light in a square head. The bell-chamber has in each wall an original window of two round-headed lights with 'long and short' jambs, imposts and central baluster-shaft; higher up are two small round openings, also original, one only surviving on the E. Flanking the larger windows are inserted round-headed windows formerly all with pendants to the key-stone; the head of the southern one on the W. has the initials and date R.P. 1586.

Fittings—*Altar-slab:* In S. aisle—part only, with three consecration-crosses, mediaeval. *Bells:* six; 1st by Robard Gurney, 1663; 2nd dated 1588; 3rd dated 1607; 4th 1825; 5th by Tobie Norris, 1610; 6th by John Draper, 1618. *Benefactors' Tables:* In N. aisle—on N. wall, two with eared architraves, semicircular heads and entablatures and aprons, gilded and marbled, made in 1735. See also monument (9). *Bier:* In N. aisle—with turned handles, turned legs and turned pendant in

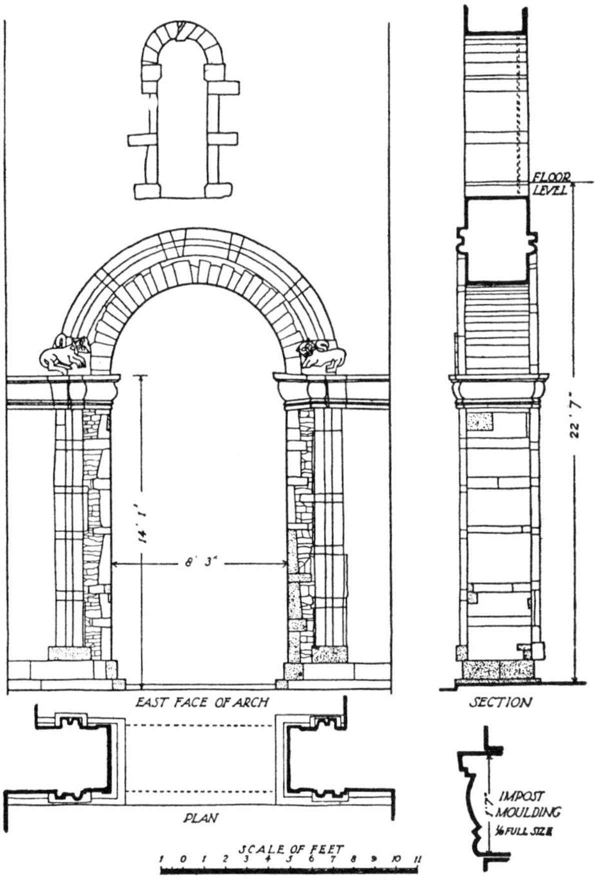

CHURCH OF ST. BENEDICT
PRE-CONQUEST TOWER-ARCH

middle of each side, 17th-century. *Books:* In N. aisle—include volume I of Erasmus' *Paraphrase* and part of a second copy; Jewell's *Defence of the Apology*, 1571, and his *Apology*, 1626; Bible of 1617, given by Thomas Hobson in 1626; Bible of 1635 bound with Prayer Book of 1635 and Metrical Version of the Psalms of 1630; Sermons or Homilies, 1635; and two old chained bindings with blank fillings. *Brass* and *Indents*. Brass: In S. aisle—to [Richard Billingford, D.D. 1442, Master of Benet's College], small kneeling figure in academic dress; inscription, perhaps angels bearing soul to Trinity, and scroll missing. Indents: In N. aisle, (1) of figure, inscription-plate and Evangelists' symbols, cut down. In S. aisle—(2) of figure, inscription-plate and Evangelists' symbols, early 16th-century. *Chest:* In N. aisle—small, ironbound, with two locks and hasps, cambered lid, late mediaeval. *Coffin-lid:* In N. aisle—tapering slab with double omega-ornament, 13th-century, broken. *Coffin-stools:* In N. aisle—two, with turned legs, 17th-century. *Communion Rails:* In chancel—modern but incorporating four carved early 17th-century panels, two with small figures of Justice and Truth, probably German or Flemish, two with arabesques and perhaps English. In S. aisle—with upper and lower rails, open arcading of six bays with balusters and end posts, incorporating some 17th-century materials, balusters mostly modern. *Fire-hook:* In N. aisle—of iron about 5½ ft. long with rings for guy-ropes, 17th or 18th-century. *Font:* In N. aisle—of marble and freestone, with round moulded bowl and baluster-stem, 18th-century. *Locker:* In chancel—in former E. wall but with rebated S. jamb only remaining, with groove for shelf, mediaeval.

Monuments and *Floor-slabs. Monuments:* In tower—on N. wall, (1) of Richard Dunthorne, 1775, and Elizabeth his wife, 1789, eared marble tablet; (2) of Mary, 2nd wife of Edward Randall, 1827, and Edward Randall, 1840, stele-shaped marble tablet on green marble backing; (3) of Pearse White, 1819, Town Clerk, a nephew with the same name, Frederick White, M.A., 1816, and Charles White, 1812, marble tablet; on S. wall, (4) of Susannah, wife of the Rev. George Coulcher, M.A., incumbent, 1842, marble tablet; (5) of Elizabeth Mary (Pershall), widow of Sir Buswick Harwood, Professor of Anatomy, 1836, marble tablet, by Tomson & Son, Cambridge. In S. aisle—on N. wall, (6) of Charles Skinner Matthews, M.A., 1811, Fellow of Downing College, marble tablet with urn, by Tomson; (7) of John Randall, D. Mus., 1799, Professor of Music, Grace his wife, 1792, and Ann (Mayor) wife of Edward his son, 1797, marble tablet on green marble backing; (8) of William Woodcock Hayward, 1838, marble tablet with pediment, Chi-Rho and urn, by R. Westmacott. In churchyard—N.E. of church, (9) flat stone slab with moulded edge recording the benefaction of John Meres, esquire-bedell, to the University and provision for a commemoration sermon; N.W. of church, (10) of Sarah, daughter of Samuel Newton, 1724–5, stone and marble pedestal-tomb (Plate 15) with gadrooned top, surmounted by urn, and achievements-of-arms of Newton at each end, one in a lozenge; (11) of Sam. Newton, 1718, Elizabeth his wife, 1723, six sons and three daughters, also Elizabeth their daughter, 1721–2, and Benjamin Watson her husband, 1717–8, and others, stone table-tomb with panelled sides and emblems of mortality on ends. In gateway in Dr. Cosyn's building, on S. wall, (12) of Thomas Felsted, 1705–6, and Dorothy his wife, 1687, stone wall-tablet with scrolls, swag and skulls; (13) of John, 1675, and Joseph, 1683, sons of Thomas Felsted, somewhat similar tablet. Against wall of Corpus Christi College, S. of church, (14) of The[ophilus] Chaplin, M.A., 1667, rector of Waram (Wareham ?), headstone; (15) of Thomas, son of Henry Woodroofe, 1689, headstone; (16) of [Thomas Grumbold, mason], 1657, shaped and scrolled headstone with panelled side-pieces and emblems of mortality; (17) of John Overton, 1696, and three children and Elizabeth his wife, 1696, headstone with carved parted drapery; (18) of Richard Daniel, 1717–8, mutilated headstone; against S. wall of church, (19) of Anthonie Milnar (?), 1666 (?), headstone. *Floor-slabs:* In nave—(1) of Mary, widow of Samuel Squire, 1732–3, and Susanna Newcome their daughter, 1763, slate. In N. aisle—(2) of John Pierse, 1652–3, with shield-of-arms of Pierse; (3) of Henry Gosling, S.T.B., 1674–5, Fellow of Corpus Christi College, with shield-of-arms of Gosling; (4) of Martha, daughter of........Bacon, and others, early 19th-century; (5) of Thomas Finch, 1773, and Sarah his daughter, 1777; (6) of John Paris, 1781; (7) of Ann, daughter of Searle and Mary Palmby, 1763 (?), and .... wife of .... Palmby, 1793; (8) of Thomas Fox, 1710; (9) of Sandys, son of Henry Peyton of Isleham, 1682, and Margaret his wife, 1687–8; (10) of Samuel Sharp, 1824. In S. aisle—(11) of John Dyer Edwards, 1833; (12) of Isaac Gallyon, 1830.

Piscinae: In chancel—recess with cinquefoiled ogee head and two square drains, blocked squint at back with quatrefoiled opening, 14th-century. In S. aisle—in staircase projection, recess with trefoiled head and quatrefoiled drain, 13th-century, reset. *Plate:* includes a late Elizabethan cup and cover-paten (Plate 24) without assay-marks, the first with rounded bowl and two engraved bands of simple strapwork ornament, similar band on the cover; a cup and cover-paten with date-letter for 1629, given by Mrs. Smith in that year; two flagons with the date-letter for 1659 (Plate 23), one given by John Preist, 1658, the other bought by the parishioners; two alms-dishes with the date-letter for 1670, given by Tobie Smith, 1670, and a brass alms-dish with repoussé figure-subject of St. George and the dragon, S. German, early 16th-century. *Seating:* In N. aisle—long oak bench with turned legs, 17th-century. *Sedile:* In chancel—with moulded jambs and ogee head, label with crockets and finial cut back, seat removed, 14th-century. *Table:* In N. aisle—with heavy turned legs, bracketed upper and plain lower rails, 17th-century. *Miscellanea:* In S. aisle—against tower-wall, reconstructed masonry with 15th-century recess or niche with four-centred head cut in pre-Conquest stones removed from the N. respond of the tower-arch; stone with incised pinnacled device and the initials I.T., probably 16th or 17th-century; on S. wall, wooden bracket with scrolls, leaves and cherub, late 17th-century. In second storey of tower—three carved oak scrolls from former reredos, 18th-century; also framed panel with names of subscribers to the new pewing, 1732; panel with note of erection of the gallery in 1823, and a third panel with the record of a peal of 720 Court Bob in 1783.

(49) PARISH CHURCH OF ST. BOTOLPH stands on the E. side of Trumpington Street. The walls are of coursed

flint and pebble rubble with dressings of freestone, Barnack stone and clunch; the roofs are covered with tiles and lead. There was a church on the site in the 12th century and of this some reused fragments remain. Structural evidence of an earlier church, which the dedication to St. Botolph might be taken to suggest, is entirely absent. The *Nave* and *Aisles* were rebuilt in the first half of the 14th century. The *West Tower* was built in the 15th century; later in the same century the *South Chapel* and *South Porch* were added and the aisle-walls heightened. The chancel was rebuilt in brick in the 18th century. The church was restored in 1841, 1872, 1874–7 and again between 1909 and 1913. The *Chancel* was rebuilt from the design of G. F. Bodley in 1872 and the *N. Vestry* and *Organ Chamber* added. An *Outer Vestry* was built in 1924.

The church has a good foursquare tower and, among the fittings, the font-case and cover and the four mediaeval bells are noteworthy. The monuments to the architects James Essex and Robert Grumbold are of some historical interest, particularly in the present context of architecture in Cambridge.

bases and, except for the S.W. respond, standing on square plinths. Reused in the bases of the W. pier on the N. and the middle pier on the S. are small mid 12th-century capitals. Both arcades have been restored and incorporate 19th-century dressings in the bases.

The *North Aisle* (8½ ft. wide) was heightened in the 15th-century and buttresses were added; two have since been demolished. It has, in the E. wall, a much restored 15th-century window of three cinquefoiled lights with vertical tracery in a segmental-pointed head with a label; below it is a modern doorway. In the N. wall are three windows similar to the foregoing. The 14th-century N. doorway, now blocked, has moulded jambs and two-centred arch with a label and one head-stop. In the W. wall is a window similar to that in the E. wall. Marks of the heightening of the aisle are visible on the outside of the N. wall.

The *South Aisle* (8½ ft. wide) was heightened in the 15th-century. It has one window in the E. wall, two in the S. and one in the W. wall, all of the 15th century and similar to those in the N. aisle. In the S. wall is a 15th-century arch opening into the S. chapel; it is four-centred and of two moulded orders, the outer continuous and the inner springing from attached shafts with moulded caps and bases; the bases are some 3 ft. above the chapel floor, which itself is higher than that of the aisle, and they probably stood on a low screen-wall now removed. Further W. is a doorway to the S. chapel with

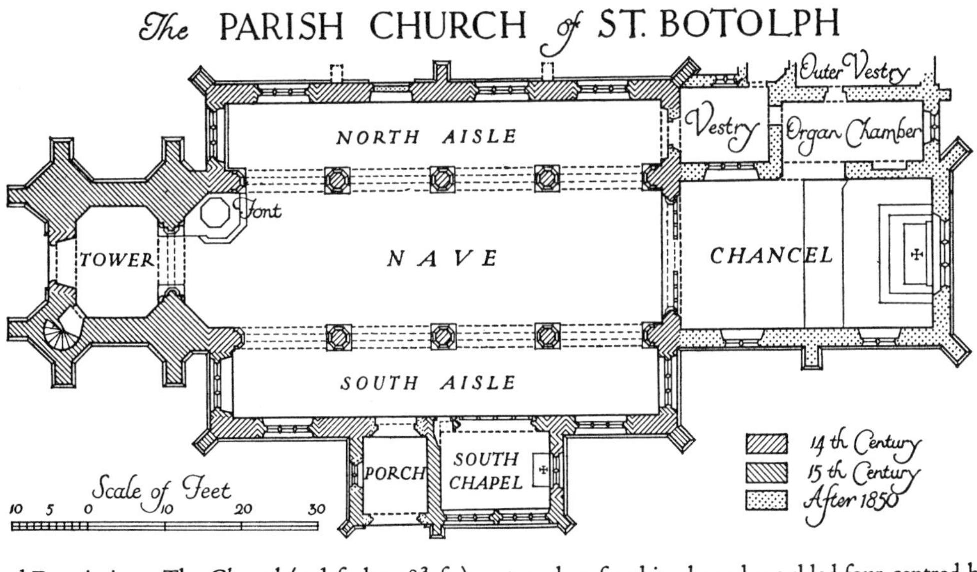

Architectural Description—The *Chancel* (33¼ ft. by 18¾ ft.) is of the late 19th century except for the 14th-century chancel-arch, which is two-centred and of two orders, the outer moulded and continuous and the inner chamfered and springing from attached shafts with moulded caps and modern bases.

The *Nave* (62¼ ft. by 17¼ ft.) has 14th-century N. and S. arcades of four bays with two-centred arches of one chamfered and one hollow-chamfered order springing from octagonal piers and semi-octagonal responds with moulded caps and

stop-chamfered jambs and moulded four-centred head. The S. doorway is modern. Marks of the heightening of the aisle are visible externally in two bays of the S. wall.

The *South Chapel* (14¼ ft. by 9¾ ft.) has a reset and partly restored 14th-century E. window of two trefoiled ogee lights in a square head with a label and defaced stops. The S. wall is almost entirely filled by two adjacent and partly restored 15th-century windows of three lights similar to those in the aisles. In the W. wall is a recess for the door-swing with chamfered four-centred half-arch.

The *South Porch* is of one build with the chapel and has an embattled parapet. The late 19th-century outer archway is four-centred and moulded and the jambs have attached shafts with moulded capitals. In the W. wall is a modern window, replacing one found blocked.

The *West Tower* (Plate 280) (10¾ ft. by 13¾ ft.) is of the 15th-century and of three stages with massive polygonal buttresses on the angles with subsidiary five-stage buttresses on their cardinal faces, a moulded plinth and a brick embattled parapet with carved stone figures of the symbols of the Evangelists at the angles; these formerly supported vanes. The tower-arch is two-centred and of two moulded and one chamfered order on the E. side and three chamfered orders on the W.; the outer and middle orders spring from attached shafts with moulded bases and capitals carved with paterae. The reset 14th-century W. doorway with two-centred head is of two continuous wave-moulded orders with a label and defaced head-stops; above it is a late 19th-century or modern window. The second stage has, in the N., S. and W. walls, a single-light square-headed window; reused in the N. and S. walls are pieces of 12th-century masonry carved with cheveron ornament. The bell-chamber has, in each wall, a much restored window of two square-headed lights; Cole's sketch (1745) shows two of them without mullions.

The lean-to *Roof* of the N. aisle is of the 15th century, much restored; it is divided into eight bays by moulded principals, the alternate principals having curved braces; braces, plates and purlin also are moulded and the rafters are exposed. The roof of the S. aisle is similar to that of the N. aisle and of the same dates. The low-pitched roof of the S. chapel is of the 15th century and in two bays with moulded principals, ridge and purlins; one wall-plate is enriched and embattled, the other renewed; at the middle intersection is a foliage-boss. The 15th-century roof of the S. porch is of two bays, with braces below the principals forming four-centred arches and wall-posts with tenons at the lower ends, for carvings now removed; all the main timbers are moulded and enriched with paterae; at the intersections and at each end of the ridge are foliage bosses.

Fittings—*Bells:* four, with the initials J.D. (for John Danyell) 15th-century; 1st inscribed "Sancte Apoline ora pro nobis"; 2nd inscribed "Sancte Andrea ora pro nobis"; 3rd inscribed "Sancta Margareta ora pro nobis"; 4th inscribed "Nomen Magdalene campana gerit melodie"; all except 1st with a stamp of the Royal arms (France modern and England); bell-frame old. *Benefactors' Tables:* In S. aisle—marble tablet in moulded stone frame recording testamentary gift of John Brewer, bricklayer, 1706. In tower, painted boards in moulded frame, recording gifts by John Lanham, 1651, and Adam Newling, 1696, given by John Peck in 1764, probably re-painted in 1836. *Books:* Bible of 1634, bound with a Common Prayer of 1636, printed by Robert Barker; Bible of 1599, printed by representatives of Christopher Barker; book of sermons, 1595, London; works of Bishop Jewel, 1621; the last three rebound; imperfect copy of *Commonplaces of Wolfgangus Musculus*, printed by Reginald Wolfe, London, 1563. *Brasses and Indents.* Brasses: In S. aisle—on S. wall (1) of John Smith, 1840, printer to the University, inscription-plate with incised Gothic ornament, mounted on stone tablet, by Cox & Sons, London. On outside of S. chapel—(2) of William Archer, 1616, formerly mayor, rectangular inscription-plate on stone tablet. Indents: In N. aisle—(1) of small figure of priest, inscription plate and shields at the corners, mid 15th-century, mutilated; (2) of figure, probably in academic dress, and inscription-fillet, slab with moulded edge from top of former altar-tomb, probably 15th-century. (See also Floor-slabs 8, 13 and 17). *Chests:* In S. aisle—(1) iron-bound, with one large and one smaller lock, 17th-century, top probably later. In S. chapel—(2) small, with three locks, late 17th-century. *Door:* In W. doorway of tower—of planks with nail-studded frame and applied mouldings forming four vertical panels, 17th-century. *Font* (Plate 32): octagonal stone bowl enclosed in timber octagonal casing with moulded skirting and capping and an arched panel on each face; cover to font with four shaped brackets supporting a ball; standing on casing, a timber canopy of four columns with caps, bands and bases, supporting a square entablature with pyramidal cresting over each face and four diagonal shaped brackets rising to a central turned finial; crestings each with a cartouche and carved swag; casing, cover and canopy painted dark green with repetitive foliate enrichments in gilt; woodwork bought in 1637 (Churchwardens' Accounts), painting and gilding added the following year, subsequently restored and with 19th-century painted inscriptions on the canopy. *Glass:* In S. aisle—in S.E. window, mediaeval and later fragments given about 1879.

Monuments and *Floor-slabs. Monuments:* In N. aisle—on N. wall, (1) of Mary, wife of Thomas Hide, 1770, white and coloured marble tablet with frame and obelisk with incised decoration; (2) of Mary, wife of the Rev. Thomas Preston, 1776, and Susanna, wife of the Rev. Anthony Fountayne Eyre, 1776, both buried elsewhere, erected by their father Kenrick Prescot, Master of Catharine Hall, oval marble tablet with shell, palms and cherub-head; (3) of William Lillie, 1788, marble wall-tablet, with side pilasters, cornice, broken pediment and cartouche with the arms of Lillie; (4) of Thomas Peacock, 1786, black and white marble tablet with pediment; (5) of Richard Hayles, 1781, surgeon, and Martha his wife, 1799, and four children, white marble tablet with pediment and shelf on brackets; (6) of Hannah, wife of Robert Roberts, 1711, clunch tablet with drapery, weeping putti and emblems of mortality; (7) of James Essex, F.S.A., architect, 1784, and his children, James, 1757, and Meliscent, wife of the Rev. John Hammond, 1787, white marble tablet with pediment; (8) of Edward Tomson, statuary and mason, 1829, and his brothers, Lewis, 1832, and Thomas, 1849, white and black marble tablet, by T. Tomson, Cambridge; (9) of Catherine, wife of Thomas Bennet, 1729–30, James, Catherine, James and Elizabeth their children, and Thomas Bennet, 1770, black marble tablet with pediment; (10) of Hannah, daughter of Peter and Sarah Middleton, 1812, white marble tablet with Greek Doric side-columns and pediment; (11) of John Sharp, 1783, for 40 years butler of Queens' College, stone slab with shaped top. In S. chapel, on W. wall, (12) of Thomas Plaifere, S.T.D., 1609–10, Lady Margaret Professor of Divinity, freestone wall-monument with bust of man in recess, flanking Corinthian columns and obelisks, entablature with enriched cresting containing a blank shield, and three crowning obelisks; monument formerly painted and on N. wall of chancel. In churchyard—on S. wall of chancel, (13) of Mary, daughter of George and Elizabeth Wilkinson, 1720, also of Thomas and Mary, children of William and Martha Swann, tablet with drapery held up by cherub; (14) of Robert Grumbold, 1720, and Bridget his wife, 1721, tablet with drapery, cherubs and emblem of all-seeing eye in radiant triangle; on E. wall of S. aisle, (15) of Judith Clay, 1664, tablet with moulded frame, scrolled pediment and emblems of mortality; on E. wall of S. chapel, (16) of Nicholas Goldsbrough, 1666, and Mary his wife, 1685, also Robart their son and two of his children, 1685, stone tablet with scrolls and skulls; on S. wall of S. aisle, (17) tablet with two panels, one with cartouche, the other skull and scroll, late 17th-century; S. of chancel, (18) of James Essex sen. and Bridget his wife, James Essex jun. and Elizabeth his wife and their two children, James Essex and Millicent Hammond, Elizabeth the last survivor died 1790, table-tomb; N. of tower, (19) of John Smith, 1840, printer to the University, pedestal-monument with panelled faces, on steps; also other 19th-century table-tombs and numerous 18th-century headstones. *Floor-slabs:* In chancel —(1) of John Hayes, 1705, Printer to the University, and Elizabeth his wife, [1705]; (2) of Thomas Walker, LL.D., F.R.S., 1764, and Elizabeth his widow, 1780. In nave—(3) of John Brewer, 1706, and Elizabeth wife of William Pitches, 1741, slate; (4) of Martha Beales, 1834, and others, slate; (5) of Hannah, daughter of Peter Middleton, 1812. In N. aisle—(6) of Thomas Cooper, 1740–1, Purbeck marble; (7) of Robert Roberts, 1778; (8) of James Barker, 1742, Purbeck slab with indent of brass inscription-plate; (9) of Herbert Raban, 1818; (10) of William Comings, 176., and Fowler and Robert Comings, infants, 1779; (11) of .... wife of .....s Soulsby, 1734; (12) of [Hannah], wife of Robert Roberts, 1711; (13) of Susannah Selby, 1739, with indent of brass inscription-plate. In S. aisle—(14) of Sarah, wife of Daniel Slack, 1788; (15) of Mary, wife of James Hinkin, 17.., James Hinkin, 1737, and Jane his second wife, 1794; (16) of Frances B[lythe], Richard [Blythe], [1722], and Frances Dehague, their daughter, 1723; (17) of John, infant son of William and Mary Seymour, 1748, and William Seymour, 1761, with indent of brass inscription-plate; (18) of Elizabeth, daughter of Robert Wright, 1685–6, and Elizabeth his wife, 1702; (19) of Richard, son of Richard Hayles, 1754, also of Richard Hayles, surgeon, 1781, Martha his widow, 1799, and Frances, their daughter, wife of the Rev. F. I. H. Woolaston, 1804; (20) of Thomas Bourn, 1741, [cook to Queens' College]; (21) of Martha, wife of John Prowett, 1834, and John their son, 1787; (22) of ...... Gotobed, ..., and others; (23) of John Prowett, 1847, and others; (24) of Edmund Curtis, 1780.

Painting: In chancel—over altar, oil painting on canvas of the Crucifixion, 18th-century copy of Van Dyck, given in 1819 by John Smith, University printer; on N. wall, copy of Madonna and Child by Raphael, after 1850. *Plate:* includes an alms-dish with the date-letter for 1712, given by John Hayes. *Pulpit:* hexagonal, of oak, five sides with fielded panels and cornice, early 18th-century, reconstituted in modern times probably from the larger structure previously here, stone base modern. *Railings:* dividing churchyard from street, plain uprights, main standards with knob-finials, late 18th-century. *Royal Arms:* In tower, framed painting on canvas, Hanoverian, 1814–37. *Screen:* Under chancel-arch—of three main bays including entrance, latter with septfoiled and sub-cusped head and pierced traceried spandrels, side bays with solid panelling below a moulded rail and, above, each of three lights with trefoiled and sub-cusped heads and tracery over, modern moulded beam and cresting, 15th-century, much restored. *Seating:* In S. chapel—two desks with shaped ends and poppy-heads incorporating a number of linenfold panels, early 16th-century and made-up. *Sundials:* On S.W. angle of tower —two adjoining painted stone dials replacing those repainted in 1614, restored in 1913. *Tables of the Creed and Decalogue:* In W. tower—on S. wall, two round-headed panels with moulded frames and scroll-brackets, painted respectively with the Creed and the Lord's Prayer, 19th-century. In S. porch—two round-headed painted panels in bolection-moulded frames containing the Decalogue, 19th-century, painting modern. *Miscellanea:* In N. aisle—wood carving in high relief of the Betrayal, probably Dutch or N. German and *c.* 1500. In outer face of S. wall of S. aisle, W. bay—fragment of 12th-century stone dressing; in outer faces of N. and S. walls of second stage of tower—stone fragments with cheveron-ornament, 12th-century. On S. wall of tower—moulded lead rainwater-head with downpipe, 18th-century. In churchyard—S.E. of S. aisle, octagonal stone structure with moulded plinth and moulded and embattled capping and low pyramidal top, 15th-century, purpose uncertain, possibly base of former cross.

(50) THE PARISH CHURCH OF ST. CLEMENT stands on the E. side of Bridge Street. The walls generally are of rubble with some brick and with freestone dressings; the chancel is of brick with stone dressings to the windows; the tower is cement-rendered. The roofs are covered with tiles, slates and lead. The church seems to have been largely built or rebuilt in the first half of the 13th century and to this period belong the four W. bays of the N. and S. arcades of the *Nave* and probably the responds and much of the arch of the chancel-arch; the wider E. bay of the nave indicates some form of transept or transeptal chapels. The E. bay of both arcades seems to have been rebuilt early in the 14th century and perhaps at this time or later the earlier piers to the W. were heightened and the arches reset; the first free pier on both sides was rebuilt early in the 16th century. In the E. wall of the N. aisle is a blocked 15th-century arch to a former N. chapel. Early in the 16th century the *North* and *South Aisles* were rebuilt and widened and the clearstorey was added. The *Chancel* was rebuilt in or about 1726 and the present capitals of the responds of the chancel-arch inserted. In 1821 the *West Tower* was built across the site of the W. wall of the nave from a bequest of the Rev. William Cole and to the designs of Charles Humfrey; the 15th-century five-light W. window and the former timber belfry standing in the churchyard to the N. of the nave were destroyed at this time.

The church was restored in 1863 and the *Vestry* built on the site of the former N. chapel in 1866; the spire formerly on the tower was removed in 1928.

Architectural Description—The *Chancel* (33¾ ft. by 17¾ ft.) is of the early 18th century and of reddish brick. Some bricks at the N.E. angle bear initials, presumably of bricklayers. There is no E. window. The N. and S. walls have both two windows of stone, of two four-centred lights in a square head outside; they have been partly blocked inside in the 19th century and now appear from within as pseudo-Gothic windows of one and two pointed lights. The partly restored 13th-century chancel-arch is two-centred and of two chamfered orders; the responds both have a chamfered inner order with an early 18th-century moulded capital.

The *Nave* (60 ft. by 16¾ ft.) has N. and S. arcades of five bays. The E. bay on both sides has an early 14th-century segmental-pointed arch of one wave-moulded and one chamfered order; the E. respond has a semi-octagonal shaft with moulded capital and base; the first pier is octagonal and of the early 16th century with moulded capital and base. The four western bays on the N. have early 13th-century arches of one chamfered and one hollow-chamfered order; the octagonal piers have moulded capitals and bases as has the W. respond; the shafts appear to have been heightened and the arches reset. The corresponding bays on the S. are similar but the arches are of two chamfered orders. The early 16th-century clear-storey has on each side five partly restored windows each of three pointed lights in a four-centred head.

The *North Aisle* (16 ft. wide) has, in the E. wall, a blocked 15th-century arch with a four-centred head and, on the N.E. external angle, a buttress, presumably of the former N. chapel. In the N. wall are four early 16th-century windows, each of four pointed lights in a four-centred head with a label. In the W. wall is a similar window but of three lights; N. of it and visible externally is a blocked doorway, with chamfered jambs and moulded four-centred head.

The *South Aisle* (16 ft. wide) has an E. wall built, apparently, immediately W. of the earlier S. transept wall, now indicated by a buttress, perhaps to give more direct support to the chancel-arch. In the E. wall is a blocked window with a four-centred head with an early 19th-century window set in the blocking and itself blocked. In the S. wall are three early 16th-century windows similar to the N. windows of the N. aisle. The reset and almost wholly restored 13th-century S. doorway has a two-centred arch of three moulded orders, the innermost continuous and the others springing from shafts with moulded capitals and bases; the label has head-stops; the restoration was the work of Poynter and is mentioned in the *Ecclesiologist* for 1843. In the W. wall is a window similar to the W. window of the N. aisle.

The PARISH CHURCH of ST. CLEMENT

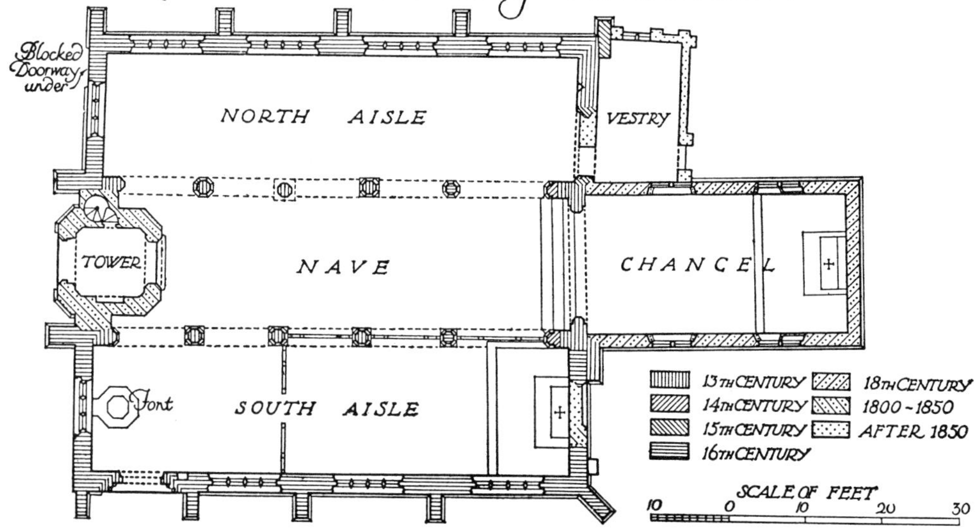

The *West Tower* (9 ft. by 8¾ ft.) is eight-sided, a square with splayed angles, and stands half within the nave. The exterior is rendered in Roman cement and has stone dressings. It was built in 1821 and is of three stages with pilaster-strips at the angles and an embattled parapet carried on an arcaded corbel-table. The low tower-arch has chamfered jambs and four-centred head. The W. doorway has chamfered jambs and a moulded four-centred arch in a square head with traceried spandrels and a label; above, on the outside, is a multifoiled diagonal panel inscribed in black-letter capitals "Deum Cole". The second stage has in the E. wall an opening with splays and two-centred head of two chamfered orders, and in the W. wall a window of two transomed ogee cinquefoiled lights with tracery in an acute two-centred head; the transom has foliage pendants over each light. Over the window just described is a circular quatrefoiled light, and in each wall of the bell-chamber a window of two trefoiled lights in a square head with a label.

The *Roof* of the N. aisle has lengths of carved and inscribed wall-plates reset against the S. wall; the inscription runs—"Orate pro bono statu Thomas Brakin Armigire et Luce 1538" and "Orate" alone.

Fittings—*Bells:* one and sanctus, former by Charles Newman, 1691, with the names of the churchwardens; sanctus by T. Osborn, 1780. *Brasses* and *Indent. Brasses:* In nave—(1) of Alan Hoberd, burgess, 1432, restored inscription. In N. aisle—on S. wall, (2) of Phoebe (Percevall), wife of Edward Withnoll, pastor, 1658, plate in modern wooden frame. *Indent:* at E. end of churchyard, of figure with marginal inscription and roundels at angles, 15th-century. *Door:* In S. doorway—of oak, battened, with applied moulded ribs, probably 16th-century, but very much restored. *Font:* octagonal bowl with shield in quatrefoil on each face, moulded underside with carved heads of two women, two men and four beasts, stem with cinquefoil-headed panels, early 15th-century, bowl probably recut.

Monuments and Floor-slabs. Monuments: In chancel—on N. wall, (1) of Sarah, wife of John Gunning, 1832, white marble tablet on black marble backing; on S. wall, (2) of William Scott, 1808, Elizabeth his wife, 1812, white marble tablet on black marble backing. In N. aisle—on S. wall, (3) of John Whittred, 1795, and Mary his wife, 1801, white marble tablet with cornice and cherub-heads below; on N. wall, (4) of Josiah Neale, 1792, Ann his wife, 1802, and Ann their daughter, 1826, white and black marble tablet, by Gilbert; on W. wall, (5) of James Burleigh, 1828, and Sarah his wife, 1824, white and black marble tablet, by Gilbert, Cambridge. In S. aisle—on S. wall, (6) of Robert Hodson, 1763, and Mary his wife, 1769, white marble tablet with pediment. In tower—on S. wall, (7) of the Rev. William Cole, A.M., 1782, formerly of Clare Hall, Vicar of Burnham, Deputy-Lieutenant for Cambridgeshire, black marble slab with triangular head, recording that his remains are in a tomb under the centre of the tower erected pursuant to his will and with money left by him for that purpose. On external W. wall of N. aisle, (8) of Joseph Gray, apothecary, 1808, slate and stone tablet. In churchyard—at E. end, (9) coped slab with seated skeleton holding hour-glass and scythe, probably 17th-century; (10) defaced headstone with cherub and drapery parted to reveal skull, 17th-century; against N. wall of vestry, (11) of Henry (?) Woolley, 1704, headstone; (12) of .... Brown, 1661, headstone; against N. aisle, (13) of Geoffrey Best, 1662, waterman, slab from table-tomb, also table-tombs to N.W. with inscriptions defaced. *Floor-slabs:* all of black marble. In chancel—(1) of Charles Filkins, 1743; (2) of ......, ..., and Anne, wife of John Hide, 1759, partly covered by organ. In nave—(3) of Charles, 1788, and Judith Martindale, 1799; (4) of Rev. Thomas Verdon, B.D., 1731–2, and his wife, 1751; (5) of Phebe, wife of William Anderson, 1762, four infant children, Elizabeth her daughter, wife of Nathaniel Vincent Stevens, 1774, and of William Anderson, 1774; (6) of Daniel Love, J.P., 1707–8, Captain of the Train Bands, and Martha his wife, 1715, with achievement-of-arms of Love impaling (unidentified 74); (7) of Ann, wife of Thomas Willett, 1774, also of Dinah his second wife, 1783, Abigail, his third wife, 1800, and of Thomas Willett, 1808; (8) of Mathew Wildbore, 1689, Francis Brackenbury, 1699–1700, and Katherine, successively wife to both, 1706, with defaced achievement-of-arms. In N. aisle—(9) of William Pedder, 1683; (10) of Adam Newling, 1696–7, alderman, Elizabeth his wife, 1686–7, Mary Smith, 1773, and Francis Smith, 1783. In S. aisle—(11) of Elizabeth, wife of Matthew Benson, 1736–7, Thomasin her daughter, 1739, and Matthew Benson, 1752.

Piscina: In N. aisle—in E. wall, plastered recess with quatrefoiled drain cut back, mediaeval. *Plate:* includes two cups and two alms-dishes, the latter plated, the first with the date letter for 1838 and all given in the same year by the Rev. George Spence, LL.B., vicar; a paten of 1674, given by Lewis Covell in memory of his daughter Joan; and a flagon made in Birmingham with the date letter for 1850. *Pulpit:* modern, with fragments of early 16th-century carved panels incorporated. *Stall:* In chancel—probably foreign and made up with 16th-century carved misericorde. *Stoup:* Immediately E. of S. door, with square jambs and chamfered two-centred head, back carved with formy cross, mediaeval. *Miscellaneous:* In tower, on N. wall, diagonal wood panel recording that the first stone of the tower was laid by Granado Pigott of Ely, legal representative of the Rev. William Cole of Milton, 6 June 1821.

(51) PARISH CHURCH OF ST. EDWARD KING AND MARTYR (Plate 285) stands between King's Parade and Peas Hill. The walls are of stone rubble, much of it re-used material, largely cement-rendered and with some Barnack stone dressings; the internal dressings are of clunch and freestone. The roofs are covered with tiles. The *West Tower* was built in the early part of the 13th century and at this time there was an aisleless nave; parts of the chancel may also be of this period, including the thicker E. end of the N. wall. The *Nave* including the chancel-arch and *Aisles* was rebuilt *c.* 1400. Consequent upon Trinity Hall and Clare Hall losing the use of the church of St. John, St. Edward's was appropriated to the use of Trinity Hall by Henry VI in February 1446, thereafter and probably before 1466 the *North* and *South Chapels* were added and the arcades of the *Chancel* built; the chapels overlap the nave by one bay and are or were known as Trinity Hall Chapel and Clare Hall Chapel. The S. wall of the W. bay of the S. chapel has an external string-course which is not present in the other bays and may indicate a slight difference in date. From Cole's drawing (1744) of the N. side of the church it appears that many windows had been altered in the late 17th or early 18th century. He refers to a new S. doorway; the N. doorway was apparently of the same date, and both have been removed, probably under a faculty of 1784, which also provided for the removal of the porches and for making a W. door. The *Vestry* and *Organ Chamber* were built in 1846. During the restoration of 1858–60 G. G. Scott redesigned the E. window, the rest of the work being done under the direction of R. Brandon; the W. door and window are of this date, and several other windows were renewed in 1869 including

the N. and S. windows of the N. and S. chapels. The chancel was restored in 1932, the nave in 1939, and the windows in the N. and S. walls of the N. and S. aisles were renewed in 1946 and 1949 respectively.

The church is of considerable architectural interest and distinguished for its wall-tablets and floor-slabs. The scale of the nave is much increased by the close inter-spacing of the piers of the arcades of *c.* 1400 and the maintenance of height in the arches, which are thus acutely pointed for their period.

Architectural Description—The *Chancel* (25¾ ft. by 18¼ ft.) has a five-light E. window of 14th-century character but of the N. wall and replacing the four windows shown in Cole's sketch are three 19th-century four-light windows of 15th-century character, of which the second is now concealed on the N. The window formerly in the third bay has been entirely cut away to make room for the organ. Under the window in the E. bay is a modern doorway; below the sill of the window in the second bay is an arcading of small blind arches with cinque-foiled heads and, in the pier immediately to the W., a recess of similar form. Across the chapel between the third and fourth bays is a chamfered four-centred arch apparently completely restored and springing from modern corbels.

The *Vestry* (26 ft. by 15 ft.) was built in 1846; the E. window is of three transomed lights with trefoiled openings under a square head. In the N. wall is a square-headed window of one light and a doorway with chamfered jambs and two-centred

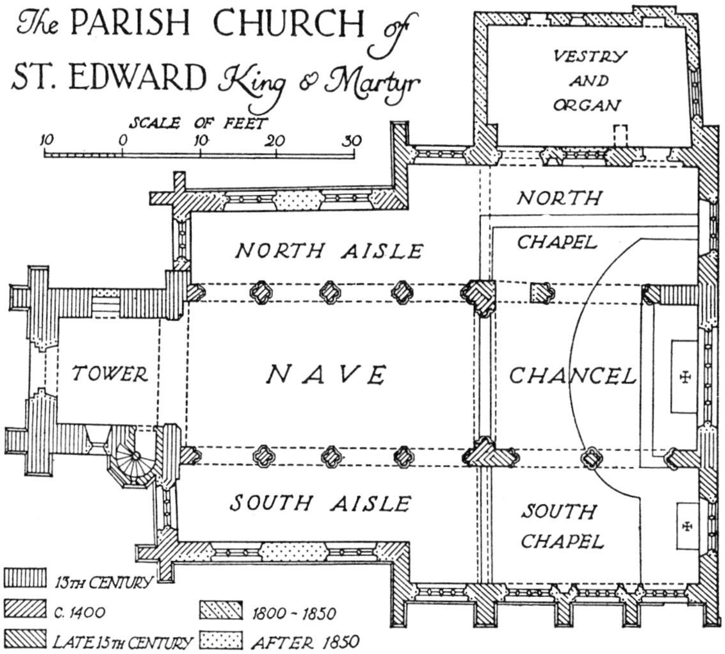

the mid 19th century. In the N. wall, which leans noticeably to the N., is a late 15th-century arch, four-centred and of two wave-moulded orders separated by a casement-moulding; the responds have three attached shafts with moulded bases and caps carved with paterae. Further W. is a small opening spanned by a modern four-centred arch. In the S. wall is a mid 15th-century arcade of two bays with responds and arches similar to those on the N.; the pier has four attached shafts. The chancel-arch of *c.* 1400 is two-centred and moulded, with two chamfers separated by a sunk chamfer; the last is continued down the responds, which have three attached polygonal shafts with moulded caps and bases and slightly concave faces. It retains the collars of an iron tie-rod removed in 1943. Above the apex of the arch is a blocked window.

The *North Chapel* or Trinity Hall Chapel (37 ft. by 14¾ ft.) has a 19th-century E. window of 14th-century character. In head with a label. The chimney has an octagonal shaft with moulded weathering and capping.

The *South Chapel* or Clare Hall Chapel (37¼ ft. by 14½ ft.) has a 19th-century three-light E. window of 14th-century character. In the S. wall are four 19th-century four-light windows of 15th-century character; below the sill of the E. bay is a blocked doorway and W. of it and below the sills of the two middle windows are blind arches similar to those in the N. chapel, with a recess of similar form in each of the piers between the three easternmost windows. Across the chapel is a completely restored arch similar to that in the N. chapel; the wider buttress outside and the form of the roofs in the two chapels indicate that this represents an ancient feature, no doubt inserted to support the chancel-arch.

The *Nave* (37½ ft. by 18¼ ft.) has N. and S. arcades of *c.* 1400 and of four bays with acute two-centred arches of two plain chamfered orders separated by a continuous sunk chamfer; the piers and responds have attached semioctagonal shafts with slightly concave faces and moulded caps and bases.

The *North Aisle* (9 ft. wide) has a N. wall with modern facing and two renewed windows; between the windows Cole's sketch shows an 18th-century doorway of which no structural evidence survives. In the W. wall is a three-light window of the 19th century externally, but the splays and rear-arch with a label are probably of *c.* 1400.

The *South Aisle* (9¾ ft. wide) is generally similar to the N. aisle. The two S. windows are modern and similar to those in the N. wall of the N. aisle. The wall-facing has been renewed and no trace remains of a S. doorway of 1735 referred to by Cole. The window in the W. wall is of similar date to the corresponding window in the N. aisle, with old internal label.

The *West Tower* (13¼ ft. square) is of the 13th century and of three stages with an embattled parapet; the floor and the surrounding ground-level have been considerably raised. Incorporated in the W. walls of the aisles are the N.E. and S.E. buttresses of the tower, indicating that the nave was aisleless when the tower was built. The stair-turret on the S.E. is a 15th-century addition with four-centred door-heads; the brick barrel-vault is sprung from the newel and the landing has a groined vault. The tower-arch is of distorted two-centred form of two chamfered orders; the responds have both a semi-octagonal shaft with a partly restored moulded capital with the abacus continued round the respond; the outer order of the respond is now flush with the side-walls of the tower indicating that the arch was built rather before the rest of the tower. In the N. wall is a recess contrived in the blocking of a 13th-century window or doorway; in the S. wall is a 13th-century lancet entirely modern externally and with a modern internal head, and the W. doorway and W. window are of 1858–60; high up in both the N. and S. walls of the ground stage is a blocked 13th-century lancet only visible from inside. The second stage has in both the N. and W. walls a round light of the 17th or 18th century set in a pointed internal recess, the head being that of a 13th-century window; in the S. wall is a 13th-century lancet, probably made narrower when the stair-turret was added and now blocked. In the E. wall is a 13th-century doorway or window, partly blocked, with rebated and chamfered jambs and two-centred head. The bell-chamber has in each wall a window of two pointed lights in a pointed head and probably of the 17th century.

The *Roof* of the chancel is of trussed rafter type and of pointed barrel form with moulded wall-plates of the 15th century and decorated with mid 19th-century stars. The *Roof* of the N. chapel, E. of the cross-arch, is of the late 15th century, almost flat-pitched and with moulded plates, principals and purlins; the principals are carved on the soffit with running foliage; under the W. end of the middle purlin is a stone head-corbel of a king, *c.* 1400 (Plate 29); the W. bay has a similar roof. The *Roof* of the S. chapel is flat-pitched and of smiliar date to that in the N. chapel, with moulded principals, ridge and plates; under the ridge over the cross-arch is a stone bearded head-corbel of *c.* 1400 (Plate 29).

Fittings—*Bells:* six, 1st by Christopher Graye, of Haddenham, 1669, 2nd and 3rd by the same, 1669, inscribed 'In timphanis laudate Dominum C.G.'; 4th inscribed 'De Buri Santi Edmondi Stefanus Tonni me fecit WL 1576,' from the Bury foundry; 5th inscribed in black-letter 'Sancta Anna ora pro nobis', by H. S., late 15th-century, from the Bury foundry; 6th inscribed 'Non clamor sed amor cantat in aure Dei', 1622(?). Bell-frame old. *Benefactor's Table:* In vestry on N. wall, Charity of Elizabeth Goodall, by will dated 1809, proved 1814, painted on boards in moulded wood frame, early 19th-century. *Book:* Bible, 1629, printed by Thomas and John Buck, printers to the University of Cambridge. *Brass-indents:* In chancel—(1) of inscription-plate, with later inscription to Owen Mayfield, 1685–6, see Monument (7). In N. chapel—(2) part of slab with two shields and later inscription to An. Ma. Crask, 1706, see Monument (2). In S. chapel—(3) of inscription-plate and shield. In nave—(4) of inscription-plate; (5) part of slab with upper parts of figures of man and wife, added inscription cut away but the date 1704 remains; (6) of inscription-plate, added inscription to Jno. Mortlock, see Monument (10); (7) of figures of man and wife, inscription-plate, scrolls, Trinity and two groups of children, with added inscription of 1729, late 15th-century; (8) of figures of man and wife, two inscription-plates, scrolls, Trinity, two groups of children, shield, added inscription to M.D. 1773; (9) of inscription-plate, added inscription to C.B.; (10) part of slab with figure of man in Doctor's cap, inscription, two Evangelist's symbols, added inscription to Frances Halfhyde, 1727; (11) of figure in shroud, scroll and inscription-plate, added inscription to S.F., 1755; (12) two pieces of slab with parts of figures of man in bascinet, feet on beast, and wife, two shields and inscription-plate, late 14th-century; (13) of inscription-plate, added inscription to Charlott, daughter of John and Margarett Heatherington, 1746, and A.H., 1748(?). *Font:* In S. aisle, octagonal bowl with upper moulding carved with paterae, a quatrefoiled panel in each face enclosing a flower, half-angels supporting angles of bowl, shafted octagonal stem with cusped panels between the shafts and moulded base with carved leaves and paterae, presented by the Cambridge Camden Society in 1842, being a complete restoration of the 15th-century font, much decayed, previously here.

Monuments and *Floor-slabs. Monuments:* In N. chapel—on N. wall, (1) of William Becke, 1614, of the Middle Temple, wall-monument with kneeling figure of a man in academic dress with ruff, enriched side-pilasters, entablature and damaged scroll-cresting; on S. wall, (2) of Judith, 1704, and Anna Maria (Wright), 1706, wives successively of Thomas Crask, doctor of physick, formerly of St. John's College, and Thomas, son of Thomas and Anna, 1707, alabaster and slate wall-tablet with cherub-head, garlands, cornice and cartouche with the arms of Crask; on W. wall, (3) of Thomas Lombe, 1800, solicitor, Ann his wife, 1789, Margaret their daughter, 1765, and Margaret his sister, 1759, white marble wall-tablet with pediment and painted shield-of-arms of Lombe. In S. chapel—on E. wall, (4) of Rev. Samuel Blythe, S.T.P., 1713, Master of Clare Hall, alabaster and black marble tablet (Plate 54) with cartouche with the arms of Clare Hall in chief and Blythe in base; (5) of Frances, widow of Edmund Halfhyde, apothecary, 1727–8, Edmund their eldest son, rector of Girton, 1739–40, Elizabeth their daughter, 1743, and Thomas their youngest son, 1745–6, scrolled white marble wall-tablet with achievement-of-arms of Halfhyde; on S. wall, (6) of Elizabeth (Buck) widow of Coniers Hatton, 1731–2, and Richard her son, 1735, scrolled white marble tablet with achievement-of-arms of Hatton; on W. wall, (7) of Owen Mayfield, 1685–6, formerly mayor, and Sarah his wife, 1684, freestone wall-monument with side-pilasters, drapery, scrolled and broken pediment and scrolled cartouche in tympanum with the arms of Mayfield. In N. aisle—on N. wall, (8) of Edward Lunn, 1813, Ann his second wife, 1809, and Susanna Turner her sister, 1818, white marble tablet, see Floor-slab (21). In S. aisle—on S. wall, (9) of John Mortlock, 1816, mayor, Elizabeth Mary his wife, 1817, and William their son, 1848, who rebuilt Knight's Almshouses, white marble tablet; (10) to John Mortlock, 1754, scrolled white marble tablet with cartouche with the arms of Mortlock; (11) of Edward Gillam, 1831, cheese-factor, Lydia (Andrews) his wife, 1793, and two children, Mary (Lunn) his second wife, 1807, and Mary, 1788, and Mark Gillam, 1809, saddler, Edward was buried at Canterbury, white marble tablet with shield-of-arms of Gillam; (12) of Robert Dawson, 1799, stonemason, plain oval marble tablet. In churchyard—against N. wall of church, (13) of E ...., daughter of James .... and Mary Mayfield (?), 1699, scrolled headstone with emblems of mortality; (14) of Elizabeth, wife of Paul (?) Goddard, 1711, headstone with cherubs and drapery, possibly displaced wall-tablet. N. of church, (15) of John Nicholson and others, late 18th-century, double headstone with cherub-heads, sun in splendour, hour-glass, etc. reused on reverse in 19th century; S. of church, (16) of William Sandars, 1767, and others, double headstone with linked urns, early 19th-century. *Floor-slabs* (see also Brass-indents): In chancel—(1) (Plate 18) of Thomas Buck, 1669–70, esquire-bedell, of black marble with shield-of-arms of Buck; (2) (Plate 18) of Hugh Martin, 1716, esquire-bedell, and Mary his widow, 1738, of black marble; (3) of Charles Morgan, S.T.P., 1736, Master of Clare Hall, black marble; (4) of Samuel Newton, 1718, alderman, Sarah his wife, 1716, and John their son, 1719, black marble, with scroll-work roundel. In N. chapel—(5) of Edward Clarke, 1726–7, Senior Fellow of Clare Hall and esquire-bedell, with long Latin inscription by Robert Greene, President of Clare Hall; (6) of Richard Thurlbourn, 1706, Elizabeth his wife, 1702–3, Mary Thurlbourn, 1702, and others; (7) of John Wood, 1742; (8) of Michael Pria ...., 1767. In S. chapel—(9) of Theophilus Dillingham, 1678, 'praefectus' of Clare Hall, and Thomas his son, 1722, black marble; (10) of Sha..ter Briggs, 1799, and Martha his wife, 1799; (11) of Elizabeth Hatton, [1731–2], black marble; (12) of Jane Kerrich, daughter of John Kitchingman, 1731; (13) of George Griffith, 1686–7, headmaster of the Perse School, added inscription to Edmund, Elizabeth and Thomas Halfhyde, 1745–6, with shield-of-arms of Griffith; (14) of John Wilcox, S.T.P., 1762, Master of Clare Hall. In nave—(15) of Robert Whiting, 1741–2; (16) of Rowland Simpson, S.T.B., 1736–7, rector of Gaywood and Aberdaron and Senior Fellow of St. John's College, black marble; (17) of Thomas Fagg, 1753, laid down by Sir William Fagg of Chartham, his brother, with shield-of-arms of Fagg; (18) of George, son of John and Mary Spen(s?), 17..; (19) of Ann, wife of John Wood; (20) of Martha ......, 1735. In N. aisle—(21) of Ann, second wife of Edward Lunn, 1809, Edward Lunn, 1813, and Susanna Turner her sister, 1818, black marble, broken.

Plate: includes a cup with the date-letter for 1568 (Plate 24), with deep bowl engraved with two bands of scroll-ornament, gadrooned stem and foot, a plain cup with the date-letter for 1627 on domed foot, a small cup with rounded bowl on low moulded foot and a cover-paten with the date-letter for 1704, both with the engraved date 1734 (Plate 23), given for the sick communicants by Mrs. Dorothy Roderick, and with engraved lozenge-of-arms of Roderick impaling Bullock, a stand-paten with the date-letter for 1707, a flagon with date-letter for 1711 (Plate 23), with straight sides, moulded foot, scrolled handle and moulded lid with finial, given by James Johnson, LL.D., and two alms-dishes, one with the date-letter for 1711, the other for 1769 and with engraved inscription of 1836. In S. chapel—pair of pewter candlesticks, 17th-century. *Pulpit:* of oak, hexagonal, four linenfold panels in each face in moulded framing, open below and with corner styles continued to form legs, solid base, early 16th-century with modern repairs and additions and some alteration to the lower part, from King's College Chapel, but originally in the church and associated with Hugh Latimer. *Seat:* In chancel, of oak, composed of linenfold panels in moulded framing, with three-sided back and box seat, incorporating early 16th-century material. *Tables:* In S. chapel—(1) with fluted and carved bulbous legs with Ionic caps, carved top and moulded lower rail, *c.* 1600, said to have been given in 1719 by Emmanuel College. In tower—(2) with reeded and fluted top rail, turned and enriched legs, and plain stretchers, late 16th or early 17th-century.

(52) Parish Church of St. Giles stands in the angle N.E. of the junction between Castle Street and Chesterton Lane. The former church, a small building consisting of chancel, nave, N. transept and S. porch, to which a large N. annexe was added early in the 19th century, was in part at least of the late 11th century. It stood just to the S. of the existing church and was pulled down when the latter was built in 1875; some portions of it were incorporated in the new building, which was designed by Healey of Bradford.

Architectural Description—The former chancel-arch, of the late 11th century, has been reset in the new church between the S. chapel and the S. aisle. It has a semicircular head of one square order with a moulded label on the E. face; the square responds have moulded and chamfered imposts with cable-ornament and a rough enrichment of network-diaper on the chamfers. The doorway, said to have been the former S. doorway, reset between the N. aisle and the Vestry in the new church, is made up of late 12th-century fragments. It is two-centred and of three orders, the inner chamfered and continued on the responds and the others moulded, the outer being enriched with cheverons on edge; the label has nail-head ornament; the jambs have detached shafts with moulded bases and carved capitals with moulded abaci continued round the inner order. Only one shaft on each side now remains and the stonework is much weathered.

Fittings, mostly from the old church—*Bell:* one, inscribed

'Cum cano busta [mori cum] pulpita vevere desi' (for 'vivere disce'), '1629'. *Chests:* in N. aisle—of oak, front of three arcaded and enriched panels with side-pilasters, enriched styles and rails, incorporating early 17th-century material. In S. aisle—of oak, front of three enriched arcaded marquetry panels with enriched styles and rails, first half of 17th-century, restored. *Clock:* works of turret clock with anchor escapement, going and striking trains of wheels mounted side by side in iron frame, locking-plate mechanism of bolt and shutter type, made by William Clement, London, 1671, with some later alterations and additions; at King's College until transferred to St. Giles in 1817; presented to the Science Museum, South Kensington, in 1925. *Communion Rails:* with moulded and carved top-rail, panelled standards and shaped carved and gadrooned square balusters, early 18th-century, brought from the English church at Rotterdam; (see also woodwork in Hall at Selwyn College). *Font:* plain octagonal bowl with moulded under-edge, octagonal stem and octagonal to square base, 15th-century, one face of bowl retooled.

Monuments: In S. chapel—on S. wall, (1) of [Nicholas] Carre [M.D., 1568, Regius Professor of Greek], Catherine Carre his daughter, who erected the monument, and William James, much restored freestone wall-monument (Plate 13) with skulls over the inscription-panels, side-columns, entablature, obelisks and elaborate strapwork cresting, with shield-of-arms of James impaling a blank shield and achievement-of-arms of James impaling Carr, early 17th-century. In N. aisle—on N. wall, (2) of Katharine, wife of Jacob Smith, 1833, white marble tablet on black marble backing; (3) of Jacob Smith, 1814, similar to (2); (4) of William Wilkins, 1815, Hannah his wife, 1815, and others, white marble sarcophagus on panelled base; (5) of Elizabeth Gifford, sister of Joseph Ivatt, 1800, white marble oval tablet; (6) of Rev. John Warter, 1802, Fellow of Magdalene College, white marble oval tablet on black marble backing. In churchyard—(7) of John Hinds, 1697–8, headstone, and twenty-eight other headstones carved with cherubs, emblems of mortality, etc., 17th–19th centuries, mostly much worn. *Paintings:* In nave—on W. wall, 18th-century copy of the Adoration of the Magi by Paolo Veronese, painted on canvas, in 19th-century gilt frame. In Vestry—Crucifixion on copper, 19th-century. *Plate:* includes a plain cup with the date-letter for 1622 and engraved with the initials of the incumbent, H.T., and the churchwardens, I.S., T.P., and a set of a cup, standpaten and flagon all with gadroon-ornament, unmarked, probably early 19th-century.

(53) Parish Church of St. Mary the Great, commonly called the University church, stands in the centre of the city, on Market Hill. The external walls are of rubble with some ashlar and dressings of oolitic limestone, with perhaps some Barnack stone reused from an earlier building. The interior is faced largely with clunch. In 1522 stone was being brought from the Weldon quarries, and again probably from the same source in 1592 for the completion of the tower; more came from the ruins of Ramsey and Thorney abbeys and Eversden and Reach clunch quarries in 1594. The chancel was refaced in 1857 with Ketton stone. The roofs are covered with lead and copper.

A stone with 12th-century cheveron-ornament is reused in the S. wall of the W. bay of the S. aisle, but in view of the sources of much of the stone no great significance should be attached to it. The *Chancel* was built or rebuilt early in the 14th century after a fire in 1290 and consecrated by Thomas de Lisle, Bishop of Ely, in 1351. In the latter part of the 15th century a general rebuilding was begun. In 1478 the foundation stone was laid, but the initial expenditure was small and little seems to have been done until 1488; then five years of activity was followed by a suspension of work until the early years of the 16th century. Over the period, the *Nave*, *Chapels* and *Aisles* were built, the nave roof being framed in 1506. John Bell, mason, appears to have been in close touch with the work and may have been the mason in charge until 1503, when records of him cease. The chancel also was extensively remodelled, and a S. porch and S.E. vestry added. William Rotherham, mason, and William Buxton, carpenter, were at work on the last in 1514 and this year probably saw the completion of the church but for the upper stages of the tower. Payments to William Burdon, mason, by the University between 1508 and 1510 and by the churchwardens, 1512–13, may indicate that he succeeded John Bell. The altar in the S. or Lady Chapel was set up in 1518; the nave seats were made and the nave opened in 1519.

The *West Tower* was begun in 1491 but by 1550 it was standing only to just above the W. window, which had been glazed in 1536. It was designed to stand free of the aisles, with N. and S. arches providing a procession-way since the W. wall bordered the western limit of the site. Early in the 16th century, it would appear, the aisles were extended to cover these arches and the bands of quatrefoiled ornament high above, which were almost certainly intended to be external, as on the W. face of the tower. In consequence the nave-arcades, which lie outside the full width of the tower, were left without W. abutment; to provide this, extra thickness of walling was added on the N. and S. faces of the tower up to the level of the aisle roofs.

The terms of an appeal (B.M. Cotton MSS. *Faustina* C III, 487–8), undated, but of the late 16th century, show that though the timber for the bell-chamber floor had been delivered it could not be placed nor the bells newly hung until the tower had been built 24 ft. higher 'besides the battlements'. The bell-chamber was begun in 1593 with Robert and William Grumbold as master-masons, and after a further appeal (Petition 28 May 1595; B.M. Lansdowne MSS. 99, 66) all the bells were rung for the first time in 1596. A spire at least 80 ft. high was projected, but the tower itself was not finished until 1608 and the spire was never built.

In 1735 the galleries in the aisles were erected, and in 1754 another gallery, 'Golgotha,' was inserted in the chancel; this last was taken down in 1863 when the interior of the church was rearranged. The *South Porch* was built in 1888 on the site of the earlier porch destroyed in 1783. The classical W. doorway of the tower erected in 1576 was replaced by the present Gothic one, designed by Gilbert Scott, in 1850–51; the tower was restored in 1892. The old vestry was demolished in 1857 and the chancel was refaced in the same year under the supervision of Anthony Salvin. Alterations to the church, particularly to the windows, were made by James Essex in 1766, and other restorations were carried out in 1784, 1805, 1812 and 1955.

The church (Plate 295) is an elegant example of late 15th-century building by masons whose work is identifiable elsewhere in the east and south-east of England, the nave having close affinities with that of Saffron Walden church for which a contract was made with Simon Clark and John Wastell, freemasons, in 1485. Among the fittings, the font, benches and remains of the 18th-century pulpit are noteworthy. Martin Bucer, who was buried here and exhumed in 1557, is commemorated by a modern brass.

Architectural Description—The *Chancel* (43½ ft. by 23 ft.) has been entirely refaced outside but retains much old ashlar facing inside. The E. window has 14th-century shafted and moulded splays; the five cinquefoiled and transomed lights with vertical tracery in a four-centred head in 15th-century style are of the mid 19th century. The N. and S. walls have each a moulded and two-centred late 15th-century arch, the outer members continuous and the inner springing from attached shafts with moulded bases and caps carved with paterae. In each of the same walls is a window of late 15th-century character but completely restored, except perhaps the splays and rear-arches. Between the arches and windows are 15th-century doorways with moulded and shafted jambs

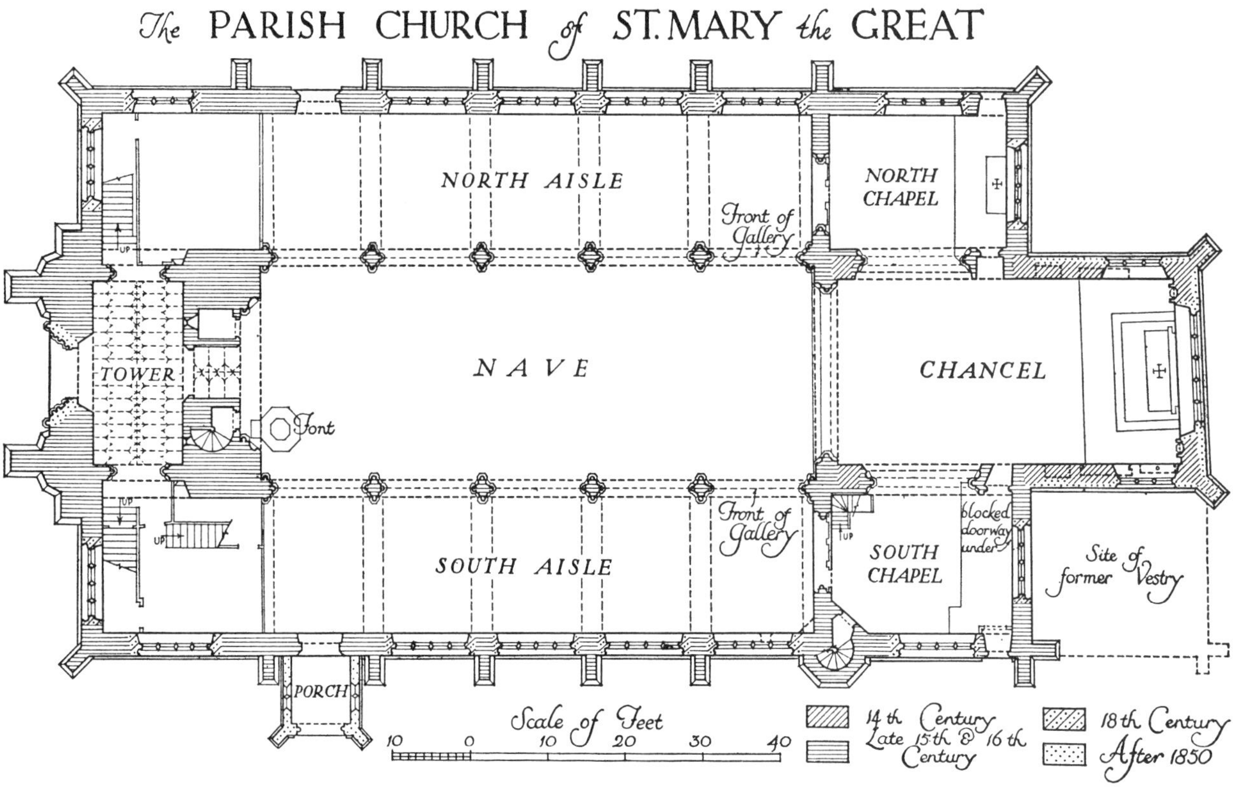

and four-centred heads; the jamb-shafts are semi-octagonal, with moulded caps and bases. Between the window and the doorway on the N. is a blocked 14th-century doorway, not visible externally except for straight joints in the footings; it has moulded splays and two-centred rear-arch and is almost entirely masked by the modern stalls. In the same position in the S. wall is another blocked 14th-century doorway, not visible externally, with damaged shafted splays and segmental-pointed rear-arch. Further W. in the S. wall is a blocked early 14th-century window with a moulded two-centred rear-arch. The chancel-arch is similar to the N. and S. arches but much taller and, on the W. face, with elaborate traceried spandrels, mostly foiled circles enclosing flowers; across the head of the arch is a deep moulded frieze of quatrefoiled squares set diagonally enclosing paterae, with small paterae on the lower member, and a cornice enriched with paterae, Tudor flowers and cresting.

The *North Chapel* (22½ ft. by 16¼ ft.) is of the late 15th century but the windows have all been restored. The E. window is of four cinquefoiled and transomed lights with tracery in a four-centred head with a moulded rear-arch. In the N. wall is a window altered by James Essex in 1766; it is of four cinquefoiled and transomed lights in a four-centred head. Further E. is a doorway with moulded jambs and four-centred arch in a square head with a label. In the W. wall is an arch similar to, but smaller than, the side arches of the chancel except that the opening is four-centred. Below the windows in the E. and N. walls is an internal string-course carved with paterae, leaves, Stafford and Bourchier knots and a leopard's face.

The *South Chapel* (23 ft. by 17¼ ft.), now a vestry, has a restored or largely modern E. window of four cinquefoiled lights with vertical tracery in a four-centred head. Below the window is a blocked doorway with moulded splays and four-centred rear-arch; indications of the outline of the former vestry remain in the external face of the E. wall. In the S. wall is a window similar to the corresponding window in the N. chapel, with an internal string-course below carved with paterae, leaves, a leopard's face and two beasts with leaves. At the E. end of the same wall is a doorway similar to that in the N. chapel but with shields with the initials I.H. and the arms of Hatcher; it was inserted by John Hatcher in 1576 and the head has been restored. In the W. wall is an arch similar to the W. arch of the N. chapel. S. of the foregoing is the lower doorway to the rood-loft stair; the upper doorway is in the S.E. angle of the S. aisle and has a four-centred chamfered head and jambs.

The *Nave* (Plates 286, 288) (71¼ ft. by 26¾ ft.) has N. and S. arcades of five bays divided by slim shafts with moulded caps and bases continued up into the clearstorey to support the main roof-trusses. The arches are two-centred and moulded, the outer members continuous and the inner springing from attached shafts with moulded caps carved with paterae and moulded bases; they have traceried spandrels, the main quatrefoiled panels having carved cusp-points, and across the head of each a string-course with paterae. The embattled clearstorey has, in each bay, two restored windows each of three cinquefoiled lights with vertical tracery in a four-centred head with moulded reveals and rear-arches; below the sills inside are bands of quatrefoiled squares set diagonally enclosing paterae.

The *North Aisle* (17 ft. wide) has an embattled parapet. The N. face of the nave-arcade has traceried spandrels similar to those on the S. face. The four eastern and the westernmost windows are similar to the N. window of the N. chapel as altered by Essex; the fifth window is similar but of three lights; below them internally is a partly restored string-course stepped over the N. doorway and carved with paterae, leaves, flowers and masks. The N. doorway has moulded and shafted jambs and a moulded four-centred arch, with panelled and traceried soffit, in a square head with traceried spandrels and a label with paterae and defaced stops; the cusped four-centred rear-arch has traceried spandrels including quatrefoils with paterae. The western end of the aisle is partitioned off and known as the Consistory Court; it is now used for parochial purposes. The tracery of the W. window was renewed in the 19th century.

The *South Aisle* (Plate 288) (17 ft. wide) is uniform in general arrangement with the N. aisle, but the rear-arch of the doorway has foliated spandrels and above it is an early 17th-century stone panel carved and painted with a shield-of-arms of Hare quartering Bassingbourn. The string-course is carved with paterae, leaves, cap or mitre, serpent, leopards' faces, cock, pelican, women's heads, double eagle-head, beast, snail, Prince of Wales' feathers, initial letter H, woolsack and two shields-of-arms, one defaced, the other of Lisle (?). The exterior of the S. doorway has moulded and shafted jambs and a four-centred opening in a square head with foliated spandrels and shields carved with a rose and a portcullis as label-stops. The tracery of the four-light W. window was renewed in 1877.

The *West Tower* (ground-stage 11¾ ft. by 22¾ ft.) is of four architectural stages and four storeys with a moulded plinth and modern embattled parapet. At each angle is an octagonal turret continued up above the parapet; against the turrets are angle-buttresses in three weathered stages finishing below the bell-chamber. The lower part, including the arches and W. window, is of 1491–1550 and the upper part was added in 1593–1608; the ashlar facing has been restored. The E. tower-arch is two-centred and of two moulded orders, the outer continuous on the E. and dying into the tower-walls on the W. and the inner springing from attached shafts with moulded bases and caps carved with paterae. The arch rises through two storeys; the lower part is filled with a contemporary but partly restored screen wall and the upper part is open to a W. gallery; no doubt this is the original arrangement. The screen-wall has a central doorway with, on the W. face, moulded jambs and two-centred arch in a square head with traceried spandrels enclosing paterae; the rear-arch is treated in a manner similar to that of the N. doorway and the soffit has cinquefoiled panels with traceried heads and paterae. Flanking the doorway, on the E. face, are doorways with moulded jambs and three-centred heads; that on the N. opens into a small chamber with a four-centred vault, that on the S. into a turret-staircase; on the W. face the chamber and stair have loop-lights.

In the N. and S. walls of the ground storey are arches generally similar in character to the E. arch but smaller and having on the outward face square heads with quatrefoiled spandrels enclosing paterae; high above them are bands of sub-cusped quatrefoils enclosing paterae and shields, on the N. of (a) (unidentified 75), (b) the abbey of Bury, (c) the See of York; on the S. (Plate 31), of (a) the See of Ely, (b) arms ascribed to Richard Barrowe. A later thickening of the N. and S. walls of the tower, added probably early in the 16th century to provide abutment for the nave-arcades, is arched over the bands of quatrefoils so framing them and the arches below. In the W. wall is a mid 19th-century Gothic doorway with shields-of-arms of the See of Ely and Trinity College. The ground storey has an original stone panelled vault of pointed segmental form running N. and S.; the panels have cinquefoiled heads with finials and tracery above. The second storey has a barrel-vault in imitation of that below but running E. and W. and apparently of plaster. The restored W. window is of four cinquefoiled lights with vertical tracery in a two-centred head with a label; below the sill is a band of quatrefoils similar to those on the N. and S. but much restored; they enclose a lily-pot, a Tudor rose, and shields carved with (a) arms of Rotherham (b) the Instruments of the Passion, (c) lily-pot, (d) arms of Bishop Alcock. The third storey has in the N., S. and W. walls a restored window of one cinquefoiled light with a label.

The bell-chamber is faced internally with brick and has in each wall a restored window of three pointed lights with intersecting tracery in a four-centred head with a label; across the angles are squinches turned in brick. The octagonal angle-turrets where they rise clear have a square-headed opening with pierced filling in each face; the former cappings have been removed. The S.W. turret, containing the stair from the second storey to the roof, is lined with hard dark bricks up to the level of the bell-chamber floor and with friable bricks of lighter colour in the late 16th-century work above.

The *Roof* of the N. chapel is of the early 16th century, flat-pitched, in two bays with moulded main timbers and with wall-posts and curved braces to the end tie-beams standing on corbels carved with foliage, a monkey holding a cup (N.W.), and a grotesque beast (S.W.). The roof of the S. chapel is similar but the ridge and plates are carved with scrolled running foliage; the wall-posts and braces have been removed and the corbels altered or removed, except the S.E. corbel, which has a carved beast. The early 16th-century roof of the nave (Plate 287) is of ten bays, flat-pitched, with moulded main timbers; the tie-beams have curved braces with traceried spandrels and spring from wall-shafts and corbels alternately. The large bosses at the intersections of tie-beams and ridge-purlin are carved as follows: (a) foliage, (b) two demi-angels holding a star or molet, (c) priest kneeling before a crucifix, (d) two demi-angels holding a shield with M.R. and a crown, (e) as (d), (f) foliage, (g) Crown of Thorns and foliage, (h) a pelican in piety, (i) St. Michael spearing a dragon, (j) Tudor rose, (k) foliage. Foliage half-bosses against the tie-beams cover the intersections with the side purlins. In the large hollow-moulding of the wall-plates are half-angels, with the wings broken off, holding scrolls, mitre, crown, blank shields, Crown of Thorns; spaced out in the sunk-chamfer above are traceried and foliated ornaments. The nave roof was repaired in 1726 and a second protective roof was built above it by James Essex in 1783. The late 15th-century roof of the N. aisle is similar to that of the N. chapel; the corbels on the N. wall (Plate 287) are carved with (a) fool, (b) half-angel holding a shield, (c) two-headed dove with a scroll, (d) half-angel holding a shield with a heart, (e) eagle with a scroll, (f) half-angel in prayer, (g) ox with scroll; on the S. side the capitals of the supporting wall-shafts are enriched with paterae. The roof of the S. aisle is similar to that of the S. chapel; the corbels on the S. wall are carved with (a) a cock and scroll, (b)–(f) foliage, some restored, (g) a monkey; on the N. side the shaft-capitals are carved with (a) a fox and a cockerel, (b) two monsters with intertwined necks, (c)–(e) foliage, (f) a ram and ewe.

Fittings—*Bells:* twelve and sanctus; 3rd, 4th, 5th, 6th, 10th by Richard Phelps of Whitechapel, London, 1722; 7th, 9th by same founder, 1723; 11th by William Dobson of Downham, 1825; 12th by Pack & Chapman, London, 1770; sanctus by John Warrin of Cambridge, 1607; all the canons, except on the sanctus, have been removed. *Benefactors' Tables:* In tower—on E. and W. walls, four, boards in moulded frames with painted inscriptions recording charities of 1648, 1652, 1679, etc., probably 18th-century and all repainted in the 19th century. In N. and S. aisles—two, painted boards in moulded framing, charities of 1809 and 1790, 1805, 19th-century. *Books:* include sermons by Henrie Bullinger, 1584, and bibles of 1611, 1706 and 1753. *Brasses* and *Indents. Brasses:* In N. chapel—on N. wall, (1) of Anne, wife of John Scott, notary, 1617, inscription-plate, largely illegible, and two shields-of-arms of Scott and Underwood; (2) of Thomas Lorkin, M.D., 1591, inscription-plate with two shields-of-arms of Professorship of Medicine impaling Lorkin and of Lorkin (Plate 6); (3) of Michael Woolf, 1614, inscription-plate with rose. In N. aisle—on N. wall, (4) of Elizabeth (Pritchard), wife of John Wickstede, 1616–7, inscription-plate only. *Indents:* In N. chapel—(1) of inscription-plate, reused as floor-slab (1). In nave—(2 and 3) defaced indents; (4) of marginal inscription and probably figures; (5) of three figures, four shields, three small plates and marginal inscription with roundels, probably early 16th-century; (6) of two figures and two shields, probably early 16th-century. In N. aisle—(7) of three half-figures, inscription-plate, two small plates and roundels at angles, reused as floor-slab (18); (8) of two figures, four shields and marginal inscription, reused as floor-slab (19); (9) probably of two figures, four shields, marginal inscription and plates at angles; (10) of inscription only. In S. aisle—(11) probably of two figures, four shields and small plate, reused as floor-slab (31); (12) defaced, reused as floor-slab (32); (13) probably of two figures, two shields and inscription-plate; (14) of two figures, much defaced. In tower—(15) slab with incised cross on calvary, indents of two figures and inscription-plate; (16) of two figures, inscription-plate and two plates, probably 16th-century.

Chest: In S.E. vestry, with five rectangular panels in front and two in each end divided by pinnacled buttresses, all except two containing flamboyant tracery and blank shields under ogee heads with finials and elaborate crockets filling the spandrels, the centre panel plain and mounted with a pierced wrought-iron lock-plate, and one end panel with a man's head in a wreath, double-headed dolphins, human masks and foliage, probably largely of the 19th century with some early 16th-century French panels incorporated, modern top. *Clock:* on W. face of tower, clock-face with spandrels carved in low relief and with painted date 1679 above, painting renewed. *Coffin-stools:* In S. chapel, organ lofts and ringing-chamber of tower, seven, with turned legs and fluted enrichment, 17th-century. *Doors:* In N. and S. doorways, two similar doors, in two leaves, with eight panels and moulded and nail-studded framing, early 16th-century, restored; in 1513–14 payment of 33s. 4d. was made to John Kale, a joiner and carver, for making the church door. In N. and S. chapels—in N. and S. doorways, two, generally similar, but in three and two heights respectively of three panels with applied hollow-chamfered mouldings and with wrought-iron strap-hinges, late 16th-century, repaired. In doorway to rood-stair, of nail-studded planks with moulded ribs applied to form three vertical panels, with strap-hinges, late 16th-century. In tower—in screen-wall, to N., plank door with applied ribs, 17th-century, to S., of moulded planks with moulded ribs and frame, nail-studded, late 15th-century.

Font (Plate 8): of freestone, octagonal, straight-sided bowl with upper and lower mouldings enriched with leaves and cable-ornament, shaped and foliated underside, pedestal carved with stylised tendrils, leaves and flowers, moulded foot on stepped base, each face of bowl carved in relief with strap-work framing to blank shields, a vase, cherubs' heads and ribbons, a vase and dancing innocents with books, and an oval panel with the date 1632; in 1631 Francis Martin gave three pounds towards the cost of a new font and in the year ended Easter 1633 two pounds was paid to George Thompson for making the font. Font-cover: of oak, a pyramidal octagon rising from an entablature to a ball-finial, with triangular moulded panels in each face, 17th-century, much restored. *Galleries:* over N. and S. aisles, with enriched moulded and panelled fronts on enriched entablatures spanning the openings of the N. and S. arcades, 1735–6, erection said to have been supervised by James Gibbs, part of testamentary gift of William Worts (died 1709). At W. end of nave, to organ-gallery, artificial stone front with arcading of ogee cinquefoil-headed panels and quatrefoiled spandrels, on cove with flanking moulded corbels, probably a remnant of the gallery built in 1819 from the designs of William Wilkins and, for the rest, demolished in 1863.

Monuments and *Floor-slabs. Monuments:* In chancel—in N. wall, (1) tomb-recess with attached jamb-shafts with moulded caps and bases, moulded flat two-centred arch and label with head-stops, early 14th-century, restored; (2) of William Butler, physician, 1617–8, alabaster wall-monument (Plate 13) with half-length figure of man in civil dress with ruff and turban, one hand on book, one on skull, in round-headed recess with obelisks and flanking putti on pedestals, one with a crutch, the other with foot on skull, on the crowning cornice a mutilated shield-of-arms of Butler in a wreath between two urns, erected by John Crane, physician, who died 1652; reset, altered and restored, (see B.M.. Cole MSS. IX. 28. for original state). In N. chapel—on N. wall, (3) of Gerrard Herring, 1703, woollen-draper, Mary his wife, 1715, and William his brother, 1722, square white and grey marble wall-tablet with gadrooned shelf on foliated corbel, cornice and painted shield-of-arms above of Herring impaling Linford. In S. chapel—on E. wall, (4) of Elizabeth and Ann, daughters of John and Sarah Mortlock, 1831 and 1838, marble wall-tablet with urn; on N. wall, (5) of Mary Turner, 1800, daughter of Mr. Hopkins, bookseller, black and white marble wall-monument; on S. wall, (6) of John Mortlock, 1775, and Sarah his wife, 1800, black, white and coloured marble wall-monument with side pilasters, pedimented entablature and shield-of-arms of Mortlock, inscription contained in wreath of foliage. In nave—on W. wall, (7) of Joseph Cooks, 1796, and Mary his wife, 1791, wall-tablet of limestone with circular inscription-panel and cherub-heads and foliage in the spandrels; (8) of Anne Theodora, wife of Charles Claydon, 1833, marble wall-tablet, by Tomson & Son, Cambridge; (9) of Elizabeth Story, 1727–8, Edward her husband, [1693], and Edward, M.B., Fellow of Magdalene College, their son, [1710], marble cartouche with smaller crowning cartouche containing painted shield-of-arms of Story impaling (unidentified 76); (10) of Thomas D'Aye, 1681, and Susanna and Anna his wives, alabaster wall-tablet with carved drapery frame and cartouche containing the arms of Day; (11) of Joseph Banks, Esther his wife, Mary their daughter and Samuel their grandson, son of Samuel and Lydia Banks, white marble oval wall-tablet, *c.* 1800; (12) of John Burrell, 1805, and other members of his family, 1812–51, marble wall-tablet. In N. aisle—on E. wall, (13) of John Crane, physician, 1652, black and white marble wall-tablet with heavy cornice and supported on console-brackets linked by fruit garland; against N. wall, (14) of Henry Balls, 1802, and Sarah his wife, 1778, and three children, double slab with shaped top and cherub-heads. In S. aisle—on E. wall, (15) (Plate 18) of William Finch, merchant, 1762, black and white marble tablet with console supports linked by flower-garland, broken pediment and cartouche with shield-of-arms of Finch; on S. wall, (16) of Jane, daughter of Swann Hurrell, 1838, marble tablet. In tower—on E. wall, (17) (Plate 18) of John Warren, 1608, square limestone wall-tablet with carved and moulded frame, repaired in 1618, and 1632 and recut after 1840; (18) of Elizabeth, wife of Gilbert Woollard, jun., 1794, and others; (19) of Gilbert Woollard, 1795, and Joanna his wife, 1788; (20) of Joseph Stuart, 1831, and others; (14) and (18–20) are headstones from churchyard, recut and painted in modern times. In churchyard—on N. wall of N. aisle, (21) of Elizabeth Goodall, 1814, stone wall-tablet with pediment; (22) of Moses Horne, Julian his wife and four children, 1658, stone wall-monument with garlands and cherub-heads. N. of the church are headstones to the following—(23) Benjamin Jeffs, 1785, and Mary his wife, 1770, double headstone carved with cherub-heads and wreaths; (24) illegible, similar to (23); (25) Thomas Adams, 1771, and Mary Adams, 1798. *Floor-slabs:* fifty-two, many partly hidden, of the 18th and early 19th century, without ornament unless otherwise described. In N. chapel—(1) Martha and Elizabeth Thurlborn, 1733 and 1736, reused brass-indent (1); (2) William Bland, 1765, and two children; (3) Richards Reynolds, 1809; (4) Sarah Steers, 1833; (5) M. T. Steers, 183.; (6) Clemency (Robinson), wife of John Coverley, 1790, and John Coverley, 1811; (7) Susannah Eliza, wife of John Smith, 1833; (8) William Bland, 1821, and Mary Ann Morton his sister, 1844. In nave—(9) Elizabeth Lamborn, 1759; (10) James Day, 1758; (11) T. N.; (12) infant son of Sam. and Eliz. Crosley, 17.5, Samuel Crosley, 1763, Elizabeth Crosley, ..., and another; (13) John Carter, 1706; (14) Ann ......, 1731; (15) .... Skinner, 1710–1; (16) John We(st?), 1744–5; (17) Samuel Frost, 1809. In N. aisle—(18) Dalby Mart, goldsmith, 1734–5, and Ann (Alpha) his wife, reused brass-indent (7); (19) John Gibson, 1767, and Jane his wife, 1756, reused brass-indent (8); (20) Thomas, Mary and William Smith, ...; (21) John Ogle, 1734–5, and others; (22) Ann, daughter of Mary Goodall, 1717, and others; (23) John ......, ...; (24) Russell Plumptre, M.D., 1793 [Regius Professor of Medicine], and Frances his wife, 1786; (25) [Thomas] Nicholson, ..., and another, 1700; (26) Eliz. Laughton, 1735–6, and others; (27) Charles Bottomley, 1823, and others; (28) Charles Bottomley, 1737; (29) William Yates, Attorney-at-law, 170.; nearby are several slabs now illegible; (30) Eliz. Lamborn, 1727. In S. aisle—(31) William H...., reused brass-indent (11); (32) John Rey ......, reused brass-indent (12); (33) Elizabeth, wife of John Gib ...., 17.., and Eliz. his second wife, 1744; (34) Francis H[icks?], 17.., Mary Hicks, 17..; (35) Edith, wife of John Smith, 1801; (36) G[eorge?] Webb, 1703; (37) William Peete Musgrave, 1817; (38) John Rudston, 1616, with long Latin inscription; (39) Ann Haselum, 1762, and another earlier; (40) .... Shut .., ..99; (41) Sime[on] Lord(?), 1764, and Ann Lord, 1779, and four others. In tower—(42) Deborah, 1761, and William Thurlbourn; (43) William Sykes, 1779, and others later; (44) Ann Crosley, 1786; (45) John Clack, 1746, Mary his wife, 1757, and William Steers, clerk of the parish, 1802; (46) William Finch, merchant, 1731; (47) W. F[inch, 1762]. In churchyard—between S. porch and gate, (48) Francis, son of Robert Scawen, 1669–70; (49) Sarah H[o?]wood, 17.3; (50) Dorothy (Plumptree) Ward, 1793, and others; (51) name illegible, 1700, with traces of achievement-of-arms; (52) .... as Rogers.

Niches: two very similar, in E. wall of chancel, flanking altar, each with fluted and pinnacled side-standards supporting cinquefoiled ogee head with sub-cusping, crockets and finial, moulded sill on corbel carved with foliage and supporting modern sculpture, remains of cusped panelling on back wall, 14th-century with much modern restoration including whole head of N. niche. *Organ* and *Organ-case:* On W. gallery, organ, three-manual, by Father Bernard Schmidt, 1698, rebuilt by William Hill & Sons, 1870; organ-case (Plate 22) with three groups of pipes appearing through openings in pierced and elaborately carved panelling divided and flanked by four towers of pipes supported on corbels carved with cherubs' heads and acanthus foliage and with tall crowning entablatures, the entablatures to the two taller central towers continuous and with scrolled side-supports, late 17th-century; Bowtell says it was bought from 'St. James's parish London', but, whilst confirmatory evidence for the case is lacking, the organ was made for St. Mary's.

Pall (Plate 68): of Florentine black cut velvet on a gold ground, the pile almost wholly decayed, with the Royal arms of Henry VII and the Tudor rose and portcullis embroidered in silk and silver-gilt thread on linen and applied on crossed bands of wine-coloured velvet, early 16th-century, by Indenture 20 Nov. 1504 (Univ. Archives) the University undertook to keep anniversaries for Henry VII in St. Mary's; now exhibited in the Fitzwilliam Museum. *Panelling:* In S. chapel—doorcase and lobby of painted pine with plain panelling, mid 18th-century. In arches at E. end of N. and S. aisles, two lengths of oak panelling, each of three bays and in two heights, the lower height with round-headed panels, one a door, divided and flanked by panelled pilasters with carved caps continued across as the base-members of the upper height of panels; the upper panels, divided and flanked by scrolled upright brackets, having moulded eared framing, scroll-pediments with shells and flanking half-round turned and carved balusters with flame-finials, early 18th-century and reconstituted, being composed of six sides of the pulpit (Plate 33) reputedly by James Essex, sen., erected in the centre of the nave *c.* 1736 and removed in 1863. In N. and S. galleries—on E., N. and S. walls, panelled dado with plain panels in ovolo-moulded framing, 18th-century with modern renewals. In tower—in ringing-chamber, quantity of linenfold panelling in three and five heights with carved frieze containing foliage and small heads, 16th-century with some modern work. *Piscinae:* In S. wall of chancel, double piscina with two two-centred and moulded arches with pierced trefoil cusping springing from a central column and attached jambshafts with moulded caps and bases, one quatrefoil and one sexfoil dishing in sill, early 14th-century, sill modern. In S. aisle, towards E. end of S. wall, with trefoiled opening in square head with carved spandrels, late 15th-century, sill modern. *Plate:* includes a pair of alms-dishes with the date-letter for 1681, given by Thomas King and Thomas Daye in that year, a spoon with pierced bowl and handle, with the mark for 1850, and eight pewter plates, four dated 1736 and with the name Capsey, two similar but unmarked, and two with gadroon borders. *Pulpit:* see under Panelling. *Recess:* At foot of stair in S. chapel, with chamfered jambs and square chamfered head, perhaps a lamp-niche, 16th-century, head modern.

Seating: In N. and S. chapels, nave, tower and N. and S. aisles, twenty-three benches (Plate 32) with poppy-heads carved with foliage, scroll-decoration under seats, early to mid 17th-century. In N. aisle—in Consistory Court at W. end, oak canopy to throne of the Chancellor of the diocese, with panelled standard flanked by pilasters with moulded bases and caps and roses carved on the shafts, coved entablature with modillions, and sounding-board with dentil-cornice, mid 17th-century. In galleries—at E. end of each, box-pew and reading-desk, seat with rounded and panelled back facing W., mid 18th-century. *Sedilia:* In S. wall of chancel, with half-round jamb-shafts with moulded caps and bases, flat two-centred arch with cinquefoiled ogee cusping, moulded and pierced, and moulded label with modern head-stops, early 14th-century, restored. *Stairs:* at W. end of N. and S. aisles and leading to galleries, of oak, with close strings, turned balusters, moulded handrails, square newels with moulded caps and, against the walls, panelled dados with moulded dado-rails, probably contemporary with the aisle-galleries, 1735–36. *Table:* In S. chapel, of oak, with turned legs on pedestals, plain stretchers, frame with ball-ornament, mid 17th-century, made up with modern work. *Miscellanea:* In tower—in ringing-chamber, painted ringers'-boards dated 1779, 1788 (Plate 59), 1790, 1791, 1793, 1797 and others later. In tower-stair—on jambs of loop-light level with bell-chamber floor, stone carved with the date 1607 and initials of the minister and churchwardens, G W [George Watts], I W and M F [John Warren and Marmaduke Frohock]. In bell-chamber—on window-splays, numerous scratchings, of initials, dates, 17th and 18th-centuries and later. On S.W. buttress of tower, incised circle, the datum-point cut in 1732 from which miles were measured along the roads from Cambridge (see MILESTONES, Monument (83)).

(54) PARISH CHURCH OF ST. MARY THE LESS stands on the W. side of Trumpington Street. The walls are of rubble, mostly ashlar-faced both inside and out in the five eastern bays and repaired in places in brick; the dressings are of Barnack stone and clunch. The roofs are covered with Collyweston stone slates and lead. The church, until 1352 called St. Peter without Trumpington Gates, is of pre-Conquest foundation as evidenced by the survival of late Anglo-Saxon fragments of interlacement. The earliest surviving structural work is of

Nave roof. 1506

N. aisle. Roof-corbel (c). c. 1500

N. aisle. Roof-corbel (f). c. 1500

(53) ST. MARY THE GREAT.

Nave; interior, looking E.

S. arcade of nave, S. side.

(53) CHURCH OF ST. MARY THE GREAT.

Late 15th and early 16th-century

Interior, looking E.

Exterior, from N.E.

(54) CHURCH OF ST. MARY THE LESS.

c. 1340–52

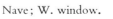

South chapel; interior, E. end.

Nave; W. window.

(56) CHURCH OF ST. MICHAEL.

(56) CHURCH OF ST. MICHAEL. Interior, looking W.

1326–27

General view of E. end of nave.

Detail, over S. nave-arcade.

Detail, over chancel-arch.

(60) CHESTERTON CHURCH. Doom painting. Late 15th-century

(61) TRUMPINGTON CHURCH. Nave; interior, looking W. *c.* 1330

(61) TRUMPINGTON CHURCH. Monument (6). *c.* 1330

(59) CHERRY HINTON CHURCH. Chancel, S. wall. 13th-century

the 12th century to which date belong the remains of the *West Tower*.

The rest of the *Church* was rebuilt between about the years 1340 and 1352 when it was finished and rededicated. It served for long as the chapel of Peterhouse and is attached to the College by a gallery S. of the chancel approached by a staircase and crossing over a gateway. The five E. bays belong to the rebuilding and the intention was to have a sixth bay of rather wider span, as is indicated by the form of the buttresses between the fifth and sixth bays. This would have given more clearance to the earlier tower-arch and the plan would then have resembled the choir and ante-chapel plan more fully developed in some of the Oxford college chapels. In the 15th-century the existing sixth bay was built, but continuing the lines of the main side-walls; at the same time the tracery of the side-windows, at the least on the N., was altered (the windows are shown in Cole's sketch of 1743), and about the middle of the century a S. porch was added by John Leedes, bursar of Peterhouse, died 1455. Two chantry-chapels were built to the N. and S. of the church, by Thomas Lane and probably by Henry Horneby, both Masters of Peterhouse; the altar in Lane's chantry was consecrated in 1443, many years before his death; Horneby died in 1517–8. The *South Vestry*, originally of the 14th century, was very largely rebuilt and an upper storey added about 1487, when the chapel of John Warkworth, Master of Peterhouse, was consecrated; in spite of some ambiguity it appears that the chapel and the vestry were the same structure.

The pulpit alone survives of a refitting of 1741. The church was restored in 1856–57 under Gilbert Scott and in 1876 and 1891; probably in 1876 the former Jacobean roof was removed. At some uncertain date the tower, shown standing in Cole's view, fell or was demolished and in 1892 the *Parish Room* and the lower part of a new *Tower* were built; the *South Chapel* was built in 1931 from the designs of T. H. Lyon.

The church is an imposing and spacious mid 14th-century building, being of some architectural pretension and without structural division from end to end. The 14th-century vaulting of the bone-hole, in part of brick, is of interest. Among the fittings, the font, the font-cover and the pulpit are noteworthy.

Architectural Description—The *Church* (Plate 289) (100 ft. by $27\frac{3}{4}$ ft.) is structurally undivided. The 14th-century E. window, with restored mullions and tracery, is of six cinquefoiled ogee lights with flowing tracery in a two-centred head with labels, shafted splays and moulded rear-arch. In the N. wall are six windows; the three easternmost and the fifth are of the 14th-century, restored and similar in detail to the E. window; each is of four cinquefoiled lights with modern tracery in a two-centred head; the tracery is copied from that surviving in the S. windows. A similar window in the fourth bay is blocked externally in red brick; below it are the blocked 15th-century doorway and tomb-arch of the former Lane chapel; the doorway has splayed jambs and moulded four-centred head and the tomb-arch a septfoiled and sub-cusped head with carved cusp-points and foliated spandrels under a moulded four-centred arch. The buttresses outside show indications of the E. and W. walls of the Lane chapel but are now finished like the other buttresses. The sixth and westernmost window is presumably of the 15th century although the

PARISH CHURCH *of* ST. MARY *the* LESS

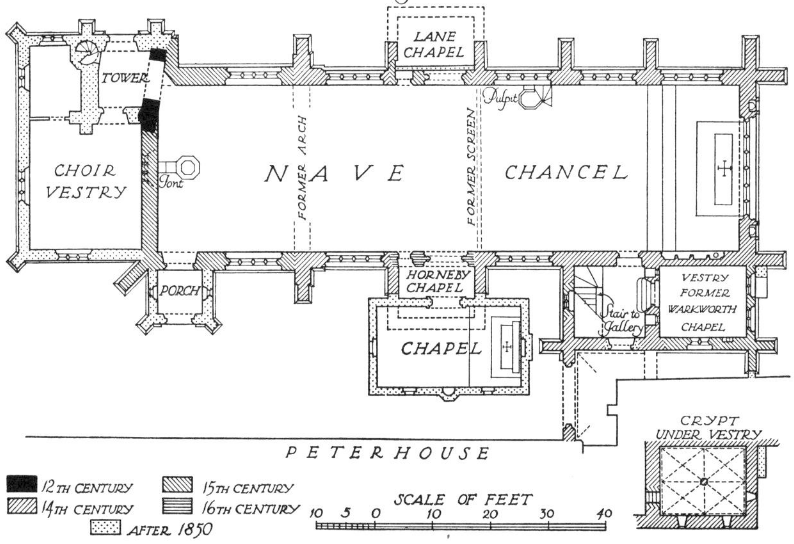

restored tracery is of 14th-century character; the internal walling in the same bay is of clunch and partly restored.

In the S. wall are six windows; the three easternmost and the fifth are similar to those in the N. wall but the first is blocked in its lower part and the second extends only about a yard below the springing; these are original arrangements. Below the second is a 14th-century doorway with moulded jambs and two-centred head, which has a high two-centred rear-arch and shafted splays with moulded capitals. In the fourth bay is a blocked window of similar outline to the others and below it are the two early 16th-century openings to the former Henry Horneby chapel; the doorway and the partly restored tomb-arch are broadly copies of those opposite in the N. wall except that the tomb-arch is semi-elliptical and has over the apex a trefoiled panel formerly in the spandrel of an ogee label with the finial now destroyed. The fifth window retains much of the original tracery. The 15th-century westernmost window is of four cinquefoiled lights with restored vertical tracery in a two-centred head; the wall in the same bay is of clunch, partly exposed internally. The 15th-century S. doorway has splayed jambs and two-centred head with a label. In the W. wall is a 15th-century window, heightened and almost entirely renewed, of three cinquefoiled ogee lights with vertical tracery in a four-centred head.

The *West Tower* (8¼ ft. by 9¼ ft.) was of the mid 12th century but only part of the E. wall and the tower-arch of this date remain; the rest of the ground-stage is modern and the superstructure has not been completed. The S.E. quoins of the E. wall are visible internally and externally the same wall is of small pebble-rubble. The semicircular tower-arch is of two square orders on the E. and the responds have quirked and chamfered imposts; the N. wall of the church impinges on the arch and is finished with a half-arch of one splayed order. Above the tower-arch is a square-headed doorway. Reset in the S.W. angle of the tower are some 12th-century stones including one with cheveron-ornament.

The *Staircase-room* (12¼ ft. by 12 ft.) S. of the chancel, has in the E. wall a 14th-century doorway with moulded jambs and two-centred head. Flanking the doorway are two 14th-century windows both of one trefoiled light and opening into the vestry. The 15th-century doorway to the bone-hole beneath the vestry has rebated jambs and four-centred head. In the N. wall is a rough recess, probably a lamp-niche, and in the S. wall is a modern doorway. The staircase up to the gallery to the College is supported on a half-arch and has a raking parapet with an old moulded coping. In the W. wall is a partly restored 15th-century window of two cinquefoiled lights in a square head. The *Gateway* (12 ft. by 15 ft.) adjoining on the S., formerly a way of access to Peterhouse and the churchyard, has had the E. half destroyed by an 18th-century extension to Peterhouse. On the W. the greater part of the walling is a 15th-century completion or rebuilding in red brick with stone dressings of the 14th-century structure. The W. archway, two-centred and of two continuous stop-chamfered orders, has been renewed except for the 14th-century lower courses of the responds. Though now built up, the W. jamb of the S. doorway to the College survives *in situ*. Only the mutilated N. and W. wall-ribs and N.W. head-corbel of the mediaeval vault of the gateway remain. On the first floor is a much restored 15th-century window of two lights with a trefoil in a segmental head. The storey above is a late 18th-century addition in yellow brick. The gallery contains no ancient features.

The *Vestry* (15 ft. by 11¾ ft.), probably the Warkworth Chapel, is of the late 15th century and has, in the E. wall, two windows, both of two pointed lights in a square head with a label. In the S. wall is a similar window but of two cinquefoiled lights, much restored and without a label. The room above has in the E. and S. walls a restored window similar to the windows below. The vaulted *Bone-hole* below the vestry has a small opening in the E. wall with a square head. The 14th-century brick vault is of four quadripartite bays with chamfered clunch ribs and stone springers, a central octagonal pier with chamfered base and moulded cap and wall-corbels tapered to a point below.

Fittings—*Bell:* one, by Tobias Norris of Stamford, inscribed 'Non sono animabus mortuorum sed auribus viventium, 1608'. *Brasses* and *Indents.* Brasses: In chancel—(1) of [John Holbrook, 1436, Master of Peterhouse and Chancellor], lower part of figure in academical dress and part of inscription, indents of scroll, marginal inscription and Evangelist-symbols at angles; (2) threequarter figure in academical dress and cap, indent of inscription, *c.* 1500. In churchyard—E. of chancel, (3) of Rev. Thomas Chubb Holmes, 1846, inscription-plate on cruciform-gabled stone tomb. Indents: In nave, (1) of small figure and inscription-plate, reused as floor-slab (8); (2) of inscription-plate on earlier coffin-lid. *Coffin-lid:* In nave—tapering slab with remains of inscription in Lombardic capitals, 13th or early 14th-century, with later brass-indent. *Font* (Plate 8): of freestone, bowl octagonal with square octofoiled panel on each face enclosing shields painted later, probably in the 17th century, with arms of the University, See of Ely, City of London (twice), Cambridge town, and Peterhouse, (two blank), and moulded underside with foiled panels, stem octagonal with ribs or shafts at angles and panel of window-tracery, of alternating designs, on each face, late 14th-century. Cover: of oak, octagonal, with moulded base with frieze-panels enriched with foliage and flowers and shields at the angles carved with the date and initials, 1632, W.C., I.B., I.D., ogee-shaped capping with scrolled ribs at the angles carved with foliage and terminal griffins' heads rising to a ball-finial on a small octagonal pedestal with half-balusters on the sides.

Monuments and Floor-slabs. Monuments etc: N. wall, (1) of [Thomas Lane, 1473, Master of Peterhouse], chantry-chapel (see Architectural Description above); (2) of the Rev. Godfrey Washington, 1729, minister of the church and Fellow of Peterhouse, white marble wall-monument with broken pediment and achievement-of-arms of Washington; (3) of Tayler Harwood, 1834, and Ann his wife, 1840, marble tablet, by Swinton; (4) of Richard, 1839, and Eliza., 1843, children of Bernard and Mary Harwood, marble tablet, by Swinton; (5) of Samuel Banks, 1788, and Lydia his wife, 1793, white and grey marble tablet with cornice; S. wall, (6) of Agnes, daughter of Gilbert Ainslie, D.D., Master of Pembroke College, and Emily his wife, 1844, and Montague their son, 1853, marble tablet, by Denman; (7) of [Henry Horneby, 1517–8, Master of Peterhouse], chantry-chapel (see Architectural Description above); (8) of Thomas Hide, 1777, grey and white marble wall-monument with side-pilasters, urns, obelisk and cherub; (9) of Thomas Southwell, 160(7?), wall-monument with double arched recess with side-pilasters supporting entablature, cresting, achievement-of-arms of Southwell quartering Witchingham, Fastolfe, Tendering and Holbrooke, and two shields of Southwell and Field, erected by Theophilus 'Feild'; on W. wall, (10) of Mary, wife of Edmund Law, D.D., Master of Peterhouse and Bishop of Carlisle, 1762, Edmund, 1758, Mary, wife of the Rev. James Stephen Lushington, 1768, Elizabeth, 1767, and Christian, 1773, their children, and Capt. Edward Christian, 1758, and Dorothy Christian, 1758, white and coloured marble tablet with cornice and broken pediment; (11) of John James Hopwood, 1842, marble tablet, by Kelsey; (12) of the Rev. Thomas Veasey, 1839, Fellow of Peterhouse and minister of the church, white marble tablet in Gothic frame; (13) of Thomas Pearne, Fellow of Peterhouse, 1827, marble tablet, by T. Tomson; (14) of William Elborne, 1824, and Sarah his mother, 1825, marble tablet; (15) of Sarah, wife of William Elborne, 1790, oval white marble tablet; (16) of Margaret Colville Borthwick, 1829, marble tablet, by T. Tomson; (17) of John James Ibbotson, 1831, marble tablet; (18) of Lydia (Amphlett), wife of John Hollingworth, minister of the parish, 1831, with shield-of-arms of Hollingworth impaling Amphlett, by T. Tomson; (19) of William Elborne, butler of Peterhouse, 1772, marble tablet; (20) of John Rickard Barker, barrister, 1843, and his mother Elizabeth (Turner), wife of the Rev. James Barker, 1847, marble neo-Greek tablet with shield-of-arms of Barker, by Denman, London; (21) of the Rev. James Barker, 1850, rector of Westley, marble neo-Greek tablet. In churchyard—E. of chancel, (22) of Ann, wife of Edward Wythie, 1703–4, pedestal-monument with gadrooned capping and part of pyramid with cherubs, skull, etc.; on N. side, (23) of Robert Goude, 1710–1, and others, carved headstone. On S. wall of parish-room, (24) of Richard Thur......, 1659, panel with incomplete inscription. (See also Brass (3)). *Floor-slabs:* In church, (1) of George Steward, son of A. H. Steward, 1804; (2) (Plate 18) of Samuel Sandys, 1676, Fellow of Peterhouse, with achievement-of-arms of Sandys; (3) of Sarah (Thompson), widow of Robert Drake, 1713, with lozenge-of-arms of Thompson; (4) of Daniel Michell, 1687, with achievement-of-arms of Michell; (5) of John James Ibbotson, 1831; (6) of Dorothy, wife of Richard Comings, 1800 (?); (7) of Dorothy Antrobus Comings, 1797, Richard Comings, 1799, and Thomas Comings, 1807; (8) of Elizabeth Margitson, 1765, reused Brass-indent (1); (9) of John Rant, 1719, Ann his first wife, 1695–6, and Jane his second wife, with achievement-of-arms of Rant; (10) of Edward Rant, 172., with achievement-of-arms of Rant; (11) of Lydia Hollingworth, 1831; (12) of Sarah, daughter of Thomas Long and Susannah his wife, 1794; (13) of Joseph Storey, early 18th-century; (14) of Margaret Colville Borthwick, 1829; (15) of R.W., 1701, with skull and cross-bones; (16) of Ann, daughter of Thomas and Ann Hide, 1773; (17) of John Rickard Barker, 1843; (18) of Thomas Halstead, 1814.

Niches: Five; below and flanking sill of E. window externally, three, middle niche with projecting shelf on attached shaft, flanking niches with tall vaulted canopies, much defaced, and pedestals with embattled capitals, 15th-century; flanking E. window internally, two, largely modern but incorporating 14th-century fragments in the vaulted canopies and crocketed spires, some with original colouring. *Piscinae:* In chancel—see *Sedilia*. In vestry—in S. wall, recess with hollow-chamfered jambs and pointed head, quatrefoiled dishing to drain, 14th-century. *Plate:* includes a flagon and a cup given by Alice Palmer, 1630, both with shield-of-arms of Palmer impaling Bradley, remodelled 1870 and with the date-mark for that year, a cup given as the foregoing but remade 1891, and the shield-of-arms reset under the foot, a paten given in 1690 and remade in 1891, a paten given by Mrs. E. B. (Elizabeth Brown) in 1630 and remade in 1876, a paten with the mark for 1685 given by Elizabeth Brown, a small cup and paten with embossed foliage ornament and the mark for 1824 on the cup only, and an almsdish with the mark for 1713, given in that year. *Pulpit* and *Sounding-board* (Plate 34): of oak, hexagonal, with enriched plinth-moulding and cornice, eared and enriched panel on each face, one with the rayed letters I.H.S. in marquetry, one side probably a door refixed, panelled standard flanked by fluted Composite. pilasters, hexagonal sounding-board with enriched entablature, frieze carved with bay-leaves and marquetry soffit; bought for the church in 1741, on later panelled base. *Royal Arms:* In Staircase-room—in carved frame, Hanoverian, formerly over the screen; according to Cole, writing in 1743, given by Valentine Ritz, a German painter (B.M., Cole MSS. ii, 49). *Screen:* Reset on W. wall, two hinged leaves of door only, close lower panels, upper panels with trefoiled and traceried heads, 15th-century; until 1857 the remains of the screen stood between the third and fourth bays. *Sedilia:* In first window-recess in S. wall and divided by continuations of the mullions from the window above into four bays, including piscina, with two-centred heads and vaults, the last now cut back, with restored or modern seats and sill to piscina, wall below divided into same number of bays by wall-shafts with moulded bases, 14th-century, much mutilated and with modern restorations. *Sundial:* On S.W. face of S.W. diagonal buttress, scratch-dial. *Miscellanea:* Reset in S. wall of parish-room, outside,—two stone fragments with late pre-Conquest carving: (a), $2\frac{1}{4}$ ft. by 6 ins., with panel of interlacement; (b), about $1\frac{1}{2}$ ft. by 10 ins., with two panels of interlacement.

(55) PARISH CHURCH OF ST. MATTHEW stands towards the E. of the city, nearly $\frac{7}{8}$ m. due E. of the church of Great St. Mary. It is a building of 1866 with an octagonal nave and contains the following:—

Fittings—*Communion Table*, of oak, with turned legs of columnar form and plain stretchers, late 17th-century, top supported on added early 18th-century console-brackets; said to be from Trinity College Chapel. *Table:* in chancel, with turned legs of columnar form, moulded stretchers, upper framing masked on one side by fascia carved with jewel-ornament, mid 17th-century, top modern; said to have come from the church of All Saints. *Miscellanea:* In chancel, at each end of W. tie-beam, cherub-heads carved in wood, late 17th or early 18th-century. In nave, over N.E. windows, two carved wood figures of angels blowing trumpets, late 17th or early 18th-century; all said to be from an organ-case once in Ely Cathedral.

(56) Parish Church of St. Michael stands on the E. side of Trinity Street near Gonville and Caius College. The walls are of rubble with dressings of Barnack and other freestone; the roofs are covered with Westmorland slates. The appropriation of the church was granted by John Hotham, bishop of Ely, to Hervey de Stanton's new foundation of Michael House, March 1324–25. At his death in 1327 de Stanton charged his executors with the completion of the church, which he was rebuilding to serve as a collegiate parish church. A surviving roll of Michael House accounts ('*Custos domorum*') at Trinity College assigned to 1326 records the expenses incurred in erecting a chancel, no doubt of the present building. The *Church* is almost entirely of this period and has been little altered. Cole's sketch of 1745 shows it much as it is now except that the lead-covered timber spire then existing was taken down and the roof covered with slate under a faculty of 1818. After a fire in 1849 the church was restored (1849–50) by Gilbert Scott; the *North Porch*, of 1850, replaces an ancient feature.

The church is of importance as a closely-dated mediaeval building of one period. Further, it is of outstanding interest for the adjustment of the normal liturgical arrangement to meet collegiate requirements, the chancel predominating in size over the nave. Among the fittings, the 14th-century sedilia, piscinae and remains of the screen to the S. chapel are noteworthy.

The Parish Church of St. Michael

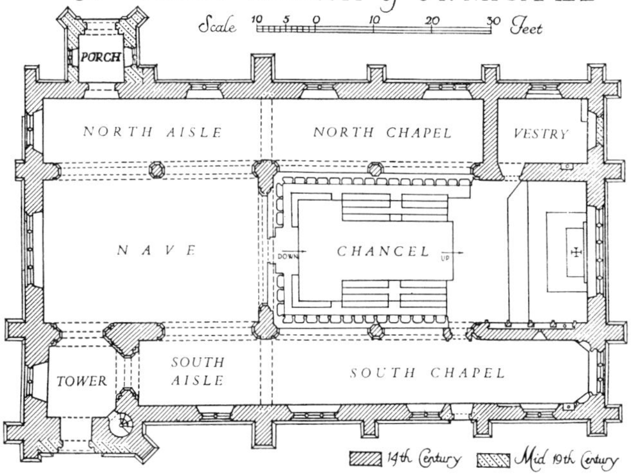

Architectural Description—The *Chancel* ($53\frac{1}{2}$ ft. by $23\frac{1}{2}$ ft.) has a restored E. window of 14th-century character of five trefoiled lights with tracery in a segmental-pointed head with labels; the soffit of the arch has a random decoration of stars in relief. In the N. wall is a 14th-century doorway with moulded jambs and two-centred head; above it is a string-course with a head-stop at the W. end. Further W. is a 14th-century arcade of two bays with two-centred arches of three chamfered orders, the middle one hollow-chamfered; the arches spring from an octagonal pier and semi-octagonal responds with moulded caps and bases; the stonework has been painted with stencil patterns in the mid 19th-century. In the S. wall is an arcade and string similar to that on the N. and a squint with a pointed loop as opening. The chancel-arch is similar to the arcades but taller and with simpler base-mouldings.

The *North Vestry* ($15\frac{1}{2}$ ft. by 11 ft.) has a blocked E. window not visible externally. In the N. wall is a two-light window similar to that in the N. chapel next described.

The *North Chapel* ($36\frac{1}{4}$ ft. by $10\frac{3}{4}$ ft.) has, in the N. wall, two restored 14th-century windows; the first is of three trefoiled ogee lights with tracery in a segmental-pointed head with labels, the internal label having head-stops; the second is similar but of two lights. The moulded sills are continued and, with those of the other windows lighting the body of the church, returned round the inside of the building as a string except in the chancel. Across the W. end is a 19th-century arch sprung from the side-walls.

The *South Chapel* (54 ft. by $10\frac{3}{4}$ ft.) has a partly restored 14th-century E. window (Plate 290) of three trefoiled ogee lights with tracery in a two-centred head with labels. In the S. wall are three partly restored 14th-century windows; the two more easterly are of two trefoiled ogee lights with a quatrefoil in a two-centred head with labels and internal head-stops, one missing; the third is of three trefoiled ogee lights with cusped spandrels in a square head and with a label. The doorway close E. of the second window has a moulded rear-arch but is of the mid 19th century externally. At the W. end is a 19th-century arch similar to that of the N. chapel.

The *Nave* (Plate 291) (37 ft. by 24 ft.) has a 14th-century N. arcade of two bays similar in detail to the chancel-arch. In the S. wall is a single arch similar to those on the N. The stonework of these arches has not been painted. In the W. wall is a window, largely unrestored (Plate 290), of four trefoiled lights with branching tracery in a segmental-pointed head with labels with head-stops, those on the outside being of the mid 19th century.

The *North Aisle* (10¾ ft. wide) has in the N. wall a window similar to the westernmost window in the N. chapel but with mid 19th-century stops to the internal label. The N. doorway has moulded jambs, two-centred arch and label with 19th-century stops. In the W. wall is a window of two trefoiled ogee lights with curvilinear-tracery in a two-centred head with labels and head-stops; the external stops are of the 19th century.

The *South Aisle* (10¾ ft. wide) has, in the S. wall, a window similar to the corresponding window in the N. aisle.

The *South-west Tower* (11¾ ft. square) is of three stages with angle and diagonal buttresses, a stair-turret projecting on the S.E. and a plain parapet. The ground stage has in the E. and N. walls a two-centred arch of three continuous chamfered orders with chamfered bases. In the S. wall is a mid 19th-century doorway. In the W. wall is a window similar to that in the S. aisle and with 19th-century stops to the external label. The second stage, has in the S. and W. walls, a window of one pointed light with a label. In each wall of the bell-chamber is a restored window of two trefoiled lights in a two-centred head with a plain spandrel.

The *Roofs* of the chancel and nave have been extensively restored; they are of king-post type and may incorporate some 14th-century timbers. The chancel roof and lean-to roofs of the chapels were painted in the mid 19th century with repetitions of the sacred monogram and stencilled leaf-patterns in red, white and black.

Fittings—*Bells:* four, 1st, 2nd and 3rd, by Christopher Graye, 1683; 4th by Charles Newman and with the names of the churchwardens, 1684. Bell-frame old. *Brass Indents:* In S. chapel—(1) of inscription-plate. In N. aisle—(2) of small figure of priest and inscription-plate, 15th-century. Under tower—(3) much worn and cut in two, of inscription-plate and marginal inscription-fillet, possibly also canopy and shield; (4) of small demi-figure and inscription-plate, 15th-century; (5) of inscription-plate; (6) of inscription-plate, in Floor-slab (16). *Glass:* In S. aisle—shield-of-arms of Warenne, 15th-century, in modern setting; below, Stuart Royal arms (Plate 53), late 17th-century, recently damaged, formerly in E. window, and fragments, 15th-century and later. In tower—in W. window, shield with symbol of the Trinity with four suns, and a rose-en-soleil, 15th-century, in modern setting.

Monuments and *Floor-slabs. Monuments:* In chancel—on N. wall, (1) of Robert Leeds, 1680, small rectangular stone tablet. In S. chapel—on E. wall, (2) of Edmund Parry, 1803, black and white marble wall-tablet with urn; (3) of Harry Brereton Passingham, 1833, black and white marble wall-tablet with pedimental head carved with Greek honeysuckle ornament, by Tomson; (4) of Humphrey, son of David and Catharine Parry of Crichel, Dorset, 1797, marble wall-tablet; (5) of [? Edward Parker, 1649], small clunch wall-tablet much damaged and worn, originally painted and gilded; on N. wall, (6) of John Horatio, son of Digby Legard, 1819, white marble wall-tablet; lying loose, (7) of [Edward Dod], 1636, framed and painted rectangular wood panel (23 ins. by 21 ins.) with Latin epitaph, shield-of-arms of Dod quartering Edge and Wollaston with a *crescent* for difference, and the crest of Dod twice, much damaged and with modern repairs. In nave—on W. wall, (8) of Richard Hovell, 1791, Mercy his wife, 1787, James their son, barrister, 1805, and Ann Triston their daughter, 1814, white marble wall-tablet; (9) of John Bowtell 'respectable book-binder of this town', 1813, black and white marble wall-tablet, by Tomson, set up by the Governors of Addenbrooke's Hospital; (10) of William Coe, 1831, D.L., Ann his wife, 1821, and Peter and Anne Wedd, their son-in-law and daughter, 1823 and 1849, black and white marble altar-shaped wall-tablet with shield-of-arms of Smyth, by R. Brown, London, erected by their daughter Mrs. James Smyth; (11) of John Shepard, B.D., 1819, Pro-Chancellor of diocese of Ely, minister of this church, white marble wall-tablet with shield containing the Pascal Lamb on a wreath; (12) of Samuel, son of Samuel and Anna Forlow, 1782, square white marble wall-tablet. In N. aisle—on N. wall, (13) of Thomas Verney Oakes, [surgeon], 1818, stone wall-tablet. In tower—on W. wall, (14) of Rev. Clement Francis, A.M., 1829, Fellow and tutor of Gonville and Caius College, black and white marble tablet, by Tomson; (15) of John Daniel Hamilton Coles, 1835, black and white marble wall-tablet, by Tomson & Son, Cambridge; (16) of Elizabeth (Smythe), widow of William Arthur Irwin, 1834, black and white marble wall-tablet with casket, all surrounded by palm wreath, by Tomson; (17) of Charles Maxey, 1837, and Sophia (Hodson) his wife, 1844, black and white marble wall-tablet, by Tomson; (18) of Francis, 1812, and Ann Hodson, 1804, and twelve children listed and dated, white marble inscription-tablet with urn on pedestal carved with Cross and palm-branch, all against black marble backing with two-centred head, by T. Tomson. In churchyard—W. of porch, (19) of William Page, 1806, and others, pedestal with urn. On aisle wall beside (19), (20) of George Francis Joseph, A.R.A., 1816, stone tablet.

Floor-slabs: In chancel—(1) of Peggy Smith, niece of the Master of Gonville and Caius College, 1786; (2) of Thomas Green, A.M., 1787, librarian of Trinity College and Woodwardian Professor; (3) of [Dorothy] Bousfield, 1766, and others; (4) of Samuel Forlow, 177(1 ?), Ann his widow, 1806, and others, much worn; (5) of Thomas Hart, 1783, and Rebecca his wife, 181.; (6) of William Coe, 1831, and Ann his wife, 1821, Peter Wedd, 1823, and Ann his wife, 1849; (7) of Ann Daw and Sara Ellis, sisters, 1799, and their mother Catherine Emly; (8) of Ann, second wife of Samuel Forlow, 1762, and Samuel her son; (9) of Margaret, widow of Joseph Smith of Coltishall, Norfolk, 1804, and her daughter, 1791; (10) of Laurence Dundas, 1818. In N. chapel—(11) of [Thomas Yorke], alderman, [1756], and others later; (12) of Richard Hovell, 1787. In S. chapel—(13) of Sarah, 1730–1, and Conyers Middleton, D.D., 1750, on same slab added later John Case, M.B., 1699–1700, Senior Fellow of Gonville and Caius College; (14) of William Henry, fifteenth child of Francis and

Ann Hodson, 1795, and others later; (15) of Charles Robert, seventeenth son of Francis and Ann Hodson, 1812, and others; (16) of Thomas Sharpe, 1788, Mary his wife, 1801, and Susan their daughter, 1799, slab with Brass-indent (6); (17) of John, son of Francis and Ann Hodson, 1789; (18) of James Bennet, 1763, Ann his wife, 1764, and Sibilla their daughter, 1763; (19) of Rev. C. R. Francis, 1829; (20) of Francis Hodson, 1812, and thirteen of his eighteen children. In N. aisle—(21) of Ludovic, eldest son of Joseph Williams of Jamaica, 1741; (22) of Thomas Burrows, 1767, Alice his wife, 1757, and Elizabeth their daughter, 1825. In S. aisle—(23) of W. Bond, 1832, Fellow of Gonville and Caius College, rector of Wheatacre, Norfolk; (24) of Edward Rogers, 1824, Fellow of Gonville and Caius College, barrister of the Inner Temple; (25) of Frances Eliza Pears (?), 1819. In tower—(26) of John Mack, 1798; (27) of William Bell, 1795.

Niches: In S. chapel—two, of clunch, flanking the E. window, with trefoiled and septfoiled sub-cusped openings and carved spandrels in ogee moulded heads with crockets and foliage finials, panelled side-standards with canopies and crocketed pinnacles, all under straight moulded embattled cornices, the N. niche with spandrels carved with foliage and a shallow cornice, the S. with rose-trees in the spandrels and a deep cornice studded with roses, moulded sills resting on corbels carved with half-angels holding books, 14th-century, lower portions much abraded. *Paving:* see Miscellaneous. *Pictures:* In N. aisle—on E. wall, large framed full-length portrait on canvas of Charles I in ermine-lined cloak and cape, with globe, reversed crown and inscription 'Mundi calco [coronam] splendidam at gravem' at feet, kneeling at altar on which is a book and crown of thorns, in background a scene of storm and shipwreck, attributed to Philippe Fruytiers, given to the church *c.* 1660, much restored 1881. In nave—on S. wall, Adoration of the Shepherds, painting on canvas, English, late 18th-century, in contemporary carved gilt frame. *Piscinae:* In N. vestry—in S. wall, with chamfered jambs and cinquefoiled head, sexfoiled dishing to drain, 14th-century. In S. chapel—in S. wall, with moulded jambs, cinquefoiled head and moulded label, round dish to drain, contemporary with the building, *c.* 1327. See also under *Sedilia. Plate:* includes two cups with the date letter for 1839 given in 1840, a late 17th-century paten with illegible marks, an almsdish of 1821 given in 1822 by John Deighton, and an almsdish of 1839 given in 1840.

Screen: Between chancel and S. chapel—stone doorway (Plate 27), probably remaining fragment of a stone screen, with jambs chamfered on the S. side and square on the N. rebated for a door, the opening with moulded ogee head, crocketed on the S. and with a crocketed label with head-stops on the N. and foliage finials, flanked on the S. by square standards with canopied and crocketed pinnacles and on the N. by walling with restored embattled coping, on the W. are remains of a moulded jamb and arch-springer of a second opening, 14th-century and with some restoration. *Seating:* In chancel—oak stalls, sixteen on the N., fourteen on the S., and six on the W. divided by a central gateway, with flat moulded and shaped tops, moulded and shaped divisions with stylised foliate-scrolled armrests and attached shafts below with moulded caps and bases, late 15th-century, misericordes mostly plain but some with carving of figures, animals and flowers probably 19th-century, gate of two leaves containing blind tracery-panels, mid 19th-century; the stalls are said to be from Trinity College Chapel. *Sedilia* and *piscina* (Plate 27): In chancel—in S. wall, in four bays, the piscina occupying the easternmost, divided and flanked by weathered and buttressed standards with embattled caps and canopied and crocketed finials, the trefoiled ogee opening in each bay with carved spandrels under a moulded and crocketed ogee head with foliage finial, 14th-century, restored and with 19th-century painting. *Miscellaneous:* green-glazed tile from the Bawsey kiln, with stamped geometrical pattern, and other shaped tiles, 14th-century, now in the Museum of Archaeology and Ethnology.

(57) Parish Church of St. Paul stands on the E. side of Hills Road. The walls are of red brick with blue brick diapering and dressings of limestone; the roofs are slate-covered. The church was built, probably on an aisled-hall plan of five bays with only a shallow sanctuary, in 1841 to the designs of Ambrose Poynter and licenced the following year. The form of the building was condemned in a critique in the *Ecclesiologist* (I, 9, 67). The aisled *Chancel* was added in 1864 and the *North Vestry* built at the same time incorporating parts of an earlier vestry; designs by H. G. Elborne for a scheme closely similar to the existing additions are preserved in the church. In 1893 the galleries over the N. and S. aisles were removed and *North* and *South Transepts* to the designs of Temple Moore added. In 1931 the fittings were rearranged. The building is in the Tudor style, and the exercise of severe economy is evident in the design of the interior.

The revived early 17th-century style for the fittings of 1841 is of interest.

Architectural Description—The *Chancel* (32½ ft. by 25¼ ft.) is of 1864. The stone chancel-arch is probably all of the same date, for the destroyed sanctuary was lit by a further clearstorey window in continuation of each of the existing ranges, as appears on the S. in J. B. Harraden's view of the exterior of 1842 (W. Day and L. Haghe litho.).

The *Nave* (61¼ ft. by 25¼ ft.) has arcades of five bays in the N. and S. walls with moulded four-centred arches springing from octagonal piers and semi-octagonal responds without caps; the mouldings are run in plaster and stop at the springings. The embattled clearstorey has ten windows on each side, each window being of two four-centred lights in a square head.

The *North* and *South Aisles* (11¼ ft. wide) have embattled parapets. In each aisle, W. of the late 19th-century transepts, which occupy the two E. bays, are three windows of three four-centred and transomed lights in a square head; the westernmost lights on both sides open into small storerooms behind partitions.

The *West Tower* (16 ft. by $15\frac{3}{4}$ ft.) is in three stages, with diagonal buttresses, an embattled parapet and corner-turrets. The tower-arch is moulded in plaster and two-centred. In the N. and S. walls are doorways with moulded jambs, four-centred openings and cusped spandrels in square heads. The W. window is of three cinquefoiled and transomed lights in a four-centred head. On each face of the second stage is a round

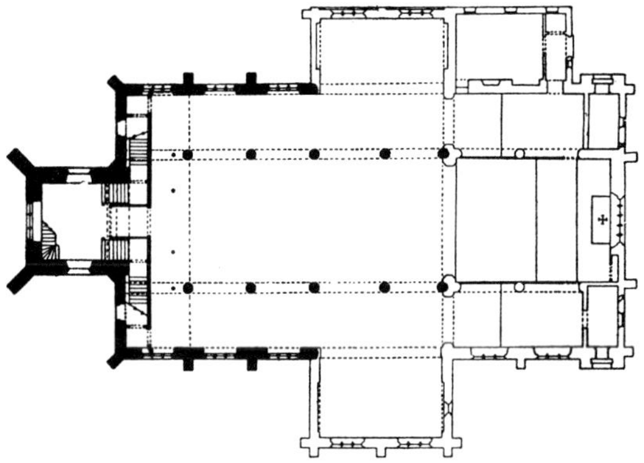

clock-face of slate in a square stone frame, one with the date 1841 cut in the spandrels. In each wall of the third stage is a three-light window with a four-centred head.

The panelled *Roof* of the nave is divided into ten bays by plain tie-beams supported on shaped brackets and each bay is divided into four main and eight subsidiary panels by plain longitudinal beams. The lean-to roofs of the aisles have trusses with plain tie-beams and a turned post in the centre of each.

Fittings—*Bell:* one, by Mears, London, 1843. *Clock:* in tower, inserted in 1843. *Font:* of limestone, hexagonal, straight-sided bowl with moulded top and lower edge and carved scrollwork in each face, square tapering stem with panelled sides and moulded base, on low square pedestal, probably 1841, in early 17th-century style. *Gallery:* across W. end of nave, supported on a timber arcade of three bays with turned columns on tall plinths and four-centred arches with panelled spandrels and turned pendants at the apices, 1841, in early 17th-century style. *Panelling:* In chancel, across E. wall and with short returns on N. and S. walls, a length of moulded panelling above a plain plank dado divided into bays by pilaster-strips carved with jewelled arabesques, with a frieze containing shaped brackets, arabesque and jewel-ornament, and a crowning dentil-cornice, 1841(?), reset and with modern painting and gilding, all in early 17th-century style; this may belong to the alterations of 1893. *Plate:* includes a set of a cup, stand-paten and flagon, presented by members of the University in 1842, with the date-letter for 1841, the cup with rounded bowl, octagonal stem with knop and flared foot, the paten with moulded rim, the flagon with scrolled handle and shaped lid surmounted by a cross.

(58) THE CHURCH OF ST. PETER stands on the S.W. side of Castle Street. The parish is now amalgamated with that of St. Giles. The walls are of flint rubble and stone with some Roman and later brick; the dressings are of Barnack and other freestone. The roof is tile-covered. The church formerly consisted of a chancel, nave, S. porch and W. tower, and is so shown in Cole's sketch of 1742. By 1760 it was very dilapidated and in 1781 much of it was pulled down, the W. part of the nave and the W. tower only being left standing. These, with reused material incorporated, form the present building. The W. parts of the N. and S. walls of the *Nave*, in pebble rubble, appear to date from the 14th century; the 12th-century N. doorway and the early 13th-century S. doorway have been reset. The *West Tower* and spire were built early in the 14th century.

The 12th-century font has unusual decoration.

Architectural Description—The *Nave* (25 ft. by 16 ft.) has an early 19th-century E. window and above it is a reset head-corbel. In the N. wall is a 12th-century doorway, now blocked, with a semicircular arch and hollow-chamfered imposts; further W. is a 15th-century window of two cinquefoiled lights in a four-centred head. Reset in the S. wall is an early 13th-century doorway with a semi-elliptical head of two moulded orders; the jambs each have two shafts with water-leaf capitals and weathered bases, but one shaft of the E. jamb has been replaced in wood; the outer face of the doorway projects beyond the main wall-face.

The *West Tower* ($7\frac{1}{4}$ ft. square) and spire were built early in the 14th century; the tower is of three stages with a moulded parapet. The tower-arch is two-centred and of two chamfered orders, the outer continuous on the E. and the inner springing from attached shafts with moulded capitals and bases. The W. window is of two trefoiled ogee lights with a quatrefoil in a

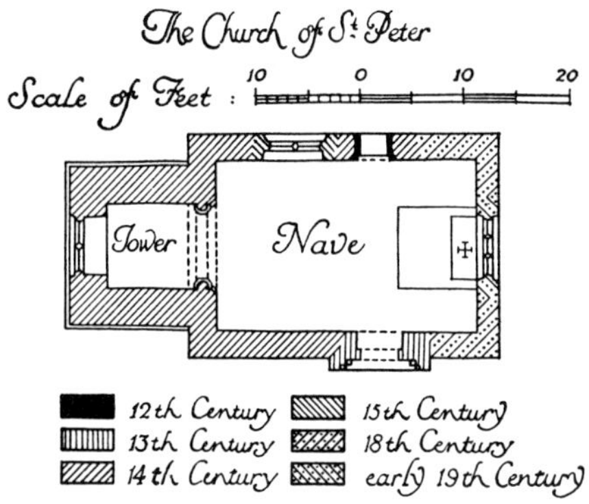

two-centred head with labels. The bell-chamber has, in each wall, a window of one pointed light. On the W. wall, below the parapet, are two carved gargoyles. The octagonal spire is of ashlar; it has, in the E. and W. sides, a trefoiled light in a defaced crocketed gable and, in the N. and S. sides, rather higher, a smaller light of similar character; at the base of the S. side is a doorway with an ogee head set in a gable.

Fittings—*Bell:* one, by Richard Bowler, 1603. *Font:* (see p. cxxix) square to circular bowl carved at the corners with tritons holding up their double tails to form a loop-pattern round the lower part of the bowl, with trefoiled spandrels in the top surface, modern circular stem and original moulded base, 12th-century. *Monuments:* In tower, (1) of Thomas Smith, 1696, also of Thomas and Isabell his parents, Mary his sister, Sarah his wife and Sarah their daughter, stone tablet with drapery and cherub-head; (2) of Thomas Smith, J.P., 1759, formerly mayor, stone wall-monument with carved flowers, foliage and scrolls forming frame. In churchyard—S.W. of church, (3) of John Wood, 1813, and Mary Ann his daughter, 1816, table-tomb with fielded side and end panels and shaped corner-pieces. *Weathervane:* pierced with initials A.P. for Andrew Perne, (1553–89), formerly on Peterhouse, blown down, and preserved by the Rev. William Cole. *Miscellaneous:* In churchyard—W. of tower, drum-stone of mediaeval pier.

(59) PARISH CHURCH OF ST. ANDREW, CHERRY HINTON, stands towards the N. end of the village, to the S.E. of Cambridge. The walls of the chancel are of clunch and Barnack stone, with the E. wall rough-cast; the aisles are of flint-rubble and the W. tower of clunch, all with freestone dressings. The roofs are lead and tile-covered. The earliest structural remains are the responds of the tower-arch of *c.* 1200. The *Chancel* was built in the second quarter of the 13th century and the arcades of the *Nave* are of the third quarter of the same century. The *North* and *South Aisles* were in all probability rebuilt in the 15th century when the *South Porch* was added. The *North Vestry* was added in the 16th century and the *West Tower*, with the exception of the responds of the tower-arch, was rebuilt about the same time. Between 1880 and 1886 the building was drastically restored, first by Gilbert Scott who rebuilt the nave, N. and S. aisles and S. porch reusing much of the old material, then by J. T. Micklethwaite, who restored the chancel more conservatively.

The 13th-century arcaded treatment of the chancel is remarkable. The rebuilt nave and, among the fittings, the piscinae, sedilia and floor-slabs are of note. The second bell is the oldest in the city and some 15th-century benches survive.

Architectural Description—The *Chancel* (45 ft. by 21½ ft.) has a mid 16th-century E. window, partly restored externally, of five cinquefoiled lights in a four-centred head with a moulded label; the whole of the upper part of the E. wall containing the window was rebuilt probably in the 15th century. In the N. wall are eight 13th-century lancet windows with moulded labels with mask-stops, mostly weathered away; they are grouped in four pairs with two-stage weathered buttresses between and, internally, are incorporated in a 13th-century wall-arcade of thirteen bays with detached freestone shafts with moulded caps, bands and bases and moulded cinquefoiled arches with a continuous moulded label shaped to the heads. The shafts stand upon a shelf with moulded edge 1¼ ft. below the window-sills. The two easternmost lights have been blocked, excepting one head, by the later vestry. The early 16th-century doorway to the vestry has chamfered jambs and a four-centred moulded head. The arrangement of the windows and wall-arcade of the S. wall (Plate 294) is similar to that of the N. wall. The 13th-century S. doorway, below the fifth light, has a two-centred arch of two moulded orders with a label,

CHERRY HINTON *The* PARISH CHURCH *of* ST. ANDREW

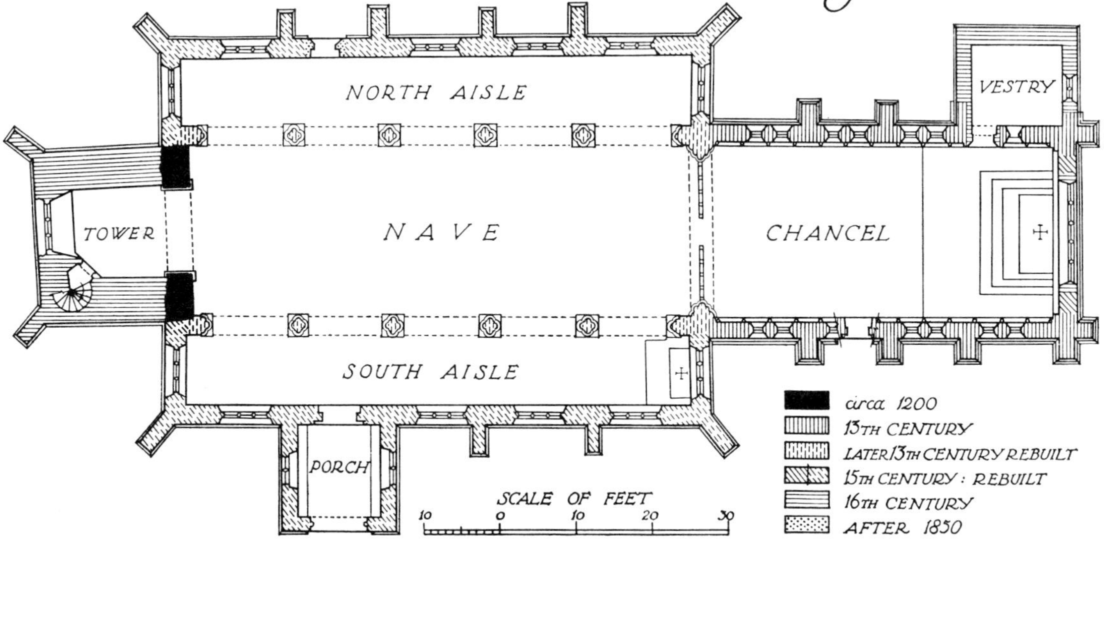

the inner order is continuous, the outer springs from detached jamb-shafts with moulded caps and bases, all much restored externally; the moulding of the segmental-pointed rear-arch is continuous. The chancel-arch is of the third quarter of the 13th century and has been rebuilt; it is two-centred and of three hollow-chamfered orders with responds comprising grouped shafts with fillets, moulded caps and bases.

The *North Vestry* (12 ft. by 10¼ ft.) was added early in the 16th century. The original E. window has been more or less restored and is of two four-centred lights in a square head.

The *Nave* (65¾ ft. by 21¾ ft.) has a rebuilt 13th-century N. arcade of five bays with two-centred arches of two moulded orders with moulded labels. The piers are quatrefoiled on plan with small keel-mouldings between the shafts and have moulded capitals and modern bases; the responds are formed as half-piers. The S. arcade is similar to the N. arcade.

The *North Aisle* (8¾ ft. wide) has been rebuilt. The parapet is perhaps entirely of 15th-century masonry reused and has three beast-head gargoyles. The E. window and the four windows in the N. wall are similar and of 15th-century character, of three lights with vertical tracery in a two-centred head. The N. doorway is entirely modern.

The *South Aisle* (8¾ ft. wide) is generally similar to the N. aisle but the parapet is modern and the windows have four-centred heads.

The *West Tower* (12 ft. by 11½ ft.) is of three stages, with a moulded plinth, embattled parapet and diagonal western buttresses in three stages stopping half way up its second stage. The responds of the tower-arch are of *c.* 1200 and have attached keel-shafts at the E. angles with plain caps, chamfered abaci, much worn moulded bases and chamfered plinths; abaci and plinths are both continued round the responds; the depressed four-centred arch is of two chamfered orders and, with the tower, is of the 16th century. The W. window, of three cinquefoiled lights in a four-centred head with a moulded label, is largely modern. In the S. wall of the ringing-chamber is a plain rectangular light with chamfered opening. Each wall of the belfry contains a 16th-century window of two four-centred lights in a square head with sunk spandrels.

The *South Porch* (11¼ ft. by 11¾ ft.) has been rebuilt. In each side-wall is a window of 15th-century character with two cinquefoiled lights in a square head with a moulded label. The entrance arch is two-centred and of two orders, the outer continuous and the inner hollow-chamfered and springing from attached shafts with moulded caps and bases; it is of 15th-century character.

The *Roof* of the chancel is of *c.* 1500, restored. It is of low pitch and in four bays; the moulded and cambered tie-beams have small curved braces, except against the end walls where they have larger braces and wall-posts. Each bay is divided into eight panels by moulded principal rafters, ridge and purlins; the common rafters are laid flat and they and the boarding are left exposed; the wall-plates are embattled. The *Roof* of the N. aisle is of *c.* 1500 in origin but rebuilt, with some of the original timber reused. It is of lean-to type, in five bays, with curved braces and wall-posts below the principals. Each bay is divided into four panels by a moulded principal rafter and purlin; the S. wall-plate is supported on shaped corbels; the corbels supporting the wall-posts are embattled and carved with half-angels holding shields-of-arms, on the N., of St. George, Lisle, See of Ely, Avenell, and on the S., of (unidentified 77), Harvey (?), Peterhouse (old), and Balsham. The *Roof* of the S. aisle is generally similar to that of the N. aisle but extensively renewed and with modern corbels.

Fittings—*Altar:* In S. aisle, stone slab with moulded edge and remains of incised crosses, mediaeval, reset on modern stone base in 1930. *Bells:* five, 1st 1727 with names of churchwardens, Walter Serocold and Francis Ellard; 2nd inscribed 'Ave Maria' in Lombardic letters, with 'Magn' on the shoulder and stamp of queen's head, 14th-century; 3rd inscribed 'Omnis populus terre jubilate Deo' in black-letter, 15th-century; 4th, 1853; 5th, by T. Mears, 1828. *Bier:* In tower, of oak, with turned legs, shaped top rail at each end, handles missing, late 17th or early 18th-century. *Brass Indents:* In chancel, (1) much defaced Purbeck marble slab for inscription-plate, and perhaps demi-figure of priest; (2) large Purbeck slab, mostly concealed by pews, of lozenge-shaped plate and marginal inscription. *Churchyard Cross:* of Barnack (?) stone, with square to octagonal moulded base, stump of square to octagonal shaft with defaced ball-flowers or heads and pyramidal stops on alternate faces of octagon, 14th-century. *Coffin-slab:* In tower, refixed in W. wall, tapering slab with sunk circular panel containing carved head of a man and tips of hands in prayer, carved rosette on each side and foliated central stem below, *c.* 1200; the upper part is more crudely cut than the foliation and suggests later reuse of the slab. *Doors:* To vestry, (1) with four-centred head, of planks, battened and with applied ribs forming four vertical panels, nail-studded, early 16th-century, restored. In S. doorway, (2) in two leaves, lattice-framed, with two-centred head and four vertical panels with restored traceried heads, 15th century, with 17th-century wood lock. *Font:* circular stone bowl with plain tapering sides, late 12th or early 13th-century, on cylindrical stem substituted in 1811 for five small shafts.

Monuments and *Floor-slabs. Monuments:* In N. aisle—on N. wall, (1) of Edward, eldest son of William Wise, early 17th-century, clunch tablet partly hidden by pews. In W. tower—on N. wall, (2) of Francis Wise, 1589, rectangular clunch wall-tablet with achievement-of-arms of Wise impaling Hutton; (3) of Mary, second daughter of Rev. Walter Serocold, 1837, white marble tablet with lozenge-of-arms of Serocold quartering Letwood, by Theakston, Pimlico; (4) of Ann, eldest daughter of Rev. Walter Serocold and widow of Rev. William Pearce, Dean of Ely, 1835, white marble round wall-tablet with bolection-moulded frame and lozenge-of-arms of Pearce with a scutcheon of the arms on Monument (3), by Theakston, Pimlico; (5) of the Rev. Edward Serocold Pearce Serocold, only son of Dr. Pearce, 1849, white marble tablet with pediment and shield-of-arms of Serocold and Pearce quarterly quartering Letwood and Little, impaling Vansittart, by H. Weekes; on S. wall, (6) of Captain Walter Serocold, R.N., only son of Rev. Walter Serocold, 1794, killed at siege of Calvi in Corsica, white marble tablet with naval trophies of war and shield-of-arms of Serocold quartering Letwood, signed by J. Flaxman; (7) of Rev. Bewick Bridge, B.D., F.R.S., 1833, white marble tablet with anthemion ornament in pediment, by Tomson & Son, Cambridge; (8) of Georgiana Elizabeth, daughter of George Smith, wife of Edward Serocold Pearce, 1828, white marble classical altar-shaped tablet with base and pediment carved with spray of lilies and honeysuckle and shield-of-arms of Pearce quartering Serocold and Letwood impaling Smith, by Theakston, Pimlico. In churchyard—several 18th and early 19th-century headstones carved with foliage scrolls and cherub-heads, the following with legible inscriptions—S. of chancel, (9) of Henry Headley, 1779; (10) Mary Headley, 1796, by Wiles, Cambridge; (11) Henry Headley, 1814, by Wiles, Cambridge; (12) Dickman Headley, 1753; (13) Mary wife of Henry Headley, 1760; (14) Jone wife of Henry Headley, 1714; (15) members of Emson family, table-tomb, 1838; S. of S. aisle, (16) Elizabeth wife of William Mason, 1702 (?), and (17) of William Mason, 1713, both with emblems of mortality; (18) Daniel North, servant to Walter Serocold, 1759; (19) Mary Rook, 1830, with portrait medallion, broken. *Floor-slabs:* In chancel—(1) of Walter Serocold, J.P., 1747, black marble slab with achievement-of-arms of Serocold; (2) of Abigail, youngest daughter of William 'Wattson' of Hull and widow of Walter Serocold, 1734, black marble slab with achievement-of-arms of Serocold impaling Watson; (3) of William Watson of Hull, 1721, 'he beautified this chancel and erected this altar' and endowed the hospital in Hull built by his brother Thomas, Lord Bishop of St. Davids, black marble slab with achievement-of-arms of Watson; (4) of Henrietta, daughter of Rev. Walter Serocold and wife of Rev. George Borlase, 1792, and Henrietta their infant daughter, black marble slab with achievement-of-arms of Borlase impaling Serocold; (5) of Rev. George Borlase, S.T.B., 1809, Casuistical Professor of Divinity, Principal Registrary of the University, black marble slab with shield-of-arms of Borlase impaling Serocold in chief and Holmes (?) in base; (6) of Rev. Walter Serocold, 1789, black marble slab with cartouche containing arms of Serocold with a scutcheon of pretence of Marshall; (7) of Mary, wife of Rev. Walter Serocold, 1782, black marble slab with cartouche of arms as on (6); (8) of Henry Hudson, 1838, and Frances King wife of his third son, Philip Samuel, 1841, stone slab; (9) of Edward Serocold Pearce, 1828, black marble slab.

Paintings: In chancel, on upper part of E. wall, N. of window, head and part of figure of bishop, possibly rising from grave, S. of window, remains of figure, 15th-century, much damaged and faded; on E. responds of N. and S. arcades of chancel, traces of polychromy, 15th-century. In N. aisle—on N. wall, framed oil-painting on canvas of the Virgin and Child with cherubim and figure of St. Simon Stock receiving the scapular from the Virgin, 17th-century, Spanish, formerly in Peterhouse Chapel. *Piscinae:* In chancel (Plate 27)—in S. wall, in two bays, with arches of two moulded orders, the inner trefoiled and the outer two-centred and enriched with dog-tooth ornament, triple central shaft and coupled side-shafts with moulded caps and bases, all under a moulded label mitred round the heads and within a rectangular moulded surround, one octofoiled and one sexfoiled dishing to drain, 13th-century. In S. aisle, with stop-chamfered two-centred head and quatrefoiled dishing to drain, 13th-century, reset and much restored. *Plate:* includes a cup (Plate 24) and cover-paten without date-letter but the paten with engraved date 1569, two stand-patens with the date-letter for 1707, given by Richard Cooke, D.D., vicar, and a brass almsdish with repoussé ornament and inscription, S. German, early 16th-century, much worn. *Recess:* in chancel, in E. wall, large, rectangular, mediaeval. *Screen:* in chancel-arch, of oak, with central opening with cinquefoiled sub-cusped two-centred head, pierced quatrefoiled spandrels and tracery above, on each side two bays with modern boarding below and open paired lights above a horizontal band of pierced trefoils and quatrefoils, the lights divided by a moulded central mullion and with traceried heads, 15th-century restored, with modern carved cornice and brattishing and buttresses flanking the central bay supporting a modern stiffening arch on the W.; some traces remain of original colouring and inscriptions, including 'S. Maria Magdalene'. *Seating:* In N. aisle, against N. wall, on raised platform, five short oak benches (Plate 26) with moulded top rails and wall-rail all carved with paterae, shaped ends with moulded borders carved with paterae, poppy-heads carved with foliage and figure with modern head, late 15th or early 16th-century with some restoration. *Sedilia* (Plate 27): In chancel, in S. wall, in three bays with stepped chamfered seats, detached shafts with moulded caps and bases and two-centred moulded arches with moulded label with mask-stops, 13th-century. *Weathervane:* On W. tower, of wrought-iron with scrolls, 19th-century.

(60) Parish Church of St. Andrew, Chesterton, (Plate 280) stands towards the S.W. of the village, to the N.E. of Cambridge. The walls are of rubble and flints with dressings of freestone and some clunch; the interior is faced mostly with clunch. The spire is of ashlar and the roofs are covered with slates and lead. The church was given by Henry III, early in his reign, to the Papal Legate, Cardinal Gualo, who bestowed it on his new foundation of canons regular, the church of St. Andrew, Vercelli (Papal confirmation 1224: *Cal. Pap. Letters* i, 97). The house was deprived of it in or shortly before 1440 when the appropriation was given by Henry VI to King's Hall. Subsequently unsuccessful efforts were made to obtain restitution.

A mid 13th-century church with aisled nave stood on the site of the present building and of it there remain the chancel-arch, except the 19th-century capitals, the lower parts of the responds of the S. nave-arcade and parts of the splays of the E. windows of the aisles. Early in the 14th century a general rebuilding of the *Nave* and aisles was begun; this extended to the present nave-arcades, the whole of the *South Aisle* and the three E. bays of the *North Aisle*, followed by the addition of the *West Tower*. In the 15th century the *Chancel* was rebuilt, the N. aisle was completed on an alignment with the work of the previous century, the *North Porch* and the clearstorey were added and a staircase inserted in the blocking of the W. window of the tower. A *North Vestry* was built early in the 16th century. The chancel was restored in 1842–44, the spire in 1847 and a general restoration took place in the second half of the same century. In 1934 the vestry was considerably enlarged and an *Organ-chamber* added.

St. Andrew's, though much restored, is a good example of a parish church of some size largely of the 14th century. It contains an important 15th-century painted Doom, now badly faded. Among the fittings, the sedilia, piscina and carved bench-ends are noteworthy.

Architectural Description—The *Chancel* (29½ ft. by 18½ ft.) was rebuilt in the 15th century but all the windows have been completely restored. The E. window is of five lights with vertical tracery in a two-centred head. The window in the N. wall is of three lights with vertical tracery in a four-centred head; a second window further W. has been destroyed except for the four-centred head, which remains over a modern moulded caps and bases to the 14th-century work; the 13th-century bases are chamfered, and of clunch, whereas the lower courses of the piers are of freestone, with clunch above. E. of the N. arcade are the remains of the entrance to the former rood-loft stair. The 15th-century clearstorey has seven windows on each side, of three cinquefoiled lights in a four-centred head, all much restored and entirely modern externally; over the easternmost window on the S. is an original brick relieving arch. The walls have restored embattled parapets continued over the E. gable and modern parapet-strings with old gargoyles.

The *North Aisle* (17¼ ft. wide) has an embattled parapet and a parapet-string with one old and two modern gargoyles. In the E. wall is a restored 15th-century window of three cinquefoiled lights in a four-centred head with a label, now opening into the modern organ-chamber; just to the S. is the S. splay of

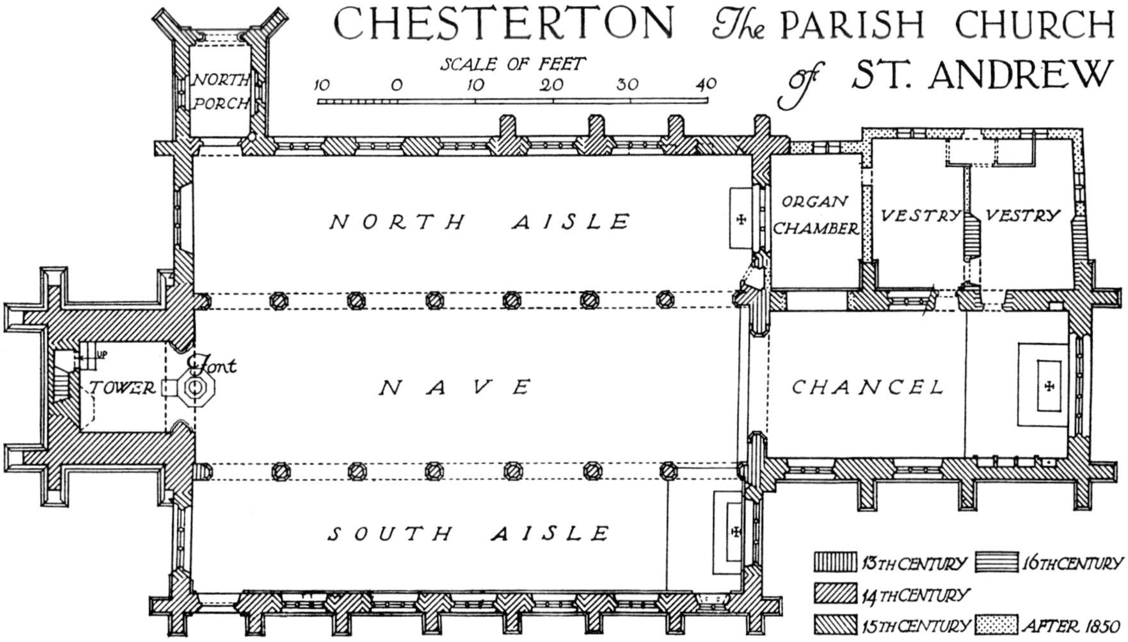

opening to the organ-chamber. The doorway to the vestry is of the early 16th century and has a plain four-centred head; the doorway further W., originally external, is of the 15th century, with chamfered jambs and four-centred head with a moulded label with carved head-stops. In the S. wall are two windows similar to that in the N. wall. The walls are plastered inside and cement-rendered outside and there may be blocked windows in the E. bays of the N. and S. walls. The mid 13th-century chancel-arch is two-centred and of two chamfered orders; the responds are semi-octagonal with moulded capitals and chamfered bases.

The *Nave* (71¼ ft. by 19½ ft.) has N. and S. arcades both of seven bays and of the early 14th century excepting the bases of the S.E. and S.W. responds, which are of the 13th century. The arches are two-centred and of two wave-moulded orders with octagonal piers and semi-octagonal responds with a destroyed window, probably of the 13th century and to a narrow earlier aisle, and across the S.E. corner is a 14th-century doorway with chamfered jambs and shouldered head to the former rood-loft stair. The three E. bays of the N. wall are divided and flanked by early 14th-century two-stage buttresses. In the E. bay are the splays and springers of the rear-arch of an early 14th-century window, now blocked and with the upper part of the head cut off at the present wall-head. The five windows further W. have three cinquefoiled lights in a square head and are of 15th-century origin but much restored internally and entirely modern externally. At the W. end of the wall is a reset early 14th-century doorway with jambs and two-centred head of two orders, the inner wave-moulded and the outer chamfered. In the W. wall is a 15th-century three-light window similar to that in the E. wall and almost completely restored.

The *South Aisle* (14¼ ft. wide) is divided externally into bays by three-stage buttresses; it has continuous moulded strings outside and inside below the windows and a moulded cornice supporting a restored embattled parapet; the gargoyles, excepting one much weathered at the W. end, are modern. In the E. wall is a wholly restored window of three cinquefoiled lights in a four-centred head with a label; to the N. of it is the N. splay of a destroyed window, perhaps of the 13th-century and to a narrow earlier aisle. In the S. wall are six windows; the easternmost is of *c.* 1330–40 with two trefoiled ogee lights with a quatrefoil in an ogee head with moulded internal and external labels, all completely renewed externally but internally original and of clunch; the remaining windows are also much restored, they are of 15th-century origin and of three cinquefoiled lights in a four-centred head. The doorway of *c.* 1340 in the westernmost bay has a two-centred head of two continuous moulded orders, the inner wave-moulded and the outer chamfered, with a label; the inner order of the head is a modern restoration. In the W. wall is a 15th-century three-light window, again much restored.

The *West Tower* (11¼ ft. square) is of the end of the first quarter of the 14th century and of three stages with angle-buttresses, a tall plinth, an embattled parapet with gargoyles and an octagonal spire. The plinths of the E. buttresses are splayed inwards presumably to clear the W. windows of the earlier and narrower aisles. The tower-arch is two-centred and of three orders with a moulded label on the E. with carved head-stops of a beast and a man; the two outer orders on the E. have wave mouldings and the innermost has a double-roll moulding; on the W. all are chamfered; the responds have attached shafts with fillets and moulded capitals and bases. The W. window has a two-centred head; in the 15th century it was blocked and a staircase inserted in the blocking and lit by three small loop-lights. The doorway to the stair has chamfered jambs and a moulded four-centred head; the lower steps rise in the thickness of the blocking, turn, and continue up as a circular vice, the extra thickness of wall to contain it being obtained by projecting a semi-hexagonal bay into the tower on the W. and supporting the projection on moulded corbelling rising from a carved lion's mask. The ringing-chamber has in both the N. and S. walls an original window, partly restored, of one cinquefoiled light in a two-centred head with a label; in the W. wall is a small recess with a two-centred head perhaps contrived in the blocking of a former window. The outline of a former nave roof of very steep pitch remains across the external face of the E. wall. In each wall of the belfry stage is an original window of two trefoiled ogee lights, the E. and W. with a quatrefoil, the N. and S. with a sexfoil in a curvilinear triangle, in a two-centred head with a label continued across the walls as a string. The *Spire* has rolls at the angles and a restored finial; in the S. face is a doorway with two-centred head under a gable opening on the parapet, and on the opposite face an inscribed panel with the date of a restoration, 1847. In each of the cardinal faces, a third of the way up, is a stone dormer-window of two trefoiled lights with a quatrefoil under a crocketed gable with side-shafts and finials; higher, in each of the intermediate faces, is a similar dormer but of one trefoiled light; all these are more or less restored.

The *North Porch* (8 ft. by 11¾ ft.) is of the 15th century, with diagonal buttresses in two stages and an embattled parapet; the buttresses have original but much weathered masks carved on the string-course at offset level and modern pinnacles. The entrance has shafted jambs and a four-centred arch in a square head with panelled spandrels and a moulded label carved with head-stops of a king and a bishop, all largely modern except the stops. On the inside of the E. wall are three cinquefoiled panels in square heads with foliated spandrels; the middle panel is pierced to form a window and completely restored except for a short length of original clunch dressing in the S. reveal. The W. window is of two cinquefoiled lights in a square head with foliated internal spandrels and a moulded label with carved head-stops, almost wholly restored except the label and stops.

The tie-beam *Roof* of the chancel, of late 15th-century design, was extensively restored in 1842–44. It is of very low pitch and in three bays. The trusses have short king-posts on the ties with longitudinal curved braces to the ridge and are supported on wall-posts and curved braces; against the walls the tie-beams are omitted and the principal rafters are so supported and braced. Each bay is divided into eight panels by principal rafters, ridge and purlins with bosses at the intersections carved with roses and human masks. All the main timbers are moulded and the wall-posts stand on semi-octagonal and embattled stone corbels with half-angels holding shields, all more or less mutilated. The tie-beam and queen-post *Roof* of the nave has a history similar to that of the foregoing, but is almost wholly of 1842–44. It is in seven bays; the ties are cambered, supported on wall-posts and stiffened with curved braces; the queen-posts have curved braces forming four-centred arches. Each bay is divided into eight panels with foliated bosses at the intersections of purlins and principal rafters. The wall-plates are carved with paterae and the stone corbels supporting the wall-posts are embattled and carved with half-angels holding shields, etc., mostly recut, as follows—on the N., (a) blank shield, (c) arms of Naylor(?), (d) book, (e) arms of Page (?), (g) blank shield; on the S., (a), (c), (e), (g) blank shields, (b) scroll.

The *Roofs* of the N. and S. aisles are of the late 15th century, also very extensively restored in the 19th century. The N. aisle has a lean-to beam roof divided into seven bays by moulded principals with curved braces and wall-posts; two purlins and intermediate principals divide each bay into six panels; the wall-posts rest on semi-octagonal embattled corbels carved with half-angels holding scrolls and shields, two with the arms respectively of Naylor(?) and Page (?), mostly recut. The roof of the S. aisle is generally similar to that in the N. aisle, but with one purlin and foliated bosses at the intersection of principals and purlin; the corbels, again much recut, are carved with, on the N., (a) head and shoulders of a grotesque, (b) half-angel with pipes, (c) as (a), (d) demi-grotesque playing gittern, (e) grotesque head, (f) as (a), (g) head and shoulders of grotesque man with tooth-ache, (h) demi-grotesque; on the S., (a) demi-grotesque, (b) woman's head, (c) angel's head, (d) half-angel holding shield, (e) head of bearded man, (f) crowned half-figure, (g) grotesque head, (h) demi-demon. The 15th-century couple *Roof* of the porch is of low pitch and in two bays, with wall-posts and curved braces forming four-centred arches, with modern solid filling in the spandrels below the principal rafters; the corbels below the wall-posts are modern.

Fittings—*Bells:* six; 1st inscribed 'Sonoro sono meo sono Deo', 1612, by Richard Holdfeld; 2nd, inscribed 'God save thy Church', same date and maker; 3rd, inscribed 'Cantabo laudes tuas Domine', 1606, with the name Richard Covington, perhaps a churchwarden; 4th, 166., by Christopher Graye; 5th, 1825, by William and John Taylor, Oxford. *Benefactors' Board:* In tower—list of charities painted on boards in moulded frame, 1729. *Brass Indents:* In N. aisle, (1) of inscription-plate, see Floor-slab (5). In tower, (2) of figures of man and woman and inscription-plate, late 15th-century. *Chairs:* In chancel and vestry, three, of oak, two with fielded panels in the backs and scrollwork above and below, turned legs and stretchers, late 17th-century, one with solid back containing enriched round-headed panel, shaped arms and turned legs, early 17th-century. In vestry, pair, of mahogany, with carved and interlaced splats, mid 18th-century with some repair. *Churchyard Cross:* N. of church—octagonal to square base only, with square socket for shaft, mediaeval. *Coffin-lids:* In churchyard, three coped slabs with foliated crosses much weathered, 13th or early 14th-century. *Communion Rails:* In S. aisle, of oak, reused panel from a set of rails with elaborate pierced carving of three cherub-heads in festoons of fruits and flowers, with moulded capping and base, late 17th-century. *Doors:* In doorway in N. wall of chancel, battened plank door with four-centred head, applied hollow-chamfered mouldings and strap-hinges, nail-studded, 16th-century with some repairs; similar door to tower-stair, with modern repairs. *Font:* plain octagonal stone bowl with moulded underedge, octagonal stem and octagonal to square base, on modern step, 13th-century. *Glass:* In S. aisle—E. window, some canopy-work in heads of main lights, perhaps 15th-century. *Lockers:* In N. wall of chancel and N. aisle, two, rectangular rebated recesses, mediaeval.

Monuments and Floor-slabs. Monuments: In chancel—on S. wall, (1) of Rev. George Adam Browne, 1843, rector, Vice-Master and Senior Fellow of Trinity College, acting Provincial Grand Master of Freemasons, Cambridge, white marble wall-tablet with pediment and masonic emblems; (2) of William Clapham, 1766, Jane his wife, 1779, oblong slate tablet; (3) of Anna Browne, widow, 1821, white marble eared tablet on black marble pedimented backing, by T. Tomson, Cambridge; (4) of Anne, widow of William Wiles, 1849, white marble sarcophagus-shaped tablet on black marble backing, by Swinton, Cambridge; (5) of William Wiles, 1827, late of Pidley Lodge, Huntingdon, tablet generally similar to (4) and by the same maker. In N. aisle—in N. wall, (6) tomb-recess with moulded ogee head and chamfered jambs, 14th-century; (7) of William Wragg, 1829, Mary his wife, 1866, and Anne Maria their child, 1832, white marble pedimented tablet, by Wiles, Cambridge; (8) of John, son of William and Hester Wragg, 1823, Isabell, daughter of John and Sophia Wragg, 1824, and others later, similar to (7) and by the same maker; (9) of William and Hester Wragg, 1804 and 1808, similar to (7) and (8); (10) of Sophia Olivia, daughter of William and Elizabeth Wragg, 1847, white marble tablet. In S. aisle—on S. wall, (11) remains of tomb-recess with moulded ogee head, 14th-century; (12) of Sir Brodrick Chinnery, 2nd Bt., of Flintfield, Cork, 1840, who erected the monument, and Diana Elizabeth his wife, 1824, white marble tablet with urn and weeping willow, by T. Tomson, Cambridge; (13) of Abraham Kaye, 1823, Susan his wife, 1829, and Ann Bracken her sister, 1821, white marble tablet with plain side-pilasters and cornice, erected to his parents and aunt by John Kaye, D.D., Bishop of Lincoln. In churchyard—N. of church, (14) of Frances, daughter of George Brigham, 167(2?), headstone carved with cherub-head, skulls and drapery and, on reverse, skeleton in round-headed panel; (15) of F.B., 1711; (16) of George Brigham, 1712; (17) of Alice, wife of William Wootton, 1713; (18) of William Wootton, 1712; (15–18) all headstones carved with cherub-heads, emblems of mortality and scrolled foliage, (17 and 18) with footstones. *Floor-slabs:* In chancel—(1) of Samuel Burton, LL.B., son of Zakariah Burton of Subsey, 1712, of grey marble with cartouche containing shield-of-arms of Burton impaling (unidentified 78). In organ-chamber—(2) of George Taylor, 1707. In N. aisle—(3) of William Wragg, 1829; (4) of John Wragg, 1823, and others; (5) of William Wragg, 1804, and Hester his wife, 1808; (6) of Ann Edwards, 1782. In nave—(7) of Mary, 176., and Christopher Benstead, 177., of grey marble; (8) of Richard Berry, LL.D., 1723, Senior Fellow of St. John's and benefactor to the library there, of grey marble with Latin inscription; (9) of Priscilla (?) Watson, 1683, grey marble; (10) of Richard Langley, 1724, Doctor of Theology and Law, son of Edward Langley of Hipperholme, grey marble, with shield-of-arms of Langley impaling (unidentified 78) in a cartouche; (11) of Jonathan Johnson, 1742; (12) of [Jonathan] Dickman, 1727(?); (13) of Alice, wife of John Dann, 1700, and Alice his second wife, 1705; (14) of Harry Pearce, *c.* 1800; (15) of George, 1803, and Catherine Pearce, 1820. In S. aisle—(16) of Sir Brodrick Chinnery, Bt., 1840, and Diana Elizabeth his wife, 1824, with winged cherubs' heads in corners; (17) of Thomas ....on, 176.; (18) of Frances (Brackenbury) Sanzter, early 19th-century; (19) of A.B., 1821, A.K., 1823, S.K., 1829.

Paintings: In nave—over chancel arch and easternmost arches of N. and S. arcades, Doom (Plate 292), much damaged and faded, on E. wall by the haunches of the arch, the dead arising and, above, eight kneeling figures presumably of the Apostles at the feet of the Almighty, but all the upper part is now destroyed; demons carrying away the damned remain clear on the S. wall and the mouth of Hell was probably here, late 15th-century. (See also under *Miscellanea.*) *Piscinae:* In chancel—in S. wall, with cinquefoiled and sub-cusped opening in a two-centred arch with sunk spandrels bringing the head to a square, small chamfered shelf just above the springing, quatrefoiled dishing, 15th-century, discovered during the restoration of 1894 and matching the sedilia. In S. aisle—in S. wall, splayed recess with modern lintel, two drains with octofoiled and quatrefoiled dishings, 14th-century. *Plate:* includes a large paten on three feet with date-letter for 1701, given in 1705 by Thomas Smith, B.D., vicar, Fellow of Trinity, a paten with date-letter for 1717, given by John Wilson, D.D., vicar, 1749, a flagon with date-letter for 1748, given by Richard Walker, D.D., a cup with date-letter for 1746, and a paten with date-letter for 1812, given by Mrs. Sarah Lonsdale. *Pulpit:* of oak, hexagonal, the sides in two heights of panels, the upper enriched with carved round-headed arches framing lozenges, with enriched frieze and simple cornice, early 17th-century, on modern stand.

Recess: In N. aisle—in N. wall, recess with pointed head, mediaeval. *Royal Arms:* In tower—on N. wall of ground stage, painted on boards in moulded frame, with initials of James II. *Seating:* In chancel, nave and aisles, twenty-one oak benches (Plate 26), with moulded rails and ends with armrests, hollow-chamfered ogee tops and poppy-heads, on the armrests carved crouching beasts, including lion, stag, antelope gorged with a crown, buck, goat, wyvern, dog, griffin, dragon, most of the poppy-heads foliated but some carved with figures (Plate 26), two with two eagles, two with standing men, head of one modern, a priest holding a staff (?), his head modern, mid 15th-century with repairs and reconstructed with modern seats. *Sedilia:* In chancel—in three bays divided by small buttresses in two weathered stages with moulded plinths, arched openings similar to that of piscina but in square moulded heads with sunk cusped spandrels, vaults with stylised ribs radiating from central rosettes and with small bosses at the extremities carved with human and beasts' heads, partitions between bays pierced with trefoil-headed loops in chamfered recesses, early 15th-century, discovered during the restoration of 1894. *Stoup:* In porch—defaced bowl on pillar with cap and necking, mediaeval, much damaged. *Miscellanea:* Loose in N. aisle—architectural stone fragments including a voussoir with a roll-moulding between two bands of dog-tooth ornament, 13th-century, and a piece of moulded clunch, 15th-century. In the Fitzwilliam Museum—stone tablet, 14½ ins. by 10 ins. by 2½ ins., now broken, painted and partly incised with three-quarter length figure of female saint, perhaps St. Sythe (Plate 68), in blue cloak lined with red over purple dress, holding in right hand a small scythe, in the left a loaf (?), and standing under a septfoiled ogee arch, background strewn with small fleurs-de-lis, early 14th-century, said to have been found in 1842 in the blocking of a window.

The *Churchyard-wall* on the E., incorporating some reused material, may in part be a mediaeval structure.

(61) Parish Church of St. Mary and St. Nicholas, Trumpington (Plate 295), stands W. of the village, to the S. of Cambridge. The lower parts of the walls are chiefly of Barnack stone with some Ketton and Ancaster stone; the greater part of the rest of the walls is of clunch refaced externally in the 19th century with Bath stone and with small areas of rubble and flint. The roofs are lead and tile-covered. The existence of an aisled nave earlier than that of the present building is indicated by the respond-base of late 12th or early 13th-century date remaining *in situ* at the W. end of the S. arcade; the existing W. responds are also of the 13th century, and contemporary with them are the lower parts of the responds of the tower-arch, the walls of the tower to a height of 3 ft. to 4 ft. and the western walls of the aisles. Later again in the 13th century the *Chancel*, with a N.E. sacristy since destroyed, was rebuilt. A general rebuilding of the remainder of the church was undertaken in *c.* 1330, a *terminus ante-quem* being given by the tomb of Giles de Trumpington (monument (6)), *ob.* between 1327 and 1332, which is inserted in the E. arch of the arcade between the N. aisle and the N. chapel. To this period belong the *Nave* and clearstorey, the *North* and *South Aisles* excepting the W. walls, the *North* and *South Chapels*, *Porches* and the completion of the *West Tower*. There were restorations in 1822, 1851, 1853, 1861 and 1876, and during the last the present nave roof replaced one put up in the restoration of 1822. The *Vestry* was rebuilt on old foundations in 1912.

The church is a fine example of a building of the second quarter of the 14th century, with clearstorey-lights set above the piers of notably lofty nave-arcades. Among the fittings, the Trumpington tomb is noteworthy and the Trumpington brass is amongst the earliest and finest in the country. Some fragments of 13th and 14th-century glass survive.

Architectural Description—The *Chancel* (37½ ft. by 16½ ft.) has an early 14th-century E. window of five trefoiled lights with geometric tracery in a two-centred head with moulded external and internal labels and shafted splays with moulded capitals and bases; the external label has carved head-stops, the inner label continues as a wall-string; the window has been restored externally except the reveals and the lower part of the head. In the apex of the E. gable is a round quatrefoiled light, probably of the early 19th century, blocked on the inner face. In the N. wall are two late 13th-century windows, almost completely restored externally, each of two trefoiled lights with a trefoil and tracery in a two-centred head with labels with mask-stops; the E. and W. external stops are covered respectively by the second buttress and the E. wall of the N. aisle, and the W. internal stop by the chancel-arch. The doorway, further E., is of the 13th century and originally opened into a N.E. sacristy; it has roll-moulded jambs and a two-centred head with a label. Externally the first two buttresses represent the stubs of the E. and W. walls of an annexe and between them are three shaped corbels which formerly supported the wall-plate; above is the weathering of the former roof. This low building formed a chapel or, more probably, a sacristy contemporary with the 13th-century chancel. In the S. chancel-wall are three late 13th-century windows and a 14th-century 'low-side' window, all much restored externally and with modern mullions; the first is of three uncusped lights with intersecting tracery in a two-centred head with a moulded label; the second and third are similar to those in the N. wall, with a modern external recess with a multifoiled cusped head and old chamfered jambs and sill below the second, and the third with a sill raised in the 14th century to allow for the insertion below it of a 13th-century doorway moved eastward to make room for the 'low-side'. This reset doorway has jambs and two-centred head of two chamfered orders with a label. The 'low-side' window is rectangular with a chamfered surround.

The *Nave* (Plate 293) ($59\frac{1}{4}$ ft. by $18\frac{1}{4}$ ft.) has a N. arcade of *c.* 1330 of five bays with two-centred arches of two double-ogee moulded orders with moulded labels, with headstops to the nave and continuous on the aisle side, and piers with double-ogee moulded attached shafts with moulded capitals and bases. The E. respond is of the same date, and similar to a half-pier. The W. respond is of the 13th century and a semi-quatrefoil in section with a contemporary base and a 14th-century cap. The S. arcade is similar to the N. arcade but the base of the 13th-century W. respond rests on the late 12th-century base of a former respond of semicircular form. The 14th-century clearstorey has in the N. wall a range of four quatrefoil lights in moulded circular surrounds; in the S. wall are four trefoiled ogee-headed lights with two-centred and chamfered rear-arches and moulded external and internal labels. All the clearstorey-windows are completely restored externally.

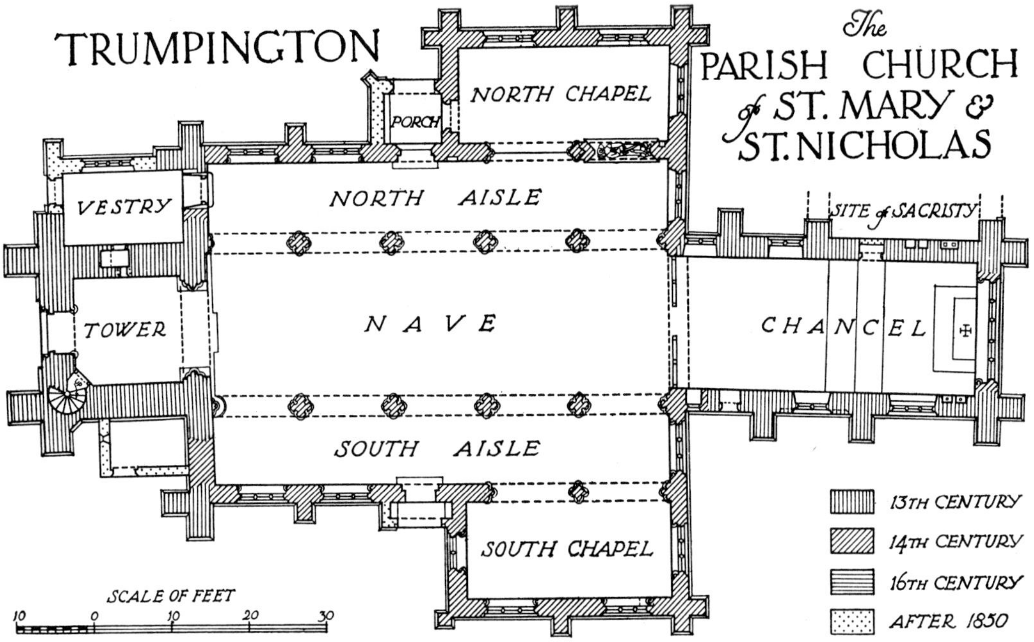

The *North Aisle* (9 ft. wide) has in the E. wall a window of *c.* 1330 of three cinquefoiled ogee lights in a two-centred head with shafted splays and labels, partly restored externally. In the eastern part of the N. wall is a 14th-century arcade of two bays opening into the N. chapel; the arches are two-centred and of two moulded orders carried on a shafted pier and responds with moulded capitals and bases; The E. bay has been in part blocked by a later canopied tomb. Further W., the N. doorway is of the 14th-century and restored externally; it has jambs and two-centred head of four wave-moulded orders, moulded splays and segmental-pointed rear-arch with a moulded label; the label is continued from the arcade on the E. and, on the W., carried down to form a string below the windows. The two windows in the western length of the wall are of the 14th-century, of three trefoiled ogee lights with net and curvilinear tracery in two-centred heads with moulded rear-arches, labels and shafted splays with moulded caps and bases. In the W. wall, below a blocked window, is a 16th-century doorway to the vestry, with chamfered jambs and three-centred head, inserted in the 14th-century blocking of an original opening.

The *South Aisle* ($8\frac{1}{2}$ ft. wide) has an E. window similar to the corresponding window in the N. aisle, much restored and with modern mullions and tracery. In the eastern part of the S. wall is a 14th-century arcade of two bays opening into the S. chapel; the arches are two-centred and of two moulded orders, the inner wave-moulded, the outer chamfered, with a moulded label; the pier and responds are shafted, with moulded capitals and bases, and the lower part of the E. respond, which is much damaged, has a square inner order rebated for a screen. The S. doorway is of the 14th century completely restored externally except the lower part of the E. jamb; the internal moulded splays and the pointed segmental rear-arch with moulded label are original. The two windows further W. are similar in date and design to those opposite and again entirely restored externally. In the W. wall are traces of a blocked window-opening; this last is curtailed by the present S. wall of the aisle, indicating that the earlier aisle was rebuilt narrower in the general 14th-century reconstruction.

The *North Chapel* ($27\frac{1}{4}$ by 12 ft.) has a restored 14th-century E. window of three trefoiled ogee lights with tracery in a two-centred head with moulded labels; only the shafted splays with their caps and bases and the internal label are original. In the N. wall are two three-light windows similar to the N. and S. windows in the aisles, completely restored externally; below the second is an original 'low-side' window, now blocked, with a surround of two wave-moulded orders. The doorway in the W. wall is of the 14th century, much restored, with jambs and two-centred head of two wave-moulded orders, a segmental-pointed rear-arch and a moulded internal label continued as a string below the N. windows.

The *South Chapel* (26½ ft. by 12 ft.) has an E. window similar to that in the N. chapel and almost entirely modern. The two windows in the S. wall are of 14th-century design but renewed except perhaps for the splays and rear-arch. The window in the W. wall is of two lights and of 14th-century origin but again only the splays and rear-arch are original.

The *West Tower* (14 ft. by 13½ ft.) belongs largely to the period of extensive rebuilding of the church in the first half of the 14th-century though the lower weatherworn courses of the walls and of the responds of the tower-arch are of the 13th century. It is of two stages externally and three storeys internally, with a plinth, angle-buttresses in four weathered stages on the N., S. and W. walls, and an embattled parapet with gargoyles on the parapet-string in the centre of each face. The parapet is of split-flint rubble; the rest of the tower has been refaced with modern ashlar and the dressings and features externally are for the most part modern. The 14th-century tower-arch is two-centred and of three continuous moulded orders on the E. and two on the W., the inner order being in the form of three shaped shafts; the latter are built up upon 13th-century responds, similar to the W. respond of the N. nave-arcade, left standing to a height of 5 ft. In the thickness of the N. wall is a small closet with a two-centred barrel-vault pierced for a bell-rope, a recess with two-centred head in the W. side and a modern opening to the tower in the S. wall replacing an earlier opening; it is entered from the vestry through an original doorway with chamfered jambs and two-centred head with a label with mask-stops. The W. doorway has jambs and two-centred head of two moulded orders with a label with decayed head-stops, shafted splays with moulded caps and bases and segmental-pointed rear-arch with a label with mask-stops. The W. window is of three cinquefoiled lights with tracery in a two-centred head with moulded labels; the inner order of the reveals and the tracery are modern. High up in both the N. and S. walls is an external recess with moulded jambs and cinquefoiled head with a label; above each recess and lighting the second storey is a single-light window with moulded jambs and trefoiled head with a label. In each face of the belfry is a window of two uncusped lights with a pierced spandrel in a two-centred head with a label.

The *North Porch* (7¼ ft. by 6¼ ft.) has been rebuilt except for the lower part of the E. jamb of the entrance; the entrance-arch is two-centred and of two continuous wave-moulded orders. The *South Porch* (8 ft. by 2 ft.) has also been almost completely rebuilt; only the plinth and lower part of the E. jamb of the entrance are old.

The *Roof* of the chancel is ceiled in plaster and of multiple canted form. It is divided into three bays by moulded wood ribs, each bay being subdivided by diagonal ribs and a central longitudinal rib, with restored bosses at the intersections; the main bosses, at the intersection of the diagonal ribs, are carved with a man's head in a quatrefoil, a grotesque face and a man's face. The roof has been reconstructed early in the 19th century, with the original 15th-century ribs and bosses reused.

Fittings—*Bells:* six; 5th, inscribed 'Celi det munus qui regnat [Trinus] et Unus', mid 15th-century, perhaps cast at Bury St. Edmunds; 6th, inscribed 'Cum cano busta mori cum pulpeta vivere desi' (disce) and 'Omnia fiant ad gloriam Dñi' (Dei), 1749, by J. Eayre. *Benefactors' Tables:* In N. aisle—painted on boards in black and gilt frame, benefactions of William Austin, tailor, of Trumpington, 1679. In S. chapel—on S. wall, charity of Thomas Allen, 1681, inscribed on black marble tablet in enriched bolection-moulded stone frame with pediment supported on reused 14th-century head-corbels, one of a woman with square head-dress. *Brasses* and *Indents:* see Monument (6). *Chest:* In tower, of deal, with domed top, iron straps, two rings at each end, lock and two hasps, late 15th-century. *Coffin-lids:* four, in S. aisle, and fragment of a fifth on outside of S. wall of chancel below a modern canopy, with foliated crosses carved in low relief, 13th or early 14th-century. *Communion Table:* with turned legs of Tuscan columnar form with pedestals, frame enriched with carved jewel-ornament, and moulded stretchers, early 17th-century. *Crosses:* Under tower-arch—freestone base only of standing-cross with square socket for shaft, octagonal to square with broaches and moulded free sides, on the square faces the following inscription in black-letter 'Orate pro animab[us] Joh[ann]is Stokton et Agnetis uxoris ei[us]', W. side illegible, late 15th-century, removed to the church from a position in the village opposite the Red Lion Inn. John Stokton was alive in 1450 and dead by 1475. Churchyard-cross: N. of church—base and part only of shaft, base square with chamfered upper edge, shaft octagonal to square with slight taper, 14th or 15th-century. *Door:* to tower staircase, of oak planks with three wrought-iron strap-hinges, 14th-century.

Font: of clunch, octagonal, straight-sided bowl, each face containing a quatrefoiled panel enclosing blank shields, Tudor roses and a patera, moulded under-edge with head corbels at the corners, of a king, a bishop, a bearded man with long hair, two of men with caps and wings, two of women with simple head-dresses, a woman with netted hair, octagonal pedestal with roll-mouldings at the angles and window-light panelling in each face, spreading base twice chamfered and with grotesque heads carved in low relief on the upper chamfer, late 15th-century style, probably entirely recut in mid 19th-century. *Glass:* In E. window—in centre light, fragments including parts of towered canopy, black-letter inscription, border of vine leaves on a red ground, crown, fleurs-de-lis, drapery and some grisaille, 14th-century. In N.W. window of chancel—in tracery light, white tricorporate leopard on red field in triangular panel (Plate 54), perhaps for Edmund Crouchback, Earl of Lancaster, (1245–1296), 13th century, and fragments of grisaille; in main lights, two reset panels containing respectively the full-length figures of St. Paul in robes holding book and sword on a red ground and St. Peter wearing mitre (?) and vestments on a red ground inscribed with his name in black-letter, both in canopied niches with cusped heads under crocketed gables and with pinnacled side-standards, 14th-century, damaged and patched with 15th-century fragments, above and below the panels are reset borders of blue with gold leopards' heads, towers, white oak leaves, etc., fragments of grisaille and two larger roundels containing leopards' heads, 14th-century. In N. aisle—in head of centre light of E. window, panel with bishop in niche with cinquefoiled ogee head, possibly *c.* 1800, and incorporated in grisaille glass of some distinction, 1853; in tracery of E. window of N. wall, shield-of-arms of Trumpington (Plate 54), 14th-century. *Hatchment:* In N. chapel—on W. wall, with shield-of-arms of Pemberton with a scutcheon of pretence quarterly Baron and Bentham, for the Rev. Jeremy Pemberton, 1800, painted on boards in a frame painted with skulls and hour-glasses. *Lockers:* in exterior of N. wall of chancel, formerly in N.E. sacristy, two, rectangular, now blocked, mediaeval.

Monuments and *Floor-slabs. Monuments:* In chancel—on N. wall, (1) of Mary, wife of John Hailstone, vicar, 1838, white marble tablet with slate backing, by Tomson & Son, Cambridge; (2) of John Hailstone, 1847, vicar, Woodwardian Professor, white marble tablet with pediment and slate backing, by Tomson & Son, Cambridge; (3) of Mrs. Isabella Telford, 1843, similar to (1) and by the same maker; on S. wall, (4) of John, second son of Christopher Anstey, 1819, one of H.M. Commissioners for auditing public accounts, white and black marble tablet with enriched cornice, draped urn and shield-of-arms of Anstey with a scutcheon of Senior; (5) of Helen, widow of John Anstey, 1837, white and grey marble sarcophagus-shaped tablet, by Denman, London. In N. aisle—see under (6). Between N. aisle and N. chapel—in E. arch partly blocked to receive it, (6) table-tomb (Plate 294) with Purbeck marble slab and brass under ogee arch; tomb-chest with freestone plinth and clunch sides with arcading of ogee cinquefoil-headed panels with blank shields in the spandrels, S. face damaged by insertion of two memorial-tablets, to Thomas Pytcher, 1[577], and William Pytcher, 1614; slab with indent of marginal inscription-fillet and brass of man in mail armour and surcoat, with ailettes and knee-cops, sword slung in front, shield on left arm, head resting on conical-topped great helm chained to waist, feet on dog, shield charged with the arms of Trumpington, ailettes and shields on sword-scabbard with the arms of Trumpington differenced with a *label*, this last perhaps cut later; arch above of clunch with multiple-shafted jambs with moulded caps and bases standing on tomb-chest, moulded ogee head, cinquefoiled and sub-cusped with carved foliage-diapering in all the spandrels, and moulded label, with head-stops of a king, a man and two women, rising to a string below the embattled parapet of the blocking which finishes in an ashlar weathered tabling; tomb-chest and arch, probably of Giles de Trumpington (*ob.* between 1327 and 1332), 14th-century; brass and slab reset, probably of Roger de Trumpington (*ob.* 1289), *c.* 1300, apparently appropriated by a later member of the Trumpington family, who amended the arms. In S. aisle—on S. wall, (7) of George Riste, J.P., 1761, alderman of Cambridge, conservator of River Cam, white marble tablet with cornice and grey marble obelisk flanked by urns, on the obelisk a laurel wreath and cartouche containing monogram, erected by his brother-in-law and sister, Joseph and Anne Bentham; (8) of M.D., 1815, stone tablet. In N. chapel—on E. wall, (9) of George, son of Thomas and Mary (Pike of Meldreth) Pitchard, 1650, grey marble slab from table-tomb, with shields-of-arms of Pitchard and of Pike impaling Gore; on N. wall, (10) of Sir Francis Pemberton, P.C., 1697, Judge of King's Bench and Common Pleas, who married Anna, daughter of Sir Jeremy Whichcote, Bt., white and black marble

wall-cartouche (Plate 16) with framing of carved drapery, cherub-heads, winged skull, and flaming urn, with shield-of-arms of Pemberton impaling Whichcote, monument reputed to have been brought here from Highgate parish church in the 19th century. In churchyard—near cross, (11)......, 1719, headstone, top shaped to cherub's head, with emblems of mortality, scrolls and foliage; S. of church, (12) of John Hailes, 1756, headstone, inscription in cartouche, with cherub-heads, scrolls and foliage; (13) of William Stacey, 1729, headstone with Corinthian side-columns, curved top with cherubs in the tympanum; (14) of Thomas Bland, 1807, and Mary his wife, 1816, headstone with low-relief carving of flowers and fine lettering and three other headstones to members of the Bland family; (15) of Joseph Harris, 1842, neo-Greek pedestal monument. *Floor-slabs:* In nave—(1) of John Maris, 1830, and Mary his wife, 1832; (2) of Richard Maris, 19th-century; (3) of William [Maris], 19th-century; (4) of James Dobson, 1759; (5) of J. Hodges, 1812, In S. chapel—(6) of Thomas Allen, 1692; (7) ......, wife of Richard Baron, 1680(?).

Piscinae: In chancel—with two trefoiled pointed openings and a sunk trefoiled spandrel in a two-centred head with continuous moulded label returned as a sill, each recess with shelf and quatrefoiled dishing to drain, late 13th-century; in exterior of N. wall, formerly in N.E. sacristy, with two-centred roll-moulded head and shafted jambs with moulded caps and bases much damaged, two square dishings to drains, 13th-century. In N. chapel—with trefoiled ogee head and plain dishing, 14th-century. In S. chapel—with cinquefoiled ogee opening in two-centred head with a label, stone shelf and sexfoiled dishing to drain, 14th-century. *Plate:* includes a cup with conical bowl and knop on stem, with date-letter for 1661, given by Herbert Thorndike in 1672, a paten given by the donor of the cup and with the same maker's mark, R.A. over a star, but without other marks, a flagon with the date-letter for 1833, given by Mary Hailstone in 1836, and a 17th-century pewter plate given by H. Thorndike. *Pulpit:* of oak, octagonal, with moulded plinth enriched with prism-ornament, deep entablature of slight projection with shaped dentils and triglyph-like brackets in the frieze, in each face one recessed panel in moulded and dentiled framing, early 17th-century, on late 19th-century arcaded pedestal-base, given by Thomas Allen in 1677, and originally at Emmanuel College.

Scratchings: In lobby to ringing-stage of tower, acrostic in 15th-century lettering, 'Dimidium pauli totum per: ultima quantas Me facit hic stare mea racio sit tibi quare' (i.e. pauper-tas); in ringing-chamber, on W. wall, 'Raiphel' and 'Michaell', 15th or 16th-century. On lead of tower-roof, scratched view of Ely cathedral, by Dobson Clarke, 1731, also scratched outline of his hand. *Screen:* Under chancel-arch—base only of wood rood-screen, with central opening and of two bays on each side divided by buttressed standards, with moulded base and plinth carved with quatrefoils enclosing roses and deep top-rail carved with grape clusters and vine tendrils, each bay subdivided into two panels with flowing tracery in two-centred heads and with flowers, fruit and foliage in the spandrels, 15th-century with modern repainting. *Stoup:* In N. aisle, by N. door, small recess with moulded surround, mediaeval, much damaged. *Miscellaneous:* In churchyard—in S.E. corner, two three-light windows with net and intersecting tracery respectively, 14th-century, from S. wall of S. chapel, which now contains modern copies.

(62) STOURBRIDGE CHAPEL, dedicated to St. Mary Magdalene, stands on the N. side of the Newmarket Road, N.E. of the railway bridge. The walls of the chancel and the E. wall of the nave are ashlar-faced; the remainder are of flint pebbles with later brick patching; the dressings are of Barnack or Weldon stone. Most of the original external and internal plastering has now gone. The roofs are tile-covered. A hospital for lepers was founded here at some uncertain date, the earliest reference to it being at the end of the 12th century. The chapel, consisting of *Chancel* and *Nave*, seems to have been built about the middle of the same century. It later came into the hands of the monastery of Ely and at the end of the 14th century indulgences were being granted for contributions towards repairs; the roofs may have been renewed at this period.

The chapel and lands were leased by the Bishop of Ely to the Corporation of Cambridge in 1544, released to them in 1597 by Elizabeth I, and in 1606 granted by James I to John Shelbury and Philip Chewte. The survival of the chapel has been attributed to secular uses connected with Stourbridge Fair. In 1816 it was bought by the Rev. Thomas Kerrich and given to the University. It was restored in 1843 and used for services for labourers building the Eastern Counties Railway. Subsequent restorations were in 1867, under the direction of Gilbert Scott, when the W. wall is said to have been remodelled, and in 1949, when the building was put into sound condition for services. In 1951 the University gave the chapel to the Cambridge Preservation Society, now the freeholders.

St. Mary's is an interesting survival of a smaller 12th-century chapel connected with a leper hospital. It contains some rather unusual architectural decoration of the date.

Architectural Description—The *Chancel* (18 ft. by 12¾ ft.) has a partly rebuilt E. gable with traces of a later blocked window and with two string-courses on the wall below, the upper with billet-ornament and the lower a simple axe-work ornament of vertical and diagonal lines. The angles both have two tiers of attached shafts, much weathered; the upper capitals still retain their scallops. The E. window of one square-headed light is probably a mid 19th-century insertion. The lower string-course on the E. wall is continued along the N. and S. walls. In the N. wall is a 12th-century window of one round-headed light with an outer order carved with conventional leaf-ornament and springing from shafts with scalloped capitals and moulded bases. The upper 2 ft. of the same wall has been rebuilt and incorporates reused 12th-century worked stones. In the S. wall is a 12th-century window generally of similar form to the foregoing, but with the inner order carved with four-leaved flowers and the outer with cheveron-ornament; the W. shaft is carved with cheveron and spiral ornament and has a moulded band carved with two rosettes; the E. shaft is missing. Further W. is a doorway, now blocked, of uncertain but post-mediaeval date, with jambs and segmental arch of two plain orders. The 12th-century chancel-arch

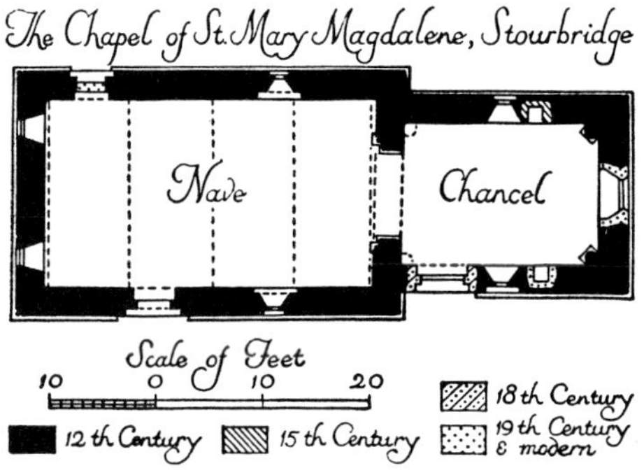

(Plate 282) is semicircular and of two orders with one roll-moulded order on the E. and beaded cheveron-ornament on the W.; the responds have attached and free circular shafts with scalloped capitals and moulded bases. The chancel was formerly covered by a quadripartite vault that sprang from vaulting-shafts in each corner about 5 ft. high. The shaft on the N.E. retains its scalloped capital, much damaged; that on the S.E. has lost its capital; the other two shafts have been removed. The marks of the vault can be seen on the E., N. and S. walls.

The *Nave* (31 ft. by 17 ft.) has two external string-courses similar to those on the chancel and, between them, the angles are shafted. In the N. wall is a 12th-century window similar to that on the N. of the chancel, but with cheveron-ornament on the outer order and cheveron-ornament on the rear-arch, and jamb-shafts with scalloped capitals and moulded bases. The 12th-century N. doorway, now blocked, has a semicircular head with cheveron-ornament and a label with billet-ornament; the order springs from modern shafts with original scalloped capitals and moulded bases; the plain inner order of the jambs supports a plain lintel. In the S. wall is a window similar to that in the N. wall. The 12th-century S. doorway has a semicircular head of two orders, the inner moulded and continuous and the outer with cheveron-ornament and springing from restored shafts with original scalloped capitals and modern chamfered bases; the label has cheveron-ornament. Between the two features in the S. wall internally is a rectangular area of blocking; Cotman's sketch of 1818 shows a fireplace inserted here. The W. wall has had the flint-pebble facing renewed. In it are three windows, the two lower round and the one above, in the gable, similar to those in the side-walls. None of the three is shown in Cotman's sketch of 1818 and the uppermost is probably of 1867, but the lower are not of this date and it is possible that they were in Cotman's time covered by rendering.

The *Roof* of the chancel is of *c.* 1400 and of three bays, with moulded principals, plates, purlins and ridge; the principals have curved braces and wall-posts, both moulded, standing formerly on stone corbels; these last have been defaced or removed except one in the S.W. corner carved with a half-angel. The roof of the nave is of similar type and construction but of four bays and with vertical ashlar-pieces; four of the corbels retain carvings of a flower and grotesques.

(J. S. Cotman, *Antiquities of St. Mary's Chapel at Stourbridge* (1819)).

Fittings—*Lockers:* In chancel—in N. wall, rectangular recess with rebated reveals, late mediaeval; in S. wall, rectangular recess without sill, of uncertain purpose and date.

(63) Augustinian Friary, founded in 1290, occupied most of the site on the N. side of Pembroke Street bounded by Corn Exchange Street, Wheeler Street and Free School Lane. In the basement of the modern Arts Schools are some reset architectural features and fragments from the buildings of the friary; Cole, born in 1714, remembered a gateway 'much like that of Trinity Hall' (see Monument (41)), comprising a large archway with a 'smaller wicket' beside it, fronting Peas Hill.

The reset material includes three clunch doorways with two-centred heads, one of two continuous stop-chamfered orders, 13th or 14th-century, another of one chamfered order within a square casement-moulding with quatrefoils in the spandrels, *c.* 1400, and the third originally of two continuous moulded orders but with only the inner order and the lower courses of the outer order surviving, 13th-century. The first two are said to be reset below the positions they previously occupied. The fragments consist of moulded stones from door-jambs and an arch-respond, 14th-century.

(64) Barnwell Priory, Augustinian canons, stood to the N. of the Newmarket Road, immediately N. of the church of St. Andrew the Less. Only a fragment of the buildings survives, comprising a single vaulted chamber standing at the corner of Priory Road and Beche Road. The walls are of clunch-rubble with dressings of Barnack stone and some clunch; brick has been used for repairs and patching; the roofs are tile-covered. Since 1886 it has been the property of the Cambridge Antiquarian Society.

Founded in 1092, the house, originally of Canons Regular, was moved here from near Cambridge castle in 1112. The church was not consecrated until 1190; the other buildings seem to have been extensively rebuilt during the first threequarters of the 13th century, including the greater part of the claustral block subsequent to *c.* 1254. The priory was surrendered in 1538 and towards the end of the century it was being used as a quarry; some of the stone for the new chapel of Corpus Christi College was from here. Between 1810 and 1812 the site was levelled and the foundations were largely destroyed. The conventual buildings lay in all probability to the N. of the church and it has been conjectured that the surviving fragment adjoined the N.W. corner of the N. and W. ranges of the cloister. The plan and details suggest that it may have been the Kitchen, forming the western part of the N. range, and the lost N. building the service stair to a first-floor Frater.

Architectural Description—The building is of the mid 13th century, much repaired and with modern buttresses; originally it continued further to the E., another building adjoined it on the S. and perhaps a second on the N. It was originally divided into double bays, of which the two westernmost pairs survive, by octagonal piers and semi-octagonal vaulting-shafts supporting two-centred quadripartite vaulting with chamfered ribs; pier and shafts have moulded capitals and bases and, with the ribs, are of Barnack stone; the vault is of clunch. The E.

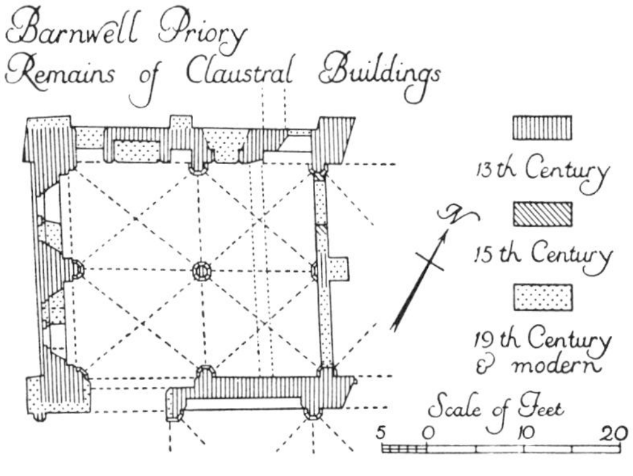

wall butts against complete vaulting-shafts in the side walls while the central pier or shaft is bonded into it; this curious arrangement suggests that the E. wall represents in part an original partition, but probably the eastern area of the vaulting and clearly the greater part of the wall have been rebuilt in modern times and therefore the central shaft may well be reused material. In the N. bay of the same wall is a doorway with four-centred head, now blocked, of uncertain date. Some 5¼ ft. to the W. of the E. wall are traces of bonding-stones remaining inside the N. and S. walls perhaps marking the position of an early partition.

The N. and S. walls both retain the W. jambs of openings at their eastern extremities. Continuing westward, the N. wall has a tall wall-arch with two-centred head embracing a doorway below and narrower two-centred window above both patched and altered, a 13th-century doorway with modern wood lintel, now blocked, and a fireplace. The fireplace occupies most of the W. bay and has chamfered jambs, a square recess on either side, a square head and a rough relieving-arch; it is of the 13th century, altered and in part destroyed. In the 19th century, evidence remained of an external wall with chamfered plinth running N. close E. of the 13th-century doorway. The S. wall has, outside, three 13th-century vaulting-shafts, with moulded bases and capitals, standing to the springing; the centre shaft is an angle-shaft and the W. shaft has been reset; a large 19th-century arched opening occupies most of the W. bay.

In the W. wall, in each bay, is a 13th-century transomed window of two paired lancet lights, rebated externally above the transom and chamfered externally and rebated internally below, with a moulded label following the heads of the lights and a segmental chamfered rear-arch; the windows are much damaged and patched and in part blocked, and the lower portion of the S. pair has been entirely destroyed for a doorway, now blocked. Fragments of a stone wall-bench survive that ran along the inside of the W. wall and the E. bay of the S. wall, now outside.

In the building are three stone coffins, one retaining part of a lid carved with a cross, 13th-century, and a number of enriched architectural fragments of the 12th and 13th centuries. See also Monuments (46) and (270) for other architectural fragments.

(65) Church of Our Lady of the Assumption and the English Martyrs (R.C.), standing at the corner of Hills Road and Lensfield Road, was built in 1887–90. It contains the following:

Fittings—An oak statue of about half life size of the Virgin suckling the Child and standing on a crescent (Plate 35), of the mid 16th century, traditionally from Emmanuel College; the connection is unknown. A statue of our Lady of Grace, which acquired some fame, is first recorded at the Dominican priory in 1515. In the Chapel of John Fisher, on the E. wall, a wood figure of St. Andrew crucified, about half life size, set against a large roundel with spandrels carved with seated angels holding St. Andrew crosses and a wide border with painted inscription: 'The Gift of A. Welby Pugin A.D. 1843 St. Andrew pray for us'. It was first in the church of St. Andrew in Union Road, Cambridge, designed by A. W. Pugin and consecrated in 1843, then of the Sacred Heart, St. Ives, and finally erected here in memory of Mgr. Canon Scott, S.T.D. (Plate 11).

(66) St. Andrew's Street Chapel (Baptist) stands on the W. side of the street, next N. of the Police Station. It was built in 1903 in replacement of the chapel of 1836, which itself replaced one of 1764. Nothing of the older structures survives but the chapel contains the following:

Fittings—*Books*: include a bible, London, 1679, in original binding with silver mounts, another in German, Minden, 1753, with original binding, six works by Robert Robinson of 1790–1812 and his MS. description of his estates at Chesterton, 1783, vellum-bound, tracts, pamphlets and other works forming a small library of some fifty books. *Chairs*: two; one with reeded horizontal bars in the back, scrolled arms, turned legs and cane seat, early 19th-century, on inscription-plate 'Chair used by the Rev. William Carey, D.D., at Serampore', the pioneer of modern foreign missions, who inspired the founding of the Baptist Missionary Society; the second in S.

vestry, of oak, with panelled back and shaped head-rail carved and inscribed 'DS 1670', shaped arms and turned legs, given in 1938. *Monuments:* On W. wall, (1) of Rev. Robert Roff, 1850, minister, oval wall-tablet of white marble. In churchyard—N. of chapel, (2) of Charles, son of Richard and Martha Foster, 1818, William Foster, 1837, and James M. Foster, 1853, table-tomb with oval inscription-panel; (3) of Katharine (Smith) Eaden Lilley, 1842, plain table-tomb; two other table-tombs and some twelve headstones of the first half of the 19th century. *Plate:* includes a pair of cups each with two scrolled handles and flared stem, the maker's mark TW JH in a square and the London assay-marks for 1819, given in that year. *Miscellaneous:* In vestry, framed medallion with modelled portrait-bust of the Rev. Rob. Hall Leicester, by T. R. Poole 'medallion modeller to the Prince of Wales', 1814.

(67) Former ZION CHAPEL (Baptist) stands on the S.E. of East Road, some 135 yds. N.E. of Parker's Piece. It is of two storeys with basement. The walls are of gault brick; the low-pitched roofs are slated. The original chapel with a schoolroom in the basement, built on the initiative of the Rev. Henry Battiscombe, former Fellow of King's College, was opened in 1838. It has been used as a hall and schoolrooms since the addition of a new chapel adjoining on the N.E. between 1877 and 1879, when also the N.W. wall was rebuilt further forward to allow the addition of a porch and staircases; at the same time minor alterations were made on the S.W. side. The later works were to the designs of William Peachey, architect, of York.

The S.W. side has a lofty shallow wall-arcade of four bays containing the ranges of four rectangular sash-hung windows on the basement, ground and first floors; the arches have semi-elliptical heads. The doorway between the two eastern bays is an insertion of 1877–9 and the additions of this date include the cornices to the ground-floor windows, the moulded string at first-floor level and the simple eaves-cornice. '1837 Zion Chapel Sunday School 1879' is inscribed on the street front over the doorway. The S.E. end is masked by 1 Petersfield, a house of 1842 given for the ministers' use in 1853 and approached through an internal doorway.

Inside, the upper floor is supported on cast-iron fluted columns with foliated capitals designed originally to carry galleries. On the ground floor, the plain timber internal porch is probably of 1837 and the enclosure of the stairs to the basement is made up of panels from the original pulpit, the latter with blind arcading of three semicircular-headed arches springing from half-round columns, early 19th-century. The baptistery bath has been removed.

(68) CHAPEL STREET CHURCH HALL, Chesterton, (former Baptist Chapel) stands at the N. end of the street, on the W. It is of one storey. The walls are of gault brick; the low-pitched roofs are slated. The original building is of *c.* 1844; it was extended E. later in the 19th century when also separate rooms were added on the W.

Both sides of the original building have a shallow wall-arcade of three bays with semicircular arches springing from plain brick responds. In each recess is a semicircular-headed window with glazing including narrow marginal panes. The interior is plain and retains no original fittings. It is now used by the Church of England.

(69) EDEN CHAPEL (Baptist) stands at the corner of Fitzroy Street and Burleigh Street, some 180 yds. E. of New Square. It is a building of 1874, replacing the original Calvinistic Baptist Chapel opened in 1825, and contains from the latter, except where otherwise described, the following:

Fittings—*Monuments:* In vestry—(1) of Lydia Tunwell Flack, 1839, plain shaped wall-tablet of stone; (2) of Susanna and Isabella Wybroe, 1836 and 1840, stone wall-tablet with black marginal line; (3) of John Cream, 1848, stone wall-tablet with cornice on black backing. In forecourt—(4) of John Stittle, 1813, plain stone tablet, from the Independent Chapel, 'Stittle's Chapel', formerly on the site of 3, 4 and 5 Green Street; (5) of Sarah Hindes, 1818, headstone; (6) of Rob. Benton, 1837, and Rebecca his wife, 1817, coffin-shaped stone in paving.

(70) Former PROVIDENCE CHAPEL stands on the S.E. of East Road, between Schoolhouse Lane and Caroline Place, 343 yds. N.E. of Parker's Piece. The walls are of gault brick; the roofs are slate-covered. It was built as a Calvinistic Baptist Chapel in 1833 on the initiative of the Rev. William Allen. The trustees mortgaged it for £400. The mortgagor died in 1834, his executors foreclosed and the chapel was sold for £577 in 1837 to become a church school. The second minister, Henry Battiscombe, then founded Zion Chapel (Monument (67)). It is now a wholesale shop.

The building consists of a rectangular block with pedimental gables to N.W. and S.E. and a single-storey porch on the N.W. below a semicircular-headed window within a wall-recess of the same shape. The walls have plain parapets above a simple stucco cornice. The sides are divided into three, and the S.E. end into two bays by continuous brick pilaster-strips. The window with flat brick arch in the upper part of each bay of the side walls is original. The porch, which is now incorporated in later additions, has an outer semicircular-headed archway of two plain brick orders.

The internal arrangement of chapel and gallery, with a basement, formerly a schoolroom, survives, but the upper floor with central opening retains nothing of the original gallery-structure. Below the chapel a small section of the basement formerly enclosed by brickwork was probably the baptistery.

EMMANUEL CONGREGATIONAL CHURCH, Trumpington Street, see Monument (71).

(71) Former CONGREGATIONAL CHAPEL, now Concert Room of the University Music School, stands in Downing Place. The walls are of white brick and the roofs are tiled. Built as Emmanuel Congregational Chapel in 1790, a single-storey porch etc. was added on the W. late in the 19th century and the interior completely modernised in 1936. The fittings from here listed below are now in Emmanuel Congregational Church in Trumpington Street, built in 1874.

The original chapel is an oblong building with hipped roofs. The entrance front, the narrow W. end, where rising clear of the later additions, has a stone plat-band at first-floor level, a simple eaves-cornice and a parapet-wall; it is in three bays, the middle bay projecting 4½ ins. and pedimented, and contained originally three tall semicircular-headed windows. These last have now been in part blocked to form six windows. In the tympanum of the pediment is a small round light. The E. end and the N. and S. walls are plain and also contain tall windows, the E. windows similar to those opposite, the others with segmental heads and in part blocked. A lead rainwater-pipe survives on the S.W. with moulded head dated 1790.

Fittings, in the new church—*Monuments:* In lobby, (1) of Rev. Joseph Sanders, 1788, white marble wall-tablet; (2) of Joseph Thodey, 1835, stone wall-tablet with cornice. *Plate:* includes a porringer (Plate 23) with foot and lower part of bowl gadrooned and two beaded scroll-handles, London assay 1698, inscribed 'CWS' and 'Given by Mrs. S. Ewens 1756', a porringer (Plate 23) similar to the first but smaller, London assay 1705, inscribed with indecipherable monogram in a cartouche and 'Given by Mr. J. Audley 1816', a porringer as before but with slighter handles and only a flange for foot, London assay 1711, inscribed 'SPF' with stars in a cartouche, and 'Given by F. Jennings 1816', and a flagon (Plate 23) 9½ ins. high with shaped body, spout, scrolled handle, shaped lid and moulded foot, London assay 1816, inscribed 'Given by Mr. C. Rutherford 1816'.

(72) FRIENDS' MEETING HOUSE, 12 Jesus Lane, stands near the junction of Jesus Lane and Park Street. It is of two storeys, with walls of brick and slate-covered roofs. It is the Meeting House built in 1777, but drastically remodelled and heightened in 1925 and now linked to a building of 1894 on the S.

The E. and W. walls and part of the S. wall of the 18th-century building stand free; all have been heightened, the first is set back 3 ins. at first-floor level. Four rectangular sash-hung windows on the ground floor on the E. may be original; all the other openings are modern.

The interior has been largely rebuilt and completely refitted.

(73) POUND HILL CHAPEL (formerly Methodist, latterly Catholic Apostolic) stands on the N.W. of Pound Hill 20 yds. from St. Peter's Street. It has a gallery and basement. The walls are of gault brick; the roofs are slate-covered. The building is shown, as 'Methodist Chapel', on Baker's map of Cambridge of 1830 and must, for stylistic reasons, have been built only shortly before that date. It is now a warehouse.

Consisting of an oblong block lengthways with the street, the N.E. and S.W. ends have low-pitched gables. The two sides both have three bays of ground-floor and gallery windows divided and flanked by lofty wall-recesses with elliptical brick heads just below the eaves and sills weathered out to the normal wall-face just above basement-level. The basement windows are symmetrically arranged but at odds with the baying above. The principal windows have flat brick arches and, on the street side, rectangular panels below the sills; they contained double-hung sashes, but are now mostly blocked. The entrance from the street is through a doorway in the northernmost wall-recess.

Inside, the gallery returns round three sides of the building in horseshoe form supported on cast-iron columns; it has a panelled front. The other fittings are of the later 19th century.

(74) CAMBRIDGE GENERAL CEMETERY lies on the E. of Histon Road, some 200 yds. N. of Huntingdon Road. Provided and administered by a Company formed by trust deed in 1843, it was opened the same year and in 1936 conveyed and assigned to the Town Council. Original buildings include an entrance lodge and a mortuary chapel, the first in the Elizabethan Tudor style, the second in mid 14th-century Gothic. The date 1833 in the chapel glass perhaps indicates the inception of the scheme.

The Lodge and the Mortuary Chapel are good examples of their kind.

The *Entrance Lodge* (Plate 309) is of two storeys. The walls are of white brick with red brick diapering and stone dressings. The roofs are covered with polygonal slates. It has acutely pointed gables to N. and S., a semi-octagonal stair-tower on the W., triangular bay-windows, and boldly projecting chimney-stacks. On the E. is a flat-roofed extension incorporating the original porch, now largely remodelled, with a stone panel over the entrance doorway inscribed '1843'. Flanking the Lodge are iron gates hung on brick and stone piers; the N. pier of both pairs of the last has on the E. face a slate panel incised with the regulations for the conduct of the cemetery.

The *Mortuary Chapel* has walls faced with flint pebbles and roofs covered with polygonal slates. It is centrally planned, in the form of a Greek cross, with transverse gabled roofs. The W. arm is extended to form a porch with a large open western arch; in the end of each of the other arms is a three-light window with curvilinear tracery in a two-centred head, and in every gable-apex a pierced curvilinear triangle or roundel. The W. doorway is contrived below the springing of an arch with two-centred head, this last containing glazed curvilinear tracery.

The crossing inside, forming the main compartment, has E., N., S. and W. arches with two-centred heads, the spandrels between the last and the gabled roofs being pierced and cusped. Original fittings include, among the woodwork, a traceried *Screen* of seven bays in the E. arch, a buttressed and traceried *Lectern*, and *Benches* with shaped ends and poppy-heads carved with foliage. In the *Glass* over the W. doorway are two roundels, one with initials EBL superimposed upon a pair of compasses, the other '1833' in ribbon-like numerals; the other windows contain 19th-century glass with geometric patterns in grisaille and colour, the arms of England and roundels, one with the initial H, another with a stag. A clunch *Monument* with crocketed gable and finials in the N.E. corner of the eastern arm, of Ebenezer Foster, 1851, and his wife Elizabeth, 1850, with a shield-of-arms of Foster below, is by Rattee. The floor is laid with 19th-century red *Tiles* with geometric and foliage patterns and EBL with a compass, as in the glass, in white slip.

A number of memorials in the Cemetery are before 1850. The following, (1–4) standing S. of the path between the Chapel and the Lodge and (5) S. of the last, are the more noteworthy: (1) of Elizabeth Headland, wife of Joel Smart, 1846, fluted demi-column with flaming urn, on pedestal, by Wiles; (2) of Eliz. Swinton, 1844, tall tapering pedestal supporting gadrooned urn with swags; (3) of Naomi Saunders, 1843, similar to (2); (4) of Thomas Foote, 1847, similar to (1) and by the same maker; (5) of William Adams, 1849, large pedestal with arabesque-enriched frieze supporting urn. The fine table-tomb in the 14th-century Gothic style, S. of (3) and (4), though recording earlier deaths, is probably shortly after 1850.

(75) MILL ROAD CEMETERY lies some 360 yds. E. of Parker's Piece. It was consecrated in 1848. The custodian's *House* in the S.W. corner was formerly the Mortuary Chapel etc. and so served until a larger chapel was built in the middle of the cemetery. The later chapel has been demolished.

The *House* has the more conspicuous walls faced with knapped flints and flint pebbles with dressings of limestone ashlar. The W. wall is of brick. The roofs, formerly covered with stone slates, are now tiled. It consists of a main E. to W. block, formerly containing the chapel open to the roof, with a two-storey W. cross-wing containing a committee-room to the S., custodian's rooms to the N. and above. In the middle of the S. wall of the first is a wide doorway sheltered by a shallow gabled porch with a stone tablet over the entrance inscribed 'Parochial Burial Ground Consecrated Nov. 7th 1848'. The wing is gabled to N. and S., the stone copings rising from shaped kneelers with cusped gablets to cusped apex-finials. The windows have timber casements of one, two and three lights in stone reveals. At the intersection of the roof-ridge is a clustered chimney-stack.

Inside, the former chapel, now with a staircase and floor inserted, has a roof divided into three bays by tie-beam trusses with wall-posts and braces and braced collars, most of the latter braces being cut away. The original floor of 9 ins. by 9 ins. tiles remains.

In the cemetery is a number of monuments dating from before 1850 but none is architecturally noteworthy.

(76) MISCELLANEOUS. Built into the Museum of Archaeology and Ethnology, in the main gallery on the second floor, is the central archway and surrounding stonework of the choir-screen designed by Inigo Jones and set up in Winchester Cathedral between the easternmost piers of the nave in *c.* 1638. The screen was demolished between 1819 and 1827 though the two bronze figures by Le Sueur, of James I and Charles I, that embellished it, were retained and are still in the nave. (John Britton, *Cathedral Antiquities*, III, pl. x (1818), shows the screen in position; *Winkle's Cathedral Churches* (London, 1838), pl. 52, shows the succeeding Gothic screen, designed by William Garbett, with the statues reused. The *Gentleman's Magazine*, 89, pt. ii (1819), 306, refers to Ingio Jones' screen still in place and *ibid*, 97, pt. ii (1827), 111, refers to it as removed.) The fragments were found between 1908 and 1910 in the triforium by Sir Thomas Jackson, Bt., R.A., consulting architect for the Cathedral and architect of the Museum, on whose recommendation the Dean and Chapter presented the middle part to the University. Much of the rest of the screen was used for patching the stonework of the Cathedral and the remainder stowed in the crypt. Many of the stones were found to be reused mediaeval dressings. (Museum Arch. and Eth., MS. note dated 3 Jan. 1914 signed T. G. Jackson).

Two 17th-century drawings of the screen are in the R.I.B.A. Library, one attributed to Inigo Jones in the Burlington-Devonshire collection (Drawer 1, no. 53), the other, differing slightly from the finished work, on the flyleaf of Inigo Jones' own copy of the Venice edition (1619) of Sebastian Serlio, *Tutte L'Opere d'Architettura* etc. (E.W. 72: 013(45), in safe). At Chatsworth are drawings for the two statues (*Sketches for Masques*, vol. I, no. 129). An agreement for the bronzes was made with Le Sueur on 17 June 1638 and witnessed by Inigo Jones; the figures were to be 5 ft. 8 ins. high, in Roman armour and to be finished by the following March for £340 (*S.P. Dom.*, Charles I, 442, 2); in the event they were fashioned in contemporary armour.

The screen, though fragmentary, is of architectural importance. When complete with the two statues, it was one of the early works of coherent and scholarly Classical design in England.

The re-erected fragment is of Beer stone, extensively restored and painted. It consists of a projecting pedimented bay containing an archway and flanked by half bays (Plate 246). Freestanding fluted Composite columns, pilaster-responds and flanking pilasters all on renewed pedestals support the enriched pedimented entablature, which has a modillioned and dentiled cornice. The attic-face above is panelled and capped by a minor dentil-cornice. The central archway has a semicircular head, a moulded archivolt with carved scrolled keystone and plain jambs with moulded imposts and bases.

(The Burlington-Devonshire drawing is reproduced in *Archl. Review* (March 1911), 130, and R.I.B.A. *Journal* xxxvi (24 Nov. 1928), no. 2; reproductions also of the Chatsworth drawings are in the second.)

SECULAR BUILDINGS, ETC.

(77) Cambridge Castle, motte, remains of bailey and Edwardian and Civil War defensive earthworks, stands on the highest ground adjacent to the city centre, on a spur called Castle Hill, some 300 yds. N.N.W. of Magdalene Bridge. For evidence of Roman occupation of the site see Monument (14). No pagan Saxon remains have been found; later Saxon finds include a number of important carved stones (see below). In 1068 William I gave orders for a castle to be raised at Cambridge (Ordericus Vitalis, *Hist. Ecc.* (ed. A le Prevost, Paris, 1835–55), II, Bk. IV, Ch. IV, 185; this passage was probably derived by Orderic from William of Poitiers, and, if so, is contemporary). Domesday Book states that twenty-seven houses were demolished to make way for it. Of motte and bailey type, this is the earliest structure of which parts survive.

A general reconstruction was undertaken by Edward I when the bailey appears to have been remodelled in a roughly rectangular form orientated diagonally N. and S. with the S. angle adjacent westward to the 11th-century motte. The evidence of the original accounts, later maps and surveys of the site and ill-recorded finds made in the 18th and early 19th centuries indicate the building in stone of a curtain-wall, a S.W. gatehouse with barbican opposite across the moat, towers at the E., N. and S. angles of the defences, the first probably to be identified with the postern, and on the motte, and a great hall in the N.W. part of the bailey. The whole was completed between 1283 and the king's death, a chapel first mentioned in the Pipe Rolls of 1 Ed. II being built or rebuilt probably during the same period. Edward I's expenditure upon it was £2,525 (W. M. Palmer, *Cambridge Castle*). It was, it seems, largely surrounded by wet moats; a moat also skirted the N. of the motte to separate the last from the bailey.

An inquest in 1367 into the defective state of wall, towers and houses, and the extensive alienation of stone from here for College buildings in the 15th and 16th centuries show the progress of deterioration, although as late as 1585 attempts were still being made to retain the curtain-wall; by 1606 the S.W. gatehouse was the only complete building left, being preserved by its use as a prison. This is the state shown in Fuller's view of Cambridge of 1634. Lyne's and Braun's views, of 1574 and 1575, are too stylised for reliable evidence and show improbably complete buildings, for, though a bridge leading to the S.W. gatehouse survived into the reign of Elizabeth I, in 1590 the castle was described as 'old ruined and decayed'.

In 1643, Cambridge being the headquarters of the Eastern Counties Association, the bailey works were reconstructed as a bastioned trace fort; fifteen houses were cleared and a brick barracks built on the site of the old great hall. In 1647 the new defences were slighted, but the three bastions, to E., N. and W., remained (see William Custance's map of Cambridge, 1798); the W. bastion was removed in 1811. The gatehouse again and the barracks were retained as prison buildings. Between 1802 and 1807 a new octagonal County gaol designed by G. Byfield was built, the surface of the bailey lowered and levelled, and the moat N. of the motte filled in with building debris.

In 1842 the S.W. gatehouse was pulled down to make way for the Court House designed by T. H. Wyatt and D. Brandon (Plate 298), which itself was demolished in 1954. In 1932 a new Shire Hall was built on the site freed by the demolition of the County gaol.

The much mutilated earthworks of Cambridge Castle, apparently mainly of the Norman and Civil War periods, with little of the Edwardian castle

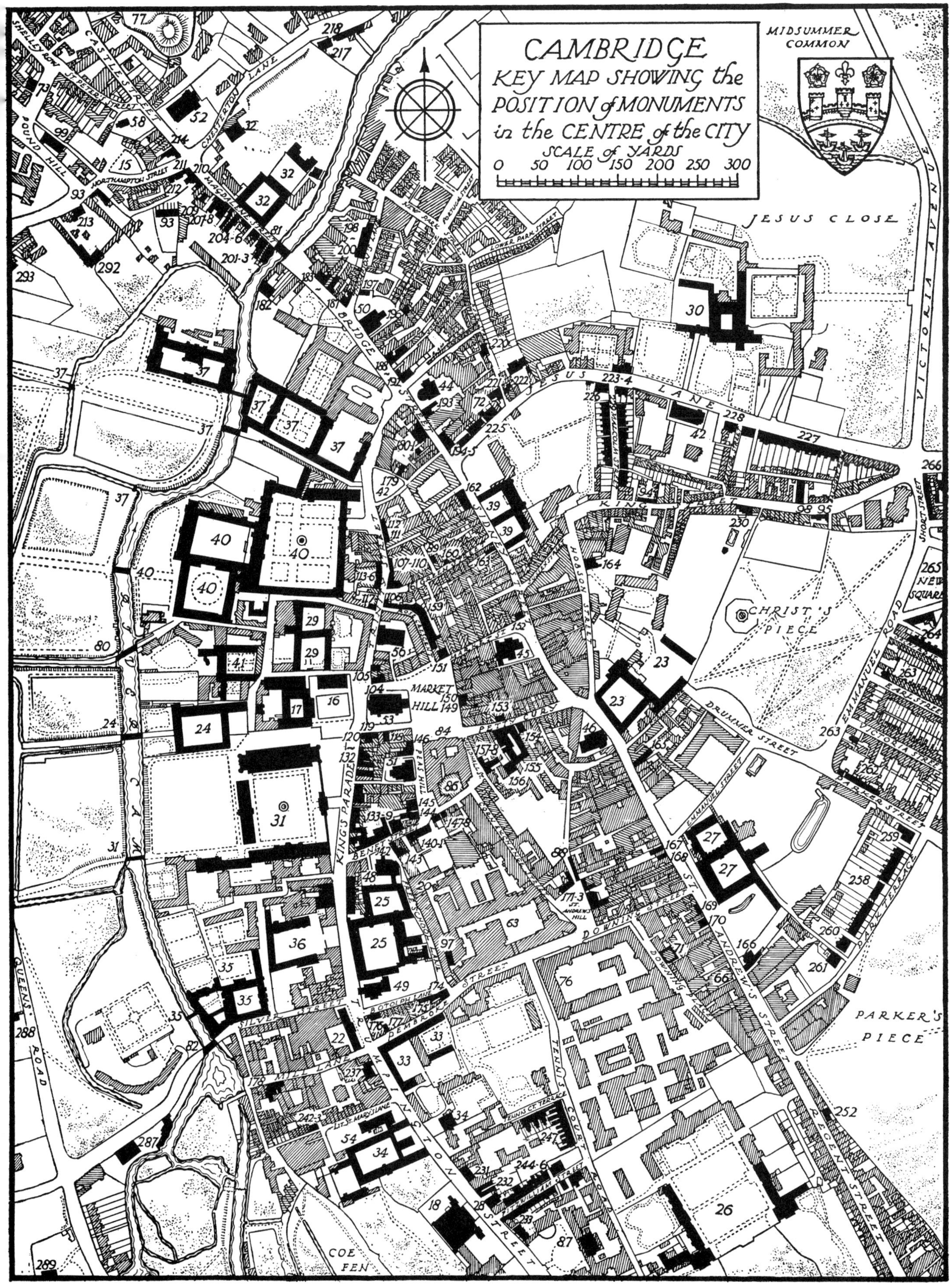
CAMBRIDGE
KEY MAP SHOWING the
POSITION of MONUMENTS
in the CENTRE of the CITY
SCALE of YARDS
0 50 100 150 200 250 300
MIDSUMMER COMMON
JESUS CLOSE
JESUS LANE
VICTORIA AVENUE
CHRIST'S PIECE
MARKET HILL
DRUMMER STREET
EMMANUEL ROAD
EMMANUEL STREET
PARKER'S PIECE
PARKER STREET
PARK TERRACE
VICTORIA STREET
NEW SQUARE
SHORT STREET
KING STREET
HOBSON STREET
SIDNEY STREET
BRIDGE STREET
KING'S PARADE
PEAS HILL
BENE'T STREET
PETTY CURY
DOWNING STREET
ST ANDREW'S STREET
REGENT STREET
TENNIS COURT ROAD
TRUMPINGTON STREET
PEMBROKE STREET
SILVER STREET
MILL LANE
BOTOLPH LANE
LIT. ST. MARY'S LANE
ST. ANDREW'S HILL
FITZWILLIAM STREET
QUEENS ROAD
COE FEN
CASTLE STREET
CHESTERTON LANE
NORTHAMPTON STREET
MAGDALENE STREET
POUND HILL
SHELLY ROW
ST PETER'S STREET
LOWER PARK STREET
PORTUGAL STREET
NEW PARK STREET
JESUS LANE
TENNIS CT. TERRACE
RIVER CAM

certainly distinguishable, are in poor condition. The motte is of interest for the traces of a berm below the summit perhaps marking the site of an apron-wall round the keep (see Sectional Preface p. lix).

The *Motte* (N.G. 44575919), a truncated cone in shape, is 200 ft. in diam. at the base, 34 ft. across the top, and rises 33 ft. above modern ground level on the N., 53 ft. on the S. The N. base is about 70 ft. above O.D. It covers some two-thirds of an acre. Paths are cut into the sides and original features are not

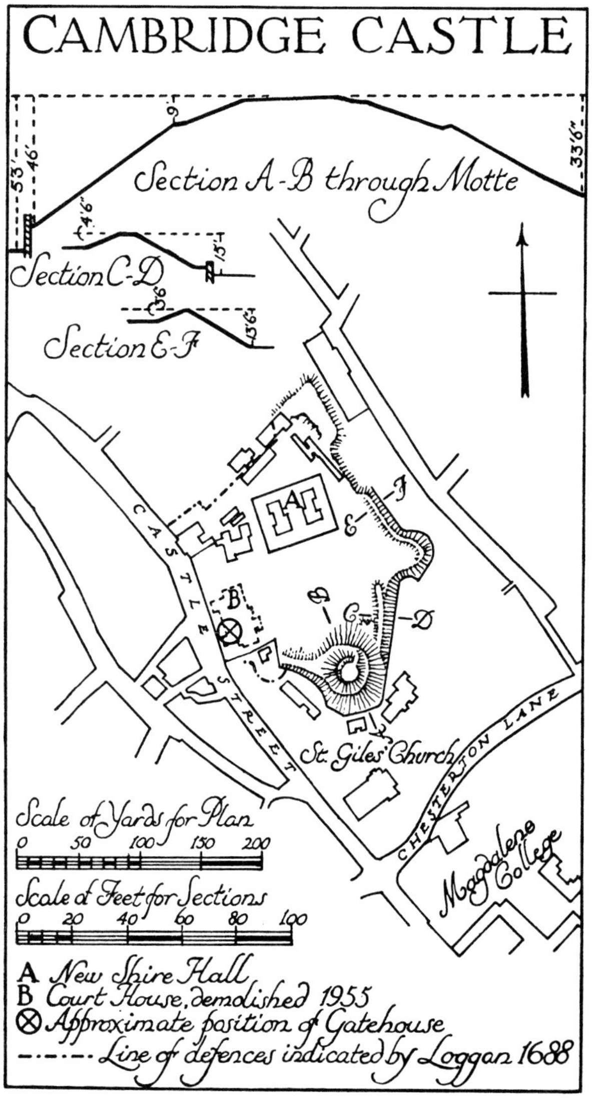

certainly identifiable, but on the S. some 9 ft. below the top a narrow terrace begins and curves downward to the E., where it is 10 ft. wide, then rises again towards the N.; it is shown clearly as a level berm in plans and elevations of 1785 (B.M. Add. MSS. 6735, 65, 68) and indicated in Fuller's view of 1634.

Leading N.E. from the motte the bank of the *Bailey*, 5½ ft. high on the inside, 8 ft. across the top, with a drop of 15 ft. to a modern wall on the outside, extends for some 40 yds. to where it is abruptly cut away down to the mutilated remains of the E. bastion of the Civil War defences. From the latter work a bank, 3½ ft. high inside and 4 ft. outside above the scarp of the old ditch, leads N.W. for some 40 yds.; it is then cut back. The N. bastion 50 yds. further on preserves more clearly the angularity of the Civil War earthwork, but is much cut into on the N. and W. The defences on the N.W. and S.W. are destroyed except for traces of the bailey bank branching N.W. from the motte. The total area enclosed was some 4 acres. (McKenny Hughes in C.A.S. *Proc.* VIII (1893), 173, and IX (1894–8), 348; W. H. St. J. Hope in *ibid.* XI (1905), 324; W. M. Palmer in *ibid.* XXVI (1923), 66, and *Cambridge Castle* (1928); J. W. Clark and A. Gray, *Old Plans of Cambridge, 1574–1798*).

The *Carved Stones* (Plate 28) referred to above were, except one, discovered 'under the ramparts of the bailey on the S.E. side of the gatehouse' early in the 19th century and included part of a wheel-cross head, five complete graveslabs and parts of two others, and a number of gravestones designed to stand upright. A sixth graveslab was found some yards outside the rampart. The gravestones and five slabs were lost, but drawings of them by the Rev. T. Kerrich exist (B.M. Add. MSS. 6735, 50–1, and *Archaeologia* XVII (1814), 228). The rest are in the Museum of Archaeology and Ethnology in Cambridge. They are of the late 10th or early 11th century and as follows: (i) wheel-cross head, diam. 14½ ins., with part of shaft, total height 17½ ins., thickness 4½ ins.; head with small central bosses, arms linked by plain ring and with marginal moulding continued down shaft, this last with interlace on front and back and key-ornament on the one surviving side; (ii) graveslab, broken across the middle, 65 ins. long, tapering from 19¼ ins. to 11½ ins. and 3 ins. to 4½ ins. thick; with symmetrical cross with U-shaped ends to longitudinal shaft, that at the head enclosing an incised cross, and four panels of interlacement; (iii) part of graveslab, 40 ins. by 18½ ins. and 4½ ins. thick; with incised wheel-headed cross and panels of interlacement flanking the shaft; (iv) part of graveslab, 31 ins. by 22 ins. and 5½ ins. thick; with upper part of cross enriched with interlacement, the ends of the horizontal arms returning vertically upwards, with interlaces on the sunk field flanking the shaft (C. Fox in C.A.S. *Proc.* XXIII (1920–4), 15).

(78) KING'S DITCH, boundary and defensive ditch to S. and E. of the old town, possibly late pre-Conquest and remodelled in the 13th century, shows only scanty surface remains. The name, loosely used in mediaeval times, by the 16th century was generally applied to the ditch shown in Richard Lyne's map of Cambridge of 1574, the course of which is traceable in the modern street-plan of the city. The ditch branched from the Cam near Mill Lane, ran along Pembroke Street, across the site of the old Botanic Gardens, where the University Laboratories now stand, along St. Tibb's Row and Hobson

Street, across the Fellows' Garden of Sidney Sussex College and along Park Street to rejoin the river nearly opposite the Pepys Building of Magdalene College (Richard Lyne's map in J. W. Clark and A. Gray, *Old Plans of Cambridge* etc. (1921)). The ditch N. of the river is described separately below.

The only surface remains consist of a slightly sunk area in the Fellows' Garden at Sidney Sussex College W. of a scarp running S.E. from the squash court. Along Park Street a ditch was open within recoverable living memory at the end of the 19th century (C.A.S. *Procs.* XI, 252), though a survey of 1629 shows that the King's Ditch was then little more than a sewer, nowhere wider than 5¼ ft. nor deeper than 2½ ft. (C.A.S. *Procs.* XI, 251).

Knowledge of the course and nature of the work was increased in the later 19th century by observation of builders' excavations. Those for the Pitt Press extensions in 1893 revealed a substantial ditch, dated by pottery finds to the late Saxon period, that ran along the N. side of Mill Lane. Some 25 yds. N. of, and parallel to, the foregoing was another ditch at least 10 ft. deep in which mediaeval pottery was found; here no Saxon ware was recorded (C.A.S. *Procs.* VIII, 255; C. Fox in Prehist. Soc. of E. Anglia *Procs.* IV, 227–30; T. Lethbridge in V.C.H. *Cambs.* I (1938), 329). Further to the N.E., excavations for the University Laboratories showed only a single ditch, which appeared to be mediaeval. Probably a prolongation of this was exposed in 1892 along the W. side of Hobson Street and in this area the earlier ditch was again found, but here inside the later alignment, an opposite topographical relationship to that found in the Mill Lane area (C.A.S. *Procs.* VIII, 263–6).

Historically, the town was 'enclosed' in 1215 (*Rot. Lit. Claus.* 1204–1224 (1833), 234). In 1267 Henry III caused ditches to be made around the town, with a walk 8 ft. wide alongside (*Ecclesie de Bernewelle Lib. Mem.* (ed. J. W. Clark), 122; *Liberate Rolls* 52 Henry III, M. 6, quoted by H. Cam in C.A.S. *Procs.* XXXV, 49–50). The Liberate Rolls also refer to compensation for houses that were pulled down to make way for the ditch and walk. In 1268 the watercourses were ordered to be opened and the 'great ditch' cleaned (*Cal. Pat. Rolls.* 1266–72, 196).

Thus the evidence, material and historical, seems to indicate that a pre-Conquest ditch was partly recut and partly superseded in the 13th century, divergences of alignment occurring demonstrably at least in the Mill Lane and Hobson Street areas.

The ditch N. of the river Cam, most often referred to as the 'ditch called Cambridge' ('le Kynges ditch' in a conveyance of 1592), now without surface remains, was possibly a stream canalised. It had an angular course; by reconstruction from the positions of narrow pieces of land belonging to the town (A. Gray in C.A.S. *Procs.* IX, 61) it branched from the Bin Brook S.E. of Merton Hall (Monument (103)), ran N.W. to turn sharply to the N.E. just short of the Hall, passed under Castle Street some 30 yds. S.E. of the Northampton Street junction, continued some 70 yds. into the Master's Garden of Magdalene College and then turned and passed W. of the Pepys Building of the same College to rejoin the Cam; the natural course of the stream seems to have continued E. to rejoin the river some yards further downstream (F. G. Walker in C.A.S. *Procs.* XV, 181–91).

The ditch has been assigned to the 7th century as affording a bridgehead for the town S. of the river (A. Gray, *Dual Origin of the Town of Cambridge* (1908), 14–15; H. Cam in C.A.S. *Procs.* XXXV, 38–9), but a date contemporary with that of the ditch S. of the river may reasonably be conjectured. About the beginning of the 13th century it seems to have been navigable as far as the church of St. Giles, then standing S.E. of the position of the present church (Monument (52)) (*Ecc. de Bernewelle Lib. Mem.*, 98–9). It had lost significance by 1278, for then in a perambulation of the castle bounds it was called 'vetus fossatum' and crossed, not followed (*ibid.* 167–8; A. Gray in C.A.S. *Procs.* IX, 63–6).

(79) Hobson's Conduit, also known as Hobson's River and Cambridge New River, includes a fountain and culverts etc., formerly and still in part supplied by the Conduit, and bridges over this last. The fountain stands at the conduit-head by the S.E. corner of the junction of Trumpington Road and Lensfield Road; the culverts etc. above and below ground distribute fresh water from the conduit-head to different places in the old town; and the position of the bridges is given below. The proposal to flush the foul King's Ditch (Monument (78)) with water brought in from Vicar's Brook was broached in a letter of 21 Nov. 1574 from Dr. Perne, Vice-Chancellor, to Lord Burghley and in the legend on Richard Lyne's map of Cambridge of the same year in Dr. Caius' *De Antiquitate*. Perne's further letter of 18 Jan. 1574–5 submits practical schemes to the Chancellor (*S.P., Dom.*, Elizabeth, 12, 103, no. 3, 1575).

The Lord of Trumpington Manor agreed to the diversion of water across the common fields by deed of 26 Oct. 1610, in which the watercourse is described as newly and lately made. This was the New River by which the water was brought from S. of Cambridge to the conduit-head and thence into the King's Ditch at the junction of Trumpington Street and Pembroke Street. A computation of levels, though necessarily approximate, seems to show that this could have scoured effectively only the westward length of the Ditch, to Mill Pit, and to explain the reason for completion, presumably before the S. range of Ivy Court of Pembroke College was begun in 1659, of a branch watercourse leading N.E. from approximately opposite the church of Little St. Mary to nearly opposite Free School Lane; the discharge of water further to the E. with increased fall may thus have been devised to scour the eastward and northward lengths of the Ditch. The N.E. branch continued to be the source of water-supply to the Old Botanic Garden until 1842.

Drinking-water was piped from the conduit-head to a new *Fountain* in Market Hill in 1614. The fountain was removed to the present position at the conduit-head in 1856, but the fountain that replaces it is supplied from the same source. In 1631 a third supply was drawn from the conduit-head for Emmanuel College and Christ's College; it now feeds the ponds and swimming-pools in the grounds there.

The cost of the scheme of 1610 was borne jointly by the town and the University. Thomas Hobson, carrier, (died 1630-1) and Samuel Potto (died 1632) left properties as endowments for the upkeep of the water-works. The New River is now administered by Trustees. For a detailed history and description see W. D. Bushell, *Hobson's Conduit: The New River at Cambridge*, etc. (1938).

Hobson's Conduit is of much interest as an early 17th-century utility supplying water for drinking, street cleansing and scouring the drains, though now a visual rather than a practical amenity. The open runnels in Trumpington Street and St. Andrew's Street are survivals of the open watercourse. The Fountain of 1614, rather later and much simpler than that at Trinity College, is a rare and pleasing survival.

The course of the New River, culverts and pipes and the positions of the dipping-holes are described by W. D. Bushell (*op. cit.*); the former are indicated on the accompanying diagram. The structures only, excepting brick culverts and piping largely concealed, are described below. At the source of Vicar's Brook, 'Nine Wells', in Great Shelford parish, is an obelisk set up in 1861. As the Brook approaches Cambridge the channel has been artificially improved to a width of 13 ft. at the top, between 8 ft. and 9 ft. at water-level, and a depth of 4 ft.. About ¼ m. N. of Long Road the entirely artificial channel, the *New River* of *c.* 1610, leads off across Empty Common, under Brooklands Avenue, and alongside Trumpington Road to the conduit-head at Lensfield Road corner where is an overflow to the sewers. N. of Brooklands Avenue the channel, 20 ft. wide and 2½ ft. deep, is raised in an embankment for some 300 yds. Spillways carry surplus water to Vicar's Brook to the W. and the pond in the Botanic Garden to the E.

The *Fountain* is a hexagonal building (8 ft. diagonal and approx. 19 ft. high), of ashlar painted, raised on a 19th-century cast-iron platform straddling the watercourse (Plate 259). It has a high moulded plinth and a full entablature with deep frieze and elaborate pierced cresting; from behind the last rises a domical ogee roof with fir-cone finial. The sides between plinth and entablature are divided into two heights by a continuous moulded string; in the lower height is a semi-circular shell-headed niche in each face; in the upper are inscription-panels in the E. and W. faces and vents of geometrical design in the other four. The renewed, and amended, inscriptions read: (E.) 'Thomas Hobson Carrier between Cambridge and London a great Benefactore to this University

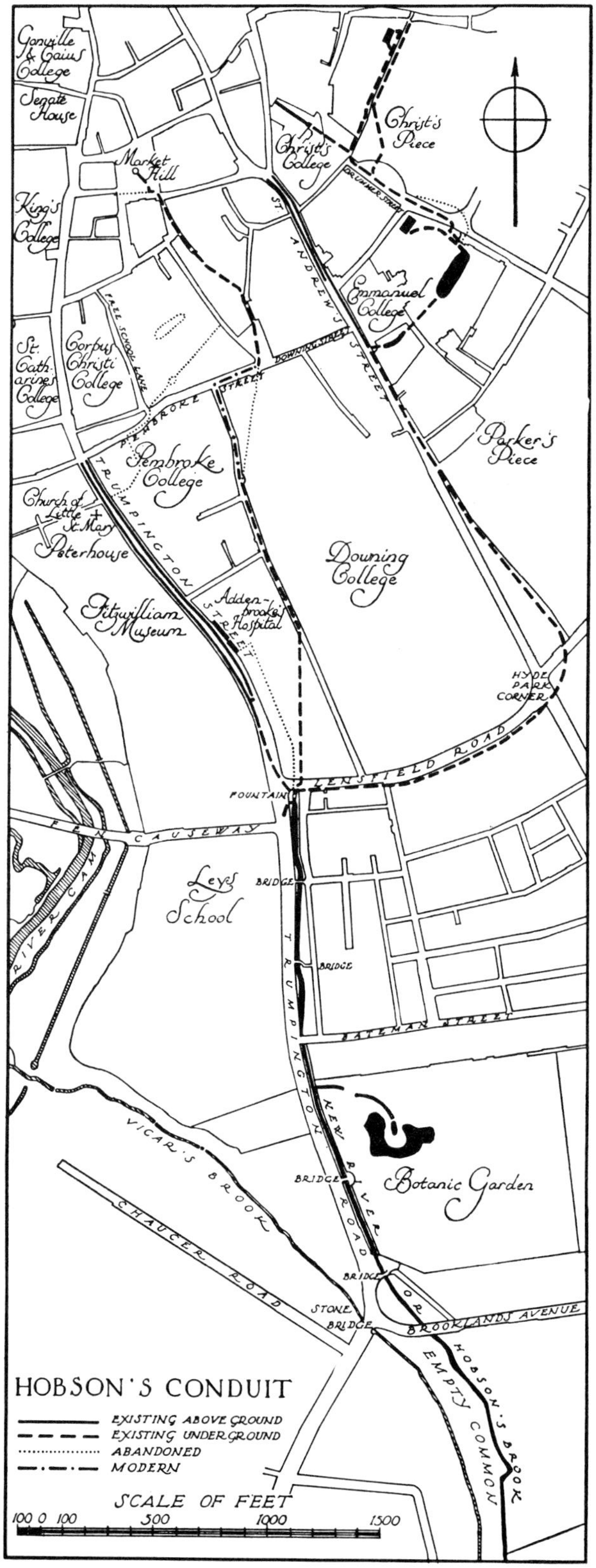

Town. Died January 1st 1630 in the 86th yeare of his age'; (W.) 'This structure stood upon the Market Hill and served as a Conduit from 1614 to 1856 in which year it was re-erected on this spot by Public Subscription'. The main cresting has putti holding gilded balls at four corners, a lion and a unicorn at the others, and between them on the W. side the Hanoverian Royal arms with lion and unicorn supporters, on the other sides plain shields in strapwork framing.

N. of the conduit-head the channel as far as Addenbrooke's Hospital has been enclosed and the water piped, though part of the open channel, with modern lining, survives in the Hospital forecourt. Thence two open runnels continue down each side of Trumpington Street to the sewer by Pembroke College; they have modern stone linings, though formed from the former single watercourse probably late in the 18th century after the decision in 1789 to widen the street.

The supply to Market Hill is now piped throughout and also the more north-easterly supply as far as Emmanuel College. There the main stream is carried in a covered brick culvert into the College grounds, but surplus water is discharged into the open gutters of St. Andrew's Street and runs into the sewer by Christ's College.

Four *Dipping-holes* survive under paving-stones, in Regent Terrace, before Emmanuel College, in Drummer Street and at the N.E. end of Milton's Walk.

Between Brooklands Avenue and Lensfield Road are four cast-iron *Bridges* and the W. bank of the river is bounded by cast-iron railings. The bridge to the Botanic Garden is of a single span of about 20 ft., of flattened arch form with pierced spandrels, the University arms in the middle and the iron-founder's name and the date, Hurrell, 1850, (Swann Hurrell succeeded his uncle Charles Finch, ironfounder of Market Hill, in 1847). The cast-iron handrails have moulded standards and two plain rails to each side; on the W. are iron gates hung between the larger W. standards and flanking railings, all with spear-headed uprights. The bridge at Brooklands Lodge (Monument (20)) is similar to the foregoing but without the shields-of-arms and the gates and with the ironfounder's name and the date obscured. The two bridges N. of Bateman Street are again similar to the first, without the gates, but the date is 1851. The mid 19th-century *Railings*, as far as the later enclosure round the Fountain, are similar to the bridge handrails but with elbowed stays.

(80) Garret Hostel Bridge carries Garret Hostel Lane, between Trinity College and Trinity Hall, over the Cam. It is of ashlar and cast-iron. William Chadwell Mylne was the designer. Tenders were invited on 3rd July 1835 (*Cambridge Chronicle*), and it was built by 1837. The contract was with the Butterley Iron Company, for £960 19s. 6d. (*ibid.* 26 Feb. 1836). The bridge is recorded to have been rebuilt six times before, in 1591, 1626, 1646, 1769, 1814, 1821. The 1769 reconstruction was by James Essex; of brick and timber, it was known as the Mathematical bridge. Until then, Trinity Hall and the town had been responsible for upkeep, but the former paid half the cost of this reconstruction to obtain future exemption.

Garret Hostel Bridge shows a horizontal use of the Gothic idiom, with an effect of breadth and dignity.

The bridge (Plate 38) is of a single depressed four-centred span of cast-iron between ashlar-faced piers. The ramped approaches are revetted in gault brick. On each side the arch has sunk spandrels and had, until recently, a heavy archivolt-moulding with a lion's mask at the apex. The cast-iron cambered parapet is elaborated with a succession of pierced trefoiled triangles. The faces of the piers contain sunk cusped panels.

(81) Magdalene Bridge, or Great Bridge, carries Bridge Street over the Cam, immediately S.E. of Magdalene College. It is of ashlar and cast-iron and carries a plate inscribed 'Arthur Browne Archt. 1823'. Browne is said to have been the contractor and one Bevan the structural engineer (*Cambridge Business Man*, 7 March 1918). The main sections were cast in Derby, the rest in Cambridge. The town contributed £150 and the University £600 towards the cost of £2,350.

The crossing is of considerable antiquity (see Monument (78)). The lands listed for pontage between 1236 and 1752 show that only landowners W. of the Cam were liable for upkeep of the bridge. The mediaeval record is one of repeated dilapidations and repairs, or rebuildings. The last timber bridge was replaced in 1754 by one in stone designed by James Essex.

Magdalene Bridge is the earliest cast-iron bridge in Cambridge. It is of interest for the linear decoration deriving from the 18th-century Gothic revival.

The bridge is of a single span built up of eight longitudinal cast-iron vertical sections between ashlar abutments. The lower edges of the sections are shaped to stilted semi-ellipses, the spaces between being filled with sheet-iron to form a solid panelled soffit. To each side, the spandrels contain fan-tracery decoration and the moulding at road-level is enriched with small trefoiled arcading. The open railings have bands of quatrefoils along the foot and trefoils below the handrails; the railings on the N.E. stop against ashlar piers with sunk quatrefoiled panels on the face and surmounted by wrought-iron lamp-standards; those on the S.W., which originally stopped against adjoining houses, now end in solid iron panels.

(82) Silver Street Bridge, or Small Bridge, carries Silver Street over the Cam immediately S.W. of Queens' College. Of cast-iron, brick and stone, it was built in 1841 in replacement of one of timber described as dilapidated in the *Cambridge Chronicle* of 5 August 1836. The iron span was cast by Charles Finch at his Market

Hill foundry (*Cambridge Business Man*, 7 March 1918). A panel with his name said to have been on the S. side is no longer visible. The total cost was £1,956 15s.

The bridge (Plate 38) is generally similar to Magdalene Bridge (Monument (81)) but the spandrels on both sides have ribbed panels enclosing shields-of-arms of the town supported by seahorses and with a castle above. The soffit is in six ribbed and panelled bays. Projecting upstream from the abutments are iron-faced cutwaters decorated with panels with two-centred heads. The approaches are bounded by short lengths of brick parapet-walling between pairs of stone piers; two of the S. piers support cast-iron lamp-standards. The bridge is strengthened with later iron ties.

(83) MILESTONES etc. are in the positions described below. From a bequest of Dr. William Mowse, Master of Trinity Hall 1552–3, supplemented by his executor Robert Hare, the latter bought the manor of Walpole as an endowment for the upkeep of highways in and about Cambridge. The estate was conveyed to the College in 1599. Within the present City, the surviving Milestones (i–iii) described below were set up under the Walpole Trust. In 1725 the first five miles along the old London Road were measured from the S.W. buttress of Great St. Mary's church by William Warren and small milestones set up; in 1726 the work was continued another five miles, and in 1727 another six to the Angel in Barkway. The total cost, with Woodward providing the stones and cutting the lettering, was £9 16s. defrayed apparently by Warren. In 1728 the first stone was replaced by Milestone (i) at a cost of £5 8s., out of the Trust fund. In 1729 the second and third stones were replaced by Milestones (ii) and (iii) of Portland stone for £2 18s. 6d. each. John Woodward seems to have been the mason again employed. In 1732 the datum mark was cut on Great St. Mary's church (see Monument (53), *Miscellanea*). For details of Milestones continuing beyond the City boundary, *Warren's Book* (ed. A. W. W. Dale, 1911), 264–8. (C.A.S. *Communications* IV (1876–80), 268, IX (1894–8), 304.)

Milestone (i), beside Trumpington Road opposite the junction of Brooklands Avenue, a tall rectangular stone with inset rounded head, is carved with the arms of Trinity Hall impaling Mowse (damaged), a pointing hand and the inscription in Roman capitals 'I Mile to Great Saint Maries Church Cambridge', 'A D' with an illegible date [1728]. 'Cambridge' has been obliterated and recut. *Milestone* (ii), beside Trumpington Road approx. 715 yds. N.E. of Trumpington church, retains traces only of a shield of the arms of Trinity Hall; it was dated 1729. *Milestone* (iii), beside the Hauxton Road approx. 1050 yds. S. of Trumpington church, is similar to (i) but with a shield of the arms of Trinity Hall and marking the third mile; the date [1729] is buried.

Stone *Wall-tablets*, two, set one above another in the street-front of no. 8 Castle Street, are inscribed 'Godmanchester Turnpike Road ends here' with an arrow, and 'To the Horse-shoe Corner Godmanchester 14 miles', late 18th or early 19th-century.

COURT HOUSE, see Monument (77).

(84) GUILDHALL stands on the S. side of Market Hill. It is a building of 1936–7, but reset in the wall on the first floor of the E. wing is the foundation-stone of the Guildhall previously on the site found during the excavations for the new foundations.

The Corporation insignia, plate and chest are described below together with the weights and measures kept here, at the Weights and Measures Office, and at the Folk Museum.

The *Foundation-stone* is tall and narrow and inscribed with a long Latin inscription, 'Faxit Deus haec nova Gilda Aula Communitatis Villae Cantabrigiae, in ipsissimo Loco veteris jam periclitantis et ruinosae, posita', etc., the date 1782 and the name of the architect, James Essex.

Corporation insignia and plate etc. (Plate 45): (i) Great Mace, 4½ ft. long, given by Samuel Shepheard of Exning, M.P., in 1710; silver-gilt, with assay-mark for 1710, maker's mark PY; of normal mace form with close-crowned bowl-shaped head, pierced scrollwork terminal figures linking the last to the first knop on the shaft, middle knop and shaped knop at end; embossed decoration on the head including the crowned arms of Queen Anne with lion and unicorn supporters and the initials A R and, round the sides, crowned rose, thistle, fleur-de-lys and harp and the arms of the town, all alternating with terminal figures flanked by the initials A and R; knops with embossed acanthus decoration; see (vii) below. (ii–v) Maces, set of four, 3½ ft. long, with assay-mark for 1723, maker's mark crowned P; all alike and generally similar to (i) but with the arms of George I and initials G. and R. and the end knops shaped to include two cartouches, one inscribed 'The Gift of Tho. Bacon Esq. Tho. Nutting Mayor 1724', the other with the arms of Bacon. (vi) Mace, 10½ ins. long, of copper-gilt, *c.* 1630; open-crowned bowl-shaped head, the top missing and the crown much damaged, divided by moulded ribs into four panels containing respectively the initials C and R, a crown and a rose modelled in relief; the shaft divided into four lengths by moulded bands; the flanges of pierced card-cut scrollwork, one broken. (vii) Mace-rest for (i) above, 1 ft. 10½ ins. tall, silver-gilt and bronze; with assay-mark for 1710, maker's mark a circle of five pellets, crowned and with P Y below; plate, with U-shaped top and embossed with an achievement of the arms of Queen Anne, mounted on a turned bronze stem with cylindrical end to fit in a socket; with red cords with two large and two small tassels knotted to the stem. (viii) Tankard, 10 ins. high, with assay-mark for 1762 and maker's mark C T W W in a circle; shaped bowl and lid with scrolled handle and pierced thumbpiece; engraved by W. Stephens with the achievement-of-arms of the town and a list of the donors, 1763. (ix) Coffee-pot, 10¾ ins. high, silver, with gadrooning, engraved with the achievement-of-arms of the town and the arms of Halsted and inscribed 'Gift of Thomas Halsted Esq. Mayor in 1767 Elected Alderman 1765 resigned 1775'. (x) Beaker, 4⅞ ins. high, with assay-mark for 1762, maker's mark JS; with nearly straight sides and moulded foot, engraved with the arms of the town and of Purchas and inscribed 'Gift of John Purchas Alderman Sept. 29 1759'. (xi) Beaker, 3¾ ins. high, otherwise similar to (x) but with the arms of Norfolk impaling Spencer and inscribed 'Gift of Wm. Norfolk Alderman Aug. 16 1759', with scratching beneath 'the cup and all the stoyps were e[n]graved by W. Stephens 1762'. (xii–xix) Salts, set of eight, 2¼ ins. high with assay-marks for 1764; with shallow rounded bowl on moulded stem and flared moulded foot; six given by Alderman James Burleigh, 1764, two by William Mott, 1764. (xx–xxvii) Spoons, set of eight, 8⅝ ins. long, with assay-marks for 1799; plain, inscribed 'Cambridge Corporation'. (xxviii–xxix) Spoons, two, generally similar to the foregoing but marks illegible; inscribed 'Gift of John Newling Alderman, Jan. 11 1763' and 'G. W. Hattersley 1915'. (xxx–xxxi) Spoons, two, generally similar to the foregoing but with assay-marks for 1813, given by Edward Goode.

Spear, 5 ft. 3¾ ins. long, with iron head and wood shaft with much-worn painting of the arms perhaps of Queen Anne and of the town and illegible inscription. Staff, 5 ft. 6½ ins. long, of wood painted with the arms of Queen Victoria and of the town, 'Rd. Foster Esq. Mayor' and '1839'; others in the Folk Museum are in better preservation. Halberds, pair, with pierced blades, tassels, and polished wood shafts, perhaps 17th-century.

Chest (Plate 46), of oak, 5¾ ft. by 2¼ ft. by 2½ ft. high, covered with sheet-iron, repaired, and iron-bound, the lid in two halves with two locks and hasps and eight hasps for locking-bars. Probably the new chest for the charters etc. made by Otte in 1531; 3 cwt. of iron, eleven iron plates and a thousand nails cost £1 9s. 4d. The total cost was £10 10s. 4d., which included carriage to London and back. (*Cambridge Borough Docs.* I (ed. W. M. Palmer, 1931) xlii).

Weights and Measure Standards: (i) Bushel Measure, of bronze, 10½ ins. high over all, 1 ft. 6¾ ins. internal diam., 8⅛ ins. internal depth, weight 69½ lbs., straight sided, with two facetted handles, three feet and band of lettering in Roman capitals with the name and titles of Queen Elizabeth interspersed with crowned initials E·R, rose, portcullis, fleur-de-lys, and date 1601. (ii) Gallon Measure, of bell-metal, 7⅝ ins. high, 17 ins. internal diam., 8¼ internal depth, with one handle, engraved with the achievements of the Stuart Royal arms and the town, 1646. (iii) Set of Cup Weights, 4 lb. to two 1 drams, fitting one inside another, the largest with a lid engraved with the arms of the University, 1822. (iv) Set of Winchester Measures, of bronze, ½ bushel, peck, ½ and ¼ peck, quart, the first three each with two handles, engraved 'University of Cambridge 1823'. (v) Imperial standard Yard and Bed, engraved 'University of Cambridge 1824', by Bate. All the foregoing Standards are obsolete. (vi) Set of Measures, gun-metal, bushel to ½ gill, the first seven with handles, and engraved with the University arms and 'University of Cambridge 1824'; the three small Measures engraved only with 'University of Cambridge 1824'. (vii) Set of spherical Weights, brass, 56 lb. to ½ dram, seven of the large weights engraved 'University of Cambridge 1824', by Bate. All the Standards in (vi) and (vii) are marked with Exchequer marks and Board of Trade Standards Department marks. They are still used by the city as local standards.

(85) Railway Station stands just over 1 mile S.E. of Great St. Mary's. It is of one and two storeys. The walls are of gault brick with stone and stucco dressings; the roofs are slate-covered. Originally the Eastern Counties Railway Station, it was designed by Sancton Wood and opened on 29 July 1845. The building was then symmetrical on plan and in elevation; an open-arcaded way on the E. matched that which survives on the W. and trains drew up in the former, vehicles in the latter (*Railway Chronicle*, 2 Aug. 1845, with sketch). To supplement the single narrow platform, about 1850 a timber island-platform reached by bridge and subway was added on the E. This was removed in 1863 and the E. arcaded way demolished to give the necessary space for the present scheme of a single wide platform with N. and S. train-bays; at the same time offices were added N. and S. of the building that remained (*Cambridge Chronicle*, 21 Nov. 1863). In 1893, with the removal of the Newmarket line take-off to Coldham's Lane, the platform was lengthened; it was lengthened again in 1908, to 1,515 ft., and again subsequently to 1,650 ft. In 1908 also more offices were added, partly in the S. end of the W. arcaded way. Encroachment upon this last has continued; the booking-hall etc. now occupies the whole of the five middle bays and a bicycle-store the four S. bays.

The Station is of interest as an early railway building and notable for the application of an Italianate style to new and entirely functional architectural requirements, with original and distinctive result.

The W. front of the original station (Plate 298) contains a continuous arcade from end to end and has a heavy unbroken crowning entablature; the roof does not show. The arcade consists of fifteen roundheaded arches, all originally open, with square brick piers, moulded plinths, imposts and archivolts. The four N. bays remain unaltered, with dwarf walls from pier to pier. The entablature has an architrave enriched with small plain roundels and a frieze with raised metopes alternating with shaped brackets under the wide overhang of the cornice. In the spandrels between arcade and entablature are original roundels containing modelled and painted arms, from the N., of St. Catharine's and King's Colleges, Trinity Hall, Pembroke College, Peterhouse, Cambridge town, Osborne quartering Godolphin for Francis Osborne, 7th Duke of Leeds (High Steward of Cambridge), Charles Philip Yorke, 4th Earl of

Hardwicke (Lord Lieutenant), Percy quartering Lucy for Hugh, 3rd Duke of Northumberland (Chancellor), Lord Lyndhurst (High Steward of the University), the University, Clare, Gonville and Caius, Corpus Christi and Queens' Colleges. Behind the arcade part of the original back-wall remains. On the ground floor the four N. bays have round windows; on the first floor are sash-hung windows in the five bays towards each end; all have stucco architraves. In the fifth and eleventh bays are open luggage-entrances with cornices.

The N. end has an archway to the W. returned from the arches on the W. front, but rather larger, for the passage of vehicles, with continuous moulded imposts and flanked on the E. by a small plain archway for foot-passengers. Close E. of the latter is the addition of 1863 with the wall rising to the height of, and capped by, a return of the impost-mouldings just described. The same arrangement, reversed, of archways was repeated originally on the E., for trains and foot-passengers; both these arches have been destroyed, but a large panel with stucco frame remains in the wall-space above impost-level flanked now only by the large W. arch. The main entablature is returned from the W. front. The roundels, as before, contain the arms of Magdalene and Christ's Colleges.

The S. end is identical in arrangement with the N. end, but the large W. archway is blocked to the springing and the small W. archway covered by later additions. The arms are of Jesus and St. John's Colleges.

The E. side comprises the back wall of the former E. arcaded way. On the ground floor are square-headed doorways and sash-hung windows, all with stucco architraves and cornices and with the window-sills continued as plat-bands; some have been blocked, altered or removed. The same design is continued across the extensions of 1863. The first floor was remodelled in the same year.

(86) PUBLIC LIBRARY, in Wheeler Street, between the Guildhall and Peas Hill, is a late 19th-century building. Reset in the Central Junior Library is a fireplace formerly in the house of John Veysy, which stood at the corner of Petty Cury and Market Hill. A second fireplace from the same place at Madingley Hall is dated 1538 and has the arms of the Grocers' Company.

The fireplace is of clunch with stop-moulded jambs and four-centred arch in a square head. The inner mouldings are enriched with carved paterae, the initials H V and a lion's mask, the outer with paterae, 'K Veysy' and 'Veysy' thrice, and the spandrels with a bird and the initial V in one, stylised foliage in the other. Over the arch is a crested frieze of tracery panels, partly defaced, with the monograms IV and KV. Early to mid 16th-century.

(87) ADDENBROOKE'S HOSPITAL stands on the E. side of Trumpington Street, E. of the Fitzwilliam Museum. Part of the original building of 1740 survives incorporated in the 19th-century and modern extensions of the Hospital. John Addenbrooke (died 1719) left £4,500 to found a hospital; land was bought in 1728 and building began twelve years later. In 1766 the hospital was transferred from the Trustees to a Court of Governors. A colonnade across the front and two wings designed by Charles Humfrey and in part paid for by John Bowtell were completed by 1825 at a cost of over £4,000 (*Cambridge Chronicle* 9 May, 26 Sept., 10 Oct. 1823, 7 Jan. 1825). The hospital at this stage is shown in C. H. Cooper, *Memorials of Cambridge* III, pl. facing p. 149.

In 1833 tenders were invited for two additional wards designed by Mr. Walter, architect to the hospital (*Camb. Chronicle* 17 April, 3 May, 4 Oct. 1833). Unspecified new buildings were completed in 1845 (*ibid.* 4 Jan.). In 1863 Matthew Digby Wyatt, in competition with A. Salvin, P. C. Hardwick and W. M. Fawcett, was appointed the architect for extensive alterations. For reasons of economy he proposed to make maximum use of the existing buildings and replied to charges of ugliness in his designs that he would be delighted to remedy it 'at an extra cost of from one to several thousand pounds according to the style adopted and the materials I might be permitted to make use of'. The building committee rejected a proposal to demolish all the old buildings and Wyatt then worked up a plan proposed by Dr. Humphry, one of the surgeons, for extending and heightening them; he prepared alternative designs for the elevations from which the committee made their selection in December 1863. Tenders for the works were invited and in May 1864 the contract was let to Messrs. Thoday & Clayton for £10,975. The work was finished in 1866. Further extensive additions have since been made. See also No. 13 Fitzwilliam Street (Monument (245)).

The fragmentary and much-altered original buildings of Addenbrooke's Hospital surviving are of little architectural significance; interest lies in their connection with a forerunner of those acts of private munificence that created and maintained the voluntary hospital movement.

Architectural Description—The surviving walls of the *Hospital* of 1740, of two storeys with a basement, form the rectangular block close behind the present main entrance. The front wall has been removed down to ground-floor level. The E., N. and S. walls are of red brickwork, the first being divided into three bays and with the middle bay projecting 9 ins.; the ground floor of the S. bay has been cut away. The original windows are sash-hung, except the two small round windows towards the E. end of the S. wall. Two walls, probably original, running E. and W. divide the interior equally into three; for the rest, no evidence of the internal arrangement survives; the staircase in the middle is modern. Two short cross-walls some 14½ ft. to N. and S. of this original block are perhaps remnants of the S. and N. walls respectively of the wings of 1823–5.

The W. *Entrance-gates* with short lengths of railing to each side are of scrolled and foliated wrought-iron and flanked by rusticated stone piers with cornices; extending thence to similar piers at the N. and S. ends of the street front are iron railings with standards with turned finials. All are of the 18th century.

The N. *Boundary-wall* of the site is of brick. It is of the 16th and 17th centuries, repaired and patched. Part is concealed by later sheds, part incorporated in the N. wall of the John Bonnett Memorial Laboratories and part, reduced to a dwarf wall, stands free behind the staff hostel in Fitzwilliam Street.

(88) Former WORKHOUSE of the parish of St. Andrew the Great, now shops, flat and store, stands at the S. end of St. Tibb's Row, N.E. of St. Andrew's Hill. It is of three storeys with a small cellar; the walls are of gault brick and the roofs are slate-covered. Built in 1829 (H. P. Stokes in C.A.S. *Procs.* XV (1911), 98) and superseded by the Union Workhouse in Mill Road (Monument (90)), it was sold by the Guardians of the Cambridge Union in 1838 (*Camb. Chronicle* 14 July 1838).

The building is a plain rectangle on plan, 89 ft. by 16 ft. The original windows are of squat proportions and sash-hung, with glazing of small panes. In the S. end is a mid 19th-century shop-front with plain pilasters dividing and flanking doorway and window. On the W. at first-floor level is a large opening with segmental head lighting and ventilating the staircase and latrines behind. The accommodation consisted of 'a sitting-room, large hall, back kitchen, cellar, yard, pump of good water and twelve good bedrooms'. The ground floor is more or less altered, but the upper floors are divided into rooms of nearly uniform size.

(89) Former WORKHOUSE of the parish of St. Michael, now in part a shop, the rest a store, stands on the E. side of Gifford's Place, 10 yds. N. of Green Street. It is of two storeys with cellars and attics; the W. wall is of brick, the other walls are timber-framed and plastered and the roofs are tile-covered. Two tenements on the site were rebuilt by the parishioners for the paupers in 1794 (H. P. Stokes in C.A.S. *Procs.* XV (1911), 118). See Monument (90).

The building is a plain rectangle on plan. The W. side to the road is more or less symmetrical, with a doorway in the middle flanked by sash-hung windows; later brickwork of adjoining properties extends into each end of the ground floor, on the N. as far as a doorway to the latrines, on the S. to include a window. Over the main doorway is a timber panel now blank but formerly inscribed S.M.P. On the first floor are three sash-hung windows, and in the roof three gabled dormer-windows. All the other walls are blank.

Inside is a large central room with an iron post in the middle supporting the upper floor and, against the E. wall, a fireplace. At the N. end and behind the latrine entered from the street is a dark closet. At the S. end is an unpierced partition to a narrow room now serving the adjoining property. The first and second floors each have three intercommunicating rooms of nearly uniform size.

(90) Former UNION WORKHOUSE, now Maternity Hospital, stands on the E. side of Mill Road, nearly opposite Tenison Road. The original building is of two storeys; the walls are of yellow brick and the roofs are slate-covered. In 1836 the Poor Law Commissioners ordered that the fourteen parishes of the Borough should be united for the administration of the laws for the Relief of the Poor under the name of the Cambridge Union. The new Guardians at first retained only six of the parochial Workhouses, St. Andrew the Less, St. Mary the Less and Holy Sepulchre, Holy Trinity, St. Andrew the Great (Monument (88)), All Saints and St. Edward, and appointed a Committee to arrange for a Central Union Workhouse to take two hundred and fifty inmates. The building was designed by John Smith and occupied in 1838; the site had cost £480. (C. H. Cooper, *Memorials of Cambridge* III, 147; *Camb. Chronicle* 2 Aug. 1837, designs on view in Mr. Smith's office.) Some alterations and extensions were made almost immediately (*Camb. Chronicle* 18 May 1839). The original lay-out included four courts with porter's-lodge, tramps' cells, bedrooms and offices, master's and matron's rooms, day-rooms, dormitories, baths, workshops, chapel and mortuary. Only the administrative block survives, amongst later buildings.

The *Administrative-block* is a long narrow building. The S.W. front is of eight bays; excluding the S.E. bay, the other bays are symmetrically arranged with a central doorway and the end bays paired under pedimented gables. At first-floor level is a continuous plat-band. The ground-floor windows are round-headed, the upper windows segmental-headed, and all contain double-hung sashes. The doorway has an architrave and a cornice supported on console-brackets. The pedimented gables have full cornices of which the lower members are continued across the building as a widely projecting eaves-cornice; each tympanum contains a small stucco panel with the date 1838. None of the other original walls contains features of note and the interior of the building has been completely modernised.

(91) Former FEMALE REFUGE stands 27 yds. S. of Christ Church to the S. of the Newmarket Road. It is of two storeys, with walls of gault brick and slate-covered roofs. An institution was established at Dover Cottage, East Road, in 1838 to 'afford to females who have been leading a sinful course of life, and express a desire of returning to the path of virtue, a temporary refuge where they may be sheltered from temptation, be provided

with proper employment, receive religious and useful instruction'. In 1839 the managing Committee advertised for fresh premises or a building-site. The site was acquired and the present building completed probably by 1841, the date on a tablet in the boundary-wall (*Camb. Chronicle* 15 June, 6 July, 26 Oct. 1839). It is now divided into flats, and partitions have been built in the larger rooms.

The Refuge is of interest as a 19th-century welfare institution of unusual character retaining the original buildings and much of the original layout.

The building is symmetrical and consists of a tall block, T-shaped on plan, sited axially upon Christ Church and midway between Napier Street on the E., Christchurch Street on the W.; single-storey ranges extend to both streets from the cross-arm of the T. The whole is enclosed on the E. and W., from the graveyard on the N. and private properties on the S. by a high wall. The entrance-front, the N. side, of the main block is in seven bays; the middle bay is partly screened by a single-storey porch; the end bays project. At first-floor level is a continuous plat-band; a second, narrower, band continues the sills of the first-floor windows. At the wall-head is a wide timber eaves-cornice with modillions. The low-pitched roofs are hipped. The porch has clasping Roman Doric pilasters at the angles with exaggerated entasis, an outer round-headed archway of brick in two orders, a modillioned eaves-cornice and a low-pitched roof. The entrance-doorway has a fanlight in a segmental head. The windows have segmental brick heads, blind recesses of similar form taking the places of windows in the end bays. Symmetrically placed at the roof-ridge are two large chimney-stacks with paired groups of flues linked by open round-headed arches. The other sides of the main block have windows and blind recesses as described above except in the S. wing where, on the upper floor, modern windows replace small windows, now blocked, probably originally barred, set high up under the eaves.

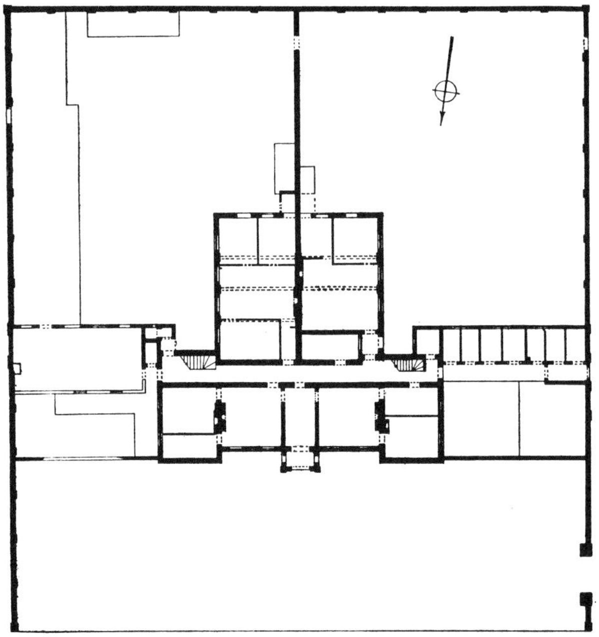

The low E. and W. ranges formerly comprised a laundry and small cells; they are now bathrooms and stores.

The interior is severely plain. The arrangement shown on the plan is, in the main, repeated on the first floor, but here some of the partitions in the S. wing are older than those elsewhere.

The brick enclosing wall is 12 ft. high with an offset and pilaster-buttresses at intervals inside. On the W., towards the N. end, is a carriage-way with massive piers and, nearer the middle, a shallow projection containing an arcade of two blind arches flanking a doorway, all uniform and with round heads; the doorway gives access through the low W. range to a side door in the main block. Symmetrically on the E. is a similar blind arch in a projection of the wall to Napier Street. A stone tablet in the S. wall is inscribed 'This wall and the ground on which it stands belong wholly to the Cambridge Refuge July 1841. This stone was replaced March 1884'.

(92) Former UNION WORKHOUSE, Chesterton, standing on the S.W. side of Union Lane, 195 yds. from High Street, is now Chesterton Hospital. It is of one and three storeys, with walls of gault brick, stone dressings, and slate-covered roofs. The purchase deed for the land is dated 17 October 1836. Mr. Bell's tender for the building for £5,716, to John Smith's designs, was accepted the same year. Completed probably in 1838, some modifications, in particular the enlargement of the N.W. end range, were made either during building or very soon after. Subsequently many of the iron casement-windows have been replaced by sashes and the kitchen has been enlarged. In modern times extensive additions have involved the destruction of most of the boundary-wall.

Much of the original building survives and is of interest in the context of social history. It is one of a number of Workhouses in England, with a remarkable plan devised for this special purpose, inspired by Sampson Kempthorne's designs accompanying the First Report of the Poor Law Commissioners of 1835. The details in the Tudor style here are Smith's applications.

The plan of the Workhouse consists of a cross with equal arms extending from a central octagon and ending in short ranges at right angles to them. The N.E. range contains the main entrance and a Boardroom above; it is flanked by low detached buildings, L-shaped on plan, bordering a forecourt. The octagon, containing the main Kitchen on the ground floor and the Master's Lodging above, is slightly higher than the three-storey wings and ends in a low-pitched pyramidal roof. The N.E. front of the entrance-range is the only one of any elaboration; it is in four bays, the middle two projecting slightly under a single gable, and has a stone plat-band at first-floor level, an eaves-cornice of oversailing courses of brickwork and a plain gable-parapet rising from moulded stone kneelers. The doorway in the middle and the windows have four-centred heads, the first having a rusticated stone architrave; the original door is in two panelled leaves. The other elevations are generally solely functional.

The interior, which is more or less altered, is for the greater part severely plain. The stone staircases have plain iron balustrades. The *Boardroom* has a cornice, moulded timber skirtings, window-surrounds and doorcases, all original. The *Kitchen* is covered with parallel segmental brick barrel-vaults on four segmental arches. The stack of the central fireplace is carried up through the middle of the *Master's Lodging* above where it is the central feature of a small square diagonally-set hall; from this last access is gained to small polygonal rooms and an entirely plain angular staircase. The fireplaces in the Lodging have fluted timber surrounds with bosses at the angles.

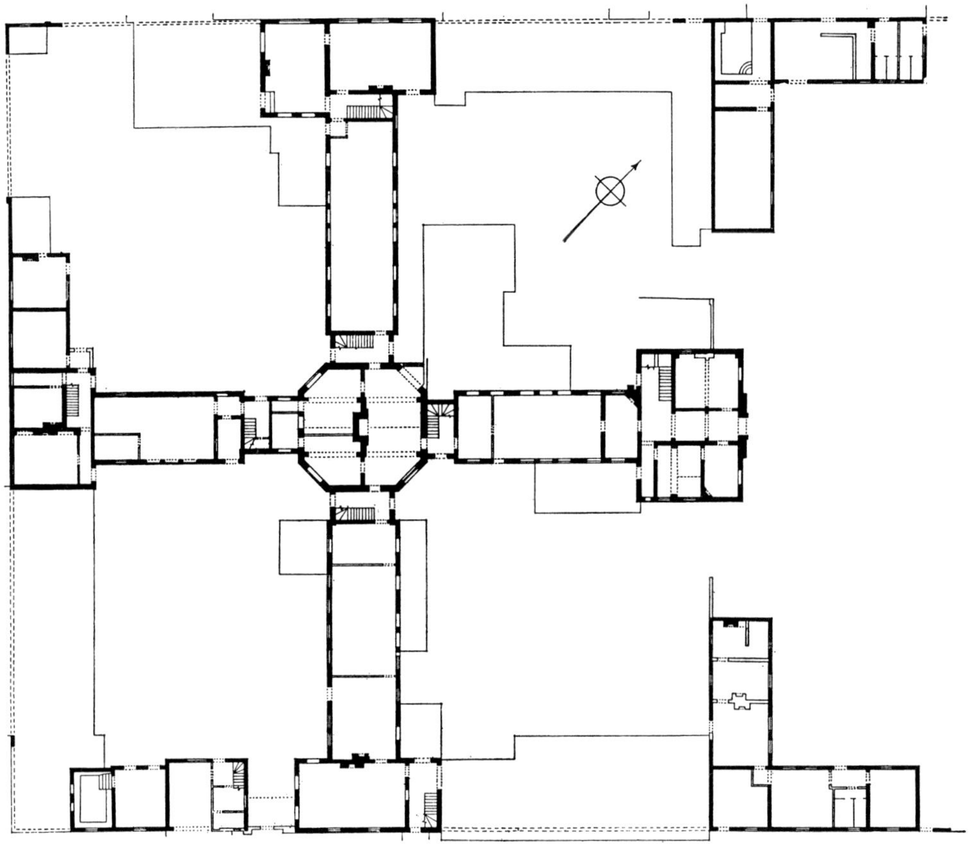

(93) Former STOREY'S ALMSHOUSES consist of two separate groups; the first group, of four dwellings, now shops and tenements, stands on the S. side of Northampton Street, 120 yds. W. of Magdalene Street; the second 60 yds. to E.S.E. of the first, in Tan Yard. They are of two storeys, the first with attics. The walls are of red brick; the roofs are tiled. The Almshouses were founded from a bequest of Edward Storey of Cambridge, bookseller, who died in 1693, for four widows of ministers of the Church of England, two widows and one maiden from the parish of St. Giles and three widows from Holy Trinity. The first group, for the clergymen's widows, was built in 1729 and the S.E. wing extended to provide an additional dwelling shortly after.

The second group consists of a range of six dwellings. It is probably in part the building, shown freestanding here in Loggan's map of Cambridge of 1688, which was a stable (31 Report of the Commissioners for inquiring concerning Charities (1837), 55). The ground floor is earlier than 1688 but the loftier upper floor was built or rebuilt in 1729. New Almshouses were provided on another site in 1844 (see below).

The group by Northampton Street is L-shaped on plan and comprises four dwellings. The wing aligned with the street is gabled at each end, though the S.W. gable-end is masked by an adjacent building; the S.E. wing is gabled at the free S.E. end. At first-floor level is a continuous plat-band, except where interrupted by a modern shop-front on the N.W.; upper plat-bands extend across both the free gable-ends at eaves-level. On the later extension the lower plat-band is deeper than elsewhere, of three courses, as opposed to two. The openings have flat brick arches and the larger windows are for the most part fitted with later sliding casements or double-hung sashes; small rectangular windows light the closets. On the roofs are four hipped dormer-windows, one of the two on the S.E. wing retaining an original leaded casement. The three chimney-stacks are largely rebuilt.

The interior retains original stop-chamfered ceiling-beams, those in the 1729 building with scroll-stops. The original arrangement seems to have provided a lobby, living-room and closet on the ground floor, and a bedroom and closet above reached by a stair flanking the chimney. The party-walls are of stud, lath and plaster. A number of 18th-century plank doors with original hinges remain.

The group in Tan Yard has a plat-band at first-floor level and to a height of six courses below this the walling is of 17th-century brickwork, the bricks being thinner and more vitrified than those above. The ground-floor openings have segmental arches with solid tympana above later rectangular timber door and window-frames, the latter with sliding casements; one S. window retains an original two-light frame. For the rest the features are generally similar to those described in the first group.

Inside, the ground-floor ceiling-beams are square and of heavy scantling. The dwellings each included an entrance and staircase-lobby to the N. and a living-room to the S. on the ground-floor, a bedroom above. The diagonal fireplaces on the ground floor have timber eared surrounds, and those above plain segmental heads; an inserted late 18th or early 19th-century surround in No. 6 Tan Yard is moulded and with paterae at the angles. The 18th-century doors are in two panels.

STOREY'S ALMHOUSES stand at the N.W. end of the site bounded by Mount Pleasant, Pleasant Row and Shelly Row. They are in two groups, of six and nine dwellings, of two storeys, with walls of yellow brick with freestone dressings and slated roofs. They were built in 1844 in the Tudor style (see above).

Each group forms a range symmetrically designed towards the front, with a plinth, a moulded string at first floor sill-level, a parapet-string and parapet-wall with moulded coping; projecting porches with plain parapets contain paired entrances with four-centred arches. At Mount Pleasant the three porches are set against slight projections of the main wall-face that are continued up to finish in small gables containing blank shields. The ground-floor windows are of three mullioned and transomed lights; the upper are of two and three lights. At the roof-ridges are chimney-stacks with grouped shafts on rectangular bases.

Inside, each dwelling has two main rooms on the ground floor and two above.

(94) WRAY'S ALMSHOUSES stand on the N. side of King Street, 85 yds. E. of the turn into Hobson Street. They are of two storeys, with brick walls, stucco-faced towards the street, and tile-covered roofs. A panel on the building is inscribed to the effect that Henry Wray, late of Cambridge, stationer, by his will proved 17 April 1629 gave these houses to be a hospital for the reception of four poor widowers and widows and gave also some lands and tenements towards the maintenance thereof; and that eight tenements here were rebuilt in 1838 by the Trustees, whose names are listed. The Almshouses now consist of a straight range of four dwellings towards the street dated 1698, but remodelled in 1838, pierced by a passage to a courtyard on the N. flanked by ranges each of four dwellings wholly of 1838.

The S. front of the earlier range has a plain plastered plinth and parapet-wall, the last with a panel inscribed 1698. It is symmetrical; the lofty archway to the through-passage in the middle has a chamfered four-centred head and the two doorways to each side have timber frames with heads of the same form with sunk spandrels. Three of the four ground-floor windows have fixed glazing of small panes with one pane hinged to open; the fourth window has a modern frame. The six upper windows are of three timber-framed lights with casements; they flank the inscription-panel referred to above. The back wall where not concealed by 19th-century additions is of red brick; the N. sides of the chimney-stacks are without rendering and the easternmost contains two sunk panels with arched heads of early 18th-century character. The ranges to the courtyard are of gault brick; they are similar to the industrial type of housing of the period and without features of note. The interiors of the dwellings are plain.

(95) JAKENETT'S ALMSHOUSES stand on the S. side of King Street opposite Belmont Place. They are of two storeys with walls of gault brick with red brick dressings and tile-covered roofs. A panel on the building has an inscription recording that Thomas Jakenett, formerly a burgess of Cambridge, and Agnes his wife founded an Almshouse in 1469 on the S. side of Great St. Mary's churchyard; that it was taken down in consequence of an Act of Parliament for paving and lighting the town, and rebuilt on this site in 1790 at the joint expense of the University and the parishioners of Great St. Mary's. In B.M. Add. MSS. 9412 f. 314 is an undated note [3 Feb. 1808?] that John Carter contracted for two tenements for the almshouses containing a room each for eight poor persons for £210.

The late 18th-century building consists of a single long range with a small gabled projection in the middle of the S. side. The street front is severely plain; it is symmetrically designed, with two doorways and four windows on the ground floor and four windows on the first floor. All the openings have flat brick arches and the windows contain timber frames of three lights with four-centred heads to the fitted casements. Midway between the floors, centrally, is the stone inscription-panel referred to above in a recess with segmental brick arch and sill; a second similar panel inserted over the E. doorway records an endowment by Joseph Merrill in 1805 of £166, the dividends to be distributed among the inhabitants of the Almshouses.

Inside are small staircase-halls flanked on each floor by bed-sitting rooms. Small extensions were made at each end of the S. side in the 19th century.

(96) VICTORIA HOMES stand on the N. side of Victoria Road, 170 yds. N.W. of the junction of Milton Road with Chesterton Road. The main building is of two storeys, with walls of white brick and slate-covered roofs. The Cambridge Victoria Friendly Society was founded in 1837 to provide almshouses for decayed members of benefit societies. The first homes were in cottages in James Street, Barnwell. In 1841 the range described below was built; it was designed by George Bradwell (C. H. Cooper, *Memorials of Cambridge* III, 177). After 1850 further accommodation was provided in separate groups of single-storey dwellings.

The building of 1841 consists of a single elongated range with a wide carriage-way through the middle. Both the N. and S. sides are symmetrically designed; each has a plinth, a plat-band at first-floor level interrupted by two colossal Roman Doric pilasters flanking the centre bay, and a deep projecting band at the wall-head representing the architrave and frieze of an entablature of which the boxed eaves form the cornice, the whole returning across the centre bay as the entablature of the order and pedimented. For the rest, the centrepiece has on the ground floor a wide archway with segmental head springing from stucco imposts, on the first floor a wide sash-hung window with tripartite timber frame, 'Cambridge Victoria Homes' painted on the entablature, and a clock in the tympanum flanked by the painted legend 'Estd. 1837'. The doorways to the dwellings have round brick arches and stucco imposts; the windows have flat brick arches, double-hung sashes and stone sills.

The interior arrangement to each side of the through-way consists of small staircase-halls the full width of the range, with doorways in both external walls, alternating with main rooms, and all intercommunicating. The whole has been modernised.

(97) OLD PERSE SCHOOL, now part of the University Department of Physical Chemistry, stands on the E. side of Free School Lane towards the southern end. It is of two storeys, with walls of brick and tile-covered roofs. The School was founded under the terms of the will of Stephen Perse, M.D., Senior Fellow of Gonville and Caius College, who died in 1615, and completed presumably by February 1623–4 when rules for governance were drawn up. The building consisted of a range running N. and S. with two W. wings, which formed three sides of a court open to Free School Lane. It was much altered in 1841–2 and bought by the University in 1890 when it ceased to be used for the original purpose.

Only the N. to S. range (22 ft. by 70 ft.) of the 17th-century School building remains identifiable. The W. front is entirely concealed by modern laboratories. The N. and S. ends have parapeted gables and are faced with 19th-century white brickwork; all the openings are of 1841 or modern. The E. side has the lower part masked, the upper faced with 19th-century brick and pierced for access to a modern E. wing.

The interior of the range is divided into two storeys by a modern floor. Recent alterations have exposed the walls in section; the original brickwork is 1½ ft. thick, with a 19th-century 9 ins. brick facing. The timber roof is divided into five bays over all by restored 17th-century hammer-beam trusses. These last spring from moulded stone corbels and have moulded pendants below the hammer-posts and centrally under each collar between arched braces; the spandrels are filled with pierced scrollwork and the bays are ceiled in plaster at collar-beam level. The trusses are copied in the modern E. wing.

(98) Former NATIONAL SCHOOL, now garage and workshop, stands on the N. side of King Street some 30 yds. W. of Belmont Place. It is of two storeys; the walls are of white brick and the low-pitched roofs are slate-covered. It was built in 1816 (*Camb. Chronicle* 23 Feb. 1816). Adjoining on the S. is a small contemporary dwelling, probably for the teacher.

The School building is rectangular on plan, gabled to N. and S. The longer sides are divided into five bays by pilaster-buttresses the height of the ground floor and have three over-sailing courses of brickwork at the eaves. Those windows unaltered here and in the teacher's dwelling are sash-hung. The whole is built with the severest economy. The interiors have been remodelled.

(99) Former POUND HILL SCHOOL with teacher's house, now a medical centre and private dwelling respectively, stand on the N. side of Pound Hill some 50 yds. N.W. of Northampton Street. The two adjoin and are of one build though separately roofed. The first is of one storey with cellars, the second of two storeys and a basement. The walls are of brick; the low-pitched roofs are slated. In 1810 tenders were invited for the supply of building materials and in March 1811 the School was described as 'lately established'. (*Camb. Chronicle* 13 July 1810, 2 March 1811). Additions were made later.

The School building is rectangular on plan, orientated S.E. and N.W., with the teacher's house on the N.W. end. The additions at the opposite end are of the later 19th and 20th centuries. The S.W. side is in five bays; the centre bay projects and has a stepped stone blocking-course inscribed 'Free School supported by voluntary contributions'. All the windows on this side have been enlarged except the one in the N.W. bay, with square head, stone sill and double-hung sashes. The end walls are masked. The N.E. side is divided into bays by pilaster-strips as shown on the plan; it retains the original entrance doorway and five original windows.

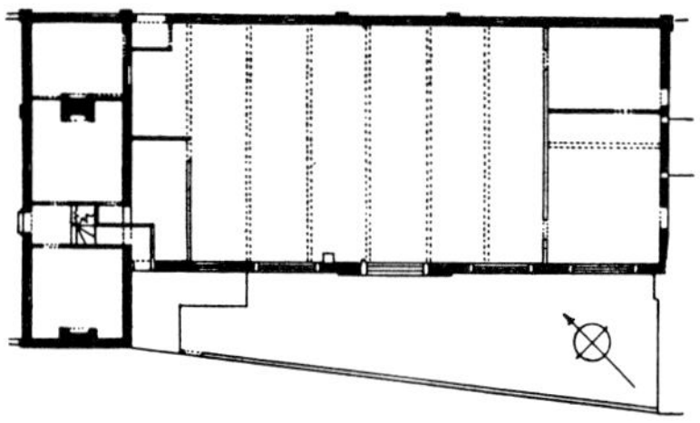

Inside, the roof of the main schoolroom is divided by trusses into seven bays; a wider eighth bay over the classroom to the S.E. is spanned by a longitudinal truss supporting the hip of the roof. Various partitions and a chimney have been inserted in modern times.

The *Teacher's House* is severely plain outside and in except for the pilaster-strips on the N.W. and N.E., as shown on the plan; the entrance doorcase is of timber, with fluted architrave, roundels at the corners and a shallow hood. The windows have double-hung sashes. The staircase is original, with plain balusters; spanning the passage behind it is a semicircular arch springing from console-brackets.

(100) Former Infant School with teacher's house, now a store, off the N.W. side of Albion Row, near Mount Pleasant, has walls of gault brick and slate-covered roofs. It is of one storey and was built probably *c.* 1825. (References to Infant Schools, *Camb. Chronicle* 28 April, 8 Dec. 1826). Later alterations and additions have been made.

The building is rectangular on plan and consists of a large schoolroom with a teacher's house on the N.W. end; the two are of one build but separately roofed. The first is lit by three sash-hung windows on each side and is open to the roof, which has three king-post trusses. The *Teacher's House*, entered from the schoolroom through a doorway in the middle of the N.W. wall of the latter, has had all the internal walls and floors etc. removed.

(101) National School stands on the S. side of Russell Street, 160 yds. from Hills Road. It is of two storeys, with walls of gault brick with stone dressings and slate-covered roofs. The School was established in 1845, presumably on rented land, for the site was given in 1847 (C. H. Cooper, *Memorials of Cambridge* III, 163–4). Subsequently two S. extensions have been made, the first replacing most of an original single-storey projection, and the boys' entrance-porch has been enlarged and heightened to two storeys. In 1952 the girls' timber staircase was replaced by one of concrete.

The original building contains one large schoolroom on each floor, a staircase across the N. end, and lateral N.W. and N.E. porches. The N. front to the street is of some architectural pretension although the narrow single-flight staircase intervenes between it and the schoolrooms. It is pedimented and has three tall round-headed arched recesses on the ground floor, blind below the returned impost-band and originally pierced above, with tall keystones rising to a brick plat-band at first-floor level interrupted in the middle by a stone panel inscribed 'National School'. The first-floor windows have segmental brick arches, stone sills and double-hung sashes. The timber cornice is continuous round the building and in the tympanum of the pediment is a round louvred opening. The entrances to the porches have low elliptical arches with stone imposts and keystones, these last rising to panels in returns of the main impost-band inscribed 'Boys' in one, 'Girls' in the other.

The schoolrooms are lit by five segmental-headed windows down each side. The original S. end is masked. The later 19th-century S. extension incorporates in the lower part of the W

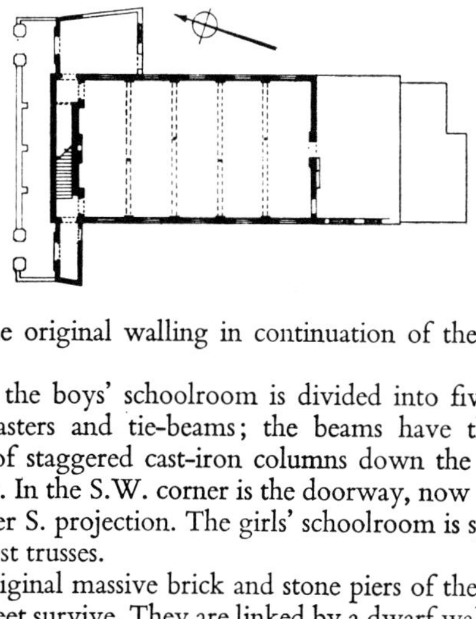

wall some original walling in continuation of the main W. wall.

Inside, the boys' schoolroom is divided into five bays by plain pilasters and tie-beams; the beams have the further support of staggered cast-iron columns down the middle of the room. In the S.W. corner is the doorway, now disused, to the former S. projection. The girls' schoolroom is spanned by queen-post trusses.

The original massive brick and stone piers of the two gates to the street survive. They are linked by a dwarf wall and have brick plinths and necking courses and stone caps with flat pyramidal tops. All the original ironwork has been removed.

(102) School, in Chesterton, on the N. side of High Street, 35 yds. N.E. of Ferry Lane, is of one storey. The walls are of brick, the roofs slate-covered. It was built in 1844.

The school is T-shaped on plan. The main cross-range is gabled and has in the S.E. gable-end a panel inscribed 'School Rooms in union with the National Society in 1844'. Additions have been made subsequently on the N.W. side of the N.E. wing. The building is severely plain.

(103) SCHOOL, in Trumpington, on the N. side of Church Lane, 86 yds. E. by N. of the parish church, is of one storey with brick walls and tile-covered roofs. A letter in the *Cambridge Chronicle* of 22 July 1843 refers to it as recently built.

The original schoolroom some 20 ft. by 36 ft. is half obscured outside by extensive later additions; it is gabled to N. and S. and has a moulded brick plinth. The E. wall is divided into three bays by weathered buttresses and in each bay is a window-opening with depressed triangular head containing a timber frame comprising three lights with trefoiled openings. The window in the N. wall is similar to the foregoing in design but larger. The position of the original entrance is not certainly identifiable. The inside has been modernised.

(104–338) Any choice of topographical sequence adopted in describing the remaining domestic buildings must be arbitrary. The following arrangement has first the area between All Saints' Passage on the N., Pembroke College on the S., Christ's Piece on the E. and the Cam on the W., then the Bridge Street and Castle Hill areas; these include the ancient parts of Cambridge, in the general sense of the name. Next come the Jesus Lane, and the Regent Street, Trumpington Street, Lensfield Road areas, the more recent developments to E., S. and W. of the old town and, last, the Cherry Hinton, Chesterton and Trumpington areas.

TRINITY STREET

E. side:—

(104) HOUSE, No. 1, on the corner of St. Mary's Street, is of three storeys with cellars and attics; the walls are of gault brick with stone dressings and the mansard roof is slate-covered. It was built early in the 19th century to contain a shop and a dwelling; the whole is now a shop and the ground floor, which probably had the entrance to and part of the dwelling in the E. part, has been altered. The S. and W. sides have a plain plinth, a plat-band at first-floor level, a small cornice, and a coping to the parapet-wall, all of stone. On the ground floor is a segmental-headed arch with rusticated stone abutments occupying the full width of the W. side and framing a modern shop-front; on the S. is an arcade of seven elliptical-headed brick arches. Of the last, the three to the E. are wall arches containing square-headed windows and a doorway, the others contain display windows with original reeded timber frames, hinged lights in the heads and renewed panelled aprons. On each of the floors above are seven windows to the S., two to the W., with flat brick arches; five on the S. are dummies; six on the first floor on the S., two on the W., have elaborate and unusual cast and wrought-iron guards with palmette and scroll ornament. Inside, on the ground floor are cast-iron columns with lotus-leaf capitals; on the first floor are original plaster cornices with lotus and acanthus foliage.

(105) HOUSE, No. 3, 15 yds. N. of St. Mary's Street, is of three storeys with cellars and attics; the walls are of brick in header bond to the W., timber-framed to the E.; the roofs are slated and tiled. It is an almost complete mid 18th-century reconstruction of possibly a late 16th-century building. On the W. the ground floor has been refaced and additions have been made on the E. in modern times. The W. front has plat-bands at first and second-floor levels, a simplified timber entablature and a parapet-wall with stone coping. The windows have flat brick arches and those on the top floor retain original double-hung sashes. Inside, the 18th-century staircase has close strings, turned balusters, moulded hand-rail and square newels with moulded caps. In the cellar is a moulded ceiling-beam, perhaps reused.

(106) HOUSE, No. 9, on the corner of Rose Crescent, is of three storeys with cellars and attics. The walls are of yellow and gault brick and the roofs slated and tiled. It is of the second half of the 18th century to Trinity Street, with an extension to the E. that is uniform in date and design with the development of Rose Crescent in *c.* 1825 (see Monument (159)). The earlier block has a modern shop-front, plat-bands at second-floor and eaves levels, a rendered parapet-wall and mansard roof. The windows have flat brick arches and contain double-hung sashes set well back from the wall-face. The later block has on the S. an early 19th-century timber shop-front divided into three bays by moulded pilasters with shaped brackets above supporting a continuous shallow cornice of wide projection; the brackets have turned acorn-shaped pendants. Two of the bays retain in the upper part the glazing-bars of the original windows; the third bay has an inserted doorway.

(107) HOUSE, No. 13, on the corner of Green Street, is of four storeys with cellars (Plate 301). The walls are of brick in Flemish bond. It was built late in the 18th century, possibly in 1783, and remodelled inside early in the 19th century when the timber shop-front on the W. was inserted. This last is in three wide bays separated by two narrow bays and all divided and flanked by plain Ionic pilasters supporting a continuous entablature with modillion-cornice, the whole standing on a tall stone plinth pierced by three cellar windows fitted with wrought-iron latticework guards. One narrow bay contains the doorway, with panelled lintel and rectangular light above, the last with a decorative pattern of radiating scalloped and scrolled metal glazing-bars; a similar lintel and light surmount a window in the other narrow bay, and windows occupy the whole of the wider bays, all with renewed thin glazing-bars framing large rectangular panes. The walling of red brick above is plain, with ranges of four windows on each floor, a

simplified brick and stone cornice and parapet-wall with stone coping. The windows have flat brick arches and double-hung sashes and those on the first floor projecting cast-iron guards of Gothic design. On one of the bricks is scratched JH 1783. The S. side is of gault brick.

(108) HOUSE, No. 14, next N. of the foregoing, is of three storeys with attics. The walls are of exposed timber-framing with pargeted infilling and the roofs are tiled. It was built in *c.* 1600; an E. wing was added and the ground floor has since been cleared and extended to the E. for a modern shop with a modern front. All the pargeting has been restored in the present century. Before 1893 it was Foster's Bank and previously the Turk's Head.

This house, though much restored, is important as one of the only two timber-framed domestic buildings of *c.* 1600 of any elaboration surviving in the city.

The street-front (Plate 305) is in two symmetrical gabled bays, with the third storey and the gabled attics projecting. Turned timber columns on head-corbels and carrying brackets carved with scrolled grotesques divide and flank the bays and support the projections. In each bay, rising the full height of each of the upper storeys is an oriel-window of three transomed lights on the face and one in each canted side. The gable-ends contain attic windows, renewed in the 19th century, and have restored moulded fascia-boards and square jewelled posts at the apices with pierced pendants and tall turned finials. The timber studs are widely spaced and the rails few, the latter moulded, and both include restorations; the modelling of the renewed pargeting is copied from the original.

Inside, the first and second floors have cross and longitudinal chamfered ceiling-beams, the latter with rebated and curved stops. On the second floor is an original timber-framed partition across the middle. The E. wing was originally timber-framed but has been cased in brick; it is loftier than the original building.

(109) HOUSE, No. 15 (Plate 303), next N. of the foregoing, is of three storeys with cellars and attics. The walls are of brick and the roofs tiled. It was built in the first half of the 18th century. Later in the same century the staircase was renewed. The shop-front is modern and low additions have been made on the E. The red brick street-front has plat-bands at both floor levels, a brick modillion-cornice returned within the frontage and low parapet-wall. An original timber casing with panelled pilasters and enriched console-brackets supporting an open pediment frames the entrance-doorway and fanlight; the last contains a Gothic pattern of glazing-bars and has a small mask on the keyblock to the semicircular arch. The windows above, three to each floor, have flat brick arches and the hipped dormer-windows moulded timber eaves-cornices. The chimney-stack is of gault brick. Inside, the staircase has cut strings, turned newels, moulded handrails and thin square balusters.

(110) HOUSE, Nos. 16 and 16a, next N. of the foregoing and adjoining the 'Blue Boar', is of three storeys with attics and cellars. The walls are of brick with stone dressings and the roofs slated. The street-front (Plate 303), built in the late Tudor style, has on the rainwater head the initials and date I.B. 1840, a date applicable to the building. It has been modernised inside. On the ground floor is a modern shop-front. The windows have chamfered stone reveals and timber frames; those on the first and second floors are of two timber-mullioned square-headed lights, the lower transomed but with the mullions below the transoms removed and the enlarged openings fitted with casements; all have contemporary scrolled wire guards. The attic storey, demarcated by a moulded string, has two parapeted gables and contains three windows.

(111) HOUSES, Nos. 20a and 22, 57 yds. N. of Green Street, are of three storeys. The W. walls are of brick, of the S. tenement of a plain dark red with lighter dressings, of the N. red with many blue vitrified headers and plain red dressings; the E. walls are timber-framed and plastered. The roofs are tiled. They are of the same date in the early 18th century and uniform in detail but the differences in the brickwork and closer spacing of the windows of the S. tenement suggest different building contracts. Short E. wings make the total plan half H-shaped. The interiors were remodelled in the 19th century; the ground floors have since been cleared and extended E. for a modern shop and the upper floors combined to serve Trinity College, together with the upper floors of the adjoining houses. The street-front has a plat-band at second-floor level and a bold timber eaves-cornice; the division between the original tenements is marked by a broad pilaster-strip that has light red brick S. quoins. The windows, of rather tall proportions, have flat brick arches and contain double-hung sashes in frames set near the wall-face. The framed E. wall has a timber eaves-cornice. In No. 20a an early 19th-century staircase, with cut strings and slim square balusters, rises from first to second floor.

(112) HOUSE, Nos. 23 and 24, next N. of the foregoing, is of three storeys with attics. The walls are of red brick with stone dressings and the roofs tiled. It was built at the beginning of the 18th century; the ground floor was subsequently cleared for a shop and the present shop-front is modern. The street-front above, after becoming unsafe, has been rebuilt in modern times with new bricks, but incorporates some original features. The E. wall is entirely masked by 19th-century additions. The W. front has rusticated quoins and a plat-band at second-floor level, all of stone, and the original timber enriched modillion-cornice. The windows, four to each floor, have flat brick arches with modern grotesque mask keystones; they contain double-hung sashes in original frames flush with the wall-face. On the roof are two 19th-century dormer-windows.

Inside, the 'Junior Parlour' of Trinity College extends the full length of the first floor and is lined with original ovolo-moulded and fielded panelling with a moulded dado-rail. The panelling above the modern fireplace has been rearranged. This room and some others retain original doors of two-fielded panels.

W. side:

(113) House, No. 29, some 55 yds. N. of Trinity Lane, is of three storeys with attics. The walls are of red brick and the roofs tiled. It was built about the middle of the 18th century and nearly doubled in depth in the 19th. The ground floor has been cleared and further extended to the W. in modern times for a shop with modern front, but the entrance to the house, with early 19th-century doorcase, remains to the S. of the last and has panelled reveals and a fanlight with intersecting tracery in a square head. The rest of the front is plain, with three double-hung sash-windows on each of the upper floors, a timber modillion-cornice returned within the frontage and two hipped dormer-windows with sliding sashes. Inside, the 19th-century staircase, with close strings, square newels and thin turned balusters, has been rearranged and now blocks the former through-passage. The plastered W. gable of the original house is visible above the staircase.

(114) Houses, Nos. 30 and 31, next S. of the foregoing, are of three storeys with attics and cellars. The walls are of red brick with vitrified headers and lighter red brick dressings. The roofs are tiled. Though separate tenements, they were built at the same time about the middle of the 18th century to a uniform design. No. 30 has been extended to the W. to link with a cottage probably of the early 18th century; No. 31 was altered inside in the 19th century. The first has a late 18th-century, the second a modern, timber shop-front. The old front has two doorways with fanlights, with a round head and a segmental head respectively, alternating with two wide segmental-headed display-windows containing a Gothic pattern of glazing-bars; the arches have moulded archivolts springing from reeded pilasters; the apron-walls below the windows are faced with panelling framed round the segmental heads of the cellar windows. The street-front has ranges of five windows over all on each of the upper floors and a continuous timber dentil-cornice returned within the frontage. The sills of the first-floor windows of No. 30 have been lowered. Between the two houses is an original lead rainwater downpipe with moulded head. Inside, No. 30 retains some good original fittings, including a staircase with cut strings, turned balusters and newels and moulded handrail, doors of six fielded panels with brass rim-locks, and moulded stone fireplace-surrounds. One room has an original dentil-cornice.

(115) House, No. 32, next S. of the foregoing and 35 yds. N. of Trinity Lane, is of three storeys with attics. The walls are of red brick, the roofs tiled. It was built about the middle of the 18th century and extended W. early in the 19th. John Bowtell, bookbinder and antiquary, lived here. The ground floor of the original house has been cleared for a modern shop with modern front. Each of the two first-floor windows has a rubbed brick arch in the form of a Venetian-window head, though without structural uprights, the opening containing a timber tripartite sash-hung frame. The plain second-floor windows are squarely proportioned. The slight cornice is of stone, and returned within the frontage, and the parapet-wall has been rebuilt. Inside, the 18th-century part contains original cornices and panelled doors and a staircase with close-strings, square newels, thin turned balusters and moulded handrail. In the addition is a good early 19th-century staircase turned in a spiral round a well; it has cut strings, slender square balusters and moulded handrail. The well is lit through a roof-lantern.

(116) House, No. 34, next S. of the foregoing, is of three storeys. The walls are of brick and, to the W., partly timber-framed. The roofs are tiled. It was built in the first half of the 18th century. The ground floor has been cleared for a modern shop with modern front. The E. wall has the remains of stopped plat-bands at first and second floor-levels, a brick dentil-cornice and modern parapet-wall. The windows, three to each floor, have flat brick arches now painted; on the first floor the arch to the middle window has a reeded and fluted keystone, those to the side windows have plain brick keys; on the second floor the keystone in the middle is rusticated. The W. wall has a brick facing to the ground floor, plastered framing above and a timber eaves-cornice. Inside is a good original staircase with cut strings, turned balusters and newels and a moulded handrail, ending in a spiral curve at the foot. The first-floor E. room is lined with fielded panelling of *c.* 1725, with dado-rail and cornice, retaining doors of two panels.

(117) House, No. 38, at the corner of Trinity Lane, is of three storeys with attics and cellars. The walls are of red and gault brick, the roofs tiled. It was built probably in the second half of the 18th century. The inside is much altered and the ground floor occupied by a shop with a 19th-century front much restored. The E. wall has a stone plat-band at eaves-level and a parapet-wall. The windows have flat brick arches and contain double-hung sashes; they are fitted with cast and wrought-iron guards. The whole is plain and only of note in that it contributes to the pleasant 18th-century aspect of the street.

St. Mary's Passage

S. side:—

(118) House, No. 3, 28 yds. E. of King's Parade, is of two storeys with cellars and attics. The walls are of brick and plastered timber-framing; the roofs are tiled and slated. The framing is probably of the 17th century but the building has been extensively modernised and the front almost entirely rebuilt in the present century in an elaboration of the style of the earlier period. Inside, except for some brickwork in the cellars, no original structural work remains visible. On the first floor is an original panelled door.

(119) House, No. 1, 14 yds. E. of King's Parade, is of two storeys with cellars and attics. The walls are of plastered timber-framing and the roofs tiled. It was built in the 17th century. In the 18th century the N. front was remodelled and heightened by means of a screen-wall to present an appearance

of three full storeys to the street. The shop-front was inserted or renewed and the first-floor windows were remodelled late in the 19th century. The ground floor has since been cleared and extended S. for a modern shop. On the N. the three first-floor windows have 19th-century architraves, brackets and cornices. The windows above retain 18th-century frames containing double-hung sashes; only the middle window is functional, being in fact a dormer-window; the flanking windows are dummies set in the screen-wall. At the wall-head is a timber modillion-cornice. Inside is a large central chimney-stack; in the cellar and on the ground floor are some stop-chamfered ceiling-beams.

King's Parade

E. side (see illustration facing p. 321 and Plate 303):—

(120) House, No. 22, at the corner of St. Mary's Passage, is of three storeys with cellars and attics. The walls are of plastered timber-framing and of red brick with rubbed dressings; the roofs are tiled. The building was framed in the 17th century; the staircase-bay was probably added and the N., W. and probably part of the S. walls were faced in brick in *c.* 1730. The interior of the ground floor has been much altered for a shop; the shop-fronts to N. and W. are of *c.* 1900. To the N., the windows on the upper floors have slightly cambered brick arches; those on the first floor have had the sills lowered in modern times. The wall is finished with a timber modillion-cornice and parapet-wall and in the roof are two gabled dormer-windows. The gabled W. wall has, above the shop-front, a colossal pilaster-strip to each side capped by a return of the modillion-cornice; between both caps the continuation of the cornice is flattened and simplified by omission of the modillions. Blind recesses take the places of windows here and the gable ends in a large rebuilt rectangular chimney-stack. The 18th-century rainwater downpipe has a moulded head. At the E. end of the building is a stack similar to that just described. The S. wing and the containing-walls of the staircase on the S.E. are timber-framed. The 18th-century oak staircase rises easily around a square well; it has close strings, square newels and a moulded handrail; the balusters are encased. The house contains a shaped and panelled stone fireplace-surround of *c.* 1700 and some reused 17th-century oak panelling.

(121) House, No. 19, 17 yds. S. of St. Mary's Passage, is of three storeys with cellars and attics. The walls are of roughcast timber-framing and modern brick; the roofs are tiled. It was built in *c.* 1700; the ground floor has been altered for a shop and the whole modernised and extended to the E. The shop-front and the fenestration above are of the late 19th century. Inside is a chamfered ceiling-beam and a reused 16th-century moulded timber, both in the cellars. The steep early 18th-century staircase has square newels and widely spaced turned balusters.

(122) House, No. 18, next S. of (121), is of three and two storeys with cellars and attics. The walls are of plastered timber-framing and the roofs tiled. It consists of a mid 16th-century block to the Parade and an E. wing of the mid 17th century. Extensive alterations have been made in modern times; part of the ground floor is a shop, with a late 19th-century front, the rest and all the upper floors are now incorporated with the next house (123). The W. front projects at second floor-level; the whole face above the ground floor has applied sham timber-framing and windows of *c.* 1900. The E. end of the E. wing has pargeting in panels of simple combed decoration and a gable with moulded bargeboards; the N. wall projects at first-floor level, and in the attic are transeptal dormers. Inside, the house contains chamfered ceiling-beams.

(123) House, No. 17, next S. of (122), is of three storeys with cellars and attics. The walls are of plastered timber-framing and modern brick; the roofs are tiled. Built in the 16th century, it has been much altered in modern times, and additions of three storeys and one storey made on the E. The ground floor has a 19th-century shop-front. The upper part, projecting at second-floor level, has added modern timbering and balustraded parapet in 17th-century styles. On the roof are three restored early 18th-century hipped dormer-windows. A projection on the E. rising the full height of the house and with a hipped roof may have contained a staircase. Inside is a chamfered ceiling-beam in the cellar. The staircase in the E. extension, in a 17th-century style, is modern.

(124) House, No. 16, next S. of (123) and 20 yds. N. of St. Edward's Passage, is of three storeys with attics and cellars. The walls are of plastered timber-framing and the roofs tiled. It was built in the 17th century and altered extensively in the 19th. The shop-front is of the late 19th century and the oriel-window rising through the two upper storeys, while perhaps representing an original feature, has sashes of the same period. The wall-face is decorated with sham timber-framing.

(125) House, No. 14, 8 yds. N. of St. Edward's Passage, is of five storeys with cellars and attics. The walls are of red brick with rubbed dressings, the mansard roofs tiled. It was built in 1787 by a Mr. York, upholsterer, on the site of 'God's House' or Driver's House (Downing College. Library: John Bowtell MSS. 3/305). The staircase was rebuilt early in the 19th century. A number of alterations have been made on the E. and the ground floor has been cleared for a modern shop with modern front.

Though the site is so restricted, building to such a height is exceptional in Cambridge houses before 1800, and rare thereafter.

The arrangement of the W. side is shown in the illustration facing p. 321. The plat-bands have oversailing courses; at eaves-level is a timber or plaster fluted frieze and cornice, with human masks on cartouches centrally over each window. The parapet-wall has been rebuilt. The windows have flat brick arches and contain double-hung sashes in slightly recessed frames. The roof is in two spans with a flat between. The E. wall has the ground floor concealed and a single original window with segmental head on each of the upper floors; the first-floor window has been altered. In the S. wall a central window to the staircase extending through the second and third storeys has been blocked by a later building; centrally above, on the third and fourth floors, are single windows.

Inside, the plan consists generally of two rooms separated by the staircase leading N. and S. A number of original fittings survive; on the first-floor landing is a dado of fielded panels; the Drawing-room on the same floor has a panelled dado and plaster cornice with acanthus enrichment; elsewhere are fitted cupboards with panelled doors and a fireplace with eared surround. In the W. part of the cellars are some stop-chamfered ceiling-beams.

(126) House, No. 12 and 12a, at the S. corner of St. Edward's Passage, probably always divided into two tenements though of one build, is of three storeys with cellars and attics. The walls are of plastered timber-framing, the roofs tiled. It was built on an irregular half H-shaped plan in the 18th-century, with the linking range to the W. and long and short E. wings, that to the N.E. hipped, that to the S.E. gabled. The ground floor has been altered for modern shops with modern fronts. On the S.E. are modern white brick and slated additions. The arrangement of the W. side is shown in the illustration facing p. 321; the window-frames are almost flush with the wall-face; the eaves-cornice is coved. The large rectangular chimney-stack at the ridge of the mansard roof is pierced on the ground floor by a passage through to the staircase adjoining on the E. The stair is modern though it may be in the position of an earlier stair. A number of posts and stop-chamfered ceiling-beams are exposed within.

(127) Houses and Shops, Nos. 10 and 11, 15 yds. S. of St. Edward's Passage, two tenements of one build, are of three storeys with cellars and attics. The walls are of gault brick, the roofs slated. They were built in 1827 (*Camb. Chronicle* 11 May 1827) and are of interest as a planned economy of shops and dwellings. No. 10 retains the original character; No. 11 is much altered. For the W. side see illustration facing p. 321. The central doorway opens to an axial through-passage giving access to the dwellings. The S. shop-window is largely original and has a recessed entrance to the S.; the N. shop-window is modern. The upper windows have flat brick arches; three contain casements opening to the floor and all have cast-iron guards. The E. wall contains segmental-headed windows. Nothing of note remains inside (plan p. 331).

(128) House, No. 9, next S. of the foregoing, is of three storeys. The walls are of gault brick, the roofs slated. It was built early in the 19th century and remodelled and extended E. in the third quarter of the same century, probably by Isaiah Deck, chemist, to whom the shop-front and the fittings may be due. On the W., the first-floor windows have early to mid 19th-century cast-iron guards. Inside, the W. room on the first floor retains an enriched plaster cornice and a marble fireplace-surround with bosses at the angles and a shallow keyblock. The staircase is in the E. extension.

(129) House and Shops, Nos. 7 and 8, next S. of the foregoing and 28 yds. S. of King Edward's Passage, are of four storeys. The walls are of gault brick, the roofs slated. They are of the second quarter of the 19th century and of interest as a planned economy originally of two shops and two dwellings. The shops have since been combined and also the dwellings above; the latter are now undergraduates' rooms. The original shop-front had paired doorways in the middle and display-windows on each side, the whole being in two bays divided and flanked by Corinthian pilasters supporting an entablature; the N. doorway has now been blocked. The W. front is illustrated facing p. 321. Inside, both tenements were planned with a W. room separated from a smaller E. room by a staircase-hall, or staircase and passage on the upper floors. The ground floor of the former S. shop has been cleared and how the staircase was approached is no longer evident. The entrance to the N. stair and tenement is from a passage intruding into Monument (128).

(130) House, Nos. 6 and 6a, next S. of the foregoing, is of three storeys with attics. The walls are of gault brick, the roofs slated. It was built in the first half of the 19th century, probably as a shop and dwelling. The shop-front is original, though altered, with a display-window in the middle and flanking entrances, the N. to the shop, the S. to a passage giving access to the dwelling over by a staircase contrived behind the next house, Monument (131). The W. first-floor windows, see illustration facing p. 321, have depressed elliptical arches turned in rubbed brick. Inside, the shop and W. ground-floor room have been combined by removal of the dividing wall. The staircase has cut strings, turned newels, square balusters and moulded mahogany handrail. On the first floor is an original reeded fireplace-surround of marble.

(131) House, Nos. 4, 4a and 5, next S. of the foregoing and 28 yds N. of Benet Street, is of four storeys. The walls are of gault brick with stucco and stone dressings; the roofs are slated. Cast in the heads of the two rainwater-downpipes on the W. is the date 1834. Stylistically this date is applicable to the building. The ground floor has since been so altered that the original plan is not recoverable. On the E. are later 19th-century additions. For the W. side see illustration facing p. 321. The wide doorway off-centre is original but has been moved; it contains a double door flanked by narrow lights with foot-scrapers below and a long light above all framed by pilasters supporting an entablature with dentil-cornice. A stone above is inscribed C.C.T.G., probably for Greef, a plumber, who lived here.

(132) HOUSE, No. 2, 12 yds. N. of Benet Street, is of three storeys. The walls are of brick, now painted, to the street and of plastered timber-framing to the E. The roofs are tiled. It was built on an L-shaped plan *c.* 1800, but has since been altered and the W. side refurbished in a revived Georgian style, though the openings may be original. The blind E. wall is covered with herringbone-patterned pargeting. The N.E. wing is similarly plastered and with sash-hung windows of *c.* 1800 or later. Inside, the ground floor has been rearranged but retains an early 19th-century reeded fireplace-surround of marble with bosses at the angles. A 19th-century staircase has been refitted with period balusters. On the first floor is an original plaster cornice and ceiling-border decorated with acanthus.

BENET STREET

N. side:—

(133, 134, 135, 136) HOUSES, Nos. 9, 8, 6, standing 11 yds. to 44 yds. E. of King's Parade, and the EAGLE INN, No. 7, adjoining No. 8 on the N., have all at one time and another been incorporated in the Inn, originally the 'Eagle and Child', and described as the Post House in Loggan's plan of Cambridge of 1688. They are of two and three storeys with cellars and attics. The walls are of plastered timber-framing, brick, and limestone ashlar with an infilling of brick. The roofs are tiled and slated. A lease of 1826 of the property, with a plan, is in the possession of Corpus Christi College; in it No. 9 is described as 'new erected', 'lately rebuilt by the Master and Fellows'. The varying thickness of the S. wall of No. 8 and the irregular ground-floor fenestration suggest the control of an earlier building, of the 16th or 17th century, upon the early 19th-century refacing conforming to that of No. 9; with this refacing may go the addition of the second floor. The first-floor assembly-room indicates the user as part of an inn. No. 6 has a history of development similar to that of No. 8, also a later addition on the N.; the carriage-way between the two houses is in much the position of that shown in John Hamond's view of Cambridge of 1592. The Inn, No. 7, was in part at least built or rebuilt probably in *c.* 1600 and the gallery-front, though now of *c.* 1800, seems to represent an original feature. All the buildings have been altered and extended in later times.

The Eagle Inn is notable for the retention of an open gallery giving access to the rooms.

(133), No. 9, has a street-front of *c.* 1825 in three bays, which varies from that of (134) only in the use of ashlar throughout and in the design of the iron guards to the cellar-windows. Inside, in the extreme N.E. corner is a doorway, now blocked, that gave access to the adjoining building.

(134), No. 8, has an early 19th-century street-front in six bays, with the ground floor ashlar-faced, the rest stucco. The plain surface is relieved by two plat-bands, at first-floor sill level and eaves level; above the last is a plain parapet-wall. The main entrance in the fourth bay has a moulded architrave and completed entablature above with wrought-iron quadrant lamp-brackets. At the E. end, in the first bay, is a large rectangular opening to the carriageway. The windows, equally spaced on the upper floors, all contain double-hung sashes. The N. side is concealed by modern additions, but a timber-framed gabled projection rising the full height probably contained a staircase.

Inside, on the ground floor are intersecting, and in the carriageway crossing, stop-chamfered ceiling-beams. One room is lined with 18th-century fielded panelling with dado-rail and cornice and round-headed arches springing from pilasters framing two recesses in the N. wall. The large room occupying the first floor has recently been partitioned; it had an open timber ceiling of intersecting moulded beams, now cased, but said to have been similar to that at the same level in the next house (135), forming ten panels. The fireplace-surround with turned paterae is of the 19th-century.

(135), No. 6, has a S. range in continuation of that of No. 8 and with a street-front similar to it in detail. The block adjoining on the N. is of the second half of the 19th century; that further to the N.E., perhaps of the late 17th century, seems to have been an annexe of No. 5 Benet Street (137), but in 1826 was a part of the inn premises. Inside, the ground floor is now a shop. On the first floor of the S. range is a cyma-moulded ceiling-beam with sunk soffit.

(136), *Eagle Inn*, No. 7, is L-shaped on plan, with E. and S. wings. The E. wing was built or rebuilt in the 19th century and has been much altered. The S. wing (Plate 304) of *c.* 1600, of two storeys with cellars and attics, has only the E. front visible; this has an open gallery of *c.* 1800 on the first floor supported on thin cast-iron columns and a later forward extension of the N. ground-floor room. Beside the central chimney-stack are paired staircases, to the cellars, to the gallery, and to the attics, that are entered through 19th-century doorways. The windows and doorways of the first-floor rooms opening on the gallery are of the same date as the foregoing. On the roof are three gabled dormer-windows, the northernmost retaining 17th or 18th-century leaded casements in a three-light timber frame. The gallery-front is divided into eight bays by slender turned timber posts linked by a latticework balustrading and supporting an eaves fascia-board cut to form shallow elliptical arches. The chamfered ceiling-beams inside the building have been encased since 1948.

(137) HOUSE, No. 5, adjoining (135) on the E., is of three and two storeys with cellars and attics. The walls are of plastered timber-framing and the roofs tiled. It was built perhaps late in the 16th century or before the middle of the 17th century, the N. wing is of the latter period, and remodelled *c.* 1700; the absence of an overhang to the second floor may indicate that the whole storey is an addition. The ground floor has since been much altered for a shop; the shop-front though mutilated is of the early to mid 19th century. The first floor projects on the S. The S. wall has two sash-hung windows on each of the upper floors, a heavy timber modillion-

cornice of *c.* 1700 at the eaves, with three iron ring attachments (see Monument (34), Peterhouse, the Master's Lodge) and two 19th-century flat-roofed dormer-windows. On the N. wing are large transeptal dormers, their ridge rising well above the main ridge. The interior retains, on the first floor, an exposed chamfered ceiling-beam; on the same floor are a door of six panels and a timber eared surround to a fireplace, both of *c.* 1700. The staircase of *c.* 1700, rising from the ground floor to the attics, has close strings, square newels, turned balusters and moulded handrail and, on the containing walls, a panelled dado up to the first floor. See also Monument (135) for a later extension of the N. wing.

(138) HOUSE, No. 4, next E. of the foregoing and 50 yds. from King's Parade, is of three storeys with cellars and attics. The walls are of gault brick and the roofs slated. It was built early in the 19th century, though red brickwork in English bond in the W. wall of the cellars and a gabled wall against the E. face of the E. wall survive from an earlier building on the site. The ground floor has a shop-front of *c.* 1825, partly altered. The house is distinguished by the wrought-ironwork fittings outside. At the entrance to a through passage is a gate with plain and spear-headed uprights linked by scrolls and, above, a scrollwork grille. To the N. and S. windows are five elaborate scrollwork guards.

(139) BATH HOTEL, No. 3, next E. of the foregoing, is of two storeys with cellars and attics. The walls are of plastered timber-framing and modern rendered brickwork; the roofs are tiled. The original building, L-shaped on plan with a small projection in the re-entrant angle, is of the 17th century. It was altered in the 18th century and extended later. In 1948 temporary stripping of the S. wall of the ground floor revealed two two-light windows, set high, with timber ovolo-moulded frames and mullions, one just W. of the present entrance, the other mutilated by the insertion of the W. window, and the original moulded timber head-rail enriched with egg-and-dart and bead ornament below the projecting first floor. But for the projection, the S. front is superficially of the late 18th century though now with applied sham timber-framing. It is in three bays and nearly symmetrical. The central doorway has flanking pilaster-strips, consoles and modillion-cornice, and the end windows on both floors contain tripartite sash-hung frames. On the roof are three 17th-century hipped dormer-windows with timber eaves-cornices. The first floor projects on the N.; similarly in the N.E. wing the first floor projects on the E. A mansard roof replaces the original roof of the wing. All the fenestration is of the 18th century. Inside are chamfered and stop-chamfered ceiling-beams. The staircase retains some 18th-century turned balusters. On the first floor, studs, wall-plates and beams are exposed, except in one room where a late 17th-century timber cornice masks the plates. In the attics are two moulded plank doors to cupboards and a reused panelled door, all of *c.* 1600; fragments of panelling of the same date are in the cellars. In 1948 the S. wall of the W. ground-floor room was seen to be partly lined with 17th-century panelling *in situ* behind the plaster.

S. side:—

(140) BARCLAY'S BANK, facing Peas Hill, is of three storeys with attics. The walls are of red-tinged yellow brick with late 19th-century stone dressings, the roofs tiled. The site, on which stood the gateway of the Augustinian friary (Willis and Clark, III, 603), was bought by William Finch, ironmonger, in 1720 who built there a house and outbuildings where he lived 'many years before his death' in 1761. In 1783 the house was bought by John Mortlock and in 1886 it was part the private house and part the bank of E. J. Mortlock (*ibid.*, 604). The outbuildings were demolished when the present Arts Schools were built. During the second half of the 19th century the two lower floors of most of the house were remodelled to form a lofty banking-hall.

The plan consists of a range to the street with shallow projections at each end on the S. and a S.E. wing; the last has been partly rebuilt and heightened but contains a lofty ground-floor room with 18th-century E. and W. walls.

On the street-front only the W. entrance, the first-floor window above it, parts of two plat-bands, and the range of second-floor windows of the mid 18th-century house survive, the first two with later stone dressings. The main entrance, tall windows, cornice and balustraded parapet, all of stone, are contemporary with the formation of the banking-hall. The back wall retains only the five 18th-century second-floor windows, but the blocking of the first-floor windows is traceable. The 18th-century roof is in two spans; on the N. it has two pedimented and two original hipped dormer-windows, on the S. a range of original dormer-windows with timber eaves-cornices.

Inside, some of the rooms on the second floor retain simple 18th-century panelling and cornices. The room in the S.E. wing, formerly the Mortlock's dining-room, was heightened and decorated in *c.* 1790. It retains a fireplace-surround, a N. door and doorcase, and a plaster entablature of this date; the plaster wall-panelling, ceiling enrichment and E. doorway are modern. The fireplace has marble slips and a surround with attenuated side scrolls supporting an enriched entablature with fluted frieze and frieze-panels containing classical figure subjects in low relief. The door is in six panels with fluted borders and enriched mouldings; the doorcase has an enriched and fretted architrave and completed entablature above, similarly enriched, with medallions in the frieze. The entablature at the wall-head has a frieze decorated with urns and garlands.

At 'Thorneycreek', Herschel Road, are other fittings removed from here in 1896. They include 18th-century panelling with moulded dado-rail and enriched modillion-cornice; a fireplace-surround with grey marble slips, eared architrave, enriched frieze with panel, and cornice-shelf; a staircase with cut and bracketed strings, fluted balusters, newels in the form of Ionic columns, and moulded handrail.

(141) HOUSE, No. 14, adjoining the foregoing on the W., is of three storeys with cellars and attics. The walls are of plastered timber-framing, the roofs tiled. It was built possibly during the 16th century and heightened by a storey late in the

17th century; in *c.* 1800 new double sash-hung windows were inserted and a new staircase added. On the S. are later and modern additions. The shop-front, the plain stucco exterior and the simple entablature and blocking-course at the wall-head are of the late 18th or early 19th century. It is now part of the adjoining bank. Inside, on the ground floor are intersecting stop-chamfered ceiling-beams. The first floor projects on the N.; this floor and the floor above have exposed chamfered ceiling-beams with scroll stops.

Free School Lane

E. side:—

(142) House, Nos. 1 and 2, at the corner of Benet Street, is of three storeys with basement and attics. The walls are of plastered timber-framing elaborated with modern applied timbering. The roofs are tiled and slated. It was built, whether as one or two tenements is uncertain, late in the 16th century; the S.E. extension projecting into the next house to the S. is probably of the following century. Extensive alterations have been made since; the present shop-front of No. 1 is of the 18th century. The house is a long rectangle on plan; it is gabled to the N. and S. and the pitch of the roof changes at the massive central chimney-stack. The first floor projects on both the W. and the N., the second floor on the W.; under the projections are 18th or 19th-century console-brackets. The N. shop-front has a doorway in the middle between two display windows with glazing of small panes. All the other windows are of the 18th century or later. Inside, the ground floor of No. 2 is completely modernised, the rest, which now comprises No. 1, retains some exposed chamfered and stop-chamfered ceiling-beams. The S. staircase, with close moulded strings, turned balusters, square newels and moulded handrail is of the early 18th century. In the S.E. extension is a bolection-moulded fireplace-surround of *c.* 1700.

(143) House, No. 3, divided in part from the foregoing by a narrow single-storey modern annexe, is of three storeys with cellars and attics. The walls are of plastered timber-framing, the roofs tiled. It was built late in the 16th century and, although all the windows have since been altered and the staircase renewed, it remains rather less altered than most of the houses of this type and date in the city. On plan, each floor has a main room to the W. divided from a smaller one to the E. by a large chimney-stack with flanking stair. It is gabled to the street with the first and second floors projecting. On the N. slope of the roof is a large dormer. The plastering has a pargeted pattern of rectangular panels; this is continued over the face of the dormer and interrupted by the late 18th-century sash-hung windows elsewhere.

Peas Hill

W. side:—

(144) House, No. 7, 10 yds. N. of Benet Street, is of three storeys with cellars and attics. The walls are of plastered timber-framing and red brick, the roofs tiled. It was built in the first half of the 18th century, incorporating parts of the framed walling of an earlier building in the western end. The ground floor of the E. block next the street has been much altered and contains shops with mid 19th-century fronts. The windows above the last are sash-hung, with stone sills and consoles; they are in four bays, with the brickwork of the N. bay largely refaced. At the wall-head is a stone cornice. The framed N. wall contains windows with twin double sash-hung frames and thick glazing-bars. Inside, three rooms are lined with original panelling with dado-rail and cornice. Reused 17th-century panelling lines a fourth room. The main staircase is of pine, with close strings, turned balusters, square newels and moulded handrail; on the containing walls is a panelled dado.

(145) Houses, next N. of the foregoing and extending 17 yds. to 30 yds. from Benet Street, now combined to form part of a King's College hostel, are structurally three distinct buildings. They are of two storeys with cellars and attics, except the S.E. four-storey block of *c.* 1800. The walls are of plastered timber-framing and brick; the roofs are tiled. The buildings have narrow frontages and extend well back from the street. Perhaps the W. part of the middle house was the first built and may have consisted of a ground-floor hall open to the roof. The W. half of the N. house followed. Both the foregoing may have extended E. to the street but were truncated by the building or rebuilding during the 16th or 17th century of their eastern parts; whether these last were together of one build or distinct is uncertain; they were however remodelled and unified in the 18th century and so now appear from the street. The W. part of the S. house was rebuilt or remodelled in 1661 and the E. part entirely rebuilt in *c.* 1800. The ground floor of the last has been cleared in modern times and forms the entrance to the Arts Theatre.

The walls of the lofty E. part of the S. house exposed to the street are of gault brick, the others framed and plastered. On the E. are plat-bands at first, second and third-floor sill-levels; for the rest the features are typical plain examples of *c.* 1800. The earlier W. part has the first floor projecting on the S., the ends of the joists being concealed by a moulded fascia-board. On the roof are transeptal dormers, that to the N. gabled, that to the S. with later hipping and supported on shaped brackets at the main eaves-level. The gabled W. end has a projecting first-floor window flush with the projecting attic-storey; this last has a moulded bressummer tenoned into extensions of the main wall-plates themselves supported on shaped brackets; these brackets had pierced pendants but the S. pendant, carved with the date 1661, alone survives. Inside the W. part, on the first floor, are hollow-chamfered pine ceiling-beams with shaped stops. In the attics original panelling and an original door enclose the S. dormer.

The E. front of the other two houses has a modern shop-front, a rectangular projecting window on the first floor of the middle house and a continuous eaves-cornice returned round the window-head. On the roof are two hipped dormer-windows. The whole, except the first, is an 18th-century remodelling. The height of the two roof-ridges differs. Of the middle house, the mediaeval W. part has later dormer-windows close to the W. end; this last is gabled and with a later chimney-stack inserted. Inside, the ground floor has been modernised. The first-floor E. room has ovolo-moulded ceiling-beams; the W. room has an exposed central longitudinal collar-purlin and, in the W. end wall, remains of a curved brace as if to a king-post.

The N. house has had the W. half reroofed. Inside, the ground floor has been modernised. In the E. half, in the S. wall of the attics, is a collar-beam truss with traces of a windbrace. It has three posts between tie-beam and collar, purlins clasped by the collar under the principal rafters, and reduced scantling of the last above purlin level.

(146) CENTRAL HOTEL, at the N. corner of St. Edward's Passage, consists of a complex of four or five small houses; some or all of these were combined at the Restoration at the latest to form an inn, the 'Three Tuns', which was closed down in 1790. They are of two and three storeys with cellars and attics. The walls are of plastered timber-framing, red brick with lighter rubbed brick dressings, and gault brick; the roofs are tiled. Most probably here Pepys 'drank pretty hard' on 25th February 1660. The ground floors have been altered and modernised and now contain a bank, shops and offices; the first floor, though partitioned, is less altered. For purposes of description, it may be divided into a N.E. range, of mid 17th-century origin and distinguished by a brick front of 1727 facing Peas Hill, a S.E. corner block rebuilt in the 19th century, a central rather later 17th-century block running N. and S. and containing the former assembly-room on the first floor, and a S.W. wing bordering St. Edward's Passage. The wing, though much altered, is probably the earliest surviving building in the complex and of the 16th century.

The Hotel is notable for the brick front of 1727. The building retains interesting mid and later 17th-century panelling and timber fireplace-surrounds.

The brick front of the N.E. range has a modern shop-window on the ground floor; above, it is in two bays divided and flanked by colossal pilaster-strips with a heavy rubbed and moulded brick dentil-cornice returned over the pilasters and a high parapet-wall, rebuilt, articulated over the returns. In each bay are two sash-hung windows on each floor with flat arches; the upper windows have shaped aprons. On the extremities are lead rainwater-pipes with square moulded heads, both cast with the date 1727 and three tuns. On the roof are two 17th-century hipped dormer-windows. The W. side is largely concealed but in the roof is an original dormer with a later roof built against it. Between the range and the S.E. corner block is a narrow gap extending from ground to roof, visible only from the attic.

The W. side of the central block, where it extends N. of the S.W. wing, has a gabled bay containing a window on the first floor in the face of a three-sided projection rising from a pent-roof over the ground floor and capped by the projection of the gable-end. The window has a timber three-light frame with casements retaining original hinges, catches and much of the original leaded glazing of small rectangular quarries. The plaster apron-wall is modelled with two human heads in panels. The gable has barge-boards with billet-ornament and pendants at the eaves; these are masked by a modern roof extending over the E. end of the hotel yard.

The whole of the S. elevation is faced in 19th-century brick. The S.W. range has projections of the first floor to N. and W. now largely concealed or obscured by brick underpinning. On the N.W. is a rainwater-pipe with 1729 and the arms of the Vintners' Company cast in the head. The mansard roof is of the 19th century.

Inside, the N.E. range has exposed intersecting cyma-moulded and ovolo-moulded ceiling-beams on the first floor; here and on the floor above are mid 17th-century timber fireplace-surrounds with side-pilasters, panelled overmantels with pilasters, entablatures with dentil-cornices, and enrichments of open flowers, bosses and bands on the pilaster-shafts, styles and architraves; the surround on the upper floor is complete, the other has lost the splayed shelf but retains in the fireplace-recess early 18th-century Dutch delft tiles decorated in manganese on a white ground. A third surround, on the second floor, of similar date and character to the foregoing, but plainer, has been mutilated. The range contains much 17th and 18th-century panelling.

The whole first floor of the central block, except the staircase and passage at the N. end, was one room with a plaster segmental barrel vault rising from a cornice. The whole survives, though the room is divided up, and retains much panelling and a projecting doorcase of *c.* 1675; the former has a dado-rail and dentil-cornice, the latter an entablature with frieze-panel, dentil-cornice, and broken pediment containing a pedestal flanked by volutes. The staircase-landing has a balustrade of *c.* 1727 with turned balusters and newels; on the landing above, in the attic, are more turned balusters perhaps of the 17th century.

In the S.W. wing, the panelling of *c.* 1670 that lined the first floor has been rearranged to form two rooms. It is divided into bays by panelled pilaster-strips and has three panels in the height and a deep entablature. This last has a panelled frieze, a heavy bedmould to the cornice, and shallow entablature-blocks at intervals enriched with silhouetted foliation. The fireplace-surround and overmantel are part of the foregoing; the first has panelled pilasters at the sides, a frieze-panel and shallow cornice-shelf, and the overmantel two panelled bays divided and flanked by panelled pilasters supporting a return of the main entablature.

S. end:—

(147) HOUSE, No. 10, 5 yds. N.E. of Monument (140), is of three storeys with cellars and attics. The walls are of gault brick with stone dressings; the low mansard roof is slated. It was built in *c.* 1830. Additions were made on the S. in the second decade of the 20th century; probably at the same time the present N. wall of the ground floor was substituted for a shop-front to form a rusticated Classical basement to the

colossal Doric order above. This last has fluted pilasters without taper or entasis dividing the front into three unequal bays, the middle bay projecting slightly, and supporting a full Doric entablature with low blocking-course. In each bay and on each floor is a sash-hung window with flat brick arch. In the roof are three squat flat-roofed dormer-windows; that in the middle is blind. Inside are two fireplace-surrounds, of white and grey marble, and a door, all of revived Greek character, and several other doors, perhaps reused, with fielded panels. In the additions are reused balusters of *c.* 1700.

(148) HOUSE, No. 11, next E. of the foregoing, is of three storeys with attics and cellars. The walls are of rendered timber-framing and brick and the roofs tiled. It was built late in the 16th or early in the 17th century; an E. wing was added later in the 17th century and a S. wing in the 18th. The whole has been much remodelled. On the N. the first and second floors both project; the lower projection is largely concealed by a modern shop-front, the upper is supported on late 19th-century console-brackets. The wall-head finishes in an unbroken horizontal parapet, probably a 19th-century alteration from plain overhanging eaves; the windows are of the same date. The S. wall has the ground floor rebuilt in brick. The S. wing is of brick up to the gable, with a plat-band at first-floor level. Inside are some exposed chamfered ceiling-beams.

MARKET HILL

E. side:—

(149) HOUSE, No. 4, 27 yds. N. of Petty Cury, is of three storeys with attics. The walls are timber-framed, the street-front being hung with tiles simulating brickwork. The roofs are tiled. It was built probably in the 16th century, the front being a remodelling of the mid 18th century when also the roof may have been reconstructed. A later E. wing links with an early 16th-century S.E. block behind the adjoining house, No. 3, and originally part of it. The W. wall has a modern shop-front and a wide passage-way to the N.; the floors above have each four sash-hung windows; at the wall-head is a timber dentil-cornice and parapet. The two 18th-century pedimented dormer-windows have sliding casements. The E. wing where not faced with modern brickwork has pargeting divided by moulded rails. The S.E. block had a first floor, now removed, projecting on the E. Inside the main block, the first-floor room has an open timber ceiling with a heavy stop-chamfered transverse beam, which is notched on the E. into a stop-chamfered post with thickened head, and longitudinal chamfered beams. The same room is lined with panelling of the early 17th century on the S. and part of the E. walls and modern elsewhere, except for two marquetry panels reset over the fireplace. The second floor has ceiling-beams and post similar to those below but the transverse beam is perhaps a replacement. The S.E. block contains an open timber ceiling with moulded longitudinal beam and wall-plates carved with folding leaf ornament and stop-moulded joists laid flat. An exposed corner-post though restored has an original shaped and chamfered head.

(150) HOUSE, No. 5, next N. of the foregoing, is of three storeys with attics. The walls are timber-framed, faced towards the street with modern tile-hanging, and the roofs slated. It was built probably in the 17th century and is older than the elaborations of 1688 described below. The ground floor has been cleared for a shop.

The house is notable for the elaborate plaster ceiling of 1688 on the first floor, which may well be the work of Henry Doogood, who was employed on Wren's City churches.

Facing Market Hill, in the W. wall, is a modern shop-front and on the first floor a doorway in the middle with a sash-hung window to each side; the doorway opens on a balcony the full width of the frontage and has a large shell-hood supported on enriched console-brackets and carved with cherubs and the date 1688. The balcony is fenced with scrolled and twisted ironwork of the same date. On the floor above are two windows and at the wall-head a timber cornice and a parapet. Inside, the first-floor room has an elaborate plaster-ceiling (Plate 63) dated 1688. It has a central and bordering panels, the first containing an oval wreath of fruit and flowers framing a sky of conventional clouds with birds and a central mask, the second with scrolled acanthus foliage including a stag hunt, a boar hunt, a monkey and other animals and birds. Cartouches interrupting the second contain the arms of the Drapers' Company and of Watson. The same room is lined with light bolection-moulded panelling with dado-rail and cornice.

It seems probable that the improvements were commissioned by William Watson, Alderman of Cambridge 1696–1702, baptised 1665, died 1722, son of William Watson, burgess and linen-draper (Registers of Great St. Mary; Day-books of the Corporation). The arms are those of Watson of Rockingham, to which possibly he had no right. Details of the ceiling are closely paralleled in the Old Library ceiling of 1690 at Pembroke College (Monument (33)), which was the work of Henry Doogood. (C.A.S. *Proc.* xli (1948), 56–9).

N. side:—

(151) HOUSE, No. 14, 5 yds. E. of Rose Crescent, is of four storeys. The walls are timber-framed and hung with tiles simulating brickwork towards the street and of brick. The roofs are tiled. The present S. front is an early 18th-century remodelling and heightening of an earlier structure that has since been much altered and in part destroyed. A N. wing was added late in the 18th century. In modern times the walls and partitions of the two lower storeys have been entirely removed and replaced by steelwork; additions mask the back of the original building. The carriageway, presumably to the Angel Inn shown in William Custance's map of Cambridge, 1798, has been destroyed, unless the E. section of the modern shop-front intruding into the adjoining house is evidence for it. The tiling of the second and third floors imitates Flemish bonding. The five windows on each of these floors have flat brick arches; the lower contain fixed frames with round heads

(53) ST. MARY THE GREAT. Exterior, from S.E.

(61) TRUMPINGTON CHURCH. Exterior, from N.E.

(305) CHESTERTON TOWER. Exterior. Mid 14th-century

(292) MERTON HALL. Exterior, from S.E. *c.* 1200 and 1374

(305) CHESTERTON TOWER. Vault. Mid 14th-century

(35) QUEENS' COLLEGE. Gatehouse, vault. 1448

(251) DOWNING TERRACE. Exterior.

(77) CASTLE HILL. Court House. 1842; demolished 1954

(85) RAILWAY STATION. Exterior, from N.W. 1845

(324) TRUMPINGTON HALL. Exterior, from E. *c.* 1710, with early 19th-century alterations

(238) GROVE LODGE. Exterior. 1795

(222) 'LITTLE TRINITY', No. 16 Jesus Lane. Exterior. *c.* 1725

(34) PETERHOUSE. Master's Lodge. Exterior, from S.W. 1702

(237) KENMARE, Late 18th-century

(28) FITZWILLIAM HOUSE. 1727

(223) No. 32 JESUS LANE. Mid 18th-century

(107) No. 13 TRINITY STREET. 1783 and later

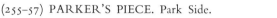

(255–57) PARKER'S PIECE. Park Side. *c.* 1835–*c.* 1850

(258–60) PARKER'S PIECE. Park Terrace, Camden House and Park Lodge. 1831–38

and carved spandrels, and the upper, double-hung sashes. At the wall-head is a timber modillion-cornice and a parapet. The N. wing has walls of yellow brick and a mansard roof.

Inside, the upper floors retain a much-damaged staircase of *c.* 1700 with turned newels and moulded handrail; all the balusters are missing.

The ironmongery here was founded in 1688. When Swann Hurrell took over the business from C. Finch, his uncle, in 1847 he moved the foundry hence to a disused brewery on Quayside. (See Monuments (79) and (82)).

Market Street

(152) House, No. 1, on the corner of Sidney Street, is of three storeys with attics. The walls are of plastered timber-framing, the roofs tiled. A building of the early 18th century in origin, containing one or two tenements, it now comprises only a part of larger shop-premises. The ground floor has been entirely reconstructed in modern times and, in the S. part, raised so that the first floor lacks headroom. The windows, where not truncated, contain double-hung sashes. At the wall-head to S. and E. is a timber modillion-cornice, with a parapet-wall to the S. part. The E. wall towards Sidney Street retains traces of pargeting. The inside has been modernised.

Petty Cury

N. side:—

(153) House, Nos. 32, 33, 34, standing 42 yds. E. of Market Hill, is of three storeys with attics. The walls are of plastered timber-framing, the roofs tiled. It was built probably in the 16th century. The ground floor has twice been reconstructed for a shop in modern times; the upper floors have been cleared and modernised. The street-front has the first and second floors projecting; the heavy moulded timber bressummer to the lower projection was revealed temporarily in 1954; the upper projection has a similar timber exposed. At the eaves is a modern timber fascia-board. All the windows, including the hipped dormer-windows, are of the 18th or 19th century. The original plan is irrecoverable but the building is in three bays, possibly of three tenements in origin. On the first floor are exposed stop-chamfered ceiling-beams and wall-plates. On the floor above, the E. bay is open to collar-beam level and the whole may have been open to the roof before attics were formed.

House, formerly at the corner of Market Hill, see Monument (86).

S. side:—

(154) House, No. 7, 60 yds. E. of Guildhall Street, between the Lion Hotel and the entrance to Falcon Yard, is of four and three storeys. The walls are of timber-framing, partly hung with tiles simulating brickwork, and of brick. The roofs are tiled. It was a part of the Falcon Inn and built in the 16th century. In the 18th century and later it was extensively remodelled. The ground floor contains a modern shop. The upper part, remodelled and heightened, is now an annexe of the Lion Hotel, the two being linked by a bridge; modern buildings span the yard-entrance on the E. The greater part of the interesting S. wing has been destroyed since 1883.

The building is notable for the survival, though altered and damaged, of a length of some 20 ft. of the original timber-framed S. wing that had open galleries on the first and second floors. The appearance of the original arrangement is preserved in drawings by Buckler (B.M., Add MSS. 36436, drwg. 177) and T. D. Atkinson (T. D. A. and J. W. Clark, *Cambridge Described and Illustrated* (1897), fig. 11).

Towards the street, the tile-hung first floor and the plastered second floor together project. At the wall-head is a 19th-century cornice and parapet. The E. side of the S. wing overlooking Falcon Yard has a modern front to the ground floor built flush with the main wall-face, so concealing the projection of the first floor. The original timber-framing of the galleries is exposed; the former-openings are disguised by blocking and inserted 18th and 19th-century windows. It is divided into bays by posts rising the full height of the two floors; rails tenoned into the posts and studs tenoned into the rails form the framing of the former solid apron-walls.

Inside, no early features remain on the ground floor. In the N. block, the first and second floors have exposed stop-moulded and stop-chamfered ceiling-beams; on the floor above is a cupboard with a damaged door of 16th-century linenfold panelling. In the S. wing the original plan-form persists in part on the upper floors, though the back wall of the first-floor gallery has been rebuilt, the longitudinal ceiling-beams being axial to the rooms not to the wing. The timber doorways shown by Buckler on the first-floor do not survive, but the second-floor gallery is still entered through a 16th-century timber doorway with continuous hollow-chamfered jambs and four-centred arch in a square head.

(155) Lion Hotel, next W. of the foregoing, 32 yds. E. of Guildhall Street, is of three and two storeys with attics. The walls are of plastered timber-framing and brick, the roofs slate and tile-covered. The buildings, of different dates and all more or less altered at different times, surround a yard, which has been covered with a modern glass roof. Called until sometime in the 19th century the 'Red Lion', it is the only inn in the city showing a continued retention of both use and courtyard-plan from at least the 17th century. None of the building complex is demonstrably earlier than this, though the probability of a mediaeval date for part has been suggested (*ibid.*, 73). Alterations have been made on the W. in the second half of the 19th century, and on the S. are long ranges of brick and tiled stables of the late 18th or early 19th century.

The range to the street, which retains a 17th-century

chimney-stack, was heightened in the 18th century and remodelled then and later. The E. range is probably of the 17th century; the E. wall and chimney-stack are both of original brickwork; the W. wall though refaced has a plaster cove of *c.* 1700 at the eaves. The yard is bounded on the W. by two buildings on different alignments incorporating late 18th-century brickwork. The S. range is of the 17th century only in the lowest storey; all above has been rebuilt.

Inside, the 17th-century part last described alone retains exposed chamfered ceiling-beams. In the S. end of the E. range is a staircase of *c.* 1700 with close strings, square newels, turned balusters and moulded handrail.

(156) HOUSE, No. 5, adjoining (155) on the S.W. some 43 yds. back from the street, is of two storeys with basement and attics. The timber-framed walls are faced with stucco; the roofs are slated. The house was built in the mid 18th century; earlier features are reset or too fragmentary to confirm the retention of any substantial part of the older structure in the new. About the middle of the 19th century the N. front was entirely remodelled; in the same century the ground-floor S. rooms were extended S., the extensions being covered with a flat lead roof. The N. forecourt is said formerly to have been flanked by a coach-house and stables.

The parapeted N. front is symmetrical; at each end are small single-storey N. wings, that to the W. to some extent altered; slight projections of the main wall-face above them to the full height of the front ensure their visual unity in the composition. The recessed central area is in three bays with a doorway in the middle and sash-hung windows with moulded architraves. The doorway is flanked by Tuscan pilasters supporting an entablature. At first-floor sill-level and below the parapet-wall are continuous plat-bands.

Inside, a central stairhall and passage are flanked by two rooms on each side separated by chimney-stacks. The N. wings contain a lobby and a closet respectively. Excepting these last, the plan is nearly square. Reused in the basement are heavy chamfered ceiling-beams. The 18th-century staircase has close strings, turned balusters, square newels and moulded handrail. On the first floor is a fireplace with marble reeded surround of *c.* 1800 with carved figure and flowers. In the attics an intermediate wall-post is exposed; the roof is of the 18th century, with the purlins cut to make way for the dormer-windows. Some 18th-century doors remain.

GUILDHALL STREET

E. side:—

(157) HOUSE, No. 9, standing 28 yds. S. of Petty Cury, is of two storeys with cellars. The walls are timber-framed, the roofs slated. It was built probably in the 16th century but has been much altered since, and perhaps shortened on the N., and the roof raised, mainly in the 19th century. The ground floor now contains two shops divided by an inserted stair. The E. wall of the N. shop has been removed for an eastward extension.

Towards the street are modern shop-fronts; the first floor projects and has modern applied timbering; the windows are of the 19th century. Some of the original timber-framed back wall remains visible. The S. chimney-stack has been rebuilt; that to the N. is modern. Inside, the ceiling of the ground floor is divided into eight panels by cross and longitudinal chamfered beams, those in the S. half alone with stops. On the first floor is an exposed wall-post with enlarged head to support a tie-beam, now removed. Only two rafters joined by a collar-beam and a tie-beam remain of the original roof, the first at the S. end, the second near the head of the stairs.

(158) FISHER HOUSE, next S. of the foregoing, is of two storeys with attics. The walls are of plastered timber-framing and of brick; the roofs are tile-covered. It consists of two small 16th or early 17th-century houses, the first lengthways with the street with the second almost at right angles to it some way to the E. The two have been linked by a later building. Late in the 17th or early in the 18th century the street-front was remodelled; in the same period the S. side of the second house was rebuilt or remodelled and the staircase renewed. Towards the street, the wall to the ground floor of the first house has been rebuilt in brick in modern times. The plastered first floor projects and has a modern cove to the soffit and a modern fascia-board; the windows and modillioned eaves-cornice are of *c.* 1700, so also are the three hipped dormer-windows in the roof. On the E. is a projecting rectangular staircase-bay cased in 19th-century brickwork. The second house has a brick S. wall with a plat-band at first-floor level, a timber eaves-cornice and sash-hung windows. The timber-framed N. side has three dormers.

Inside, a room on the first floor of the first house is lined with early 18th-century panelling removed from 58 St. Andrew's Street (demolished 1955), with an eared panel over the fireplace. The second house, consisting of two rooms on each floor divided by a great central chimney-stack, has beside this last a staircase with close strings, turned balusters, square newels with moulded caps and moulded grip-handrail. One of the dormers has been reconditioned but is still used as a bed-recess.

ROSE CRESCENT

(159) HOUSES and SHOPS, Nos. 1–11, all on the N. and E. sides of the footway between Trinity Street and Market Hill, are of three storeys with basements. The walls are of brick, the roofs slated. The Crescent occupies the yard and approaches to the former Rose Tavern, which are shown in William Custance's plan of Cambridge of 1798. Nothing of the structure of the inn survives. The terrace, a planned economy of shops and dwellings, was built at one time to a uniform design; it was described as 'newly erected' in the *Cambridge Chronicle* of 4 August 1826.

Rose Crescent is of interest as an early 19th-century commercial development of small shops, the timber shop-fronts being built to a repetitive design of some distinction. The whole survives remarkably complete with only a few late intrusions, though much of the original glazing of the display-windows and fanlights has been destroyed.

The frontage has a doorway and a display-window alternately almost continuously from end to end of the terrace, the single unit consisting of a shop-doorway flanked by windows and a house-doorway to the side. The bays are

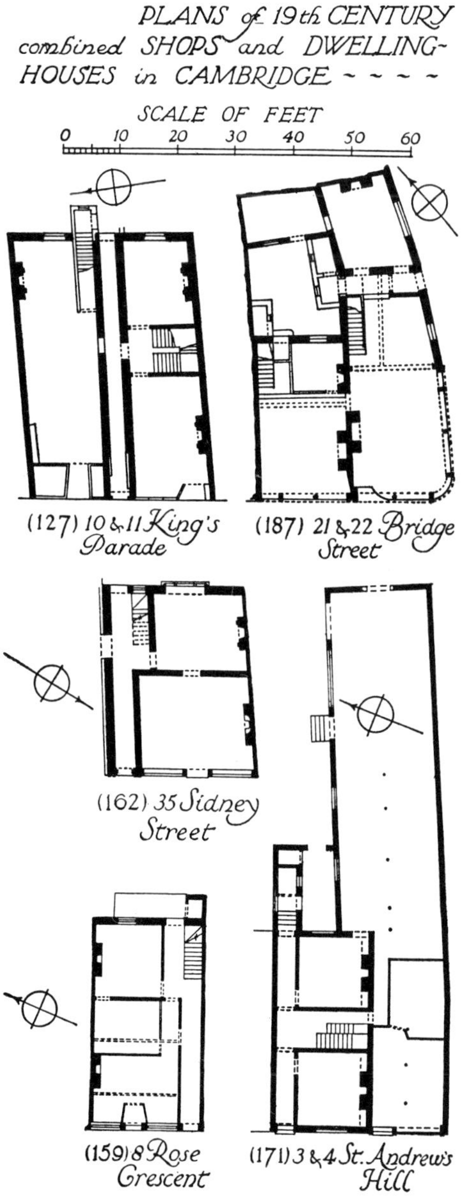

separated by moulded pilasters supporting an architrave-like fascia under a cornice projecting about 1 ft. Over the doorways are square lights with lead glazing-bars forming a geometrical pattern with scrolls in the spandrels. Little of the original glazing of small panes remains in the display-windows; under the windows are wrought-iron grilles to the basements. Above, the windows have flat brick arches and contain double-hung sashes; those on the first floor have stone sills continued as a plat-band and some plain and scrolled wrought-iron guards. At the wall-head is a continuous cornice, of slight projection, and a parapet. A number of the original wrought-iron lamp-brackets survive, projecting from the first floor. The more conspicuous variations in, or alterations to, the fronts, apart from damage already described, are as follows: No. 2, modern shop-front, leaded lights inserted in upper windows; 3, carriage entrance at side with original panelled gates; 4, attics added; 5 and 6, Rose Inn, ground floor entirely refronted; 7, survives largely intact; 8, shop door and frame renewed; 11, timber front altered in part, attics added.

On plan, Nos. 1 to 3 are very shallow and only the last has lighting from the back; Nos. 4–11 are two rooms deep and, except 5 and 6, have a passage leading straight from the house-doorway to a staircase. The interiors were probably always plain.

Green Street

N. side:—

(160) House, No. 10, some 77 yds. from Trinity Street, is of three and four storeys with attics. The walls are of brick with vitrified headers, the roofs slated. It was built *c.* 1700 and refronted later in the 18th century. The shop-front is of the late 19th century and the window-frames and sashes are renewals of the same period. The plain parapet is presumably an alteration, of uncertain date. The street-front is entirely plain, with two window-openings with flat brick arches on each of the two upper floors. The N. side has three plat-bands and a brick dentil-cornice. The E. party-wall is timber-framed.

Inside, the S. ground-floor room is lined with original bolection-moulded panelling with dado-rail and cornice; the similar panel in the overmantel is flanked by panelled pilasters. The fireplace-surround is of the late 18th century, with enriched architrave, composite pilasters at the sides enriched with swags and stylised foliage, a frieze with central panel carved with dancing figures and flanked by festoons and musical trophies, and a dentilled cornice-shelf. The contemporary cast-iron grate has oval garlanded medallions containing figures. The original staircase has close moulded strings, twisted balusters, square newels with ball-finials and moulded pendants, and broad moulded handrail; it rises in six flights to the attics where a slighter balustrade has wavy plank balusters. The upper floors contain original bolection-moulded panelling, fireplace-surrounds and overmantels, panelled window-shutters, and some original white hearth-tiles. A first-floor fireplace contains carved slips and a cast-iron grate of neo-Greek design.

N. and S. sides:—

(161) Houses, from end to end of the street, excepting No. 10 (Monument (160)), are nearly all part of a single rebuilding scheme probably of the second quarter of the 19th century. Nos. 8 and 9, which were older houses, have been largely, and

Nos. 14 to 20, 22 and 24, entirely, rebuilt since; the rest have been more or less altered. Some original shop-windows survive but most are of the late 19th century or modern.

The houses are of two, three and four storeys, some with attics and basements. The walls generally are of gault brick, the roofs slated. The fronts are plain, most with parapet-walls. The windows have flat brick arches and stone sills and contain double-hung sashes. Nos. 3 to 5 have elliptical-headed shop-windows and round-headed doorways with stone imposts; over the doors are fanlights with festooned radiating glazing-bars of some elaboration. Nos. 26 and 27 form a unified group at the W. end of the S. side. On the corners of Nos. 12 and 28 are respectively curved windows and a curved doorway. The rest call for no particular comment except that the corner-treatment is one popular in Cambridge, with minor variations, throughout the century; here the variant is an inset convex quadrant.

Sidney Street

W. side:—

(162) Houses, three, Nos. 35 (plan p. 331), 36 and 37, standing 43 yds. to 66 yds. N. of Green Street, are of three storeys with cellars. The walls are of gault brick, the roofs slated. They form a terrace of one build of the early 19th century; from the first they comprised shops and dwellings. Subsequent alterations to the shop-fronts have broken the initial architectural uniformity. No. 37 retains the original character and plan though the staircase has been removed. The others have had the ground floor cleared and new shop-fronts inserted in the present century. The upper floors have all been converted for use as an undergraduates' hostel.

The original shop-front has a doorway between large display-windows and a doorway to the dwelling to one side, all divided and flanked by Roman Doric pilasters on square bases continued as a plinth and supporting a bold entablature; paired pilasters flank the doorway to the dwelling. The windows above are of lofty proportions, with flat brick arches and, where unaltered, stone sills. At the wall-head is a stone cornice and a parapet-wall. In the W. wall of No. 37 is a french window set slightly in front of the wall-face. Inside is a doorway into the shop from the back room, not from the passage at the side as in the usual terrace-house plan.

(163) House, No. 48, standing 4 yds. S. of Green Street, is of three storeys. The walls are of plastered timber-framing, tile-hung towards the street to simulate brickwork. The roofs are tiled. Built in the 17th century, and altered in the following century, it has now been incorporated with the shop on the corner of Green Street by removal of the dividing wall on the ground floor. On the E., the shop-front is modern; the upper floors project at first-floor level; the timber window-frames have been renewed and the whole wall-head remodelled in modern times. Facing a passage on the S. side is the only original window left; it is of two lights with timber frame and mullion. The roof is H-shaped; the link, which runs E. to W. with half of straight pitch and half mansard, has dormers on the N. and dormer-windows on the S. Inside, the only ancient features remaining visible are some ceiling-beams.

Hobson Street

E. side:—

(164) House, No. 32, next S. of County Hall, is of two storeys with attics. The walls are timber-framed, the W. wall being hung with tiles simulating brickwork, the rest plastered; the roofs are tiled. It was built early in the 17th century and remodelled in the 18th. Subsequent single-storey brick additions have extended the original L-shaped plan to the rectangle.

The house has remarkably accomplished 18th-century 'mathematical' tiling on the front to Hobson Street.

The street-front, now to all appearances of the 18th century, has a stucco plinth, tiling above resembling brickwork in Flemish bond and including the simulated rubbed brick flat arches over the window-openings, and a timber modillioned eaves-cornice. The doorway in the middle contains a door of six fielded panels and has a fanlight with interlacing glazing-bars flanked by console-brackets supporting an open pediment with dentil-cornice; N. of it are two windows and S. of it paired windows, all sash-hung. The three sash-hung windows on the first floor are nearly symmetrically arranged. All the openings have boarded reveals concealing the tile-hanging. On the roof are two modern dormer-windows. The E. side has the plastering scored to resemble ashlar, 18th-century windows and a gabled dormer; the E. wing is similarly treated and has transeptal dormers.

Inside, in the S.W. room on the ground floor are stop-chamfered ceiling-beams. All the rooms on this and the first floors are lined with 18th-century panelling, some fielded, some entirely plain; the contemporary doors are of two panels. All the fireplaces have been renewed. The lower part of the staircase is of the 19th century, the upper part of the 18th century, with close strings, turned balusters and square newels.

St. Andrew's Street

E. side:—

(165) House, Nos. 68 and 68a, standing 17 yds. S. of Christ's Lane, is of two storeys with attics. The walls are of plastered timber-framing and brick, the roofs slated and tiled. It consists of a short early 17th-century range to the street with a short E. return and a carriageway on the S., all remodelled in the 19th century when a room was added or rebuilt over the last. Later in the 17th century the E. return was extended by the addition of an E. to W. range fronting the cobbled through-way.

The street-front has a modern shop-window, a projecting three-sided sash-hung window above and a hipped dormer-window. The E. return has a large gabled S. dormer-window and E. chimney-stack with original square base and the upper part with channelling of 17th-century character though rebuilt in the early 19th century and subsequently heightened. The back range has a timber eaves-cornice and two large gabled dormer-windows on the S.; the N. side is masked. Inside the W. range is a stone bolection-moulded fireplace-surround with a similarly moulded panel in the overmantel, the latter flanked by panelled pilasters, all of the early 18th century.

(166) BELMONT, No. 55 and 55a, next N. of the New Theatre, is of two storeys with cellars. The walls are of gault brick with stone dressings, the roofs slated and tiled. It was built probably in 1822 but incorporates part of an early 18th-century structure forming the E. wing; the S.W. block is self-contained and seems to have contained separate offices from the first. Particulars of sale in 1838 describe it as held of the Dean and Chapter of Ely on a lease of forty years from 1822, being in private occupation, with a suite of solicitor's offices adjoining.

Belmont is a neo-Classical building of some originality in composition.

The street front is asymmetrical; four recessed bays front the dwelling, a single wider bay projecting obtusely defines the office-block. A uniformity of treatment is maintained throughout. The dwelling-entrance in the third bay is beneath an open porch with Ionic columns and pilaster-responds supporting a roofed entablature. The tall ground-floor windows have flat brick arches. The first-floor windows, of the same form as the foregoing but shorter, are contained in a wall-arcade with broad piers based upon a stone plat-band in continuation of the sills, stone imposts and segmental brick arches. At the wall-head is a stone capping in the form of a simplified and flattened cornice and blocking-course. The horizontal features are continued across the office-block and in the front wall, on the ground floor, is a segmental-headed wall-arch containing a window and, on the first floor, one bay of arcading as before. The other walls are plain; in the S. wall is a large modern window. The service-doorway in the E. wall is in a round-headed wall-arch and a window of the same form lights the main staircase. The older E. wing has brick plat bands at first and second-floor levels to the S., several blocked windows, and a dormer-window; the E. end and N. side are plastered and with later windows.

Inside, the original main staircase has cut strings, moulded handrail and slight square balusters, grouped at the foot in place of a newel, and turned newels above. In the E. wing are exposed chamfered ceiling-beams.

W. side:—

(167) HOUSE, No. 22, opposite Emmanuel Street, of two storeys with attics, has walls of gault brick and tiled roofs. It was built *c.* 1730. The ground floor has since been cleared for a shop. Towards the street, the shop-front is of the late 19th century; on the floor above are two windows with flat-rubbed brick arches and sash frames flush with the wall-face. At the eaves is a timber modillion-cornice and on the roof are two large dormer-windows with pedimented gables. The back wall is gabled and has two deep plat-bands; it contains a doorway with a fanlight in a doorcase with panelled pilasters and console-brackets supporting a broken pedimental hood with modillion-cornice. The windows here have high segmental heads.

Inside, access to the first floor is now by a stair in the adjoining building. At this level the E. room is lined with original simple panelling; all the rooms have cornices, and the original staircase surviving up to the attics has cut and bracketed strings, turned balusters, columnar newels and moulded and ramped handrail.

(168) HOUSE, No. 24, next but one S. of the foregoing, of three storeys, has walls of dark brick in header bond with dressings of lighter brick. The roofs are tiled. It was built early in the 18th century; the E. room on the ground floor has since been converted into a shop. The brickwork of the street-front is of some note.

Towards the street, the shop-window is modern. The two windows on each of the upper floors have flat rubbed brick arches, the lower with projecting stepped brick keys, and contain sash frames set nearly flush with the wall-face. Below the parapet is a brick dentil-cornice, stopped and returned well within the width of the frontage, with every fifth dentil shaped. The back wall is cement-rendered. Inside, are two rooms in the depth, divided by the staircase, the former with corner-fireplaces against the staircase-walls; flanking the ground-floor front room is an original passage to the stairhall. The front room on the first floor is lined with original fielded panelling. The staircase has cut and bracketed strings, turned balusters, moulded handrail, and turned newels with square caps and pendants.

(169) HOUSE, Nos. 33 and 34, standing 14 yds. S. of Downing Street, of two storeys with attics, has walls of brick, where visible, and tiled roofs. It is of 17th-century origin and may originally have been timber-framed. In the 18th century a W. wing was added, and other additions have been made since. The E. wall, rebuilt with a parapet in the first half of the 19th century or later, has a modern shop-front the full length and height of the ground floor. The inside has been modernised.

(170) HOUSE, No. 36, standing 33 yds. S. of Downing Street, is of two storeys with cellars and attics. Where the old walls survive they are of plastered timber-framing; the roofs are tiled. It was built in the first half of the 17th century but the street-front has been entirely rebuilt and the ground and first floors cleared inside in modern times. On the roof are two 18th-century hipped dormer-windows to the E., an original dormer-window to the N., and an original dormer to the S.

ST. ANDREW'S HILL

E. side:—

(171) HOUSE etc., standing 20 yds. to 29 yds. N. of Downing Street, house No. 4, with shop, No. 3, and warehouse adjoining on the S. (plan p. 331), the last behind the premises of Messrs. Barrett & Son, china and glass dealers, 25 St. Andrew's Street, the three forming a domestic and business unity. The walls are of gault brick, the roofs slated. Barrett's warehouses in Jesus Lane were offered for sale as building materials in 1831 and R. Barrett was 'of St. Andrew's Hill' in 1836. (*Camb. Chronicle* 15 April 1831, 29 April 1836). Probably therefore the present

group was built *c.* 1830; uniform with it, and doubtless part of the same capital development, to produce an annual rent income, are houses Nos. 5 and 6; the four buildings, Nos. 3–6, together form a single terrace, the front of No. 3, above the shop, being like the rest.

The terrace, of three storeys with basements, has a stone plat-band continuing the sills of the first-floor windows, a brick plat-band at eaves-level and a parapet-wall; the two rainwater downpipes between the houses are inset. The entrance-doorways to the houses have round heads and plain stone imposts and the wide ground-floor windows contain tripartite timber frames with double-hung sashes. No. 3 retains an original timber shop-front with wide display-window and doorway to one side divided and flanked by moulded pilasters supporting a simplified entablature with broad cornice; window and overdoor contain glazing of small panes. All the sash-hung windows on the upper floors have plain flat arches of rubbed bricks.

The warehouse is of two storeys with basement. The walls have horizontal timbers at intervals; to these the staging for the china was, and still is, fixed. The upper floors extend over the shop. The lay-out of the whole group is little altered, except that the partitions and small workroom between the shop and warehouse are later insertions.

Nos. 5 and 6, see Monument (171).

(172) House, No. 7, adjoining the foregoing on the N., of two storeys with attics, has walls of brick and tiled roofs. It was built late in the 18th or early in the 19th century together with outbuildings on the E.; the E. wing N. of the latter is modern. The first floor has been extended S. to bridge a carriageway. Severe economy in the building appears in the plainness of the exterior; the openings are rectangular; the doorway has a simple plaster architrave; the windows contain light double-hung sashes in frames set flush with the wall-face.

N. side:—

(173) Houses, Nos. 9 and 10, on the corner of Tibb's Row and extending towards Corn Exchange Street, of two storeys with attics, and cellars in part, have walls of plastered timber-framing and brick, and tile-covered roofs. They consist of a long range of one build to St. Andrew's Hill, with additions along the N. side, and a N.E. wing at an angle bordering the Row. The first retains no firmly dateable features but the plan suggests a 16th-century origin. The earliest of the additions, to the W., is of *c.* 1700. The wing, probably once a separate building, is of the 17th century. The whole was remodelled and the main range refronted early in the 19th century, probably by Charles Humfrey and in 1818 when the ownership of the land on which two porches were being built was in dispute (*Camb. Chronicle* 17 July 1818). Humfrey evidently established his right, for the porches survive and the space between them is enclosed with railings. Later 19th-century alterations, including the addition of a bay-window, and modern additions have been made.

The S. front is of red brick; at each end is a plain porch, with one now closed, and near the middle a window with tripartite timber frame set in an elliptical-headed wall-arch. On the first floor are seven rather irregularly spaced sash-hung windows in frames flush with the wall-face, and on the roof six 19th-century dormer-windows. The E. and W. ends are gabled; the first is of plastered framing, the second faced with brick. The W. addition on the N. side is timber-framed. The N.E. wing has the walls of the ground floor rebuilt in brick, weatherboarded above. To the E. are two plastered dormers. The railings of *c.* 1818 bordering St. Andrew's Hill have plain wrought-iron uprights and standards with urn finials.

Botolph Lane

S. side:—

(174) Botolph House, at the E. end, on the corner of Free School Lane and Pembroke Street, of four storeys with basement, has walls of gault brick. It was built *c.* 1790 and has lower annexes on the S. flanking the projecting staircase-bay. The N. front and E. end have continuous stone plat-bands at first-floor level and below the parapet-wall. The original entrance-door of six panels has a fanlight above with radiating glazing-bars; the doorcase has panelled reveals and side pilasters with stylised acanthus-leaf capitals supporting an entablature with garlands on the frieze and an enriched modillion-cornice. The three windows on each floor above, irregularly spaced horizontally, have flat brick arches, stone sills and sash-hung frames set flush with the wall-face. The S.E. annexe, of the same build, is of three storeys with a timber cornice and parapet. The single-storey S.W. annexe may be a slightly later addition.

Inside, the passage-hall is ceiled with quadripartite plaster vaulting in four bays with foliage bosses at the intersections. The principal rooms have enriched plaster cornices and typical late 18th-century marble fireplace-surrounds with figures carved on frieze-panels flanked by foliage swags and with enriched cornice shelves. The staircase is elliptical, with a roof-light over the well. The building is misshapen by uneven settlement.

The adjoining houses, Nos. 14, 15 and 16, on the W., of rather earlier date and with plastered timber-framed walls to the S., have been refronted at the same time as, and in similar materials to, (174) though in simpler style and with a timber modillion-cornice.

(175) House, now two dwellings, Nos. 12 and 13, adjoining the foregoing on the W., of two storeys with cellars and attics, has timber-framed walls faced in part with later brickwork, and tiled roofs. It was built on a T-shaped plan in the 16th century; E. and W. of the S. wing are modern additions. The modern brick-faced street-front contains modern windows; on the roof are three 18th-century hipped dormer-windows. To the S., the first floor of the main range projects. The central chimney-stack has a base of original red brickwork; the upper part has been rebuilt. The roof of the S. wing has been raised and given mansard form; the attics are approached from No. 11 Pembroke Street adjoining. Inside, No. 12 has

chamfered ceiling-beams in the main range, moulded wall-plates in the S. wing; No. 13 has intersecting chamfered beams and plates in the one ground-floor room. On the first floor are exposed wall-posts with enlarged heads to carry tie-beams; in both posts and ties are mortice-holes for braces now removed.

(176) House, Nos. 1, 1a and 1b, standing 5 yds. E. of Trumpington Street, of two storeys, with rendered timber-framed walls and tiled roofs, was built in the 16th century. It has been much altered. The street-front, probably originally with a projecting first floor, was remodelled in the 18th or 19th century and has two modern shop-windows, two sash-hung windows on the first floor and a parapet. Inside, the W. shop has exposed moulded and stop-moulded intersecting ceiling-beams and wall-plates and a wall-post with shaped head; on the first floor are chamfered beams.

(177) House, No. 3 Pembroke Street, on N. side, 20 yds. from Trumpington Street, is of two storeys. The walls are of plastered timber-framing, the roofs tiled. It was built in the 16th century and probably originally consisted of two rooms on each floor divided by a central chimney-stack; the W. part was rebuilt as a separate tenement in the 19th century. The street-front has had the ground floor reconstructed in modern times to include a shop-window in the late 18th-century style. The first floor projects. The roof is of high pitch, with the chimney-stack emerging close behind the ridge. The back wall is obscured. No old windows survive.

Inside, the ground-floor room has a chamfered longitudinal ceiling-beam. An original wall-plate is visible on the upper floor.

Mill Lane

S. side:—

(178) House, No. 12, now a club for women graduates, stands 111 yds. W. of Trumpington Street. It is of two and three storeys with walls of timber-framing and brick and tile-covered roofs. Various dwellings, altered and extended at different times, form the present building-complex. They include, to the Lane, a 16th-century house on the W. with a house of *c.* 1775 adjoining on the E., the latter with a contemporary kitchen-wing extending S. A S. range abutting the foregoing kitchen-wing and with a stair-hall and open court interposed between it and the earlier house on the N., and itself with a S. wing, is of *c.* 1800. On the E. and S.E. are later 19th-century and modern additions.

The ground floor of the 16th-century house is cased in 18th-century brick; the windows are of the later date. The first floor projects to both N. and S. and the high-pitched roof ends in a rebuilt brick parapeted gable on the W. The E. end abuts the taller building of *c.* 1775. At the roof-ridge is a tall brick chimney-stack rebuilt in the 18th century with round-headed recessed panels on the face; added on the S. is a later flue.

The E. house has a brick facing to the Lane; this returns short of the full frontage on the second floor. It is in four bays and has a stone plat-band at first-floor level, a timber cornice, and a parapet-wall. The round-headed doorway in the W. bay has a fan-light with cast-iron radiating glazing-bars and anthemion-ornament and is flanked by timber Ionic pilasters supporting an entablature; the door of eight panels is original. All the windows have flat brick arches and contain double-hung sashes in frames nearly flush with the wall-face; those at each end of the second floor have scrollwork cut in the brickwork of the arches. The W. gable-end, above the adjoining building, is plastered; the E. is in gault brick. In the E. wall of the kitchen-wing is an original timber-framed window of archaic pattern with mullion and transom and wrought-iron casements.

The S. range is of yellow brick with red brick dressings. It has an open arcade to the court on the N. with round-headed red brick arches and piers faced with stucco.

Inside, the entrance-hall has a plaster quadripartite vault and a dado of reset early 17th-century panelling. Most of the late 18th-century fittings of the Dining-room to the E. survive; the walls are divided into panels by plaster mouldings and have a frieze enriched with swags and roundels and a dentil-cornice; the fireplace-surround is of marble with an enriched architrave, flanking scrolls, a frieze carved with acanthus foliage and an enriched cornice-shelf. On the floor above are 18th-century two-panel doors. The fittings in the 16th-century house include an 18th-century overmantel with dentil-cornice and foliated scrolls at the sides and a fitted cupboard of the same period with round head and open shelves. On the first floor parts of an original moulded wall-plate are visible and a room is lined with 18th-century fielded panelling, with an eared architrave to the fireplace.

All Saints' Passage

(179) Lichfield House, No. 1, to N.E. of the old churchyard, is of two storeys with cellars and attics. The walls are of plaster and tile-covered timber-framing and brick, the roofs tiled. It consists of a long rectangular block framed in the 17th century lying N.E. to S.W., with a brick N.W. wing and a small N.E. addition both of the second quarter of the 19th century, the period when the rest was superficially remodelled. The entrance-front, to the N.W., has a timber doorway in the middle of the original length of wall, with round head, side pilasters and pediment with dentil-cornice; at the wall-head is a timber cornice with added timber parapet; on the roof are three hipped dormer-windows. These last are transeptally arranged with three gabled dormers opposite on the S.E. roof-slope. The S.E. side of the building is entirely masked. The S.W. end has a stone plinth, plaster rendering up to the level of the first floor and tiling simulating brickwork above; the shaped bargeboards are of the 19th century. The windows generally, both 19th-century casements and sashes, have glazing-bars forming two-centred arches in the heads of the lights.

Inside, the ceiling-beams are now cased. The N.E. ground-floor room has a wide opening to the N.E. addition, with four-centred arch springing from pilasters. A cast-iron fireback dated 1697 seems always to have been in the house.

Bridge Street

S.W. side:—

(180) Lindum House, No. 70, behind No. 71 and 15 yds. N.W. of All Saints' Passage, of two and three storeys, is in the main an early 19th-century building incorporating part of an 18th-century structure on the S.; projecting eastward is a lower 17th-century wing. The oldest walls are of plastered timber-framing; the roofs are tiled. The house was formerly the 'Freemasons' Tavern'; within living memory the name and 'Livery Baiting Stables' was painted in the passage to it from Bridge Street. The old part retains no ancient features outside. Inside are stop-chamfered ceiling-beams on the ground floor and on the first floor where also the wall-posts are exposed. The roof has collar-beam trusses.

(181) House, No. 69, 22 yds. N.W. of All Saints' Passage, of three and two storeys with cellars, has brick walls and tiled roofs. It is mainly of the early 18th century; the tall range to the street appears to be a reconstruction of an earlier building and parts of the cellar walls are of 16th or 17th-century brickwork. The kitchen at the N.W. end and the rooms over are part of No. 68, a 17th-century building refaced in the 19th, formerly the 'Bell'. The house, previously the property of the Ewin family, was bought for Sir Isaac Pennington, M.D., in 1793 for £2,000. During the 19th century it was divided into two; though now one house again, two 19th-century staircases remain.

The street-front has plat-bands at first and second-floor levels and below the parapet-wall. This last is panelled and has a moulded stone coping; it is probably a reconstruction of the late 18th century; two elaborately moulded lead rainwater-heads bear the date 1791. The entrance-doorway has a plain square-headed opening with a late 18th or early 19th-century stone architrave and the windows contain double-hung sashes nearly flush with the wall-face; the glazing-bars and most of the frames have been renewed. The lower S.W. range, parallel with the street range and divided from it by the staircase-hall, has a plain parapet and early 19th-century windows with tripartite sash-hung timber frames; part of the S.W. wall has been rebuilt.

Inside, the Dining-room N.W. of the entrance-passage is lined with 18th-century fielded panelling with dado-rail. The window at landing-level in the N.W. wall shows that, of the two 19th-century staircases, that to the N.W. is in the position of the earlier staircase. The ceilings of the S.W. rooms have been raised. The house contains some early 17th-century panelling reset as a dado to the stairs. (J. A. Bullock in *Cambridge Public Library Record* (April 1939)).

House, No. 45, now demolished, see Monument (214).

(182) Warehouse, on the river bank 37 yds. S.W. of Magdalene Bridge, of three storeys and attics, with walls of white brick and timber and with slated roofs, was built in 1820. It is nearly rectangular on plan, the N.W. end following the turn of the river. The N.E. front has been remodelled in the later 19th century. Original windows remain in the N.W. and S.W. walls; they are small, of greater breadth than height and have segmental brick heads. Circular wall-anchors bear the initials and date I.E. 1820. The walls are 2 ft. thick on the ground floor, 1 ft. above; floors are supported on 1 ft. by 1 ft. beams resting on pilaster-like projections of the brickwork.

N.E. side:—

(183) House, No. 30, standing 40 yds. S.E. of Magdalene Bridge, of three storeys with attics, with walls of brick and timber-framing, was built in the first half of the 18th century. The ground and first floors have been altered. The street-front, of brickwork faced with stucco, has a shop-window of *c.* 1900 occupying the whole of the ground floor and a large window of *c.* 1840 on the first floor. The features above are original: a plat-band at second-floor level, two sash-hung windows, a brick cornice returned within the frontage, and a parapet-wall. On the roof are two hipped dormer-windows with casements. The N.E. wing has a plastered timber-framed gable. Inside, on the second floor is some 18th-century fielded panelling. Doors of two and six panels survive, and some of the rooms retain original cornices. The staircase has close moulded strings, slender balusters and a moulded handrail.

(184) House, No. 29, adjoining the foregoing on the S.E., of three storeys with cellar and attics, has walls of plastered timber-framing and tiled roofs. It was built in the 16th or 17th century and much altered and heightened in the early 19th when a range was added on the N.E. The street-front has a 19th-century shop-window on the ground floor. The first and second-floor windows are both of the 19th century and the dormer-window in the mansard roof is of the same period. The chimney-stack on the N.E. is of the 18th century. Inside, the shop contains a chamfered ceiling-beam; a later beam close to the street frontage suggests that the shop-window masks an original projection of the first floor, an arrangement confirmed by the evidence of the building-lines of the later adjoining houses. The 17th-century staircase from ground to second floor has close strings, turned balusters, square newels and a square handrail; the continuation to the attics is of the 19th century.

A kitchen in the yard on the N.E. is weather-boarded and has 19th-century sliding windows.

(185) House, No. 28, next S.E. of the foregoing, of three storeys with attics, has walls of timber-framing and tiled roofs. No evidence remains to suggest that the building is earlier than the late 18th or early 19th-century date of the mansard roofs. The stone-mullioned windows are modern. Inside, in one of the upper rooms, is an early 19th-century cast-iron grate of elaborate design.

(186) House, Nos. 25 and 26, standing 61 yds. S.E. of Magdalene Bridge, of two storeys with basement and attics, has walls of plastered timber-framing and tiled roofs. It consists

of a 16th-century range to the street, with a 17th-century N.E. wing. The interior has been much altered. Late in the 17th century the first-floor rooms in the earlier range were heightened. Early in the 19th two sash-hung windows were inserted on the first floor towards the street; later in the same century the ground-floor front was rebuilt flush with that of the first floor, which formerly projected. In recent years the ground-floor front has again been rebuilt and parts of the earlier structure have been either demolished or rebuilt in brick.

Towards the street, in addition to the features already mentioned, the stucco-faced front has a late 17th-century plaster cove at the eaves; on the roof are two hipped dormer-windows. On the N.E. side is a later 17th-century chimney-stack with moulded brick string and a round-headed recess in two of the faces. The timber-framed walls of the wing have been almost wholly rebuilt, but on the first floor is a 17th-century oak-framed, transomed and mullioned, three-light window.

Inside, the basement walls are built of thin bricks, and the ceiling-joists carried on longitudinal beams supported by a moulded cross-beam; the N.W. fireplace has a segmental head, the N.E. a chamfered timber bressummer. On the ground floor, the ceiling-beams are stop-chamfered and the N.E. fireplace has an 18th-century eared architrave. The passage through the building on the S.E. is an alteration. On the first floor stop-chamfered ceiling-beams of pine and a new partition were inserted in the 17th century. Early timbers are exposed in the attics including the original framing of the S.E. gable-end, posts with enlarged heads supporting a tie-beam, collar-beam and studding.

The 17th-century deal staircase to the N., from ground floor to attics, has close moulded strings, heavy turned balusters, chamfered grip-handrail, and square newels with ball finials and some pendants; a continuation, of the same period, leads down to the basement. The second staircase, from basement to attics, has pine treads and risers housed into a central square newel; it is of the late 18th century.

The attics of the N.E. wing contain two original trusses with tie-beam, high collar, queen-posts and two horizontal struts from the last to the purlins. A number of simple 18th-century fittings survive in the house.

(187) Houses, Nos. 21 and 22, on the corner of Thompson's Lane, of three storeys, with walls of gault brick and slated roofs, are most probably those described as 'recently erected' in the *Cambridge Chronicle* for 14 August 1835, and by James Walter, architect. Though apparently built as social-economic unities of shops and dwellings, they have been combined; now much of the ground floor has been cleared for a modern shop and the rest is a hostel of Magdalene College. To Bridge Street and round into the Lane the original timber shop-fronts remain little altered; they have panelled pilasters supporting an entablature with a deep frieze; across the window-heads are ventilators consisting of metal strips pierced with continuous palmette ornament. The building has rectangular sash-hung windows with stone sills, more or less regularly spaced, and a plat-band below the parapet-wall, this last with a stone coping; the corner is contrived as a slightly recessed quarter-round. The interior has been altered and access to part is now through an adjoining house in the Lane (plan p. 331).

The adjoining houses, Nos. 23 and 24, on the N.W. are of the same style and period but lower and presumably built as dwellings only; they now contain shops with late 19th-century and modern fronts.

(188) Houses, Nos. 15 and 16, on the corner of Jordan's Yard, of three storeys, have plastered timber-framed walls and tile-covered roofs. They were built early in the 16th century and a new staircase was added to No. 16 in the 17th century. In spite of insertion of 19th-century and modern shop-fronts, later windows, attics in part, modifications to the roofs, and clearance of partitions from the lower floors, the original arrangements remain distinguishable. See also Monument (189).

Nos. 15 and 16 Bridge Street are good examples of a type of late mediaeval town house, of which few now survive in Cambridge; they retain much of their original detail. The upper floors are in part derelict.

The street-fronts (Plate 307) project at first and second-floor levels, the upper projection, the only one unmasked by later fascia boards, being supported on curved timber brackets. The sash-hung oriel-windows and others are of the 18th or 19th century. The roof is gabled at each end. The rear wall is botched after the collapse of an adjoining building.

No. 16, on the evidence of the disposition of ceiling-beams now cased, may have had the ground and first floors each divided into two, into a large and a narrow compartment, the latter across the width of the N.W. end and comprising, on the ground floor, an entrance-passage. No evidence survives to show the position of the original stair; a projecting timber-framed staircase-bay on the N.E., beside the chimney-stack in the rear wall, was an addition, probably of the mid 17th century; it is now largely demolished and access to the first floor is by ladder. The fireplace in the former main room on the ground floor is blocked; that on the first floor is fitted with a 19th-century grate and surround. The second floor is divided by an original partition *in situ* into two compartments, the arrangement postulated for the lower floors. The large room was originally open to the roof and was ceiled probably in the 17th century; the small room has always been ceiled and has an original stop-chamfered ceiling-beam. The structural wall-posts are chamfered and have thickened heads to support the tie-beams of the roof-trusses. The timber-framed partition incorporates curved braces to the tie-beam, chamfered only towards the large room. The roof has king-posts on the ties supporting a purlin under the collars of the pairs of trussed rafters; the longitudinal braces from posts to purlin have all been removed and replaced by props in other positions. At this level the original chimney-stack is seen to be of $8\frac{1}{4}$ by $4\frac{1}{2}$ by 2 ins. bricks; it is disused; the part rising clear has been removed and the roof continued down over the stump.

No. 15 is generally similar to the foregoing; the modern passage and staircase against the N.W. party-wall may perpetuate the original arrangement. The chimney-stack, at the S.E. end of the rear wall, has a fireplace on the first floor with chamfered bressummer though the opening has been reduced and an 18th-century fireplace with eared surround inserted. The oriel-windows overlooking the street are in the positions of earlier windows. The fireplace on the second floor is also an insertion of the 18th century, with moulded surround, key-block, and cornice-shelf with simple geometrical decoration.

(189) HOUSES, Nos. 1, 2, 3, 4 and 4a Jordan's Yard, forming a range of dwellings of three storeys with cellars, with plastered timber-framed walls and tiled roofs, continue and are of the same build as Nos. 15 and 16 Bridge Street, described above. In the 18th century the upper floors were newly fronted in lath-and-plaster above the projection of the first floor on the S., so obliterating any projection that may have existed higher, and a stair and kitchen built flanking the chimney-stack at the eastern end. The two upper floors of No. 1 and the second floor of No. 2 have been demolished.

Towards the Yard, the first-floor projection is supported on small curved brackets. All the doorcases and windows are of the 18th or 19th century. The E. end has near the middle a large original chimney-stack weathered back at the eaves and rebuilt in white brick above.

Inside, the cellar under No. 3 has walls of thin bricks and communicates with another later cellar with four-centred brick vault under the Yard. A chamfered ceiling-beam supports some original joists under the ground floor. On the ground floor of Nos. 1 and 2 moulded wall-plates and a central longitudinal moulded ceiling-beam support moulded joists with leaf-stops; one of the supporting wall-posts visible has an enlarged head. Shaped posts and moulded and chamfered beams are exposed in No. 3, and chamfered beams in No. 4. On the first floor a room in No. 3 is lined with 17th-century pine panelling in four heights of panels with plain pilasters; the overmantel comprises two oval panels in two rectangular panels divided and flanked by pilasters; one of the doors is contemporary. Much of the structural timber-work is exposed on the upper floors throughout. Generally the dwellings contain a quantity of 16th and 17th-century panelling, some in No. 1 *in situ*, and plain 18th-century fittings.

(190) HOUSE, No. 5 Jordan's Yard, adjoining the foregoing on the E., of two storeys with attics, has plastered timber-framed walls and tiled roofs. The E. part is of the 17th century; in the 18th century the W. part was built between the foregoing and No. 4a Jordans's Yard, incorporating an older wall at the back, and a staircase and offices were added behind the first building. To the S. is now a plain cement-rendered 18th-century front with flat timber hood to the entrance-doorway and sash-hung windows with all the glazing-bars removed. Inside, on the ground floor is a stop-chamfered ceiling-beam in the E. part; the W. room has an 18th-century cornice, a cased beam, and chamfered wall-posts exposed in the N.E. and N.W. corners. On the first floor, the middle room is lined with reset mid 17-century panelling, four panels high and with a fluted frieze under an 18th-century cornice; the contemporary door is of eight panels. A number of 18th-century doors remain in the house. The roof is in three bays; the earliest truss, to the E., has a collar-beam and principals of heavy scantling.

(191) HOUSE, No. 12, standing 9 yds. N.W. of Round Church Street, of two storeys with cellar and attics, with stucco-fronted timber-framed walls and tiled mansard roofs, was built *c.* 1600. It was refashioned and probably heightened in the 19th century. In modern times the ground-floor has been cleared and a garage-entrance made through it, shop-windows have been inserted and the original back wall demolished, a new wall being built further E. Towards the street the first floor projects and is supported on curved brackets carved with strapwork and foliation; the same floor contains three 19th-century windows with architraves, friezes and cornices, the last supported on console-brackets. At the wall-head is a plain parapet and on the roof are three 19th-century dormer-windows.

Inside, the cellars continue eastward where they served a range now demolished. On the ground floor the wall-plate of the original back wall remains *in situ*. On the first floor, the N. room retains original moulded panelling, four panels high, with a strapwork frieze; exposed in the ceiling are intersecting chamfered beams. Similarly the S. room has some original panelling, the N. wall being built against it, and exposed beams; below the window is 19th-century panelling. The framing of the original back wall shows in an E. room. The late 18th-century staircase has slender square balusters and a moulded mahogany handrail.

(192) HOUSES, Nos. 10 and 11, and No. 16 Round Church Street, stand on the corner N.W. of the church of Holy Sepulchre. No. 11 is of one build with No. 12 (Monument (191)) but now united internally with No. 10, which itself is of one build with No. 16 Round Church Street. The last two were built in the 17th century and are of two storeys with attics; the walls are of plastered timber-framing and the roofs slated and tiled. No. 11 was refronted on the S.W. in the first half of the 19th century and in modern times the ground floor has been cleared, a shop-window inserted in both street-frontages, and the rear party-wall demolished. The S.W front is now flat, with sash-hung windows, a cornice and parapet-wall, but the first floor probably projected originally. The gabled S.E. end has, on the projecting first floor, an early 19th-century three-sided bay-window that is constructed round one of the structural wall-posts. Inside, on the ground floor the rear wall-plate in continuation from that in Monument (191) remains *in situ*. On the first floor is an original door of six panels.

No. 10 and the adjoining house, also with modern shops and shop-windows on the ground floor, have 18th-century windows on the first floor, four in all, plain eaves and gabled dormer-windows. At the E. end is a large brick chimney-stack weathered back above ridge-level and rebuilt above. Inside, chamfered beams are exposed in the ceilings. The staircase is of the 18th century, with square paired balusters and moulded handrail. On the first floor of No. 10 much of the main room is lined with 17th-century panelling, of three patterns, some probably *in situ*, four panels high and with a carved frieze in part misplaced. Loose in the attic is a 16th-century bargeboard carved with leaf and vine ornament.

(193) House, No. 9, the first building S. of the church of Holy Sepulchre, of three stories with cellars and attics, has plastered timber-framed walls, with some clunch in the cellars, and tiled roofs. It is L-shaped on plan. The street range has 16th-century cellars, but above ground it is an 18th-century rebuilding. The N.E. range is of the 17th century, with a staircase inserted in the 18th century. The whole has been partly refitted at later dates, a modern shop-front inserted and additions made in the re-entrant angle. The S.W. front, above the ground floor, is severely plain, with sash hung windows and simple eaves; two of the upper windows are fitted with early 19th-century voluted wire guards. The N.W. side has two large brick chimney-stacks, both of the 18th century except for the rebuilt upper courses, at the N. angles of the 17th and 18th century ranges respectively; the windows are of the 19th century.

Inside, the cellar under the N.E. range contains a 16th-century door with linenfold panels. The wall between the two rooms above has been removed and the whole is one room, with the staircase structure projecting into it; exposed in the ceiling are chamfered beams; on the walls is reused 17th and 18th-century panelling, including an elaborate overmantel to the more westerly fireplace with a moulded panel superimposed on a horizontal fielded panel and flanked by foliated scrolls all below a dentil-cornice.

On the first floor, a room in the front range is wainscoted throughout with fielded panelling of *c.* 1730 in two heights with dado-rail and cornice; it is *in situ*. The staircase, of the same date, has close strings, turned balusters and newels and square moulded handrail. A cambered tie-beam is visible in the attics of the N.E. range. The house contains many reset lengths of 17th and 18th-century panelling and several panelled doors of the same periods.

(194) House, No. 4, standing 20 yds. N.W. of Jesus Lane, of three and two storeys with cellars and attics, has walls of red brick now painted yellow and slate and tile-covered roofs. L-shaped on plan, it was built in 1729. In the 19th century the middle flights of the staircase were refashioned and the first-floor windows to the street modified. In modern times the ground floor has been altered, a shop-window inserted and new stairs built from ground to first floor. The front is the width of a brick in advance of the front of the adjoining house, No. 3 (Monument (195)), though the two are generally similar in character; Nos. 3 and 4 together once formed part of the Hoop Inn, earlier the Bell Inn; it has a plaster plat-band at second-floor level and a timber modillioned eaves-cornice returned at the extremities and fitted with metal rings. The windows, three on each of the upper floors, have flat arches of rubbed bricks with mask keyblocks; those on the first floor are now without glazing-bars. The mansard roof is a 19th-century rebuilding. The N.E. wing, of red brick in Flemish bond, retains two original dormers.

Inside, a first-floor bedroom has a moulded wood fireplace-surround of *c.* 1800 with paterae at the angles, another a white marble arched surround with keystone. The 19th-century staircase has square balusters and a mahogany handrail; the early 18th-century upper flights, from the second floor to the attics, except where rebuilt at the head, have moulded strings, twisted pine balusters, a newel with moulded pendant, and moulded handrail. (A. B. Gray, *Cambridge Revisited* (1921), 43; *Cambridge Public Library Record* XI, No. 42, April 1939.)

(195) House, No. 3, standing 9 yds. N.W. of Jesus Lane, with walls of red brick in Flemish bond with vitrified headers, now all painted yellow, and tiled roofs, is of three storeys with cellars and attics. It was built in 1729 (see Monument (194)) and towards the middle of the century the first-floor rooms were panelled. Early in the 19th century a large N.E. wing was added. The ground floor now contains a modern shop with display-windows occupying the whole of the street-front up to first-floor level. At second-floor level is a brick plat-band. Of the timber modillion-cornice and parapet-wall, similar to those on the later wing and perhaps early 19th-century renewals, the former was removed in 1956. The five windows on each of the upper floors towards the street have flat rubbed brick arches with mask keyblocks; four retain later 18th-century glazing. On the roof are three dormer-windows with timber pedimented cornices and sliding casements. The grey brick N.E. wing has, projecting on the S.E. side, a three-sided bay-window rising through the three floors and with a crowning cornice.

Inside, the ground floor is supported on stop-chamfered beams exposed in the cellars. The two large rooms on the first floor are lined with mid 18th-century panelling with dado-rail and dentil-cornice, the dentils being of some elaboration. The fireplaces have plain surrounds, cornice-shelves and overmantels each containing a large fielded panel. The doors are of six fielded panels. The staircase from the second floor to the attics is of the early 19th century and has square balusters, newels in the form of small columns with moulded caps and bases, and a moulded handrail.

Portugal Place

(196) House, No. 8, standing 20 yds. due E. of St. Clement's Church and formerly the vicarage, of two storeys with attics, has rendered timber-framed walls and tiled roofs. It was built in the 17th century, improved in the 18th, and has since been modernised. The windows, of the late 18th century, have sliding casements; the timber eaves-cornice is of the same date, so is the hipped dormer-window to the N.E. Inside, on the ground floor the ceiling-beams are cased; the S.E. room contains an 18th-century fitted oak corner-cupboard with a cornice and doors consisting of fielded panels. The late 18th-century staircase has slender turned balusters and moulded handrail. On the first floor the ceiling-beams are chamfered,

and the partitions are of the 18th century, with doors of two fielded panels hung on angle-hinges. The timber-framing is exposed throughout; it has plain square angle-posts and wall-plates.

THOMPSON'S LANE

E. side:—

(197) OLD VICARAGE, at the N. corner of St. Clement's churchyard, of two storeys with cellars and attics, has walls of plastered timber-framing and brick and tiled roofs. It was built in the 16th century and, despite minor changes in the 18th century, retains much of the original form and character. Most notable is the large chimney-stack in the N. external wall, which has been pierced in modern times for passages on the first and second floors.

The walls to the ground floor are largely of red brick, that to the W. being a modern reconstruction in vitrified brick and timber-framing; the S. wall has a slight plinth; the E. is plastered where not concealed on the N. by a timber addition. The first floor and attics together project on the W. and S. and probably formerly did on the E.; they are of timber-framing, which is continued round on the N. as far as the great brick chimney-stack. The bressummers under the projections are supported on brackets. The W. and the S.E. doorways, the second now blocked, have late 18th-century timber cases and all the windows are of the 18th or early 19th century, those on the ground floor to the S. with contemporary shutters. The chimney-stack, some 26 ft. wide, is rectangular and forms a great base, about at ridge height, for freestanding chimneys, in part rebuilt, set diagonally; it is weathered back at eaves-level and has a square-headed opening above pierced through the centre for a downward continuation of the main roof to provide drainage to the eaves; the converging corbelling of the flanking flues appears in the thickness of the opening.

Inside, the original square beams and joists supporting the ground floor are visible in the cellar. On the ground floor the ceiling-beams are exposed, including two dragon-beams, to S.W. and S.E., continued to support the projecting upper floors; they are chamfered, except the S.W. dragon-beam, which is moulded on one side. Chamfered ceiling-beams occur on the floor above. The open fireplaces have all been altered, but the original shaped oak lintel of that on the first floor is visible above a plain 18th-century surround. The doors, door-cases and fireplace-surrounds generally are of the 18th century and plain.

W. side:—

(198) HOUSE, No. 29, standing 93 yds. from Bridge Street, of two storeys with cellars and attics, has walls of gault brick and tiled roofs. The almost symmetrical block centred on the entrance doorway and extending to the back wall of the stairhall in depth was built early in the 19th century, before No. 30 (Monument (199)). An original N.W. wing of this last overlaps, concealing the S. end of the W. wall; the ground floor is now a part of No. 29. Later in the 19th century an extension including a carriage-way was made on the N. and offices were added on the W. The E. front has a plinth and a timber eaves-cornice. The doorway and fanlight have a continuous splayed plaster reveal and architrave, all contained within a round-headed arch. The windows have flat brick arches and stone sills. On the roof are three dormer-windows. The N. extension has a window with segmental head on the ground floor. On the W., in the earlier block, above the later offices, is a staircase-window with semicircular head; at the eaves is a cornice similar to that on the E., and on the roof are three more dormer-windows. An original rainwater head remains.

Inside, on the ground floor, the S. room has a moulded fireplace-surround with paterae at the angles and a cornice. The staircase has moulded strings, slender square balusters, moulded mahogany handrail and, in part, a dado of fielded panelling. The secondary staircase has turned newels. On the first floor is a dado of fielded panels in one room, and in another a glazed door with the bars forming a Gothic pattern. Other original fittings remain but they are plain.

(199) HOUSE, No. 30, adjoining the foregoing on the S., of two storeys with cellars, with walls of gault brick with stone dressings and tile-covered roofs, was built *c.* 1820.

No. 30 is a particularly good and well-preserved example of a type of town house of which there are many much less elaborate in Cambridge.

The street-front is symmetrical, with an elliptical-headed doorway in the middle, two windows to each side and five on the first floor, the last contained within a wall-arcade, a brick plinth, stone plat-bands at first-floor and eaves level, and a low parapet-wall with stone coping. The monumental doorway is of two square orders with plain stone imposts and the returns and soffit of the inner order lined with wood panelling; the door is of enriched fielded panelling in two leaves, and the fanlight has radiating foliated and festooned metal glazing-bars. All the windows have flat brick arches and retain their shutters. The wall-arcade on the first floor, rising from the lower plat-band, has elliptical arches springing from moulded stone imposts continued across the piers.

The W. side is longer than the E. and overlaps No. 29 (Monument (198)) where it is obtusely gabled to the N. It has a continuous brick plat-band at eaves-level and a parapet-wall. An original doorway, now blocked, and the staircase-window, set high, have round brick arches; the windows where open have double-hung sashes, but some are dummies and others have been blocked. A small modern annexe has been built against the staircase-wall.

Inside, some of the 'period' decoration is obvious modern pastiche; thus the antiquity of much of the enriched architectural elaboration here described is in doubt, this however is correct for the period *c.* 1820, though in pristine condition. The entrance-hall has an open round-headed archway to the stairhall and two round-headed recesses in the N. and S. walls, that to the W. in each containing a doorway with timber case with architrave, frieze and pedimented cornice; frieze and pediment are both enriched, the former with an urn on a panel in the middle and roundels containing paterae to each side; the corresponding doorcases on the reverse, in the N. and S. flanking rooms, are generally similar but without pediments; the doors, of six moulded panels, are original. The main N. room has a wood and composition fireplace-surround with slender paired columns at the sides, a

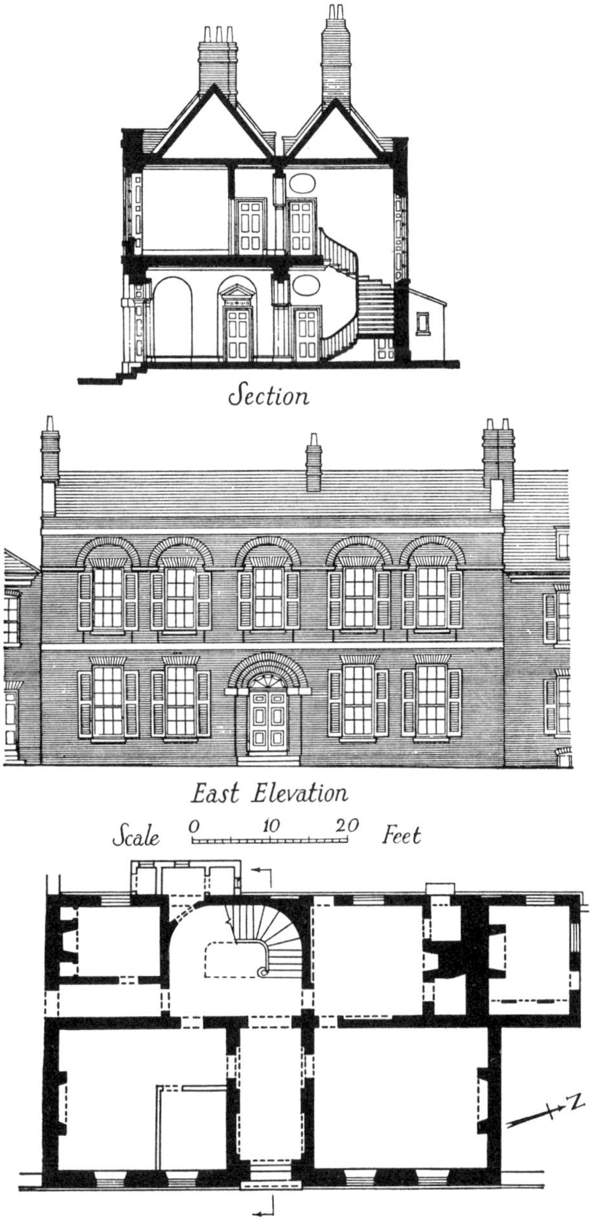

No. 30 Thompson's Lane

frieze with central panel and panelled blocks over the columns modelled with female figures, cupid, lion and lamb, and roundels similar to those on the doorcases described above, and an enriched cornice-shelf. In the S. room is a fireplace-surround with Ionic side-columns and enriched frieze and cornice, with a frieze-panel of Cybele in a chariot. Both the foregoing rooms have heavy skirtings and dado-rails, enriched plaster cornices, and panelled window-reveals with architraves; the S. room has a second enriched doorcase, on the W. wall, of similar character to that on the N. described above.

The stairhall is oblong, with rounded N.W. and S.W. corners. In the N. and S. walls are doorways and oval panels above; of the latter, one is glazed, the other blind. Standing against the S. wall is an enclosed stove cased with tiles, probably German and of *c.* 1700 (Plate 51). The stone cantilevered staircase rises from first to second floors in one curving flight against three walls, the front edge of the landing across the fourth wall being enriched with an urn and swags. The stairs have returned moulded edges to the treads, moulded soffits, plain iron balusters and a mahogany handrail.

On the first floor, a N. room has a fireplace-surround similar in character to those on the ground floor, but with pilasters at the sides, their shafts enriched with scrolled foliation, urns on the entablature-blocks, and a central frieze-panel modelled with figures personifying perhaps Love before Minerva extolling Health, Wealth and Happiness. The wall-niches flanking the foregoing, and the fittings and painted decoration in Adam style in the bedroom E. of the stairhall were certainly added in the present century by craftsmen in the tapestry works formerly housed here. See also Monument (200).

(200) House, No. 31, adjoining (199) on the S., 50 yds. from Bridge Street, of two storeys with cellars, has walls of gault brick and tiled roofs. On the E. it has a continuation of the plinth of No. 30 (Monument (199)), but a straight joint above between the two houses suggests different building phases; general stylistic similarities and the fact that the N. half at least of No. 31 was originally an annexe of No. 30, which it still is, suggest that the lapse of time between the two phases was short. The street-front is asymmetrical; the round-headed main doorway is of two continuous square brick orders and flanked on both sides by a wide window with segmental head and a narrow one with flat head; one of the last is a dummy. On the first floor are six sash-hung windows and one dummy window. At the eaves is a timber frieze and slight cornice.

Inside, the cellars have five parallel brick barrel-vaults running E. to W. and a passage on the W. The main ground-floor room in the N. half, formerly the kitchen of No. 30, has a dado of fielded panelling, cased ceiling-beams, and a wide segmental-headed fireplace in the S. wall, formerly open but now partly blocked, with a timber surround. The staircase in the S. half is original, with plain square balusters, turned newels and moulded handrail. Some original fireplace-surrounds with dentilled cornice-shelves remain on the first floor.

Magdalene Street

S.W. side:—

Monuments (201–211) form a notable row of plastered timber-framed town houses dating from late mediaeval times to the 18th century and, except for later windows almost throughout, comparatively little altered structurally. It is the only frontage of its age surviving in the city of sufficient length to give any impression of the earlier street scene. The houses belong to, or are being bought by, Magdalene College mainly for further accommodation for undergraduates. The alterations are now being made (1955–7). The aspect to the street is being retained but most of the W. extensions, of various dates, are being demolished, except the notable W. range of Monument (205). The interiors are being modernised. In the following descriptions, for simplicity, the street-front is taken to be orientated facing due E.

(201) House, No. 31, adjoining Madgalene Bridge, of two storeys with attics, has plastered timber-framed walls and tiled roofs. It consists of a 16th-century range to the street with a nearly contemporary building on the N.W., perhaps originally separate, that was subsequently extended to the W. The S.W. re-entrant was built up in *c.* 1800 when the E., S. and W. return faces of the E. range were remodelled, the last two including the addition and so presenting a unified front to the river. The house seems once to have formed an annexe to the Pickerel Inn (Monument (202)).

The street-front has, on the ground floor two early 19th-century display-windows and doorways, originally to two shops, three sash-hung windows on the first floor, a cornice at eaves-level, and a high parapet-wall. The S. front is built out over the river revetment; the last is of ashlar and rubble, and white and red brickwork, coextensive respectively with the original range and addition of *c.* 1800; in the older range is a projecting three-sided bay-window, two storeys high, contemporary with the refacing; the horizontal features return from the street-front. The W. range has some brick underpinning but in general is of framing with heavy horizontal timbers in the walls at first-floor level; the first floor does not project. In the N. wall is an ovolo-moulded oak doorway and, close up under the eaves, a blocked two-light window, both of the 16th century; in the roof is an unaltered 17th-century dormer-window with leaded quarries. A small 18th-century extension spanning the through-way links the W. range with the Pickerel Inn.

Inside, in the E. range, the N. room originally continued as far S. as the S. wall of the middle passage, and here the partition between the head-beam and the chamfered sill is of late 16th or early 17th-century panelling, three panels high, with a fluted frieze. Some of the ceiling-beams are exposed; one cased at the N. end is at a higher level than the others in consequence it seems of the remodelling of the Pickerel Inn, for it continues over the adjoining entry. The S. room was remodelled in *c.* 1800 and has a fireplace-surround with enriched frieze and dentilled cornice-shelf. On the first floor the N. party-wall with the Inn is modern. The S. room, also remodelled, has a W. fireplace with marble slips and eared wood surround of *c.* 1800; beside it, behind a cupboard-door, are oak stairs. In the W. range, on the ground floor, the W. wall of the early part has been replaced by two supporting posts; a passage-width E. of the latter is a partition with original studs about 1½ ft. apart containing a later doorway, now blocked, incorporating a 16th-century bargeboard carved with running vine ornament. In the later part are square cross and longitudinal beams supported at the intersection by a post that seems to have been a partition-stud. Three 18th-century cupboards remain on this floor. In the attics the lath and plaster E. gable end of the W. range survives.

(202) Pickerel Inn, No. 30, adjoining the foregoing on the N.W., of three and two storeys with attics, has walls of plastered timber-framing and of brick; the roofs are tile and slate-covered. It is L-shaped on plan, with a long range projecting W. from the southern part of the E. range. The oldest structure is that half, approximately, of the W. range adjoining the E. range; it is of the 16th century. In the 17th century the E. range was built, or more probably rebuilt, and the W. half of the W. range added. Early in the 19th century the street-front was rebuilt in brick, the range heightened and the interior and the carriage-way on the N. were altered; at the same time a brewery was built in the yard to the W., but this has been demolished. Late in the 19th century a large single-storey addition was made in the re-entrant angle.

The early 19th-century E. front has a plat-band at second-floor level and a cornice of oversailing brick courses. The wall-openings generally, except the modernised ground-floor windows, have segmental-arched heads. The carriage-way to the N. extends well up into the first floor and the framing inside shows this to have been heightened at the sacrifice of the first-floor rooms above; the E. entrance has an early 19th-century timber frame, but the S. post masks a chamfered oak post of the 17th-century building; above is a contemporary wrought-iron scrollwork lamp bracket. The W. side of the E. range where visible is plastered and probably timber-framed. In the S. end wall is a modern doorway to the adjoining entry.

In the W. range, the early E. part is lower than the rest and largely concealed on the N. On the S. side some much patched original timber-framing is exposed; it incorporates towards the E. end a doorway, now blocked, with one oak post, and towards the W. end of the first floor a blocked window with an ovolo-moulded mullion and head; further W. again are three small blocked windows close up under the eaves. The outside of the rest of the range is plastered and the open fenestration throughout the whole building is of the 18th century and later.

Inside, the ground floor of the E. range has been opened out to form one room, S. of the carriage-way; it has a large chimney-stack in the W. wall, a smaller in the N. wall, both altered, and intersecting ceiling-beams; these last are encased; the original W. wall-plate, in part exposed, is moulded. The 16th-century E. half of the W. wing has most of the wall-posts and ceiling-beams cased, but one exposed original post is chamfered. Original chamfered longitudinal beams and wall-plates are exposed in the later W. half; here the fireplaces are of the 18th and 19th centuries. On the upper floors are exposed wall-posts, chamfered ceiling-beams and wall-plates but otherwise the rooms have been modernised. The roof of the W. half of the W. range is now older than that of the E. half.

Many of the doors and door-frames are of the 18th century and some 17th-century panelling remains S. of the doorway to the staircase in the W. range.

(203) HOUSE, No. 29, adjoining the foregoing on the N.W., 26 yds. from Magdalene Bridge, of two storeys with attics, has walls of plastered timber-framing and of brick; the roofs are slate and tile-covered. It was built in the 16th century and remodelled late in the 18th century when the shop-windows were inserted and a small wing was added on the S.W. The ground floor and the N. shop-window have been altered and the E. slope of the roof slated in modern times; with these exceptions the house remains practically as it was at the end of the 18th century. On the E. are two display-windows flanking the shop doorway, and a second doorway to the N. The 18th-century S. window contains a glazing of forty small panes; the N. window is largely modern. The first floor projects but the bressummer is concealed; symmetrically placed in it are three 18th-century sash-hung windows. The N. end contains some rough ashlar but, for the rest, is of later gault brick to the ground floor, plastered above; the N.W. oak corner-post is exposed. The W. side has a forward extension of the ground floor with a lean-to roof and a modern brick addition towards the S. The rebuilt chimney-stacks on the N. and S. walls rise just behind the ridge.

Inside, on the ground floor a heavy chamfered ceiling-beam spans the whole building longitudinally; a second beam to the W. supported on an iron column is the original wall-plate. Similar beams and plates and wall-posts with thickened heads are exposed on the first floor. A stair to the attic flanks the N. chimney-stack; the main staircase is now near the middle of the range. The S. room has an original N. partition wall with studs about 1½ ft. apart and plaster infilling; in the S. wall is a fireplace with segmental brick head. Only the N. end of the roof-space has been used as an attic bedroom, which has a N. fireplace similar to that just described; the use may be an innovation of the early 17th century, a period of severe overcrowding in the town. The roof has been altered and renewed, but heavy oak purlins remain in the S. roof-space and many original rafters survive.

(204) HOUSE, Nos. 26, 27, 28, 28a, next N. of the foregoing, of two storeys with attics, has walls of timber-framing and brick to the street range, of gault brick to the parallel W. range, and tile-covered mansard roofs (Plate 305). It was built in the 16th century, but largely remodelled and entirely reroofed in the late 18th century when the walls, except that to the street, were rebuilt or refaced in gault brick and the W. range was added. To the E., the ground floor, largely refaced with 19th-century brickwork, contains three separate shop-windows with doorways; two are of the early 19th century, that to the N. is later. The first floor projects and contains three 18th-century windows. Inside are chamfered and square ceiling-beams exposed on the ground floor, mostly spanning from E. to W.

(205) HOUSE, Nos. 25, 25a, adjoining (204) on the N.W., 54 yds. from Magdalene Bridge, once the Cross Keys Inn, of three storeys to the street and two storeys with cellars and attics westward, has plastered timber-framed walls and tiled roofs. It is L-shaped on plan. The long W. range is of the early 16th century, the street range of the early 17th century. Dormers were added on the W. side of the last later in the 17th century and in the 18th the N.E. ground-floor room was extended internally to W. and S.

Nos. 25 and 25a comprise a notable timber-framed town house of the early 17th century with a late mediaeval rear wing; the street-front though simpler than that of No. 14 Trinity Street is much less restored.

The street-front (Plate 305) has the first and second floors projecting boldly. On the ground floor is a large entrance to a carriage-way in the S. end, with restored timber posts carrying an original nail-studded oak gate in two leaves, each of six vertical panels with moulded and chamfered muntins and rail, strap-hinges and locking-bar. The rest is occupied by a late 19th-century shop-front. N. of this last an original wall-post survives; it has a pilaster on the face with foliate capital beneath a bracket to the first-floor projection; the bracket is elaborately carved with a crouching man, jewelled strapwork and volutes. Four such features existed but this is the only one complete; a second bracket only, carved with a satyr, survives N. of the carriage-way. The first floor is in two bays divided by posts and brackets to the second floor similar to those just described, but with tapering Ionic pilasters and the brackets carved with a seated man, a naked woman and a centaur respectively. In each bay to the full height is a projecting three-sided window; though modernised and sash-hung, they represent original features. Extending between their flanking wall-posts and the enriched posts described above, approximately at the level of the Ionic caps on the last, are rails that originally formed the sills of small two-light windows close up under the upper projection. All are now blocked and only the sills and the mullion of the southernmost window remain visible outside; but, inside, those flanking the N. bay-window survive almost complete, with ovolo-moulded frames and mullions and iron stanchions. The face of the second floor is plastered and contains two 18th-century windows but the undulations of the plaster indicate the framing of other windows. The wall-posts at each end are exposed; they also have pilasters on the face, with moulded bases on rusticated pedestals, but much mutilated and lacking the caps and the brackets to the eaves.

The N. end has a moulded pendant at the gable-apex, and the S. end moulded bargeboards meeting a similar pendant; in the S. gable is an original two-light window, now blocked. The W. side has the N. half concealed by the adjoining W. range, but on the roof above and above the carriage-way are two large 17th-century dormers; both were blind and plastered, but a window was inserted in the latter in 1956.

The W. range (Plate 306), all of one build, has most of the timber-framing exposed on the S. side; the N. wall is of narrow bricks, white to the E., red to the W. On the S. is a blocked doorway towards the E. end retaining original posts;

the other doorways and windows are later. The first floor projects, the projection being carried on the protruding ends of the floor joists, which are divided into four bays by joists of heavier scantling; three of the last are supported by curved and chamfered brackets and the ends of all the joists are rounded. The sill resting on the joist-ends is plain; the studs are about 12 ins. apart and the infilling is of lath and plaster. One original window now blocked and a second containing an 18th-century frame remain on the first floor, both close up under the eaves. The other windows are later and on the roof are two 17th-century dormer-windows. At the ridge is an original chimney-stack heightened in the 18th century. On the N., towards the E. end, alterations in 1956 revealed an ovolo-moulded two-light window in an apparent heightening of this part of the range; it has been cut down to form a doorway to No. 24. The timbers hereabouts were seen to be badly charred behind the facing of 19th-century brickwork. Further W., the chimney-stack in the stretch of original red brickwork has moulded bricks below the eaves. The W. end was refaced in 1956.

Inside, the longitudinal chamfered ceiling-beams and wall-plates are exposed in the carriage-way and the room to the N., on the floors above, and on both floors of the W. range. The beams in the N. first-floor room in the street range are moulded; the panelling from this room is now in the Small Combination Room at Magdalene College. The studding on the second floor of the same range is so arranged and moulded as to show the positions of the earlier windows. In the W. range some of the wall-posts have enlarged heads, and the E. framed gable-end is visible from the top landing of the E. staircase; it has a collar-beam with studding below. Trusses further W. have deep collars, chamfered and slightly curved; visible in a cupboard is apparently a principal at a lower level, suggesting that the E. part of the N. slope of the roof was once of steeper pitch.

(206) House, No. 23, next but one N.W. of the last, 67 yds. from Magdalene Bridge, of two storeys with cellars and attics, has plastered timber-framed and brick walls and tiled roofs. It was built late in the 16th century; the slightly later W. wing, extended in the 18th and 19th centuries, was demolished in 1955. In the 17th century the roof-space of the E. range was made habitable by the addition of the large gable towards the street.

The E. side (Plate 305) has a modern shop-front and a carriage-way on the N. with modern gates. The projecting first floor is supported by three brackets carved with stylised leaf-ornament, rosettes and paterae; the middle bracket has been mutilated. On the first floor is a 19th-century window with sliding casements; the surrounding pargeting in large panels is of the 17th or 18th century. The plastering and window to the gable are of the 19th century.

Inside, the carriage-way has original chamfered ceiling-timbers, the N. wall-plate containing mortice-holes in the underside for studding, which was replaced with red brick-work in the 17th century. The S. wall is of 18th or 19th-century timber-framing with white brick infilling. Chamfered ceiling-beams and wall-plates are exposed in most of the rooms. In the attics the original chamfered roof-purlins remain and the gable is seen to be fitted in between original rafters.

(207) House, Nos. 21 and 22, next N.W. of the foregoing, 52 yds. S.E. of Northampton Street, of two storeys with attics, has plastered timber-framed walls and tiled roofs. The range to the street was built in the 16th century and a small cottage some yards to the W. in the first half of the 17th century; the two were then linked by an 18th-century block, and a kitchen was added on the W. in the following century. The cottage, the kitchen and other minor 18th and 19th-century additions were demolished in 1956. The roof-space of the street range seems to have been made habitable in part in the 17th century, but the whole of the interior has now been modernised.

Towards the street the ground floor is taken up by modern shop-fronts flanking a small open entry and concealing the former projection of the upper floor. On the first floor are 18th and 19th-century windows, and under the eaves is a moulded fascia in part covering an old wall-plate. The W. side and the outside of the 18th-century building are largely concealed by modern additions, but the second has an oak corner-post exposed in the S.W. angle and a plaster eaves cornice.

The interior of the ground floor is much altered. In the street range longitudinal chamfered ceiling-beams and wall-plates are exposed. The positions of the stops to the chamfers suggest that the range may have comprised two tenements divided on the line of the S. wall of the entry and that in the S. tenement, No. 22, a narrow room or lobby intervened between the N. end wall and the internal chimney-stack. A small rectangular addition, probably of the 17th century, projecting from the W. wall outside may have housed the stair to this lobby; it contained the stairs from the first floor to the attics; the position of the original stairs is unknown. On the first floor some of the structural timbers are exposed.

(208) House, No. 20, next N.W. of the foregoing, of two storeys with attics, has walls of brick, replacing timber-framing, and tiled roofs. The shape of the building and the way it conforms to the row of 16th-century houses in which it stands are the main evidence for suggesting a 16th-century origin for it, though it is built against, and therefore later than, No. 21 (Monument (207)) adjoining; it was extended to the W. in the 18th century and a new staircase added. In the following century a single-storey annexe was built against the extension; this has since been altered. The house has been extensively modernised inside and out and now communicates with No. 21. The N. wall of the extension retains a plat-band at first-floor level. Inside the street range are exposed longitudinal chamfered ceiling-beams. The posts and tie-beam visible in the S. end of the attics belong to the adjoining house. In the extension the 18th-century roof with square purlins and chamfered rafters survives.

(209) House, No. 18a, on the N. side of the entry next (208), 10 yds. from Magdalene Street, of two storeys with attics, has plastered timber-framed walls and tiled roofs. It consists of

(108–110) TRINITY STREET. E. side.

(120–125) KING'S PARADE. E. side.

(336) TRUMPINGTON. 'The Green Man'. Exterior. 15th-century

(136) EAGLE INN. Exterior. *c.* 1600 and *c.* 1800

(204–6) Nos. 23–28 MAGDALENE STREET.
16th-century and later

(108) No. 14 TRINITY STREET. *c.* 1600

(210–12) Nos. 13–16 MAGDALENE STREET, No. 1 NORTHAMPTON STREET and CORY HOUSE.
16th-century and later

(317) CHESTERTON. Range in Water Street. 16th-century

(292) MERTON HALL. Exterior, from W. 16th and 17th-century

(205) No. 25 MAGDALENE STREET. Exterior of W. range. 16th-century

(188) Nos. 15 and 16 BRIDGE STREET.
Early 16th-century

(329) TRUMPINGTON. The Old House.
Late 16th-century

(309) CHESTERTON HALL. Exterior. *c.* 1630

(270) ABBEY HOUSE. W. gable. 1678

(240) SCROOPE TERRACE. Trumpington Street. 1839 and 1864

(266) MAIDS' CAUSEWAY. Doll's Close. 1816

(249) Nos. 2 and 3 BENET PLACE, Lensfield Road. Exterior c. 1820

(322) ROUND HOUSE. Exterior. *c.* 1830

(321) CHESTERTON. Railway dwelling (a). *c.* 1845

(321) CHESTERTON. Railway dwelling (b). *c.* 1847

(280) HILLS ROAD. Rattee's house. *c.* 1845

(20) BOTANIC GARDEN. Brooklands Lodge.
Early 19th-century

(74) GENERAL CEMETERY. Lodge. 1843

(264) ORCHARD TERRACE. *c.* 1825

(218) Nos. 4–10 CHESTERTON ROAD. *c.* 1795

(265) NEW SQUARE. N. Terrace. 1834–35

(227) RADEGUND BUILDINGS. Jesus Lane. 1816

two small adjoining houses combined; that to the E. is of the 16th century, the other may be of the same period though of a different building phase, but it has been much altered. Large houses stand to E. and W., of the 19th and 18th centuries respectively, a ground-floor room of the latter providing a sitting-room for No. 18a. Though the S. front has modern plastering and fenestration, the first floor of the E. building projects boldly on protruding joists with quarter-rounded ends. The first floor of the other building projects only slightly, but this may be the result of later remodelling.

Inside, the E. ground-floor room has a ceiling-beam and wall-plate, both moulded. At the head of the stairs is part of an original roof-truss, with tie-beam and small curved brace to a wall-post. In the attic, though the W. gable-end of the E. house has been destroyed, a fragment of a curved brace belonging to it remains.

(210) Houses, Nos. 15, 15a, 16, standing 10 yds. from Northampton Street, of two storeys with cellars and attics, have timber-framed walls and tiled roofs. They comprise a long early 16th-century E. range differing from tenement to tenement but all contemporary and uniform towards the street. In the 17th century a shorter parallel range was added on the N.W., which was extended by the addition of a W. wing at right angles to it late in the same century. The two-storey annexe on the S.W. of the early range is of the 18th century. Alterations and additions in and between the extensions have been made subsequently. The building is now divided into flats, with a separate tenement at the S. end.

Towards the street (Plate 305) are two shop-fronts, a door and a window, all modern, on the ground floor. The first floor projects and is supported on seven curved brackets; the windows are of the 19th century. On the roof are three 18th-century dormer-windows with 19th-century casements. The N. and S. ends are concealed. Little of the W. side is visible; towards the N. is a large dormer-window. The short parallel block has been generally underpinned in brick and stiffened with a S.W. angle-buttress; the framed upper floor has been heightened at the S. end; between the two storeys is a cornice. In the W. wing, of brick below and timber-framing above like the foregoing, the first floor has a cornice at the level of the base sill and three original casement windows with leaded quarries.

Inside, in the cellar under the middle part of the street range, is an original longitudinal chamfered ceiling-beam of heavy scantling; the joists and floor are modern. The room above the same, now a shop, has an original doorway in the N. partition-wall with a four-centred head, and, at the S. end, evidence of the former existence of a through passage. Throughout the ground floor the chamfered ceiling-beams and wall-plates are exposed, and similarly on the first floor, including wall-posts with forward-curving thickening to the heads. On the upper floor is a 17th-century door of six panels in moulded framing with 'cock's-head' hinges. In the attics two purlins and an original truss with chamfered collars are visible.

(211) Houses, Nos. 13, 14, and No. 1 Northampton Street, forming the corner block, of two storeys with cellars and attics, has timber-framed walls and tiled roofs. It consists of two 16th-century ranges nearly at right angles to one another (Plate 305), all of one build, though now divided, and later than the adjoining range (Monument (210)). In the 17th century the attics were reconstructed and in the 18th century the N. to S. roof was replaced by the present mansard roof. The ground floor now contains shops. In *c.* 1900 various partitions and stairs were inserted. The panelled pargeting, most of the windows and the shop-fronts are of the 18th and 19th century.

The ground floor to the streets is almost wholly altered by the insertion of shop-windows and brick underpinning. The first floor projects and the studding, indicated by undulations of the pargeting, is of narrow timbers, widely spaced. Of the six windows at this level, the easternmost on the N. and the

two on the E. are in their original setting though the frames are renewals. The second floor also projects on the N. and on the E. return to a distance equivalent to the width of the E. to W. range, being supported on a diagonal bracket at the corner and a straight bracket at the S. end. Above the projection are attics with half their height with vertical walls, half in the roof; they have two N. dormer-windows and an E. window in an eccentric gable, the roof flanking the last rising fantastically to a high ridge. The eaves of the adjoining mansard roof are level with the second-floor projection. The rear walls of the ranges are without distinctive features.

The cellars are built of clunch and narrow red bricks. In the N. wall are two deep round-headed garderobe recesses. Many of the original chamfered joists to the ground floor survive. The ground floor has some exposed original ceiling-beams and plates; the longitudinal beams are housed into a diagonal beam at the turn. The entry in the N. to S. range is not an original feature of the plan. On the first floor the ceiling-beams and plates are arranged as below and show structural continuity throughout. Two rooms contain 17th-century panelling with the frieze carved with arabesques, and some panelled doors of the same date survive. In the attics some original framing is exposed at the W. end of the N. range.

Northampton Street

S. side:—

(212) Cory House, 40 yds. from Magdalene Street, a long narrow range bordering the street, of two storeys with attics, has walls of brick and plastered timber-framing and tile-covered roofs. Two distinct 16th-century structures are linked by a narrow early 18th-century building (plan p. 345). The last represents the infilling of a through carriage-way. Subsequent additions have been made on the S. and the whole has been modernised. Towards the street (Plate 305) the ground floor of the older buildings has been underpinned in brick; their framed upper floor projects; the mansard roof of the W. building is an early 18th-century reconstruction. The middle building has a flat front and a mansard roof; the floors, front and roof are higher than those to each side. On the roof are five 18th-century dormer-windows. On the S. the E. addition, of the 17th century, is steeply gabled; further W. is a large projecting chimney-stack. The windows throughout are of the 18th and 19th centuries.

Inside are exposed wall-posts, chamfered wall-plates and ceiling beams, the last intersecting in the E. building; the beams in the W. building are 18th-century renewals. A number of 18th-century doors and fireplace-surrounds remain. Visible in the attic of the E. building is the N. wall-plate and part of the studding below; the plate is a rough pole and the studs are spaced 12 ins. apart.

(213) Pythagoras House, No. 26, standing 140 yds. from Magdalene Street, of three storeys and one storey with attics, has walls of gault brick and tile-covered mansard roofs. It was built *c.* 1800 and formed the prototype for the continuation of the row westward very shortly afterwards, the addition being marked by a straight joint in the brickwork, though the roof-covering is now continuous. A S.E. wing also of *c.* 1800 was built as a separate tenement, but subsequently remodelled and combined with the first. The additions in the re-entrant angle are of the late 19th or early 20th century. The street-front is symmetrical with a doorway in the middle; the two wide ground-floor windows contain tripartite timber frames and retain their shutters. Inside, the N.E. room has round-headed recesses flanking the chimney-breast in the outside wall. The original staircase has square balusters and turned newel.

See Monument (211) for No. 1 Northampton Street.

Castle Hill Area

The area N.W. of Northampton Street and Chesterton Lane and intersected by Castle Street is, excepting the few public and institutional buildings, predominantly a humble residential district. In contrast with the New Town and Barnwell, development here has been piecemeal; single houses, pairs and groups including irregular terraces make up the bulk of the buildings. The few planned terraces are of relatively unambitious character. Gault brick and slate are the prevalent materials, though plastered timber-framing and tiles occur, often all in the same structures.

Monuments (214) and (215) are the only houses of any note earlier than *c.* 1800.

For the rest, the Castle Hill area retains little building earlier than the 18th century, though parts of the boundary-wall to the Phoenix Nursery, at the N.W. end of Castle Street, and near Storey's Almshouses (Monument (93)) may be of the 17th century, and some of the terraced cottages on the N.E. side of Shelley Row may incorporate walling of the same age though otherwise built very largely of reused 18th-century material. Late 17th and 18th-century maps (Surveys by David Loggan, 1688, and William Custance, 1798) show an open space, Pound Green, in the area of the present Albion Row, Pound Hill and Haymarket Road; this was gradually built up after inclosure of the parish of St. Giles in 1805. By 1850 the district was largely covered with the heterogeneous buildings still existing, though additions continued to be made later in the century; some of the houses suggest the private enterprise of small freeholders who benefited under the inclosure, for example, Nos. 7, 19, 20 St. Peter's Street, the first dated 1839, and No. 8 Kettle's Yard.

The Almshouses apart, the most formal terrace is the L-shaped range of small houses Nos. 109 to 121 (odd numbers) Castle Street and 1 to 4 Collin's Buildings of one storey with attics in the mansard roofs; of similar character though even less ambitious are Nos. 1 to 3 Miller's Passage, formerly of five dwellings, and Nos. 8 to 14 (even numbers) Pleasant Row; Bell's Court is less formally planned than the foregoing but not entirely haphazard. The whole area has a down-at-heel aspect though, in its variety, not without quaint and picturesque vistas. Seen from Northampton Street, the chance grouping of Nos. 8 to 11 Kettle's Yard with St. Peter's church behind is of much character.

(214) Folk Museum, house, No. 2 Castle Street, formerly the White Horse Inn, on the corner of Northampton Street, of two storeys with cellars and attics, has walls of plastered timber-framing and brick and tile-covered roofs. The range to the street was built in the 16th century. In the following century a loftier addition, more than doubling the size of the house, was made on the W. and to this a W. wing was added in *c.* 1700, when also a number of windows and partitions were inserted. The most notable feature of the house, apart from the visual stimulus of its form, varied roof-line and texture of building materials, is the very large chimney-stack in the S.W. wall of the original range; the use of pine structural timbers in the 17th-century work is a feature of some interest and is found in other Cambridge houses (e.g. Monument (145)). Mainly elm is used in the earlier work.

The street front of the E. range has been largely modernised. It has the entrance to a carriage-way in the S. end. The three large dormer-windows are of the 17th or 18th century. The high gable-end of the W. block is advanced to rise from the ridge. On the W., the only part of the range visible is that, framed and plastered, over the carriage-way. The S. side of the W. block has a small brick annexe with a plat-band between the storeys and a lean-to roof under the main eaves; the rest of the main wall is of later brickwork than the foregoing and an 18th-century reconstruction; it returns on the W. The large framed S. dormer-window contains 18th-century sliding casements. The W. gable is framed, and in the middle of the roof is a large chimney-stack with three diagonal and two later oblong shafts. The brick W. wing has a discontinuous plat-band between the storeys and inserted later 18th-century windows. Throughout the house, doorways and windows have been inserted or renewed in the 18th and 19th century.

Inside, in the E. range, the cellars are built of narrow red bricks and contain chamfered ceiling-beams. The ground floor, which has an original small room flanking the chimney-stack on the N. now bereft of lighting by adjoining buildings, has exposed plates and beams in the ceiling. The 18th-century square staircase-bay flanking the chimney-stack on the S. contains stairs turning round a central newel; on the landing is an opening for access to the chimney-flue fitted with a 17th-century oak door found elsewhere in the house. On the first floor many of the wall-posts, studs, plates and beams are exposed, including the entire original framing of the N. and S. walls and the partition with diagonal struts, central posts, studs and head-rails. In the W. block the original two ground-floor rooms are now combined in one and the necessary support provided by an iron pillar. The large open fireplace in the E. wall, in the back of the earlier chimney-stack, has a chamfered oak bressummer and small recesses in the N. and S. returns. The ceiling-beams and most of the wall-plates here and in the room above are of pine; the latter room contains an early 18th-century bolection-moulded fireplace-surround of wood. In the W. wing, the ground-floor room contains a fixed corner-cupboard of the 18th-century with fielded and glazed panels in the door; in the room above, the S. and W. walls retain traces of original blue and red painted marbling on the plaster, and in the W. wall is a fireplace with a plain 18th-century wood surround flanked on the N. by a deep cupboard beside the chimney-stack.

In the attics a doorway has been cut through the roof of the street range to open to the W. block. In the W. side of this last is a dormer enclosed by an 18th-century partition. The staircase inserted in the N. end of the street range and rising from cellar to attics is of the late 18th century with plain strings, slender square balusters and simple moulded handrail.

Preserved in the yard is exhibited a shop-front of some elegance removed from No. 45 Bridge Street (now destroyed). It has a central doorway with a cornice supported on flat-faced brackets, the cornice being continuous over the flanking segmentally-bowed windows.

(215) HOUSE, No. 83 Castle Street, on the S.W. side, beyond the Castle, about 330 yds. from Northampton Street, of two storeys with attics, was built with timber-framed walls in the 16th or 17th century. Early in the 19th century the walls were entirely faced with gault brick, a room added on the S.E. and a shop-window with flanking door inserted in the street-front. The roofs are tile covered. Although it consists of a range at right angles to the street, the part N.E. of the central chimney-stack, containing one room on each floor, is roofed with the ridge parallel with the street, suggesting that the house originally was one of a row, like the houses in Magdalene Street.

HUNTINGDON ROAD

(216) THE GROVE, standing 113 yds. S.W. of the road, rather over ½ m. N.W. of Magdalene Bridge, is of two storeys, in part with cellars and attics. The walls are faced with gault brick with some stone dressings, except those of the cellars and outbuildings, which are of soft red brick. The low-pitched roofs are slated. The original early 19th-century building forms about two-thirds of the present house-block; 1813 is cut in the cellar brickwork; 1814 is on the rainwater-heads. The S.E. third was added in the mid 19th century, incorporating part of an original kitchen-yard, and the original dining-room remodelled and enlarged by the addition of a three-sided S.W. bay. The gault brick and stonework are of the date of the addition, probably facing soft red brickwork in the original walls. The interior fittings are largely of the late 19th century.

The outside has a plat-band at first-floor level and paired dentils of brick below the timber eaves-cornice. For the most part the wall-openings are regularly and widely spaced. The main entrance, on the N.E., is in a recess with added plain Doric columns *in antis* supporting a straight stone lintel below the tympanum of a segmental-headed arch. The ground-floor windows generally are in segmental-headed shallow wall-recesses; the upper windows are plain. Both the N.E. and N.W. fronts to the original building are symmetrical; in the middle of the second is a large semicircular bay the full height of the

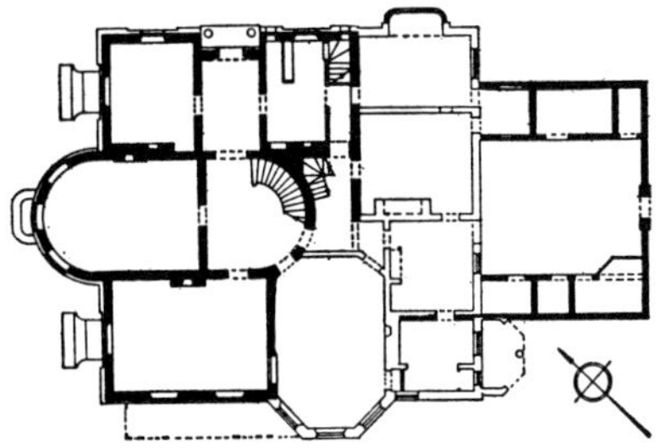

house flanked by reset rainwater-heads with the initials and date W.C. probably for William Custance, and 1814. On the S.W. side the angular bay of the dining-room and the flanking building on the S.E. are of the mid 19th century; the earlier part, to the N.W., has two french windows behind a verandah of the later period, with trellis-work supports to a low-pitched lean-to roof. The S.E. side has a low pedimented gable facing the kitchen-yard; here the fenestration is irregular and two of the first-floor windows are in segmental-headed wall-recesses tall enough to include the attic windows; at the S.W. end is a modern addition with an arbour on the ground floor.

Inside, the arrangement and form of the rooms on the N.W. and of the stairhall are original. The service staircase is an insertion. The Drawing-room has an early 19th-century moulded and enriched surround of white marble to the fireplace, and another room a reeded surround. Most of the earlier doorways retain their reeded architraves and the doors their applied mouldings on the reverse sides, though the fronts have been remodelled. The main staircase, of the form shown on the plan, has plain square balusters of wood, two to a step, but alternating at every third step with wrought-iron scroll-work between two uprights. The front edge of the landing is curved on plan. In the roof is a glazed light over the well. On the first floor are original fireplace-surrounds of simple design in marble and wood.

The small Kitchen-yard S.E. of the house is flanked by low red brick and slated buildings; in the S.E. wall is a doorway between brick piers. Some 17 yds. to the S.E. is an early 19th-century coach-house of similar materials, with a two-storey block in the middle under a low pyramidal roof, and single-storey wings. A contemporary brick wall extends further S.E. to form the N.E. side of a small farmyard some 15 yds. away.

Chesterton Road

S. side:—

(217) Wentworth House, No. 2, adjoining the Fellows' Garden of Magdalene College, of two storeys with cellars and attics, has stuccoed timber-framed walls on a brick plinth and tiled mansard roofs. It was built at the end of the 18th century. The road front is symmetrical, in three bays, with the middle bay projecting slightly; it has a central doorway in a shallow round-headed recess, two ground-floor windows with tripartite timber frames containing double-hung sashes, and three plain sash-hung windows on the first floor. At the wall-head is a small cornice and boxed eaves-gutter. On the roof are three dormer-windows. The timber doorcase has recessed pilaster-strips at the sides and an entablature with dentil-cornice; the door is original, of four fielded panels.

Inside, the base of the cellar walls is of clunch with some narrow bricks and may be earlier than the rest of the house; reused in the ceiling is a 17th-century moulded beam. The N.E. room on the ground floor contains an 18th-century fireplace-surround of wood with plain pilasters at the sides and an enriched cornice-shelf. The original staircase has moulded strings, slender square balusters, square newels and a moulded handrail. On the first floor, in the N.E. room the fireplace has an early 19th-century white marble surround with paterae at the corners. Other original or early 19th-century fittings surviving include panelled doors and a cast-iron basket firegrate.

(218) Range of cottages, Nos. 4, 6 (plan p. 365), 8, 10 (Plate 310), close E. of the foregoing and some 225 yds. from Magdalene Street, of one storey with attics, has walls of plastered timber-framing on stock brick plinths, chimney-stacks of gault brick, and tile-covered mansard roofs. It was built at the end of the 18th century, at much the same time as the houses to E. and W. The covering of pantiles on the low pitch, plain tiles on the steep pitch of the roofs seems to be original. The unit design is constant, later minor alterations alone breaking the repetition. The main windows are sash-hung, the doors at the entrances in four plain panels, the dormer-windows gabled and fitted with casements.

Each tenement has two main rooms; the staircase and kitchen are in S. annexes. A number of original fittings survive; the staircases have square balusters and newels and moulded hand-rails.

The *House*, No. 12, adjoining on the E. though of the date of the foregoing, has been entirely modernised.

(219) Fort St. George, inn, on the S. bank of the river Cam, on Midsummer Common, ½ m. E.N.E. of Magdalene College, is of two storeys. The walls are of plastered timber-framing in part refaced or rebuilt in brick; the roofs are tiled. It was built in the 16th century on a T-shaped plan, the cross range being to the S. In the 19th century and since, additions have been made flanking the small N. wing and on the E. A sketch dated 1827 in the inn shows that it stood on an island between the river and a cut to a lock close S.E. On the S., the ground floor is brick-faced and the first floor projects on curved timber brackets; the windows are modern. The gabled E. and W. ends and wing are partly refaced with brick where not obscured.

Inside, access is into a staircase-lobby on the S. side of the great central chimney-stack. In the E. room are exposed chamfered ceiling-beams; the longitudinal beam in the W. room is cased.

Park Street

Park Street, known until *c.* 1830 as Garlic Fair Lane, contains houses predominantly of the first half of the 19th century; only two are exceptional in any way and they are described separately below (Monuments (220) and (221)). Upper Park Street follows the line of King's Ditch, and Lower Park Street leads off at right angles eastwards from the N. end of it. The whole area appears undeveloped in William Custance's *Survey* of 1798.

Nos. 49–57, irregular terraces, and No. 59, an oddly-shaped three-storey house, on the W. of Upper Park Street, probably rose soon after the sale of the Blackmoor Head estate in 1825 (*Cambridge Chronicle*, 6 May 1825). Nos. 5–18 on the E. are of rather later in the same decade and are shown in R. G. Baker's map of Cambridge of 1830; they have round-headed doorways, sash-hung windows, and plain overhanging eaves and possess some architectural quality deriving from an entirely utilitarian simplicity combined with good proportions; some have been heightened from two to three storeys. Nos. 19–42, a terrace some 120 yds. long on the S. side of Lower Park Street, are of *c.* 1834; twelve of the houses were advertised for sale in the *Cambridge Chronicle* in that year. The terrace is of two storeys, with continuous eaves throughout, and plainly the severest economy was exercised in its construction. Both streets are drab in general appearance.

(220) House, No. 61, on the W. side 65 yds. from Jesus Lane, is of three storeys with basement. The walls are of gault brick,

the roofs slate-covered. It was described as 'modern built' in the *Cambridge Chronicle*, 16 Feb. 1850; by comparison with closely dated houses in the city it may be of *c.* 1840. The more notable feature of the house is the street-front. This has a wall-arcade of three bays on the ground floor, with plain plinth and imposts, a plat-band above the elliptical arches, at first-floor sill-level, and a stucco cornice and blocking-course. In the arcade is a doorway in the middle, containing an original door with four rectangular and two round reeded panels, and a sash-hung window with shutters in each of the side bays. On the floors above are sash-hung windows with scrolled ironwork guards. The extremities of the front for some 2 ft. are slightly recessed, with the horizontal features returned across them.

Inside, the entrance-hall is divided from the stairhall by an elliptical-headed archway with reeded pilaster-responds; a similar archway is on the first floor. The stairs are slight, with square balusters and turned newels.

(This house was demolished in 1956.)

(221) ANNEXE, with shop, to No. 13a Jesus Lane, on the E. side and 10 yds. from the corner, is of two storeys. It incorporates plastered timber-framed walls of the 16th or 17th century; for the rest, the walls are of 19th century gault brick. The roofs are tiled. The only feature of note is a tall dormer with a modern casement-window in the S. side, at right angles to the street.

JESUS LANE

The N. street-frontage of Jesus Lane was already in part built up between Bridge Street and the Fellows' Garden of Jesus College late in the 16th century (see J. Hamond's view of Cambridge, 1592). The density of building along the same frontage increased during the following century and then remained apparently substantially as shown by David Loggan (Survey of Cambridge, 1688) until the present century when some houses were demolished to make way for Wesley House. On the S., Hamond and Loggan both show building restricted to the frontage approximately opposite the Fellows' garden of Jesus College, with the manor house of St. Radegund standing back in gardens opposite the 'Chimney' and the Master's Garden; building has since extended eastward to the corner of King Street and Short Street. Yet the only houses now in Jesus Lane with any substantial parts earlier than *c.* 1800 are 'Little Trinity' and No. 32.

(222) 'LITTLE TRINITY', No. 16, standing back on the N. side 117 yds. from Bridge Street, of three and two storeys with cellars, has the main walls of grey brickwork in header bond with gauged red brick and ashlar dressings, and those of the kitchen and S.E. ranges of gault and red brick and timber-framing. The roofs are tiled. The principal block was built *c.* 1725; the humbler kitchen range adjoining on the E. is probably of much the same age. A S.E. block, formerly separate, but now linked to the latter by a 19th-century staircase building, may have a 17th-century origin and be indicated in D. Loggan's map of Cambridge of 1688, but it was remodelled, if not largely rebuilt, in the mid 18th century. Both it and the kitchen range have since been superficially remodelled to present a uniform appearance. An annexe N. of the kitchen is of the 19th century. At an unknown date fireplaces of *c.* 1760 were inserted in the principal block. The 18th-century *Boundary-wall* is of gault brick; it indicates the extent of the property from at least an early stage in the history of the present buildings. The N. part and the S.E. corner are now in commercial use, but in the latter are remains of walling that may well have been of stables.

'Little Trinity' is an outstanding small 18th-century house containing fittings of the same period.

The main front (Plate 300) of *c.* 1725 is symmetrical and approached axially from the Lane through a gate in contemporary wrought-iron railings with iron finials flanked by tall brick and stone piers surmounted by enriched urns. It has a

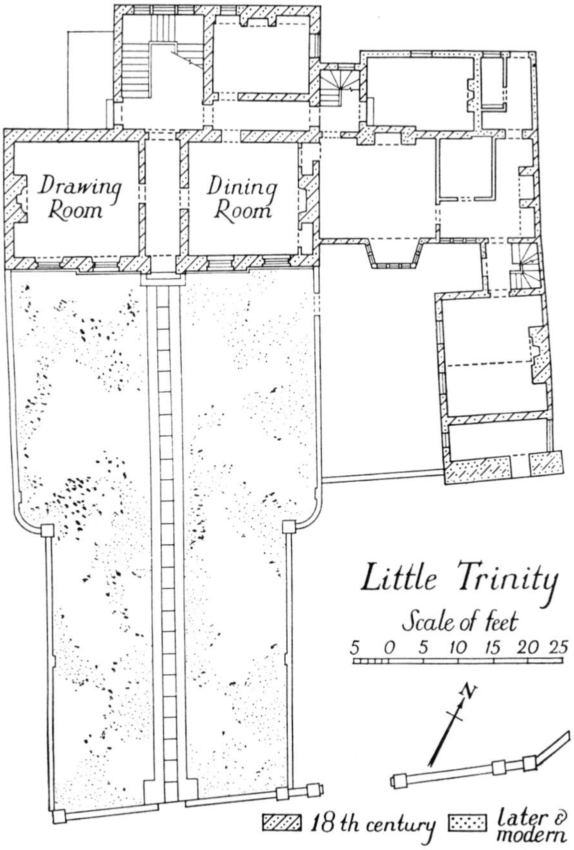

plinth, plat-bands at first and second-floor levels, a stone cornice and a brick parapet-wall with stone coping surmounted by urns. The middle three of the five bays project slightly and are pedimented, the pediment having a plain tympanum and an urn standing on the apex. The central doorway and semi-elliptical fanlight are framed in a rectangular recess in a timber doorcase with fluted Ionic pilasters supporting a pedimented entablature with pulvinated frieze and dentilled modillion-cornice. The windows have rubbed brick flat arches and contain double-hung sashes.

The E. and W. ends have low gables with stone copings and rebuilt chimney-stacks at the apices. On the N. the large staircase-bay has a Palladian window high in the N. wall, with keyblock and cornices over the side lights; against the W. wall is a low modern annexe. On the roof are three dormer-windows, the largest modern.

The kitchen range is rendered on the S. and has a modern three-sided bay window to the ground floor and a wave-moulded timber eaves-cornice, possibly a modern renewal. The N. wall is masked. The S.E. wing has a white brick plinth, plastering above, a timber eaves-cornice similar to the foregoing, and casement and sash-hung windows; it is without features of note. Most of the window-frames are modern. In the screen-wall between the garden and the kitchen-yard is an 18th-century wrought-iron gate.

The *Interior* of the main block has a timber doorcase at the entrance, with panelled pilaster-responds and a round head with moulded archivolt and keyblock carved with a bearded male mask. The E. room is lined from floor to ceiling with fielded panelling in two heights, with dado-rail and cornice; the fireplace in the E. wall has an original timber surround with enriched eared architrave, pulvinated frieze and moulded cornice-shelf; in the overmantel is a large plain panel with moulded and eared surround; at the corners of both the foregoing are carved rosettes. Doorways flanking the chimney-breast have cases similar to that described above but with plain keyblocks of bold projection; the doors are each of eight fielded panels, two being shaped to the semicircular head. The doorways in the N. and W. walls have moulded architraves and six-panel doors. The window-linings, shutters and window-seats are also panelled. The W. room has a timber dado-rail and dentil-cornice; the fireplace-surround (Plate 50) is of *c.* 1760, with grey marble slips, an enriched eared frame, and entablature with elaborate carved rococo decoration on the frieze and frieze-panel and a dentil-cornice; set in the overmantel is an 18th-century romantic landscape painting in an eared surround with rosettes at the corners and foliage pendants at the sides. The window-linings and shutters are panelled.

The stairhall has two flanking doorcases at the southern end, similar to that described above inside the entrance-doorway, framing fanlights over six-panel doors; the open archway in the S. wall is similarly cased. Round the walls is a panelled dado and a modillion-cornice; the floor is paved with original diagonal stone slabs with small black marble squares at the angles. The original staircase of oak and deal has cut strings with carved scrolled brackets, turned balusters, newels in the form of fluted Roman Doric columns, and moulded ramped handrail; the dado has pilasters corresponding to the newels and a rail moulded and ramped to match the handrail. The room next E. of the stairhall contains panelling, cornice and fireplace-surround, etc., similar to those described above in the E. room; set in the overmantel is an 18th-century landscape painting.

On the first floor, the E. room is lined from floor to ceiling with fielded panelling in two heights with dado-rail and cornice; the fireplace in the E. wall has a plain white marble surround and cornice-shelf and is flanked by cupboards with six-panel doors; opposite the last are two doorways in the W. wall. The room S. of the staircase has perhaps been refitted in modern times; it contains a remarkable rococo fireplace-surround of *c.* 1760 (Plate 50) with plain veined white marble slips framed in a riot of C-scrolls, stalactites and foliation supporting three small shaped brackets. Other rooms in the main block contain contemporary panelling and fireplaces of a simple type; the secondary staircase adjoining it on the E., also contemporary, has close strings, turned balusters and moulded handrail.

In the Kitchen is a large fireplace, now reduced in width, with an early 18th-century stone surround with supports for two spits; the surround has chamfered reveals and four-centred head with keystone and a square hollow-chamfered outer margin. The fireplace in the room above has a bolection-moulded surround. Other simple 18th-century fittings remain here and in the S.E. wing.

(223) HOUSE, No. 32, adjoining the Fellows' Garden, Jesus College, of three storeys with cellars and attics, has walls of red brick in header bond and dressings of brighter red gauged and rubbed brickwork and stone; the mansard roofs are slated. It was built probably shortly before the middle of the 18th century. In the 19th century new kitchen-offices were added on the N., the lower part of the staircase was remodelled and large double doors were inserted in the partition between the main first-floor rooms. Since 1899 the entrance-hall has been differently apportioned. It was the home of C. H. Cooper, F.S.A.

The classically proportioned front of No. 32 Jesus Lane is of note as an example of 18th-century street architecture of much dignity.

The front (Plate 301) has a weathered brick plinth, a plat-band at first-floor level and a cornice, with heavy ogee bed-mould, both of stone, and a low parapet-wall; it is in five bays, the second from the E. containing the entrance. This last has a stone surround with eared architrave and console-brackets supporting a cornice; the door is of six fielded panels and the fanlight contains radiating and concentric iron glazing-bars. The windows, four on the ground floor with panelled shutters, ranges of five above, have stone sills, dressed reveals and flat arches of gauged and rubbed bricks; they contain renewed double-hung sashes with slight glazing-bars. On the roof are two renewed dormer-windows. The N. side, originally symmetrical, is much altered and in part concealed by the later additions. The house is two rooms deep and the ends are twice gabled but walls screen the valley between; the E. end is without windows and has brick plat-bands in continuation of the horizontal features of the main front.

The *Interior* retains some clunch in the cellar walls. Many of the rooms throughout the 18th-century building contain contemporary wainscoting, generally of fielded panelling in two heights with dado-rail and cornice; the social importance of the rooms is differentiated by reduction in the degree of elaboration, by omission of dado-rails, fielding, etc.; the modern panelling inserted matches the old. The entrance-hall originally included the main E. room and extended to the W. wall of the entrance, with the present lobby in the S.W. corner. The lobby is wainscoted throughout and the original inner door is of six fielded panels, it now opens to a small room with a modern E. partition-wall and an original archway in the N. wall to the stairhall. The archway has panelled pilaster-responds and a round head with panelled soffit, moulded archivolt, and keystone. The staircase has moulded strings, turned balusters, square newels and moulded handrail; it is original from the first floor upwards. Some of the rooms contain original fireplace-surrounds, several with 19th-century cast-iron grates of some elaboration. The surrounds in the E. ground-floor room and a N.E. room on the first floor are much alike, of clunch, with enriched eared architraves with flowers at the angles; those in the W. ground-floor room and the E. first-floor room are of marble and of the early 19th century, reeded and with roundels at the angles.

(224) HOUSE, No. 31, adjoining the foregoing on the W., of three storeys with cellars, is of two periods; the S. half beside the Lane, with walls of white brick and slated roofs is of *c.* 1830, the N. half, with plastered timber-framed walls and tiled roofs, of the late 17th century. A small 18th-century N.E. wing was until recently part of a range of stables. The W. wall has been entirely rebuilt in the present century in consequence of the demolition of adjoining houses to make way for Wesley House. The S. front is of three bays; though the features are symmetrically disposed, the whole is made eccentric by the inclusion in the W. bay of windows double the width of the rest and with tripartite timber frames. The round-headed doorway is of two square brick orders with plain imposts. At first-floor level is a brick plat-band and, at the wall-head, a timber modillioned eaves-cornice. The windows have stone sills, yellow brick flat arches and contain double-hung sashes.

Inside, the floors of the earlier N. half are one step higher than those of the S. The staircase rises in straight flights between parallel containing-walls athwart the later half and is contemporary with it.

The greater part of the rest of JESUS LANE was rebuilt in the first half of the 19th century and contains numbers of terrace-houses, in particular Radegund Buildings, showing much ingenuity and originality in the design of their fronts while conforming to the generally unobtrusive aspect of the street. More or less in order of date, RADEGUND BUILDINGS (Nos. 50–61 Jesus Lane) were begun in 1816 largely on the initiative of Jesus College (*Chanticleer*, CXLVI (1948)), No. 49 in much the same style was built in *c.* 1820 (*Cambridge Chronicle*, 2 Nov. 21); Nos. 1–4 at the W. end, probably of the same build as the adjoining two houses in Bridge Street, and their near contemporaries Nos. 5–10 are of *c.* 1825, so also are Nos. 62, 63 at the E. end, but they were refronted and heightened ten or twenty years later; Nos. 47, 48 were built in the N.E. corner of the grounds of St. Radegund in *c.* 1833 after the manor house had been demolished and the materials offered for sale in 1832, No. 46 behind them being added later; All Saints' church and vicarage now occupy the greater part of these grounds. The houses near the middle of the Lane, by Malcolm Street, are not closely dated by documents; some of those on the N. side are probably later than 1850. Beyond Belmont Place all except the two at the E. end have been rebuilt in the second half of the 19th century. In modern times a block of eight houses 'newly erected' in 1814 (*Cambridge Chronicle*, 29 April 1814) has been cleared away for Westcott House.

For purposes of brief architectural description the houses in Jesus Lane may be grouped as follows:—

(225) HOUSES, Nos. 1 to 10, standing on the N. side at the W. end, mostly of three storeys, have brick walls with some stone dressings and slated roofs. They were built in *c.* 1825 for a class of professional status. Towards the front they have round-headed doorways, stone plat-bands, windows with double-hung sashes, some with cast-iron guards, and parapets with stone copings. The rainwater downpipes are recessed and at the junction with Bridge Street is a recessed rounded corner. An entry between Nos. 4 and 5 is closed by a wrought-iron gate of scrolled wheel pattern made by one Audley (A. B. Gray, *Cambridge Revisited* (1921), 56). The ground floors of Nos. 5 and 7 have been converted into a garage.

(226) HOUSES, Nos. 33, 34, and 35–37, standing on the S. side flanking the entrance to Malcolm Street, are of about the date of this last, *c.* 1840. The first two are of three storeys, the rest of two, with walls of grey brick with stone dressings and slate-covered mansard roofs. The round-headed entrance-doorways are of two plain orders with stone imposts and contain four-panel doors and fanlights with radiating metal glazing-bars. The first two have a stone plat-band at first-floor sill-level and all simple stone cornices with parapet-walls. The windows contain double-hung sashes and some are fitted with scrolled wire guards. Inside they retain many plain original fittings.

(227) RADEGUND BUILDINGS (Plate 310), No. 49, a double-fronted detached house, and Nos. 50 to 61, terrace-houses, standing opposite the tennis-court of Jesus College, the first of three storeys, the others of two, have walls of grey brick and slate-covered roofs. Begun in 1816, they are distinguished by a surface modelling of tall and narrow recessed panels dividing the bays and stopping in stepped courses close above the plinth and below the eaves. Nos. 54 to 57 are rather higher than the flanking houses, to accentuate the middle of the

terrace, and have recessed panels between the upper window-heads and the eaves. The entrance-doorways have plain rectangular openings, six-panel doors and oblong fanlights with latticework glazing bars; before them are small paved landings approached by steps on one side and both with wrought-iron latticework balustrading, the whole forming an original composition of much sensibility. The windows contain double-hung sashes with thin glazing-bars.

(228) HOUSES, Nos. 46 to 48, next W. of the foregoing, are perhaps a decade later than Radegund Buildings but of similar building materials. They have plain rectangular wall-openings, latticework fanlights over the doors, boxed eaves-gutters and notable cast-iron railings with spear-headed uprights.

MALCOLM STREET

(229) HOUSES, five terraces, Nos. 1 to 6 (plan of No. 2, p. 365), 7 to 11 on the W. side, Nos. 16 to 18, 19 to 25, 26 to 29 on the E. side, are of two storeys with basements and attics. The walls are of gault brickwork and the mansard roofs slate-covered. They were probably built by James Webster, a local builder, soon after 1842 (*Chanticleer*, CXLVI (1948)); some later additions have been made at the backs. The design is generally uniform throughout. They have plain rectangular wall-openings and a deep stylised brick entablature, the architrave being represented by two projecting courses, the cornice by a plain low parapet without projection and the dentils by bricks laid diagonally. The doorways, approached up three steps, have four-panel doors and fanlights with rectangular intersecting glazing-bars. The windows contain double-hung sashes; some are fitted with scrolled wire guards. Fencing the basement-areas are wrought-iron railings with standards surmounted by small urns and plain intermediate uprights. Inside, a narrow entrance-passage flanking the front room widens out beside the back room to take a dog-leg staircase. The small gardens behind, each in area about equal to that occupied by the house, are enclosed by brick walls.

(230) HOUSE, No. 66 King Street, on the S. side some 13 yds. E. of Manor Street, of two storeys with attics, has brick walls and tiled roofs. It was built on a T-shaped plan early in the 18th century. The street-front is symmetrical, in three bays. The doorway in the middle has a timber case with pilasters, which until recently supported entablature-blocks and an open pediment framing a blind fanlight. Projecting at first-floor level are short horizontal brick panels that spanned the former windows below, now replaced by larger modern shop-windows. The upper windows are sash-hung and on the roof are three hipped dormer-windows, that in the middle now blocked, with timber eaves-cornices. Inside, the original staircase has close strings, turned balusters and square newels.

TRUMPINGTON STREET

E. side:—

(231) LITTLE ROSE, inn, nearly opposite the Fellows' Garden of Peterhouse, 180 yds. from Pembroke Street, of two storeys with attics, has walls of plastered timber-framing and brick and tile-covered roofs. The long rectangular range bordering the street was built in the 16th century; the structure includes a gabled N. bay, now in separate occupation, and a gabled S. bay containing an open carriage-way. In the following century the N.E. wing was built, and in modern times the free length of the original range has been nearly doubled in width by a low addition on the W. Towards the street the ground floor has been faced with brick and contains 19th-century doorway and windows towards the middle and a modern shop-front under the N. gable. The first floor is plastered and contains 18th-century windows. The bargeboards to the N. gable are moulded; the S. gable, which has bargeboards carved with flowers within cheveron ornament, springs from above general eaves-level, necessitating higher wall-plates; of these last, that to the N. is supported by a square carved and moulded strut from the projecting end of the E. to W. tie-beam within. On the roof are two hipped dormer-windows and rising at the ridge is a great central chimney-stack with weathered offset.

To the W. are three gables, two behind those on the E. and one near the middle to give headroom over the staircase against the E. side of the chimney-stack; the rest of the wall is masked. The wing is without features of note.

Inside, chamfered cross and longitudinal ceiling-beams with plain and geometrical stops are exposed on the ground and first floors; one beam upstairs in the room N. of the stack is in an early 17th-century enriched casing. Other structural timbers visible include a wall-post with enlarged head; the tie-beam spanning the N. side of the S. gabled bay with one of two original curved braces surviving; two collar-beams and two windbraces in the middle bays, and, in the N. gabled bay, rafters of heavy scantling sawn square and halved and pegged together, without a ridge-piece. Some reset fragments of panelling of *c.* 1600 remain in the inn.

(232) TUNWELLS COURT, 5 yds. N. of Fitzwilliam House (Monument (28)) and 38 yds. N. of Fitzwilliam Street, of one and two storeys with attics, has walls of plastered timber-framing and tiled roofs. It consists of a long and narrow quadrangular plan extending far back from the street. Down the middle is a carriage-way passing through the E. and W. buildings. It is the creation of four building phases: the street range and its S.E. wing probably in the 16th century, the two easterly blocks with the link between them containing the second carriage-way in the 17th century, and the formation of the N. and the S. lateral ranges by linking the earlier buildings in the 18th century and modern times respectively, the modern S. link being no more than outbuildings and screen walls.

On the W., the shop-window to the N. is of the first half of the 19th century, the shop-window to the S. of later in the same century; the latter encroaches upon the carriage-way between the two. To judge by the adjoining frontage and by the eccentricity of the longitudinal ceiling-beams within the range, the first floor may have projected originally. At the eaves is a timber dentil-cornice of the 18th or early 19th century, the period when the first-floor windows and hipped dormer-windows were inserted or renewed. The gabled N. and S. ends are largely masked. Large projecting chimney-stacks flanked by staircases are symmetrically arranged against the back wall of the range to each side of the carriage-way; the staircases each show a heightening covered by a lean-to roof against the side of the stack, suggesting the conversion, perhaps early in the 17th century, of the roof-space into habitable rooms. The N. stair is largely destroyed. The S.E. wing is of one storey with attics and refaced with brick.

The 18th-century N. range is lower than those adjoining on the E. and W. The ground floor is refaced on the S. with brick; the doorway in the middle contains an original door of four fielded panels. The windows contain sliding casements, and on the roof is a small gabled dormer-window, partly blocked. Inside is a reset ceiling-beam and a plank door.

The E. range has both the blocks flanking the carriage-way gabled to E. and W. The E. wall of the S. block is refaced with brick on the ground floor; it projects slightly and is gabled well above main eaves-level. The N.E. gable is at the level of this last. The way through the range is spanned by a room on the first floor with the roof running N. to S. The old windows have been renewed and others inserted in the 18th century and since. Inside, the staircase with square newels with turned half-balusters planted on them is an insertion of *c.* 1700; it passes close in front of one of the fireplaces on the upper floor. The bolection-moulded panelling lining a room on the first floor is of the same period.

(233) Houses, Nos. 25 to 27, three, by the grounds of Addenbrooke's Hospital, 20 yds. S. of Fitzwilliam Street, forming a terrace, are of three storeys with basements. The walls are of white brick with stone and rubbed brick dressings; the roofs are tiled. One seems to be included on R. G. Baker's map of Cambridge, 1830, and a parish boundary-mark at the N. end appears to read '1834'; their style agrees with a date *c.* 1830. They have a continuous stone plat-band at first-floor level, a simplified stone cornice and a parapet-wall. In six bays over all, of the entrance doorways originally in the first, third, and fifth from the N., only the first remains; it is approached up stone steps and has jambs and a semicircular head of two plain brick orders with stone imposts, a fanlight with lobed pattern of glazing-bars and a panelled door; the other two have been converted into windows and the steps removed. On the first floor are french windows, some retaining their sunblind-boxes with shaped side-pieces, opening to original cast-iron balconies with balustrading comprising scrolls and Greek honeysuckle ornament. The other windows contain plain double-hung sashes. The basement-area is fenced with railings with plain intermediate uprights, cast lattice panels, and standards with urn finials; the length before No. 27 has been removed. The interiors retain nothing of note.

(234) House, No. 21, standing 92 yds. southward from the foregoing, of two storeys with attics, has walls of plastered timber-framing and tiled roofs. It is the remnant of a larger house built probably in the 17th century and consists of one room on each floor, with a late 19th-century extension to the E. The doorway, windows and gabled dormer-window to the W. are renewals or insertions of the 19th century. Inside, part of the ground-floor room has been lost to the shop adjoining on the N., the modern N. wall being some 2 ft. further S. than the earlier wall. The ceiling-beams on the ground floor are cased; those above are stop-chamfered.

(235) House, No. 17, St. Bonaventure's Priory, 123 yds. N. of Lensfield Road, of three storeys with basement, has walls of white brick with dressings of stone and rubbed brick and slate-covered roofs. It was built early in the 19th century and has an unusual entrance-doorway. The street-front is asymmetrical, in four unequal bays; but the three S. bays are symmetrical in themselves, centring on the doorway. This last, approached up stone steps, consists of a broad opening, with shallow elliptical head, containing a timber screen in three bays divided and flanked by panelled pilasters supporting a full entablature below the glazed tympanum. The screen contains a four-panel door in the middle bay and glazing above panelled dadoes in the side bays; in the tympanum the glazing-bars form a pattern of interlacing four-centred arches. Over the arch is a wrought-iron lamp bracket. The windows generally contain plain double-hung sashes. At the wall-head is a cornice and blocking-course, both of stone. Fencing the basement-area are wrought-iron railings with plain uprights.

Inside, the interesting feature is the form of the plan. The rectangular entrance-hall has flanking rooms; behind these, extending the full length of the building, is a long narrow stair-hall parallel with the street containing two symmetrically-planned staircases, the principal one, though of only slightly greater elaboration, being at the N. end. The stairs are lit by oval glazed domes in the roof. Beyond the stairhall are further rooms.

(236) Brook House, No. 10, standing 75 yds. from Lensfield Road, of three storeys with basement, has walls of gault brick and slate-covered roofs of low pitch. It was built *c.* 1840; some refitting was undertaken later in the century. In modern times the dividing wall between the two N. main rooms has been removed. The street-front is in four bays. The entrance-doorway is in the southernmost bay and set in a round-headed wall-recess continued up to include the first-floor window above, so to accentuate a principal feature in a weak position architecturally; covered approach to it is up a flight of stone steps between low brick and stone piers and wrought-iron balustrades under a wrought-iron scrollwork arch of ogee form fronting a ramped flared roof of sheet-metal. The piers, arch and roof may be rather later additions. All the windows contain plain double-hung sashes, some with their glazing-bars removed; those on the ground and first floors have slatted shutters, those on the second floor wrought-iron guards with C-scrolls and plain uprights. On the E. is a projecting bay towards the S. end with a large ground-floor window containing a tripartite timber frame and double-hung sashes. N. of the bay is a raised verandah, no longer covered.

Inside, entry is directly into a large stairhall, nearly square. The cast-iron balustrading to the staircase is probably a part of the later 19th-century refitting, when also white marble fireplaces were set up in some of the rooms.

W. side:—

(237) KENMARE, house, and No. 74a, annexe, 10 yds. S. of Mill Lane, of two storeys with basement and attics, has walls of gault brick and tile-covered roofs. Known in the 18th century as Randall House, it occupies the site of Cotton Hall, which was sold in 1768 to John Randall. It consists of a long range, parallel with the street, some 15 ft. back from the present building-line, that was built in the third quarter of the 18th century; incorporated is a small central W. wing of earlier date, possibly a part of the building shown in Loggan's survey of 1688. Later in the 18th century an annexe was built between the range and the street, covering the northern part of the E. front; subsequently, towards the end of the century, the free southern part was re-fronted to present a symmetrical composition within its length. On the W. are 19th and 20th-century additions.

The street-front of Kenmare presents an interesting and unusual composition including four Palladian windows. The admirable contemporary railings enclosing the small forecourt were taken for scrap metal during the 1939-45 war.

The E. front (Plate 301) has a plain plinth containing very broad basement windows, a timber cornice and a parapet-wall. The second-floor windows light attics and the wall at this level and above is in fact only a screen. In the middle, approached up a flight of stone steps with plain railings, is a doorway with flanking Tuscan pilasters supporting a pedimented entablature with dentil-cornice; above it on the first floor is a sash-hung window with architrave and pediment. To each side of the foregoing, on each floor, is a Palladian window, again of the Tuscan order, with a moulded archivolt to the middle light. The three attic windows are square, with continuous architraves. All the surrounds described are of timber painted white. Further N., the upper part of the wall of the same range shows above the annexe; it has an 18th-century eaves-cornice of bricks set diagonally. This last is continued across the N. end of the range and the W. side as far S. as the early wing; S. again is a remodelled projection to the staircase and a projecting chimney. The early wing has red brick quoins, a plat-band at first floor-level, and a projecting chimney on the W.; the ground-floor windows are modern, those above 18th century.

The interior has been much modernised. The hall retains late 18th-century paving of stone slabs with small slate squares at the angles. Some 18th-century doors of six fielded panels remain, and a first-floor room in the early wing has an original plaster cornice. The staircase is modern.

(238) GROVE LODGE, house, standing well back from the street in its own grounds 85 yds. S.E. of the Fitzwilliam Museum, of two storeys in part with cellars, has walls of gault brick and slate-covered roofs. Christopher Pemberton took a building lease of the site from Peterhouse in 1795. The house is shown on William Custance's map of Cambridge of 1798; the representation shows a building equating with the present main E. block; the rest is a building or rebuilding of the second half of the 19th century. Further, the original part has been so rearranged that entrance is now from the S. instead of under the E. portico. The house now contains lecture rooms and two flats.

Pemberton's Grove Lodge is a late 18th-century villa of simple and gracious design. The architect was probably William Custance, surveyor and builder.

The late 18th-century E. block has the E. front in five bays (Plate 299). The middle three project slightly and are pedimented, the horizontal and raking cornice-members being of stone; coextensive with the projection and on a stylobate of three steps is a single-storey tetrastyle Ionic portico with an uninterrupted entablature, all of wood painted white, and with a flat roof; in the back wall is a round-headed doorway in the middle bay, now blocked, with a fanlight with radiating and scrolled metal glazing-bars and an original door hung in two leaves each of four fielded panels; in the side bays are french

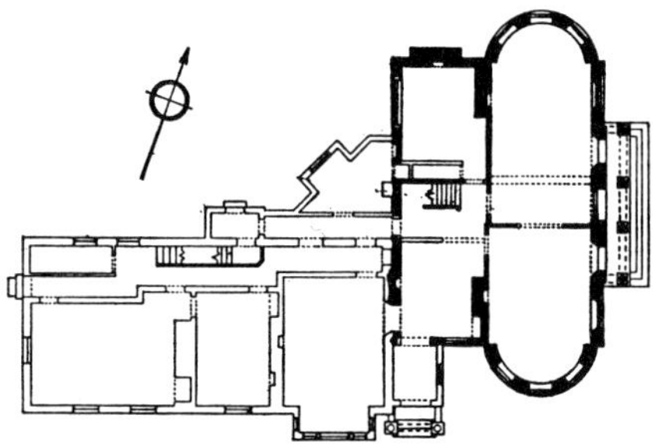

windows with later frames. Flanking the portico are rectangular windows with flat brick arches in round-headed wall-recesses. At first-floor sill-level is a stone plat-band; the overhanging eaves are plain. All the windows, except under the portico, contain double-hung sashes with thin glazing-bars. The apsidal bays on each end of the E. block, now of the height of the last, but possibly originally of one storey only, each contain windows similar to those last described, and wall-recesses simulating windows. W. of the S. apsidal bay is a later 19th-century porch and entrance; all westward again is of the same period and later.

Inside, the original entrance-hall has been eliminated and the N. main room extended S. The present entrance-hall has been extended to include the stairhall by removal of much of the partition-wall between them; it contains a reset mid 18th-century fireplace-surround with enriched eared architrave and cornice-shelf and contemporary panelled overmantel with scrolls at the sides and pedimented entablature carved with flowers. The staircase has cut strings, slender square balusters, without newels, and a moulded handrail, curved at the landing. In the stairhall are three doorways with late 19th-century enriched friezes and semicircular overdoors containing scrolls and foliation in relief. On the first floor, the N.E. room contains an original white marble fireplace-surround with fluted lintel and rosettes at the angles; the marble slips are modern.

Two of the *Outbuildings* to S. and W. of the house are of late 18th-century brickwork. They are shown in Custance's map. Of two storeys, they are quite plain.

(239) St. Peter's Terrace, houses Nos. 1 to 7, standing 30 yds. S.E. of the foregoing some 27 yds. back from the street fronting a private road, of three and four storeys with basements, has walls of gault brick, faced in part with stucco, with dressings of stone. The roofs are slated. The site was advertised to let on building leases for a term of forty years in the *Cambridge Chronicle* for 30 Nov. 1850, plans and elevations being prescribed; application was to be made to Elliot Smith.

In St. Peter's Terrace the revived Roman and the contemporary styles are combined with virtuosity and much logic in a street-front of architectural distinction.

Towards the street, the terrace is a carefully designed symmetrical unity of twenty-one bays from end to end. The fronts of the first, fourth and seventh houses, of three bays each, project slightly and have open Tuscan porches, the middle porch having the architectural emphasis of an enclosed upper storey with superimposed pilasters; the first and last houses have attics rising above the continuous main eaves-cornice. The ground floor is faced with rusticated stucco and contains round and segmental-headed openings, the doorways having continuous concave reveals. The main rooms being on the first floor, their windows are given appropriate predominance by architraves and full entablatures, pedimented in the second, fifth and eighth bays from each end; the openings extend down to the floor and have cast-iron balconies. The second-floor windows have simple stone architraves and sills continued across the front as a plat-band. All the windows contain double-hung sashes. The basement-areas are fenced by cast-iron railings with spear-headed uprights. The two ends of the terrace and the W. side are solely functional in design.

(240) Scroope Terrace (Plate 308), houses Nos. 1 to 12, standing between St. Peter's Terrace and Coe Fen Lane, of three storeys with basements, has walls of white brickwork and stucco dressings; the roofs are slate-covered. The N. part of the site was let by Gonville and Caius College on building leases for forty years in 1839 and houses Nos. 1 to 7, forming a symmetrical block, were then built. Nos. 8 to 12 were added by the College, in uniform style, in 1864 at a cost of £8,704 (*Cambridge Chronicle*, 7 Sep. 1850, 12 Nov. 1847; E. J. Gross in J. Venn, *Biographical History of Gonville and Caius College*, IV, pt. 2, 21).

The front is a dignified and well-proportioned example of formal street architecture, though dependent for effect more upon a regular repetition of parts than upon any special subtlety of design.

The terrace is some 120 yds. long and in thirty-six bays, each house comprising three bays. Towards the street the fronts of the two houses at each end and the two in the middle are accentuated by slight projection and slightly greater height; in the long view they are further emphasised as entities in a unified composition by their low-pitched hipped roofs. This architectural strengthening of the middle and ends, though slight, is entirely adequate to correct the optical illusions inherent in so long a block of comparatively low, uniform buildings. The ground floor is faced with rusticated stucco; the openings have square heads, the doors being hung between timber pilaster-responds supporting a lintel below a glazed panel. At each extremity is a single-storey rectangular annexe containing the doorway to the end house. The first-floor windows have moulded architraves, those of the projecting bays with plain entablatures, and extend down to the floor for access to small cast-iron balconies; they and the rest of the windows contain double-hung sashes. The second-floor windows have architraves similar to the foregoing and sills continued as a plat-band. At the wall-head is a stucco cornice and a low parapet.

Inside, Nos. 1 to 3 have been remodelled for the University School of Architecture; Nos. 9 to 12 have been more or less altered to form the Royal Hotel. In No. 3 is a white marble fireplace-surround of much refinement in design with twin pilaster-strips at the sides supporting an entablature; it contains a contemporary cast-iron grate with rococo ornament and mirror slips. Another fireplace-surround of white marble, in the School library, has tapering turned balusters at the sides supporting a debased entablature decorated with lions' masks. Many of the rooms have original plaster cornices with neo-Greek enrichment.

(241) Scroope House, now part of the University Engineering Laboratories, standing 75 yds. W. of Scroope Terrace (Monument (240)), of two storeys with basement, has walls of gault brick with stone dressings and slated roofs of low pitch. The site was let on a building lease for forty years in 1837 and the house completed the same year, when the father of John Willis Clark, the antiquary, moved in from Wanstead House (Monument (279)) in Hills Road (J. Venn, *Biographical History of Gonville and Caius College*, IV, pt. 2, 21). It now contains lecture-rooms and laboratories. The servants' wing has been demolished.

The house has a plinth, a deep plat-band at first-floor level, a shallower one at first-floor sill level, a brick dentil-cornice, and a boxed eaves-gutter. The N. front, originally symmetrical and of five bays, has the middle bay projecting slightly; the entrance doorway in the latter is protected by an open stone porch with Ionic columns supporting an entablature concealing a flat roof. The two ground-floor windows to either side have been replaced in the later 19th century by a large square bay-window to the E. and a single window to the W. On the first floor the five windows contain original double-hung sashes; the middle window is wider than the rest, has a cambered head and contains a tripartite timber frame. On the W. are two windows similar to the last, but with flat arches, on the ground floor and three windows, like the others, on the first floor. On the S. side is a large segmental bay with windows lighting the dining-room and a bedroom above.

Inside, between the entrance-hall and stairhall is a large round-headed archway with panelled responds and soffit and a moulded archivolt. The two rooms extending the full depth of the building on the W. are closely alike; in the party-wall between them is a large opening with a panelled architrave and fitted with doors, the two leaves being of eight panels each and divided by a removable pilaster. The woodwork is grained to resemble walnut and gilded. The dining-room has the service end defined by responds supporting a trabeation across the ceiling with panelled soffit and enriched cornice. Most of the rooms on this floor and above retain their original skirtings and cornices, both plain and enriched, and white and grey marble fireplaces. The staircase has cut and bracketed strings, turned ash balusters and a moulded handrail.

Little St. Mary's Lane

N. side:—

(242) House, No. 12, on the W. corner of the entry 100 yds. from Trumpington Street, of two storeys with cellar and attics, has timber-framed and brick walls, the former with modern rendering, and tile-covered roofs. It was built late in the 16th or early in the 17th century and extended N. late in the 18th century. The ground floor has been rebuilt in brick but the first floor still projects to the S. On the roof is a gabled dormer-window. The windows have all been renewed. Inside, the fireplaces and chimney-stack are at the W. end and the staircase is in the recess to the N. of the chimney-breast. On the first floor, the planks with fluting and scale enrichment surrounding the fireplace are probably reused material of *c.* 1600; of the same period is the panelling with carved frieze forming a cupboard S. of the chimney-stack, the door being hung on 'cock's-head' hinges.

(243) House, Nos. 13 and 14, adjoins the foregoing, is generally similar to it and probably of the same build. It was separated into two tenements and a chimney-stack inserted in the N. wall of the W. tenement in the 18th century or later; the stack contains older reused bricks. The fireplaces and stack at the E. end back against those in No. 12 and also have a stair in the recess to the N.

Fitzwilliam Street

(244) Houses, Nos. 1 to 24, excluding Nos. 13 and 15 (see below), and No. 29a Trumpington Street, consisting of two terraces on the N. and S. sides of Fitzwilliam Street, which leads from Trumpington Street from nearly opposite the Fitzwilliam Museum to Tennis Court Road, are contemporary and broadly of uniform character. They and the street comprise a single early 19th-century development. The street does not appear on William Custance's plan of Cambridge of 1798, and the building of the terraces in 1821–2 (*Cambridge Chronicle*) give the terminal date for the formation of it. The N. terrace is of three storeys, the S. of two, with basements and attics. In the main the walls are of gault brick and the roofs slate-covered. The original minor divergencies in the designs have not been unduly widened by subsequent alterations and by the remodelling of many of the roofs to mansard form.

Fitzwilliam Street comprises well-proportioned unpretentious houses designed for the professional classes and is of note as a product of one period, the third decade of the 19th century, surviving without substantial alteration or decline in status.

The houses generally are of two or three bays, with round-headed entrance doorways, plain window-openings containing double-hung sashes, and parapet-walls. Fencing the basement-areas are railings with plain sharpened uprights and standards with urn finials. On the N. side, Nos. 16 to 24 have scrolled wrought-iron balconies to the first-floor windows. On the S. side, No. 29a Trumpington Street has a pilastered front towards the last. Nos. 3 and 4 have their front doors deeply recessed in round-headed openings with moulded and panelled reveals. Nos. 5 and 6 are similar to the foregoing but built after them; the former is of three storeys. Nos. 7 and 8 are a pair, but the former has been heightened; they have shallow hoods to the doorways below the tympana of the containing arches and No. 8 has panelled parapets.

(245) House, No. 13, standing detached on the S. side of the street, towards the W. end, was built after the terrace houses described above (Monument (244)), in *c.* 1830; it is now part of Addenbrooke's Hospital. It is of three storeys with basement and substantially built of gault brick; the roofs are slate-covered. Large modern E. additions mask the E. end. The E. part of the house may be rather earlier than the W. The entrance doorway has flanking pilasters and entablature in the neo-Greek style. The W. side is symmetrical, with ranges of three windows on each floor. On the S., a balcony to the first floor has a scrollwork balustrade and trellised timber standards supporting a lean-to roof.

(246) House, No. 15, standing detached on the N. side of the street, towards the E. end, of two storeys, in part with basement, has walls of gault brick with stone dressings and slate-covered roofs. It was built in *c.* 1825; the authority for the tradition that it was designed by William Wilkins has not been discovered, circumstantial evidence points rather to Charles Humfrey (see Monument (247)). Some minor alterations, including the insertion of further windows, have been made since and most of the first-floor fireplace-surrounds are later

19th-century replacements. The house has many points of similarity with Scroope House (Monument (241)).

The house, though inspired by the Greek revival, presents a functional composition to the street, while the E. front is remarkable for the original use of the stylistic

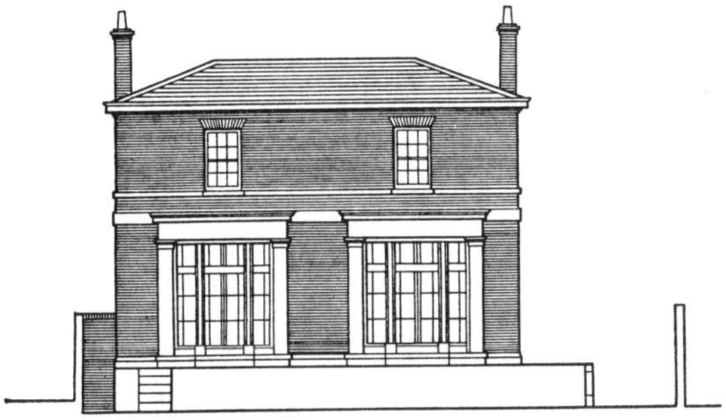

East Elevation

South Elevation

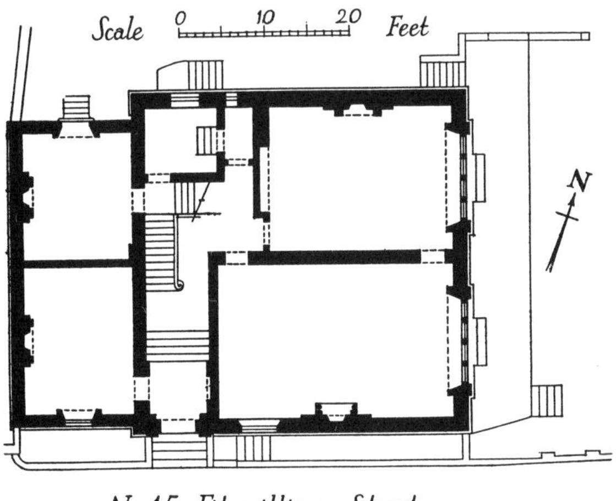

No.15 Fitzwilliam Street

convention and an uncompromising duality in the design.

The building consists of a tall square block with a lower W. annexe; the former has a high plinth, two plat-bands, a wide one at first-floor level, a narrow one at first-floor sill level, and a cornice consisting of two oversailing courses of brick as a bedmould to a deep boxed eaves-gutter; these features are continued across the free faces. The annexe, which has the floors at levels lower than elsewhere, has a plat-band at first-floor level; the plinth and cornice are similar to those just described. The roofs are of very low pitch. A monumental effect redolent of the revived Greek style is achieved by this horizontal accentuation.

In the S. wall, the entrance-doorway has flanking Doric pilasters without taper supporting a plain entablature, a door with reeding down the middle and a light above the lintel-rail. The two chimney-stacks, on the same plane as the S. wall, rise well above the eaves and are linked by a semicircular flying arch. The E., or garden, front is in two bays and entirely symmetrical. The comparatively very large ground-floor windows consist of four timber-mullioned and transomed lights in a neo-Greek surround of flanking Doric pilasters supporting a plain entablature, all similar in detail to the S. doorcase described above; the tall casements below the transoms open to the ground.

Inside, the Hall and Drawing-room and Dining-room to the E. have original cornices enriched with variations upon the classical egg-and-dart ornament with, in the Dining-room, heavy dentils. All the ground-floor rooms, including the kitchen to the N.W., contain original white marble fireplace-surrounds, one with tapering turned balusters at the sides, another with anthemion ornament. The staircase has cut strings with enriched brackets, plain square balusters and a moulded mahogany handrail.

Tennis Court Road

W. side:—

(247) Houses, Nos. 4 to 12, extending from 20 yds. to 77 yds. N. of Fitzwilliam Street, and Nos. 1 to 6 Tennis Court Terrace returning W. from the latter point, form two terraces. They are modest buildings of *c.* 1825 of two storeys, with walls of gault brick and slate-covered roofs. In 1822 (*Cambridge Chronicle*, 19 May) Fitzwilliam Street was described as linking Trumpington Street with 'the proposed New Square belonging to Peterhouse'; the proposal was short-lived, for four months later building leases were advertised of ground belonging to the Master and Fellows of Peterhouse 'situate near the east end of Fitzwilliam Street and fronting Tennis Court Road' where was 'space sufficient for sixteen houses, which must be erected according to a plan of elevation already determined by the Society', particulars being obtainable from 'Mr. Humfrey, the architect' (*Cambridge Chronicle*, 17 Sept. 1822). The two terraces comprise only fifteen houses, if Tennis Court Terrace may be accepted as on ground 'fronting Tennis Court Road', which in the general terms of the advertisement it probably may. Only by including No. 15 Fitzwilliam Street (Monument (246)), still the property of Peterhouse, or the detached house at the W. end of Tennis Court Terrace, both of *c.* 1825 but of individual design, is the requisite number of houses reached. Thus some slight doubt remains about the precise origins of the existing terraces.

The houses of the first terrace, which was built in two phases, have plain eaves, round-headed entrance-doorways, some with stone imposts, and slightly moulded reveals, four-panel doors and fanlights, and windows containing double-hung sashes, those on the ground floor originally with solid shutters. The houses of the second terrace are similar to the foregoing but even plainer.

Further S. in Tennis Court Road, 130 yds. from Lensfield Road, KELLETT LODGE is of the date of the foregoing and of similar materials and character except that it is double-fronted and the doorway in the middle has a more elaborate gadroon-pattern of glazing-bars in the fanlight.

LENSFIELD ROAD

N. side:—

(248) HOUSES, pair, Nos. 4 and 5 Benet Place, next W. of Tennis Court Road, of three storeys with basements, have walls of gault brick and low-pitched slate roofs. They were built in *c.* 1820 and, though distinct dwellings, form a single block of unified and symmetrical design.

Nos. 4 and 5 are good examples of large town houses of their period, with notable ironwork. The whole of Benet Place (Monuments (248–250)) is a spacious early 19th-century development of much dignity.

The S. front is in eight bays, with lower and recessed flanking annexes containing porches on the ground floor; it has a widely projecting eaves-cornice. The regularly spaced windows on each floor have flat brick arches and contain double-hung sashes with very thin glazing-bars; those on the top floor are fitted with scrolled wire guards. The most conspicuous feature is the elaborate cast-iron balcony extending the length of the first floor; it has latticework balustrading and standards between the bays supporting four-centred arches with scroll-work in the spandrels and a continuous frieze below a flared sheet-metal roof; the whole is inspired by the Chinese phase of taste of the mid 18th century.

Inside many original fittings remain, including plaster cornices and ceiling-borders with Greek ornament, doors with reeding in the middle and fireplace-surrounds. The staircases though original are of no particular distinction. The principal room of each house is on the first floor, with three windows overlooking the road.

Ramped screen-walls flanking the building extend to Tennis Court Road on the E. and on the W. to the house next described, though that to the W. is interrupted in the middle by the opening for a carriage-way with square moulded stone cappings to the responds.

(249) HOUSES, Nos. 2 and 3 Benet Place (Plate 308), next W. of the foregoing are generally similar to them and of much the same date, but of six bays and without the balcony; other variations include the presence of paired brick dentils to the eaves-cornice and a round-headed wall-recess containing the first-floor window at each end of the S. front. On the top floor the middle S. window in each house is blind. A ramped screen-wall extends, as on the E., to the house next described.

(250) HOUSE, No. 1 Benet Place, 22 yds. from Trumpington Street, stands next W. of the foregoing and again is of similar date and character to them, but of two bays only and without the annexes. Late in the 19th century a two-storey bay-window has been added on the S. The round-headed entrance-doorway, approached up a flight of steps with plain iron balustrades, has a fanlight with original glazing-bars forming a gadroon pattern and a semicircular wrought-iron hood, the last possibly added later.

S. side:—

(251) DOWNING TERRACE (Plate 298), 13 houses, extending some 85 yds. W. from Panton Street, is generally of two storeys with basements, except where altered, with walls of gault brick and slate-covered roofs. It was built to a symmetrical design over all, in 1819 (*Cambridge Chronicle*, 10 Dec.). The four houses at the W. end were remodelled and heightened to three storeys late in the same century.

Downing Terrace presents an original architectural composition to Lensfield Road, which despite inconsistency in scale between the centrepiece and the rest, and ill-advised alterations, makes a valuable contribution to the interest and variety of the street architecture in Cambridge.

The terrace comprises a narrow double-fronted house forming the centrepiece, with a wall-arcade of lofty narrow arches embracing the openings on basement, ground and first floors, and six houses to each side, each house being of one and a half bays under the modular control of a continuous wall-arcade, as shown on the diagram facing p. 362; the tripartite grouping of the arches is related to the party-walls within containing the fireplaces. The upper part of the centrepiece has been altered, possibly heightened, but the original form is not recoverable. The doorway in the middle is round-headed, with a fanlight; the other doorways have reeded doorcases and shallow hoods. All the windows have double-hung sashes except those describing sectors of a circle; they have hinged casements. Many of the panelled shutters to the ground-floor windows have been removed. The accompanying diagram shows the original features of the four W. houses that have survived the remodelling, including the imposts of the wall-arcade and the doorcases, though the latter have been heightened by the insertion of lights over the doors.

REGENT STREET

E. side:—

(252) GLENGARRY HOTEL, No. 41, some 34 yds. S.E. of the entrance to Downing College, of three storeys with basement, with walls of gault brick and slate-covered roofs, was built *c.* 1830. The outside has since been painted white with red dressings. It was the first home, from 1871 to 1875, of the Society that later became Newnham College. The street-front

is symmetrical and in three bays, the openings being set in large expanses of brickwork; it has a plat-band at first-floor sill-level and widely projecting eaves. The roofs are of low pitch. The doorway in the middle is of two plain orders with a semicircular head containing a fanlight with radial glazing-bars. The E. side is in part masked; the part free has a shallow plinth, a later bay-window on the ground floor and other windows including one with a semicircular head lighting the staircase.

Inside, on the ground floor are two original fireplace-surrounds, one moulded, the other of reeded marble, and both with paterae at the angles; three more remain on the upper floors. The staircase has cut strings, slender square balusters, newels in the form of attenuated columns, and a moulded ramped handrail.

Parker's Piece

S.E. side:—

(253) Gresham House, standing in its grounds on the corner of Gonville Place and Gresham Road, of two storeys with cellars, has walls of gault brick and slate-covered roofs of low pitch. It was built *c.* 1830, the dining-room perhaps being an addition of slightly later date, and is an example of the villa-type of house of the period. It consists of a roughly square main block, with a smaller block clasping the N. angle and a lower S.E. range containing the dining-room and kitchen parallel with one another; the kitchen-offices were extended S. later in the same century. The house has a symmetrical S.W. front to the main block, of greater breadth than height, with slight projections towards the ends, a shallow plinth, a plat-band at first-floor level, and widely projecting eaves with coupled brackets. In the middle is a doorway with a semicircular head protected by an open timber porch with free-standing Ionic columns supporting a plain entablature. The only fenestration to the S.W. consists of an original window over the porch and a modern round window further N. The horizontal features are continued across the other sides, which have more regular fenestration including a three-sided bay-window on the N. and a french-window to the dining-room in the S.E. range. Round windows have been inserted in the S.E. wall of this last in modern times.

Inside, between the hall and stairhall is an archway with a segmental head springing from enriched cornices supported on brackets. A number of original fittings remain, including doors and doorcases. The staircase has cut strings with scroll-brackets beneath the returns of the moulded edges to the treads, one slender turned newel and a mahogany moulded handrail; the balusters in the 17th-century style are modern replacements.

N.E. side:—

(254) House, No. 44 Park Side, now flats, 45 yds. from East Road, of two storeys, with battered walls of gault brick and slate-covered roofs of low pitch, was built late in the second quarter of the 19th century and extended N.E. later in the same century. The street-front is symmetrical and in three bays. The entrance in the middle has stone freestanding Ionic columns and pilaster-responds at the sides supporting an entablature to form a shallow outer porch; the doorway is in the back of a shallow inner porch. The flanking ground-floor windows are large and have stucco surrounds comprising side-pilasters and an entablature; they contain tripartite sash-hung frames, the middle light being wider than the side lights. On the first floor are three normal sash-hung windows. In the back wall is a large round-headed window lighting the staircase; the bay-window is an addition.

(255) Houses, Nos. 38 to 40 and 41 Park Side (Plate 302), comprising two blocks, standing respectively either side of Warkworth Terrace, originally of three storeys with basements, have walls of gault brick with stone and stucco dressings and slate-covered roofs; a mansard containing attics has been added to Nos. 38–40. They are not in R. G. Baker's map of Cambridge of 1830, but date from the same decade for they are shown in the print of the Coronation Dinner of 1838 (Litho. by G. Scharf. R. Ackermann, London). Clearly a moderately ambitious scheme for two unified and symmetrical blocks, each containing three houses, flanking the entrance to the Terrace was proposed, each with a recessed centre screened on the ground floor by an open colonnade extending between the flanking wings. The N.W. block was completed. The S.E. block only progressed as far as the first wing; structural provision for the recessed continuation remains visible in the S.E. wall.

To the S.W. the buildings have stone plat-bands at first-floor sill level across the two-bay wings, a stucco cornice at second-floor sill level across the five recessed bays and stopping against the wings, continuous stone plat-bands at eaves level, and parapet-walls. The stucco colonnade has square columns supporting an entablature surmounted by the balustraded parapet to a first-floor balcony. The entrance-doorways to Nos. 38 and 39 are plain, those in Warkworth Terrace to Nos. 40 and 41 have stucco pilasters at the sides and entablatures. The windows contain double-hung sashes and many of those on the ground and first floors retain slatted shutters; rectangular recesses mostly take the place of windows in the end walls. Inside, the plans of all the houses differ; in No. 40 the layout of the staircase at right angles to the entrance-lobby is unusual and visually successful.

No. 39 is equipped with an outside bell and heavy bars in a number of the windows, suggesting an institutional purpose. Before 1850 the Rev. James Scholefield, Regius Professor of Greek, established in Park Side a 'Female Servants' Training Institution' (C. H. Cooper, *Memorials of Cambridge*, III, 186).

The two-storey *Coach-houses* some 17 yds. behind the houses are original; they are of brick with slate-covered roofs.

(256) Houses, Nos. 36, 37 Park Side, a pair, close N.W. of the foregoing, of three storeys with basements, have walls of gault brick and slate-covered roofs. They are shown in the lithograph of the Coronation Dinner of 1838 and form a single symmetrical block similar in general character to the houses in Benet Place (Monuments (248–50)). Small single-storey projections at each end contain stucco-faced porches.

Towards Parker's Piece the lateral entrance-doorways have square attached Doric columns without taper at the sides supporting a plain entablature concealing the flat roofs behind. The main block has ranges of four double-hung sash-windows on each floor, a plat-band at first-floor sill-level and a timber eaves-cornice. The pyramidal roof is of low pitch. All the glazing-bars have been removed from the windows. The other sides of the building are of no particular note.

(257) House, No. 27, standing 65 yds. from Clarendon Street, of two storeys with basement and attics, has walls of gault brick in part faced with stucco and slate-covered roofs. It was built about the middle of the 19th century to an eclectic Classical design of some monumentality. An addition has been made subsequently on the N., the original plan being symmetrical in outline. The Park front is in three bays, the middle bay projecting boldly. The whole of the ground floor has a rusticated facing of stucco; at the wall-head is a simplified entablature with stucco cornice pedimented over the projection, and a low parapet-wall. The entrance-doorway in the middle has a surround in low relief with straight Doric pilasters supporting a plain entablature with a blocking-course surmounted by a shaped panel. The ground-floor window in each of the side bays has a tripartite sash-hung timber frame set in a shallow rusticated projection rising from basement-level and finishing in a cornice just below the first-floor window. The three main first-floor windows have stucco surrounds consisting of strip-pilasters standing on sills resting on shaped brackets and supporting simplified entablatures with segmental pediments. In the sides of the central projection are plain windows and blind recesses. In the mansard roof are three dormer-windows.

To the N.E. is a projection larger than that described to the S.W.; here and across each end a simple brick cornice continues the stucco cornice described above.

The *Coach-house* standing free some 5 yds. to the N.W. is contemporary with the house. It is of two storeys but low, with brick and tile Doric pilasters clasping the angles and supporting a continuous simplified entablature pedimented over the N. and S. ends. The carriage-entrance has a segmental head.

N.W. side:

Park Terrace (Plate 302) includes sixteen houses overlooking Parker's Piece built at different times in the second quarter of the 19th century under a single comprehensive scheme. It consists of five blocks of buildings: in the middle two houses, Nos. 7 and 8, set back behind the building line and designed as a unit; two long terraces of taller houses, Nos. 1 to 6 and 9 to 14, on the building line and linked to the first by screen-walls, and, pavilion-like on the extremities, two freestanding houses, Park Lodge and Camden House, complete in themselves; only the two terraces are alike, the other three blocks differ from them and from one another, though the end houses balance in mass and form.

The first leases from Jesus College (in College Muniment Room) indicate more or less the building sequence: Nos. 7 and 8 in 1831; Nos. 1 to 6 in 1835; Nos. 11 and 12 in 1839; Nos. 9 and 10 in 1840. Thus the middle block was completed first, then the S.W. terrace followed by the opposite terrace; the original lease of Nos. 13 and 14 has not been traced (*Chanticleer* CXLVI, May 1948). But all, including Park Lodge and Camden House, were standing and roofed by 1838 for they are shown in the lithograph of the Coronation Dinner in that year on Parker's Piece. In the following description the buildings are grouped architecturally under Monument Nos. 258–60.

In Park Terrace a controlling ownership, a long-term plan, and sensibility have created an extensive group of town houses, symmetrical in lay-out and mass, of much distinction.

(258) Houses, Nos. 1 to 14 Park Terrace, all of three storeys with basements, and some with attics, have walls of gault brick and slate-covered roofs. Their disposition and history is described in the introduction to Park Terrace above.

The block comprising *Houses* Nos. 7 and 8 was linked originally to the flanking terraces only by screen-walls; it has since been extended E. and W. and No. 7 now joins the S.W. terrace. The original building is of four bays with small projections at each end, of the same height, containing the entrances. At first-floor sill-level is a plat-band, continued as the capping to the screen-walls, and at the eaves a frieze and boxed gutter on brick dentils; these last occur only over the brickwork between the windows. The entrance-doorways have rectangular lights above the panelled doors; the steps up to No. 8 retain original cast-iron railings with latticework panels. All the windows are sash-hung; only those on the first floor of No. 7 retain their slatted shutters and only those in the basement their glazing-bars.

The two terraces, *Houses* Nos. 1 to 6 and 9 to 14, are loftier than the foregoing, have taller sash-hung windows and parapet-walls. Their most prominent feature is a cast-iron covered balcony extending the full length of the first floor of each terrace. It is supported on cast-iron foliated scroll-brackets and has a balustrade, standards and frieze all decorated with a free adaptation of the Greek honeysuckle ornament; the sheet-metal pent roof is flared. Fragments of balustrading similar to the foregoing remain fencing some of the basement areas and No. 2 has an elaborate scrollwork balustrade to the steps up to the entrance, with a newel in the form of an enriched column. Many of the houses have small additions at the back. Inside, generally the entrance-passage widens out towards the back to contain the staircase. This last has slender square balusters and curves, without newels, between the flights. On the ground floor is one front and one back room; the main room is on the first floor, the full width of the front and lit by three windows.

The small front gardens were originally fenced by railings on dwarf walls between brick piers; the railings have been removed and a general unkempt appearance mars the dignity of the terraces.

(259) PARK LODGE, on the corner of Parker Street and flanking Monument (258), of two storeys, has walls of gault brick with some stone dressings and slate-covered roofs. It was built in the second quarter of the 19th century (see the introduction to Park Terrace above). Of the villa type of house typical of the period, it consists of a rectangular main block, broader than tall, with widely overhanging eaves on slender shaped brackets and a low-pitched hipped roof. The front is strictly symmetrically designed, in five bays, the entrance-doorway having a stone surround with antae supporting an entablature and console-brackets under the cornice. At first-floor sill-level is a continuous stone plat-band and all the windows contain double-hung sashes with their glazing-bars. A N.W. wing extends beside Parker Street; it is of two storeys but lower than the main block.

(260) CAMDEN HOUSE, flanking Monument (258) on the S.W. and balancing the foregoing, is of two storeys with walls of gault brick and slated roof. It was built in the second quarter of the 19th century (see the introduction to Park Terrace above). Like Park Lodge, it is of the villa type of house of the period, consisting of a rectangular main block, broader than tall, with low-pitched roof and wide eaves. Strict symmetry governs the more conspicuous sides, necessitating the use of blind window-recesses to preserve it. The Park front is in three bays, the three rectangular ground-floor windows being set in round-headed wall-arches. The entrance is from the side street on the N.E.; the doorcase has side-pilasters supporting an entablature all of stucco. A N.W. wing contains the kitchen. Inside, most of the fittings are original; the principal rooms have enriched cornices and white marble fireplace-surrounds, moulded and with bosses at the corners. The entrance-hall is spanned by two arches springing from pilasters and the staircase has slender square balusters, no newels.

(261) FURNESS LODGE, next S.W. of Monument (260), of two storeys with basement, has walls of gault brick and slate-covered roofs. It was built about the middle of the 19th century and forms no part of the unified lay-out of Park Terrace described above. The design is more pretentious and less successful than that of the earlier 19th-century 'villa' exemplified by Camden House or Park Lodge (Monuments (259, 260)). The front is in five bays, with plat-bands at ground and first-floor sill-levels. The doorway in the middle has a neo-Greek surround with square Ionic pilasters *in antis* supporting an entablature with wreaths in the frieze; the broad first-floor window above it has strip-pilasters at the sides, console-brackets supporting a square cornice and a cast-iron balcony of ogee profile. Under the deep boxed gutter are small brackets, and pendants at the corners. The roof is of low pitch and at the ridge are two chimney-stacks. At the back are two gables with shaped barge-boards and a large round-headed window lighting the staircase.

(262) TERRACE, Nos. 1 to 6 Parker Street, on the N.E. side, extending from 67 yds. to 127 yds. from Parker's Piece, of two storeys, has walls of gault brick and slate-covered roofs. Cut in the brickwork at the back of No. 5 (plan p. 365) are the initials and date E N 1838. On stylistic grounds, the six houses may well be of this age. Two through-passages group the houses in pairs and the whole street-front, from end to end, is divided into unequal bays by colossal pilasters supporting a severely simplified entablature. Three bays define the separate houses, two extra bays the passages; the entrances to these last are of two plain orders, with round heads and stone imposts, the imposts being continued as strings down the passages, and hung with simple iron gates. The doorway in the middle bay of each house has a small oblong light above the door. Inside are two rooms, one behind the other, to each side of the entrance passage, the width of one of the back rooms being reduced to leave space for a square staircase. Behind the houses are small square yards enclosed by brick walls and containing privies in one corner.

CHRIST'S PIECE

E. side:

(263) HOUSES, a pair, Nos. 5 and 13 Emmanuel Road, standing some 78 yds. apart symmetrically between Parker Street and Orchard Street, facing Christ's Piece, are of two storeys and have walls of gault brick with stone dressings and slate-covered roofs. They were built as grooms' houses between 1826 and 1828 and architecturally devised as the small pavilion-like terminal features to a long range on the

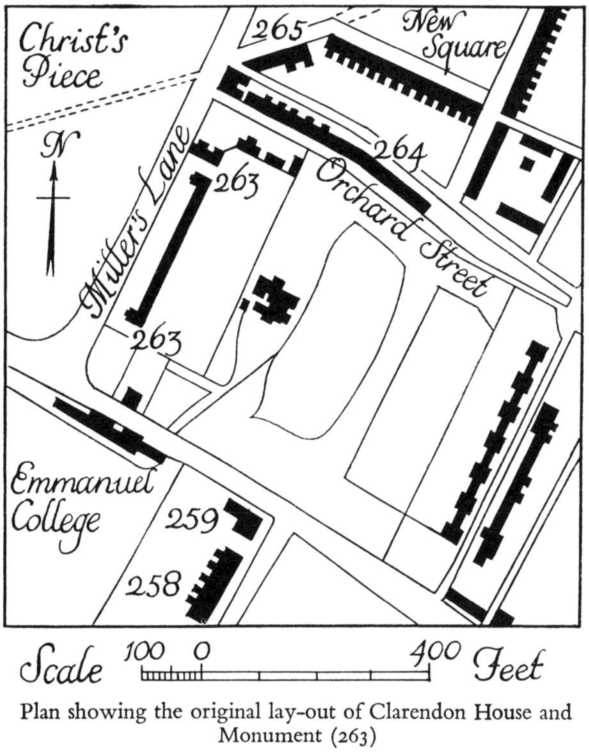

Plan showing the original lay-out of Clarendon House and Monument (263)

N.W. boundary of the grounds of Charles Humfrey's house, Clarendon House, which stood between Clarendon Street, Victoria Street and Earl Street. The range was built by Humfrey for letting as mews but the middle part was leased to the Borough and adapted for use as a police station. It is shown on R. G. Baker's map of 1830. (Plans for lease of police station: University Library, Maps 53 (2) 84.13; *Cambridge Chronicle* 6 Jan. 1837, 5 May 1838, 18 July 1846.)

The N.W. end of each house has the middle part recessed, so to suggest broad pilaster-strips at the sides supporting a pediment spanning the whole. Bay-windows have been added, of two storeys to No. 5, concealing most of the face, of one storey to No. 13, leaving visible the original first-floor segmental-headed window, which interrupts the horizontal members of the pediment and extends into the tympanum. The refaced S.E. half of the S.W. side of No. 13 shows where the main linking range adjoined; the corresponding N.E. side of No. 5 is masked. The other walls contain segmental-headed openings.

In the boundary-wall to Emmanuel Road are original octagonal gate-piers of brick to carriage-entrances to N.W. and S.W. respectively of the two houses. Piers have subsequently been inserted between them to restrict the entrances to foot passengers.

264 ORCHARD TERRACE (Plate 310), fourteen houses, Nos. 1 to 13 and 16, on the N.E. side of the street, of one storey with attics, have walls of gault brick and tile-covered mansard roofs. The terrace appears on R. G. Baker's map of 1830 but not on S. I. Neale's of 1820. It was continuous for some 140 yds. until in the middle of the 19th century Nos. 14 and 15 were demolished to make way for Clarendon Street, leaving No. 16 isolated. (*Cambridge Chronicle* 7 June 1845 refers to the Terrace 'built about twenty years'.)

The buildings of Orchard Terrace are of very humble character, but the small scale of the fronts and the repetition of their features, the low eaves, the unbroken extent of the mansard roofs and great chimney-stacks produce a most striking effect, enhanced by the fortuitous curved lay-out of the street.

Towards the street each house has a front door in the middle, with timber doorcase with side pilaster-strips supporting a simplified pedimented entablature, and a plain sash-hung window to each side; no windows break the roof surfaces facing this way. Offices have been added along the back and the attics are lit by dormer-windows above. No. 16 shows how the houses may be modernised without destruction of their external character.

NEW SQUARE

(265) NEW SQUARE (Plate 310), a large open space (approximately 150 yds. by 80 yds.) extending from Emmanuel Road opposite the N.E. corner of Christ's Piece, bounded on the E. and the greater part of the N. and S. by terrace-houses, Nos. 1 to 47 and No. 2 Fitzroy Street, was an entirely new development, to a single coherent design, in the second quarter of the 19th century. Only two houses, Nos. 34 and 35, have since been rebuilt. The terraces are of two storeys, in part with basements, with 9 in. walls of gault brick and slate-covered roofs (plan of No. 16, p. 365).

The first notice of a resident in New Square appears in 1825 (*Camb. Chronicle* 1 April) although the earliest leases in the books of Jesus College, the landlords, are of 1829 and 1830. The S. terrace, Nos. 1 to 20, was built first, from the E. end. The E. terrace, Nos. 21 to 33 and No. 2 Fitzroy Street, was built in 1834, and the N. terrace, Nos. 34 to 47, in 1834–35 (*Chanticleer*, Jesus College House Mag., CXLVI, Summer 1948). Though generally uniform except for the pedimented centrepiece to each terrace, the houses have minor variations on plan for they were evidently built by different persons on building leases from Jesus College and some by the Society itself. A house in the middle of the E. terrace was advertised for sale in 1838 because, 'built in the best possible manner, the outlay has so far exceeded the owner's capital' (*Camb. Chronicle* 30 June). The lease for the same house was forty years from 1834; similarly the leases for Nos. 21 to 23, and 31 and 32 on the E. and Nos. 35 and 36 on the N. are known from sale advertisements to have been from 1834 (*Camb. Chronicle* Sept. and Nov. 1843). Thus though there are consistent differences in the houses, for example in the two halves of the E. terrace, they must indicate the progress of building rather than significant differences in date.

R. G. Baker's map, 1830, shows the S. terrace only; R. Harwood's map, 1840, shows three terraces. Most of the houses are now University lodgings.

New Square is a spacious urban development of the first half of the 19th century given coherence by the control of the external appearance of the houses and distinction by the application of architectural principles, though the simplest, to the project. The visual effect of the whole is obscured by the bus and car park occupying the Square and in 1956 the E. terrace was marred by demolitions.

The *South Terrace* (see illustration opposite), of *c.* 1825 is in two separate lengths, the four W. houses, Nos. 1 to 4, being set at an angle towards the S.W. and of these the first and last are rather larger houses than the rest. Nos. 12 and 13 are distinguished as the centrepiece by four brick pilasters on the front supporting a pediment, now lacking its horizontal members. In the pediment is the shield-of-arms and crest of Brand. All the houses have doorways with round heads, without imposts, panelled doors and fanlights with radiating glazing-bars, where the original glazing survives. All the windows are plain, with double-hung sashes. At the back are small two-storey projections. *East Terrace* (see illustration facing p. 362) and *North Terrace*, of 1834–35, are generally similar to the foregoing, but Nos. 27 and 28 and Nos. 41 and 42 being the respective centrepieces are rather more elaborate. They are distinguished by slightly greater height and have five pilasters to each, dividing the front into two wide central and two narrow flanking bays. The wide bays are pedimented and in the tympanum is a small light, in one round, in the other round-headed. The doorways have imposts and some of the original window-shutters remain; weathering of the brickwork shows that once all the windows had shutters. Most of the houses in the S. half only of the E. terrace have original two-storey projections at the back like those in the S. terrace; Nos. 27 to 33, that is, the rest northward, and the N. terrace are the houses with basements. Inside, the houses are well fitted. The original fireplace-surrounds have moulded architraves with roundels at the angles. The staircases have cut strings, turned newels and plain balusters.

Maids' Causeway[1]

(266) Houses, thirty-nine, Nos. 4 to 20 on the S. side at the western end, and Nos. 2 to 17 Willow Walk, Nos. 1 to 5 and the hostel Fair Street, and Nos. 1 to 8 Short Street, generally of two storeys with basements, some with attics, have walls of gault brick and slate-covered roofs. They stand on a site, bounded by the streets named, formerly known as Doll's Close, which was bought by Charles Humfrey, architect and builder, in part from James Burleigh in 1809 and in part from Downing College in 1810, and developed by him, the lay-out of the houses being to a carefully balanced and integrated plan. Building was started in 1815 and finished by 1826. The principal houses on the site are those in Maids' Causeway (see Plate 308 and illustration facing p. 321) overlooking Butt Green consisting of five large detached and two pairs of semi-detached houses set well back from the road, symmetrically disposed, uniform in design and linked by straight screen-walls. On the extremities of the foregoing, linked to it originally by curved screen-walls, the end houses of the smaller terrace-houses returning at right angles down Fair Street and Short Street form pavilion-like terminal features. The same two terraces return at their S. end a short way along Willow Walk where, centrally between the returns but originally separated from them by open spaces, is the Willow Walk terrace of still smaller houses, which are shown overlooking an open space, now New Square, in R. G. Baker's map of 1830. The accompanying diagrammatic plan, though in some minor respects necessarily conjectural, indicates the original scheme.

In November 1815 Humfrey promised to offer for sale in the spring of 1816 'skeleton shells' and 'sites' of houses here. In 1816 one of the houses was advertised as 'newly erected and unfinished'. They were usually

[1] For the ancient usage, see the introduction to the Barnwell Area, p. 366.

Monument No. 266 DOLL'S CLOSE *Conjectured original layout*

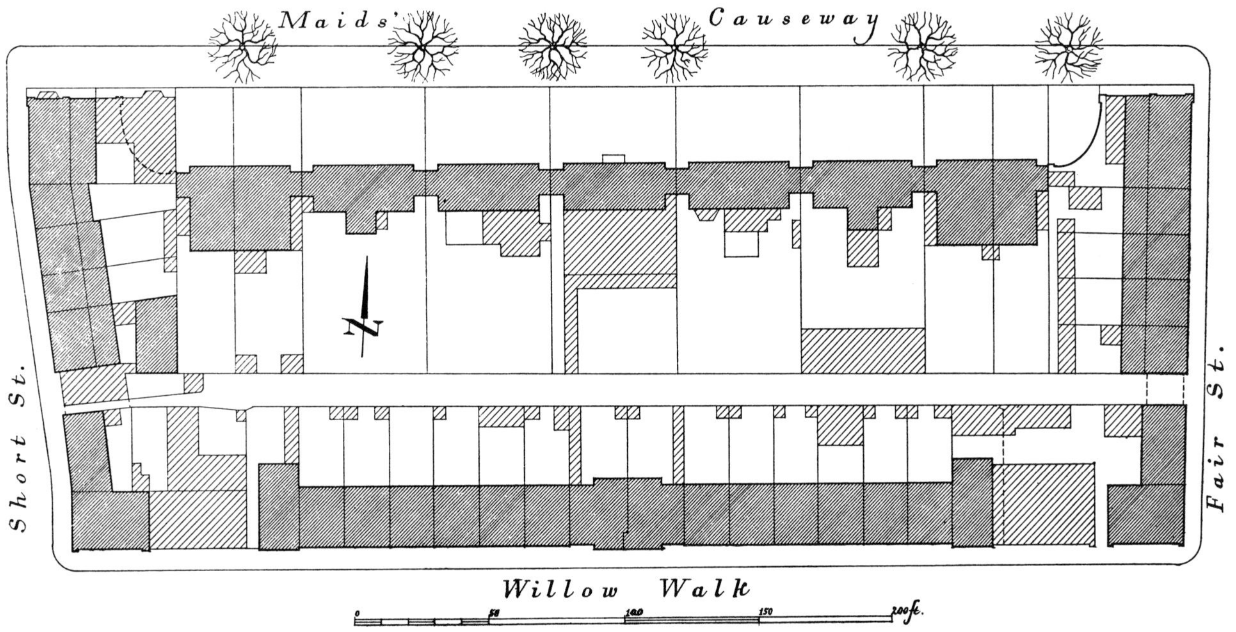

sold on forty-year leases, Humfrey retaining the freehold. After raising a mortgage of £7,000 on Doll's Close in 1842, he was obliged to sell out in 1846. (*Cambridge Chronicle* for 22 Sept. 1815, 6 Sept. 1816, 2 Oct. 1820, 6 April 1821, 9 Aug. 1822, 7 Oct. 1825, 7 April 1826, 11 Aug. 1826, 24 July 1847; University Library, Maps 53 (2) 84.13).

The Causeway houses were built 37 ft. wide on plots 46 ft. wide. The Willow Walk houses are 22 ft. wide. Nearly all the spaces originally between the houses have subsequently been filled by extensions and outbuildings; the curved wall at the W. end of the Causeway houses has been replaced by later dwellings, and other alterations are noted below.

The Doll's Close buildings are of much interest as an example of a social and economic urban development of the early 19th century. They include dwellings proportioned in fact and appearance to two independent classes of society and, presumably, in Willow Walk, for the outside staff of the wealthier of the two. It is of note as a development designed and controlled and completed by an architect who was a speculative builder; further, the aspect to Maids' Causeway despite alterations is one of architectural distinction.

Maids' Causeway: Nos. 4 to 20 (plan of No. 16 p. 365), nine houses (see illustration facing p. 321), are of two storeys with basements and attics. Houses Nos. 4 and 6, 18 and 20 are semi-detached, entrance to the end houses being in concealed projections at the side. The building-history is given above; the later alterations other than those described include the addition of a storey to Nos. 4 and 6, and a S. extension nearly doubling the size of No. 12; the same houses have been more or less damaged by alterations to their principal fronts. With these exceptions the street-fronts are uniform in design, each is in three bays, the wall-openings being set in large areas of brickwork. They have plinths, plat-bands at first-floor sill level, simple cornices of slight projection, parapet-walls and mansard roofs. The entrances in the middle have timber doorcases with panelled and horizontally fluted strip-pilasters at the sides and simplified pedimented cornices. The windows are plain and sash-hung, except the pedimented dormer-windows, which contain casements. Screen-walls the height of the ground floor, with low buildings concealed behind them, link all the houses. The backs are without elaboration; Nos. 8 and 16, a symmetrical pair, were planned with large central projections; the end semi-detached pairs were given greater depth than the rest, the latitude in planning so gained making it possible to maintain elevational uniformity with the other houses. Curved screen-walls, so far as they survive, similar to those already described but with widely-spaced pilaster-strips, link the foregoing to the 'pavilions' terminating Fair Street and Short Street. The neo-Greek porch of No. 12 is a mid 19th-century addition.

Inside, a typical house has a central entrance passage leading through to a staircase. To each side is a large room, one with a window at the back as well as at the front. On each of the floors above is a room over the entrance passage. The simple staircase has cut strings. All the fittings are quite plain.

Bounding the gardens to Maids' Causeway are timber fences, largely original, with top and bottom rails, the former with iron spikes, square standards and latticework infilling.

Fair Street: houses Nos. 1 to 5 and an unnumbered continuation to the S., now a Church Army hostel, equivalent to two houses, are of two storeys with basements. They form a terrace of uniform design backing on the gardens of the foregoing; the small original annexes at the rear have all been heightened to two storeys in the later 19th century. No. 1 has the N. end pedimented above a broad wall-arch with elliptical head embracing the single windows on basement, ground and first floors; between the two upper windows is a brick panel and the square head of the top window extends up behind the soffit of the wall-arch, which is rebated to receive it. The rear annexe, heightened and with windows inserted, is no longer disguised by the screen-wall to the Maids' Causeway houses, and an original doorway in the wall has been blocked. The street-front of Nos. 1 to 5 is regular, with a brick plat-band at first-floor sill level, plain eaves-gutters and timber doorcases with side-pilasters and simplified entablatures. Between the foregoing and the even plainer S. continuation containing the hostel is an open archway with segmental head occupying the whole of the ground floor and giving access for carriages to a service road behind (see diagrammatic plan). The houses are each of two bays, the hostel of five, and all the windows are plain with double-hung sashes. The S. wall of the short return towards Willow Walk has flanking strip-pilasters of brick and ranges of three windows on each floor, those in the middle blocked.

Short Street: houses Nos. 1 to 8 repeat, in reverse, the Fair Street houses described above though the alterations and additions have been more extensive. The N. end now has a two-storey bay-window filling most of the wall-arch, and the screen-wall originally extending E. from it has been replaced by houses; No. 1 has a mid 19th-century door-surround; No. 5 has been remodelled as a public-house, No. 6 combined with it, the carriage-way it incorporated being reduced to a narrow footway, and extensive additions made at the back.

Willow Walk: houses Nos. 2 to 17 (plan of No. 10 p. 365) are of two storeys with basements. They form a symmetrical terrace, architecturally accentuated in the middle and at the ends, placed centrally between the S. returns of Fair Street and Short Street; the latter, though of the simplest character, as described above, are devised as detached terminal features to the terrace, but the spaces between have now been built up. The centrepiece projects slightly and is in three bays divided and flanked by brick pilasters supporting a pediment with timber cornice. The end houses also project, and have the entrances in the return walls. The doorways on the front have elliptical brick arches, all but the two centremost being paired under embracing arches, and the doors are panelled. The windows generally are plain, some retaining shutters, but those on the ground floor in the end houses are set in elliptical-headed recesses. The small gardens at the back are enclosed by brick walls. The interior arrangement varies slightly from that of the typical terrace-house.

(267) Terrace-Houses, formerly Brunswick Place, extending on the N. side of Maids' Causeway some 165 yds. E. from Brunswick Walk, interrupted by Brunswick Gardens and Brunswick Terrace, and on the S. side between Fair Street and Causeway Passage, of two storeys mostly with basements and attics, are of gault brick with slate-covered roofs. They were built in the 19th century before 1830, being shown in R. G. Baker's map of that year, and have many minor alterations and additions. The houses vary, within a restricted range; they differ in height, some have plat-bands and parapet-walls; the entrance-doorways are round-headed or square, some being approached up steps with iron balustrades; and several houses have cast-iron balconies or guards to the upper windows. Only Nos. 24, 26, 28, eastward from Fair Street, are designed as a single composition in seven bays with the middle five recessed, but they are much altered. Nos. 49, 51 and 53 have a particular grace. The houses are in general plain but of some dignity and accord more with the residential district close W. than with the Barnwell area of development next described, in which they stand. The interior arrangement provides a hall-passage.

The terraces, *Brunswick Walk*, including *North Terrace* and *Brunswick Terrace*, N. of the foregoing, though of much the same date are less distinguished but pleasant in their simplicity and lack of ostentation. An exception is No. 12 Brunswick Terrace, with a street-front in three bays, that in the middle projecting, a central doorway with moulded architrave, a dentil-course, parapet-wall and mansard roof; it appears to have been the beginning of a terrace of some individuality never carried further. *Willow Place* and *Causeway Passage*, close S. of Maids' Causeway, are even less distinguished than the foregoing though again of much the same date.

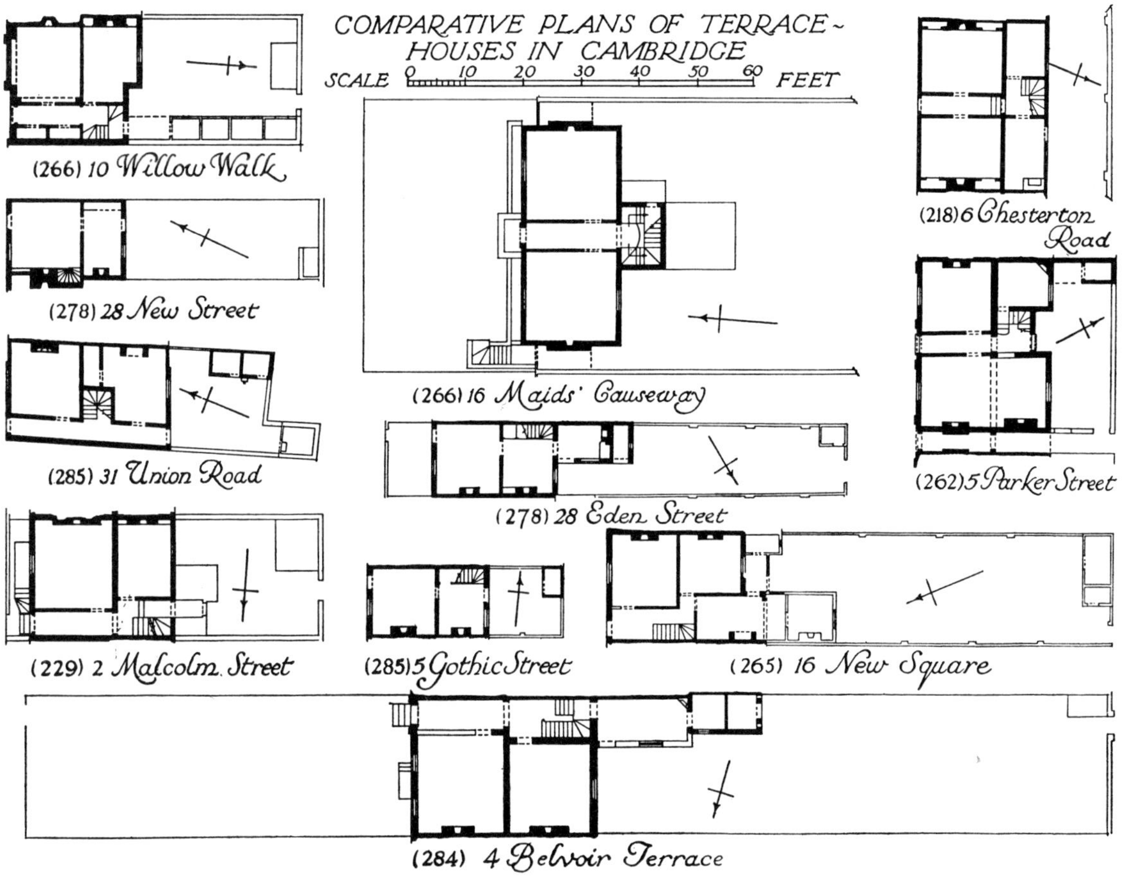

Barnwell Area

The buildings described below stand S. of the river Cam and E. and N.E. of the line Brunswick Walk, Fair Street, Jesus Terrace, Orchard Street, Prospect Row, and Petersfield, an area intersected by Newmarket Road and East Road. The greater part of the development is of the first half of the 19th century and of mixed industrial and residential character, but in so far as the former village of Barnwell is the nucleus of the area and the Newmarket Road the successor in part of the former Barnwell Causeway several older houses occur; these and the more noteworthy houses are singled out below before describing in general terms the prevailing character of the built-up area. The rather more distinguished terrace-houses at the W. end of Newmarket Road though within the area are numbered with Maids' Causeway (see Monument 267)). On the S. side of this last the raised footway is the only vestige of the Causeway built under the terms of the will of Dr. Perse (died 1615); the present appellation seems comparatively modern, deriving possibly from the Knight and Mortlock almshouses for 'poor godly, ancient maidens' formerly on the site of Nos 64–7 Jesus Lane, for it is still Barnwell Causeway on William Custance's map of 1798.

NEWMARKET ROAD

North Side:—

(268) BURLEIGH HOUSE, No. 13, nearly opposite Christchurch, of two storeys with cellar and attics, has walls of gault brick with stone dressings and slate-covered roofs. It was built in the 18th century but in the second half of the 19th century the front was extensively remodelled and a cross wing added on the E. Of the original S. front only the walling with flush quoins, a plat-band at first-floor sill level, a cornice and parapet-wall survive. The stonework of the doorway and windows is all later and disguises the original appearance of the building. The original horizontal features are continued across the free sides of the house; the W. end has twin parapeted gables and the back a later Doric porch; modern offices have been added on the N.W. All the sashes are renewed. The interior is divided into four by a spine wall containing the fireplaces and cross walls. The staircase in the N.E. quarter is of the 19th century. Some of the rooms retain original bolection-moulded panelling, with dado-rail and cornice, and bolection-moulded overmantels. The eponym is James Burleigh, F.S.A., carrier and landowner, of Cambridge, died c. 1830.

(269) HOUSE, No. 61, N.E. of the opening to Wellington Street, of two storeys with cellar and attics, has walls of yellow and red brick and slate-covered roofs. It was built in the first half of the 18th century and probably comprised a main range with a single-storey kitchen behind; subsequently in the same century the latter was extended E. and a second storey added over the whole. Early in the 19th century the interior was remodelled. The 18th-century S. front, of yellow brick, is symmetrical and in five narrow bays; it has a discontinuous plat-band at first-floor level and a timber eaves-cornice. The entrance-doorway in the middle has an early 19th-century timber doorcase, panelled and with weathered hood. The window-openings have segmental heads and contain double-hung sashes in frames flush with the wall-face. The gabled and parapeted ends of the front range are also of yellow brickwork. The red brick range behind has an eaves-cornice of the same material and 19th-century and modern windows. Inside, the staircase up to the first floor, is of the early 19th century, the original N. wall of the stairhall being cut away for it; it has slender square balusters, no newels. From the first floor to the attics the original staircase remains; it rises round a rectangular well and has close strings, square newels and turned balusters.

N.E. of the house is a large timber-framed and brick outbuilding, much altered but probably of the late 17th century, with a massive central chimney-stack. The ground floor now forms garages.

(270) ABBEY HOUSE, some 33 yds. back from the Road, 17 yds. E. of Abbey Road, of one and two storeys with cellars and attics, has plastered timber-framed and brick walls and tile-covered roofs. In the main it is the work of three periods, the late 16th, the late 17th and the early 18th century, but many minor alterations and additions have been made since and most of the windows are renewals or insertions of the later 18th or 19th century. The original timber-framed building is T-shaped and comprises the S. half of the house. In 1678 a large brick addition almost doubling the size of the foregoing was made on the N. In c. 1700 the original building was faced in brick and both it and the addition slightly extended on the W. and on the E. and W. respectively; at the same time the interior was extensively refitted. Later 18th-century additions are on the N. and N.E. In the present century the house has been divided into three dwellings. It was given to the Cambridge Folk Museum by Lord Fairhaven in 1946.

Abbey House, though with many botched alterations, is a building of much character with a dated 'Dutch' gable. It contains panelling of c. 1700.

Architectural Description—The W. side has towards the S. end the projecting staircase-wing of the original building. The wing is refaced in the lower part but, above, the N. wall retains some old pargeting and the W. gable has original moulded bargeboards with a shaped pendant at the apex; it is flanked by large brick chimney-stacks projecting from the W. wall of the main range. Both stacks are original, with square clustered shafts; the lower part of that to the N. is masked by an 18th-century and modern single-storey addition. Brick walls of c. 1700 have been built flush with the projecting face of the S. stack, up to the eaves, leaving a narrow space between them and the original external wall of the main range; remaining on the old external face is an area of original pargeting enriched with strapwork and jewel ornament. The E. face of the late 16th-century house has two framed and plastered gables separated by a short length of plain eaves. The first floor and probably the gable-ends originally projected, but in *c.* 1700 the front wall of the two main floors was rebuilt in red brick; the whole is now flush and in advance of the original eaves. The brickwork has a plat-band at first-floor level and windows with flat heads; the three-sided S. bay-window is an early 19th-century addition. Both gables retain original moulded bargeboards and pendants; in the N. gable is a 19th-century window; the S. gable is blind and comprises a dormer. A lead moulded rainwater-head of *c.* 1700 is modelled with two churchwarden's pipes in saltire; (this came in modern times from No. 11 Sidney Street, now

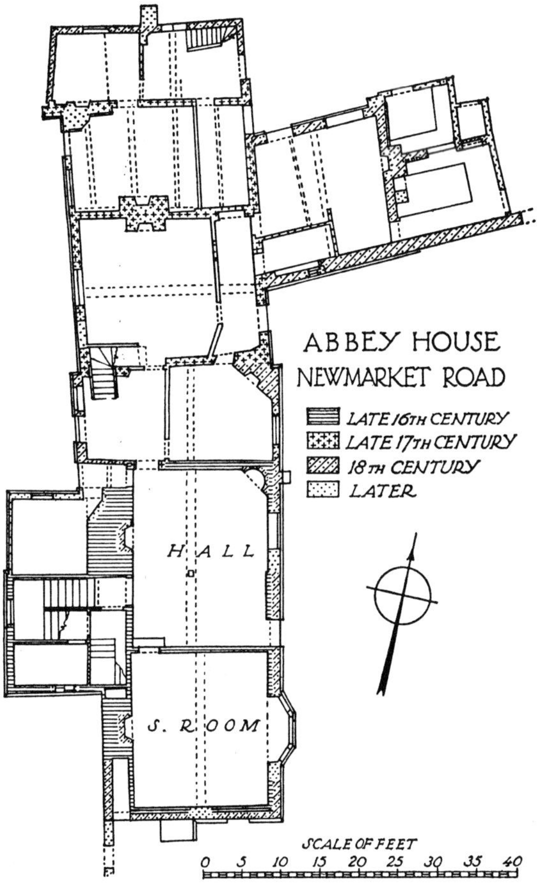

gone, associated by A. B. Gray (*Cambridge Revisited*, 40) with Joshua Lee's pipe-works). The brick work of *c.* 1700 is returned across the S. end of the house below the gable and includes the doorway to the narrow space flanking the chimney-stack described above; again this gable-end is of plastered timber-framing and retains original bargeboards and a pendant at the apex. A lead rainwater-head contemporary with the brick-work is decorated with fleurs-de-lys and a rose.

The 1678 N. addition was originally more or less symmetrical; it is defined by a moulded brick plinth, so far as it survives. The main gabled bay in the middle of the W. side (Plate 307) has plat-bands at first and attic-floor levels and a shaped parapet consisting of concave quadrants rising to an inset semicircle. The parapet has an oversailing capping of tiles on bricks projecting in dentil-like fashion. The windows on the ground and first floors are in new positions but the original pairs of windows with flat brick arches, though blocked, are visible; the original attic window, with renewed frame, in the gable-end has a short brick plat-band immediately above the arch. In the semicircular head of the gable under a square label is a sunk panel containing the date 1678. Of the flanking bays, that to the N. has the eaves at first-floor level; the moulded plinth continues without break from the gabled bay suggesting that the wall was originally in this position, unless the whole is a reconstruction, with reuse of original material, some 4 ft. forward, the original position being marked by a ceiling-beam inside. The front wall of the S. flanking bay is clearly an 18th-century reconstruction well in advance of the gabled bay; it is of two storeys, now with a flat roof and has a plat-band at the level of the doorheads. The corresponding bay on the opposite side of the house has similarly been rebuilt further out contemporaneously with the underbuilding of the E. front of the late 16th-century house, which it continues; the two late 17th-century bays N. of the foregoing, so far as they are not concealed by the later N.E. addition, have a moulded brick plinth. This last returns round the N. end of the house until concealed by the later N. addition. These two 18th-century additions have plinths of brick and reused mediaeval ashlar, presumably from the ruins of Barnwell priory close by, and timber-framing above. The S. wall of the N. addition projects westward to form the E. respond of a gateway now destroyed; the projection has a reused chamfered ashlar plinth and retains a hinge-pin on the N.

Inside the original house are longitudinal ceiling-beams, chamfered where exposed, now rather to the W. of centre. The Hall, originally perhaps a room and a passage, is paved with flagstones brought from the ruins of Barnwell priory by a Mr. Bullen some years before 1812 (C.A.S. *Proc.* VII, 235); it is wainscoted throughout with bolection-moulded pine panelling of *c.* 1700 in two heights with a dado-rail and cornice; some mutilation of the panelling was caused by the insertion of the 18th or 19th-century sash-window in the E. wall. The overmantel consists of a horizontal panel flanked by wide pilasters. The two broad two-panel doors are contemporary with the foregoing. The S. room is lined with panelling generally similar to that in the Hall, but of oak, with later panelling above and below the 19th-century bay-window; the fireplace has a bolection-moulded surround. The staircase-wing has much of the timber-framing exposed inside, including the studs etc. of the containing partitions to the cellar stair and to the main stair, wall-plates and a braced tie-beam with studding above in the W. gable-end. The main staircase has been renewed in the lower part, where are slender square balusters, turned newels and a moulded mahogany handrail, but the original position and form are retained; the upper part is original and has a contemporary newel with shaped head.

On the first floor, a bedroom over the hall is lined with reset early 17th-century oak panelling, five panels high, with a fluted frieze; the doors are contemporary and hung on old hinges. The S. room is lined with pine panelling of *c.* 1700 similar to that in the ground-floor rooms, with a bolection-moulded fireplace-surround and similarly moulded panel in the overmantel between plain pilasters; the door-panelling is mounted on an older door. In both these rooms insertion of the sash-windows has involved some rearrangement of the panelling. In the attic the framed N. gable-end of the 16th-century house survives. Enclosure of the dormer in the S.E. gable is provided by early 17th-century panelling.

In the 1678 extension are longitudinal ceiling-beams in the flanking bays and a cross-beam in the middle, gabled, bay. The N. and the middle rooms on the ground floor were remodelled in *c.* 1800 and the second contains a moulded fire-place-surround with paterae at the angles. Of the two rooms in the S. bay, that to the W. is now the hall of dwelling No. 2 and contains the first flight of a 19th-century staircase, that to the E. is lined with plain 18th-century wainscoting, two panels high, with a dado-rail and cornice; the overmantel is of *c.* 1700, with a bolection-moulded panel flanked by panelled pilasters, and the moulded fireplace-surround with roundels at the angles is of *c.* 1800. On the first floor are two rooms lined with plain 18th-century panelling, one having a bolection-moulded fireplace-surround and overmantel of *c.* 1700 similar to those already described. The roof is visible in the attics; much of it is of the late 17th century but very rough, with pine rafters and purlins and ash or elm collar-beams. Many of the rooms throughout the house contain 18th-century fitted cupboards with contemporary panelled doors and hinges.

The old *Boundary-wall* running E.N.E. towards Beche Road from the N.E. addition is for much of the length built on a plinth of 15th-century walling *in situ* of limestone rubble with flint galleting, which retains a run of some 14 ft. of original moulded stone weathering. The outward face is to the S. and the wall is probably part of the precinct wall of Barnwell priory. The only surviving building of the priory (Monument (64)) stands some 30 yds. away to the N.

In the garden are numerous wrought stones presumably from the priory. They include incorporated in two rustic arches parts of engaged and detached shafts, 12th-century moulded voussoirs and fragments carved with cheveron ornament, a small arch of three chamfered orders, the middle order with rudimentary leaf ornament, and a 13th-century moulded Purbeck stone base used as a capital, etc., elsewhere miscellaneous moulded dressings and, built into the wall flanking the entrance gateway, two mediaeval carved heads.

(271) OYSTER HOUSE, on the S.W. side of Garlic Row, some 233 yds. from Newmarket Road, of two storeys with cellars and attics, has walls of red brick, except where rebuilt in gault brick, and slate-covered roofs. It is a building of the early 18th century and stands near the middle of the site of Stourbridge Fair. Extensive alterations were made in the late 19th century when the N.W. and N.E. walls were entirely rebuilt and the roof was raised and the pitch reduced. It is associated with the feast succeeding the ceremony of proclaiming Stourbridge Fair by the University Registrary described by H. Gunning (*Reminiscences of Cambridge* (1885), I, 148–151), and thereafter with the Court House during the Fair. A plan of 1725 names it 'Mr. Jenyngs's House' (A. B. Gray, *Cambridge Revisited* (1921), 88 and fig.).

Reset in the rebuilt N.E. front is a stone panel inscribed A.I.L. 1707 and retained to tie back the brickwork are wrought-iron wall-anchors inscribed J. Lee. The S.W. wall has a plat-band at first-floor level and five bays of wall-openings compressed towards the southern end. The doorway and four ground-floor windows have segmental heads; the heads of the first-floor windows have been renewed; three of the windows are now blocked. Such original features as remain on the S.E. are similar to those just described. Inside, a timber partition containing the doorway to reputedly the old oyster-bar is flanked by turned and twisted posts supporting a timber grille the whole width of the room composed of small turned and twisted balusters between head and base rails, all of the early 18th century. A second doorway also has a section of similar balustrading above. The original staircase has close strings, turned balusters, square newels with round finials and turned pendants, and square moulded handrail. For the rest, the interior has been much altered.

S. side:—

(272) HOUSE, now two tenements, Nos. 172, 174, standing 100 yds. W. of Coldham's Lane, of two storeys and with attics in the back wing, has red brick walls and tile and slate-covered roofs. It was built in the first half of the 18th century on a T-shaped plan; in the following century the street range was extended E. and the wing lengthened. The N. front has a brick plinth, a timber cornice and parapet-wall. The ground-floor openings have been altered at different times. On the first floor are three symmetrically-placed windows with double-hung sashes in frames nearly flush with the wall-face. The wing has a plat-band at first-floor level and plain eaves. Inside, the room occupying the whole of the ground floor of the original wing is partly lined with original ovolo-moulded panelling; in the ceiling is a chamfered beam. This room and two on the first floor contain 18th-century fireplace-surrounds of wood with some enrichments.

(273) HOUSE, No. 158, temperance hotel, formerly the 'George and Dragon', 14 yds. E. of Leeke Street, of two storeys with cellar and attics, has walls of plastered timber-framing, partly faced with later brick, and tile-covered roofs. The deeds of the house include indentures of 1737 for the land where 'lately stood the . . . tenement known as the Magpie'. The house built presumably soon afterwards consisted of a rect-angular block beside the road with a staircase bay projecting at the back. Towards the end of the same century the front was rebuilt or cased in brick and a large wing added on the S. A lower E. extension by the road containing a carriage-way and shop is comparatively modern. On the N. is a plat-band at first-floor level stopping short of the full width of the frontage. The ground-floor openings have been altered; the three first-floor windows are symmetrically arranged and have high segmental brick arches. On the roof are two hipped dormer-windows. The interior has been altered; beside the

chimney-breast is a cupboard with 18th-century panelled doors on original hinges. The staircase has close strings, square newels and widely spaced turned balusters. In the wing is a late 18th-century wood fireplace-surround with pilasters and entablature, the enriched frieze having figure subjects in the centre panel.

(274) House, now three tenements, Nos. 152, 154, 156, next W. of the foregoing, of three storeys, has walls of brown brickwork with red brick quoins and window-dressings. The roofs are covered with pantiles. It was built early in the 18th century on a comparatively ambitious scale, consisting of a rectangular block to the road. Later 18th-century and modern additions along the back may include original projections no longer identifiable. The ground floor was drastically remodelled and shop-windows were inserted late in the 19th century, when also the E. and W. gable-ends were rebuilt and presumably the roof, which is now of low pitch with plain eaves. On the N. are two moulded brick bands stopping short of the full width of the frontage. The windows, five on each floor, have flat arches of rubbed brick and stone sills; the sash-frames are flush with the wall-face. The free W. end is blind.

(275) House, now three tenements, Nos. 146, 148, 150, next W. of Leeke Street, of two storeys, have timber-framed walls faced with later brickwork and tile-covered roofs. Built perhaps in the late 16th century, it was remodelled early in the 19th century when also additions were made all along the back. No original features remain outside and the central chimney-stack has been rebuilt above roof-level. Inside the E. tenement a post and intersecting chamfered ceiling-beams are exposed on the ground floor and a post and tie-beam on the first floor. In the middle tenement all the timbers are concealed. Each tenement has one room on each floor cut into for a modern staircase.

(276) House, No. 38, standing 22 yds. W. of Wellington Street close N.E. of the former theatre, of three storeys with basement, has walls of gault brick and slate-covered roofs. In 1831 a sale advertisement described it as part of the estate of the late George Peacocke and 'built . . . by the late William Wilkins Esq., architect, for his own occupation' (*Cambridge Chronicle* 9 Dec.). William Wilkins sen. (1751–1815) had built for himself Newnham Cottage (Monument (288)) by *c.* 1805 and the house may be assigned to the end of the 18th century. It is therefore an early example of a type of house usually associated with the Regency. The E. and W. sides have since been more or less concealed, the former by another house, the latter by an entrance to the former theatre (Monument (277)); minor additions have been made at the back. Inside, the arrangement is little altered; the ground floor is now storerooms; the upper floors are flats.

The walls are of plain brickwork with oversailing courses at the eaves. To the front, the openings are formally though not symmetrically disposed and the doorway is in the western of the three bays; they have flat rubbed brick arches. The first-floor windows open to wrought-iron balconies. The openings at the back of the house, probably not all original, vary in size and are more at random. Inside, 'the entrance-hall, capital dining-room, breakfast room or study, butler's pantry' remain on the ground floor though the partition between the main rooms has been reduced to a dwarf wall. One original plain black fireplace-surround remains. The staircase, now damaged, has winders, slender square balusters and a moulded handrail. In the basement are 'two capital kitchens', on the first floor 'a noble drawing-room, best bedroom adjoining, store room or china closet', on the floor above 'four good rooms'. The drawing-room, now divided, has a slight plaster cornice and an original fireplace with cast-iron grate in a wood surround with reeded convex strip-pilasters at the sides and a plain shelf. (See also the following Monument.)

(277) Former Theatre Royal, known originally as Barnwell Theatre, subsequently as the Festival Theatre, now a store, stands back on the S. side of Newmarket Road, between Wellington Street and Napier Street. The walls are of gault brick and the roofs slate-covered. It was built to replace an earlier theatre in Barnwell in 1814 (*Camb. Chronicle* 11 Feb., 10 Oct. 1814), 'the fronts of the boxes are painted in arabesque and the proscenium which is supported by four Giallo Antiquo marble pilasters is really simple and magnificent . . . the frieze is ornamented with figures in rechausée d'or representing Apollo and Minerva visiting the Muses; the design of the proscenium is carried through the Act Scene . . .'. In 1815 William Wilkins sen., 'eminent builder in this town', appeared in a lawsuit as owner and in 1832 a Mr. Wilkins owned six theatres, at Norwich, Bury, Cambridge, Ipswich, Yarmouth and Colchester (*ibid.* 1832). In 1878 it became a Mission Hall; between the last two wars it was again used as a theatre.

The blocks E. and W. of the stage and along the E. side of the auditorium are early additions. In modern times additions have been made on the N.E. and W. of the auditorium, the first containing an entrance-hall, box-office etc., and a secondary entrance has been contrived on the E. The roof of the stage has been rebuilt and the cyclorama is modern. The original proscenium-opening with its doors and most of the original decoration have been destroyed in the present century.

The Theatre is of interest for the retention of the early 19th-century arrangement of the auditorium.

The exterior of the Theatre is quite plain. Original windows are either blocked or concealed by additions. In the back wall of the stage is a modern window in the blocking of a larger opening. Modern iron staircases give additional means of exit from the auditorium.

Inside, the auditorium has lower, middle and upper circles, U-shaped on plan, extending laterally close up to the proscenium-opening. The circles have solid fronts, the upper two with applied cornice-mouldings, and plain cast-iron supporting columns. Separating the lower and middle circles from the crush-rooms behind are polygonal U-shaped walls pierced by numerous doorways. These last may have opened upon separate boxes. The auditorium floor is stepped in the clear.

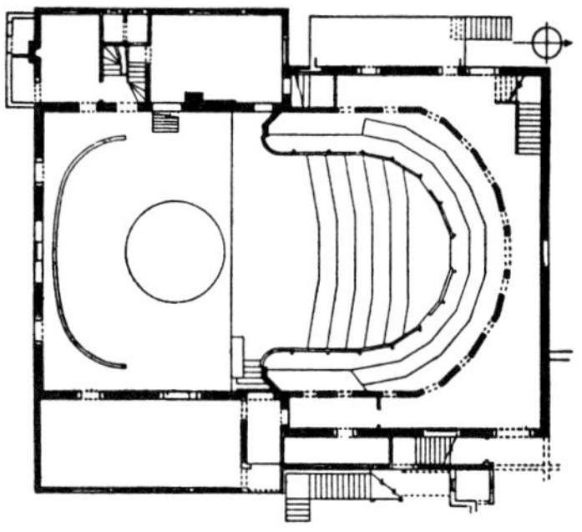

The proscenium-opening now extends the full width of the stage and is spanned by a timber truss; above, in a framing the shape of the tympanum of a curved pediment, are painted the Royal arms of Queen Victoria with supporters and attendant putti. Old candelabra with five branches remain on the front of the upper circle.

(278) HOUSES (excluding Monuments (267–276)), several hundreds, in the Barnwell area specified above, are mostly built in terraces, often of great length, and of two storeys with gault brick walls and slate-covered roofs. The greater part of the area lay in the parish of St. Andrew the Less. The Inclosure Act of 1807[1] and the Award of 1811[2], by making possible the sale and division of the open fields, resulted in the extensive building development here described. The original award and map (copy in Town Clerk's Office) shows Barnwell as a village with houses bordering the main street E. and W. of the church. Few of these could have antedated the fire of 1731, which destroyed fifty dwellings (Bowtell MSS, Downing College IV/821). Notices in the *Cambridge Chronicle* confirm that houses were built soon after the inclosure; their position is not exactly determinable but some were beside or near NEWMARKET ROAD. New tenements are noted in 1814 near the Theatre, then under construction, and Nos. 32 and 34 are of about this date (see below). The age of the earliest buildings in FITZROY STREET, on the N. towards the E. end, is indicated by the death in 1811 of Augustus Henry Fitzroy, Duke of Grafton, Chancellor of the University. The rapid expansion of the street westward followed the close of the Napoleonic War; its other name, Blücher Row, and that of Wellington Street nearby are themselves historical data. Soon after 1820 BRUNSWICK PLACE (Monument 267)), now the E. part of Maids' Causeway, and the terraces N. and S. of it were built, filling the area between Cambridge and the Barnwell suburb.

The earlier references to EAST ROAD in the *Cambridge Chronicle* (e.g. 8 May 1818) suggest a residential road of some distinction; the present piecemeal development must be the result in part of parcelling out relatively large private gardens at a rather later date. Architectural continuity obtains only in the long terrace, Nos. 50 to 69, on the S.E. side. Much of NEW STREET was built between 1818 and 1822 (*Cambridge Chronicle* 26 June 1818, etc.). By 1825 the parish church was found inadequate for the population, which, including New Town, was 4,845, with sixty-seven new houses under construction (*ibid* 1 July, 26 Aug., 9 Sept. 1825). Five years later, R. G. Baker's map of Cambridge of 1830 shows PROSPECT ROW, ADAM AND EVE ROW and BURLEIGH STREET enclosing the 'Garden of Eden' on the S.W., S.E. and N.E. respectively; behind the first, BRANDON PLACE is rising. N.E. of Burleigh Street Baker shows GOLD STREET and, across East Road, STAFFORDSHIRE STREET and the adjoining GAS LANE; houses are shown also in ABBEY STREET.

In the following decade EDEN STREET was built and PETERSFIELD begun, so too, at the end of the decade, were BROAD STREET, off East Road, and MELBOURNE PLACE, in continuation of Eden Street. After the opening of Christ Church Church in 1839 (Monument (43)), CHRISTCHURCH STREET, JAMES STREET and NAPIER STREET were developed.

Most of the streets named above were still receiving additions at the end of the period under review, 1850: the infilling of the former 'Garden of Eden', CITY ROAD and its subsidiaries, and the development of the area E. of Zion Chapel (Monument (67)), BRADMORE STREET for example, were proceeding. But speculative interest was then shifting to other parts of the town, notably to the Mill Road and railway station areas. The extensive development N. of the Newmarket Road in the Abbey Road area took place after 1850.

Architectural Description—NEWMARKET ROAD contains E. of Maids' Causeway two relatively stylish houses, Nos. 51 and 83. The first, of 'villa' type, of two storeys with stucco-faced walls and low-pitched roofs, is of the early 19th century; the second, a square block, of two storeys with attics, with gault brick walls and slate-covered mansard roofs, is of *c.* 1820, with later bay-windows. Nos. 32 and 34 referred to above, of *c.* 1814, of two storeys with gault brick walls and very low pitched slate-covered roofs, comprise a symmetrical block with elliptical-headed wall-recesses under pedimental gables. E. of the few houses of individual character (Monuments (269, 270, 272 to 275)) near the church of St. Andrew the Less,

[1] Stat. 47 George III. Sess. 2, c. 60.

[2] The area of land involved was just over 1156 acres; Parker's Piece, Jesus Green, Midsummer Common, Butt Green, Stourbridge Fair Green, Coldham's Common, etc., were excepted from the Act.

some of which antedate the fire of 1731, and E. of Godesdone Road–Coldham's Lane is some 'ribbon-development' of *c.* 1800 and later, mostly of poor type, that extends, with interruptions, to the Barnwell Junction railway bridge.

In NEW STREET, Nos. 18 to 28 (evens) of *c.* 1820 have a central carriage-entrance, now blocked, under a pediment, timber door-frames with four-centred heads, and openings of the same form to the two-light windows, which have vestigial labels and contain casements with glazing-bars themselves forming four-centred arches (plan p. 365).

EDEN STREET is lined with lengthy terraces, incomplete on the E., of the fourth decade of the 19th century, with centrepieces and a succession of elliptical-headed doorways alternating with plain sash-hung windows (plan p. 365); the two centrepieces, reminiscent of those in New Square, each have three brick pilasters and a pediment. To E. and S.E. of Eden Street, the slightly earlier terrace Nos. 7 to 36 PROSPECT ROW, originally facing an open space, entirely utilitarian except for a brick dentil-cornice, is relieved from monotony by the boldly projecting timber window-bays of the public-houses at either end. BRANDON PLACE and ADAM AND EVE STREET are devoid of such relief.

Nos. 4–7 GRAFTON STREET of *c.* 1850 have an exotic arrangement of pilasters and half-pilasters and chamfered openings, the doorways with four-centred timber heads under flat arches, the windows with timber mullioned casements; on the first floor are panels containing stucco blank shields, Renaissance grotesques in oval medallions and wooden crosses *flory*. Opposite the foregoing, Nos. 37 to 39 are distinguished by elliptical-headed doorways, a carriage-entrance, now blocked, and a timber dentil-cornice.

While occasional deliberate efforts seem to have been made to soften the asperities of the uniform brick terraces, in the simple economy of BRANDON PLACE the minor variations in doorways, from elliptical to square heads, some with timber doorcases, and in window design may be due to vagaries of limited individual choice; some such explanation must also cover the sporadic irregularities in SOUTH STREET, for instance, where No. 19 is slightly bigger than its neighbours, No. 21 exceptionally set back behind a garden; but the E. end of FITZROY STREET dates from a period, *c.* 1810, when the technique of wholesale terrace-building was not yet general at this social level. The disorders of PETERSFIELD, overlooking its small park, with variations in height, eaves and parapet-walls, plat-bands and plain wall-surfaces, etc., may owe something to a co-ordinating mind remotely influenced by the Romantic movement.

Nos. 35–39 BROAD STREET, though of the simplest utilitarian aspect, show an interesting arrangement of semi-detached houses with side-entrances behind short screen-walls linking the blocks. Nos. 5a to 19 NAPIER STREET have a similar arrangement. A lay-out designed to reduce the street frontage to a minimum and exploit the hinterland is exemplified by Nos. 13–16 JAMES STREET with Nos. 1–4 JAMES COTTAGES, two parallel ranges with a passage through both that gives access to the front doors of the rear range, which faces away from the street; the front houses have gardens behind, the rear have gardens in front. Nos. 3–9 PORTLAND PLACE back on the street and front their gardens.

The condition of many of the buildings in the area is poor. Much of the development is ill-planned, even where it is not ill-built. Some parts in the New Street neighbourhood are slums, and Caroline Place and Eden Place are examples of socially bad, if economically interesting, back-to-back houses.

HILLS ROAD

W. side:—

(279) WANSTEAD HOUSE, on the N. side of Union Road, of two and three storeys with cellars, has walls of gault brick and slate-covered roofs. It incorporates fittings from Wanstead House, Essex, which were offered for sale in 1824. On the bankruptcy of Richard Woods, the builder and occupant, in 1826 the 'new-built' house was sold (*Cambridge Chronicle* 1 Sept.) and a plan of it in that year is in the University Library (MS. plans 174). Shortly afterwards a drawing-room was added on the N.W. and, later in the century, a kitchen range.

The house is notable for the important fittings it contains from Colen Campbell's first major work, Wanstead House, in Essex, which was built between *c.* 1715 and 1721 for Sir Richard Child, Bt., later Earl Tylney of Castlemaine, and is illustrated in *Vitruvius Britannicus* (I, pls. 23–26; III, 39, 40).

The street-front is in three bays, the openings being widely spaced in large expanses of brickwork; at the wall-head is an enriched early 18th-century timber modillion-cornice with dentils. The central doorway has an imposing timber doorcase, also of the early 18th century, with an eared architrave with carved swags and urns in relief above and flanking attached Corinthian columns with short returns supporting a full entablature with enriched pulvinated frieze and dentilled modillion-cornice (Plate 47). The windows have simple 19th-century architraves and contain double-hung sashes. The rest of the original house has a simple contemporary eaves-cornice and most of the windows are segmental-headed. The later additions are plain.

Inside, all the more elaborate fittings are of the early 18th century. The walls of the entrance-hall and stair-hall are divided into bays by Ionic pilasters supporting trabeations across the ceilings; in the N. wall of the former is a doorcase with enriched eared architrave with swags of oak leaves and acorns pendent from volutes below the ears. The Dining-room, N. of the entrance-hall, has the most fittings from Campbell's Wanstead, which are large for the room. They include two timber doorcases with pedimented entablatures with foliated and banded pulvinated friezes and modillion-cornices with all the members enriched; a similarly enriched ceiling cornice; a low panelled dado with carved skirting and rail, the latter with key-ornament; large wall-panels with enriched architraves rising from oval foliated volutes; an elaborately carved white marble fireplace-surround with paired foliated side-scrolls projecting forward and laterally supporting an architrave and pulvinated frieze both interrupted by a central green scagliola panel and by flanking console-brackets supporting an enriched cornice returned over the last; from a different architectural context is the double-eared panel in the overmantel with the head mitred round a shell flanked by swags and surmounted by an enriched cornice, the members being picked out with gilding. The window has an enriched architrave with keyblock and shutters containing enriched fielded panels. The room opposite to the S. has an enriched dado and a modillion-cornice, an eared fireplace-surround with console-brackets above supporting a dentil-cornice and flanking a frieze carved in bold relief with a female mask and scrolled acanthus foliation and, above, an overmantel similar to that described in the Dining-room and also from a different architectural context. Other rather plainer doorcases on the ground floor are also of the early 18th century, but the Drawing-room has original panelled shutters, of *c.* 1825, to the windows.

The staircase has 19th-century cut and bracketed strings, risers and treads, an elaborate early 18th-century wrought-iron scrollwork balustrade with sheet-cut foliation and a 19th-century moulded mahogany handrail. On the first floor the N. room has a 19th-century white marble fireplace-surround flanked by contemporary wall-recesses with architraves and simple broken-pedimented cornices. The early 18th-century fireplace-surround (Plate 50) in the S. room is of white marble, with eared architrave, side scrolls, console-brackets supporting a cornice-shelf with the bedmould carved with acanthus-leaves, and an enriched pulvinated frieze interrupted by a faun's mask flanked by foliage scrolls; the cast-iron firegrate decorated with wheatears and convolvulus is of the 19th century. Of the latter date are the surround and grate in the room over the Drawing-room; the first is of wood with roundels at the corners, the second of cast-iron with slender shafts at the sides and scrolls and foliage above.

E. side:—

(280) House, on the S. corner of Station Road, part of the premises of Messrs. Rattee and Kett, builders, of two storeys, has walls of red and white brick and slate-covered roofs. The site was bought by Rattee, who founded the business there in 1843. The house was built probably within the decade; the porch is an early addition. It was subsequently extended to the S.E. and has now been divided into flats. The workshops stand to the E. and S.E.

The house is a remarkable example of virtuosity in bizarre pattern and colour composition by a builder (Plate 309).

The free sides show a prodigal use of rustication in white brickwork, the variously shaped panels so formed containing red brickwork in 'herringbone' courses of headers. At the wall-head is a timber cornice with modillions and dentils. The balanced elevations are thrown out of symmetry by two-storey bay-windows; these are three-sided, with moulded brick labels over the ground-floor windows and moulded shafts at the angles of the frames; the double-hung sashes contain narrow marginal panes of coloured glass. The added white brick porch on the N.W. has a round-headed entrance and a shaped gable with stone coping and an urn at the apex. Over the porch is a round-headed window with rustications and keyblock. On the main pyramidal roof are polygonal slates and at the apex is a cluster of chimney-stacks rising from a square base with brick brattishing; the stacks have a continuous capping of oversailing brickwork.

Inside, many of the fittings also show an individual eccentricity in design. In the hall are the initials I.R. in plaster. The Drawing-room to the W., with its two bay-windows linked by an alcove in the corner, has a panelled fireplace-surround of wood adorned with rosettes. The staircase has twisted balusters.

Brooklands Avenue

(281) Brooklands, house, on the S. side some 185 yds. from Trumpington Road, of two storeys, has walls of gault brick and slate-covered roofs. The site was bought from James Burleigh by Richard Foster in 1825. Foster's will of 1831 mentions the 'new-built' messuage in which he lived; he died in 1842 and his son Richard inherited (Foster family deeds with Ginn & Co., Cambridge). It is now in Government use.

The house consists of a large rectangular block with semi-octagonal bays the full height of the building near the middle of the N. and S. sides. It has low-pitched roofs with boxed gutters and is generally severely plain. In *c.* 1900 were added a stone porch on the W. end and a low block, presumably for a billiard-room, on the N.; a new staircase was inserted and the S.W. ground-floor room refitted. The N. side has been altered, the interior subdivided, and a single-storey office-block added on the E. in more recent times.

The W. end is symmetrical, in three bays, the middle bay slightly recessed. In the centre is the modern porch; the S. bay has glazed sham windows and a functional chimney-stack flush with the wall-face, the N. bay real windows and a sham chimney-stack. The S. side is divided into unequal bays by breaks in the plane of the wall, and the E. end into three bays, that in the middle pedimented. Inside, the S. room with the window-bay has a fireplace with enriched architrave flanked by columns supporting a dentil-cornice. The panelled overmantel follows the Palladian window design, with attached columns and an enriched cornice surmounted by urns; in the side panels are floral pendants. Other original fittings include elaborated doorcases, and brown and white marble fireplace-surrounds. In the garden, to the E. is a large *Greenhouse* of *c.* 1850 and, to the N., a brick-built *Coach-house* with segmental-headed openings.

Trumpington Road

E. side:—

(282) House, standing in spacious grounds on the S. side of Bateman Street, of two storeys with cellars and attics, has walls of gault brick and slate-covered roofs. It is not shown on R. G. Baker's map of 1830 but must have been built very shortly afterwards. A large semi-octagonal bay was added on

the W. and the interior subdivided late in the same century. Further alterations have been made inside in modern times to provide offices for the Director of the Botanic Garden and for flats.

The house though of composed 'villa' type shows a departure from strict symmetry towards a picturesque composition.

The S., garden, front is asymmetrical with a plat-band at first-floor sill level and a large semicircular bay projecting rather E. of centre. The roofs are comparatively low-pitched, with a widely overhanging timber eaves-cornice and gutters studded with leopards' masks. The bay has french-windows on the ground floor, protected by a flared sheet-metal roof supported on wrought-iron brackets, plain double-hung sash-windows above. The flanking wall-faces are of one bay and three bays respectively. The E. end of the house is gabled, the W. hipped.

Inside, the stairhall is entered from the S. and W. through round-headed arches with panelled pilaster-responds and panelled soffits. The wide curved staircase has straight balusters and a turned newel; the curved enclosing wall contains two semidomed niches. Some of the rooms retain original enriched plaster cornices.

W. side:—

(283) The Leys School, headmaster's house, standing in spacious grounds 83 yds. back from the road and 100 yds. S. of Coe Fen Lane, of two storeys with cellars and attics, has walls of gault brick and slate-covered roofs. The land was enclosed in 1811; the house is traditionally dated 1815, which is possible on stylistic grounds, and shown on R. G. Baker's map of 1830. Subsequently a bay-window has been added on the E. and a large single-storey wing on the N. Later school buildings adjoin on the W. The original house is almost square on plan with a three-sided bay projecting from the W. end of the S. side. It has a stone plinth and a continuous widely projecting eaves-cornice of shallow section on slender shaped brackets. The entrance-front to the E. is symmetrical. It is in three bays with the side bays projecting and pedimented; the latter are connected by a single-storey stone screen across the recessed centre bay. The screen comprises two Doric columns *in antis*; this, with a flat roof behind the entablature, forms a porch to the entrance-doorway in the recessed wall. The windows all contain double-hung sashes; those on the ground floor open down to the plinth and the taller lower sashes slide up in part into the wall. The original S.W. projecting bay rises the full height of the house. The chimney-stacks have separate round flues linked by their capping.

Inside, many original fittings survive, including plain and enriched plaster cornices. The doorways have panelled architraves with paterae at the corners and panelled doors with extra mouldings applied on the panels. The windows have architraves similar to the foregoing and panelled shutters. The fireplace-surrounds generally are of white or gray marble, panelled or moulded and with roundels at the corners, but one has flanking pilaster-strips containing an incised linear decoration, another a fluted frieze. Segmental barrel-vaulted cellars extend under the whole house. The staircase has bracketed strings, square fluted balusters, a turned newel and a moulded mahogany handrail.

(284) Belvoir Terrace, Nos. 1 to 5 (plan of No. 4 p. 365), opposite the N.W. corner of the Botanic Garden, of three storeys with basements, has walls of gault brick and slate-covered roofs. The five houses were built probably *c.* 1825 on plots some 63 yds. deep, leaving comparatively large gardens at front and back. A two-storey bay-window has been added to No. 1. Small W. projections that may have existed from the first have been so altered that their original form is not recoverable. The flatness of the front is relieved by vertical recessed panels rising through the two upper floors and demarcating the separate houses; the houses are each of two bays, except No. 5, which extends over a carriage-entrance. The entrance-doorways have round heads with continuous moulded stucco architraves with plain imposts and keyblocks, and fanlights with radial glazing-bars, where these survive. The windows have double-hung sashes, those on the ground floor with slatted shutters. At the eaves is a boxed gutter to roofs of fairly low pitch.

Inside, the houses show a normal terrace-house type of plan, with one room behind another alongside an entrance passage that widens at the expense of the width of the back room to contain a staircase; but they are more spacious than others of the period in Cambridge.

New Town

(285) New Town area is bounded on the N. by Lensfield Road, on the E. by Hills Road, on the S. by the University Botanic Garden, on the W. by Trumpington Road. Excluding the few more important secular buildings here already described (Monuments (101), (251), (279), (282)), it comprises in the main building development of a humble residential character, with two-storey terrace-houses (plans p. 365) with gault brick walls and slate-covered roofs predominating. Exceptions are the few early 19th-century villas built before the general development of the area. Of these by far the most important was Lensfield standing back from Lensfield Road, built by William Wilkins for his own use, which was demolished in 1955 and the site and gardens covered by the huge new University Chemical Laboratory. Panton Hall, a noncomformist chapel, and a brewery both originated before 1850 but retain nothing of the period.

Downing Terrace (Monument (251)) and probably Gothic Cottage (*Cambridge Chronicle* 2 June 1820, 14 Jan. 1825), now incorporated in the 'Cross Keys' inn (see below), were just finished before the intensive building of New Town, called New Zealand prior to

1822 (*ibid* 18 May 1822), was begun about 1820, though some houses already existed beside Hills Road (e.g. *ibid* 12 May, 6 Oct. 1820). UNION ROAD is mentioned in 1821 and Nos. 9–14 GEORGE IV STREET bear the same date. In 1822 Wilkins sold the W. part of his garden for a terrace, Annesley Place, now part of PANTON STREET; the terrace in the same street, just S. of Union Road, followed (*ibid* 19 Aug. 1825) and Nos 42–44 (evens) Panton Street are dated 1851 though in appearance rather earlier. By 1825 CORONATION STREET, PRINCES STREET, QUEEN STREET had been begun (*ibid* 11 June 1824, 13 May 1825); R. G. Baker's map of 1830 shows most of the S. side of the first built, SAXON STREET behind Downing Terrace and DORIC STREET off it, and a beginning of the N. end of GOTHIC STREET. TERRACE LANE must have been built soon afterwards. RUSSELL STREET is first heard of in 1835 under the name of Gwydir Street when an ambitious scheme was announced for development near the 'new Botanic Gardens' (*ibid* 13 Feb. 1835); a start may have then been made but little was done before the end of the decade and most of the buildings in the street are of 1840 to 1850 and later; Nos. 77–81 are dated 1846, Nos. 84 and 85 1849; RUSSELL PLACE was built before 1840 (*ibid* 18 July 1840). Development of the area continued after 1850.

Much of New Town was ill-built, and as early as 1850 the condition of Terrace Lane and Annesley Place was unfavourably commented upon by the Board of Improvement Commissioners (*ibid* 21 Dec.). The area immediately S. of Saxon Street is now a slum.

Architectural Description—The design of most of the terrace-houses follows something of a standard pattern. It is of two bays, with a doorway and window on the ground floor and two windows symmetrically above; brick dentil-cornices occur and the eaves are continuous across adjoining houses; the fireplaces are in the party-walls and the flues emerge at the ridge in plain rectangular stacks. Those doorways with flat arches usually have fanlights with latticed glazing and shallow hoods; others are round, elliptical or, mostly in poorer building, segmental-headed with stone imposts and fanlights; many have moulded timber doorcases with roundels, panels or paterae at the angles. Where basements occur the main doorway is often approached up stone steps with simple wrought or cast-iron balustrades. Window-openings contain double-hung sashes and have flat or segmental heads; some have a marginal arrangement of glazing. Inside, the houses are two rooms deep, and the doorway leads into a passage, but in some, generally of poorer type, the door opens into the front room. Projections at the back containing the offices are sometimes original; many have been enlarged or added, individually, or wholesale to a uniform plan.

Improvements upon or modification of this standard type are to be found. Nos. 30 and 31 UNION ROAD (plan p. 365) are a three-storey pair with a round-headed wall-arch rising their full height as a dominating feature in the street-front. No. 6, FARCET HOUSE, is exceptional, being double-fronted and of individual design, symmetrical, with a timber doorcase and high panelled parapet-wall rising well above the adjoining terrace-houses. Nos. 15 to 17 GEORGE IV STREET are a trio with the ground floor and the cornice and blocking-course stucco-faced, the whole of Greek Doric inspiration, ponderous but well-proportioned. In PANTON STREET, Nos. 3–11 (odds), formerly Annesley Place, and Nos. 27–41 (odds) have some architectural pretensions, the former with elaboration in the doorcases, the latter with a refreshing if perhaps restless break in the symmetry, the round-headed doorways of adjoining houses being paired and the first-floor windows, regularly spaced from end to end of the terrace, being out of alignment with the ground-floor openings. No. 32 is a very simple double-fronted house of a status slightly different from the foregoing, retaining a modest coach-house in the garden at the back. In CORONATION STREET, Nos. 36–41 are plain but present a balanced composition of four low terrace-houses flanked by slightly projecting taller gabled houses with shop-windows. Though the houses further from the main through roads are the more featureless, exceptions are Nos. 77–81 and 99–103 RUSSELL STREET; here effective use is made of brick panelling and pilasters, combined in the second group with timber features. These last include doorcases with plain strip-pilasters, rusticated friezes with roundels towards the ends and hood-like cornices, the caps of the colossal pilasters rising the full height of the fronts, and the eaves-cornices.

The 'Cross Keys' in Brookside, 22 yds. from Lensfield Road, incorporates the former GOTHIC COTTAGE, a house of *c.* 1820 with windows and timber cusped decoration below the eaves of the low-pitched W. gable that justify, if they were not the reason for, its name. The windows have four-centred heads and a pattern of frame and glazing of the same form. In mass and silhouette the building is a typical 19th-century villa.

(286) OLD NURSERIES, house, No. 2 Latham Road, on the N. side at the corner of Trumpington Road, of two storeys, with stucco-faced brick walls and slate-covered roofs, was built in the first half of the 19th century, before 1830, being shown in R. G. Baker's map of that year standing in the corner of the 'Cambridge Nursery'. It seems to have been designed to provide two tenements though very soon made into one, when the W. annexe was added. The E. bay-window is later. The S. side has six original two-light windows with four-centred heads to the openings, to the lights and to the glazing-bars in the casements; two other ground-floor windows and the doorway are modern insertions. The roof is hipped at both ends and the central chimney-stack rises at the ridge. In the annexe are windows with pointed heads to match those in the main house.

The inside is much modernised but retains an original moulded fireplace-surround of wood with bosses at the angles. In each half of the house and in the annexe is a staircase rising steeply in a small enclosed space. On two of the window-panes are scratched the name and date Brewer 1839. Between 1830 and 1840 Brewer, nurseryman, was advertising and in 1832 opened a bulb shop in St. John's Street (*Cambridge Chronicle* 26 Oct. 1832).

Newnham

(287) Newnham Grange, on the S.E. side of Silver Street, 140 yds. S.W. of Silver Street Bridge, of two storeys with cellars, has walls of gault brick with stone dressings and tile-covered roofs. The house was built early in the 19th century, before 1830, for the Beale family, corn and coal merchants, and included a large irregularly-shaped yard to the E. largely surrounded by stables, offices, coal-stores and granaries. The property was bought by the Darwins in the last quarter of the 19th century and a plan and elevation as it was in 1885 are in the possession of Sir Charles Darwin. Some outbuildings were then removed, the projecting N. wall of the stables adjoining on the E. was rebuilt in line with the front wall of the house and to the remodelled E. gable was added an aedicule framing the date, 1885. In the last decade of the century large bay-windows were added on the N. and S. sides of the house, other outbuildings were demolished and the remainder, at the E. end of the yard, were reconstructed. These last now form a separate house, the Old Granary.

Newnham Grange is an early 19th-century house of gracious aspect containing fittings of the period.

The N. front is in five bays with the two flanking bays on each side slightly advanced, leaving a recessed middle bay and very short lateral returns; against these last the stone platbands at first-floor and eaves level stop. It has a low parapet-wall with a stone capping, which is continued up the slopes of the E. and W. gable-ends of the house. The doorway in the centre is in a semicircular arch of two orders of gauged brickwork with plain stone imposts. The door is of six panels, with a fanlight with radial glazing-bars above the moulded lintel-rail. The three-sided bays projecting symmetrically to each side are both late 19th-century additions. The five first-floor windows contain double-hung sashes. The E. end is masked by a return of the outbuildings, remodelled and containing the kitchens, etc.; it is of two storeys with a hipped roof and has a walk on the ground floor behind an open screen of Roman Doric columns; in the roof are two gabled dormer-windows each of two lights with two-centred heads and glazing-bars. The W. end has wall-recesses, original and modern windows and, in the middle, a tall round-headed staircase-window with stone imposts. The S. side has two added bay-windows on the ground floor, the one to the W. being built within part of an early 19th-century verandah with flared metal roof. Symmetrical on the first floor are three original windows; those to the sides are double the width of the other, with segmental heads and containing tripartite sash-hung timber frames.

Inside, the main house-block is nearly square on plan. The entrance-hall and stairhall have a T-shaped arrangement, the latter extending centrally across the full width of the house, and with the principal stair at the W. end, the service stair at the E.; the square bay at the junction has round-headed archways on the E., N. and W., a blind arch of similar form on the S., and a groined plaster vault. The archways have pilaster-responds and moulded archivolts. One of the doorways has a pedimented entablature, with a frieze containing ovals, garlands and swags. The ground-floor rooms retain original cornices, that in the S.W. room elaborated with acanthus foliation. Also in the S.W. room is a moulded architrave to the doorway with roundels at the angles and, moved from the first floor, an original fireplace-surround of wood with green marble slips, with Ionic side-pilasters supporting an entablature with central frieze-panel and stylised cornice all enriched with delicate decoration of leaves, swags, an urn, writing trophies and paterae. In the N.W. room the fireplace has an original white marble reeded surround with foliated roundels at the angles; this room and that to the N.E. retain reset in the late 19th-century bays the sashes and panelled linings of the four windows originally here. Another original reeded marble fireplace-surround remains in the S.E. room.

The staircase has cut and plainly bracketed strings, slender square iron balusters and a square moulded iron newel under a spiral-return of the moulded handrail; this last is of mahogany. The cellars under the main house are barrel-vaulted. On the first floor the openings to the stairwell and landing are generally similar to those in the hall below. Most of the fittings, dadoes, doorcases and cornices are original, and also five of the fireplace-surrounds; these last are of wood, with elegant enrichments of foliage pendants, swags, urns, ovals, and roundels containing stylised foliage, honeysuckle-ornament, etc. A reeded surround in the N.W. room is probably modern.

The *Old Granary*, though remodelled to form a separate house, incorporates the fabric of the original business offices, with an upper storey added, and the E. block of the store buildings; the rest of the granary was demolished. The N. wall of the offices has small rectangular windows, those on the ground floor in two round-headed wall-arches with stone imposts, those above in the blocking of two larger windows. Across the W. wall is a plat-band with modern openings below and a round-headed arch and a segmental-headed recess above. The E. side is much altered; three blocked windows are visible on the first floor.

The Old Granary, see Monument (287).

(288) Newnham Cottage, house, on the W. side of Queens' Road 87 yds. S. of West Road, is of two storeys with gault brick walls and slate-covered roofs. The site, part of Butcher's Close, was let on a building lease to William Wilkins sen. (1751–1815) by Gonville and Caius College in *c.* 1800 (E. J. Gross in J. Venn, *Biog. Hist. of Gonville and Caius College*, IV, pt. 2, 27). The house, so far as it remains unaltered, does not entirely agree in shape with the house shown on the Inclosure Award map of 1804, but in 1816 and 1836 it was advertised for sale and on the second occasion described as 'erected about thirty years since by the late William Wilkins' (*Camb. Chronicle* 27 May, 3 June,

1836). The present N.E. wing replaces a narrower wing pulled down *c.* 1900; the N.W. wing is later again. Lesser additions include a covered way extending to the road, and a mid 19th-century glazed cast-iron verandah on the S. The covered way existed in 1836 but the entrance to it was rebuilt and the timber balustrading and supports on the open S. side were renewed late in the 19th century.

Newnham Cottage is an 'Italian villa' type of house that demonstrates a successful synthesis of rational values and the neo-Classical style.

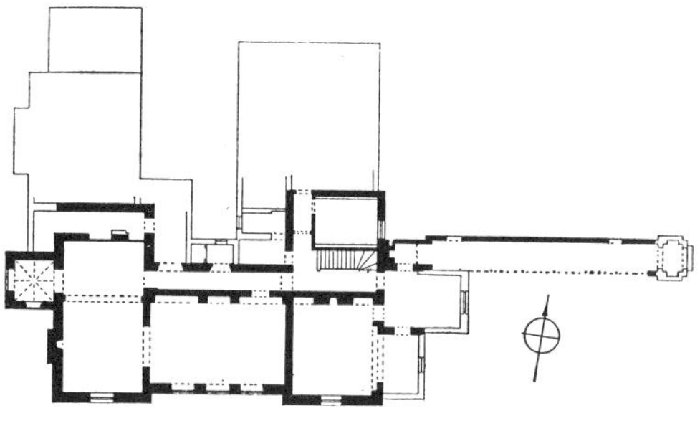

The S. front has the middle part recessed 1½ ft. though the eaves-cornice is continued straight across from the side bays. On the ground floor are five french-windows, that in the centre an insertion; on the first floor are four casement-windows, two in the recess, one in each side bay. To the E. are two small additions. On the W. is a small projection, probably an addition, described as an 'oriel' in 1816, with S. and W. windows, the last converted from a doorway.

Inside on the ground floor are three main rooms facing S. to the garden: a study to the E., a central room and a W. room of greater depth than the foregoing and crossed by a trabeation supported on pilasters with enriched caps. Leading from the last room, the 'oriel' has a ribbed quadripartite two-centred plaster vault springing from foliated corbels in the angles and with foliage bosses; the S. window has plaster shafted splays and a moulded rear-arch; in 1816 it was 'glazed with ancient stained glass'. The plain staircase has cut strings and slender balusters with a mahogany handrail. The 1816 advertisement says the building was 'erected under the immediate direction of Mr. Wilkins for his own residence, whose taste and judgement in architecture have made it combine all the conveniences and advantages to be expected from the possession of such abilities' (*Camb. Chronicle* 5 Jan.). It may be added that it possessed 'two water-closets, one on each floor, and a hot bath'. The fines on renewal of the lease of the property and the rents charged up to 1907 are set out in the Sectional Preface p. xcvi.

(289) NEWNHAM HOUSE, on the W. side of Newnham Road, just N. of Malting Lane, opposite the Mill Pit, of two storeys with gault brick walls and low-pitched slated roofs, was built *c.* 1820. It was L-shaped on plan, with S. and W. wings; a range of outbuildings stood N. and S. further W. Late in the 19th and in the present century the house was extended to include the outbuildings, which were remodelled to provide extra living-accommodation. It is now a hostel of Corpus Christi College. The E. side is of five bays; the three in the middle are divided by plain brick pilaster-strips. The flanking bays projected slightly and contained ground-floor windows set in segmental-headed wall-arches, but only the N. bay remains unaltered. The continuous widely overhanging eaves-cornice has a plastered soffit. The severe N. front has plain fenestration and an entrance doorway in the second of the five bays with semicircular head and fanlight. The other sides are largely masked.

Inside, rooms have been subdivided. Original simple cornices and a panelled dado remain. One original panelled fire-place-surround has roundels at the angles. The staircase has cut strings, slender turned balusters and turned newels; on the W. containing-wall is a semicircular-headed panel with fluted pilasters supporting a moulded archivolt with a keyblock.

(290) LITTLE NEWNHAM and FROSTLAKE COTTAGE, house, opposite the foregoing Monument (289), to the S., of two storeys, has brick walls and slate and tile-covered roofs. It occupies the W. end of a range of buildings along the S. side of Malting Lane of 18th-century origin but very much altered, comprising houses, cottages, maltings, oast-houses and stables; *Malting House* at the E. end has been so extensively remodelled that it is virtually a modern building. The house was built early in the 19th century, enlarged later in the first half of the same century, and subsequently divided into two tenements: Little Newnham to the W., Frostlake Cottage to the E., the latter incorporating a lower range of early 18th-century buildings on the E., probably originally stables, for the kitchen, etc.

The house is not of particular architectural note but the original windows have high four-centred heads with interlacing glazing-bars in the double-hung sashes; several of the frames and sashes have been reset in the later 19th-century addition along the W. side of the building. A large bay-window has been added on the E.

Inside Little Newnham one pointed window remains *in situ* in the wall, originally the outside wall, between the Drawing-room and Study and four blocked openings of similar form are visible in the same wall on the floor above. The 19th-century staircase has slender turned balusters. The rooms have 19th-century plaster cornices, and one on the first floor contains a cast-iron grate of the same age with foliage decoration. In Frostlake Cottage the 19th-century staircase has turned newels and slender square balusters.

(291) CROFT LODGE, on the S. side of Barton Road, 237 yds. from the corner of Newnham Road, of two storeys with basement, with gault brick walls and slate-covered roofs, was built *c.* 1822 (*Cambridge Chronicle* 16 April 1824). It is almost square on plan. The E. front is symmetrical, in three widely spaced bays, with an open porch in the middle composed of freestanding Doric columns and pilasters of Ketton

stone supporting a simplified entablature of timber with wrought-iron railings above forming a balcony before a french-window on the first floor. The flanking ground-floor windows are set in segmental-headed wall-arches and open on small balconies with wrought-iron scrollwork balustrading. The flanking first-floor windows have similar ironwork guards. The eaves have a wide overhang and the roofs are of low pitch. The N. and S. ends are almost wholly blind. The W. side has three wall-arches on the ground floor, similar to those described above, containing a central doorway and french-windows, the latter also with scrollwork balconies; the windows above have guards of similar design. All the larger windows contain casements opening in two leaves and with a marginal arrangement of panes.

Inside, some original fittings remain, including plaster cornices, two white marble fireplace-surrounds, doors and doorcases. The second are moulded and with roundels at the angles. The original staircase has cut strings, slender square balusters and a moulded mahogany handrail ending at the foot in a spiral over a slender shaped newel. On the first floor the division between landing and stair-well is marked by an archway with segmental head, square responds and moulded imposts; the plaster cornice to the stair-well is boldly enriched.

(292) MERTON HALL or the School of Pythagoras, house, stands well back from the junction of Queens' Road with Madingley Road and Northampton Street, 110 yds. N.W. of the New Court of St. John's College. It is the property of Merton College, Oxford. The building is L-shaped and so orientated that the external angle points due S.; in accordance with the precedent of a contract of 1374, in the following account the wings are described as if extending due E. and due N. The E. wing and a short return of the N. wing are of two storeys, the latter with an attic, with walls of clunch and other rubble, much decayed and patched with brickwork, and Barnack stone dressings. The rest of the N. wing is of two storeys with attics, with timber-framed and brick walls. All the roofs are tiled.

In 1271 Richard Dunning conveyed the house to Merton College and in deeds of 1270 relating to the transfer it is described as the stone house in which Eustace, father of Richard Dunning, formerly dwelt (Merton Records nos. 1556, 1574). It consisted of a *Hall* raised on a vaulted *Undercroft*, comprising the present E. wing of *c.* 1200; the hall fireplace being well to the E. suggests, on the analogy of Boothby Pagnell Manor, Lincolnshire, that space for a solar was left at the W. end, but the architectural evidence, so far as it is ascertainable in the present damaged state of the stonework, shows that the N.W. return is also an original feature. In the following account the last is called, without prejudice, the *Solar Wing*. In 1374 an agreement was made with Adam Mathie and John Meppushal, masons, to rebuild the W. wall and a length of 18 ft.

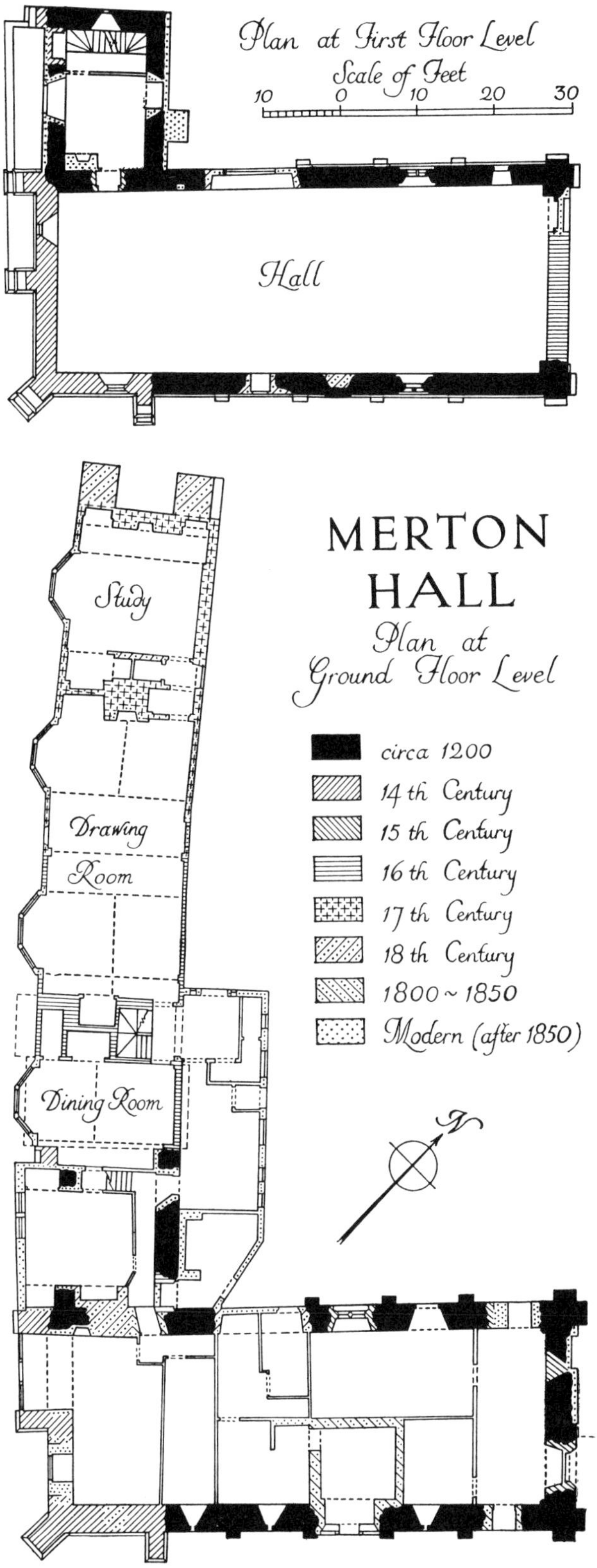

of the S. wall from the foundations to the height of the old walls, to build four buttresses, two being at the angles and two according to the usage and discretions of masons, and to rebuild the broken vault, the door ('hostium') under the vault and the steps leading up to the hall ('aula'), all in the sum of £30 13s. 4d. (Merton Records No. 1639). The stone house was in disrepair in the 16th century and suffered much destruction in the 18th and 19th centuries. The piers and vault of the undercroft have been almost entirely destroyed and the hipped roof of the hall is of the 19th century.

The *North Wing*, in extension of the Solar wing, was built in the 16th century and lengthened in the second half of the following century. The interior has been altered and modernised and the plaster stripped from the outside of the 16th-century walls to reveal the timbers.

Merton Hall of *c.* 1200 though much damaged and in part rebuilt is important as one of the few domestic buildings of so early a period surviving in this country. Only about a dozen houses of the kind remain in town and country, all more or less altered. (See also Sectional Preface, p. xc.)

Architectural Description—The main block of the early stone house is rectangular on plan. Outside, it has a moulded string across the free faces, except on the E., original two-stage angle pilaster-buttresses on the N.E. and S.E. corners, 14th-century three-stage buttresses towards the W., all stopping just below the eaves, and original single-stage pilaster-buttresses, the height of the undercroft only, along the N. and S. walls, except where destroyed on the N. and rebuilt in *c.* 1375 on the S.; the rebuilt S. buttress is similar to its contemporaries on the W. The surrounding ground-level has risen 3 ft. to 4 ft. concealing any plinths that may have existed.

The N. wall is in four free bays. The walling of most of the fourth bay has been removed from ground to eaves and a thin rubble wall and weatherboarding substituted; the rest is covered by a modern addition. To the lower storey in the first bay is a modern doorway with, some 1½ ft. to the W., indications of the W. jamb of a blocked opening possibly of the late 15th century, or later, with a short horizontal return of the head; the rear-arch of the last is traceable. In the second bay is a doorway with original jambs and chamfered segmental head, the last perhaps rebuilt; it rises only some 3½ ft. above present ground-level. In the third bay is a 15th-century window of two cinquefoiled lights with a quatrefoil in a four-centred head with a restored label. To the upper storey, over the E. bay is a short lancet window with patched chamfered jambs. Over the second bay is an original two-light window similar to that opposite, described below with the S. wall, but more damaged, the mullion being replaced by a post, the head, bereft of the outer order, extending into a large 19th-century brickwork patching, and the shafts of the shafted splays inside removed.

The E. wall is much refaced and rebuilt, except the buttresses, from first-floor level upward; only a short length of the return of the first-floor string remains, against the S. buttress. The lower part of the N. half has been faced with 19th-century brickwork, but, inside, the rear-arch of a blocked loop appears. In the S. half is a blocked 15th-century doorway with four-centred head. Just N. of the doorway, at springing-level, is an impost-moulding to the stone springer of a destroyed arch projecting at right angles from the wall. On the floor above, at the N. end, is a doorway, now blocked, with some original dressings but, for the rest, rebuilt and altered in form.

The S. wall (Plate 296) is original in the five E. bays and of *c.* 1374 in the W. bay. In the lower storey it has in the E. bay a doorway of *c.* 1800 with brick jambs and stone two-centred head, and in the second, fourth and fifth bays original rectangular chamfered loops with segmental rear-arches. In *c.* 1800 the whole of the walling to this storey in the third bay was removed and the opening spanned by a segmental arch and fitted with a glazed screen incorporating a doorway and windows all with two-centred heads to the timber frames. In the upper storey, over the second bay is an original though much decayed clunch window of two trefoiled lights divided by a shafted mullion with cap and base, with a small pierced re-curved quatrefoil in the spandrel and all within a slight recess with semicircular head forming an outer order; the semicircular rear-arch sprang from shafted splays with capitals carved with stiff-leaf foliage and moulded bases, but the shafts have been destroyed. Corbelled out over the third bay and interrupting the string is a shallow ashlar pilaster-like projection containing the flue from the fireplace in the hall: it is much patched with tiles and now stops at the eaves. The walling over the fourth bay has been refaced in brick and contains an 18th-century window. In the W. bay is a late 14th-century window of two trefoiled lights in a square head; the mullion has gone and the rebuilt wall above is carried on a modern timber lintel.

The W. end of *c.* 1374 is in two bays divided and flanked by buttresses, the S.W. buttress being diagonal. The lower walling of the N. bay has been removed and a glazed timber screen containing a doorway and windows set flush with the front of the buttresses. In the S. bay is a modern window cutting through the brick segmental head of an 18th-century blocked opening. To the upper storey in the N. bay is a small late 14th-century rectangular window with chamfered dressings and altered head with four-centred chamfered rear-arch.

Inside the E. wing the former *Undercroft* is divided by later partitions; of the original wall-shafts and five freestanding columns down the middle that supported quadripartite vaulting, only the vaulting-shafts in the N.E. and S.E. angles, with mutilated caps and three-sided abaci, survive. All the rest have been destroyed since the middle of the 18th century, though a rise in floor-level may conceal ancient bases.

The former *Hall* (62¾ ft. by 23¼ ft.) on the upper floor is undivided and open to the modern roof; the modern timber floor is some 2 ft. below the original floor-level. A continuous moulded string at sill-level is almost entirely destroyed. In the S. wall the relieving-arch and some dressings of the original fireplace, now blocked, survive; corbel-stones, now hacked flush with the wall, show that it had a hood. Towards the W.

end of the N. wall are traces of an original doorway with semicircular head and S. label; it is blocked and in the blocking is a 15th-century stone doorway with stop-chamfered jambs and four-centred head; some 8 ft. to the E. is a rectangular locker, also blocked.

The *Solar wing* has a 14th-century buttress on the N.W.; for the rest, the rubble walling where exposed has been refaced. No original features survive in the lower storey; most of the N. and W. walls at this level have been removed, and modern additions conceal the E. wall; this last has a blocked 16th-century brick doorway at the S. end. On the first floor in the N. wall is an original window with semicircular head, wide splays and semicircular rear-arch; though blocked by the 16th-century additions beyond, it is open to the S. and has chamfered and rebated reveals. A similar window is said to be in the E. wall (J. M. Gray, *The School of Pythagoras* etc. (1932), C.A.S. 4to. series N.S. IV, 33) though now entirely concealed and represented only by a recess inside and a blocking outside. In the W. wall is a 14th-century locker with square rebated jambs and two-centred head. This wing is now partitioned and contains a modern staircase.

The rest of the *North Wing* (Plate 306) is of the 16th century for about half the length, to where the exposed timber-framing on the W. ends and the roof-height changes. The 17th-century extension is of brick and timber-framing and has two large 18th-century sloping buttresses against the N. end. The W. front has at the S. end two gabled bays jettied at the first floor. The southernmost bay has the ends of the projecting joists exposed and small curved brackets at each end, that to the S. having been renewed. The second gabled projection is modern. All the timber studs are closely spaced. The windows throughout and in the 17th-century extension to the N. are comparatively modern; on the roof are five 18th or 19th-century dormer-windows. The E. side of the 16th-century building, partly concealed by modern additions, is pargeted in two heights of rectangular panels and has the S. bay projecting at the first floor and gabled. Two doorways, the southernmost blocked, have 18th-century timber cases with panelled pilasters and entablatures. The 17th-century brick N. end of the wing has two plat-bands between the buttresses and a shaped gable surmounted by a rectangular chimney-stack.

Inside the N. wing, the party-wall between the 16th and 17th-century buildings has been removed. On the ground floor are exposed chamfered and stop-chamfered ceiling-beams, the Dining-room ceiling being cambered, and two old fireplaces, restored. On the first floor are exposed posts and beams and an early 17th-century door panelled on the face and of planks on the back. The E. to W. framing of part of the roof exposed in the first-floor room in the S. end bay retains two wind-braces; in the same room is an original fireplace with timber stop-chamfered bressumer.

Queens' Road

E. side:—

(293) Merton House, 27 yds. S. of the junction with Madingley Road, of two storeys with basements and attics, has walls of gault brick and slate-covered roofs. It was built by Professor the Rev. W. Farish, vicar of St. Giles, and, on stylistic grounds, early in the 19th century. Though said to have been built in 1790 (C.A.S. 4to N.S. IV (1932), 19), it does not appear on the Inclosure Award map of 1804. The N.W. and S.E. sides are each symmetrical; the ends are gabled; the first has a plat-band at first-floor level and a simple timber eaves-cornice, a doorway in the middle and a tall window above, both with round heads. The flanking windows have slatted shutters. The S.E. side has a timber cornice and shuttered windows similar to those described on the N.W.

Inside, many of the fittings are original, including marble fireplaces with paterae at the corners, doors and doorcases, skirtings and plaster cornices. Between two of the ground-floor rooms is a large door raised by pulleys. The original staircase has a mahogany string and moulded handrail, turned newel and slender square balusters. The first-floor landing has round-headed archways to the passages to N.E. and S.W.

(294) Merton Cottage, 25 yds. S.W. of the foregoing, of two storeys, has gault brick walls and slate-covered roofs. It was described in 1823 as a modern house (*Cambridge Chronicle* 3 Jan.). Soon after 1850 a N. extension was made and later again two-storey bay-windows were added on the W. The original building has a brick plinth and a high parapet-wall with flat stone coping. The W. front was symmetrical, with a wall-arcade of three bays, rising through the two storeys and embracing the ground and first-floor openings; the arches had segmental heads and stone imposts level with the top of the upper windows. Only the middle bay remains unaltered though most of the imposts and the segmental heads of the flanking arches survive behind the two added bay-windows. The entrance-doorway in the middle is protected by an open trelliswork porch. On the E. also the windows are embraced in tall wall-recesses but here with square heads, creating a pilaster-like effect. The inside has been modernised.

Mill Road

(295) The Limes, house, standing back on the N.E. side, 100 yds. E. of Kingston Street, of two storeys, with walls of gault brick with stone dressings and slate-covered roofs, is dated 1846 on a stone panel in the S. gable-end. It is of some interest as an early example of the lofty, irregularly-planned house of indeterminate Gothic inspiration that was soon to appear in great numbers in suburban development in most parts of the country. The tall gabled projections, asymmetrical on the S. and N. sides, have stone quoins and elaborate barge-boards to the steeply pitched roofs. The open timber porch has similar bargeboards and pointed openings. The windows have chamfered stone jambs and flat heads, some with moulded labels; the marginal pattern of panes in the glazing are the sole link with earlier 19th-century fashion of less stylistic pedantry. Inside, the doorway to the stairhall is flanked by Gothic niches with mirror-glass in the backs.

Cherry Hinton

(296) Cherry Hinton Hall, nearly ¾ m. S.W. of the parish church, of two storeys with cellars, has gault brick walls with

stone dressings and slate-covered roofs. It was built for John Okes and the title to the property begins with the purchase of plots of land in 1834 (University Library, Map Room: sale advertisement, 1870). Scratched on the roof-lead is the date 1839, to which the house would approximate on stylistic grounds. Late in the same century a billiard room was added on the W. Since 1948 it has been converted into a day-nursery and clinic involving alterations and additions inside and out. The coach-house and stabling standing nearby to the N.W. have been drastically remodelled to provide living-quarters. The *Lodge* some 210 yds. to the S.W. is contemporary with the house.

Cherry Hinton Hall is a large and rather bald building of the first half of the 19th century in the late Tudor style.

The elevations generally have moulded strings at first-floor sill and eaves levels, tall parapet-walls carried up in gablets with moulded copings and apex-finials and stone-mullioned windows of one, two and three square-headed lights with labels; the ground-floor windows are transomed. The S. front is asymmetrical on plan and in height, the porch and the E. part being slightly higher than the rest westward. The doorway has continuously moulded jambs and four-centred head.

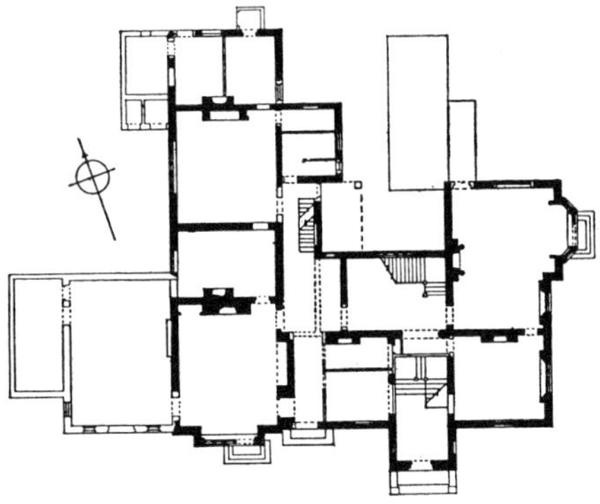

The rectangular bay-window towards the W. end is an early addition. On the N. side is a four-light transomed window lighting the original staircase; to the kitchen is another of five lights on the W. side. The lights in several windows have been cut down for doorways and french-windows, others retain the original glazing of lozenge-shaped quarries. The chimney-stacks have separate octagonal shafts with oversailing brick cappings.

Inside, the staircase in the entrance-hall is a modern insertion involving the blocking of the four-centred archways in the N. and W. walls. The principal rooms have doorways with architraves and six-panel doors all with roll-mouldings; another period allusion is the heavy moulding of the plaster-cornices. The E. part of the house retains two original fireplace-surrounds of gray polished stone, with moulded jambs and four-centred arches, sunk spandrels and moulded shelves; they are flanked, one by pilaster-like responds with roll-moulded angles and moulded caps, the other by octagonal projections with trefoil-headed sunk panels in the faces. The main staircase has close moulded strings, grip handrails, square panelled newels and pierced strapwork balustrading of gilded woodwork. The back staircase has cut strings, a turned newel and slender square balusters.

The *Lodge*, of one storey, with gault brick walls with stone dressings and tile-covered roofs, of uniform character with the house, has been much enlarged. It has large gables, and a smaller gable to the porch, all with moulded stone copings rising from corbelled kneelers. The windows have stone mullions and the tall chimney-stacks octagonal shafts.

(297) RED LION INN, near the corner of High Street and Millend Road, ¼ m. E. of Monument (296), of two storeys, has walls of plastered timber-framing and tile-covered roofs. It consists of a main range with a slightly lower wing across the western end, all of the 16th century. If an E. cross wing ever existed it has left no trace; an 18th-century brick addition is now in this position. More modern additions are on the back towards both ends, and on the wing, the last involving the removal of the front wall on the ground floor, though without destroying the evidence for the original projection of the first floor. The doors and windows are modern. The main chimney-stack at the E. end of the range is of 18th-century brickwork; the stack in the wing is of modern brick.

Inside, the main range has a longitudinal chamfered ceiling-beam stopped at the W. end where supported on an inserted brick wall. The structural framing visible on the upper floor is of heavy scantling, with enlarged heads to the wall-posts. The roof is not accessible.

(298) HOUSE, No. 75 High Street, 122 yds. N.N.E. of Monument (297), of two storeys, with red brick walls and tile-covered roofs, was built early in the 18th century and is now two tenements. It is a rectangular building, with gabled ends containing the chimney-stacks. The street-front is symmetrical with a plat-band at first-floor level, plain eaves, a central doorway, a window with rubbed brick flat arch to each side, three windows above, and two gabled dormer-windows. The door opens on a lobby and staircase flanked by living-rooms. Longitudinal axial ceiling-beams are exposed. In the N. room are remnants of a panelled dado.

(299) HOUSE, No. 81 High Street, 23 yds. N.N.E. of the foregoing, is a rectangular timber-framed and plastered 17th-century building of one storey with attics. Two gabled dormer-windows rise off the S. wall. The two rooms are divided by a large internal chimney-stack with diagonal clustered shafts of thin yellowish bricks. The stair is in the S.W. angle of the house. In the S. wall is a clunch panel inscribed 'July 25 1·17'.

(300) HALL FARM, house, 15 yds. N.N.E. of the foregoing and 660 yds. S.S.W. of the parish church, comprises a late 17th-century two-storey wing extending S. from an early 18th-century E. to W. range of one storey; the latter has a modern S. extension further towards the W. The walls are of red brick, the roofs tile-covered. The wing has a moulded

brick plinth, a plat-band at first-floor level and moulded kneelers to the S. gable; the chimney-stack at the gable-apex is largely rebuilt. The range has a plat-band across the E. gable-end and, on the N., a course of diagonal brickwork below the eaves; the central chimney-stack has conjoined diagonal shafts. The window-openings here have segmental heads, those and the doorways in the wing having been renewed.

(301) Glebe Cottages, house, now three tenements, Nos. 232–236 High Street, 170 yds. S.S.E. of the parish church, of two storeys, have timber-framed walls faced in the 19th century with gault brick. It was built probably in the 16th century; in the mid 19th century a two-storey range was added along the E. side. The outside was remodelled when refaced; the only earlier feature unaltered is the central chimney-stack, some 8 ft. by 6 ft. at first-floor level, of thin dark red bricks. The stack against the N. end wall is of the 19th century.

Inside are chamfered and stop-chamfered ceiling-beams exposed on the ground floor and wall-posts with enlarged heads on the first floor. In the middle tenement a steeply cambered tie-beam passes close in front of the stack and the fireplace in the same room has a stop-chamfered timber lintel, only slightly cambered.

(302) Uphall, 173 yds. N. of the parish church, of two storeys with timber-framed and gault brick walls and slate-covered roofs, consists of a long range of different dates bordering the road. A 16th-century timber-framed house with central chimney-stack was encased in brick, heightened and extended N. and S. in *c.* 1830, the S. extension nearly doubling the size of the earlier building and being given architectural predominance. In the 19th century, and since, the N. extension was much enlarged. The outside is now of early 19th-century character, with double-hung sash-windows and low-pitched roofs with widely overhanging eaves on shaped brackets. The doorway in the S. extension and a french-window at the S. end have side-pilasters supporting flat hoods with panelled soffits.

Inside, the timber-framing of the original house is exposed, including stop-chamfered ceiling-beams and the wall-plates, these last now some feet below the eaves; the building was of three bays, that in the middle narrow and containing the stack with a flanking staircase. In the Drawing-room is an early 19th-century circular cast-iron grate simulating a sea-shell, with original ashpan and modelled shells and scrolls in the spandrels; it is set in a contemporary moulded stone surround with roundels at the angles and a plain cornice-shelf. A similar grate at Great Hundridge was cast at Berkhamsted in 1827 (*Country Life* 15 Feb., 5 April 1941); a number survive throughout the country.

A small outbuilding close N.E., now cased in gault brick, has timber-framed walls and a tie-beam roof with curved braces between the wall-posts and ties and a ridge-piece.

(303) House, No. 146 Rosemary Lane, 400 yds. N. by W. of the parish church, of two storeys with attics, has walls of timber-framing, with the ground floor underbuilt in modern brick, and tile covered roofs. It is a small building of the early 18th century with a central chimney-stack flanked on one side by the entrance, on the other, until removed during recent alterations, by a stair. On the N.W. is a modern addition. During renovation in 1949 the fabric was stripped down to the framing and the latter seen to be of slight scantling, mostly sawn, with sills, studs interrupted by diagonal braces, and head-rails supporting a simple roof-structure, this last with rafters, purlins two-thirds up the slopes supported on collar-beams, and a ridge-piece. On the timber lintel of the fireplace in the E. ground-floor room are the initials and date W M 1708.

(304) Mafeking Cottage, 47 yds. N. of the foregoing, of two storeys, has timber-framed walls faced with modern rendering and thatched roofs. The S.W. half with a projecting first floor is of the 16th century; the N.E. half may be a slightly later addition; the two were once separate dwellings. A 19th-century cottage adjoins on the S.W. The building has chimney-stacks in the end walls, one off-centre, flanked by stairs. No original doorways or windows survive. Inside are chamfered ceiling-beams on the ground floor and exposed wall-posts with enlarged heads on the upper floor. Two of the doors are old, one of planks, the other incorporating panelling of *c.* 1600. Two early 19th-century *Outbuildings* have walls built of a single thickness of clay bats, 18 × 11 × 6 ins. with 1½-in. joints, incorporating chopped reed; the outside rendering of lime-wash has largely gone.

Chesterton

(305) Chesterton Tower (Plate 296), house, standing in the Vicarage garden 177 yds. N. of the parish church, is of two storeys with walls of rubble patched with brick and with clunch and Ketton stone ashlar dressings; the roofs are tile-covered. It was built about the middle of the 14th century probably for the procurator of the abbot of Vercelli (see Sectional Preface, p. lxviii). The circumstances of the gift of the church of St. Andrew, Chesterton, to the church of St. Andrew, Vercelli, are described above (Monument (60)); in 1440 the appropriation was granted to King's Hall and this last was subsequently merged in Henry VIII's foundation of Trinity College, to which Chesterton Tower belongs. (C.A.S. *Proc.* XIII (1909), 185.) From time to time the building has been repaired, but in 1949 a restoration was made with the advice of the Ministry of Works involving the renewal of nearly all the decayed dressed clunch in Ketton stone, some in a form that has destroyed archaeological evidence.

The Tower is a rare survival of a dwelling for the representative in England of a foreign appropriator and of much architectural interest despite the recent restoration. (See also Sectional Preface, p. xc.)

Architectural Description—The building is rectangular on plan with the entrance in the N.E. side, and octagonal turrets and a rectangular garderobe projecting on the N., W. and S. angles respectively; the N. turret contained a circular stair. The shallow projection by the E. angle contained the fireplaces. The roof is half-hipped and has plain eaves, the turrets rising some 2 ft. to 3 ft. above them. On the N.E., the entrance has chamfered jambs and a two-centred head; further S.E. is a loop-light; above the former is a comparatively modern blocked opening, and further S.E. an original but mutilated trefoiled light in a two-centred head. Modern renewals include the quoins at the E. angle from $6\frac{1}{2}$ ft. above ground upward and rubble patching above the doorway. The N.W. side has on the ground floor two windows each of two cinquefoiled lights with a quatrefoil in a two-centred head with a label, both almost completely renewed in the 19th century; below the S.W. jamb of the more northerly is a small loop-light. On the floor above is the blocking of a modern doorway cut through a former opening, of which the S.W. splay survives, and further S.W. a small blocked light.

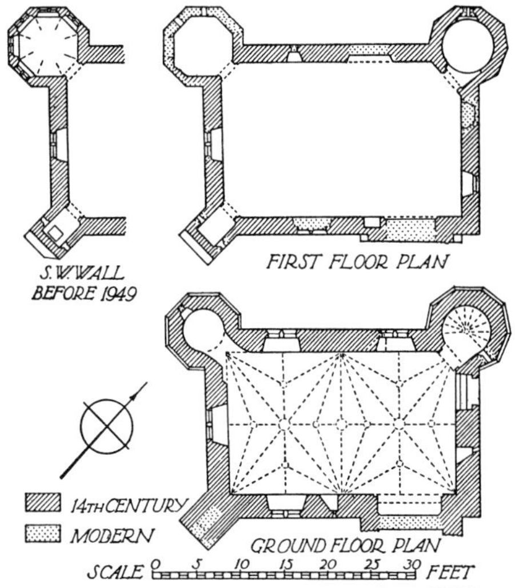

CHESTERTON TOWER

The N. stair-turret has a chamfered plinth, modern quoins from about 7 ft. above ground level upwards, and two loop-lights now with surrounds of reset bricks. The W. turret has a chamfered plinth and a corbel-table supporting the projecting first floor; this last contained in each face the remains of a window of two trefoiled lights with a two-centred rear-arch, three of which were blocked and all more or less defaced, but all excepting one rear-arch were obliterated in the recent restoration when the upper stage was largely rebuilt with reused bricks; most of the quoins and corbel-table were also renewed, the quoins being bonded in the usual manner where the original quoins stopped short to leave space for the window-dressings.

The S.W. end has on the ground floor a window of two cinquefoiled lights with a quatrefoil in a two-centred head with a label; below is a blocking where the window was once cut down to form a door; on the floor above is a window of two trefoiled lights; both windows are entirely renewed outside. The garderobe structure has a weathered offset and stands as high as the eaves; nearly all the dressings have been renewed, those below the weathering being brought to a right angle where previously was a broad chamfer, and the upper courses rebuilt. On the S.E. side, the projection of the chimney-stack long since truncated at the eaves, is in two stages with two weathered offsets at the sides; the outer face was rebuilt, the lower part in rubble, the upper part in brick, prior to the 1949 restoration, and appears originally to have projected further. Between it and the garderobe is a window on each floor and a loop-light low down; the ground-floor window is similar to that opposite and as much restored; the upper window of two trefoiled lights is blocked and remains unrestored and much weathered. Most of the windows described above retain their original inner splays and segmental-pointed rear-arches.

Inside, single rooms (26 ft. by $15\frac{3}{4}$ ft. and $27\frac{1}{2}$ ft. by $17\frac{1}{4}$ ft.) occupy the two floors of the main block. The W. turret provides a small circular closet off the hall on the ground floor and an octagonal chamber off the room above. The garderobe is entered from the first floor. The ground-floor room is covered by an original stone vault (Plate 297) in two equal bays with hollow-chamfered cross, diagonal, intermediate and ridge ribs with bosses at their intersections, except at the centre where the ribs mitre round a small open circle. The ridge-rib is horizontal from end to end. The bosses are carved as follows: N.E. bay (middle) defaced, (intermediate, a) foliated, (b, c) man's face, (d) hooded man's face; S.W. bay (middle) lion's mask, (a) bearded man's face, (b) grotesque face, (c) stylised flowers, (d) hooded man's face. The fireplace in the S.E. wall has a shouldered lintel but only a fragment remains; the opening has been heightened and has a chamfered segmental-pointed head. The doorway to the N. turret has chamfered jambs and two-centred head. None of the original steps of the vice survives. The closet in the W. turret is covered by a roughly domed ceiling and entered through an opening with a rough two-centred head.

The first-floor room is open to the roof. In the S.E. wall, the fireplace, blocked with brick in 1949, has rebated jambs and lintel and, just to the S.W., a small recess, partly blocked, with a chamfered segmental head. In the N.W. wall is a large modern brick patching. The doorway to the garderobe has rebated jambs and a two-centred head. The doorway to the vice is similar to the foregoing but with chamfered jambs and, in the adjoining wall of the turret, a recess with a half-arch for the doorswing. The chamber in the W. turret was originally vaulted, but only the springers of the vaulting-ribs remain rising directly out of the angles between the walls. The garderobe has a loop-light in each side wall and retains the shaft and an outlet at ground level.

The roof is comparatively modern, incorporating reused timbers. It is in three bays with tie-beams braced from the side walls and struts from the ties to the purlins.

(306) Vicarage, 100 yds. N. of the parish church, of two and three storeys, with gault brick walls and slate-covered

roofs, was built *c.* 1820, with the principal front to the S.E. and the entrance on the N.W. Later in the century a single-storey addition was made at the back, on the N.W., the adjacent part of the house being remodelled to contain three storeys. In the present century a porch was built on the N.E., the original doorcase being reset.

The uncompromising expression in the simplest architectural terms of the vertical and horizontal features of the S.E. front is of interest as a forerunner of the panel-treatment seen in the most modern buildings. The front is of constant height with a plain stone capping to the parapet. At each end are vertical projecting strips rising the full height without a break; extending horizontally between them across the recessed wall-face is a plain square stone cornice. The contained rectangle so formed has graduated ranges of four windows on each floor, the lower unusually tall. The design is enhanced by the upper windows being so placed that a considerable height of brickwork intervenes between their sills and the window-heads below and only four or five courses between their heads and the cornice.

The reset entrance-doorway in the modern porch has timber pilasters at the sides supporting an entablature with an enriched frieze containing a panel carved with a draped urn in low relief. The N.W. side is irregular; a doorway has timber side-pilasters supporting a shallow flat hood; a large round-headed window lights the staircase. Inside, many of the fittings are modern, but the doorways to the principal rooms have reeded linings to the reveals.

(307) Manor House, in Church Street, 40 yds. N. of the parish church, of two storeys with attics, has red brick walls with modern stone dressings and tile-covered roofs. It was built late in the 17th century and comprised a straight range with a staircase-projection at the back. In the 19th century a W. wing was added, which incorporates 17th-century brickwork, probably a former boundary-wall. In modern times the main, S.W., side has been entirely refaced, the staircase-bay heightened and single-storey additions made on the N.E.

The street-front, with parapet, central doorway, two windows to each side and five on the first floor, is modern though perhaps perpetuating the earlier design. The gabled S.E. end has plat-bands at first and second-floor levels and contains blocked windows. The inside is much altered. The entrance-hall, now extending to more than half the ground floor of the original house, has an original open fireplace, restored, and a carved overmantel brought from elsewhere. The original staircase has close strings, turned balusters and square newels.

The boundary-wall running N.W. from the house, of 17th and 18th-century brickwork, extends to an early 18th-century brick-built *Barn* of two storeys bounding the house-yard on the N.W.; it is now in part converted into a dwelling.

In the E. corner of the garden, beside the N.E. arm of Church Street and built partly on the boundary-wall, is an 18th-century *Summer-house*. It is of two storeys, with walls of brown brick with red brick dressings and roofs covered with pantiles. At first-floor level is a plat-band and at the eaves a brick dentil-cornice; the latter and the chimney-stack are of the 19th century. A modern doorway in the S.E. side opens to the street; on the floor above are a sash-hung window and a blind recess; the other walls contain similar windows. Access from the garden is through a plain doorway.

(308) Old Manor House, 23 yds. S.E. of the parish church, of two storeys with attics, has plastered timber-framed walls and tile-covered roofs. It was built in *c.* 1700 on a T-shaped plan and subsequently extended and modernised. The range beside the street has fireplaces in the gabled end walls; the old S.W. stack is of red brick and projects, that to the N.E. is of modern brick. In the back wing are the only two original windows remaining; they have unmoulded timber frames and wrought-iron casements. Inside, the ceiling-beams athwart the range are cased. The original staircase has close strings and turned balusters.

(309) Chesterton Hall, 317 yds. W.N.W. of the parish church, of two and three storeys with attics, has walls of red brick and tile-covered roofs. It was built in the second quarter of the 17th century on an L-shaped plan with a small block in the re-entrant angle and an octagonal tower on the N.W. angle of the N. wing. In the 19th century a rectangular stair-tower and porch were added on the N. of the W. wing alongside the re-entrant projection and the whole was much restored. In the present century the N. wing was extended N. The house is now the property of the city; it has been modernised and converted into flats.

Chesterton Hall though altered and much restored is of interest as a comparatively large work of the period when much brick building was going forward in Cambridge.

The S. side to Chesterton Road is symmetrical (Plate 307); it has a plain plinth, a moulded brick string at first-floor level and plain eaves. The wall is continued up flush to form the face of three dormer-windows with inset semicircular parapeted gables. All the mullioned windows, of five, three and two lights, those on the lower floors transomed, are of 19th-century stonework, including the small oriel-window in the middle of the first floor. The W. end of the W. wing has plat-bands and finishes in a shaped parapeted gable springing from kneelers composed of oversailing courses of brickwork. The N. side is largely obscured by the 19th-century additions, but rising clear are three old chimney-stacks with twin square shafts. In the N. face of the re-entrant projection E. of the square tower is a modern doorway.

The W. side of the N. wing has been heightened and completed with a fretted parapet in the 19th century. The N.W. tower is divided into three stages by weathered brick strings and has a rebuilt parapet-wall; in the top stage are 19th-century pierced stone panels. All the N. end is masked, except the chimney-stack, similar to those already described but with a modern shaft added. The E. side of the wing has a plain brick string at first-floor level. It has been heightened and the windows have been renewed. No original features remain inside.

(310) Chesterton House, at the corner of Chesterton Road and Church Street, was built at the very end of the 18th century, but the original house has been almost completely obliterated by late 19th-century alteration and extension. It retains linked to outbuildings to the S.E. an 18th-century *Pigeon-house* of brick with a tiled roof; this is square on plan, and of two storeys, with a plat-band, pilaster-like projections clasping the angles and on the sides, and a doorway on each floor. The alighting platform on the roof survives but not the nesting-boxes.

(311) House, now two tenements, Nos. 25, 27 High Street, on the N. side just N. of the end of Church Street, of two storeys with attics, has brick walls and a slated mansard roof. Though of the 18th century, the building has been drastically altered and a N. wing added in the 19th century. The street-front is of 18th-century brown brick to the top of the first-floor windows; all above, in gault brick, and the roof, are of the 19th century. The front was symmetrical, with a central doorway, two windows to each side and five above; the original doorcase has gone; one of the windows has been converted into a second doorway and the rest contain 19th-century sashes. The other walls are of 19th-century gault brick. No original features survive inside. No. 27 is the 'Bowling Green' public-house.

(312) House, now two tenements, Nos. 26, 28 High Street, on the S. side between Church Street and Chapel Street, of two storeys, with attics, is a late 17th-century timber-framed building mostly cased in 18th-century and modern brickwork and with some weatherboarding. The framing is exposed at the E. end and inside on the first floor.

(313) Hill House, No. 81 High Street, on the N. side opposite Chapel Street, of two storeys with gault brick walls and slate-covered roofs, was built early in the 19th century. At the back is a late 19th-century wing. The street-front is symmetrical, in three bays, with a projecting glazed porch in the middle. This last is comparatively modern but the reset doorcase is of the early 18th century, with enriched architrave, flanking engaged Ionic columns, and pedimented entablature; the frieze contains arabesque ornament and the soffit of the pediment is enriched, but the dentil-cornice has been restored without the dentils to the slopes. The windows have slightly cambered brick arches. Inside, the staircase with plain square balusters and turned newels rises in a narrow stairhall between two rooms on each floor.

(314) Westcroft and The Elms, two terrace-houses, Nos. 13, 14 Church Street, on the N. side, near the corner of Chapel Street, of two storeys, have walls of brick and plastered timber-framing and tile-covered roofs. They were built early in the 19th century on a symmetrical half H-shaped plan. The two houses have identical fronts, each with a central doorway with a fanlight set in a round-headed recess of two orders, a window to each side and three on the first floor, and a plat-band below a continuous parapet-wall. In the bay obstructed by the party-wall between the houses are blind recesses uniform with the window-openings. The brickwork is returned only about half-way along the gabled ends of the main range; for the rest, the exterior walls are of plastered framing.

Adjoining the foregoing on the S.W., *No. 5 Chapel Street*, forms a part of the same development but is less distinguished. It has a stucco surround to the round-headed doorway and an eaves-cornice with bricks projecting diagonally.

(315) House, now two tenements, Nos. 225, 227 High Street, on the N. side, 17 yds. N.E. of the School (Monument (102)), of one and two storeys with attics, has walls of rendered brickwork, presumably encasing timber-framing, and tile-covered roofs. It was built probably in the 17th century, comprising a range with a lower cross wing at the S.W. end, the latter projecting only a short way beyond the main frontage, further at the back. Against the back of the main range are modern additions and the chimney-stacks are rebuilt or modern. The timber-mullioned windows to the street are of three lights, some, and the plain entrance-doorway, having stucco labels, all dating from an early 19th-century remodelling. The free end of the main range is faced with 19th-century brickwork; the N.W. end of the cross wing is of older brick, the stack and the rest of the walling being of different builds. Inside, athwart range and wing are exposed chamfered ceiling-beams. No. 225 is derelict (1952).

(316) Roebuck House, opposite the corner of Ferry Lane and Water Street, ¼ m. N.E. of the parish church, of two storeys in part with cellars and attics, has walls partly timber-framed, partly of brick, with some stucco-facing, and tile-covered roofs. The house presents a thick rectangular block on plan. The south-eastern part comprises a nearly symmetrical unit of the early 18th century designed with a room on each side of a central through-passage. An earlier range parallel with and adjoining the foregoing on the N.W. was rebuilt, with reuse of much material, by Robert Robinson when he bought the property in 1775; it then projected north-eastward beyond the early 18th-century range and in the mid 19th century the N.E. re-entrant was filled.

Robert Robinson, Baptist minister and farmer, wrote a brief account of his alterations and repairs; the MS. is preserved in St. Andrew's Street Baptist chapel (Monument (66)).

To the S.E. the stucco-faced front of the early 18th-century house has, approached laterally up flights of steps, a central doorway with a flat hood flanked by two windows to each side, and five windows on the first floor; the two northernmost windows are dummies containing smaller openings. On the roof are two hipped dormer-windows. The 19th-century

N. continuation is in gault brickwork, the N.E. return, to the street, rising in an obtuse gable; beyond, flush with the latter, is the red brick gabled end of the earlier block, with a projecting brick course and headers at first-floor level and a plat-band below the gable. The openings are quite plain, the windows containing double-hung sashes. The N.W. side has the upper part of the more northerly end built of reused orange-red bricks, red below, and the rest with a predominance of late 18th-century gault brick. The S.W. end, in large part of timber-framing, is faced with stucco.

Inside, the early 18th-century building contains cased intersecting ceiling-beams and some original doors of two panels. In the rebuilt range, in the N. corner room, are two exposed ceiling-beams, one moulded, of the 17th century and reused, the other chamfered. In the same room an 18th-century cupboard door has two fielded panels and original hinges; another in the room above has doors of early 17th-century panelling.

Outbuildings S.W. of the house, in part of timber-framing probably of the 17th century, include a stable; according to the MS., Robinson rebuilt a stable, barn and wash-house in 1779. The *Garden-wall* leading S.E. from the E. angle of the house is largely of 17th-century bricks, averaging 1¾ ins. thick.

(317) Range of four tenements, the 'Green Dragon' inn, Nos. 7, 9, 11 Water Street (Plate 306), on the N. side, 500 yds. N.E. of the parish church, of two storeys with attics, has plastered timber-framed walls and tile-covered roofs. It was built in the 16th century, with two wings at the back; additions have since been made beside and on the ends of the wings.

The building is of note as a long timber-framed range of the 16th century.

Towards the street the first floor projects and at the eaves is a timber cornice. The window-frames, containing sliding casements or double-hung sashes, are all of the 19th century including the two three-sided bay-windows to the inn at the south-western end. Between Nos. 7 and 11 is a carriage-way the full height of the ground floor, and providing access to No. 9, which occupies the wing at the rear of No. 11. The latter wing is of miscellaneous materials including squared stones but with timber-framing to the first floor except at the N.W. end; this last is all of brick, the upper floor incorporating 18th-century lacing-courses and therefore presumably rebuilt. The central chimney-stack of the 'Green Dragon' is original below but rebuilt with old bricks in the clear; the S.W. stack in No. 11 is original, with two diagonal shafts; the other stacks are modern or rebuilt.

Inside, the long street range and No. 9 contain longitudinal chamfered ceiling-beams. In No. 11 studded partitioning is exposed. In the inn is an early 18th-century fixed cupboard with doors in two heights of fielded panels, the upper arched, hung between side panels.

(318) House, No. 15 Water Street, on the N. side, 13 yds. N.E. of the foregoing Monument (317), of two storeys, has timber-framed walls, faced with modern brick towards the street, plastered at the back, and tile-covered roofs. It was built probably early in the 17th century, but has been much altered and extended to the N.W. The S.W. gabled end and the base of the chimney-stack at the apex are of original brickwork; in the back wall is a second original chimney-stack, also rebuilt at the top. All the windows have been renewed. The interior has been modernised and the large fireplace to the S.W. cut back; the stair flanking the latter remains presumably in the original position.

(319) House, No. 43 Water Street, on the N. side, 60 yds. N.E. of the foregoing Monument (318), of two storeys, has timber-framed walls cased in modern brickwork and tile-covered roofs. It is of the 16th century with a 19th-century wing on the back, to the N.W. The only original feature remaining visible outside is the great chimney-stack rising from behind the roof-ridge towards the south-western end of the building; the top few courses have been rebuilt. The stack at the junction with the wing is of the 19th century. Inside are intersecting stop-chamfered ceiling-beams on the ground floor. Exposed on the first floor are chamfered wall-posts with enlarged heads under the roof-trusses.

(320) House, on the N. side of Scotland Road, ¼ m. N. by E. of the parish church, of two storeys with attics, has brick walls and tile-covered roofs. It is a 17th-century timber-framed structure remodelled in the 18th century when the S.W. side and the ends were cased in gault brick. A wing was added on the E. in the 19th century. The brick walls have a plat-band at first-floor level. The S.W. side has a central doorway flanked by a wide window on each side, five windows on the first floor and a timber eaves-cornice. The S.E. end has in the lower part red brickwork in continuation of the adjoining garden-wall; the gable-end and that at the opposite end are plastered, probably over framing. The N.E. side, where free, is faced with pargeting in large rough-faced panels. Inside, the entrance is into a lobby beside the central chimney-stack. The S.E. ground-floor room is lined with reset panelling, mostly of the early 17th century. Some doors are of the early 18th century, of two panels.

(321) Railway Dwellings near the Chesterton Junction of the Cambridge–Ely, Cambridge–St. Ives railway-lines, consist of (a) and (b) two detached houses, (c) two symmetrical blocks containing six tenements. They are of gault brick with low-pitched, slate-covered roofs. The Eastern Counties Railway from Bishop's Stortford to Ely was opened in 1845, the St. Ives branch line in 1847.

(a) *House* for the crossing-keeper (Plate 309), close S. of Fen Road, built *c.* 1845, is of one storey and cruciform on plan with porches and some later additions in the re-entrant angles. The window-openings have round heads and brick imposts continued round the building as plat-bands; they contain double-hung sashes. The boxed eaves project widely, the roofs are hipped and the ridges run into a central square chimney-stack.

(b) *House*, perhaps incorporating a former signal-box (Plate 309), in the angle between the junction, 100 yds. N. by E. from the Fen Road crossing, built *c.* 1847, is of two storeys and comprises, on plan, a rectangle to the N. joined by a recessed bay to an octagon to the S. It has a continuous plat-band at first-floor level. The openings are plain; some windows contain double-hung sashes, several others are blind. The roofs are hipped and have boxed eaves with a continuous bedmould consisting of an oversailing brick course. The rebuilt chimney-stacks are eccentric.

(c) *Tenements*, 37 yds. N. of (b), built *c.* 1847, of two storeys, comprise two symmetrical blocks, H-shaped on plan, with the link and the cross-wings each containing a tenement. They have rusticated brick quoins and plat-bands at first-floor level. Some of the windows are blind, others contain double-hung sashes.

(322) THE ROUND HOUSE (Plate 309), former toll-house, on the N. side of Newmarket Road, 70 yds. E.S.E. of Stourbridge Chapel (Monument (62)), originally of one storey, has gault brick walls and low-pitched slate-covered roofs. The decision to build a new toll-house at the end of the turnpike at the 'Paper Mills' (Monument (323)) is recorded in the *Cambridge Chronicle* 29 Aug. 1828. It was symmetrical, comprising a narrow rectangular block with a semi-octagonal bay projecting on the S. as far as the road, but a modern two-storey addition has been made on the N.E. The openings are plain. The windows have stone sills and those flanking the bay are set in segmental-headed recesses. The roofs are hipped and have bracketed boxed eaves supported on slender freestanding cast-iron columns at the angles of the bay.

(323) 'PAPER MILLS', house, on the E. bank of Coldham's Brook, 33 yds. E. of Monument (322), of two storeys with attics, has gault brick walls and tile-covered roofs. It was built early in the 18th century and consists of a long rectangular range at right angles to the Newmarket Road. Alterations were made early in the 19th century and subsequently a wing and various small additions were built on the E. The mill adjoining on the N., presumably a rebuilding of an older mill, is dated 1871. Fuller writing in 1662 (*Worthies*, 149) says paper was made here 'in the memory of our fathers'. Subsequently it seems to have been used as a flour-mill until affected by reduction in the flow of the brook resulting from extraction by the Waterworks Company, who bought the freehold (A. B. Gray, *Cambridge Revisited* (1921), 91).

The house has a continuous plat-band at first-floor level, another across the base of the S. gable-end and a brick dentil-cornice at the eaves. The W. front is given early 19th-century character by the addition of a trelliswork porch with flared roof to the main entrance and slatted shutters to the windows; the whole is in six bays and on the roof are two dormer-windows with 19th-century bargeboards. At the S. end is a projecting chimney-stack and the gable springs from moulded brick kneelers. The E. side is masked.

Inside were originally three rooms divided by two partitions. The N. partition to the entrance-passage through the house is an early 19th-century insertion; the original S. partition has timber-framing and brick nogging exposed to the S. Where visible the ceiling-beams athwart the range are chamfered. The middle room was remodelled in the early 19th century and the fireplace, stack and cornice are of this date.

TRUMPINGTON

(324) TRUMPINGTON HALL, 245 yds. N.W. of the parish church, of three storeys with cellars, has walls of red brick and slate-covered roofs of low pitch. It is approached along an avenue of elms leading E. and W. from the Trumpington Road. The estate was bought from the Pytcher family in 1675 by Sir Francis Pemberton, 1625–97, Lord Chief Justice 1681, in whose family it has remained, the Pemberton name being retained on descent through the female line. The hall was built in *c.* 1710 on a half H-shaped plan with the wings extending E., incorporating an earlier building of *c.* 1600 in the northern end. It was reroofed early in the 19th century, the date 1826 is scratched on one of the slates, and this seems to have involved heightening the earlier attic storey to a full storey. Probably at the same time a porch was added in the middle of the main, E., front, all the windows were resashed and kitchen-offices added on the N.W. Modern work includes the addition in 1900 of a rectangular window-bay on the W., the insertion of a staircase from first to second floor, various other minor alterations inside and, in 1905, a new Library wing on the N. The open walk against the S. wall of the kitchen-offices is an addition of 1929. Part of the house was converted into three flats in 1947.

Trumpington Hall, though too much altered to be an outstanding example of building of the early 18th century, is a house of gracious dignity in a fine, spacious architectural and natural setting.

Architectural Description—The building has a plinth, plat-bands at first and second-floor levels and widely projecting early 19th-century eaves to contemporary low-pitched hipped roofs. The entrance front (Plate 299) is symmetrical; the recessed face was originally of seven bays but the ground-floor windows S. of the central doorway have been altered and the original northernmost window on the same floor blocked; for the rest the original window-openings remain on the ground and first floors and have comparatively high segmental heads. The top-floor openings with shallower heads are probably of 1826. The early 19th-century porch with pilasters and entablature is stucco-faced. The wings have two windows to the front on each floor; their inward-facing returns are each in three bays mostly of blind recesses maintaining the rhythm of the fenestration already described, but the centre bays each contain a doorway on the ground floor, that in the N. wing, cut in 1922, hung with a glazed door, that opposite having a doorcase with a crowning entablature with the moulded architrave ramped up in the frieze, the door being of eight fielded panels. The S. end has a projecting three-sided bay, probably a rather later addition, near the middle with a window in each face on each floor; these and the windows and recesses in the flanking wall-faces are similar to those already described but the easternmost ground-floor window has been cut down to form a doorway and the westernmost blocked. The W. side is in part concealed by a rectangular two-storey bay to the S. and a kitchen annexe to the N., both modern, but a change in colour of the brickwork of the top storey shows a heightening; the windows, where visible, are similar to the rest at the same respective levels. The same holds for the N. end, but here a ground-floor window retains original box-framing and hung sashes with thick glazing-bars.

Inside, the '*Justice Hall*' in the S.E. wing is lined with reset panelling of *c.* 1600 above an 18th-century panelled dado. The fireplace has a flat moulded stone surround of the early 18th century with a contemporary cast-iron fireback and S. of it within the depth of the chimney-breast is a small winding stair rising to the second floor. In the *Dining-room* is an early 19th-century reeded fireplace-surround of white marble with roundels at the angles. The *Kitchen* has an early 18th-century fireplace-surround with marble slips, timber eared frame, pulvinated frieze and cornice. In the passage W. of the Kitchen is a dado of reset panelling of *c.* 1600 in two heights with a fluted frieze. Early 17th-century stop-chamfered ceiling-beams span the *Servants' Hall* at the N. end of the house, the cross-beam extending over the service-passage adjoining on the W.; the same room contains an early 18th-century flat moulded stone surround to the fireplace. In the *Study* in the N.E. wing is a stop-chamfered ceiling-beam and an overmantel incorporating reused early 17th-century enriched panelling; the dado-panelling is of the same period. The Butler's pantry in the N.W. corner of the house retains some early 18th-century panelling. Beside the fireplace in the main *Stairhall* is a small round-headed alcove with panelled side-pilasters and moulded archivolt. The staircase from ground to first floor is of *c.* 1710, of oak, with alternate turned and twisted balusters two to a step, cut strings with carved scroll-brackets, moulded ramped handrail and columnar newels.

On the first floor the bedroom, formerly the Drawing-room, over the present Drawing-room is lined with 18th-century fielded panelling in two heights with dado-rail and cornice; the fireplace has marble slips, an enriched timber architrave, pulvinated frieze and cornice and a bolection-moulded panel forming the overmantel. Two other E. bedrooms are panelled similarly to the foregoing; in one is a flat stone, in the other a marble, surround to the fireplace. The bedroom over the servants' hall and the adjoining corridor on the W. though subdivided by later partitions are lined from floor to ceiling with early 17th-century panelling in five heights with a fluted frieze; part of the chimney-stack of the earlier house is visible in a cupboard in the S. wall; the contemporary fireplace-surround and overmantel are now loose in the stables. The fireplace has fluted Ionic pilasters at the sides standing on pedestals enriched with arabesques; the overmantel comprises three bays of enriched arched panels divided by acanthus-leaf brackets and a frieze containing carved lions' masks. The flat moulded marble surround to the fireplace in the bedroom over the Kitchen is of the early 18th century.

The deep segmental-ended E. *Forecourt* is the same width as the Hall; adjoining the latter in the high brick lateral walls are small wrought-iron gates between piers. The E. end is circumscribed by a dwarf wall and has in the middle a large wrought-iron gate in two leaves between tall brick piers with stone cornices surmounted by gadrooned urns; the lateral curves are divided into bays by square brick piers set diagonally and contain restored white painted palings.

The *Stables* N.E. of the Hall are contemporary with it and of similar materials. They have a plinth, a plat-band at first-floor level, a brick dentil-cornice and a renewed low-pitched roof. Modern double doors have been inserted. On the S. wall is an early 18th-century lead rainwater-pipe with shaped head.

(325) ANSTEY HALL, 133 yds. S.E. of the parish church, of two storeys with cellars and attics has walls of dull red brick, with freestone dressings towards the front, and tile-covered roofs. It was built late in the 17th century probably by Anthony Thompson (Deputy Lieutenant for Cambridgeshire 1698–1701) on a half H-shaped plan, the wings extending back to the S., with small square projections, that to the W. perhaps containing a staircase, in the re-entrant angles. (Cf. Magdalene College, plan of Pepys Building.) In the second half of the 19th century the house was made nearly half as large again by an addition on the E. and in 1909 the original building was extensively remodelled inside. This later work included the removal of the re-entrant projections on the ground and first floors, an addition filling most of the depth of the S. recess between the wings, removal of the main staircase from the W. re-entrant projection and reconstruction where it now is, removal of partition-walls from the present Hall and Library and rearrangement of the N.E. ground-floor rooms. Low additions were also made on the W. The panelling, now painted, and fireplace-surrounds in many of the rooms are of late 17th-century character, but the interior alterations and refitting have been so extensive that some uncertainty remains of their antiquity.

Anstey Hall though extensively altered inside retains a notable late 17th-century N. front with pedimented centrepiece.

The N. front is symmetrical, in nine bays, with the middle bay projecting slightly and elaborated with rusticated stone quoins and inset lofty attached Ionic columns on rusticated pedestals supporting a pediment with a modillion-cornice; in the tympanum is a cartouche carved with the arms of Thompson. The wall continues up above the pediment as an attic with two pedestals on the face surmounted by pineapple finials. The central doorway approached up steps has a stone surround with scroll-brackets supporting a segmental pediment. The rest of the front flanking the centrepiece has a plinth with moulded weathering, rusticated quoins, a plat-band at first-floor level and a modillion-cornice all of stone with lead-covered box guttering simulating a blocking-course. The window-openings are uniform throughout, with stone architraves and sills, and contain double-hung sashes with thick glazing-bars. On the roof are six dormer-windows with segmental and triangular timber pediments alternating outwards from the centrepiece. The roof is hipped at each end, though a later roof adjoins on the E.

The S. side has a continuous brick plat-band at first-floor level. The two wings have coved eaves-cornices and hipped roofs. Emerging above the modern addition in the recessed centre are the upper parts of the two original re-entrant projections; these have cornices and roofs similar to those of the wings. The window-openings are plain, with double-hung sashes. Rising from the S. wall of the main range are two lofty chimney-stacks, in part rebuilt.

The W. end is partly concealed by small single-storey modern additions. The plat-band and eaves-cornice are continued from the S. side. The projecting chimney-stack is modern but links with an original stack at eaves level; the former impinges upon the stone architrave of a small casement-window on the first floor; the upper courses of the latter have been rebuilt. The E. end is entirely covered by later building.

Inside, the *Hall* is lined with bolection-moulded panelling in two heights of panels with dado-rail and cornice. The fireplace has a bolection-moulded wood surround with pulvinated frieze and cornice-shelf and an overmantel with a similarly moulded panel flanked by broad panelled pilasters under a deep panelled frieze and a return of the main cornice. The whole has been painted. The *Library* W. of the foregoing is lined with similar panelling and contains two restored fireplace-surrounds, etc., also similar to that just described but of marble and wood and without the panelled frieze. The elaborate plaster ceiling is of 1909. The room in the S.E. wing has exposed intersecting moulded oak ceiling-beams and is lined in large part with reset early 17th-century panelling, seven panels high, but in the N. wall is an early 18th-century recess with elliptical head flanked by round-headed doorways with panelled side-pilasters and moulded archivolts with scrolled keyblocks. The early 18th-century fireplace has a flat panelled surround of stone with a keyblock.

The main staircase incorporates some original turned balusters. On the first floor some of the rooms contain bolection-moulded panelling and fireplace-surrounds of *c.* 1700 in character. The room in the S.E. wing has an enriched plaster ceiling, fireplace-surround and, between the windows, a pier-glass in an elaborate rococo frame, all of the mid 18th century. In the attics are two old plank doors and one reused eight-panel door of *c.* 1600. In the cellars are some chamfered ceiling-beams and a reused 16th-century moulded beam.

(326) VICARAGE, 20 yds. S.E. of the parish church, of two storeys with cellars and attics, has walls of purple-brown brick with red brick dressings and tile-covered roofs. A faculty was granted on 21 July 1733 to the Rev. John Barwell, D.D., to rebuild the vicarage (C.A.S. *Proc.* XXXV (1935), 62). The new building was nearly square on plan with an annexe on the N. Early in the 19th century a two-storey window-bay was added on the E. In modern times the house has been increased about a third in size by a S. extension uniform in height and style with the 18th-century work; the N. annexe has been demolished and replaced by a lower addition.

The outside is plain, with a plinth and a continuous plat-band below the parapet-wall. The rectangular window-openings contain double-hung sashes. On the roof are hipped dormer-windows. To the W. the original house was of four bays with the entrance-doorway in the second from the N., but the two windows S. of the latter have since been remodelled. The semi-octagonal window-bay added on the E. is of gault brick; in each face on each floor is a window.

Inside, the Dining-room and Study are lined with original panelling in two heights with dado-rail and cornice. The fireplaces have flat moulded stone surrounds, the lintels with small quadrants springing from the side-pieces, and later enriched friezes and cornice-shelves. The Bedrooms over the foregoing contain rather similar fireplaces and the second is lined with plain original panelling with one of the doors hung on cock's-head hinges. The staircase is original, with moulded strings, turned balusters, columnar newels, a moulded handrail, and a panelled dado from ground to first floor.

(327) ANSTEY HALL FARM, house, barns, dovecote, stands close W. of the parish church. The house, of two storeys and one storey with attics, has walls of plastered timber-framing and brick and slate-covered roofs of low pitch. It is roughly half H-shaped on plan. The main N. and S. range may be of 17th-century origin but it has since been widened by reconstruction of the W. wall further out and heightened. The N.W. wing was added in the late 18th century, the S.W. wing in the late 19th century. The main E. side is of rural simplicity, of three widely-spaced bays, with a central doorway and wide sash-hung windows on the ground floor, narrower above. In the N. gable-end is a two-light window with two-centred head containing leaded quarries. Inside are cased ceiling-beams and some 18th-century doors of two fielded panels.

The large 17th or 18th-century thatched *Barn* S.W. of the house has a brick plinth to weather-boarded timber-framed walls. It is of four bays with an aisle on the W. side and returned across the S. end. The trusses have tie-beams with straight braces from the wall-posts and struts to the principals, single collar-beams, two purlins to each slope under the principals and a ridge-piece. The double-framed aisle roof has ties with struts to the principals. The threshing-floor has double doors to E. and W., the last in a transeptal bay. On the N. end is a narrower and lower extension of three bays.

The small *Barn* of *c.* 1700 standing 60 yds. S. of the house is of brick. It has been much altered and reroofed. The 17th or 18th-century *Dovecote* 50 yds. W. of the foregoing is of two storeys, square on plan, with a gault brick plinth, plastered timber-framed walls and a half-hipped roof covered with tiles. Though now without nests, it is so identified by analogy with the otherwise similar building at Long Stow (R.C.H.M., *Huntingdonshire*, 262, pl. 166).

(328) HOUSE, 37 yds. N.N.E. of the parish church, of two storeys with attics, has plastered timber-framed walls and tile-covered roofs. It is dated 1654. The plan is L-shaped, consisting of a main range with a N.W. wing. The doorways and windows were renewed in the 18th and 19th century and the whole of the framed W. side of the wing is modern. The date is on the plaster facing to the S. side of the main range and doubtless renewed. It retains two original central chimney-stacks, one in the main range flanked by a stair, the other at the junction with the wing; the former has the upper part rebuilt; the latter has four shafts set diagonally.

Inside are stop-chamfered and ovolo-moulded ceiling-beams running longitudinally and athwart the main range and exposed framing. Doors include one of mid 17th-century moulded panelling, and others of the early 18th century of two and three fielded panels. The E. *Boundary-wall* of the garden is of 17th or 18th-century red brick.

(329) THE OLD HOUSE on the S.E. side of Church Lane, 127 yds. E. by N. of the parish church, of two storeys with attics, has brick walls and tiled roofs. It was built as a rectangular range late in the 16th century, early enlarged by the addition of a N.E. wing in the following century, and restored in 1924 when an extension on the S.W. end was entirely rebuilt. During the restoration the lower part of the N.E. gabled end of the original range and the ground-floor fireplace collapsed and were rebuilt. The interior has been reconditioned.

The Old House is a good example of late 16th-century local brick building.

The outside has a restored continuous plat-band at first-floor level, plat-bands across the base of the gables and plain eaves. The gables to each end of the original range bordering the street and the paired gablets of the N.E. wing have crow-stepped parapets; those to the former are properly contrived with coped brickwork weatherings, to the latter botched. In the brickwork are several ties with wrought-iron S-shaped wall-anchors. The street-front (Plate 307) has a blocked doorway at the extreme southern end, two windows on the ground floor, the southern modern, and three on the first floor, the last with labels. The windows, except the one, are original and of three lights with moulded timber frames with simple gouged enrichment. A fascia to the wall-plate has enrichment similar to the foregoing and iron rings. The N.E. gabled end is surmounted by a rebuilt chimney-stack with square shafts rising from a rectangular base and linked by their capping; in the base is a recessed oval stone panel carved with a swag tied with a ribbon now weatherworn. The windows are similar to those to the N.W. but of two lights. The opposite end is largely masked; the stack is similar to that already described but with a square diagonal brick panel in the base. The S.E. side of the range is largely remodelled but on the roof are two old gabled dormer-windows. The N.E. wing is much patched and restored; the window-frames are old but may be reset; in the gablets are small oval windows.

Inside, are exposed longitudinal chamfered ceiling-beams supporting joists of slight scantling. At the head of the stairs from the ground to the first floor is a length of oak balustrading with shaped plank balusters and a moulded grip-handrail. The reset early 17th-century staircase from the first floor to the attics has close strings, moulded square balusters tapering to the base, a moulded grip-handrail and square newels with shaped finials. The doorways opening off the first-floor landing have original moulded timber frames; towards the rooms they had late 17th-century pedimented hoods on shaped brackets, but the pediment of one is now missing.

(330) MARIS HOUSE, on the N.E. side of Maris Lane, 150 yds. E.S.E. of the parish church, of two storeys with attics, has red brick walls and roofs mainly tiled. It is a rectangular house of *c.* 1800 with a roof in two spans; on the N. is a contemporary annexe subsequently heightened and now with a slated lean-to roof. On the N.E. is a small modern addition. The street-front is symmetrical. The doorway in the middle has a timber case with a moulded architrave with roundels at the angles and a flat hood with panelled soffit; the casement-windows to each side and the three on the first floor have segmental heads; on the roof are three gabled dormer-windows. The tall chimney-stacks rise behind the ridge, from the valley between the roofs. In the side walls are two casement-windows with two-centred heads and glazing-bars similarly curved; one is of two lights, the other of one light.

The inside has been altered but parts of an original panelled dado remain in the kitchen and an exposed chamfered ceiling-beam in the N.W. room. Off the N.W. corner of the house is a small cellar with a brick barrel vault; the upper surface of this last is now exposed.

(331) HOUSE, set back on the W. side of Trumpington Road, 273 yds. E. by N. of the parish church, is of two storeys with attics. The N. and W. brick exterior walls only are old, of the 17th century. The N. wall retains a three-light window on the first floor with ovolo-moulded timber frame and mullions, probably reset. In the W. wall is a boldly projecting chimney-stack weathered back just above a plat-band at first-floor level and with two original diagonal shafts.

(332) MANOR FARM, on the E. side of Trumpington Road, 20 yds. N. of the Village Hall, of two storeys with cellars and attics, has red brick walls and tiled roofs. It was built early in the 17th century and probably consisted of a hall and inner room on the ground floor. In the 18th century a new staircase and attics were inserted and the whole refronted in brick. A 19th-century single-storey extension to the E. contains the kitchen. A wing projecting from the N. side has been demolished; against the N. wall is now a 19th-century passage with a small modern addition at the W. end. The outside is plain, the only features in any way unusual are the staircase-windows in the S. wall placed midway between the storeys and the pitched brickwork to the parapet of the W. gable. Inside are early 17th-century stop-chamfered ceiling-beams of elm and pine. The staircase has plain strings, slender turned

balusters and newels and a moulded handrail. In the roof a tie-beam is cut through for a doorway, another is breast high; the studs of a partition are exposed.

(333) HOUSE, on the E. side of the road, 20 yds. N. of the foregoing, of two storeys, has plastered timber-framed walls and tiled roofs. It was built in the early 17th century, with a central chimney-stack flanked by an entrance lobby giving access to a hall and parlour and by a stair, since removed. At the back, on the S., is a later addition with a lean-to roof. The plinth wall has been faced or rebuilt in gault brick; the framing above is exposed on the S. where it has a sill and studs 1½ ft. apart. Rafters, plates and purlins are exposed in the W. gable-end. The window-openings contain sliding and hinged casements. The chimney-stack dividing the rooms, originally two on each floor, rises at the ridge in a large square shaft of red brick.

Inside are longitudinal chamfered ceiling-beams. The open fireplace facing N. has a chamfered timber bressummer. One stair is in the S.W. corner, a second in the S.E. corner; both are later insertions, presumably of the time when the house was divided into two tenements. Much of the timber-framing of the walls, including the N.W. corner-post, is exposed. On the first floor is an 18th-century pine plank partition dividing the E. room into two.

(334) HOUSE, the Old Police Cottage, now two tenements, on the W. side of Trumpington Road, 50 yds. N. of the entrance to Trumpington Hall, of two storeys with cellars, has brick walls and thatched roofs. It comprises a main range with a projecting staircase-bay on the S.W.; the N. part, consisting of two rooms with a central chimney-stack, is of the 17th century, extended S. and the whole reroofed early in the 18th century. On the W., bringing the plan out to the rectangle, is a modern single-storey addition containing kitchens for the two tenements. A continuous plat-band at first-floor level returns upward in label-like form over the original doorways and three ground-floor windows in the E. front; a fourth window has been blocked and a 19th-century doorway broken through beside it. Three ground-floor windows have segmental heads, those above square heads, and all contain early casements. On one of the bricks of the chimney-stack at the ridge are scratched the initials T (or I) P said to be for a Pemberton.

Inside, the cellar-stair has solid oak treads and turned balusters. To the fireplace in the N. ground-floor room is a bolection-moulded clunch surround. The S. room has an early 19th-century moulded fireplace-surround with roundels at the angles. Chamfered and stop-chamfered ceiling-beams and square joists are exposed throughout most of the ground floor. The staircase has original square newels, plain and waved plank balusters and a later handrail. The partitions of the S. bedroom are of exposed timber framing. The numerous plank doors are original.

(335) HOUSE, now two tenements, on the W. side of the road, 27 yds. N. of the foregoing, of one storey with attics, has brick walls and thatched roofs. It was built *c.* 1700 and consisted of a range of three rooms with fireplaces at each end. The middle room was smaller than the others and perhaps once a dairy with an entrance passage to one side, but any partition has been removed and a party-wall built across the middle of the house. The division into two tenements was made probably in the late 18th century when sculleries were added on each end of the range. The outside has a plat-band at first-floor level; the windows are of two and three lights with timber frames and leaded quarries. The gabled dormer-windows rise flush with the main wall-face and their casements retain original wrought-iron fittings. One of the W. doorways retains an original moulded plank door.

Inside are longitudinal chamfered ceiling-beams and the framing of some of the partitions is exposed. In a bedroom a partition is seen to consist of studding between the tie-beam and collar of a roof-truss.

(336) 'GREEN MAN', inn, on the E. side of Trumpington Road, 47 yds. S. of Alpha Terrace, of one storey with attics and two storeys, has walls of timber-framing and brick and tile-covered roofs. It was built in the 15th century with a ground-floor hall open to the roof in the middle and a cross-wing at each end. In the following century a floor was inserted in the hall and the S. wing was extended eastward; the N. wall of the extension has been rebuilt since and a further extension made in modern times. A large bay-window was added on the road side of the hall and a small annexe on the S.W. corner of the house in the early 19th century. The inn was modernised and most of the mediaeval work concealed in 1954.

The 'Green Man' is a late mediaeval house of much interest, but the structural timberwork inside is no longer visible.

Towards the road (Plate 304) the eaves of the original hall are low and the great expanse of roof is broken by an inserted hipped dormer-window. The original doorway to the screens-passage was remodelled early in the 19th century and has a timber doorcase of this period with side-pilasters and entablature; filling most of the wall northward is an inserted bay-window. In the opposite wall of the hall some of the original framing shows outside but the screens doorway and the window beside it are renewed.

The N. cross-wing projects only slightly to the W. and is flush with the hall wall on the E. It is gabled to E. and W.; in the W. gable-end is a modern pargeted panel; the E. gable-wall is underpinned in brickwork, which is returned across the N. wall. The chimney-stack projecting from this last is of 18th-century bricks in the lower part, modern above. The windows and doorways are renewed or later insertions. The original S. cross-wing is similar in form and general appearance to the foregoing, also with later brick underpinning, but the E. wall and the S.W. angle are concealed by the later additions. The form of the S. slope of the roof has been modified but the earlier rafters remain.

The E. wing has a large projecting chimney-stack on the S. with a weathered offset at first-floor level and a moulded brick base to an original diagonal shaft.

Inside, are central longitudinal beams from end to end of the ground floor. The upper floor has been modernised but in 1948 the original roofs were seen largely to survive. The hall roof consisted of tie-beam trusses with collar-beams and a collar-purlin; the purlin extended further N. and S. to be supported on braced king-posts integral with the tie and collar-beam roofs of the cross-wings, themselves with collar-purlins.

(337) 'Coach and Horses', inn, on the W. side of the road, N.W. of the foregoing, of two storeys with cellars and attics, has walls of plastered timber-framing and brick and tile-covered roofs. The N. part of the main range was built early in the 17th century; soon afterwards it was enlarged by the addition of a small gabled wing on the W. and a long S. extension. In the 18th century a square staircase-bay was added in the re-entrant angle; then single-storey annexes were built round the wing, involving the removal of the lower walling, and against the stair and the whole reroofed, and last, in the early 19th century, a large extension was made to the N.E. The walls have since been extensively faced and underbuilt in gault brick. The road-front is largely of the 19th century and modern but retains an early 18th-century timber dentil-cornice at the eaves supported on reused 17th-century curved brackets. The large chimney-stack of red brick in the back wall of the S. extension has a plinth, pronounced weatherings and a 19th-century heightening. In the doorway into the single-storey annexe to the W. wing is a reset early 17th-century panelled door with strap-hinges. The windows have for the most part been renewed.

Inside, the N. room in the main range has a large blocked fireplace in the back wall, exposed wall-plates and a longitudinal chamfered ceiling-beam. The middle room has the E. and S. walls lined with mid 17th-century panelling, four panels high, with a frieze of guilloche ornament; on the W. wall is some early 17th-century panelling carved with arabesques. The S. room is lined with 17th-century panelling, four panels high, with a plain frieze, and the overmantel comprises four enriched panels flanked by Doric pilasters. Both the latter rooms have 18th-century stone fireplace-surrounds and exposed longitudinal ceiling-beams. The staircase-bay has the timber-framing exposed inside; the stairs turn round a central newel and on the top landing are slender turned balusters. Much of the timber-framing, with chamfered wall-plates, is exposed in the bedrooms. The S. bedroom contains 17th-century panelling with a fluted frieze. Many of the rooms retain minor 18th-century fittings.

(338) Clay Farm, S. of Long Road, ⅝ m. N.E. of the parish church, comprises four buildings ranged round a square yard N.W. of the farmhouse. The arrangement and some of the buildings are of the 17th or 18th century; of the latter the following are more noteworthy:

(a) *Barn*, on the N., with walls of weatherboarded timber-framing on a brick plinth and thatched roofs, is aisled and of five bays, the middle bay containing the threshing-floor. The freestanding posts have enlarged heads supporting braced tie-beams with struts to the purlins and raking struts to the principals; at regular intervals are lower and upper collars to the common rafters, the upper collars clasping purlins immediately below the ridge.

(b) *Barn*, on the W., with walls of cob faced with tar on a brick plinth and thatched roofs, is of three bays.

(c) *Granary*, on the E., of two storeys with walls of cob, partly rebuilt in brick, and tile-covered hipped roofs, is square on plan. The bins on the upper floor may be original.

EARTHWORKS, MEDIAEVAL AND LATER

(339) Moat, remains of, in Chesterton, N. of Scotland Road, at the centre of the circle described by Eastfield (O.S. 25 ins. XL 15; N.G. 465603), is on flat ground approx. 27 ft. above O.D. It was square on plan, enclosing an island 37 yds. wide and level with the ground outside. The ditch survives along the S.E. side; it is dry, 24 ft. wide and 3 ft. deep. The cutting elsewhere is filled in but faint traces of the scarp of the island are discernible. Condition, poor.

(340) 'Mount Ararat', raised enclosure, in Chesterton, on the N. side of Water Street, 250 yds. W.S.W. of the level-crossing (O.S. 25 ins. XL 15; N.G. 472602), stands on flattish ground under 20 ft. above O.D. It is an irregular rhomboid in shape covering approx. 1 acre, raised from 1 ft. to 3½ ft. above the surrounding ground, scarped on the W., N. and E. sides, and with a low bank on the S. This last has a deep drain outside continuing E. some 40 yds. beyond the enclosure before turning N. at the field angle; from the angle a causeway 1½ ft. high leads back into the S.E. corner of the enclosure. The ditch continues N. and may have turned W. to form a N. boundary where is an apparently modern drainage channel. The enclosure is only some 60 yds. from the river and may have provided a cattle-fold in time of flood. Condition, much disturbed, with gravel pit on the N.

(341) Worts' Causeway, remains of raised roadway leading from Cambridge to the Gog Magog Hills S.E. of the city by way of Red Cross. It coincides in part with a more ancient way (see Roman Roads, Monument (10c)).

William Worts, dying in 1709, left £1,500 for building a causeway from Emmanuel College to the Gog Magogs and an annual sum for upkeep (C. H. Cooper, *Annals of Cambridge* IV, 86). The convenience of the causeway is referred to in *Cantabrigia Depicta* (1763) 'gentlemen ride out [the 4 miles to the Hills] clean in the depths of winter'.

The Causeway is visible leading E. by S. from the Hills Road at Red Cross for nearly 1½ m., in part along the city boundary; it then passes out of the city and continues as an unnamed country road in Fulbourn parish. The embankment is about 17 ft. wide and stands 2 ft. to 3 ft. high.

See also:—

CAMBRIDGE CASTLE, Monument (77);

KING'S DITCH, Monument (78);

MAIDS' or BARNWELL Causeway, p. 366.

CLARE COLLEGE. Main Gate.

MOULDINGS IN CAMBRIDGE CITY

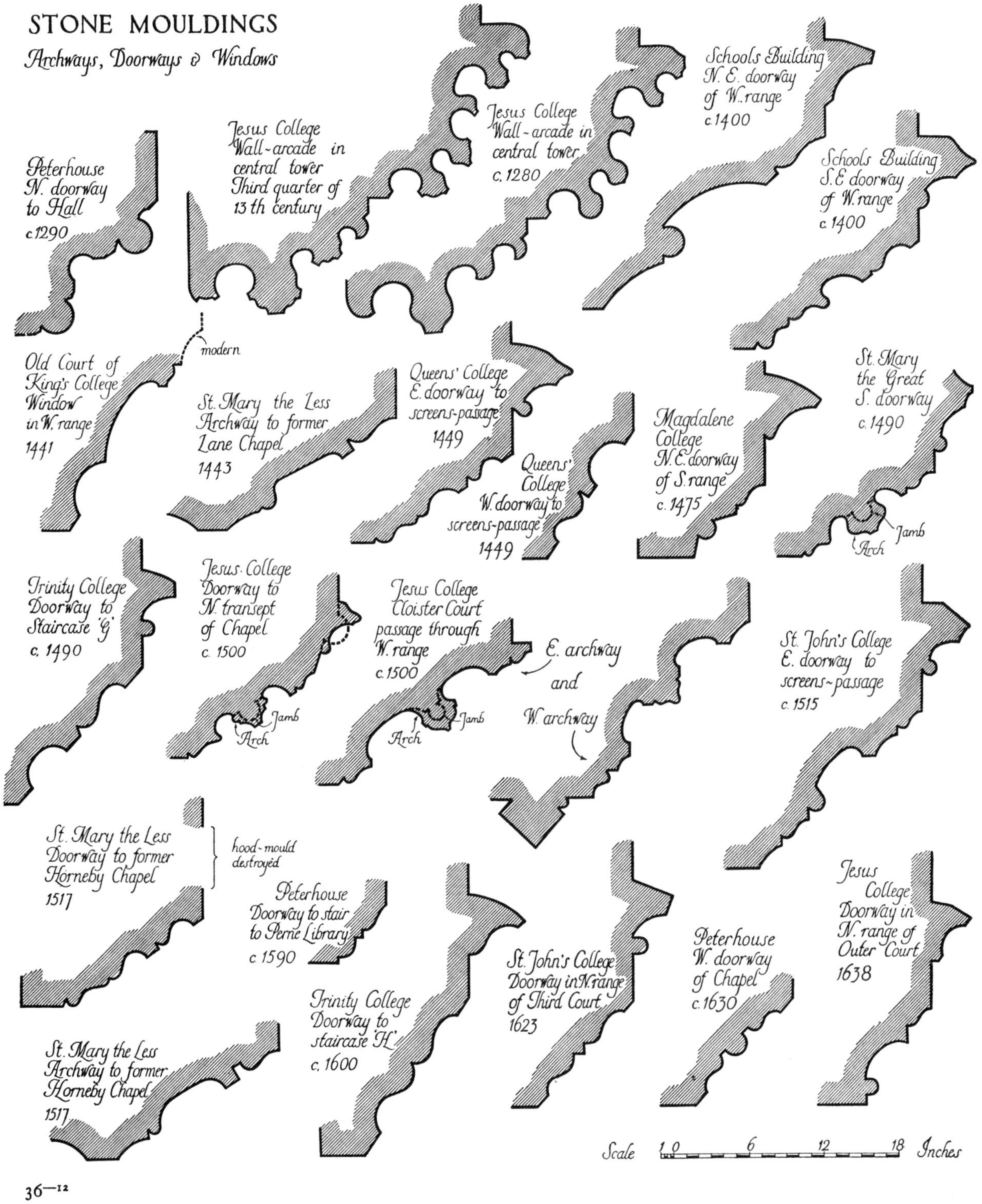
STONE MOULDINGS
Archways, Doorways & Windows
Peterhouse N. doorway to Hall c.1290
Jesus College Wall-arcade in central tower Third quarter of 13 th century
Jesus College Wall-arcade in central tower c.1280
Schools Building N. E. doorway of W. range c.1400
Schools Building S.E doorway of W. range c.1400
modern
Old Court of King's College Window in W. range 1441
St. Mary the Less Archway to former Lane Chapel 1443
Queens' College E. doorway to screens-passage 1449
Queens' College W. doorway to screens-passage 1449
Magdalene College N.E. doorway of S. range c.1475
St. Mary the Great S. doorway c.1490
Jamb
Arch
Trinity College Doorway to Staircase 'G' c.1490
Jesus College Doorway to N. transept of Chapel c.1500
Jamb
Arch
Jesus College Cloister Court passage through W. range c.1500
Jamb
Arch
E. archway and W. archway
St. John's College E. doorway to screens-passage c.1515
St. Mary the Less Doorway to former Horneby Chapel 1517
hood-mould destroyed
Peterhouse Doorway to stair to Perne Library c.1590
St. John's College Doorway in N. range of Third Court 1623
Peterhouse W. doorway of Chapel c.1630
Jesus College Doorway in N. range of Outer Court 1638
Trinity College Doorway to staircase 'H' c.1600
St. Mary the Less Archway to former Horneby Chapel 1517
Scale 1 0 6 12 18 Inches

COLLEGE GATEWAYS

ARCH - MOULDINGS

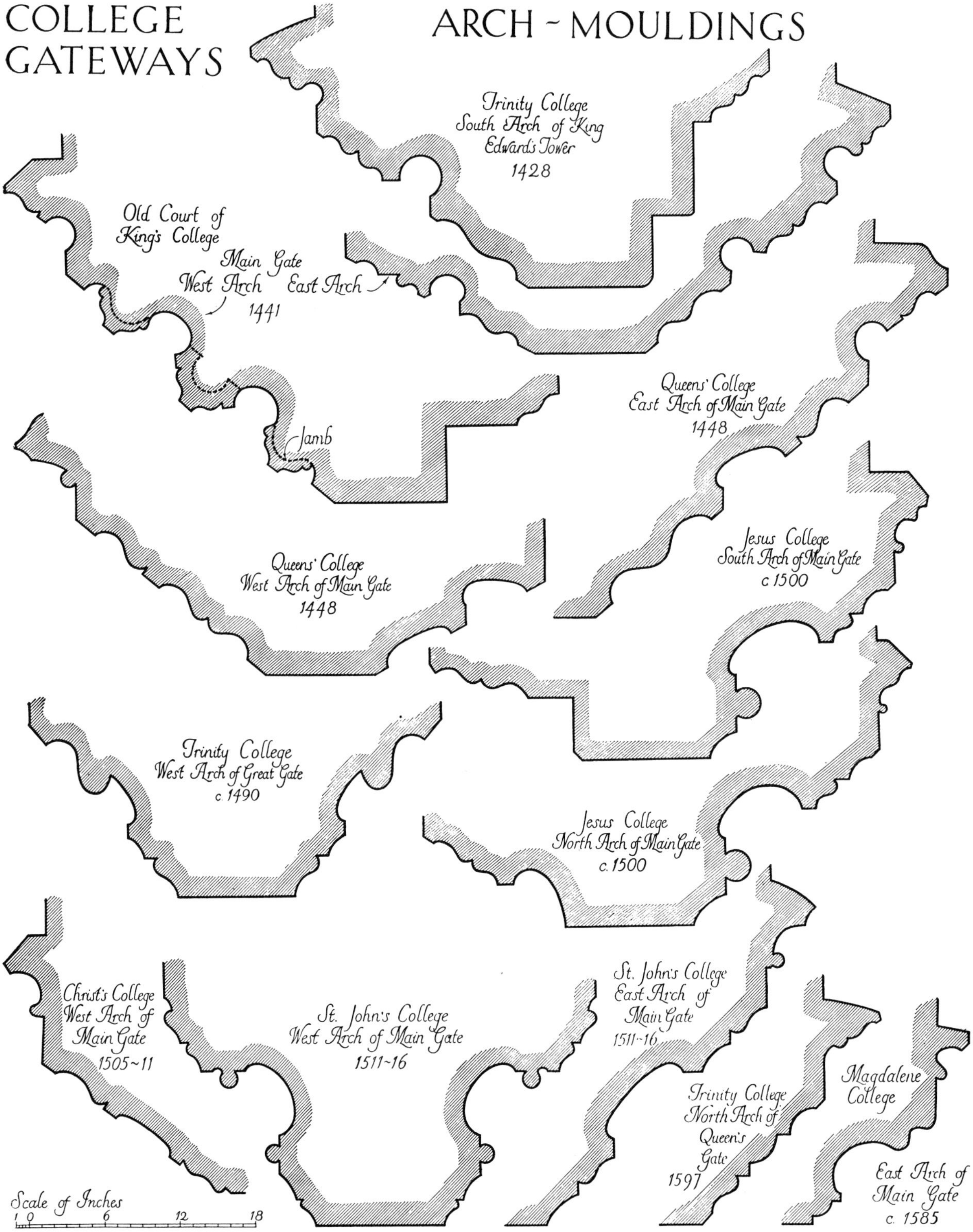
Trinity College
South Arch of King
Edward's Tower
1428
Old Court of
King's College
Main Gate
West Arch
East Arch
1441
Jamb
Queens' College
East Arch of Main Gate
1448
Queens' College
West Arch of Main Gate
1448
Jesus College
South Arch of Main Gate
c. 1500
Trinity College
West Arch of Great Gate
c. 1490
Jesus College
North Arch of Main Gate
c. 1500
Christ's College
West Arch of
Main Gate
1505~11
St. John's College
West Arch of Main Gate
1511~16
St. John's College
East Arch of
Main Gate
1511~16
Trinity College
North Arch of
Queen's
Gate
1597
Magdalene
College
East Arch of
Main Gate
c. 1585
Scale of Inches
1 0
6
12
18

STONE MOULDINGS

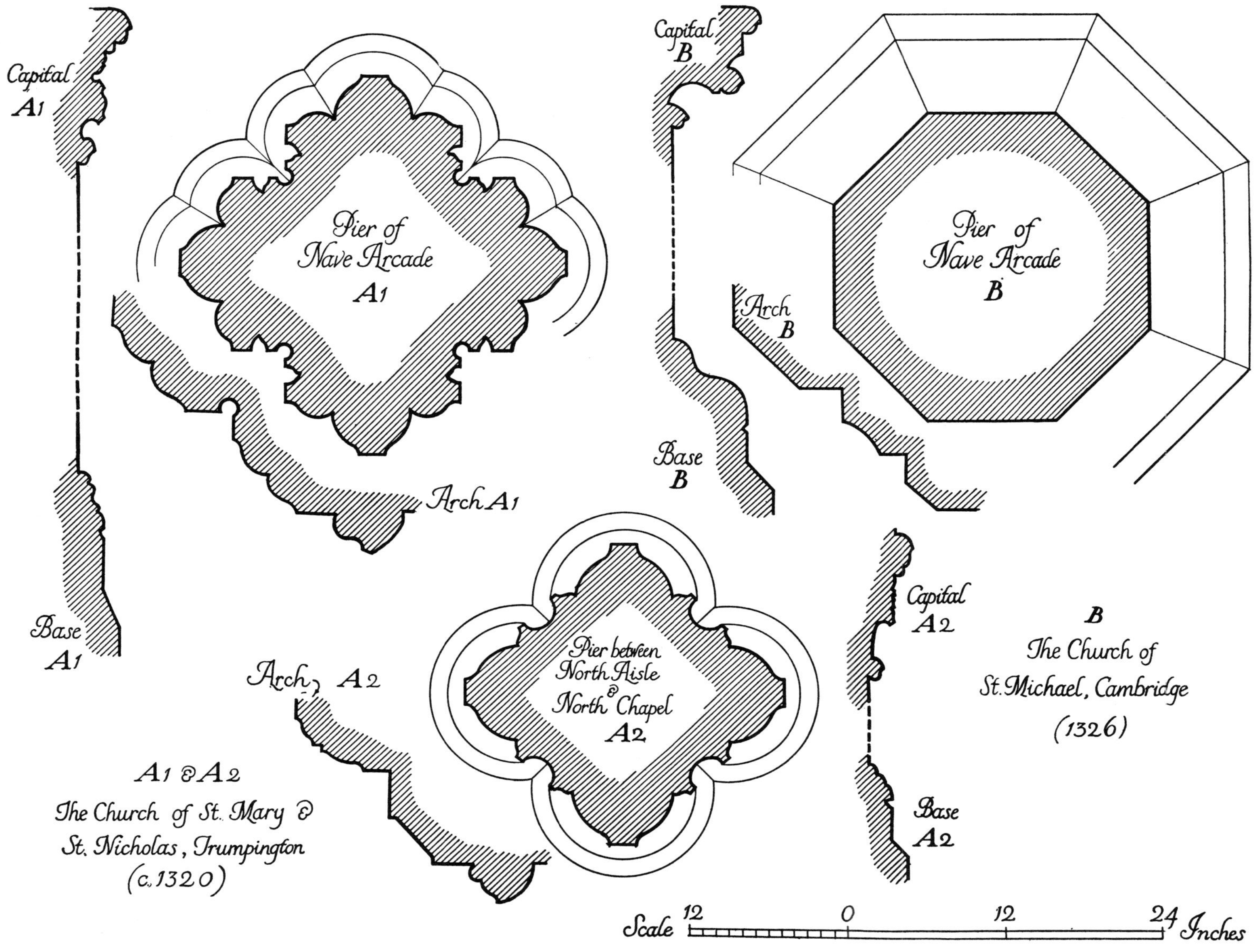
Capital A1
Base A1
Pier of Nave Arcade A1
Arch A1
Arch A2
A1 & A2
The Church of St. Mary & St. Nicholas, Trumpington (c.1320)
Capital B
Base B
Arch B
Pier of Nave Arcade B
Pier between North Aisle & North Chapel A2
Capital A2
Base A2
B
The Church of St. Michael, Cambridge (1326)
Scale 12 0 12 24 Inches

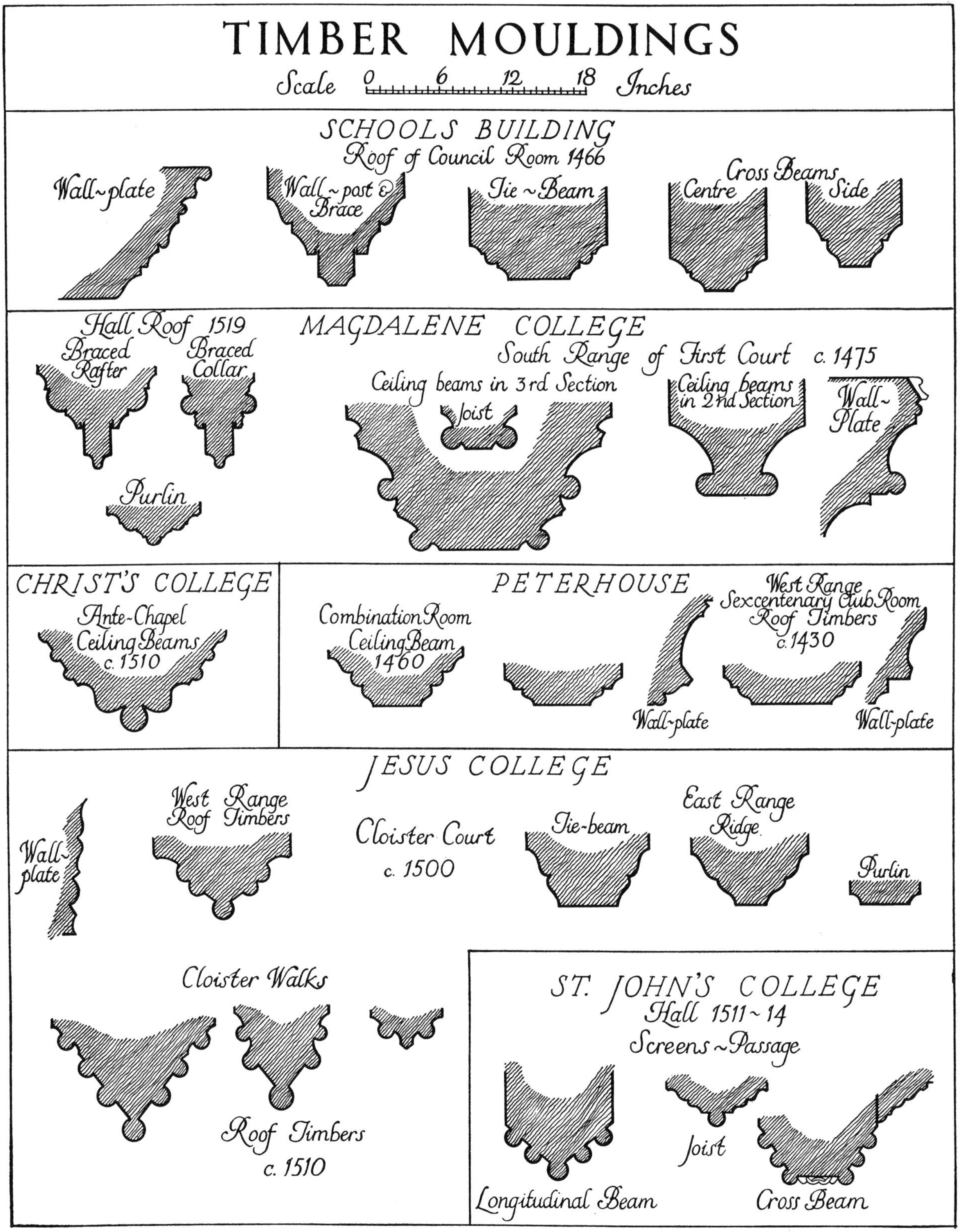
TIMBER MOULDINGS
Scale 0 6 12 18 Inches
SCHOOLS BUILDING
Roof of Council Room 1466
Wall~plate
Wall~post & Brace
Tie~Beam
Cross Beams
Centre
Side
Hall Roof 1519
Braced Rafter
Braced Collar
Purlin
MAGDALENE COLLEGE
South Range of First Court c. 1475
Ceiling beams in 3rd Section
Joist
Ceiling beams in 2nd Section
Wall~Plate
CHRIST'S COLLEGE
Ante~Chapel Ceiling Beams c. 1510
PETERHOUSE
Combination Room Ceiling Beam 1460
West Range Sexcentenary Club Room Roof Timbers c. 1430
Wall~plate
Wall-plate
JESUS COLLEGE
Wall~plate
West Range Roof Timbers
Cloister Court c. 1500
Tie-beam
East Range Ridge
Purlin
Cloister Walks
Roof Timbers c. 1510
ST. JOHN'S COLLEGE
Hall 1511~14
Screens~Passage
Longitudinal Beam
Joist
Cross Beam

ARMORIAL INDEX

OF ROYAL, CIVIC AND ACADEMIC, AND OTHER HERALDRY BEFORE 1850

The blazons given are those that appear on the monuments surveyed. They are not necessarily the generally accepted blazon. Where a coat-of-arms occurs several times and in varying forms the commonest form is blazoned, and the variants are indicated by enclosing their page references in brackets. Where variants are equally common the one in the form generally accepted by Heralds is blazoned and the others have their page references in brackets. Where variants are equally common and no one is the more generally accepted the variations are indicated in the blazon.

The suffixes 'a' and 'b' in the index signify respectively the first and second column of the page.

ROYAL ARMS

ENGLAND. (*Gules, three lions passant gardant or*).
EDWARD II (impaling Old France). 222b.
EDWARD III. 222b.
SOVEREIGN NOT IDENTIFIED. 222b.

BROTHERTON, Thomas of, Earl of Norfolk. England *with a label argent*. 129a, 133b, 143a, 146b, 198a, 226b, 227a.
CROUCHBACK, Edmund, Earl of Lancaster. *Sable, a tricorporated lion or*. 52b, (296b).
HOLLAND, Earls of Kent. England *with a border argent*. (171b), 177a, 226b.
LANCASTER, Henry, 1st Duke of. England *with a label of* France. 53a.

ENGLAND AND FRANCE. 1340 – *c*. 1405. (*Azure flory or*, for Old France, quartering England).
EDWARD III. 216b, (222b).
RICHARD II. 97a.

CLARENCE, Lionel, Duke of. Old France quartering England, *with a label argent charged on each point with a canton gules*. 216b.
GAUNT, John of, Duke of Lancaster. Old France quartering England, *with a label ermine*. 68b, 216b.
WALES, Edward, Prince of. Old France quartering England, *with a label argent*. 216b.
WOODSTOCK, Thomas of, Duke of Gloucester. Old France quartering England, *with a border argent*. 69a, 142b, 146b, 175b, 216b, (226b).
YORK, Edmund, Duke of. Old France quartering England, *with a label argent charged on each point with three roundels gules*. 216b.

ENGLAND AND FRANCE. *c*. 1405–1603. (*Azure, three fleurs-de-lys or*, for France Modern, quartering England).
HENRY VI. Supporters: *two antelopes; a lion and an antelope*. 130b, 133b, 171b, 177a.
EDWARD IV. 177a.
HENRY VII. Supporters: *a dragon and a greyhound*. 85a, 130b, 227a, 280a.
HENRY VIII. Supporters: *a dragon and a greyhound; a lion and a dragon*. 129a, 130b, 230b.
MARY. Supporters: *a lion and a crowned eagle*. 130b.
TUDOR (Sovereign not identified). 106b, 109a, 109b, 113b, 116b, 118a–124a, 125b, 126b, 129a, 129b, 130a, 131b, 132b, 133a, 141b, 230b, 231a, 233a, 243a.
DYNASTY NOT IDENTIFIED. 14b, 106b, (125b), 141a, 216b, 230a, 268a.
BEAUFORT, Margaret, Countess of Richmond and Derby. France Modern quartering England, *with a border gobony argent and azure*. Crest: *a demi-eagle in a coronet*. Motto: *Souvent me Souvient*. Supporters: *two yales*. 27a, 33a, 189a, 192b, 193a, 193b, 194a, 194b, 198a, 198b, 200a, 200b.
CLARENCE, George, Duke of. France Modern quartering England, *with a label argent*. 141b, 226b.

STUART. 1603–1707. (Quarterly: 1 and 4, France Modern quartering England; 2, *Or, a lion within a double tressure flory and counterflory gules*, for Scotland; 3, *Azure, a harp or stringed argent*, for Ireland. Supporters: *a lion and a unicorn*).
JAMES I. 160b, 189b, 217a.
CHARLES I. 130b, 311a.
CHARLES II. 14b, 127b.
JAMES II. 294a.
WILLIAM and MARY. Stuart Royal Arms, *over all on a scutcheon azure billetty or a lion or*, for Nassau. 151b, 240a.
ANNE, before the Union with Scotland. Motto: *Semper Eadem*. 226a, 240a.
SOVEREIGN NOT IDENTIFIED. 51b, 78a, 94a, 129a, 193b, 242b, 254b, 285a.
FITZROY. Stuart Royal Arms, *over all a couped baton sinister gobony azure and argent*. 227b, 228a.

STUART. 1707–14. (Quarterly: 1 and 4, England impaling Scotland; 2, France Modern; 3, Ireland).
ANNE, after the Union with Scotland. Motto: *Semper Eadem*. 142b, 310b.

HANOVERIAN. 1714–1800. (Quarterly: 1, England impaling Scotland; 2, France Modern; 3, Ireland; 4, Per pale and per cheveron: i, *Gules, two lions passant gardant in pale or;* ii, *Or semy of hearts gules, a lion azure;* iii, *Gules, a horse courant argent,* for Hanover. Supporters: as Stuart).
GEORGE I. 24a, 149a, 310b.
SOVEREIGN NOT IDENTIFIED. 11a, 283b, 309a.

HANOVERIAN. 1800–37. (Quarterly *with a scutcheon of Hanover ensigned with an Electoral hat over all:* 1 and 4, England; 2, Scotland; 3, Ireland. After 1814 the Electoral hat replaced by the Hanoverian crown).
SOVEREIGN NOT IDENTIFIED (after 1814). 52a, 260b, 269b.

GLOUCESTER, William Frederick, Duke of. Hanoverian Royal Arms of 1814–37, *with a label of five points argent, on the middle point a fleur-de-lys azure, on the others a cross gules.* 228a.
SUSSEX, Augustus Frederick, Duke of. Hanoverian Royal Arms of 1814–37, *with a label argent, on the middle point an ermine spot, on the others a cross gules.* 227b.

VICTORIAN. 1837–50. (As Hanoverian 1800–37 without the scutcheon etc., of Hanover).
VICTORIA. 257b, 261b, 311a.

CAMBRIDGE CIVIC AND ACADEMIC ARMS

CAMBRIDGE, City of. *Gules, a bridge in fesse with three turrets, in chief a fleur-de-lys or between two roses argent, in base on water barry wavy argent and azure three ships sable.* 282b, 310a, 310b, 311a, 311b.
CAMBRIDGE, University of. *Gules, on a cross ermine between four lions passant gardant or a book gules garnished and clasped or.* 11a, 18b, 21a, 35b, 36a, 116b, 130b, 178a, 282b, 309a, 311a, 312a.
CAMBRIDGE, University of, Regius Professor of Divinity. *Gules, on a cross ermine between four doves argent a book gules garnished and clasped or and charged with the letter θ.* (127b), 193b.
CAMBRIDGE, University of, Regius Professor of Law. *A cross moline, on a chief a lion passant gardant charged on the flank with a capital letter L.* 252b.
CAMBRIDGE, University of, Regius Professor of Medicine. *A fesse ermine between three lozenges, on a chief a lion passant gardant charged on the flank with a capital letter M.* 278b.
CHRIST'S COLLEGE. France Modern quartering England, *with a border gobony argent and azure* (for Margaret Beaufort). 35b, 37a, 261a, 312a.
CLARE COLLEGE. *Or, three cheverons gules* (for Clare) impaling *Or, a cross gules* (for De Burgh), *all within a border sable gutty or.* 40b, 42a, 42b, 48a, 273b, 312a.
CORPUS CHRISTI COLLEGE. *Gules, a pelican in piety argent* quartering *Azure, three fleurs-de-lys argent.* 49b, 50b, 51a, 51b, 52a, 52b, 53a, 312a.
DOWNING COLLEGE. *Barry of eight argent and vert, a griffin segreant or within a border azure charged with eight roses argent.* 59a, 59b, 61b.
EMMANUEL COLLEGE. *Argent, a lion azure holding in the dexter paw a wreath of laurel vert.* 63b, 68a, 71a, 261a.
GONVILLE AND CAIUS COLLEGE. *Argent, on a cheveron cotised indented sable three escallops or* (for Gonville) impaling *Or semy of flowers gentle, two serpents erect with their tails tied together and resting upon a square slab of green marble all proper, between their breasts a book garnished gules and studded or, in centre chief resting upon their heads a sengrene proper* (for Caius). 74b, 312a.
JESUS COLLEGE. *Argent, a fesse between three cocks' heads erased sable combed and wattled gules within a border gules semy of crowns or.* 95b, 98a, 312a.
KING'S COLLEGE. *Sable, three roses argent, barbed vert, seeded or, on a chief per pale azure and gules a fleur-de-lys or dexter and a lion passant gardant or sinister.* 125b, 126b, 127a, 127b, 128a, 129b, 130b, 131b, 132a, 132b, 133a, 133b, 136b, 311b.
MAGDALENE COLLEGE. *Quarterly per pale indented or and azure, with an eagle displayed or in 2 and 3, and over all on a bend azure a fret between two martlets or.* 142b, 312a.
PEMBROKE COLLEGE. *Barry argent and azure, an orle of martlets gules* (for Valence) dimidiating *Gules, three pales vair and on a chief or a label of five points azure* (for St. Pol). 149a, 149b, 151b, 152b, 153b, 311b.
PETERHOUSE. *Or, three pales gules within a border gules semy of crowns or.* 157b, 158b, 159b, 163a, 164a, 166a, 282b, 311b.
PETERHOUSE, First Arms. Ely, See of. 166a.
PETERHOUSE, Second Arms. *The crossed keys of St. Peter.* 166a, 289b.
QUEENS' COLLEGE. Quarterly of six: 1, Hungary; 2, Naples; 3, Jerusalem; 4, Anjou; 5, Bar; 6, Lorraine, (for Margaret of Anjou). 171b, 172a, 172b, 175a, 177a, 178a, 312a.
QUEENS' COLLEGE, Third Arms. *Sable, a processional cross and crozier in saltire or and over all a boar's head argent.* 173a.
REGIUS PROFESSORS. See CAMBRIDGE, University of.
ST. CATHARINE'S COLLEGE. *Gules, a Catharine wheel or.* 181a, 182b, 183a, 183b, 186a, 311b.
ST. JOHN'S COLLEGE. France Modern quartering England, *with a border gobony argent and azure* (for Margaret Beaufort). 195a, 196b, 198b, 199b, 201a, 202b, 312a.
SIDNEY SUSSEX COLLEGE. *Argent, a bend engrailed azure* impaling *Or, a pheon azure* (for Frances Sidney, Countess of Sussex). 207a, 208b.
TRINITY COLLEGE. *Argent, a cheveron between three roses gules, on a chief gules a lion passant gardant between two books or.* 222b, 224b, 226a, 231a, 231b, 233a, 242b, 243a, 244a, 277b.
TRINITY HALL. *Sable, a crescent within a border ermine.* 248a, 248b, 249b, 250b, 251a, 251b, 253a, 253b, 254b, 310a, 311b.

GENERAL ARMORIAL

ABARROW. *Sable, two swords saltireways between four fleurs-de-lys or.* 76a.
ADDENBROOKE. *A fesse wavy between three crescents.* 181b.
ADDISON. *Ermine, on a bend gules three annulets or, on a chief azure three leopards' faces or.* 52b.
AINSLIE. *Or, a cross flory in a border gules.* Crest: *a wyvern's head.* 18b.
ALBANY. *Gules, a lion or.* 226b, 227a, (227b), 231b.
ALCOCK. *Argent, on a fesse between three cocks' heads erased sable combed and wattled gules a mitre or.* 85a, 94a, 95a, 95b, 97a, 166b, 278a.
ALDEBURGH. *Gules, a lion argent.* 252b.
ALEYN. *Sable, a cross potent or.* Crest: *a demi-lion gules holding a scaling ladder.* 262a.
ALLEN. *Per bend sinister indented argent and sable, six martlets three and three counterchanged.* 52b.
ALLOT. *A fesse double-cotised.* 254b.
ALSTON. *Azure, ten estoiles or.* 193b.
AMPHLETT. *On a fesse between three lozenges a rose.* 283a.
ANDREW. Quarterly: 1 and 4, *Gules, a saltire or surmounted by another vert, a crescent or for difference in chief;* 2 and 3, *Ermine, two bars sable each with three fusils or.* Crest: *a blackamoor's head.* 249b.
ANGERSTON. *Argent, on a bend sable three lozenges ermine.* 257b.
ANGOULÊME. Old France *with a label gules.* 129a.
ANJOU. Old France *with a border gules.* See: ANJOU, Margaret of; QUEENS' COLLEGE.
ANJOU, Margaret of. Quarterly of six: 1, Hungary; 2, Naples; 3, Jerusalem; 4, Anjou; 5, Bar; 6, Lorraine. 171b, 177a.
ANSTEY. *Or, a cross engrailed between four birds gules.* Crest: *a bird.* Motto: *Esse quam videri.* 297a.
ARCHDEACON. *Argent, three cheverons sable.* 141b.
ARCHES. *Gules, two single arches and a double arch in base argent.* (29b), 227a.
ARDAGH, See of. *Argent, a cross gules between twenty trefoils vert.* 68a.
ARGENTEIN. *Three covered cups.* 116a.
ASCHAM. *Gules, a fesse between three dolphins argent.* 194a.
ASHE. *Argent, two cheverons sable, on the upper a martlet for difference.* 68a.
ASTLEY. *Azure, a cinquefoil ermine.* 143a, 227b.
AUDLEY. *Gules, a fret or.* 227a.
AUDLEY of Walden. *Quarterly per pale indented or and azure, with an eagle displayed or on the blue, over all on a bend azure a fret between two martlets or.* Motto: *Garde ta foy.* Supporters: *two Audley beasts chained and collared or; two lions couchant gardant.* 142b, 143a, 143b, 146b.
AVENELL. *A fesse between six annulets.* 289b.
AYLOFFE. *A lion between three crosses formy.* Crest: *a demi-lion.* 221b.
BABINGTON. *Ten roundels in pile, a label with a crescent for difference.* 220b, 240b, 244b.
BACKHOUSE. *Per saltire or and sable, a saltire ermine.* Crest: *on a torse an eagle proper.* 227b.
BACON. *Gules, on a chief argent two mullets sable.* 52b, 221b.
BACON. *A cheveron between three trefoils.* 310b.
BACON of Baconsthorpe. *Gules, a bacon pig or with a martlet sable on the shoulder.* 53a.
BADLESMERE. *Argent, a fesse double-cotised gules.* 53a, 141b.
BAINBRIG. *On a cheveron between three martlets three stags' faces.* Crest: *a stag's head full face and erased.* 221a.
BAINES. *Two shank-bones crossways.* 31a.
BAKER. *Argent, on a saltire engrailed sable five escallops argent, on a chief sable a lion passant argent.* Crest: *an arm holding an arrow.* 133b, 191b, 194a, 197a, 198a.
BALDRY. *Sable, on a cheveron engrailed or between three demi-griffins ermine three martlets gules.* 227a.
BALSHAM. *Three pales.* 289b.
BAME. *Ermine, on a chief indented sable a trefoil between two annulets argent.* 68a.
BANCROFT. *Or, on a bend between six crosses crosslet azure three garbs or.* Motto: *Volente Deo.* 226b.
BANGOR, See of. *Gules, a bend or gutty sable between two pierced mullets argent.* 133b, 177a.
BANKES. *Sable, a cross engrailed ermine between four fleurs-de-lys argent.* 51b, 52b, (228a).
BANKS. *A cross between four fleurs-de-lys.* 221b.
BANNING. *Or, on two bars sable four escallops or two and two.* 227b.
BAR, Duchy of. *Azure crusily fitchy, two barbels erect addorsed or.* See: ANJOU, Margaret of; QUEENS' COLLEGE.
BARKER. *Sable, on a cross paty or five annulets sable.* 68a.
BARKER. *Three bears' heads erased and muzzled, a chief.* 283a.
BARNACK. *Argent, a fesse azure between three horse-barnacles gules.* 226b.
BARNARD. *A bear erect.* Crest: *a demi-bear.* 262b.
BARNARDISTON. *Azure, a dance ermine between six crosses crosslet argent.* 53a.
BARNETT?. *Gules, on a sinister canton or two lions passant sable.* 68a.
BARON. *Argent, three bends sable.* 297a.
BARRINGTON. *Argent, three cheverons gules and a label azure.* 226b.
BARRINGTON. *Three cheverons, a baronet's badge in chief.* 221b.
BARROW. *Two swords in saltire between four fleurs-de-lys.* Crest: *a squirrel eating a nut.* 239a, 240b.
BARROW. *Gules, on a chief argent three lions' heads erased sable.* 227b.
BARROWE. *Two swords saltirewise, in chief the letter P.* 277b.
BARTON. *On a canton an owl.* 29b.
BASSET. *Or, three bars wavy gules.* Supporters: *two unicorns each with a shield of Basset hung from the collar.* 133b.
BASSETT. *Or, three piles gules, on a canton argent a griffin sable.* 226b.
BASSINGBOURN. *Gyronny of twelve.* 277b.
BATEMAN. *Sable, a crescent ermine within a border engrailed argent.* (77b), 81a, (126a), 248b, 251b.
BATH AND WELLS, See of. *Azure, a saltire per saltire argent and or.* 194a, 226b.
BATHURST. *Two bars and in chief three crosses formy.* 221b.

BATTIE. *Sable, a cheveron between three goats argent, on a chief or a demi-woodhouse holding a club argent between two cinquefoils gules.* Crest: *a kingfisher holding a fish in its mouth.* 133b.

BAUX. Quarterly: 1 and 4, *Gules, an estoile of sixteen points argent;* 2 and 3, Old France. See WOODVILLE, Elizabeth.

BEADON. *Sable, three mantigers ermine with faces proper between four crosses formy in pale argent.* 194a.

BEAUCHAMP of Warwick. *Gules, a fesse between six crosses crosslet or.* 52a, 52b, 53a, 141b, 226b.

BEAUCHAMP of Powyck. *Gules, a fesse between six martlets or.* 227a.

BEAUCHAMP of Hache. *Vair.* 141b, 240b.

BEAUMONT. *Flory, a lion.* Crest: *on a chapeau a lion statant.* 158b.

BEDEL. *Sable, on a fesse between three saltires argent an escallop between two mullets azure.* 68a.

BEKE. *Gules, a millrind cross argent.* 227a.

BEKENSAW. *Gules, a saltire engrailed and voided between four fleurs-de-lys or.* 175a.

BELLASIS. *Argent, a cheveron gules between three fleurs-de-lys azure.* 226b, 227a.

BELLINGHAM. *Argent, three hunting horns sable mounted or.* 89a, 227a.

BELVOIR. *Azure, a Catherine wheel or.* 52a, 53a.

BENDLOSE. *Quarterly per fesse indented gules and or, on a bend or a cinquefoil azure between two martlets argent* (sic). 52b.

BENDLOWES. *Quarterly per fesse indented gules and or, a bend or.* 198a.

BENTHAM. *Quarterly ermine and gules, four roses respectively gules and or.* 297a.

BENTLEY. *Or, three bends sable.* 193b, 221b.

BERG or MONS. *Argent, a lion with tail forked in saltire gules, crowned or.* 125b.

BERKELEY. *Gules, a cheveron between six crosses formy argent.* 52a, 53a.

BETHEL. *Argent, on a cheveron between three boars' heads couped sable an estoile or.* 133b.

BEVERIDGE. *Argent, a saltire engrailed between four escallops sable.* 193b.

BIGOD. *Per pale or and vert, a lion gules.* 175b, 226b.

BILL. *Or, a fret gules and on a canton argent five martlets sable all within a border azure.* 227b.

BILLINGHAM. *Barry argent and gules, on a canton sable a lion passant argent.* 226b, 227a.

BINGHAM. *Azure, a bend cotised between six crosses formy or.* 227b.

BLANCHMAN. *Gules, a cinquefoil ermine.* 226b.

BLAND. *On a bend three pheons.* 127b.

BLOMFIELD. *Quarterly argent and azure, a bend gules.* 227b.

BLUNDEVILLE. *Azure, three garbs or.* 209a.

BLYTH. *Ermine, three roebucks trippant gules.* 216b.

BLYTHE. *Argent, a cheveron gules between three lions sable.* 273b.

BOHUN of Hereford. *Azure, a bend argent cotised or between six lions or.* 142b, 175b.

BOHUN of Northampton. *Azure, on a bend argent cotised or between six lions or three mullets gules.* 142b, 226b.

BOLDERO. *Per pale or and azure, a saltire counterchanged.* Crest: *a couched greyhound.* 96a.

BOLEYN. *Argent, a cheveron gules between three bulls' heads couped sable.* 198a.

BOLEYN, Anne. Quarterly: 1, Lancaster; 2, Angoulême; 3, Guienne; 4, Butler quartering Rochfort; 5, Brotherton; 6, Warenne. 129a.

BOLLAND. *Gules, on a fesse ermine between three bezants three spearheads sable.* Crest: *an eagle's head erased argent, collared ermine, edged or, with a spearhead in mouth or.* 227b.

BONVILLE. *Sable, six pierced mullets argent.* 143a, 227b.

BOOTH. *Argent, three boars' heads couped and erect sable.* 171b, 175a, 227b.

BORLASE. *Ermine, on a bend two cubit arms in armour issuing out of clouds and rending a horseshoe or.* 290a.

BOSUN. *Gules, three bird-bolts argent.* 227a.

BOTETOURT. *Or, a saltire engrailed sable.* 68a.

BOTREUX. *Argent, a griffin gules.* 141b.

BOURCHIER. *Argent, a cross engrailed gules between four waterbougets sable.* 69a, 175b, 226b.

BOWSTEAD. *Vert, on a cross between four roses argent a rose vert.* 52a.

BOYLE. *Per bend embattled argent and gules.* 228a.

BOYS or COPLAND. *Argent, two bars and a canton gules, over all a bend sable.* Crest: *an old boy's head in a cap.* 68a, (262b).

BRADFORD. *Argent, on a fesse sable three stags' heads erased or.* 52b, 53a.

BRADLEY. *A cheveron checky between three ducks.* 283b.

BRADSTON. *Argent, on a canton sable a rose or.* 177a.

BRAND. *Two swords in saltire within a border engrailed.* Crest: *a leopard's head issuing from a coronet.* 362b.

BRANDON. *Gules, four bars argent, and over all a lion or crowned per pale argent and gules.* 193b.

BRANTHWAITE. *Or, a bend sable.* 76a.

BRANTHWAITE. *Argent, on a bend sable three lions passant or.* 76a.

BRANTHWAITE. *Or, two bars engrailed sable.* 77b.

BRAY. Quarterly: 1 and 4, *Argent a cheveron between three eagles' legs erased sable;* 2 and 3, *Gules, three bends vair.* 94a.

BRAY. *Argent, a cheveron between three eagles' legs sable.* 227a.

BRAY. *Vair, three bends gules.* 227a.

BREREHAUGH. *Argent, a cross potent gules between four roundels sable.* 227a.

BRERETON. *Argent, two bars sable.* 206b.

BRETON. *A bend between six mullets.* 66b.

BREWES. *Argent crusily, a lion or.* 227a.

BREWSTER. *A cheveron ermine between three estoiles argent.* 220b.

BRISTOL, Deanery of. *Azure, a saltire between three fleurs-de-lys in flanks and base and a portcullis in chief argent.* 52b.

BROCKETT. *Or, a cross paty sable.* 227a.

BROWNLOW. *Or, an escutcheon in an orle of martlets sable.* 51b, 52b, 143a, 228a.

BRUGES. *Nine pieces ermine and ermines.* 141b.

BRYANT. *Or, three piles azure meeting in base.* Crest: *a greyhound courant looking backwards.* 133b.

BUCK. *A bend between two bucks statant looking backwards ermine.* 274a.

BULBECK. *Vert, a lion.* 141b.

BULLOCK. *Gules, a cheveron ermine between three bulls' faces argent.* 127a, 274b.

BULMER. *Billetty, a lion.* 231b, 242b.

BURGH. *Argent, on a fesse indented sable three bezants.* 177a.

BURGON. *Azure, a talbot argent.* 227a.

D'OYLY. *Or, two bends azure.* 52b.
DRAKE. *A firedrake.* Crest: *a demi-firedrake.* 240b.
DRAPER. *Argent, on a fesse engrailed between three annulets gules three covered cups or.* Crest: *a stag's head gules charged with a fesse between three annulets or.* 133b.
DRAPERS' COMPANY. *Three clouds radiated in base, each surmounted by a triple crown.* 328b.
DRAYTON. *Per pale gules and azure, a lion or.* 198a.
DRYLAND. *Gules gutty, a fesse nebuly in a border argent.* 68a.
DRYLAND. *Gules, a cheveron argent between three garbs and three crosses crosslet fitchy argent.* 68a.
DUCKETT. *Sable, a saltire argent.* Crest: *a horse surmounted by a garb.* 89a, 175a, 227a.
DUFFIELD. *Sable, a cheveron between three doves argent with a label argent.* 198a.
DUNDAS. *Argent, a lion within a double tressure flory and counter-flory gules.* Crest: *on a torse argent and gules a lion's face argent crowned or looking from an oak thicket proper.* 227b.
DUNNE. *Azure, a wolf rampant and a chief argent.* 248b.
DUNSTAVILLE. *Argent, a fret gules, on a canton gules a lion passant or all in a border engrailed sable.* 133b, 198a.
DUNSTAVILLE, Reginald de. *Gules, two lions passant or and over all a bend sinister.* 133b.
DURHAM, See of. *Azure, a cross or between four lions argent.* 18b, 157b, 193b, 198a.
DYNHAM. *Gules, a fesse of fusils ermine.* 29b, 227a.
EACHARD. *Ermine, on a bend three millrinds or.* 181b.
EASTON. *Gules flory argent, a lion or.* 227a.
ECHINGTON. *Sable, three towers triple-turreted or with a roundel argent in the fesse point.* 227a.
ECHINGTON. *Argent, on a bend cotised gules three cinquefoils or.* 227a.
EDEN. *Argent, on a fesse gules between two cheverons azure each charged with three escallops argent three garbs or.* Crest: *a wingless dragon charged with a crescent and holding a rose-branch.* 221b, 248b, 249b, 253a.
EDGE. *Per fesse sable and gules, an eagle displayed argent.* 285b.
EDMUND the MARTYR, ST. *Three crowns.* 105b, 106b.
EDWARD the CONFESSOR, ST. *Azure, a cross paty between five martlets or.* 53a, 97a, 105b, 106b.
EGERTON. *Argent, a lion gules between three pheons sable.* 226b.
EGREMONT. *Argent, three bars gules.* 68a, 227b.
EKINS. *A bend of six lozenges between two crosses crosslet.* Crest: *a hand holding a cross crosslet.* 221b.
ELAND. *Barry argent and gules, six martlets or, three, two, one, on the red bars.* 227a.
ELLISTON. *Per pale gules and vert, an eagle displayed or.* 208a.
ELTISLEY. *Argent, on a bend azure three lilies argent.* 52b.
ELWES. *Or, a fesse azure and over all a bend gules.* Crest: *on a torse or and azure a sheaf of five arrows or entwined by a serpent vert.* 227a.
ELY, Deanery of. *Gules, three keys or.* 49b, 52b, 127a, 193b, 201a, 261b.
ELY, See of. *Gules, three crowns or.* 49a, 50b, 52b, 76b, 85a, 92a, 94a, 95a, 95b, 97b, 133b, 142b, 154a, 157b, 166a, 177a, 193b, 197a, 226b, 261b, 277b, 282b, 289b. See PETERHOUSE.
EMPIRE, Holy Roman. *A double eagle.* 230a.
ENGLAND. *Gules, three lions passant gardant or.* 71a, 130a, 130b, 303a. See ROYAL ARMS.
ENGLEFIELD. *Two bars and on a chief a lion passant.* 29b.
ENGLETHORPE. See INGLETHORPE.
ENGLISH. *Ermine, three lions passant sable, tongues and claws or.* 68a.
ERRINGTON. *Argent, two bars azure and in chief three escallops azure.* 226b, 227a.
ESMERTON. *Argent, on a bend cotised sable three mullets argent.* 227a.
ESPEC. *Gules, three cartwheels argent.* 52a, 53a.
ESTON. *Ermine, a cross pommy fitchy sable.* 227a.
ESTURMI or ESTURMY. *Argent, three demi-lions gules.* 141b, 240b.
ETON COLLEGE. *Sable, three lilies slipped and leaved argent, on a chief per pale azure and gules, a fleur-de-lys and a lion passant gardant or.* 116b, 125b, 129b, 130b, 132a, 132b, 133a, 133b.
EUDO. *Ermine, a crescent in chief.* (231b), 242b.
FAGG. *Two bends vair.* 274a.
FAIRMEADOW. *Gules, three trefoils sable in a border engrailed.* 262a.
FALCONER. *Sable, three falcons argent beaked and legged or, a crescent for difference or.* 227b.
FANE. *Azure, three gauntlets or.* 68a, 69a.
FARMAN?. *Paly wavy argent and azure, on a cheveron three martlets or.* 175b.
FASTOLFE. *Quarterly, on a bend three escallops.* 283a.
FELBRIGG. *Or, a lion salient gules.* 175a.
FERNE. *Per bend indented.* 233a.
FERRAR. *Or, on a bend cotised sable three horseshoes or.* 145b.
FERRERS. *Vairy or and gules.* 175b, 226b.
FIELD. *Sable, a cheveron between three garbs or.* 283a.
FIELD. Quarterly: 1 and 4, *Sable, on a cheveron between three garbs three doves rising;* 2 and 3, *Per pale, a fesse ermine between two fleurs-de-lys in chief and a snake in base.* Crest: *a hand issuing from a cloud and holding a globe.* Motto: *Probitas Verus Honos.* 208a.
FINCH. *Argent, a cheveron between three griffins passant sable.* Crest: *a griffin.* 31a, 36a, 279b.
FISHER. *On a cheveron between three demi-lions three roundels.* 181b, (201a).
FISHER. *Argent, a dolphin embowed between three ears of corn in a border engrailed or.* 177a, 192a, 193a.
FISHER. *Argent, three eel-spears sable and on a chief sable a lion passant or.* 192a, 193a.
FISHER. *Sable, two stags combatant argent, collared with coronets and chained and attired or.* 194a.
FITZHERBERT. *Gules, three lions or.* 226b.
FITZWALTER. *Or, a fesse between two cheverons gules.* 68a, 204b, 227b. See SIDNEY, Frances.
FITZWARREN. *Quarterly per fesse indented argent and gules.* 69a.
FITZWILLIAM. *Lozengy argent and gules.* Crest: *a plume of ostrich feathers.* Motto: *Deo Adjuvante non Timendum.* Supporters: *two ostriches argent each holding in the beak a horseshoe or.* 21a.
FLEETWOOD. *Per pale wavy, six martlets counterchanged, a crescent for difference in chief.* 128b.
FLETCHER. *Argent, a cross paty between four escallops.* 52b.
FLYER. *A cheveron between three arrows points downwards.* Crest: *a stag's head erased with an arrow in the mouth.* 127b.
FOSTER. *A cheveron between three buglehorns.* Crest: *a stag passant.* 303a.

FOTHERBY. *Gules, a cross of lozenges flowered at the ends or.* Motto: *Fato non Fortuna.* 227a.

FOWLER. *Ermine, on a canton gules an owl argent.* 29b, 262a.

FOXLEY. *Gules, two bars argent.* 228a.

FRANCE, Old. *Azure flory or.* 222b. See ROYAL ARMS.

FRANCE, Modern. *Azure, three fleurs-de-lys or.* 71a, 130a, 130b. See ROYAL ARMS.

FRANCIS. *Argent, a cheveron between three spreadeagles gules.* 170b, 227b.

FRAY. *Ermine, a fesse sable between three fig-frays.* 68a.

FRECHVILLE. *Sable, a bend between six escallops or.* 227b.

FREEMAN. *Azure, three lozenges argent, a crescent for difference.* 126b, 127b.

FROXMORE. *Sable, a griffin between three crosses crosslet fitchy argent.* 53a, 226b.

FULLER. *Three bars and a canton.* 221b.

FUNDIN. *Bendy azure and or.* 227a.

FURTHO. *Gules, a lion crowned or charged with a crescent argent on a crescent sable for difference.* 227a.

GACHES. *Azure, three escallops argent, on a chief gules a fleur-de-lys between two mullets or.* Crest: *an owl.* 133b.

GAELL. *On a fesse between three saltires three lions' heads erased.* Crest: *on a wreath a lion holding a saltire.* 127b.

GARBETT. *Gules, a griffin segreant holding a banner argent charged with a double-headed eagle sable.* 227a.

GARDINER. *Azure, on a cross or between four griffins' heads erased argent a rose gules.* 248b.

GATWARD. *A cheveron ermine between three storks argent.* 260a, 260b.

GEARING. *Two bars each charged with three voided lozenges, on a canton a leopard's face.* 127b.

GEORGE. *A fesse between three birds.* 127b.

GEORGE, ST. *Argent, a cross gules.* 33b, 216b, 289b.

GERARD. *A saltire.* 127b.

GERARD. *A lion.* 127b.

GERNON. *Vairy argent and gules.* 29b.

GESTINGTHORP. *Argent, a cheveron sable between three cushions sable ermined argent.* 227a.

GIBBS. *Argent, three battle-axes sable.* Crest: *a right arm in armour holding an axe.* 133b.

GILLAM. *Sable, a horse's head erased between three hands proper.* 274a.

GISBORNE. *Or ermined sable, a lion sable collared argent, on a canton vert a garb or.* 166a, 198a.

GISSING. *Argent, on a bend sinister gules three eagles.* 227a.

GLANVILLE. *Nine crosses crosslet, three crescents for difference.* 231b.

GLOUCESTER, See of. *Azure, two keys in saltire or.* 52b, 227b.

GLYN. *Argent, three saddles proper with stirrups or.* 177a.

GLYNN. *Gules, three salmon spears or.* Crest: *a demi-talbot.* 133b.

GOADE. *Gules, a cheveron or between three lions with forked tails argent.* 125b.

GODOLPHIN. *Gules, a double-headed eagle between three fleurs-de-lys argent.* 311b.

GOLDINGHAM. *Argent, a bend wavy gules.* 220b.

GONVILLE. *Argent, on a cheveron cotised indented sable three escallops or.* 81a. See GONVILLE AND CAIUS COLLEGE.

GOOCH. *Per pale argent and sable, a cheveron between three talbots counterchanged, on a chief gules three leopards' faces or, a baronet's badge in the fesse point.* 76b.

GOODALL. *Gules, an eagle displayed argent, on a canton argent a chaplet vert.* Crest: *an eagle displayed argent.* 133b.

GOODKNAPE. *Sable, a lion passant or and in chief two helms or, on a canton argent a Lombardic capital G.* 248b.

GOODYEAR. *Gules, a fesse between two cheverons vair.* 227b.

GORE. *A fesse between three crosses crosslet fitchy.* 297a.

GOSLING. *A cheveron between three crescents ermine with a mullet for difference in chief.* 266b.

GOSTLIN. *Gules, a cheveron between three crescents ermine.* 76a.

GOWER. *Azure, a cheveron between three wolves' heads erased or.* 191b, 193b, 198a.

GRAY. *Barry argent and azure, three roundels gules in chief, a label ermine.* Crest: *a unicorn argent amid sun-rays.* 227b.

GRAY of Groby. *Barry argent and azure.* 227b.

GREEN. *Gules, a lion per fesse or and sable.* 171b.

GREEN OR GREENE. *Azure, three stags tripping or.* 52b, 195a.

GREVILLE. *Sable, on a cross engrailed in a border engrailed or five roundels sable.* 227a.

GREY. *Barry of six argent and azure.* 171b, 175a.

GREY. *Barry of six argent and azure, in chief three roundels gules.* Crest: *a wyvern.* Motto: *Foy est tout.* Supporters: *two wyverns.* 143a, 206b, 209a.

GREY. *Gules, a lion in a border engrailed argent.* Crest: *on a torse argent and gules a scaling ladder or.* 227b.

GREYSTOKE. *Barry argent and azure, three chaplets gules.* 133b.

GRIFFIN. *Sable, a griffin argent.* Motto: *Ne vile velis.* Supporters: *two lions regardant argent maned sable.* 139b, 143b, 146b.

GRIFFITH. *Gules, a cheveron between three stags' faces argent attired or.* 197a, 198a.

GRIFFITH. *Gules, a cheveron ermine between three old men's heads in profile couped at the neck proper.* 274a.

GRINDALL. *Quarterly or and azure, a cross quarterly ermine and or between four doves counterchanged.* 53a.

GUIENNE. *A lion passant gardant.* Supporter: *a greyhound with a crown about its neck and a chain.* 129a.

GULICK. See JULICK.

GUNNING. *Gules, on a fesse between three doves argent three crosses formy gules.* 52b, 193b, 198a.

GUNSON. *Argent, three bars wavy sable bezanty, on a chief gules a culverin between two anchors or.* 68a.

HACKET OR HACKETT. *Argent, three piles sable, on a chief gules a lion passant or.* 198a, 221b, 240b, 242a.

HADLEY?. *Argent, a fesse and a cheveron interlaced sable.* 227a.

HALE. *A cheveron embattled and counter-embattled and in chief a mullet for difference.* Crest: *a serpent entwined around five arrows.* 166b.

HALFHYDE. *Argent, two cheverons sable the upper reversed and interlaced, on a chief azure three cinquefoils or.* 274a.

HALL. Quarterly: 1 and 4, *Argent, on a cheveron engrailed between three talbots' heads erased sable a mullet or;* 2 and 3, *Argent, two bars nebuly sable, on a chief sable three crosses trefly argent.* 227b.

HALSTED. *An eagle displayed and a chief checky.* 311a.

HAMMOND. *Or, three crescents azure, on a chief azure three ostrich feathers argent.* 227b.

HARCOURT. *Gules, two bars or.* Crest: *a demi-lion with a crown or about the neck.* 227a.

HARE. *Gules, two bars and a chief indented or.* Crest: *from a torse or and gules a demi-lion argent holding a lozenge charged with a cross gules.* 133b, 193b, 198a, 277b.
HARLOW. *Per saltire or and azure, two martlets in pale and two pierced cinquefoils in fesse all counterchanged.* 220b.
HARRINGTON. *Sable, a fret argent.* 143a, 204b, 206b, 207a, 227b.
HARRISON. *Argent, on a chief or three martlets gules.* 171b.
HART. *Sable, a cheveron argent between three fleurs-de-lys or.* Crest: *a hart's head encircled by a coronet.* 206b.
HART. *Per cheveron azure and gules, three harts tripping or.* 227a.
HARTISHORN. *Azure, a cheveron between three bulls' heads couped argent.* 227a.
HARVEY. *Or, a cheveron and in chief three leopards' faces gules.* 248b.
HARVEY. *On a bend three trefoils.* 289b.
HASTINGS. *Argent, a maunch sable.* 141b, 209a. *With a martlet gules for difference.* 68a.
HASTINGS. *Or, a maunch gules.* 143a, 227b.
HATCHER. *A cheveron between four escallops three and one.* 277a.
HATFIELD. *Ermine, on a cheveron sable three cinquefoils or.* 170b, 227b.
HATTON. *Azure, a cheveron between three garbs or.* Crest: *a hind or.* 274a.
HAWTREY. *On a bend cotised three lions passant gardant.* Crest: *a lion passant gardant.* 127b.
HAZELWALL. *Argent, a chief azure.* 228a.
HEBBLETHWAITE. *Argent, two pales azure, on a canton or a pierced mullet sable.* Crest: *out of a coronet or a wolf's head ermine.* 193b.
HENGHAM. *Azure, on a saltire argent five martlets sable.* 227a.
HERBERT. *Per pale azure and gules, three lions argent.* 141b, 193b.
HEREFORD, Deanery of. *Argent, three cheverons azure.* 52b.
HEREFORD, See of. *Gules, three leopards' heads reversed jessant de lys or.* 227b.
HERINGALD or HERRING. *Gules, three herrings haurient in fess argent.* 53a, 226b.
HERRING. *Azure crusily of crosslets, three herrings argent.* 279a.
HERRING. *Gules, three herrings between nine crosses crosslet argent.* 52b.
HERRIS. *Or, on a bend engrailed sable three cinquefoils or, in chief a mullet gules for difference.* 151b.
HETON. *Argent, on a bend sable three bulls' heads cabossed argent.* 226b.
HEWKE. *Or, on a pile gules between two trefoils vert three crescents or.* 248b.
HEYFORD. *Gules, a maunch or.* 227a.
HEYNES. *Gules, a cinquefoil in an orle of crosses crosslet or.* 175a.
HIDE. *Argent, a cheveron between three lozenges azure, on a chief gules an eagle displayed or.* 226b.
HIGGS. *Azure, a cheveron or between three roses argent barbed and seeded or.* Crest: *on a torse argent and azure a hart's head proper antlered or.* 228a.
HILDYARD. *Three mullets, in the fess point a baronet's badge.* Crest: *a cock.* 240b.
HILL. *Gules, two bars ermine and a lion argent in chief.* 53a.
HINCHLIFFE. *Or, a wyvern between three fleurs-de-lys vert.* 227b, 228a.
HINTON. *Gules, three martlets argent.* 194a.
HIPPISLEY. *Or, on a bend cotised three mullets.* 133b.
HITCH. *A bend vair cotised dancetty sable and a label argent in chief;* in pretence, *Gules, a cross paty with a roundel in dexter chief argent.* 228a.
HITCHAM. *Gules, on a chief or three roundels gules.* Crest: *a beast* (unidentifiable). 151a, 156a.
HOBART. *Sable, an estoile with seven rays or between two flaunches ermine.* Crest: *on a wreath or and sable a bull passant per pale gules and sable gutty or.* 116a, 136b.
HODGSON. *Gules, three targes argent between nine bezants.* 18b.
HODSDON. *Argent, a bend nebuly gules between two horseshoes sable.* 68a.
HOLAND. *Azure flory, a lion argent.* 52a, 53a.
HOLBECHE. *Five escallops in saltire.* 66b.
HOLBROOKE. *A cheveron between ten crosses crosslet.* 283a.
HOLLES. See CLINTON.
HOLLINGWORTH. *On a bend three holly leaves.* Crest: *a hart couched.* 283a.
HOLMES. *Three bars and on a canton a chaplet.* 290a.
HOOPER. *Gyronny of eight, a tower triple-turreted.* 244a.
HORTON. *Gules, a lion argent with a crescent or in chief, all in a border engrailed argent.* 228a.
HORTON. *Per bend sinister ermine and sable ermined argent, a lion argent.* 228a.
HOTHAM. *Barruly, on a canton a cornish chough.* 166b.
HOUGH. *Argent, three bars gules and on a canton or a martlet azure.* 227a.
HOVELL. See SMITH.
HOWARD. *Gules, a bend between six crosses crosslet fitchy argent.* Mottoes: *Non quo sed quomodo; Uni et uni voce.* 226b, 227a.
HOWARD, with Flodden Augmentation. Howard, *with an escutcheon or on the bend charged with a demi-lion with an arrow through the mouth within a double tressure flory and counter-flory gules.* 133b, 143b, 146b, (198a).
HOWARD, Queen Katherine, Marriage Augmentations. 1, *Azure, three fleurs-de-lys or between two flaunches ermine each with a rose gules;* 2, *Azure, two lions of England within a border of four demi-fleur-de-lys issuing from the flanks or.* 125b.
HOWARD DE WALDEN. Howard with Flodden Augmentation *and a crescent sable for difference.* Motto: *Non quo sed quomodo.* Supporters: *a lion proper collared argent and a lion argent.* 142b.
HUBBARD. *Sable flaunched ermine, an estoile of eight rays or.* 68a.
HULSE. *Argent, three piles sable, one from the chief between two from the base.* 194a.
HUMBURLTON. *Or, on a pale gules three eagles displayed or.* 172a.
HUMFREY. *Gules, a cross trefly or.* Crest: *a harpy.* 262a.
HUNGARY, Kingdom of. *Barry gules and argent.* See: ANJOU, Margaret of; QUEENS' COLLEGE.
HUNGERFORD. *Sable, two bars argent and in chief three roundels argent.* 141b.
HUSSEY. *Gules, two bars ermine.* 227a.
HUTCHINSON. *Per pale, a lion in an orle of crosses crosslet.* Crest: *a wyvern in a crown.* 201b, 221b.
HUTTON. *Three roundels, each charged with a bird, on a chief an eagle displayed, all within a border engrailed.* 289b.
IBBETSON. *Gules, on a bend cotised argent between two golden fleeces three escallops or* (sic). 228a.
INGLETHORPE. *Sable, a cross engrailed argent.* 177a.
INGLOSS. *Argent, a bend cotised sable.* 227a.

PENDARVES. *Argent, a falcon volant between three mullets or.* 133b.
PENNINGTON. Quarterly: 1 and 4, *Or, a fesse of five fusils azure;* 2 and 3, *Gules, two gemel-bars between three escallops argent.* 194a, 198a, 201a.
PEPYS. *Sable, on a bend or between two nags' heads erased argent three fleurs-de-lys sable.* 145b.
PERCY. *Or, a lion azure.* 18b, 193b, 198a, 201a, 260a, 312a.
PERCY, Ancient. *Azure, a fesse of five fusils or.* 18b, 198a.
PERNE. *Or, on a cheveron between three pelicans' heads erased azure a mullet or.* 17b.
PERRY. *A fesse of five lozenges.* 221b.
PERSE. *Sable, a cheveron ermine between three cockatrices' heads erased argent.* Crest: *on a torse argent and sable a pelican in piety sable.* 76a.
PETER, ST. *Two crossed keys.* 166a. See PETERHOUSE.
PETERBOROUGH, Deanery of. *Two swords in saltire points upwards between four crosses crosslet fitchy.* 242b.
PETERBOROUGH, See of. *Gules, two keys in saltire or between four crosses crosslet fitchy argent.* 193b, 194a, 201a, 227b, 228a.
PEVEREL. *Azure, three garbs argent and a chief or.* 141b.
PIERPOINT. *A lion in an orle of cinquefoils.* Crest: *on a torse a lion.* Motto: *Pie Repone te.* 221b.
PIERSE. (*? A crown between three crosses*), *a chief.* Crest: *a cross crosslet.* 266b.
PIGOTT. *Sable, three miners' picks argent.* 227a.
PIKE. *Sable, three pitchforks argent.* 218b, 297a.
PILKINGTON. *Argent, a cross trefly voided gules and on a chief vert three suns, a crescent argent in the dexter canton.* 193b.
PITCHARD. *A fesse between three escallops.* 297a.
PITT. *Sable, a fesse checky argent and azure between three bezants.* Crest: *on a torse a stork argent beaked and legged or supporting an anchor argent with beam and cable gules.* Motto: *Benigno Numine.* 227b.
PLATT. *Or fretty sable nailed argent.* 194a.
PLUMTRE. *Argent, a cheveron between two pierced mullets in chief and an annulet in base sable.* 175b.
POLE. *Per pale sable and or, a saltire engrailed counterchanged.* 141b.
POLLARD. *Argent, a cheveron sable between three escallops gules.* 193b.
PORCHER. *Barry of eight argent and gules per pale counterchanged, a cinquefoil or.* 53a.
POSSLETHWAITE. *Gules, a fesse counter-gobony or and azure between three hawks argent.* CREST: *on a torse or and gules a hawk proper with a bell and flower gules.* 228a.
POWLETT. *Sable, three swords in pile argent, hilts or, and on a canton argent a scutcheon sable charged with a salmon haurient argent.* Motto: *Aimez Loyauté.* 133b.
POWYS. *Or, a lion's paw in bend between two crosses crosslet fitchy gules.* 50b.
POYNTZ. *Barry of eight or and gules.* Crest: *a clenched fist.* 133b.
PRATT. *Sable, on a fesse between three elephants' heads erased argent three mullets sable.* Crest: *out of a coronet an elephant's head erased argent.* Motto: *Judicium Parium aut Lex Terrae.* Supporters: *a griffin sable and a lion or each with a collar argent charged with three mullets sable.* 18b, 133b, 227b.
PRESTON. Quarterly, *with a crescent for difference in the first quarter:* 1 and 4, *Two bars and on a canton a cinquefoil;* 2 and 3, *Three mullets.* 249b.
PRIOR. *Vert, a bend cotised argent.* 198a.
PRYNNE. *A fesse engrailed between three escallops.* 240b.
PUCKERING. *A bend lozengy.* Crest: *on a coronet a boar's head between two ostrich feathers.* 240b.
PURCHAS. *A lion and on a fesse over all three roundels.* 311a.
PURRY. *Argent, on a fesse between three martlets sable three mullets argent.* 220b.
PYKE. See PIKE.
QUALE. *Ermine, on a quarter vert a Latin cross argent.* 228a.
QUINCY. *Gules, seven voided lozenges three, three and one or.* 143a, 226b, 227a, 227b.
RADCLYFFE or RATCLYFFE. *Argent, a bend engrailed sable.* Supporters: *two bulls sable crowned and chained or.* 68a, 204b. See: SIDNEY SUSSEX COLLEGE; SIDNEY, Frances. *With a crescent gules for difference.* 227b.
RADCLIFFE. *Argent, two bends engrailed sable with a crescent for difference.* 227a.
RAMSEY. *Sable, on a cheveron between three rams' heads couped argent a mullet sable.* 68a.
RANT. *Ermine, on a fesse three lions.* Crest: *a lion sejant.* 283a.
RAVENSBERG. *Argent, three cheverons gules.* 125b.
REDESHAM. *Argent flory or* (sic). 227a.
REDMAN. *Gules, three cushions ermine.* 252b.
RENNELL. *Argent, on a cross moline or a roundel gules.* Crest: *a demi-wolf.* 133b.
REPPES. *Ermine, three cheverons sable.* 227a.
RICH. *Gules, a cheveron between three crosses trefly or.* 227a.
RICHARDSON. See WILLIAMS.
RICKMAN. *Three piles surmounted by three bars and over all a buck passant.* 201b.
ROBSON. *Or, on a fesse between two cheverons sable three billets argent.* Crest: *a demi-lion issuing from a mural crown checky.* 262a, 262b.
ROCHESTER, Deanery of. *Argent, on a cross gules the letter 'R' argent.* 193b.
ROCHESTER, See of. *Argent, on a saltire gules an escallop or.* 52b, 53a, 177a, 192a, 193b, 201a.
ROCHFORD. *Or, a chief indented azure.* 198a.
ROCHFORT. *A lion crowned.* 129a.
RODE. *A lion or.* 227b.
RODERICK. *Or, a lion passant gardant gules.* 127a, 274b.
ROLFE. *Or, three ravens.* 171b.
ROOS. *Gules, three bougets argent.* 52a, 53a, (172a), (177a).
ROTHERAM or ROTHERHAM. *Vert, three bucks* (sometimes *stags*) *trippant or* (sometimes *argent*). 18b, 133b, 221a, 278a.
ROWLAND. *Sable, a pile wavy ermine.* 260a, 260b.
ROWSE. See LE ROWSE.
RUD. *Five martlets and a canton.* 221b.
RUSHBROOKE. *Sable, a fesse between three roses or.* 227a.
RUSSELL. *Argent, a lion gules and on a chief sable three escallops argent.* 53a, 226b.
RUSTAT. *On a saltire between four crosses crosslet fitchy an annulet.* 89b.
RYDER. *Argent, three crescents or each charged with an ermine spot.* 194a.
ST. ASAPH, See of. *Sable, two keys in saltire argent.* 133b, 193b.
ST. AUBYN. *Or, on a cross sable five bezants.* 172a.
ST. BARBE. *Checky sable and argent.* 227a.
ST. DAVID'S, See of. *Sable, on a cross or five cinquefoils sable.* 77b, 193b.

St. Leger. *Azure fretty argent, on a chief or a crescent sable.* 53a.

St. Maur. *Argent, two cheverons gules and a label sable.* 227a.

St. Pol. *Gules, three pales vair and on a chief or a label of five points azure.* 149a, 151b. See: Pembroke College; Woodville, Elizabeth.

Salisbury, See of. *Azure, the Virgin and Child or.* 77b, 177a, 194a.

Salmon. *Gules, three spearheads argent.* See Canning.

Sancroft. *Argent, on a cheveron between three crosses formy gules three doves argent.* Crest: *a snake with a twisted tail.* 66b, 68a, 70b.

Sandiford. *Per cheveron sable and ermine, in chief two boars' heads or.* 52b, 53a.

Sandys. *Or, a dance between three crosses crosslet fitchy gules.* Crest: *a griffin erect.* 193b, 283a.

Sanford. *Barry wavy argent and azure.* 141b.

Sapcott. *Sable, three dovecotes argent with a mullet or for difference in chief.* 53a.

Sawyer. *Gules, a cheveron between three birds argent and a chief ermine.* See Parris.

Scales. *Gules, six escallops argent.* 175a.

Scarlett. *Checky or and gules, a lion argent and a canton azure.* Crest: *a column gobony gules and or supported by two lion-paws erased argent.* 228a.

Scawen. *A cheveron between three griffins' heads erased, the two in chief facing each other.* Motto: *Respiciendo et Prospiciendo.* 127b.

Schwarzenberg. *Argent, a lion crowned or.* 125b.

Sclater. *Or, a cheveron between three trefoils and a baronet's badge over all.* Crest: *a wreath of laurel tied with a ribbon.* 221a, 236a, 240b, 244b.

Scotland. *Or, a lion within a double tressure flory counterflory gules.* 130b. See Royal Arms.

Scotland, David of. *Or, three piles gules.* 209a.

Scott. *Per pale indented, a saltire counterchanged.* 278b.

Scott. *Vert, three tripping stags or.* 228a.

Scrope. *Azure, a bend or.* 52b.

Seamark. *Argent, on a cross gules five mullets argent* (sometimes *or*). 53a, 226b.

Seckford. *Ermine, on a fesse gules three escallops or.* 220b.

Sedgwick. *Argent, on a cross gules five hawks' bells argent.* 175b.

Segrave. *A lion crowned or.* 226b, 227a.

Segrave. *Sable, three garbs argent.* (226b), 227a.

Selioke. *Or, a saltire gules between four eagles displayed azure.* 170b, 227b.

Selwyn. *On a bend cotised three annulets.* 242b.

Senior. *A fesse ermine between two lions' heads in chief or and a dolphin naiant in base argent.* 297a.

Sergeaux. *Argent, a saltire sable between twelve cherries proper.* 141b.

Serocold. *Per cheveron argent and sable, in chief two fleurs-de-lys azure and in base a tower or.* Crest: *a fleur-de-lys issuing from a tower.* 289b, 290a.

Seymour. *Gules, a pair of wings conjoined or.* Crest: *a demi-phoenix in flames, issuing from a coronet.* Supporters: *a unicorn and a bull crowned and chained.* 141b, 193b, 240b.

Seymour, Marriage Augmentation granted to Jane Seymour. *Or, on a pile gules between six fleurs-de-lys azure three lions of England.* 141b, 193b, 240b.

Shales. *Six escallops argent.* 262b.

Shaxton. *Azure, a sword and key in saltire or and on a chief or three lozenges gules.* 77b.

Shelford. *Azure, a fesse of five fusils or.* 50b.

Shelley. *Sable, on a fesse engrailed between three whelk-shells or a mullet gules, in fesse point a baronet's escutcheon.* Crest: *a griffin's head collared with a coronet.* 206b.

Sherlock. *Per pale, three fleurs-de-lys counterchanged.* Crest: *a pelican in piety.* 183a.

Sidney. *Or, a pheon azure.* Crest: *a porcupine azure, quilled, chained, collared or.* Motto: *Dieu me garde de calumniez.* Supporters: *two porcupines azure, quilled, chained, collared or.* 204b, 206b. See Sidney Sussex College.

Sidney, Frances, Countess of Sussex. Radclyffe quartering Fitzwalter all impaling Sidney. 204b, 206a, 206b, 208a, 208b.

Simeon. *Six pieces sable and or, three trefoils and three ermine spots counterchanged.* Crest: *a tree stump encircled with ivy.* 133b, 260a.

Skaiffe. *A cheveron between three roundels and a chief.* 65b.

Smith. *Azure, on a bend sable between two unicorns' heads erased or three lozenges argent.* 65b.

Smith. *Vert, a castle argent on a mount sable and on a chief or three storks' heads erased sable.* 191b.

Smith. *A cheveron cotised between three demi-griffins, the two in chief facing each other.* 290a.

Smith. *On a cheveron between three roundels three crosses formy.* 76b.

Smith. *A cross between four peacocks.* 221b.

Smith. *A fret and on a canton a lion.* Crest: *on a torse a bird.* 220b.

Smith of Suffolk. Quarterly: 1 and 4, *Barry wavy argent and azure and on a chief gules three horse-brays or;* 2 and 3, *Argent, a cheveron between three pheons azure and on a chief sable a running greyhound argent.* 227a.

Smith alias Hovell. *A crescent within a border.* 127b.

Smyth. *Ermine, on a bend between two unicorns' heads erased azure three lozenges or.* Crest: *out of a gold coronet a demi-bull argent horned or.* 228a.

Smyth. *On a fesse between three crosses formy fitchy three eagles.* Crest: *an arm holding a dagger, with a ribbon around the wrist.* 285b.

Solers. *Or, a fesse vair.* 68a.

Somerset. *Or, a fesse of Beaufort.* 141b.

Southwell. *Three cinquefoils each charged with six annulets.* 283a.

Sparke. *Checky or and vert, a bend ermine.* 257b.

Sparrow. *Ermine, three roses argent.* 177a.

Spencer. *Quarterly argent and gules, with a fret or on the red and over all a bend sable.* Motto: *Dieu défend le droit.* Supporters: *a griffin per fesse sable and or and a wyvern ermine, each with a collar sable charged with three escallops argent.* 69a, (141b), 226b, 227b. *With the bend charged with three mullets or.* 171b, 172a, 177a. *With the bend charged with three escallops argent.* 311a.

Spencer. *Sable, two bars nebuly ermine.* 194a, 198a.

Spencer. *Azure, a fesse ermine between six seamews' heads erased argent.* Crest: *a pelican in piety.* 49b, 51b, 52b.

Spencer. *Argent, a fesse engrailed and in chief three lions gules.* Crest: *a panther's head erased argent semy of roundels azure and gules with fire issuing from its mouth and ears.* 228a.

WALCOT. *Argent, a cheveron between three chessrooks sable ermined argent.* 227a.
WALGRAVE. *Per pale argent and gules.* 68a.
WALKER. *A cheveron ensigned with a cross-bar and ring between three crescents.* 221b.
WALPOLE. *Or, on a fesse between two cheverons sable three crosses crosslet or.* Crest: *an old man's head with a pointed and tasselled cap issuing from a crown.* 133b, 221a.
WALSINGHAM. *Paly of six argent and sable, a fesse gules.* 68a.
WALSINGHAM. *Gules, a couped cross checky argent and azure between twenty bezants.* 68a.
WARCOP. *Sable, three covered cups argent.* 228a.
WARD. *Azure, a cross formy or.* 228a.
WARDE. *Azure, a bend argent in a border engrailed argent.* 170b, 227b.
WARREN or WARENNE. *Checky or and azure.* 129a, 133b, 198a, 226b, 227a, 285a.
WARWICK, Earl of. *Checky azure and or, a cheveron ermine.* 52a, 52b, 53a, 141b.
WASHINGTON. *Argent, two bars sable and in chief three mullets.* Crest: *out of a crown or a demi-eagle sable.* 282b.
WATERS. *Per pale argent and sable, on a saltire a saltire wavy all counterchanged.* 68a.
WATSON. *Argent, on a cheveron azure between three martlets sable three crescents or.* Crest: *a wolf's head erased holding a trefoil.* 209a, 328b.
WEBB. *Gules, a cross engrailed between four falcons or.* Crest: *on a torse an eagle's head and wings issuing from a coronet.* 76a.
WEBB. See KELLAWE.
WELBY. *Sable, a fesse between three fleurs-de-lys argent.* 227a.
WELD. *Azure, a fesse nebuly between three crescents ermine.* 227a.
WELLS. *Argent, a cheveron gules between three pierced mullets sable.* 175b.
WENTWORTH. *Sable, a cheveron between three leopards' faces or.* 171b, 193b.
WESTMINSTER, Deanery of. *Azure, a cross paty between five martlets or, on a chief or a pale of France Modern and England quarterly between two roses gules.* 198a.
WESTWOOD. *Gules, three pierced mullets or and a canton ermine.* 208a.
WHALLEY. *Three whales' heads erased.* Crests: 1, *a whale's head erased and erect;* 2, *a cockatrice displayed.* 170a, (227b).
WHICHCOTE. *Ermine, two boars courant gules langued azure tusked and bristled or.* Crest: *a boar's head erect sable.* 125b, 298a.
WHISTLER. *A bend of five voided lozenges between two talbots passant.* 128a.
WHITAKER. *A fesse between three voided lozenges.* Crest: *a statant horse.* 65b.
WHITAKER. *Sable, a cheveron between three voided lozenges argent.* 193b.
WHITE. *Sable, a dove argent and on a chief argent three crosses formy gules.* 193b.
WHITGIFT. *Argent, on a cross paty azure five bezants.* 231a, 231b, 233a.
WHYTEHEAD. *Azure, a fesse argent between three fleurs-de-lys or.* 198a.
WICKINGHAM or WITCHINGHAM. *Ermine, on a chief three crosses formy.* 283a.
WIDDRINGTON. *Quarterly, a bend with a crescent thereon for difference.* 31a.
WIDWORTHY or WILDYARD. *Argent, five bendlets azure in a border or.* 127a.
WILDYARD. See WIDWORTHY.
WILKINS. *Ermine, on a bend sable three martlets argent and on a canton or a rose gules.* 50b, 52b, 53a.
WILKINSON. *Gules, a fesse vair and in chief a unicorn courant gules.* 175a.
WILLIAMS, apparently derived from RICHARDSON. *Argent, three wreaths of roses and leaves.* Crest: *from a torse argent and gules a bent arm brandishing a scimitar.* Motto: *Tutela Legum.* 228a.
WILLIAMS. *Gules, a cheveron ermine between three men's heads cut off at the neck proper.* 193b, 195b, 198a.
WILLOUGHBY of Eresby. *Or fretty argent* (sic). 193b.
WILMER. *Gules, a cheveron argent between three eagles or.* 226b.
WINCHESTER, See of. *Gules, two keys in bend respectively or and argent with a sword in bend sinister passed between them.* 248b.
WINDESORE. *A saltire between twelve crosses potent.* 89a.
WINGFIELD. *Argent, on a bend gules three pairs of wings argent.* 52b.
WINGHAM. *Azure, a fesse between three wings or.* 227a.
WINSTON. *Per pale gules and azure, a lion argent ramping against a tree eradicated proper.* 127a, 227a.
WISE. See WYSE.
WISEMAN. *Sable, a cheveron ermine between three cronels or.* Crest: *a wyvern couchant.* Motto: *Sapit qui Deum sapit.* 158a, 262b.
WISHART. *Argent, three piles gules meeting in base.* 52b.
WITCHINGHAM. See WICKINGHAM.
WOLLASTON. *Argent, three pierced mullets sable.* 285b.
WOOD. *Sable, a lion argent and a chief gules.* 193b, 197a, 198a, 201a.
WOOD. *Argent, on a cheveron sable between three trees eradicated vert three trefoils argent.* 228a.
WOOD. *Argent, a cheveron between three bulls' faces sable.* 227a.
WOODLARK. *Per bend indented gules and azure, in sinister chief a fleur-de-lys and in dexter base a lion passant gardant or.* Crest: *a lion passant gardant.* 133b.
WOODVILLE. *Argent, a fesse and a canton gules.* 141b, 143a, 175b, 226b, 227b.
WOODVILLE, Elizabeth. Quarterly of six: 1, Luxemburg; 2, Baux; 3, Cyprus; 4, Orsini; 5, St. Pol; 6, Woodville. 171b, 177a.
WORCESTER, See of. *Argent, ten roundels gules.* 128b, 193b.
WORDSWORTH. *Three bells.* 244a.
WORSLEY. *Argent, a chief gules.* 18b, 191a.
WORSLEY. *Argent, a cheveron between three falcons sable beaked, legged and belled or.* 191a.
WRAY. *Azure, on a chief or three martlets gules.* Motto: *Juste et Vrai.* 142b, 145b.
WREN. *Argent, a cheveron sable between three lions' heads erased azure and on a chief gules three crosses crosslet or.* 154a.
WRIGHT?. *Sable, a cheveron between three bulls' faces argent attired or.* 227a.
WRIOTHESLEY. *Azure, a cross or between four falcons close argent.* 198a.
WRITLE. *Sable, on a bend argent a bendlet wavy sable.* 68a.
WROTH. *Argent, on a bend sable three lions' heads erased argent crowned or.* 227a.

WYNNE. *Gules, a lion argent.* 228a.

WYNSTON. See WINSTON.

WYSE. *Sable, three cheverons ermine.* 53a, 226b, 289b.

YARRINGTON. *Gules, a cheveron ermine between the letters S and C in chief and Y in base.* 53a.

YATE. *On a fesse between three gates a crescent.* Crest: *a goat's head issuing from a crown.* 262a.

YORK, See of, Ancient. *Gules, an archbishop's cross or surmounted by a pallium proper.* 18b.

YORK, See of, Modern. *Gules, two keys in saltire with a crown in chief or.* 52b, 133b, 193b, 233a, 277b.

YORKE. *Argent, on a saltire azure a bezant.* Crest: *on a torse argent and gules a lion's head erased argent with a collar gules charged with a bezant.* Supporters: *a lion gardant or and a hart argent, horned or, each with a collar gules charged with a bezant.* 52b, 53a, 227b, 311b.

ZOUCH of Leicester. *Azure, ten bezants, four, three two, one.* 226b.

ZOUCHE. *Gules, ten bezants, four, three, two, one, and a canton ermine.* 191a, 227a.

UNIDENTIFIED COATS

1. *Three lions rampant.* 31a.
2. *Sable, on a fesse or three lions gules.* 36a.
3. *Three woolsacks each charged with a crescent.* 66b.
4. *Gules, a cheveron between three fleurs-de-lys argent.* 68a.
5. *Argent, a fesse or.* 68a.
6. *Gules, a cross paty argent.* 68a.
7. *Argent, a cross engrailed sable between four roundels gules.* 76a.
8. *Argent, on a fesse sable three eagles displayed or.* 76a.
9. *Gules, three lions argent.* 76a.
10. *Argent, a cheveron gules between three bulls' heads couped sable.* 77b.
11. *Five gouttes in saltire.* 89a.
12. *Gules, a fesse argent between three leopards' faces or.* Crest: *a leaping leopard argent powdered with roundels.* Motto: *Vix ea Nostra.* 94a.
13. *Argent, a lion gules crowned.* 125b.
14. *On a bend cotised three roundels.* 127b.
15. *Ermine, on a saltire a crescent in a border engrailed.* 128a.
16. *Argent, a cheveron or between three roses gules.* 133b.
17. Quarterly of five: 1, *Argent, a griffin sable;* 2, *Azure, three boars argent bristled or;* 3, Bruges; 4, *Azure, on a chief gules two crosses crosslet or;* 5, France Modern quartering England. 141b.
18. *Argent, a cheveron ermine between three bunches of grapes proper.* 171b.
19. *Argent, a double-headed eagle displayed gules.* 175a.
20. *Gules, three crosses crosslet or and on a canton argent a lion passant gardant azure.* 177a.
21. Quarterly: 1 and 4, *Gules a pale between dexter a cross and sinister three roundels or;* 2 and 3, *Argent, three chess-rooks sable.* 218b.
22. *Sable, two cheverons argent between three lions or.* Crest: *on a torse argent and sable a lion or.* Motto: *Moriar ut vivam.* 218b.
23. *Argent, three mullets sable.* 220b.
24. *On a cheveron sable three roses.* 226b.
25. *Or, a fesse argent* sometimes *sable between three roundels gules.* 226b, 227a.
26. *Argent, a cheveron gules between three bugle-horns sable.* 226b.
27. *Argent, on a bend cotised sable three martlets argent.* 226b.
28. *Argent, a cheveron azure between three chaplets gules.* 226b.
29. *Sable, a cheveron argent between three lions' heads or.* 226b.
30. *Gules crusily fitchy, a griffin or.* 226b.
31. *Or, a cross quarterly argent and gules.* 226b.
32. *Gules, two lions passant argent.* 226b.
33. *Gules, a bend argent.* 226b.
34. *Gules, three escutcheons argent.* 226b.
35. *Gules, a chief indented or.* 226b.
36. *Or, two lions passant gules.* 226b.
37. *Gules, a lion or.* 226b.
38. *Azure, a fesse between three stags' faces.* 226b.
39. *Argent, a fesse between three inverted crescents sable.* 226b.
40. *Barry of ten argent and gules, over all a lion or.* 226b.
41. *Azure, a millrind cross or.* 226b.
42. *Lozengy ermine and gules.* 226b.
43. *Or, a cross paty azure.* 227a.
44. *A lion crowned or.* 227a.
45. *Or, a saltire engrailed sable.* 227a.
46. *Ermine, on a fesse three crosses formy or.* 227a.
47. *Gules, two bars argent.* 227a.
48. *Gules, a pelican in her nest or.* 227a.
49. *Per cheveron embattled azure and sable, in chief dexter a crescent argent, sinister an estoile or, in base a lion or.* Crest: *on a torse sable and argent a bird.* 227a.
50. *Argent, three cheverons sable, each charged with a bezant.* 227a.
51. Quarterly: 1 and 4, *Lozengy sable and or,* impaling *Or, a lion azure;* 2 and 3, *Azure, on a fesse gules between six crosses crosslet or three escallops or,* impaling *Vert, a lion or.* 227a.
52. *Argent, a lion azure.* 227a.
53. *Gules, a pierced cinquefoil ermine.* 227a.
54. *Gules, a pale or.* 227a.
55. *Sable, four voided lozenges argent.* 227a.
56. *Gules, two bars argent.* 227a.
57. *A saltire argent between four crosses crosslet or.* 227a.
58. *Ermine, on a bend gules three leopards' faces or.* 227a.
59. *Or, two bends gules.* 227a.
60. *Azure, three bends or.* 227a.
61. *Gules, a lion crowned or.* 227a.
62. *Argent, a ragged Tau cross gules.* 227b.

BADGES

GLOSSARY

OF THE MEANING ATTACHED TO THE TECHNICAL TERMS USED IN THE INVENTORIES

ABACUS—The uppermost member of a capital.

ACANTHUS—A plant represented in Classical and Renaissance ornament, used particularly in the Corinthian and Composite Orders.

ACHIEVEMENT—In heraldry, the shield accompanied by the appropriate external ornamants, helm, crest, mantling, supporters, etc. In the plural the term is also applied to the insignia of honour carried at the funerals and suspended over the monuments of important personages, comprising helmet and crest, shield, tabard, sword, gauntlets and spurs, banners and pennons.

ACROTERIA—In Classical architecture, blocks on the apex and lower ends of a pediment, often carved with honeysuckle or palmette ornament.

AEDICULE—A small temple or similar shrine, or a miniature representation of the same. A surround to a doorway, niche or window having a pediment or canopy resting on pillars and suggestive of a small and exquisite building.

AGGER—The earthen ridge carrying a Roman road.

ALABASTER TABLE—A panel or series of panels of alabaster carved with religious subjects and placed at the back of an altar to form a reredos. The manufacture was a distinctively English industry of the 14th, 15th and early 16th centuries, centred at Nottingham.

ALB—Long linen robe, with close sleeves; worn by clerks of all grades.

ALERION.—In heraldry, an eagle without beak or feet.

ALTAR-TOMB—A modern term for a tomb of stone or marble resembling, but not used as, an altar.

AMESS—Fur cape with hood, and long tails in front; worn by clerks of the higher grades.

AMICE—A linen strip with embroidered apparel (*q.v.*) placed upon the head coifwise by a clerk before vesting himself in an alb, after which it is pushed back and the apparel then appears like a collar.

ANNULET—In heraldry, a ring.

ANTA-AE—In Classical architecture, a pilaster terminating a range of columns in the manner of a respond, with base and capital differing from those of the columns. *In antis*—Placed in a line between paired anta-responds.

ANTEFIXES—In Classical architecture, small ornamental blocks fixed at intervals along the verge of a roof to conceal the ends of the roofing-tiles.

ANTHEMION—Honeysuckle or palmette ornament in Classical architecture.

APPARELS—Rectangular pieces of embroidery on alb, amice, etc.

APSE—A projection from the wall of a church, hall or other building, semicircular or polygonal on plan, usually covered with a semi-dome or vault.

ARABESQUE—A kind of highly stylised fret-ornament in low relief, common in Moorish architecture, and found in 16th and 17th-century work in England.

ARCADE—A range of arches carried on piers or columns. *Blind arcade*, a series of arches, frequently interlaced, carried on shafts or pilasters against a solid wall.

ARCH—The following are some of the most usual forms:—
Equilateral—A pointed arch struck with radii equal to the span.
Flat or straight—Having the soffit horizontal.
Four-centred, depressed, Tudor—A pointed arch of four arcs, the two outer and lower arcs struck from centres on the springing line and the two inner and upper arcs from centres below the springing line. Sometimes the two upper arcs are replaced by straight lines.
Lancet—A pointed arch struck with radii greater than the span.
Nodding—An ogee arch curving also forward from the plane of the wall-face.
Ogee—A pointed arch of four or more arcs, the two uppermost being reversed, *i.e.*, convex instead of concave to the base line.
Pointed or two-centred—Two arcs struck from centres on the springing line, and meeting at the apex with a point.
Relieving—An arch, generally of rough construction, placed in the wall above the true arch or head of an opening, to relieve it of most of the superincumbent weight.
Segmental—A single arc struck from a centre below the springing line.
Segmental-pointed—A pointed arch, struck from two centres below the springing line.
Skew—Spanning between responds not diametrically opposite.
Squinch—*See* SQUINCH.
Stilted—An arch with its springing line raised above the level of the imposts.
Three-centred, elliptical—Formed with three arcs, the middle or uppermost struck from a centre below the springing line.

ARCHBISHOP'S VESTMENTS—Buskins, sandals, amice, alb, girdle, stole, maniple, tunic, dalmatic, chasuble, pall, gloves, ring, mitre; an archbishop carries a crosier but, in later times, holds a cross-staff for distinction.

ARCHITRAVE—The lowest member of an entablature (*q.v.*); often adapted as a moulded enrichment to the jambs and head of a doorway or window-opening.

ARCHIVOLT—In Classical architecture, the moulding round an arch.

ARGENT—In heraldry, white or silver.

ARMET—A close-helmet. Restricted in modern usage to the type in use in the 15th century with hinged cheek-pieces overlapping on the chin.

ARRIS—The sharp edge formed by the meeting of two surfaces. *On arris*—Set diagonally.

ASHLAR—Masonry wrought to an even face and square edges.

ATTIRED—In heraldry, applied to the antlers of a buck, stag, etc. when of a different tincture from the body.

AUMBRY—Cupboard in a church for housing the sacred vessels.

AVENTAIL OR CAMAIL—A tippet of mail attached to the bascinet to protect the throat and neck, and falling to the shoulders.

AZURE—In heraldry, blue.

BAILEY—The courtyard of a castle.

BALDACCHINO—A canopy, suspended or on pillars, over an altar or throne.

BALL-FLOWER—In architecture, a decoration, peculiar to the first quarter of the 14th century, consisting of a globular flower of three petals enclosing a small ball.

BALUSTER—A vertical support to a rail.

BAR—*See* FESSE.

BARGE-BOARD—A board, often carved, fixed to the edge of a gabled roof, a short distance from the face of the wall.

BARONET'S BADGE—In heraldry, an escutcheon argent with the Red Hand of Ulster borne upon a baronet's shield.

BAROQUE—A style of architecture and decoration emerging in the 17th century which uses the repertory of classical forms with great freedom to emphazise the unity and pictorial character of its effects. The term is also applied to sculpture and painting of a comparable character.

BARREL-VAULTING—*See* VAULTING.

BARROW—Burial mound.
Disc—A small burial mound separated from its encircling ditch by a relatively wide space.
Bell-disc—Similar but with a larger mound and relatively lesser space.

BARRY—In heraldry, an even number of horizontal divisions in a shield, normally six, but sometimes four or eight. When a greater and indefinite number of divisions appear the word *Burely* or *Barruly* is used.

BASCINET—Steel head-piece, egg-shaped with pointed apex, usually worn with an aventail, and fitted with a vizor.

BASTION—A projection from the general outline of a fortress or work from which the garrison is able to see, and defend by a flanking fire, the ground before the ramparts.

BASTION-TRACE FORT—A 17th-century type of fort with projecting angles or bastions.

BATTLEMENTED—*See* EMBATTLED.

BAYS—The main vertical divisions of a building or feature. The divisions of a roof, marked by its main trusses.

BEADING—A small round moulding.

BEAKER—A type of pottery vessel of the early second millenium B.C. representing a British variant of the Continental Bell-Beaker and Corded-Ware ceramic traditions.

BEAKER PEOPLE—The brachycephalic physical type associated with pottery of Beaker type (*q.v.*).

BEAVER—A defence for the lower part of the face.

BELL-DISC BARROW—*See* BARROW.

BEND—In heraldry, a diagonal band crossing the shield from dexter chief to sinister base; a bend sinister runs from sinister chief to dexter base. *Per bend*—Applied to the field or to a charge divided bendwise with a difference of tincture on either side.

BENDWISE—In the direction of a bend.

BERM—In earthworks, the level strip of ground between a bank and its accompanying ditch or scarp.

BEZANT—In heraldry, a gold roundel or disc.

BILLET—In architecture, an ornament used in the 11th and 12th centuries consisting of short attached cylinders or rectangles with spaces between. In heraldry, a small upright oblong charge.

BILLETY—In heraldry, a field or charge powdered with billets.

BISHOP'S VESTMENTS—Similar to an archbishop's (*q.v.*) but without a pall, and a bishop carries a crosier and not a cross.

BOLECTION-MOULDING—A bold moulding of double curvature raised above the general plane of the framework of a door, fireplace or panelling.

BOND, ENGLISH OR FLEMISH—*See* BRICKWORK.

BORDER—In heraldry, an edging of a different tincture from the field.

BOSS—A projecting square or round ornament, covering the intersections of the ribs in a vault, panelled ceiling or roof, etc.

BOUGET OR WATER-BOUGET—A pair of leather bottles, borne as a heraldic charge.

BRACE—In roof construction, a subsidiary timber inserted to strengthen the framing of a truss. *Wind-brace*, a subsidiary timber inserted between the purlins and principals of a roof to increase resistance to wind-pressure.

BRATTISHING—Ornamental cresting on the top of a screen, cornice, etc.

BRESSUMMER—A spanning beam forming the direct support of an upper wall or timber-framing.

BRICKWORK—*Header*—A brick laid so that the end only appears on the face of the wall.
Stretcher—A brick laid so that one side only appears on the face of the wall.
English Bond—A method of laying bricks so that alternate courses on the face of the wall are composed of headers or stretchers only.
Flemish Bond—A method of laying bricks so that alternate headers and stretchers appear in each course on the face of the wall.
English Garden Wall Bond—Bricks laid with three courses of stretchers to one of headers.

BROACH—*See* SPIRE.

BROACH-STOP—A half-pyramidal stop against a chamfer to effect the change from chamfer to right angle.

BURGONET—An open steel head-piece, lighter than the close-helmet, and usually with a peak over the eyes and hinged ear-pieces.

BUTTRESS—A mass of masonry or brick-work projecting from or built against a wall to give additional strength.
Angle-buttresses—Two meeting, or nearly meeting, at an angle of 90° at the corner of a building.
Clasping-buttress—One that clasps or encases an angle.
Diagonal-buttress—One placed against the right angle formed by two walls, and more or less equiangular with both.
Flying-buttress—An arch or half-arch transmitting the thrust of a vault or roof from the upper part of a wall to an outer support.

CABLE-MOULDING—A moulding carved in the form of a rope or cable.

CABOSSED—In heraldry, applied to the head of a beast shown full-face and without a neck.

CAMAIL—*See* AVENTAIL.

CAMBERED—Curved so that the middle is higher than the ends or sides.

CANONICAL CHOIR-HABIT—Surplice, amess, cope.

CANONS (of a bell)—The metal loops by which a bell is hung.

CANOPY—A projection or hood over a door, window, etc., and the covering over a tomb or niche.

CANTON—In heraldry, a rectangle in the corner of the shield in dexter chief.

CARTOUCHE—In Renaissance ornament, a tablet imitating a scroll with ends rolled up, used ornamentally or bearing an inscription or arms.

CARYATID—Sculptured female figure used as column or support.

CASEMENT—1. A wide hollow moulding in window-jambs etc.
2. The hinged part of a window.

CASSOCK—Long, close-sleeved gown; worn by all clerks.

CASTOR WARE—A colour-coated ware made in potteries near Castor (Northants.) and elsewhere from the late 2nd century A.D.

CHALICE—The name used in the Inventory to distinguish the pre-Reformation type of Communion cup with a shallow bowl from the post-Reformation cup with a larger bowl.

CHAMFER—The small plane formed when the sharp edge or arris of stone or wood is cut away, usually at an angle of 45°; when the plane is concave it is termed a *hollow chamfer*, and when the plane is sunk a *sunk chamfer*.

CHANTRY-CHAPEL—A chapel built for the purposes of a chantry (a foundation, usually supporting a priest, for the celebration of masses for the souls of the founder and such others as he may direct).

CHARGE—In heraldry, the representation of an object or device upon the field.

CHASUBLE—A nearly circular cape with a central hole for the head worn by priests and bishops at mass. It is put on over all the other vestments.

CHECKY—In heraldry, a field or charge divided into squares or checkers.

CHEVAUX-DE-FRISE—Iron spikes, originally set in timber to repel cavalry, now usually along the tops of walls to protect property.

CHEVERON—In heraldry, a charge resembling an inverted V; *per cheveron* is applied to a field or charge divided cheveronwise with a difference of tincture on either side. In architecture, a decorative form similar to the foregoing and often used in a consecutive series.

CHIEF—In heraldry, a division occupying the upper part of the shield. A charge is said to be *in chief* when placed in the top third of a shield.

CHIMAERA—A fabulous monster with a lion's head, a goat's body and a serpent's tail.

CHIP-CARVING—Architectural enrichment of sunk triangular form resembling chip-carved woodwork.

CHOIR-HABIT—In secular churches: for boys, a surplice only over the cassock; for clerks or vicars, the surplice and a black cope-like mantle, partly closed in front and put over the head, which was exchanged for a silk cope on festivals; canons put on a grey amess over the surplice. In monastic churches: for all classes, whether canons regular, monks, friars, nuns, or novices, the ordinary habit with a cope on festivals.

CINQUEFOIL—1. *See* FOIL.
2. A heraldic flower of five petals.

CLEARSTOREY—An upper storey, pierced by windows, in the main walls of a church. The same term is applicable in a domestic building.

CLOSE—Enclosure. In earthworks, an area enclosed by banks.

CLOSE-HELMET—A helmet fitted with vizor etc., completely enclosing the head and face.

COCKATRICE—In heraldry, usually drawn as a wyvern with a cock's head, but occasionally as a cock with a dragon's tail.

COFFERS—Sunk panels in ceilings, vaults, domes and arch-soffits.

COIF—Small close hood, covering head only.

COLLAR-BEAM—In a roof, a horizontal beam framed to and serving to tie together a pair of rafters some distance above the wall-plate level.

COLONETTE—A small column.

COMB—The keel-shaped ridge on the top of a helmet.

CONSOLE—A bracket with a compound curved outline.

COPE—A processional and choir vestment shaped like a cloak, and fastened across the chest by a band or brooch; worn by clerks of most grades.

COPED SLAB—A slab of which the upper face is ridged down the middle, sometimes hipped at each end.

COPS, ELBOW—A modern term for elbow defences of leather or plate, *see* COUTER. *Knee-cops*, in modern usage applied to the leather or plate defences of the knees at all dates, *see* POLEYN.

CORBEL—A projecting stone or piece of timber for the support of a superincumbent weight. *Corbel-table*—A row of corbels, usually carved, and supporting a projection.

CORNICE—A crowning projection. In Classical architecture, the crowning or upper portion of the entablature.

CORONA—The square projection in the upper part of a Classical cornice with vertical face and wide soffit.

COTISES—In heraldry, pairs of narrow bands, in the form of bends, pales, fesses, or cheverons, and accompanying one of those charges, on each side of it.

COUNTER-CHANGED—In heraldry, a term applied where the field and charges exchange tinctures on either side of a dividing line.

COUPED—In heraldry, of a head or limb cut off with a straight edge. *See also under* CROSS.

COURTYARD TYPE OF HOUSE—*See* HOUSES.

COUTER—Elbow defence of leather or plate.

COVE—A concave under-surface of the nature of a hollow moulding but on a larger scale.

COVER-PATEN—A cover to a communion cup, used as a paten.

CRENELLES—The openings in an embattled parapet.

CREST, CRESTING—1. A device worn upon the helm or helmet.
2. An ornamental finish along the top of a screen etc.

CROCKETS—Carvings projecting at regular intervals from the vertical or sloping sides of parts of a building, such as spires, canopies, pinnacles, hood-moulds, etc.

CRONEL—The crown-like head of a blunt tilting-lance.

CROP-MARK—A trace of a levelled or buried feature revealed by different growth of crops, especially after drought.

CROSIER, OR PASTORAL STAFF—A tall staff ending in an ornamental crook carried as a mark of authority by archbishops, bishops, and heads of monastic houses, including abbesses and prioresses.

CROSS—In its simplest form in heraldry, a pale combined with a fesse, as the St. George's Cross; of many other varieties the following are the most common: *Couped*—with the four arms not extending to the edge of the shield; *Crosslet*—with a smaller arm crossing each main arm; *Fitchy*—having the lowest arm spiked or pointed; *Flowered* or *flory*—having the arms headed with fleurs-de-lis; *Formy*—arms widening from the centre, and square at the ends; *Moline* (or *mill-rind*)—with the arms split or forked at the ends; *Paty*—as a cross *formy*, but with the arms notched in two places at the ends, giving them a form which may approach that of a blunt head of a fleur-de-lis; *Pommy*—with the arms ending in a ball like the pomme or pommel of a sword or walking-cane; *Potent*—having a small transverse arm at the extreme end of each main arm; *Quadrate*—with a small rectangular projection at each angle as though the crossing was surcharged with a square; *Saltire* (or *St. Andrew's*)—an X-shaped cross; *Tau* (or *Anthony*)—in the form of a T; *Trefly*—with the arms terminating in a trefoil.

CROSS-STAFF—Staff terminating in a cross; carried before archbishops. On effigies, brasses, etc., the figures are usually shown holding it.

CRUCK (OR CRUTCH) TRUSS—*See under* ROOFS.

CRUSILY—In heraldry, covered or powdered with crosslets.

CURTAIN—The connecting wall between the towers or bastions of a castle.

CUSHION-CAPITAL—A capital cut from a cube with its lower angles rounded off to adapt it to a circular shaft.

CUSPS (*cusping, sub-cusps*)—The projecting points forming the foils in Gothic windows, arches, panels, etc.; they were frequently ornamented at the ends (*cusp-points*) with leaves, flowers, berries, etc.

CYMA—A moulding with a wave-like outline consisting of two contrary curves.

DADO—The separate protective or decorative treatment applied to the lower parts of wall-surfaces to a height, normally, of 3 to 4 feet. *Dado-rail*, the moulding or capping at the top of the dado.

DALMATIC—The special vestment at mass of a deacon; a loose tunic of moderate length, slit up the sides, with wide sleeves and fringed edges.

DANCE—In heraldry, a fesse or bar drawn zigzagwise, or *dancetty*.

DEACON'S VESTMENTS (MASS)—Amice, alb, stole (worn over left shoulder), dalmatic, and maniple.

DENTILS—The small rectangular tooth-like blocks used decoratively in Classical cornices.

DEXTER—In heraldry, the right-hand side of a shield as held.

DIAPER—All-over decoration of surfaces with squares, diamonds, and other patterns.

DIE—The part of a pedestal between the base and the cornice.

DIMIDIATED—In heraldry, applied to the halving of two shields vertically and joining a half of each to make a new shield.

DISC BARROW—*See* BARROW.

DOG-LEGGED STAIRCASE—*See* STAIRCASES.

DOG-TOOTH ORNAMENT—A typical 13th-century carved ornament consisting of a series of pyramidal flowers of four petals; used to cover hollow mouldings.

DORMER—A sleeping recess contrived as a projection from the slope of a roof and having a roof of its own, usually unlighted but occasionally with small lights in the cheeks.

DORMER-WINDOW—A vertical window on the slope of a roof and having a roof of its own.

DORTER—A monastic dormitory.

DOUBLE-OGEE—*See* OGEE.

DOVETAIL—A carpenter's joint for two boards, one with a series of projecting pieces resembling doves' tails fitting into the other with similar hollows; in heraldry, an edge formed like a dovetail-joint.

DRAWBAR—A wooden bar or bolt, inside a door, fitted into a socket in one jamb and a long channel in the other jamb, into which it slides back when not in use.

DRESSINGS—The stone or brickwork used about an angle, window, or other feature when worked to a finished face, whether smooth, tooled or rubbed, moulded, or sculptured.

E TYPE OF HOUSE—*See* HOUSES.

EAVES—The under part of a sloping roof overhanging a wall.

EMBATTLED—In architecture, a parapet with *merlons* separated by *embrasures* or *crenelles*. In heraldry, having an outline like a battlement.

EMBRASURES—The openings or sinkings in embattled parapets, or the recesses for windows, doorways, etc.

ENGRAILED—In heraldry, edged with a series of concave curves.

ENTABLATURE—In Classical or Renaissance architecture, the moulded horizontal superstructure of a wall, colonnade or opening. A full entablature consists of an *architrave*, *frieze*, and *cornice*.

ENTASIS—The convexity or swell on a vertical line or surface, to correct the optical illusion of concavity in the sides of a column or spire when the lines are straight.

ERASED—In heraldry, a head or limb torn off, leaving a jagged edge.

ERMINE—The fur most frequently represented in heraldry; white powdered with black tails. *Ermines*—black powdered with white tails.

ESCARBUNCLE—In heraldry, an ornamental elaboration of the metal reinforcement of a shield, drawn as eight batons tipped with fleurs-de-lis radiating from a central boss.

ESCUTCHEON—*See* SCUTCHEON.

ESTOILE—In heraldry, a star-like charge with wavy rays. Unless otherwise described it has six points.

FAN-VAULTING—*See* VAULTING.

FASCIA—A plain or moulded facing board.

FESSE—In heraldry, a broad horizontal band across the shield. Where more than one fesse is borne they are known as *Bars*. *Per fesse*—applied to the field or to a charge divided fessewise with a difference of tincture on either side.

FIMBRIATED—In heraldry, applied to a bend, cheveron, etc., with a narrow border of a different tincture.

FINIAL—A formal bunch of foliage or similar ornament at the top of a pinnacle, gable, canopy, etc.

FITCHY—*See* CROSS.

FLANCH or FLAUNCH—In heraldry, the segmental area formed at the sides of a shield by curved lines drawn from the corner of the chief to near the base.

FLORY—In heraldry, applied to a field or charge powdered with fleurs-de-lis. *See also under* CROSS.

FOIL (*trefoil*, *quatrefoil*, *cinquefoil*, *multifoil*, etc.)—A leaf-shaped space defined by the curves formed by the cusping in an opening or panel.

FOLIATED (of a capital, corbel, etc.)—Carved with leaf ornament.

FOUR-CENTRED ARCH—*See* ARCH.

FRATER—The refectory or dining-hall of a monastery.

FRET—In modern heraldry, a charge formed of a voided lozenge interlaced with two narrow pieces in saltire. *Fretty*—applied to a field or charge covered with three or more narrow bends and as many bends sinister interlaced in a lattice pattern.

FRIEZE—The middle division in an *entablature*, between the *architrave* and the *cornice*; generally any band of ornament or colour immediately below a cornice.

FUNERAL-ARMOUR—*See under* ACHIEVEMENTS.

FUSIL—In heraldry, an elongated lozenge.

GABLE—The wall at the end of a ridged roof, generally triangular, sometimes semicircular, and often with an outline of various curves, then called *curvilinear* or *Dutch*. A *stepped* gable has an outline formed of a series of steps.

GADROONED—Enriched with a series of convex ridges, the converse of fluting, and forming an ornamental edge or band.

GARB—In heraldry, a sheaf, usually of wheat.

GARDEROBE—Wardrobe. Antiquarian usage applies it to a latrine or privy chamber.

GARGOYLE—A carved projecting figure pierced or channelled to carry off the rain-water from the roof of a building.

GAUGING—In brickwork, bringing every brick exactly to a certain form by cutting and rubbing. Specially made soft bricks are used for the purpose.

GEMEL-BAR—In heraldry, a pair of narrow bars lying close to one another.

GNOMON—The rod of a sundial, showing the time by its shadow.

GOBONY—In heraldry, applied to a border or charge made up of a row of segments of alternating tinctures. *Counter-gobony* is used for two such rows.

GORGET—The plate-armour protecting the neck.

GRIFFIN—In heraldry, a winged monster with the fore parts of an eagle and the hinder parts of a lion.

GRISAILLE—Painting, decorative or on glass, in greyish tints.

GROINING, GROINED VAULT—*See* VAULTING.

GUIGES—Suspension straps of a shield.

GUILLOCHE-PATTERN—In Classical or Renaissance architecture, a geometrical ornament consisting of two or more intertwining wavy bands forming a series of circles.

GULES—In heraldry, red.

GUTTAE—Small stud-like projections under the triglyphs and mutules of the Doric entablature.

GUTTY—In heraldry, applied to a field or charge shown as though sprinkled with drops of liquid.

GYRONNY—In heraldry, applied to a field divided into eight triangular segments by two lines drawn quarterly and two drawn saltirewise.

H AND HALF-H TYPES OF HOUSE—*See* HOUSES.

HALL—The principal room of a mediaeval house, often open to the roof. Also the Dining-room of a College.

HALL AND CELLAR TYPE OF HOUSE—*See* HOUSES.

HAMMER-BEAMS—Horizontal brackets of a roof projecting at the wall-plate level, and resembling the two ends of a tie-beam with its middle part cut away; they are supported by braces, and help to diminish lateral pressure by reducing the span. Sometimes there is a second and even a third upper series of these brackets.

HATCHMENT—Now used for the square or lozenge-shaped tablet displaying the armorial bearings, usually painted, of a deceased person, first hung outside his house and then laid up in the church.

HAUBERK—Shirt of mail.

HAURIENT—In heraldry, applied to a fish represented standing on its tail.

HELM—Complete barrel or dome-shaped head-defence of plate. No longer used in warfare after the middle of the 14th century; it continued in use in the tilt-yard into the 16th century.

HELMET—A light head-piece. *See* ARMET, BURGONET, CLOSE-HELMET, POT, SALLET.

HEXASTYLE—A portico having six columns.

HIPPED ROOF—A roof with sloped instead of vertical ends. *Half-hipped*, a roof whose ends are partly vertical and partly sloped.

HOOD-MOULD (*label, drip-stone*)—A projecting moulding on the face of a wall above an arch, doorway, or window; it may follow the form of the arch or be square in outline.

HORSE-BARNACLE—In heraldry, the nose pincers used by farriers to curb a horse.

HOUSES—These are classified as far as possible under the following heads:—

1. *Hall and Cellar Type*—Hall on first floor; rooms beneath generally vaulted; examples as early as the 12th century.
2. *H Type*—Hall between projecting wings, one containing living-rooms, the other the offices; the usual form of a mediaeval house, employed, with variations, down to the 17th century.
3. *L Type*—Hall and one wing, generally for small houses.
4. *E Type*—Hall with two wings and a middle porch; generally of the 16th and 17th centuries.
5. *Half-H Type*—A variation of the E type without the middle porch.
6. *Courtyard Type*—House built round a court, sometimes only three ranges of buildings with or without an enclosing wall and gateway on the fourth side.
7. *Central-chimney Type*—Rectangular plan, in small houses only.

IMPALED—In heraldry, applied to the marshalling side by side on one shield of the arms of a husband and wife, or of a dignity and its holder.

IMPOST—The projection, often moulded, at the springing of an arch, upon which the arch appears to rest.

INDENT—The sinking in a slab for a monumental brass.

INDENTED—In heraldry, notched like the teeth of a saw.

INFULAE—The tasselled labels or strings of a mitre.

INTAGLIO—A design cut into any substance leaving the pattern sunk below the surface of the material.

INVECTED—In heraldry, edged with a series of convex curves.

JAMBS—1. The sides of an archway, doorway, window, or other opening.
2. In heraldry, legs of lions etc.
3. In armour, (greaves) plate-defences for the legs below the knees.

JESSANT-DE-LIS—In heraldry, applied to a leopard's face with a fleur-de-lis issuing from the mouth.

JETTY—The projection of the upper storey of a building beyond the plane of a lower storey.

JOGGLING—The method of cutting the adjoining faces of the voussoirs of an arch with rebated, zigzagged or wavy surfaces to provide a better key.

JUPON—Close-fitting surcoat, worn over armour *c.* 1350 to *c.* 1410; sometimes called a *gipon.*

KEYSTONE—The middle stone in an arch.

KING-POST—The middle vertical post in a roof-truss. *See under* ROOFS.

KNEELER—The stone at the foot of a gable.

L TYPE OF HOUSE—*See* HOUSES.

LABEL—*See* HOOD-MOULD. In heraldry, a narrow horizontal strip (fillet) across the upper part of the shield from which hang broader oblong tags (points or pendants); unless otherwise specified the points are three in number. Later it was often cut short at each end and the pendants were dovetail-shaped instead of rectangular.

LANCET—A long, narrow window with a pointed head, typical of the 13th century.

LANGUED—In heraldry, applied to the tongue of a beast when of a different tincture from the body.

LENTEN VEIL—A hanging suspended before the altar during Lent and taken down on the Wednesday or Thursday before Easter.

LIERNE-VAULT—*See* VAULTING.

LINENFOLD PANELLING—Panelling ornamented with a conventional representation of folded linen.

LINTEL—The horizontal beam or stone bridging an opening.

LION—In heraldry, shown with the face in profile and (unless otherwise blazoned) always rampant.

LOCKER—A small cupboard formed in a wall. *See also* AUMBRY.

LOOP—A small narrow light, often unglazed.

LOUVRE—A lantern-like structure surmounting the roof of a hall or other building, with openings, for ventilation or the escape of smoke, usually crossed by sloping slats (called louvre-boards) to exclude rain. *Louvre-boards* are also used in church belfries, instead of glazing, to allow the bells to be heard.

LOZENGE—In heraldry, a charge like the diamond in a pack of cards.

LUCE—In heraldry, a fish (pike).

LYNCHETS—Indications of cultivation-terraces on hillsides.

MANDORLA—A glory in the form of an oval surround. Also VESICA PISCIS (*q.v.*).

MANIPLE—A strip of embroidery, probably at one time a handkerchief or napkin, held in the left hand, or worn hanging from the left wrist by bishops, priests, and deacons.

MANNERIST—A use of the repertory of revived antique forms in an arbitrary way.

MANSARD—*See under* ROOFS.

MANTIGER—In heraldry, a monster with the face of a man and the body of a tiger.

MANTLE OR MANTLING—In heraldry, a cloth hung over the hinder part of the helm; the edges were often fantastically dagged and slit.

MARTLET—A bird, always shown in heraldry without feet.

MASK-STOP—*See under* STOPS.

MASS VESTMENTS—These included the amice, alb, and girdle (which were worn by all clerks), to which a sub-deacon added the tunicle and maniple, a deacon the dalmatic, maniple, and stole (over one shoulder only), and the priest the maniple, stole (over both shoulders), and chasuble. Bishops and certain privileged abbots wore the tunicle and dalmatic under the chasuble, with the mitre, gloves, and ring, and buskins and sandals. Archbishops used the pall in addition to all the foregoing. Bishops, abbots, and archbishops alike carried crosiers, and in the same way, but an archbishop had likewise a cross carried before him for dignity, and he is generally represented holding one for distinction. The mass vestments were sometimes worn over the choir-habit, and the hood of the grey amess may often be seen on effigies hanging beyond the amice apparel at the back of the neck.

MAUNCH—In heraldry, an old-fashioned sleeve with long hanging end.

MERLON—The solid part of an embattled parapet between the embrasures.

METOPES—The panels, often carved, filling the spaces between the triglyphs of the Doric entablature.

MILL-RIND (*Fer-de-moline*)—The iron affixed to the centre of a mill-stone. A common heraldic charge; in early heraldry, the name given to the cross of this form, or *cross moline*.

MINIM—An unofficial Roman coin of very small size.

MISERICORDE—1. A bracket, often elaborately carved, on the underside of the hinged seat of a choir-stall. When the seat is turned up the bracket comes into position to support the occupant during long periods of standing.
2. In monastic planning, a small hall, generally attached to the Infirmary, in which meat and better food than the ordinary was supplied for special reasons.

MITRED ABBOT'S VESTMENTS—Similar to a bishop's.

MODILLIONS—Brackets under the cornice in Classical architecture.

MORSE—Large clasp or brooch fastening the cope across the breast.

MOTTE—In earthworks, a steep mound, flat-topped, forming the main feature of an 11th or 12th-century castle; originally often surmounted by a timber tower; associated with a BAILEY (*q.v.*).

MULLET—In heraldry, a star-like charge with straight points. Unless otherwise described it has five points.

MULLION—A vertical post, standard, or upright dividing an opening into lights.

MUNTIN—In panelling, an intermediate upright, butting into or stopping against the rails.

MUTULES—Shallow blocks under the corona of the cornice in Classical architecture.

NAIANT—In heraldry, applied to a fish represented swimming.

NAIL-HEAD—Architectural enrichment of small pyramidal form used extensively in 12th-century work.

NEBULY—In heraldry, applied to an exaggeratedly wavy outline.

NECKING OR NECK-MOULDING—The narrow moulding round the bottom of a capital.

NEWEL—The central post in a circular or winding staircase; also the principal posts at the angles of a dog-legged or well-staircase.

NODDING ARCH—*See under* ARCH.

OCTASTYLE—A portico having eight columns.

OGEE—A compound curve of two parts, one convex, the other concave; a *double-ogee* moulding is formed by two ogees meeting at their convex ends.

OR—In heraldry, gold.

ORDERS OF ARCHES—Receding concentric rings of voussoirs.

ORDERS OF ARCHITECTURE—In Classical or Renaissance architecture, the five systems of columnar architecture, known as Tuscan, Doric, Ionic, Corinthian, and Composite. *Colossal Order*, one in which the columns or pilasters embrace more than one storey of the building.

ORIEL-WINDOW—A projecting bay-window carried upon corbels or brackets. In Colleges and great houses a special usage is for the large projecting windows generally lighting the Hall dais.

ORLE—In heraldry, a term used to describe a voided scutcheon, or a number of small charges arranged in this form.

ORPHREYS—Strips of embroidery on vestments.

OVERSAILING COURSE—A brick or stone course projecting beyond the one below it.

OVOLO MOULDING—A Classical moulding forming a quarter round or semi-ellipse in section.

PALE—In heraldry, a vertical band down the middle of a shield. If more than one, they are called *Pallets*. *Per pale*—applied to the field or to a charge divided palewise with a difference of tincture on either side.

PALIMPSEST—1. Of a brass; reused by engraving the back of an older engraved plate.
2. Of a wall-painting; superimposed on an earlier painting.

PALL—1. In ecclesiastical vestments, a narrow strip of lambswool, having an open loop in the middle, and weighted ends; it is ornamented with a number of crosses and forms the distinctive mark of an archbishop; it is worn round the neck, above the other vestments.
2. A cloth covering a hearse.

PALLADIAN WINDOW—A three-light window with a tall round-headed middle light and shorter lights on either side, the side lights with flanking pilasters and small entablatures forming the imposts to the arch over the centre light.

PALY—In heraldry, a shield divided by lines palewise, normally into six divisions, unless otherwise blazoned.

PARLOUR—In a monastery, a passage-way, usually through the east range of the cloister; the talking place. The principal private room in 15th-century and later houses.

PASSANT—In heraldry, of beasts, etc., walking and looking forward with head in profile. *Passant gardant*—with head turned to the onlooker. *Passant regardant*—looking backwards.

PASTORAL STAFF—*See* CROSIER.

PATEN—A plate for holding the Bread at the celebration of the Holy Communion.

PATERA-AE—A flat ornament applied to a frieze, moulding, or cornice; in Gothic work it commonly takes the form of a four-lobed leaf or flower.

PATY—*See* CROSS.

PEDIMENT—A low-pitched gable used in Classical and Renaissance architecture above a portico, at the end of a building, or above doors, windows, niches, etc.; sometimes the gable angle is omitted, forming a *broken pediment*, or the horizontal members are omitted, forming an *open pediment*. A curved gable-form is sometimes used in this way.

PELICAN IN PIETY—A pelican shown, according to the mediaeval legend, feeding her young upon the drops of blood she pecks from her breast.

PHEON—In heraldry, the barbed head of an arrow or dart.

PILASTER—A shallow pier of rectangular section attached to the wall.

PILE—In heraldry, a wedge-shaped charge issuing from the chief of a shield and tapering to the base.

PISCINA—A basin for washing the sacred vessels and provided with a drain, generally set in or against the wall to the S. of the altar, but sometimes sunk in the pavement.

PLAT-BAND—A flat projecting horizontal band of masonry or brick-work across the face of a building, as distinct from a moulded string.

PLINTH—The projecting base of a wall or column, generally chamfered or moulded at the top.

PODIUM—In Classical architecture, a basis, usually solid, supporting a temple or other superstructure.

POLEYN—Knee defence of leather or plate.

POPPY-HEAD—The ornament at the heads of bench-standards or desks in churches; generally carved with foliage and flowers, somewhat resembling a fleur-de-lis.

PORTCULLIS—A movable gate, rising and falling in vertical groves in the jambs of a doorway.

PORTICO—A covered entrance to a building, colonnaded, either constituting the whole front of the building or forming an important feature.

POT—Colloquial term for an open helmet in the 17th century.

POWDERED OR SEMY—In heraldry, strewn with an indefinite number of small charges.

PRESBYTERY—The part of a church in which is placed the high altar, E. of the choir.

PRETENCE—In heraldry, a scutcheon 'of pretence' or 'in pretence' is a scutcheon bearing the wife's arms placed by the husband of an heiress upon the centre of his own shield.

PRIEST'S VESTMENTS (*Mass*)—Amice, alb, girdle, stole crossed in front, maniple, chasuble.

PRINCIPALS—The main as opposed to the common rafters of a roof.

PROCESSIONAL VESTMENTS—The same as canonical (*q.v.*).

PROPER—In heraldry, of the natural colour.

PULPITUM—A screen in a monastic church, dividing the monastic choir from the nave.

PULVINATED FRIEZE—In Classical and Renaissance architecture, a frieze having a convex or bulging section.

PURLIN—In roof construction, a horizontal timber resting on the principal rafters of a truss, and forming an intermediate support for the common rafters. For *Collar-purlin*, see *King-post* under ROOFS.

QUARRY—In glazing, small panes of glass, generally diamond-shaped or square set diagonally.

QUARTERED OR QUARTERLY—In heraldry, applied (1) to a field divided chequerwise into four quarters, those diagonally opposite to each other having the same tinctures; (2) to four or more coats of arms marshalled chequerwise on one shield. When there are more than four quarters the number is specified.

QUATREFOIL—In heraldry, a four-petalled flower. *See also* FOIL.

QUEEN-POSTS—A pair of vertical posts in a roof-truss equidistant from the centre line of the roof. *See also under* ROOFS.

QUOINS—The dressed stones at the angle of a building, or distinctive brickwork in this position.

RAFTERS—Inclined timbers supporting a roof-covering. *See also under* ROOFS.

RAGGED, RAGULY—In heraldry, applied to a charge whose edges are ragged like a tree trunk with the limbs lopped away.

RAIL—A horizontal member in the framing of a door, screen, or panel.

RAMPANT—In heraldry, of beasts etc., standing erect, as if attacking or defending.

REAR-ARCH—The arch on the inside of a wall spanning a doorway or window-opening.

REBATE—A continuous rectangular notch cut on an edge.

REELS—Ornament resembling a line of bobbins, used in Classical architecture.

RELIQUARY—A small box or other receptacle for relics.

REREDORTER—A monastic latrine.

REREDOS—A screen of stone or wood at the back of an altar, usually enriched.

RESPONDS—The half-columns or piers at the ends of an arcade or abutting a single arch.

REVEAL—The internal side surface of a recess, especially of a doorway or window opening.

RIDGE (or RIG) AND FURROW—Remains of old cultivations.

RIDGE-ROOF—*See King-post and Ridge under* ROOFS.

RISER—The vertical piece connecting two treads in a flight of stairs.

ROCOCO—The latest (18th-century) phase of Baroque, especially in Northern Europe, in which effects of elegance and vivacity are obtained by the use of a decorative repertory further removed from antique architectural forms than the earlier phases and often asymmetrically disposed.

ROLL-MOULDING OR BOWTELL—A continuous prominent convex moulding

ROOD (*Rood-beam, Rood-screen, Rood-loft*)—A cross or crucifix. The *Great Rood* was set up at the E. end of the nave with accompanying figures of St. Mary and St. John; it was generally carved in wood, and fixed on the loft or head of the rood-screen, or on a special beam (the *Rood-beam*) reaching from wall to wall. Sometimes the rood was merely painted on the wall above the chancel-arch or on a closed wood partition or tympanum in the upper half of the arch. The *Rood-screen* is the open screen spanning the E. end of the nave, shutting off the chancel; in the 15th century a narrow gallery was often constructed above the cornice to carry the rood and other images and candles, and it was also used as a music-gallery. The loft was approached by a staircase (and occasionally by more than one), either of wood or built in the wall, wherever most convenient, and, when the loft was carried right across an aisled building, the intervening walls of the nave were often pierced with narrow archways. Many of the roods were destroyed at the Reformation, and their final removal, with the loft, was ordered in 1561.

ROOFS—*Collar-beam*—a principal-rafter roof with collar-beams connecting the principals.

Cruck (*or Crutch*)—having a truss with principals springing from below the level of the wall-plate. The timbers are usually curved but examples with straight timbers are recorded.

Hammer-beam—hammer-beams instead of tie-beams, braced from a level below the wall-plates, form the basis of construction.

King-post and Collar-purlin—a trussed-rafter roof with king-posts standing on tie-beams to carry a centre purlin supporting collars.

King-post and Ridge—in which king-posts standing on tie-beams or collar-beams directly support the ridge.

Mansard—characterised in exterior appearance by two pitches, the lower steeper than the upper.

Principal-rafter—with rafters at intervals of greater scantling than the common rafters and framed to form trusses; normally called by the name of the connecting member used in the truss, *tie-beam* or *collar-beam*. Later, as opposed to mediaeval, roofs of this kind often have queen-posts.

Queen-post—with two vertical or nearly vertical posts (queen-posts) standing on the tie-beam of a truss and supporting a collar-beam or the principal rafters.

Scissors-truss—as Trussed-rafter, but with crossed braces instead of collars.

Tie-beam—a principal-rafter roof with a simple triangulation of a horizontal beam linking the lower ends of the pairs of principals to prevent their spread.

Trussed-rafter—in which each pair of common rafters, all the timbers in the slopes being common rafters of uniform size, is connected by a collar-beam, which is often braced. At intervals pairs of rafters may be tenoned into a tie-beam.

Wagon—a trussed-rafter roof with curved braces forming a semicircular arch springing from wall-plate level.

ROPING—Ornament resembling a rope or cable.

ROUNDEL—A circular unit of decorative or figure composition. In heraldry, a round plate or disc of any tincture; a gold roundel is called a *Bezant*.

RUBBLE—Walling of rough unsquared stones or flints. *Coursed Rubble*—rubble walling with the stones or flints very roughly dressed and levelled up in courses some 12 to 18 inches in height; in *Regular Coursed Rubble* the stones or flints are laid in separate courses and kept to a uniform height in each course.

RUPILATION—*See* RUSTICATION.

RUSTICATION—Primarily, masonry in which only the margins of the stones are worked, also used for any masonry where the joints are emphasised by mouldings, grooves, etc.; rusticated columns are those in which the shafts are interrupted by square blocks of stone or broad projecting bands. *Rupilation*—Masonry faced to resemble a waterworn rock surface.

SABLE—In heraldry, black.

SACRISTY—A room generally in immediate connection with a church, in which the holy vessels and other valuables are kept.

SALIENT—In heraldry, applied to a beast in a leaping position.

SALLET—A light helmet. The form varied but, in English representations, it is usually characterised by a short tail. Often fitted with a vizor and worn in conjunction with a beaver.

SALTIRE—In heraldry, an X-shaped cross. *Per saltire*—applied to the field or to a charge with alternating tinctures in the four parts formed by two lines drawn saltirewise across it.

SAMIAN Ware—A common table ware of the Roman period, mostly of Gaulish origin, with a glossy surface, generally red in colour. Also known as *terra sigillata*.

SCALLOPED CAPITAL—A development of the cushion-capital in which the single cushion is elaborated into a series of truncated cones.

SCARP—In earthworks, an artificial cutting away of the ground to form a steeper slope.

SCREEN—In College chapels, the wooden partition separating the main compartment from the Antechapel. In secular buildings, that separating the main space of a hall from the service end. *Screens-passage*, the space at the service end of a hall between the screen and the end wall; *Screens* is sometimes used to describe the whole arrangement of screen and screens-passage. *See also under* ROOD.

SCUTCHEON or ESCUTCHEON—1. A shield; a charge in heraldry. *Voided Scutcheon*, a scutcheon that has had the middle part cut away leaving only a border.
2. A metal plate pierced for the spindle of a handle or for a keyhole.

SEDILIA (sing. *sedile*, a seat)—The seats on the S. side of the chancel, choir, or chapel near the altar, used by the ministers during the Mass.

SEGREANT—In heraldry, applied to a griffin when rampant.

SEMY—In heraldry, applied to a field or charge powdered or strewn with small charges.

SEXPARTITE VAULT—*See* VAULTING.

SHAFT—A slender column.

SHAFTED JAMBS—Jambs containing one or more shafts either engaged or detached.

SHERD—A scrap or broken piece of pottery.

SILL—The lower horizontal member of a window or door-frame; the stone, tile or wood base below a window or door-frame, usually with a weathered surface projecting beyond the wall-face to throw off water. In timber-framed walls, the lower horizontal member into which the studs are tenoned.

SINISTER—In heraldry, the left-hand side of a shield as held.

SLIP-TILES—Tiles moulded with a design in intaglio which was then filled in, before burning, with a clay of a different colour.

SOFFIT—The under-side of an arch, staircase, lintel, cornice, canopy, etc.

SOFFIT-CUSPS—Cusps springing from the flat soffit of an arched head, and not from its chamfered sides or edges.

SOIL-MARK—A trace of a levelled or buried feature revealed by differences in colour or texture of the soil, usually in ploughed land.

SPANDREL—The space between the outside curve of an arch and the surrounding rectangular framework or moulding, or the space between the outside curves of two adjoining arches and a moulding above.

SPIRE, BROACH-SPIRE, NEEDLE-SPIRE—The tall pointed termination covered with lead or shingles forming the roof of a tower or turret. A *Broach-spire* rises from the sides of a tower generally without parapets, the angles of the tower being surmounted by half-pyramids (broaches) against the facets of the spire to effect the change from the square to the polygon. A *Needle-spire* is small and narrow, and rises from the middle of the tower-roof well within the parapet.

SPLAY—A sloping face making an angle of more than a right angle with another face, as in internal window-jambs etc.

SPRINGING-LINE—The level at which an arch springs from its supports.

SPURS—*Prick*—in the form of a plain goad, an early type.
Rowel—with spiked wheel, came into general use about 1325.

SQUINCH—An arch thrown across the angle between two walls to support a superstructure, such as the base of a stone spire.

SQUINT—A piercing through a wall to allow a view of an altar from places whence it could otherwise not be seen.

STAGES—The divisions (*e.g.* of a tower) marked by horizontal string-courses externally.

STAIRCASES—A *close-string* staircase is one having a raking member into which the treads and risers are housed. An *open-string* staircase has the raking member cut to the shape of the treads and risers. A *dog-legged* staircase has adjoining flights running in opposite directions with a common newel. A *well-staircase* has stairs rising round a central opening more or less as wide as it is long.

STANCHION—The upright iron bars in a screen, window, etc.

STOLE—A long, narrow strip of embroidery with fringed ends worn above the alb by a deacon over the left shoulder, and by priests and bishops over both shoulders.

STOPS—Blocks terminating mouldings or chamfers in stone or wood; stones at the ends of labels, string-courses, etc., against which the mouldings finish, frequently carved to represent shields, foliage, human or grotesque masks; also, plain or decorative, used at the ends of a moulding or a chamfer to form the transition thence to the square.

STOUP—A receptacle, normally by the doorway of a church, to contain holy water; those remaining are usually in the form of a deeply-dished stone set in a niche, or on a pillar.

STRING or STRING-COURSE—A projecting horizontal band in a wall, usually moulded.

STRUT—A timber forming a sloping support to a beam etc.

STUDS—The common posts or uprights in timber-framed walls.

STYLE—The vertical members of a frame into which are tenoned the ends of the rails or horizontal pieces.

STYLOBATE—The podium or architectural base of a temple or other Classical building.

SUB-DEACON'S VESTMENTS (Mass)—Amice, alb, tunicle, maniple.

SURCOAT—Coat, usually sleeveless, worn over armour.

SURPLICE—A white linen vestment with wide hanging sleeves.

SWAG—An ornament; a festoon suspended from both ends and carved to represent cloth or flowers and fruit.

TABARD—Short loose surcoat, open at the sides, with short tab-like sleeves, sometimes worn with armour, and painted or embroidered with arms; distinctive garment of a herald.

TALBOT—In heraldry, a hound with drooping ears.

TAS-DE-CHARGE—The lower courses of a vault or arch, laid in horizontal courses and bonded into the wall, forming a solid mass; as they project forward they lessen the span.

TERMINAL FIGURE—The upper part of a carved human figure growing out of a column, post, or pilaster diminishing to the base.

TESSERA-AE—A small cube of stone, glass, or marble, used in mosaic.

TETRASTYLE—A portico having four columns.

THUMB-GAUGING—An ornamental top-edge to a ridge-tile, made with the thumb before the tile is baked.

TIE-BEAM—The horizontal transverse beam in a roof, tying together the feet of pairs of rafters to counteract thrust.

TIERCED IN PALE—In heraldry, a division of the shield into three vertical pieces. *Tierced per pale and cheveron*, division of the shield into three pieces, the two uppermost per pale and the lowest per cheveron.

TIMBER-FRAMED BUILDING—A building of which the walls are built of open timbers and the interstices filled in with brickwork or lath and plaster ('wattle and daub'), the whole often covered with plaster or boarding.

TINCTURE—In heraldry, the generic name for the colours, metals and furs used on coats-of-arms.

TOOLING—Dressing or finishing a masonry surface with an axe or other tool, usually in parallel lines. (A change from diagonal tooling to vertical has been noted at Wells Cathedral *c.* 1210 (*Arch. Jour.* LXXXV).)

TOOTHING—*See* TUSKING.

TORSE—In heraldry, the wreathed ring upon which the crest is placed; often shown as a short stiff rod of two tinctures twisted together.

TORUS—In Classical architecture, a convex moulding, generally a semicircle in section.

TOUCH—A soft black marble, quarried near Tournai and used in monumental art.

TRABEATION—The use of horizontal beams in building construction; descriptive in the Inventory of conspicuous cased ceiling-beams.

TRACERY—The ornamental work in the head of a window, screen, panel, etc., formed by the curving and interlacing of bars of stone or wood, grouped together, generally over two or more lights or bays.

TRANSOM—An intermediate horizontal bar of stone or wood across a window-opening.

TREAD—The horizontal platform of a step or stair.

TREFOIL—In heraldry, a three-lobed leaf with a pendent stalk.

TRELLIS, TREILLAGE—Lattice-work of light wood or metal bars.

TRESSURE—In heraldry, a narrow band formed by a voided scutcheon. A *double tressure*, two such charges one within the other. *Tressure flory*, with fleurs-de-lis issuing from the outer band. *Tressure flory and counter flory*, with fleurs-de-lis issuing from the outer and inner bands.

TRIBUNE—*See* TRIFORIUM.

TRIFORIUM—In the larger churches, an arcaded wall-passage at about mid wall height, between the aisle arcades and the clearstorey. A large gallery the full width of the aisle below is termed a *Tribune*.

TRIGLYPHS—Blocks with vertical channels, placed at intervals along the frieze of the Doric entablature.

TRUSS—A number of timbers framed together to bridge a space, to be self-supporting, and to carry other timbers. The *trusses* of a roof are generally named after a peculiar feature in their construction, such as *King-post, Queen-post, Hammer-beam, Crutch*; see under ROOFS.

TUFA (Calcareous)—Spongy deposit formed by the action of water on limestone and resembling volcanic lava. Often used in vaulting on account of its lightness.

TUSKING—Bricks or stones in alternate courses left projecting beyond the wall-face of a building to facilitate the bonding in of an extension. Also *Toothing*.

TYMPANUM—The triangular or semicircular field in the face of a pediment or in the head of an arch.

VAIR—In heraldry, a pattern imitating grey squirrels' skins, usually shown as an alternating series, often in rows, of blue and white bell-shaped patches. If of other tinctures it is called *vairy*.

VAULTING—An arched ceiling or roof of stone or brick, sometimes imitated in wood and plaster. *Barrel-vaulting* is a continuous vault unbroken in its length by cross-vaults. A *groined vault* (or *cross-vaulting*) results from the intersection of simple vaulting surfaces. A *ribbed vault* is a framework of arched ribs carrying the cells that cover in the spaces between them. One bay of vaulting, divided into four quarters or compartments, is termed *quadripartite*; but often the bay is divided longitudinally into two subsidiary bays, each equalling a bay of the wall-supports; the vaulting bay is thus divided into six compartments, and is termed *sexpartite*. Increased elaboration is given by *tiercerons*, secondary ribs springing from the wall-supports and rising to a point other than the centre, and *liernes*, tertiary ribs that do not spring from the wall-supports, but cross from main rib to main rib. In *fan-vaulting* numerous ribs rise from the springing in equal curves, diverging equally in all directions, giving fan-like effects when seen from below.

VENETIAN WINDOW—*See* PALLADIAN.

VENTAIL—*See* VIZOR.

VERT—In heraldry, green.

VESICA PISCIS—A pointed oval frame generally used in mediaeval art to enclose a figure of Christ enthroned. *Also* MANDORLA (*q.v.*).

VESTMENTS (Ecclesiastical)—*See* alb, amess, amice, apparels, archbishop's vestments, bishop's vestments, canonical choir-habit, cassock, chasuble, choir-habit, cope, crosier, cross-staff, dalmatic, deacon's vestments, maniple, mitred abbot's vestments, morse, orphreys, priest's vestments, processional vestments, stole, subdeacon's vestments, surplice.

VEXILLUM—A scarf on a pastoral staff.

VICE—A small circular stair.

VIZOR—A defence for the eyes, sometimes for the whole face. The close-helmet of the 16th century was fitted with a vizor consisting of three separate plates: the vizor proper, the ventail or upper beaver covering the face, and the chin-piece or lower beaver.

VOIDED—In heraldry, a voided charge has the middle part cut away, leaving a margin.

VOLUTE—An ornament in the form of a spiral scroll, *e.g.* in the Ionic capital.

VOUSSOIRS—The stones forming an arch.

WAGON-ROOF—*See under* ROOFS.

WALL-PLATE—A timber laid lengthwise on the wall to receive the ends of the rafters and other joists. In timber-framing, the studs are tenoned into it.

WATER-BOUGET—*See* BOUGET.

WAVE-MOULDING—A compound moulding formed by a convex curve between two concave curves.

WEATHER-BOARDING—Horizontal boards nailed to the uprights of timber-framed buildings and made to overlap; the boards are generally wedge-shaped in section, the upper edge being the thinner.

WEATHERING (to sills, tops of buttresses, etc.)—A sloping surface for casting off water.

WEEPERS—Small upright figures, generally of relatives of the deceased, placed in niches or panels round the sides of mediaeval tombs; occasionally also represented on brasses.

WELL-STAIRCASE—*See* STAIRCASES.

WIMPLE—Scarf covering chin and throat.

WOODMAN OR WOODHOUSE—A wild man of the woods, generally represented naked and hairy.

WYVERN—In heraldry, a two-legged dragon.

YALE—In heraldry, a composite animal resembling a spotted deer, with swivelling horns.

INDEX

Part I of the Inventory contains pages i–cxxix and 1–136, the frontispiece and plates 1–197. Part II contains pages 137–392, the Armorial Index and plates 198–310.

The Armorial Index (pages 397–414) contains the references to heraldry throughout both parts of the Inventory. The heraldic references in the General Index are only to those arms that can be identified with the individual who bore them.

In the Indexes references to the left and right columns on the page are identified by 'a' and 'b' respectively after the page numbers.

The classified lists chronologically arranged in the following Index are necessarily selective.